DEGAS

THE UNCONTESTED MASTER

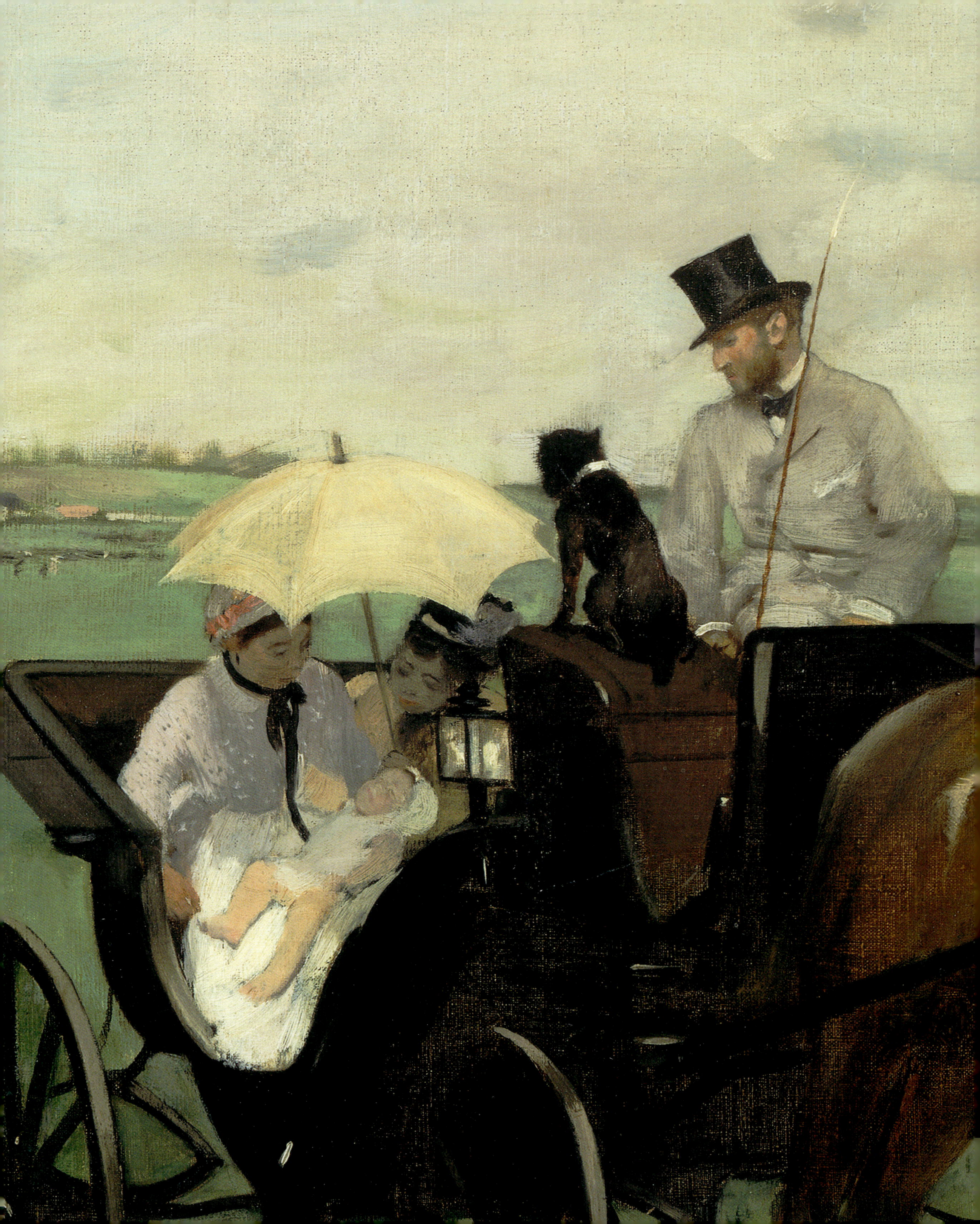

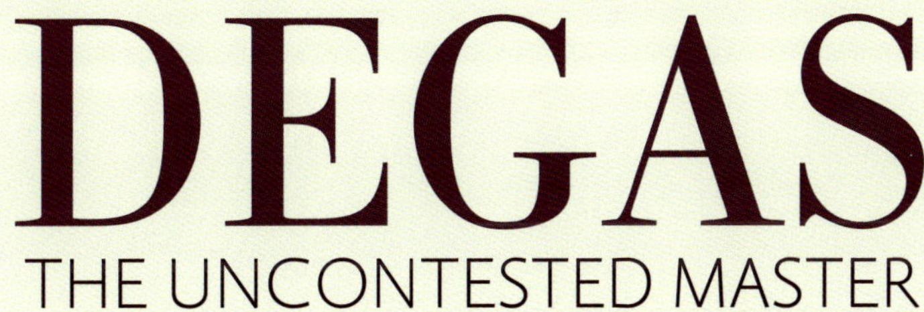

DEGAS
THE UNCONTESTED MASTER

Jane Kinsman
with Michael Pantazzi

■ national gallery of **australia**

The National Gallery of Australia is an Australian Government Agency
nga.gov.au

Produced by NGA Publishing
National Gallery of Australia, Canberra
Research assistance: Pauline Green
Editing: Pauline Green and Paul Cliff*
Designer and production coordinator: Kirsty Morrison*
Photography: NGA Imaging Services*
Rights and permissions: Nick Nicholson*
Index: Sherrey Quinn
Publishing manager: Julie Donaldson*
Pre-press and printing: Blue Star Print (Vic)
* National Gallery of Australia

Cataloguing-in-Publication data:
Kinsman, Jane
Degas: the uncontested master
ISBN 9780642541932 (pbk)
Includes index
Subjects: Degas, Edgar, 1834–1917 – Exhibitions.
Painting – France – Exhibitions.
Other authors/contributors: Pantazzi, Michael; Maxwell, Simeran
National Gallery of Australia
Dewey Number: 750.90944

Published in conjunction with the exhibition
Degas: master of French art, at the National Gallery of Australia, Canberra
12 December 2008 – 22 March 2009

Principal Partners

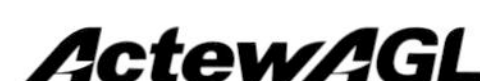

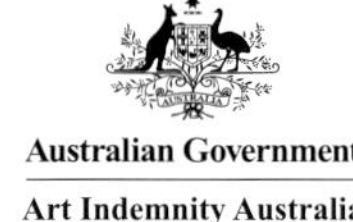

(frontispiece)
At the races in the countryside
(Carriage at the races)
1869 (detail cat 13)

CONTENTS

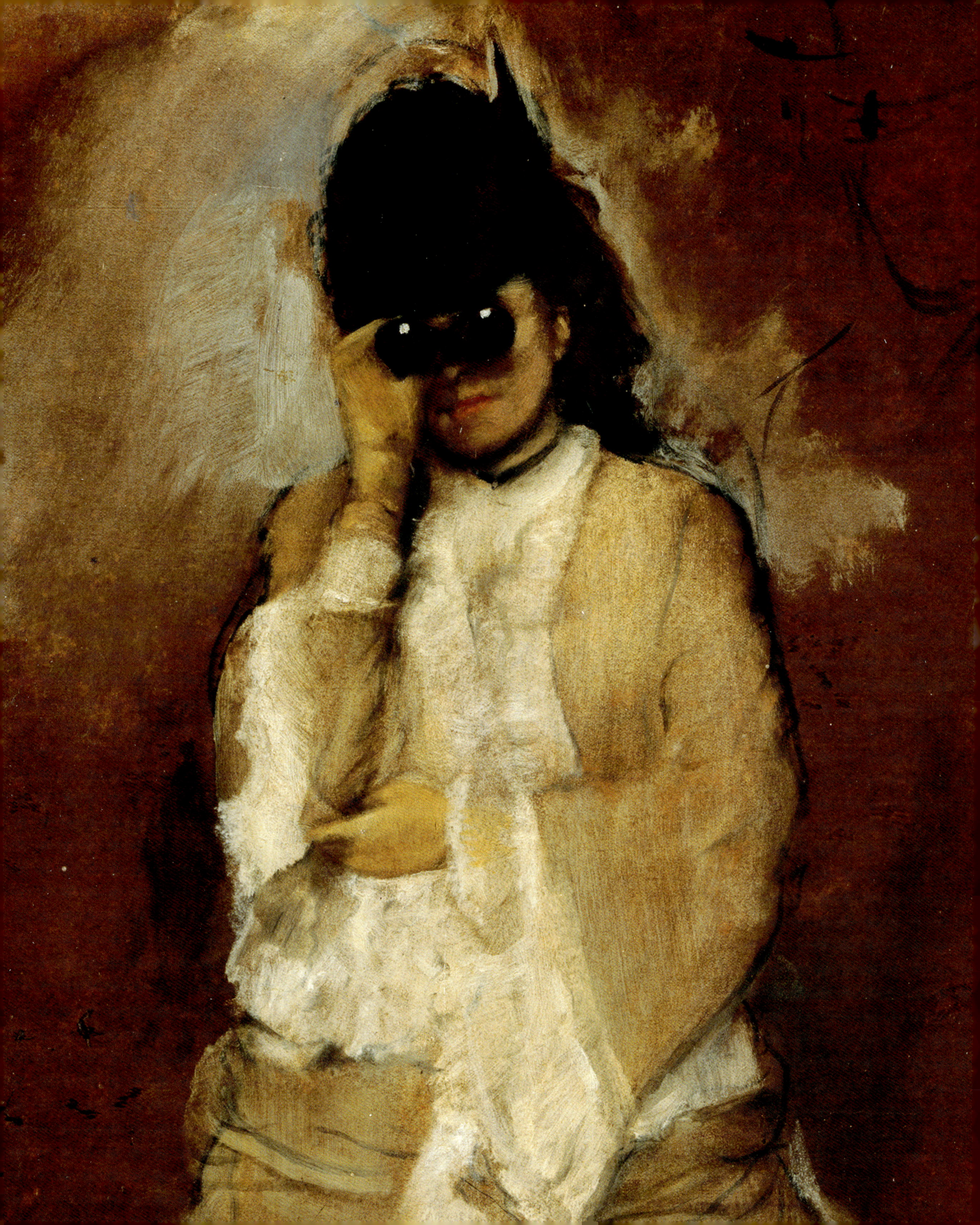

SPONSOR'S FOREWORD

ActewAGL is delighted to be the Principal Partner of the National Gallery of Australia's exhibition, *Degas: master of French art.*

ActewAGL values greatly our partnership with the National Gallery of Australia as a means of directly contributing to the local and national community. Through supporting this exhibition we reaffirm our commitment to promoting and celebrating the vital role that the arts play in our national identity and to ensure that Australians have access to some of the world's most breathtaking works of art.

This is the first time in Australia that audiences have had the opportunity to see an exhibition on Edgar Degas, one of the most important and admired French Impressionist artists. We are honoured to give Australians the opportunity to be inspired by the diverse art of this French master.

ActewAGL and its predecessors have been serving the Canberra region since 1915 and supporting the National Gallery of Australia for over a decade. Our vision is to connect with our customers. Our mission is to ensure that the best interests of our customers, owners and staff are considered in everything we do. As the Principal Partner of this exhibition we are demonstrating that along with providing excellent services we are committed to the cultural and creative wellbeing of our community through supporting art exhibitions and programs that stimulate the senses and enliven the spirit.

It is our wish that as many people as possible will take this opportunity to visit Canberra and enjoy the magic and creative genius of Edgar Degas.

ActewAGL would like to congratulate the Council and staff of the National Gallery of Australia for organising this truly awe-inspiring exhibition.

Michael Costello
CEO ActewAGL

(opposite)
Woman with field glasses 1875–76
(detail cat 14)

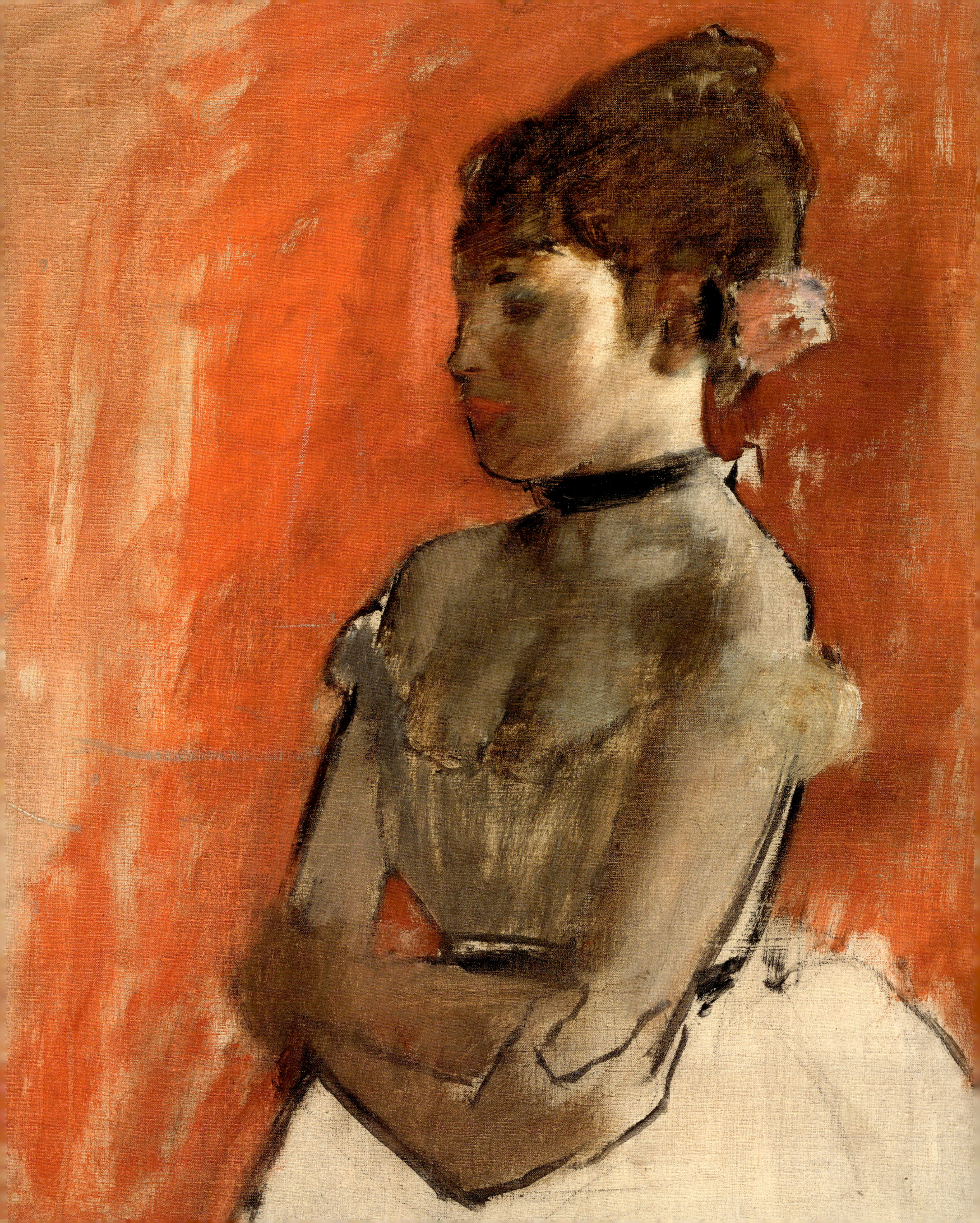

PRIME MINISTER'S FOREWORD

Congratulations to the National Gallery of Australia for the outstanding *Degas: master of French art* exhibition, the highlight of the Gallery's exhibitions program this summer. This is the first time Australians have had the opportunity to see in an Australian gallery such a range of work by this important French artist. The exhibition traces Edgar Degas' development as a pioneering and influential artist through an ensemble of artworks drawn from galleries and museums across the globe. The exhibition charts the evolution of Degas' distinctive style through decades of experimentation with subject matter, media and technique, and features painting, sculpture, drawings, prints and photography. This exhibition also demonstrates the Australian Government's ongoing support for the arts. *Degas: master of French art* has been made possible by Art Indemnity Australia, through which the Commonwealth indemnifies major exhibitions of significant cultural material. Almost 22 million visitors have enjoyed over 100 exhibitions covered by the scheme since it was established in 1979. The National Gallery of Australia is one of our leading national institutions, making a significant contribution to the cultural life of the nation. I encourage everyone to take this opportunity to visit this exhibition and experience the work of one of the most significant and celebrated artists of his era.

The Honourable Kevin Rudd MP
Prime Minister of Australia

(oposite)
Ballet dancer with arms crossed
c 1872 (detail cat 52)

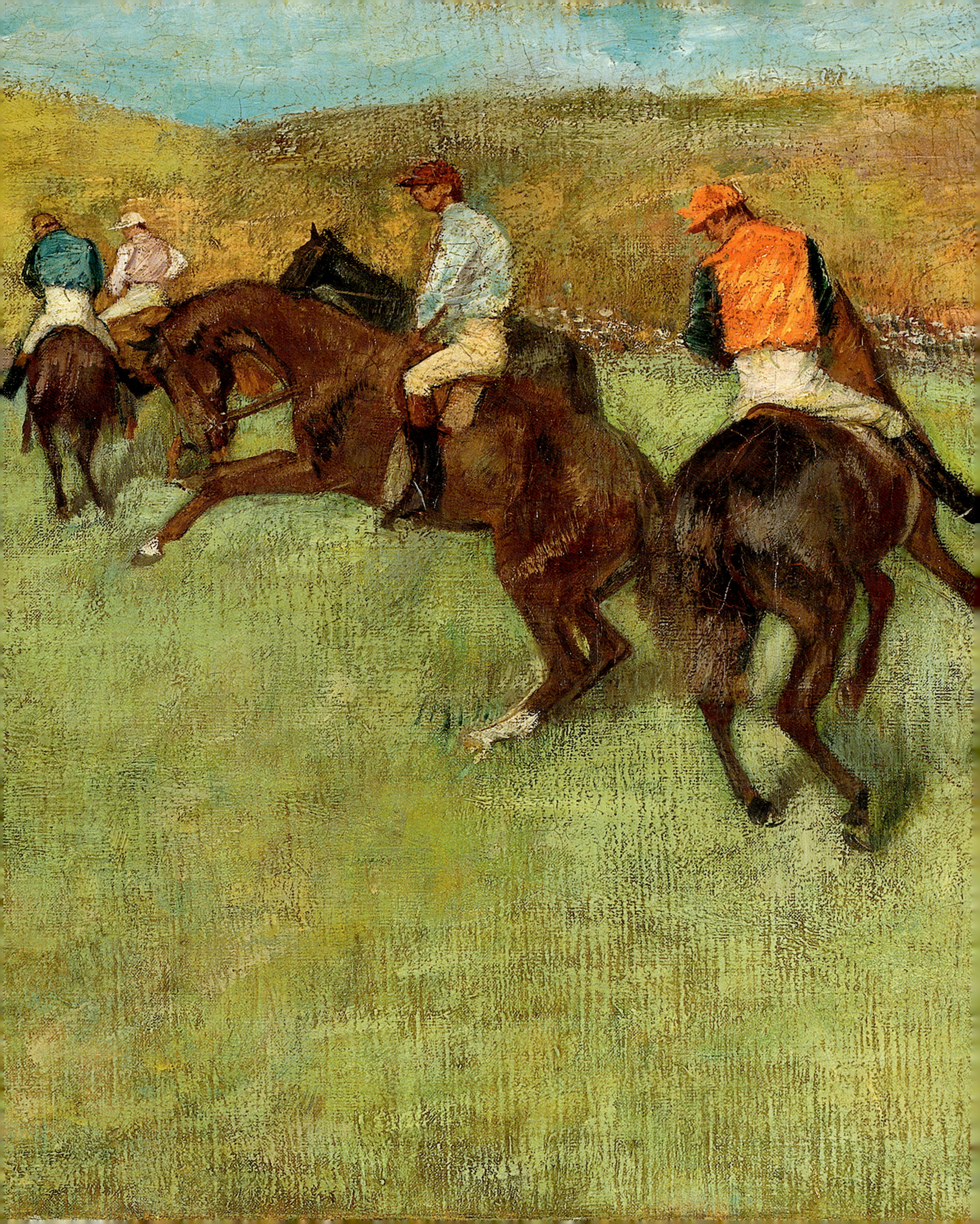

DIRECTOR'S INTRODUCTION

EDGAR DEGAS CREATED some of the most recognised and loved images of late nineteenth- and early twentieth-century art. So popular are his figure compositions that we can easily forget not only his astonishing originality, but also the fact that he was a creative pioneer in many areas. A painter, draughtsman, sculptor, printmaker and photographer (all well represented in this exhibition), Degas' impact on his contemporaries and successors was as far-reaching and as broad as his art practice. He not only influenced some of his famous peers, such as Whistler, but had a very significant impact on his younger followers such as Gauguin, Toulouse-Lautrec, Bonnard, Vuillard, Matisse and Picasso, all of whom acknowledged their debt to Degas.

His paintings and drawings of ballet dancers, the racetrack, café culture, laundresses and prostitutes are very familiar to us. It is as though they have always existed such is their iconic power. However, this exhibition delves further than these admittedly stunningly original works to uncover the lesser-known Degas, whose highly innovative practice was perhaps nowhere more evident than in his intimate monotypes, of which we include 21 in the exhibition. From the mid 1870s to mid 1880s, his experiments with the spontaneity of monotypes heavily influenced the way he approached other techniques and mediums as well as his subjects and compositions. Similarly, his experiments in photography of the mid1890s led the way to later innovations in his paintings. This exhibition, then, goes well beyond any conventional image we may have of Degas.

In his insightful biography of Degas in this publication, Michael Pantazzi concludes that Degas may have appreciated an epitaph, 'He captured the elusive moment that passes.' But the need to be spontaneous in creating his monotype prints by brushwork and finger-marking directly on the metal plates, was as close as Degas got to real spontaneity. In his later adventurous oil paintings he strived and laboured for months, sometimes longer—he was famous for revisiting and modifying his paintings years after their initial conception, much to the annoyance of their owners—to achieve the so-called look of spontaneity and movement, to show that 'elusive moment that passes'. This is where he differs from the Impressionist landscape painters who attempted to capture the fleeting, momentary light of the motif before them.

Although Degas is widely regarded as one of the first and most important Impressionists, and exhibited in and was a driving force behind seven of the eight Impressionist exhibitions held between 1874 and 1886, he found the term distasteful. Indeed, his work sometimes goes to the point of being anti-Impressionist. He preferred, instead, to be seen as extending the tradition of Realism from which Impressionism had stemmed in the 1860s and 1870s. Degas was an artist who recorded modern Parisian life truthfully, potently, not fleetingly.

Degas: master of French art has been curated by Jane Kinsman, a Senior Curator of International Art at the National Gallery of Australia. I wish to thank and congratulate Jane on her three years of work dedicated

(opposite)
At the races: before the start
c 1885–92 (detail cat 22)

(opposite)
Prostitutes in their camisoles
1876–77 (detail cat 33)

to the exhibition and on her essays in this publication. Mark Henshaw, Curator in the Gallery's department of International Prints, Drawings and Illustrated Books, has curated a parallel print exhibition entitled *Degas' world: the rage for change,* showing both the influences on Degas, and conversely and particularly, Degas' own influence on artists of the second half of the nineteenth and early twentieth centuries. Mark Henshaw has also assisted Jane Kinsman by providing fresh translations to many of the contemporary French reviews of the Impressionist exhibitions to which Degas contributed.

The major biographical essay here is by Michael Pantazzi, a distinguished Degas authority who was an important contributor to the major international Degas retrospective of 1988. Until 2006, he was Curator of European and American Art at the National Gallery of Canada, Ottawa, and is currently preparing a catalogue raisonné of Degas' drawings with a group including Henri Loyrette, Director of the Musée du Louvre. We very much appreciate this new biography of Degas, which includes much new information.

Unfortunately, Degas is not well represented in Australian collections, which makes this exhibition especially important to Australia. It may at first seem surprising that this non-touring exhibition is the first Degas exhibition to be held in Australia and indeed the first comprehensive Degas exhibition in the Southern Hemisphere. Degas' paintings are amongst the most appreciated works in the art museums where he is represented and since there is no single large collection of his paintings, loans of his works are often difficult to secure. They are the works the public wants to see in their respective institutions. His works are also fragile.

We are therefore grateful to all 45 generous lenders from around the world who have parted with their Degas works for our exhibition. Importantly we record our special appreciation of the Musée d'Orsay, Paris; the Bibliothèque nationale de France, Paris; the Bibliothèque de l'institut national d'histoire de l'art, Paris; the Metropolitan Museum of Art, New York; the National Gallery of Art, Washington; the British Museum, London; and the J Paul Getty Museum, Los Angeles, for the substantial number of loans they have each made to the National Gallery of Australia for this Degas exhibition. All other lenders are individually thanked in my formal acknowledgments.

We trust that Australians are stimulated and excited by this first exhibition of Degas' work in Australia.

Ron Radford, AM
Director, National Gallery of Australia

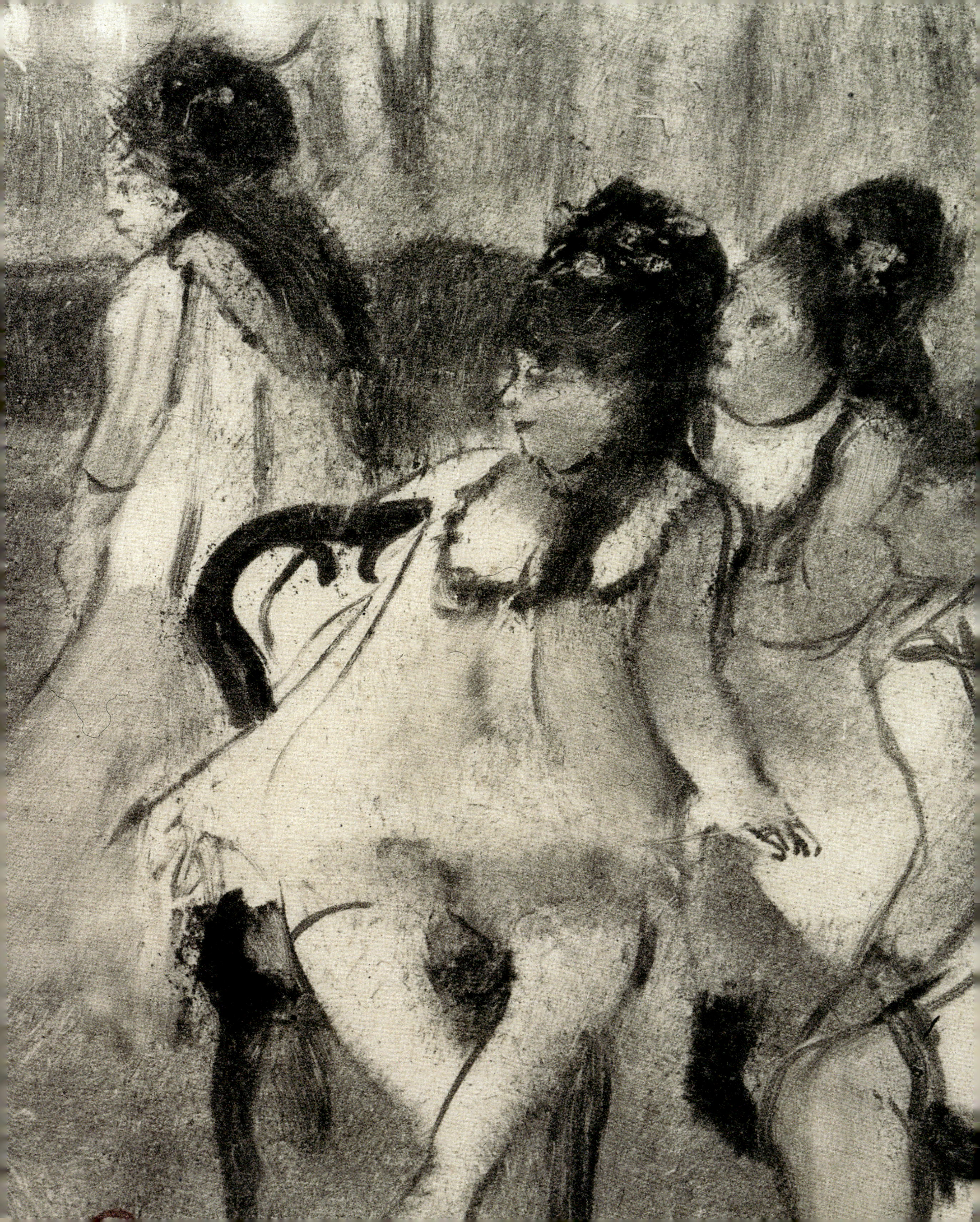

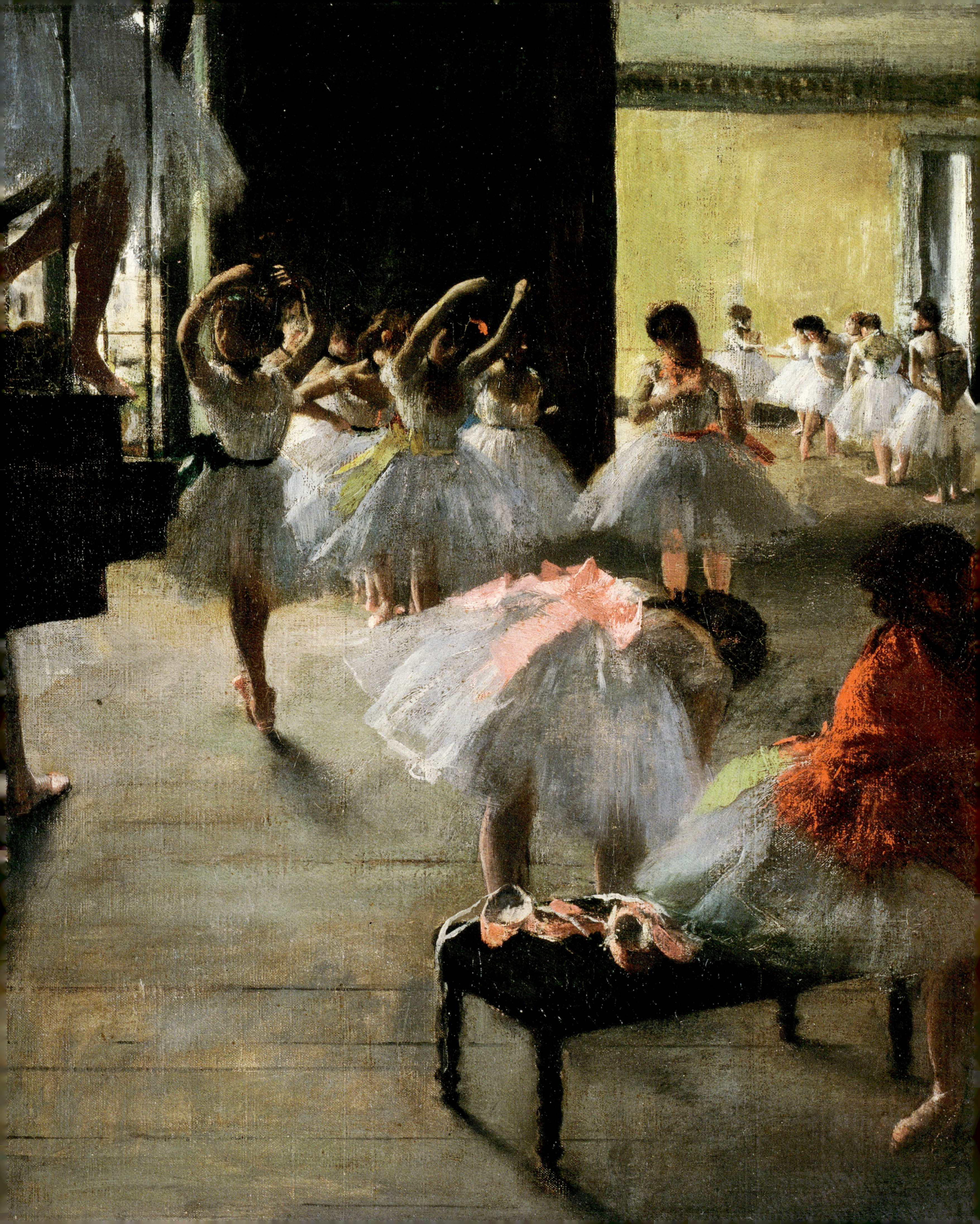

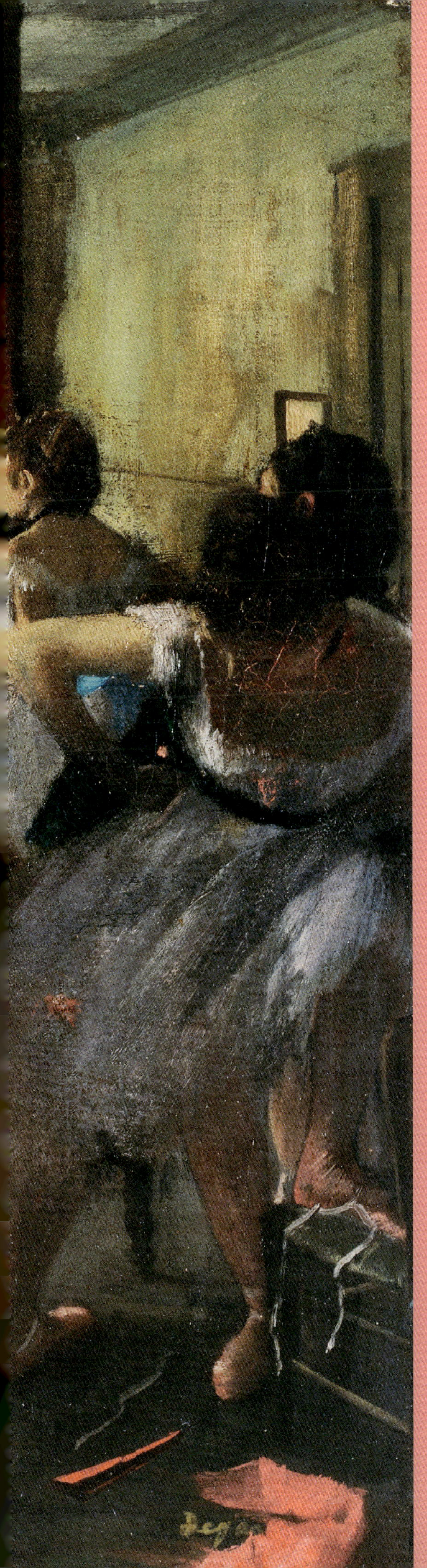

DEGAS AND THE IMPRESSIONISTS

Jane Kinsman

They're Impressionists in the sense that what they depict is not the landscape itself, but the effect or sensation that the landscape produces on us.

Jules-Antoine Castagnary, *Le Siècle*, 29 April 1874

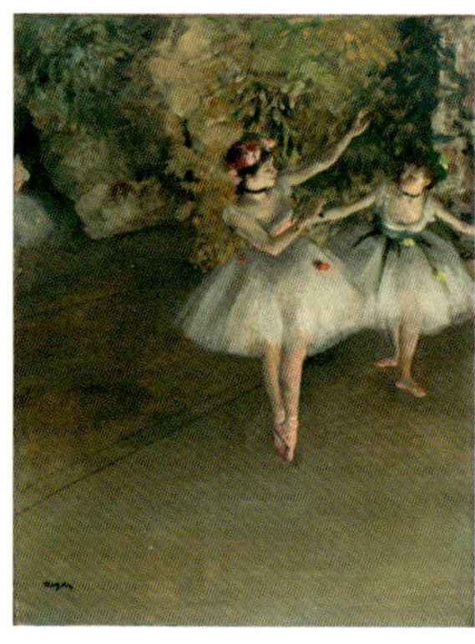

(above)
Two dancers on a stage (Deux danseuses en scène) c 1874
oil on canvas, 61.5 x 46.0 cm
Courtauld Institute of Art Gallery, London
Gift of Samuel Courtauld 1934
Lemoisne 425

(previous pages)
The dance class
c 1873 (detail cat 51)

EDGAR DEGAS was a leading figure in the development of French art in the latter part of the nineteenth century. As a young artist in his mid-twenties he turned his interest to contemporary subject matter to become one of the great artists of 'modern life', increasingly innovative and exploratory in the composition and execution of his work.

Although he exhibited with a group of other young artists who came to be known as the Impressionists—which included Claude Monet, Pierre-Auguste Renoir and Camille Pissarro—Degas was seen to stand apart from them, both in his choice of subject matter and his skill as a draughtsman. As one contemporary critic noted: 'Horses, ballerinas, laundresses are his predilections and of all the things in the world which surround him seem to preoccupy him exclusively. But what truth there is in his draughtsmanship, and how astute is his understanding of colour.'[1]

'These works are all new'

On 15 April 1874, a group of avant-garde artists opened an exhibition in Paris. Degas had been involved in the formation of the group, who came together as the Société Anonyme (coopérative à capital variable) des Artistes, Peintres, Sculpteurs, Graveurs etc[2], in order to show their work independently, free from the restrictions and clutter of the official Salon.

Thirty artists participated in the exhibition, the first of eight group-shows to be held between 1874 and 1886. The contributing artists would change the face of French art—and profoundly influence the practice and perception of art worldwide, well into the twentieth century. Degas remained a driving force behind these ventures and showed his own work in all but one of the eight exhibitions.

The wide-ranging articulate and, for the most part, informed commentary associated with these events, as it appeared in contemporary daily newspapers, journals and pamphlets, reveals the rich life of art criticism in France at the time. Writers were sometimes scathing, often witty, and frequently perceptive and illuminating—but whatever the course of such criticism, there was a general understanding that a new art was in the making.

The timing of the Société Anonyme exhibition in mid-April 1874 was crucial; held earlier than the annual Salon of the Ecole des Beaux-Arts, it could not be considered just another Salon des Refusés—an exhibition of work rejected by the Salon jury.[3] But, despite their efforts to avoid such assessments, inevitably comparisons were made. The *Revue de France* published the criticism that: 'except for a small number of paintings ... All of the works put together ... would have been vehemently rejected by the jury of the official Salon.'[4]

Jules-Antoine Castagnary, in *Le Siècle*, was more discerning, and keen to make the point that the art on display had not already been overlooked by the Salon, and was therefore untainted:

> So let's make it clear to the public—you will absolutely not find here any canvases that have already been stigmatised or compromised by being rejected. These works are all new. They've never been judged by any jury, never been subject

to any decision designed to keep them out of contention. They present themselves to the art lover unsullied, virgin, and as a consequence the public's freedom to make up its own mind remains intact.[5]

These events came to be known as the 'Impressionist exhibitions', although alternative names to identify the group were considered—including Intransigents and Independents.[6] Degas himself found the term 'Impressionist' distasteful, preferring the term 'Realist'. In a letter written to his friend James Tissot in 1874, Degas commented that he hoped for the establishment of a new salon, one with relevance to the times—a Realist salon: 'The realist movement no longer needs to fight with the others, it already is, it exists, it must show itself as *something distinct*, there must be a *salon of realists*.'[7]

'The Salon show of 1863 doesn't signify anything'

The first 'Impressionist' exhibition had been many years in the making, and arose from a growing dissatisfaction with the government-sponsored Salon exhibitions. While it was to their great advantage to be shown at the Salon, these emerging artists resisted the rigid selection process, which was strongly tied to the academic tradition. The often lamentable quality of the work chosen for exposure at the Salon, and its presentation—works jammed together, tier upon tier—contributed to a general view that the Salon was out of touch with contemporary life.

In 1863, the selections of the Salon jury were so controversial that the year came to mark a watershed in the evolution of modern art in France. Both in content and method of execution, the standard of the art exhibited had reached an all-time low. The critic and art historian Théophile Thoré, known for his admiration of Realism, lamented:

> On entering the Salon you have to forget about any aspiration for real art to be overly ambitious in terms of its ability to express anything profound about what it is to be human—to have ideas, feelings, or passions—or even with respect to the splendours of nature—its beauty, light, form or its colours …
>
> The French School such as it appears in the Salon show of 1863 doesn't signify anything. It is no longer religious, or philosophical; there's absolutely no history, and there's no poetry. It simultaneously lacks any reference to the traditions of the old, or the imagination of the new.[8]

From a field of more than 5000 entries in 1863, the Salon jury chose less than half for exhibition, and the outcry against the extremely conservative selection spurred Emperor Louis-Napoléon Bonaparte to establish a separate venue where works rejected by the jury could be shown—the Salon des Refusés. Among the works hung in the inaugural Salon des Refusés, Edouard Manet's *Luncheon on the grass* caused a sensation.[9] Although he took inspiration from great Italian and Spanish old masters, Manet's subject was thoroughly modern and broke with conventions for painting the female nude. The image of a young woman, completely naked, casually picnicking with two fully clothed male companions shocked Parisians; while hostile critics attacked Manet's painting style.

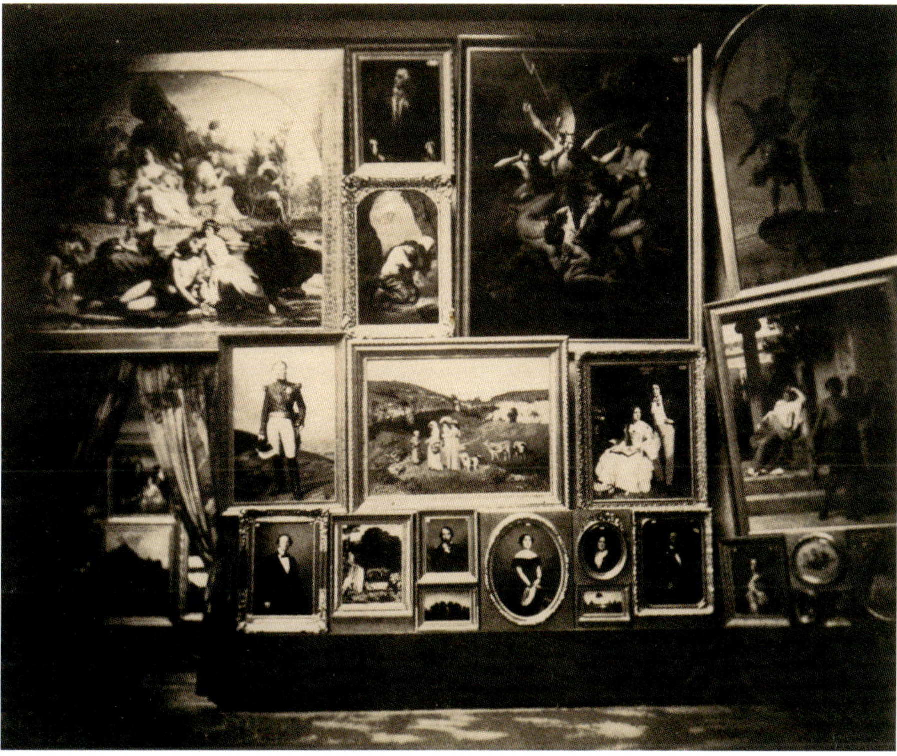

Gustave le Gray
Salon of 1852, large north gallery (centre: 'The village girls' by Gustave Courbet) (Salon de 1852, grand salon, mur nord (au centre: 'Les demoiselles de village' de Gustave Courbet)) 1852
salted paper photograph, glued on card, 19.4 x 23.6 cm
Musée d'Orsay, Paris

Up to that time in the early 1860s, the work shown at the Salon was the chief subject of French art criticism. With the establishment of the Salon des Refusés, and the later independent exhibitions, the role of the art critic and writer broadened significantly: their commentary constitutes a mise en scène against which to view events and understand attitudes surrounding the emergence of the new art.

In an extended essay published in 1876, a prominent observer of events in Paris, the writer and art critic Edmond Duranty, a friend of Degas, commented on the dire state of mid nineteenth-century French art—that it was reactionary and barren of ideas, supported by official channels, and out of touch with society. Referring to his earlier treatises on Realism,[10] Duranty eloquently articulated his vision of contemporary life in all its variety as ready subject matter for artists. He began by quoting the comment he'd made on painting, 20 years earlier:

> 'I saw a society, its actions, its events, its professions, its personalities, and its various milieux. I saw a veritable comedy of manners and facial gestures which were just made to be painted. I saw en masse the formation of groups brought together by their interactions when they encountered each other in different contexts: at church, in the dining room, in the lounge room, at the cemetery, on the battlefield, in the studio, in the Houses of Parliament. Everywhere, the different way people dressed competed with their differences in physiognomy, posture, feelings, or actions. To me, everything seemed arranged as if the world were made purely for the enjoyment of painters, purely for the delectation of their eyes only.'

Duranty added:

> I saw painting undertaking vast series of works devoted to the peoples of the world—priests, soldiers, peasants, farm workers, shopkeepers—series in which the people depicted varied according to their place in society. Here they would be brought together in scenes which were common to them all—marriages, baptism, births, deaths, festivities, the intimacies of family life. In other words, in those activities which repeated themselves over and over and which, as a consequence, expressed the social fabric of a country.[11]

'Our wits sharpened'

In Paris in the late 1860s, at the Café Guerbois, near Manet's studio in the outer neighbourhood of Batignolles, and at the Café de la Nouvelle-Athènes in Montmartre, a new generation of artists passionately debated the importance of fostering a different, more relevant art for their time. Years later, Claude Monet recalled the ardent nature of their exchanges:

Honoré Daumier
Artists subjecting the work of a rival to scrutiny (Artistes en train d'examiner le tableau d'un rival), from the series *The public at the Salon (Le public du Salon)*, published in *Le Charivari*
14 May 1852
lithograph, 34.6 x 26.4 cm (sheet)
National Gallery of Australia, Canberra
Purchased 1980

> It was only in 1869 that I saw him [Manet] again. At our first meeting he invited me to join him every evening at a café in the Batignolles district, where he and his friends gathered at the end of the day to talk. There I met Fantin-Latour, Cézanne, Degas, who had recently returned from Italy, the art critic Duranty, Emile Zola, who was then making his first foray into literature, and several others. For my part I used to take Sisley, Bazille and Renoir there. Nothing could be more interesting than the discussions we had, with their perpetual clash of opinions. They kept our wits sharpened, encouraged us to press ahead with our own experiments, provided us with enough enthusiasm to keep at it for weeks on end until our ideas became clear and coherent.[12]

These artists and writers had further cause to press ahead with their experiments following the catastrophe of the Franco–Prussian war of 1870–71.[13] In the aftermath of this calamitous period there was an upsurge of nationalism and conservatism in French society and the official art world became even more reactionary. Philippe de Chennevières, Director of the Académie des Beaux-Arts, commissioned murals for the Panthéon celebrating the life of Sainte Geneviève,[14] the patron saint of Paris who is said to have averted an attack on the city by Attila the Hun—with obvious allusion to recent times.[15] The Salon too became the venue for 'the reassertion of the country's cultural prowess, while Salon critics focused on whether that prowess was present or not'.[16] The time was ripe for a new art.

In April 1874, the artists of the Société Anonyme displayed their work in the large studios formerly belonging to the photographer and balloonist Nadar (Gaspard-Félix Tournachon) at 35 boulevard des Capucines. Along with Degas, contributors included Claude Monet, Camille Pissarro, Alfred Sisley, Berthe Morisot, Pierre-Auguste Renoir, Paul Cézanne and Armand Guillaumin. While the work of these artists varied in style, all were keen to create an art that related to their own day. This was the first of what became known as the Impressionist exhibitions.

It was a condition of participation in the group-shows that the artists did not also submit work to the Salon in the same year—a condition that Degas would consistently advocate. (Manet chose to continue to present his art for Salon selection, and so didn't exhibit with the group for this reason.) In previous years, Degas had regularly and successfully submitted works to the Salon, but he'd developed serious misgivings about the process in terms of the quality of the work chosen and the presentation, leading to his writing an open letter to the *Paris Journal* in 1870 suggesting improvements.[17]

In the catalogue for the group's first venture in 1874, Degas listed 10 of his works (six of which have now been identified, with a possible seventh).[18] Five were paintings featuring dance (at the theatre, and ballet practice behind the scenes); there was a depiction of a washerwoman, and a scene at the provincial races. He also contributed drawings with similar contemporary themes, including one pastel, as well as an image of a woman bathing.

The immediate critical response to the exhibition included a satirical review published in *Le Charivari* of 25 April, where the great proponent of academic art Louis Leroy famously and derisively called the artists 'Impressionists'.[19] Several members of the group were to adopt the title as a badge of honour.

Degas had persuaded some of his friends to participate in the exhibition—Félix Bracquemond, Ludovic Lepic, Léopold Levert and Henri Rouart, all of whom had previously exhibited at the Salon. He wrote to Bracquemond: 'We are getting an excellent recruit in you. Be assured of the pleasure you give and the good you are doing us.'[20] Degas had argued that the participation of these artists would enhance the standing of the exhibition and widen its appeal,[21] but there was ill feeling among other members of the Société Anonyme at the inclusion of work they considered to be conservative in style and of limited artistic merit.

'This fireworks display'

A series of astute commentators identified the Société Anonyme exhibition as a turning point in French art—whether for better or worse was another question and the subject of much debate. Within days of the exhibition's opening, Armand Silvestre noted: 'For a week now, they are all we've heard about …'[22] The groundbreaking nature of the event was recognised by one critic urging his readers to visit 'this fireworks display of riotous colour':

> You'll come away with a sense of something new and maybe you'll come back again, convinced that these painters who are exploring their talents outside the confines of the Academy will find in such exhibitions the most favourable conditions for the development of their strengths, and their originality.[23]

Philippe Burty, the noted promoter of Japanese art and the etching revival, saw the exhibition as marking a way forward for French artists—an assault undertaken by the avant-garde: 'A battalion of young people have broken through. They have already won over—and this is the important thing—those who love painting itself.'[24]

The great upholder of the Salon system, Emile Cardon, reacted caustically in his essay 'Avant le Salon', published on 28 April 1874:

> It's a great occasion. The exhibition at the boulevard des Capucines is another event that people who like the ridiculous and the grotesque will not want to miss. In fact, it's in Nadar's studios at the boulevard des Capucines that new art has found refuge, and not after having suffered the ignominy of rejection by any official jury. Instead, disdainfully, scornfully refusing to submit themselves to the judgment of those whom they say are incapable of either understanding or appreciating their work, or who might have admitted them purely out of pity, they have got in ahead.[25]

Warming to his criticism, a day later Cardon published a further lengthy riposte. Arguing that some of the participants were talented enough to be selected at the Salon and 'could not justly be considered as adepts of the new School', he turned his criticism to the representatives of that school:

> There thus remain MM. Degas, Cézanne, Monnet [sic], Sisley, Pissarro, Mlle Berthe Morisot etc. etc., the disciples of M. Manet, the pioneers of the painting of the future, who are the most convinced and authoritative representatives of the *School of Impressionism*. This school does away with two things: line, without which it is impossible to reproduce any form, animate or inanimate; and colour, which gives the form the appearance of reality … When it comes to the human figure it's something else altogether. The aim is no longer to render its form, its contours, or its expressiveness; all that's necessary is to render the impression without defining lines, without colour, with neither light nor shade. By trying to realise some crazy theory one descends into an insane mess, something mad and grotesque which fortunately has no precedent in art because, put quite simply, all we have here is nothing but the negation of the most fundamental rules of draughtsmanship and of painting … The famous Salon des Refusés which one can hardly recall without laughing, where one could see women the colour of Spanish tobacco, with green hair, in the middle of a forest of blue trees, well, this Salon des Refusés is a Louvre compared to the exhibition on show at the boulevard des Capucines.[26]

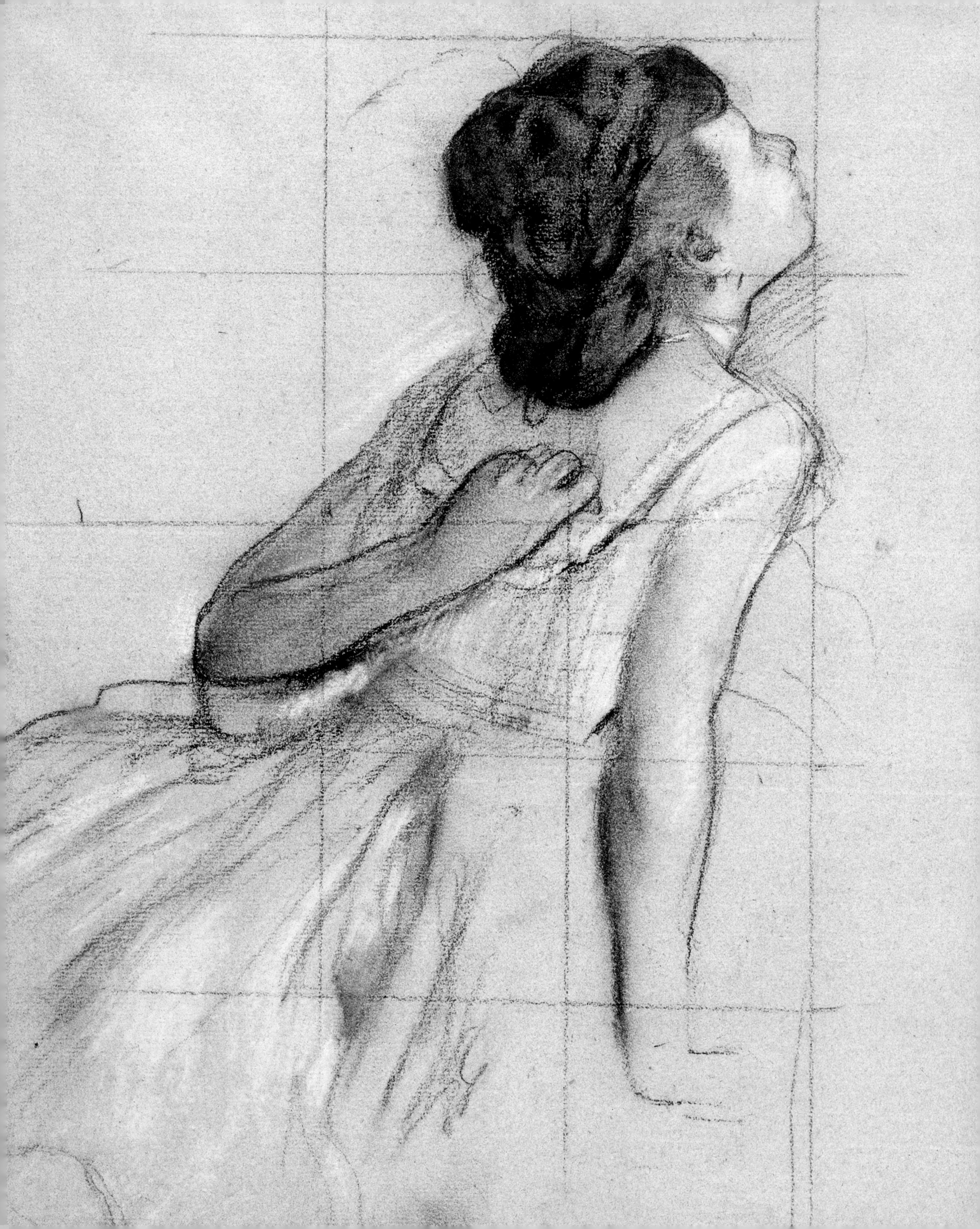

'I swear … there's talent here'

Jules-Antoine Castagnary, the noted elder of French art criticism, proponent of Naturalism and admirer of both Jean-Auguste-Dominique Ingres and Eugène Delacroix, wrote a lengthy and considered response on the occasion of the Société Anonyme exhibition:

> A couple of years ago there was a rumour getting around artists' studios about the birth of a new school of painting. What was their aim, how did they go about things, what was their territory? In what way did what they produce distinguish itself from any school that preceded them, and what effect would they have on contemporary art. It was difficult at first to tell. The members of the [Salon] jury, with their usual intelligence tried to block the way of these newcomers. They closed the Salon doors to them, prevented them from getting any publicity and by every idiotic means which egotism, stupidity or envy has at its disposal in this world to express itself, did their best to make them the object of ridicule.
>
> To get some idea of what these newcomers want, what they dream about, what they're trying to do, to get some measure of just how much distance separates them and their way of seeing things from the way things have been seen in the past, you need to go and stand in front of the canvases by Pissarro, Monet, Sisley, Renoir, Degas, Guillaumin, and those of Mlle Berthe Morisot. These are the major players in the new school—if indeed it is a new school, something which we will soon see … Let's have a little look then at what these terrible revolutionaries have to say that is so monstrous, so subversive, so undermining of our social order.
>
> Well, I swear to you on Cabanel's ashes, and those of Gérôme, that there's talent here, and a lot of it. These young people have a way of apprehending nature that has nothing dull or banal about it. It's alive, agile, light. It's ravishing. How quickly an object has been perceived, how intelligent has been its execution. Yes, it is a kind of summary, but how true the details are.[27]

In contrast to Leroy's expression of abuse, Castagnary adopted the term 'Impressionist' as an affirmation of this new art style and practice:

> If one tried to characterise them in a single word that would explain them, one would have to invent the new term Impressionists. They're Impressionists in the sense that what they depict is not the landscape itself, but the effect or sensation that the landscape produces on us. The word itself has passed into their lexicon, it's not landscape that is used to describe M. Monet's *Soleil levant* in the catalogue, but Impression. In this way, they leave reality behind and enter into pure idealism.[28]

'Degas has been amongst the most remarked upon'

Degas was singled out from others in the group for his ability to depict figures in movement—an aspect of his art practice that he would constantly develop throughout his career. In a review of the exhibition published in *Le Patriote français*, the photographer Etienne Carjat noted: 'M. Degas has been amongst the most remarked upon. And justifiably so.' Carjat described Degas' ballet dancers as 'delectable', and his figure groups, 'back arched, hips swaying, stretching in various poses' as 'keenly observed and intelligently rendered'.[29]

The notorious anti-clerical author and art critic Marie-Amélie Quivogne, writing under the nom de plume Marc de Montifaud, observed that Degas was exceptional in the directness and intimacy of his anatomical observation:

> *The dance class* is also a subtle and profound study, out of which comes something that one would never encounter in the work of certain painters who blush to depict an unclothed figure on a couple of square inches of canvas: which is to say, the study of a woman in all her naked opulence, her anatomically elegant or meagre form. M. Degas shows, with equal brilliance, the boniness of a shoulder blade, how it sticks out beneath the skin; or the sinewed back of a knee, below which a stocking is so fully pulled up that it is stretched as tight as a tambourine.[30]

What also distinguished Degas was his ability to distil lessons from the past and to absorb these into his everyday subjects—leading him to inscribe in his notebook: 'Ah Giotto! Let me see Paris, and you Paris, let me see Giotto!'[31] His fascination with the old masters was a trait Degas shared with Manet; and neither artist was concerned to capture only surface qualities. Nor was Degas interested in creating landscapes out-of-doors, and in different conditions—a key concern of his fellow participants.

Carjat, in his review of 27 April 1874, sounded a note of caution in response to the work of other members of the Société Anonyme, whom he recognised as moving in a different direction, and he warned against the possibility that their art might become mere decoration:

> MM. Monet, Pissarro, Cézanne, Sisley and Guillaumin form a separate group in this exhibition of which they have been the principal initiators. What they seem to be striving to achieve above all is Impressionism, a word which was specifically invented to meet the needs of their cause. We are certainly not going to advise them—that would be to insult them—to imitate the award winners of the [Ecole des] Beaux-Arts or the people who tie those pretty little bows in fabric shops, or other makers of trinkets. But if they are not careful,

(opposite)
Dancer scratching her back
c 1873–74 (detail cat 54)

> if they get it into their heads to go off in the wrong direction only to get more and more lost, then they'll inevitably end up in some sort of dubious competition with those painters of shop signs who work for Mr. Coal-Deliverer or Mr. Contract-Removalist.[32]

Despite the considerable controversy surrounding the first 'Impressionist' show, and a lack of sales,[33] a second was planned. Degas was one of 19 contributors to this follow-up exhibition, which opened on 15 April 1876 at the premises of the dealer Durand-Ruel, 11 rue le Peletier, Paris—near the newly established Opéra Garnier, in a fast developing quarter of Paris. Degas noted: 'The premises are less big than we need but admirably situated.'[34]

Degas had hoped that the impact of the first exhibition would prompt the Salon to be more inclusive and modern in its own selection. While this proved a vain hope, the second Impressionist show received widespread attention, including perceptive analysis by some of the most significant writers of the day—Edmond Duranty, Emile Zola and Stéphane Mallarmé—who commented that the work on display strongly reflected the influence of Manet.[35]

Among the detractors, Bertall (Charles-Albert, Vicomte d'Arnoux, Compte des Limoges-Saint-Saëns)—a prolific printmaker and one-time collaborator with Honoré de Balzac—fed the Parisians' appetite for satirical caricature by likening the artists to inmates in a madhouse:

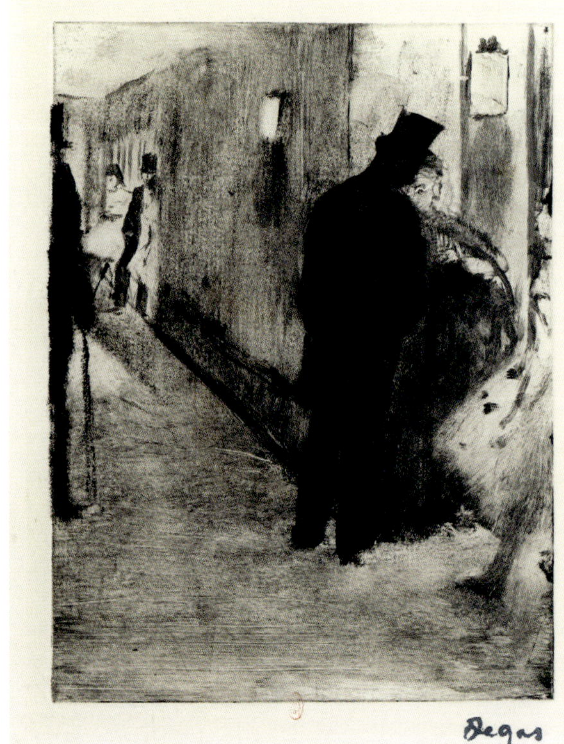

Ludovic Halévy talking to Madame Cardinal (Ludovic Halévy parlant á Madame Cardinal) 1876–77
monotype in black ink on white laid paper
first impression of two,
15.8 x 11.8 cm (plate)
Bibliothèque nationale de France, Paris Janis 200 / Cachin 59

(opposite)
A cotton office in New Orleans
1873 (detail cat 11)

> I've heard it said that on the rue le Peletier there's a mental asylum … It's mostly painters who are admitted there. Theirs is a sweet madness—it consists of taking up a brush that has been feverishly loaded up with the most garish of colours and rubbing it willy-nilly onto a series of white canvases … they wander around together, never like common, everyday artists arguing amongst themselves. Instead, while standing in front of each others' works, they affectionately shake each others hands, with tears of delight in their eyes as they plunge, headlong, into that sacred bliss of mutual admiration. These people … are called *the impressionists.*[36]

Charles Bigot, in *La Revue politique et littéraire,* considered the change in style more as a changing of the guard than a radical break with the past. To characterise it as anything else, such as a new art, was overstating the matter, and pretentious:

> I confess that it is not scandal that the artists of the rue le Peletier should be worried about. France is quick to be scandalised, and not so long ago it was Delacroix, Decamps, Corot, Rousseau and Millet who were scandalising the bourgeoisie. But the real question, as always, is to know whether one is a Rousseau, a Millet, a Corot, or a Delacroix, or not … The pretension of these newcomers is to claim that theirs is nothing less than the painting of the future. Their friends call them the impressionists because what they are trying to do above all is to render the impression of nature. Those less favourably inclined call them the intentionists, insinuating that their talent is made up of the same good intentions that pave the way to hell.[37]

The participants listed on the catalogue cover included Degas, Lepic, Renoir, Morisot, Monet, Pissarro, Sisley, Alphonse Legros and Gustave Caillebotte. This was the first inclusion of the independently wealthy Caillebotte, who was to become active in the organisation of the exhibitions and provide considerable financial support.

Degas' contributions again focused on modern life subjects: the café, the orchestra, washerwomen and dancers, as well as portraits, including a depiction of Edouard Manet's brother Eugène relaxing in a landscape.[38] He also showed his remarkable painting *A cotton office in New Orleans* 1873, illustrating the cotton business of his relatives with whom he stayed during a trip to New Orleans in 1872–73.

The emerging writer Emile Zola was ambivalent about Degas' ability to rival literature in the exploration of contemporary themes, and was critical of the artist's method of execution. While he acknowledged Degas as 'very taken with modernity, life indoors, and everyday models', Zola wrote disparagingly of *A cotton office in New Orleans,* finding the style 'half-way between a seascape and a plate from an illustrated

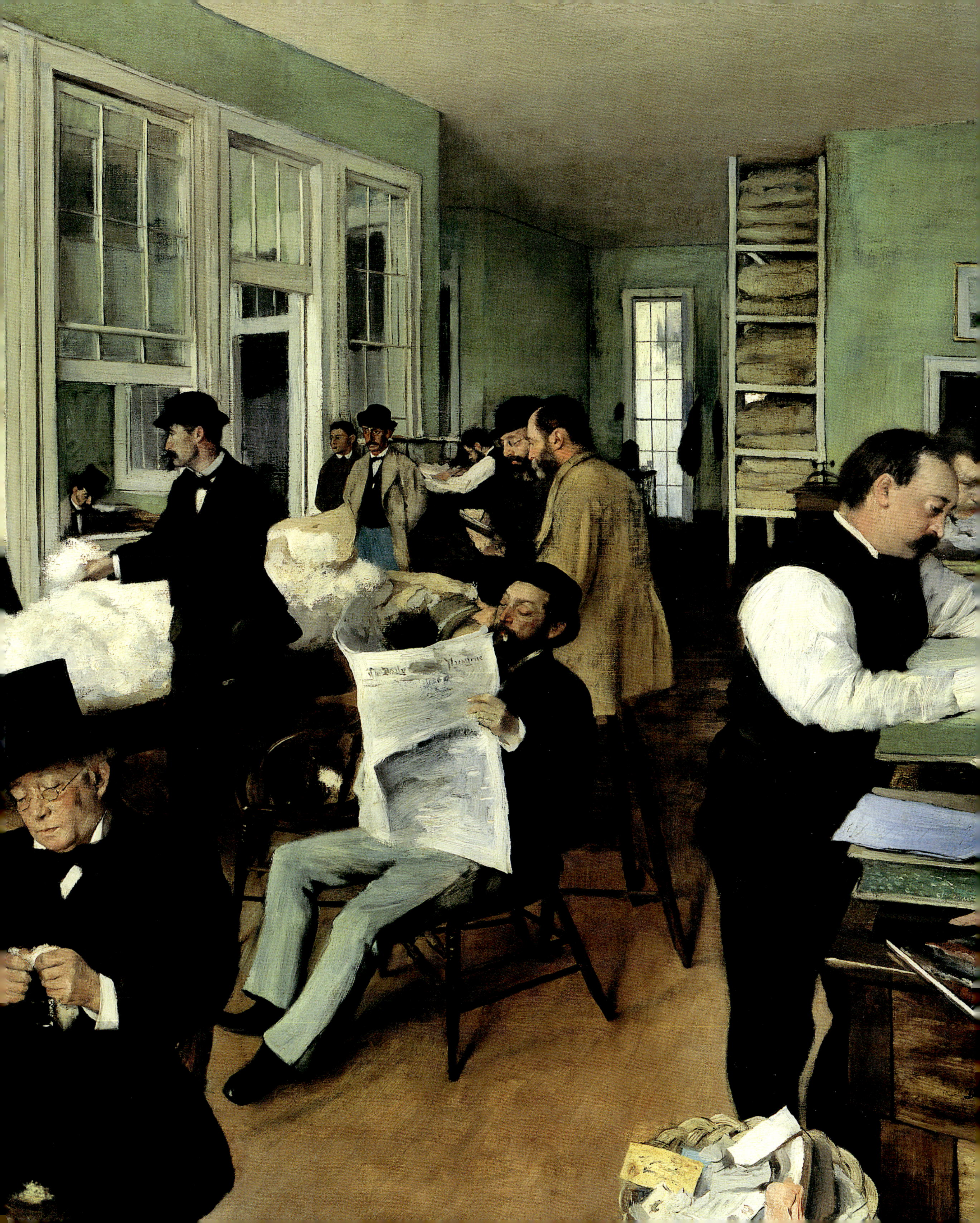

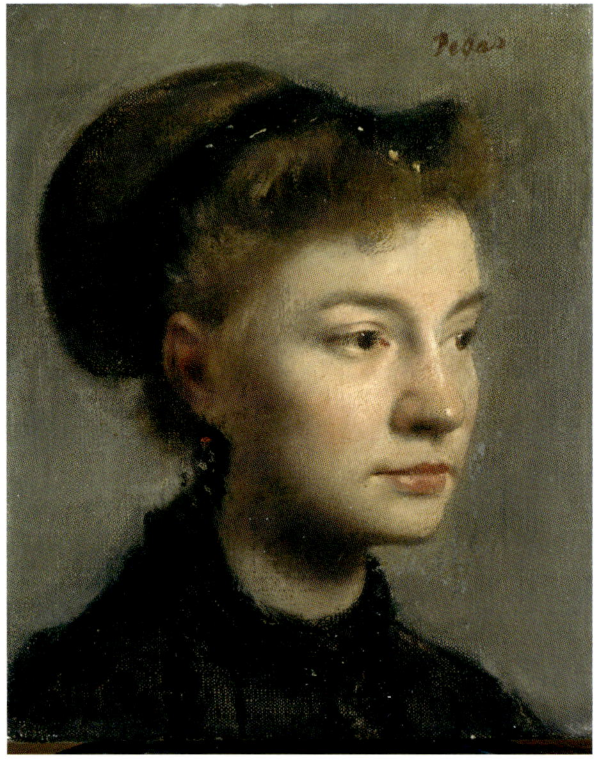

Portrait of a young woman (Portrait de jeune femme) 1867
oil on canvas, 27 x 22 cm
Musée d'Orsay, Paris
Acquisition: coll Georges Viau
Lemoisne 163

journal.'[39] He also judged Degas harshly for the finish of his work: 'What is annoying, though, is the way he spoils everything just at the moment he puts the finishing touches on a work … he has excellent artistic perceptions, but I'm afraid as a painter, he will never make it.'[40]

The critic Marius Chaumelin was dismissive of the Impressionists' rapid technique, which he termed the 'school of spots'. He considered Degas as distinct from this group, observing that his figures were not posed but portrayed as in everyday situations: 'They are grouped—or rather scattered just as you would see them in a wholesaler's shop on the rue du Sentier.'[41]

'Proximity does not create kinship'

A year later, in April 1877, the group exhibited again. In this third venture the title 'Impressionists' appeared above the entrance to their exhibition premises, although not in the catalogue itself.

Caillebotte, who was providing financial support to the group, had arranged for Monet, Renoir, Sisley, Manet, Pissarro and Degas to dine with him at his home in advance of the exhibition—a diplomatic triumph in itself given the differing views held by these artists. Nonetheless Manet continued to disappoint, preferring to continue submitting his work to the Salon.[42] Caillebotte also organised the venue, an apartment at 6 rue le Peletier, the same street as the second installation.

Despite the artists' differences, this venture proved the most stylistically coherent of the three exhibitions to date, with a number of large cityscapes providing a focus. Degas, however, was displayed in a gallery space of his own rather than being shown as part of the group. This arrangement may have been partly due to the smaller scale of his works compared to the imposing dimensions of some of the other compositions, particularly Caillebotte's *Paris street: rainy day*, Renoir's *Ball at the Moulin de la Galette* and Monet's *Interior view of the Gare Saint-Lazare*.[43] The separation was also perceptible in Degas' choice of subject, and manner of execution. Degas contributed some 23 works, including *Portrait of Monsieur H.R.*—a depiction 'in front of his factory' of Henri Rouart, a friend since their student days;[44] and, for the first time, he showed some recent monotypes and pastels over monotypes.

The subjects of the monotypes relate to Ludovic Halévy's satirical short stories about the Cardinal family—Monsieur and Madame Cardinal and their daughters Pauline and Virginie—and their unsavoury encounters backstage at the Paris Opéra.[45] In response, the writer Jules Claretie was fulsome in his praise of Degas, commenting that his drawings were 'life itself':

> Of all of those in this exhibition there is one interesting exception, a man of real talent, an artist of high esteem. And that man is M. Degas. His work is truly unique. He doesn't resemble anyone. The only thing he resembles is the truth. It wouldn't be necessary to show him on his own to have him noticed, or for him to create an *impression*, to cause a sensation. He knows, and captures, what goes on in the wings of a theatre, and in the dance halls, the heady seduction of these little bits of girls learning to dance with their skirts aswirl … His drawings have an extraordinary quality. They are life itself. Both Goya and Gavarni are present in such an artist.[46]

Why Degas also chose to show in this exhibition a painting from 1867—the wistful and accomplished *Portrait of a young woman*—is unclear.[47] The historian and critic Paul Mantz pondered on its inclusion, and the relationship of Degas to the other artists:

> It is hard to understand why exactly Edgar Degas categorised himself as an Impressionist. He has a distinct personality and stands apart from the group of so-called innovators … Presented on an easel and under a carefully chosen ray of light is the portrait of a woman that evidently was not painted for the good cause, as it is dated 1867. The work is serious, with some Italian reminiscences … We will not ask ourselves

how the Florentine of ten years ago has become today's Impressionist. Proximity does not create kinship.[48]

'There is someone who feels as I do'

It would have irritated Degas that others in the group were identifying themselves as Impressionists and that the designation was beginning to appear regularly in reviews and other commentaries. For the fourth Impressionist group-exhibition, he was determined that the term 'Independents' should appear on the poster advertising the event. In his notebook he had drawn poster designs: the second draft included the title 'The fourth exhibition of Independent, Realist and Impressionist artists', but this was edited back to 'Independents' in the final draft.[49]

Caillebotte, Pissarro and Degas organised this exhibition, in which the work of 16 artists was included. A newcomer, Paul Gauguin, was invited to exhibit by Pissarro and Degas just days before the opening. He accepted with pleasure, and agreed to abide by the conditions that precluded exhibiting at the Salon that year.[50] At such short notice, Gauguin submitted an accomplished and rather conventional marble bust of his young son Emil.[51] Degas was keen to extend the stylistic range of the exhibition and again invited Bracquemond to join the group, as well as Madame Marie Bracquemond and Federico Zandomeneghi—all devotees of Degas.

This fourth exhibition took place in 1879, though Caillebotte, who had promised to fund it, had argued for a date in 1878 to take advantage of the drawing power of the *Exposition Universelle* in Paris, from May to November of that year. Pissarro agreed that this timing would be helpful to their cause;[52] but Degas argued that an exhibition in 1878 would be overlooked, and he successfully held out for the following year. The show opened on 10 April 1879 in a new exhibition space at 28 avenue de l'Opéra.

Several members of the group who had exhibited previously did not take part. Berthe Morisot, who had contributed to the first three exhibitions, excused herself because she was pregnant—although this may have been a polite way of declining to exhibit that year. Sisley and Renoir also broke ranks, so as to be able to submit work to the Salon. Monet, too, seemed to be having doubts. Just one month before the exhibition opened he wrote to his wealthy patron, the art collector Dr George de Bellio: 'I am absolutely sickened and demoralised by this life I've been leading for so long … I hear that my friends are preparing another exhibition this year but I must discount the possibility of participating in it since I have nothing worth showing.'[53] As it turned out however, with Caillebotte's emotional, organisational and financial support, Monet did participate, though he remained aloof and disengaged from the event itself.[54]

Another newcomer, American-born Mary Cassatt, joined the group in 1879 at the request of Degas—who was to become something of a mentor to her. On seeing her painting *Ida* at the Salon of 1874, Degas had commented: 'There is someone who feels as I do.' For her part, Cassatt greatly admired Degas: '[H]ow well I remember … seeing for the first time Degas' pastels in the window of a picture dealer on the boulevard Haussmann. I used to go and flatten my nose against that window and absorb all I could of his art. It changed my life. I saw art then as I wanted to see it.'[55]

'Parisian wit and Impressionist audacity'

The art on display in the 1879 exhibition was diverse in style, making for an exhibition that lacked coherence; the new themes and techniques of earlier exhibitions were largely absent. Degas contributed some key works as well as some painted fans, but he failed to deliver all the works he had

Paul Gavarni
Edmond et Jules de Goncourt 1853
lithograph, 19.2 x 16.2 cm (comp), 37.4 x 26.4 cm (sheet)
National Gallery of Australia, Canberra
Purchased 1986

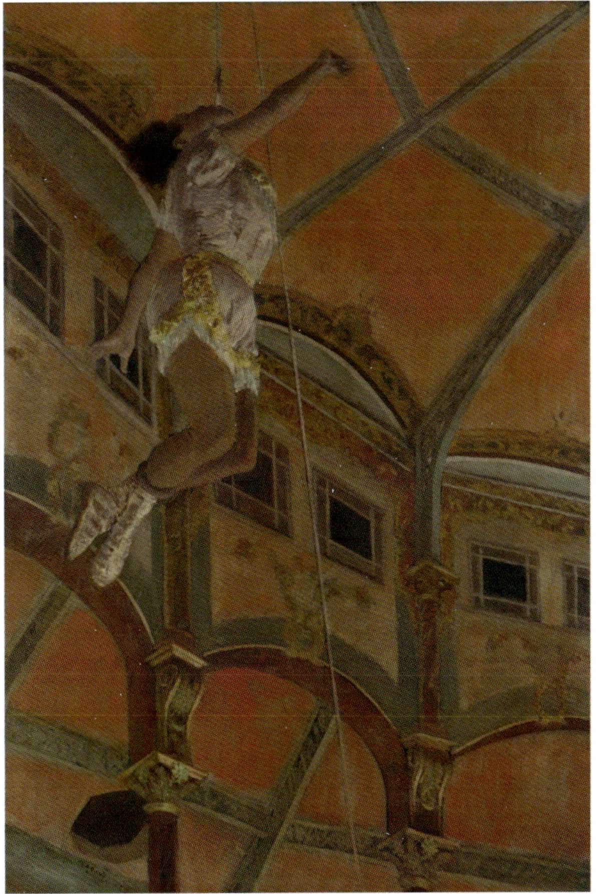

Miss La La at the Cirque Fernando (Mlle La La au Cirque Fernando) 1879
oil on canvas, 117.2 x 77.5 cm
The National Gallery, London
Lemoisne 522

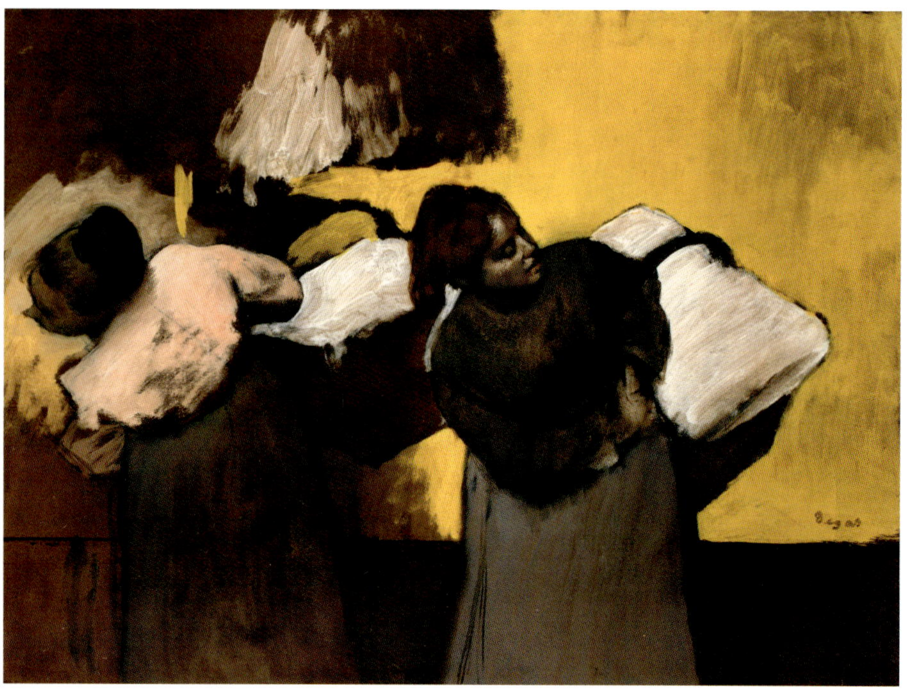

Laundresses carrying linen (Blanchisseuses portant du linge)
1876
peinture à l'essence on paper laid on canvas 46 x 61 cm
Christie's London, 28 March 1988, lot 16
Lemoisne 410

promised. His fellow-organiser, Caillebotte, complained to Monet: 'Don't believe … that Degas sent in his twenty-seven or thirty items. This morning there were eight canvases by him on hand. He is indeed vexing. But you have to admit that he has a lot of talent.'[56]

Degas' growing obsession with the depiction of movement and three-dimensional form was evident in his painting *Miss La La at the Cirque Fernando*[57]—a thoroughly modern subject. In fact, he was instrumental in the adoption of the circus as an appropriate subject for art. In this he followed Honoré Daumier, and was to lead the way for other artists—including Jules Chéret, Georges Seurat, Henri de Toulouse-Lautrec and, later, Pablo Picasso.

Miss La La captivated the critic Arsène Houssaye (writing under the nom de plume F.-C. de Sèyne in the journal *L'artiste*), who praised the 'very individual originality' of her creator and his new brighter palette:

> Parisian wit and Impressionist audacity vigorously set off by a fanciful Japanese touch: such are the elements that Degas is able to combine to create very marked, very individual originality. Degas searches out mysterious and wild effects. No one knows better than he how to use silvery sparkling lights, pale opalescences, glowing incandescent reds, coppery radiations and twilit half tones.[58]

Degas also took inspiration from Daumier in another painting on display, *Laundresses carrying linen*,[59] both in the subject of the washerwomen and in the bold lines of the forms. While he had absorbed the style and theme of Daumier—a favourite caricaturist, along with Paul Gavarni—Degas was sufficiently artistically mature to have developed his own style, one of refinement and simplicity, which stood him apart from the Impressionist group. In a review of the exhibition, Amand Silvestre observed this contrast:

> Let's move on to something significant. Where we'll find this to its highest degree is in the all too few canvases of M. Degas. With M. Degas, we always find the same process of synthesis united with a feeling for truth that is wholly admirable. Look at his laundresses bent under the weight of their baskets. There is a distant echo of Daumier here. But on closer inspection there is more than just Daumier. These paintings reflect a kind of mastery, the influences of which are difficult to define. They are the most eloquent refutation of the mishmash of colour and the confusion of effects that painting does to death these days.[60]

'The holy phalanx is no longer up to strength'

The fifth of the group's exhibitions opened on 1 April 1880, at 10 rue des Pyramides—which was to all intents and purposes a building site, busy with workmen. Eighteen artists contributed works—but now it was Monet's turn to decline, choosing to submit to the Salon instead: 'It is not my inclination to do this, but it is unfortunate that the press and the public have not taken seriously to our exhibition, preferring instead the official emporium.'[61]

The disintegration of the group was now evident, and there was a clear split between the Impressionists and the supporters of Degas. The fifth exhibition was resultantly a disorderly affair, with the artists showing their work individually rather than in a group display as on earlier occasions. The sense of momentum seemed to have dissipated, and much of the work was criticised as lacklustre, less provocative and more conventional. Henry Havard, writing for *Le Siècle*, predicted the demise of the new painting: 'Let us acknowledge that Impressionism is dying. The holy phalanx is no longer up to strength. Degas is still without disciples, and Pissarro generates no pupils. In addition, the former leaders are deserting. Claude Monet has gone over to the enemy; this year he exhibits at the Salon.'[62]

In contrast, Joris-Karl Huysmans provided the most perceptive and favourable assessment of the exhibition in a lengthy essay, republished in 1883 in a collection of his exhibition commentaries, *L'art moderne*. A large part of his commentary concerning the 1880 exhibition was devoted to Degas, who he compared to the Naturalist writers

Jules and Edmond de Goncourt. Huysmans characterised Degas as 'a painter of modern life … a painter who does not draw from others, who does not mimic anybody, who carries the taste of a completely new art and develops an execution completely new.'[63]

Ten works by Degas, and some etchings (the number not specified), were listed in the catalogue for this fifth exhibition, including his early enigmatic masterpiece, the classically inspired *Young Spartans exercising* c 1860–62 (reworked 1880), and his wax sculpture, *Little dancer aged fourteen* of 1880—neither of which however appeared.[64] Degas installed a glass display case that remained empty for the duration of the exhibition, for some reason not seeing fit to show the sculpture that year. (The glass case would reappear in 1881, in the sixth exhibition—at first empty again, before Degas installed the *Little dancer* with dramatic effect.)

'When on earth will they stop the headlines?'

Behind the scenes of the 1880 exhibition, a schism had developed between Degas and Caillebotte. Mutual ill feeling came to a head in an argument over the listing of artists' names on the exhibition poster. Degas considered this to be unseemly self-aggrandisement on the part of the artists;[65] Caillebotte disagreed, and won the day. This rankled with Degas, and in a letter to Bracquemond he complained:

> [The exhibition] is opening on April 1st, the posters will be up tomorrow or Monday. They are in bright red letters on a green ground. There was a big fight with Caillebotte as to whether or not to put [up] the names. I had to give in and let him put them up. When on earth will they stop the headlines? … Next year, I promise you, I shall take steps to see that this does not continue. I am miserable about it, humiliated.[66]

With the planning for the sixth exhibition, the two artists were at loggerheads again. An infuriated Caillebotte wrote to Pissarro: 'Degas has brought disorganisation among us … He spends his time orating at the Nouvelle-Athènes, when he would be much better occupied in turning out a few more pictures. No one denies that he is a hundred times right in what he says and that he talks about painting with infinite wit and good sense.'[67]

While acknowledging the older artist's intellect and artistic skills, Caillebotte remained unforgiving over Degas' denying his fellow impecunious artists the chance to achieve further sales by exhibiting at the Salon or elsewhere while participating in the group-shows. Degas was adamant in this view, despite his own financial problems. (His brother René had accumulated considerable debts, which Degas and his brother-in-law Henri Fevre had to repay.[68]) Caillebotte also argued against Degas' inclusion of artists who he considered second-tier, believing their work diminished the quality of the exhibitions: 'Today he says he needs to earn a living, and he will not grant that Renoir and Monet have such a need … He pretends to have Raffaëlli because Monet and Renoir had defected and we had to have someone. But he has been tormenting Raffaëlli to join us for the past three years … In 1878 [sic] he brought in Zandomeneghi, Bracquemond, Madame Bracquemond.' With some irony, Caillebotte declared: 'What a phalanx of fighters for the cause of Realism.'[69] The virulence of these complaints caused the more measured Pissarro to remind his colleague that Degas in earlier years had invited the then unknown Caillebotte to join their exhibitions. Pissarro's attempt at conciliation failed, however, and Caillebotte would withdraw from the sixth exhibition.

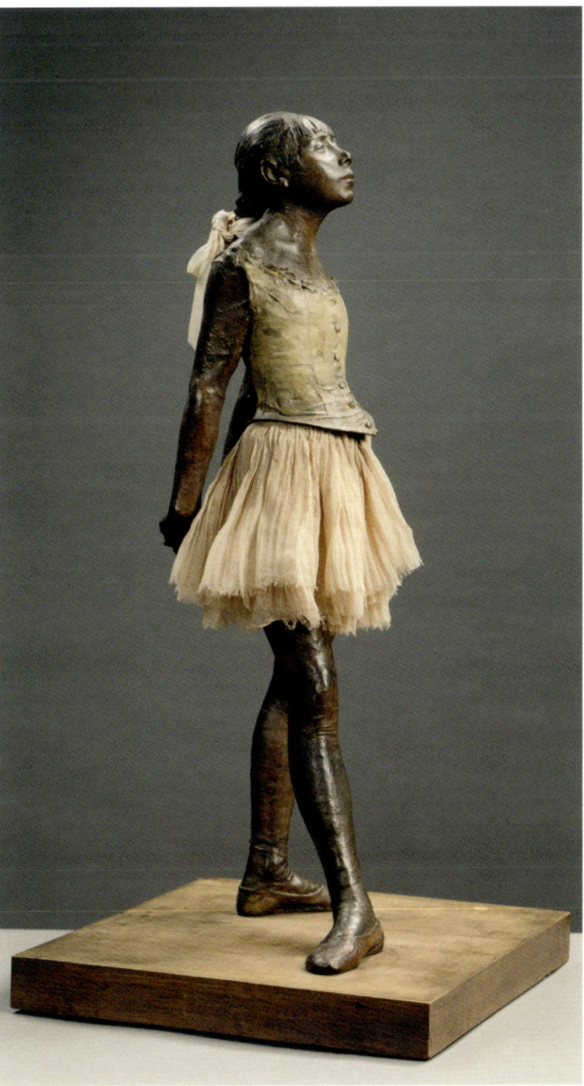

Little dancer aged fourteen
(La petite danseuse de quatorze ans)
modelled 1880–81; cast 1920–21
bronze, gauze and satin
cast P of 29
98 x 35.2 x 24.5 cm
Musée d'Orsay, Paris
Czestochowski and Pingeot 73

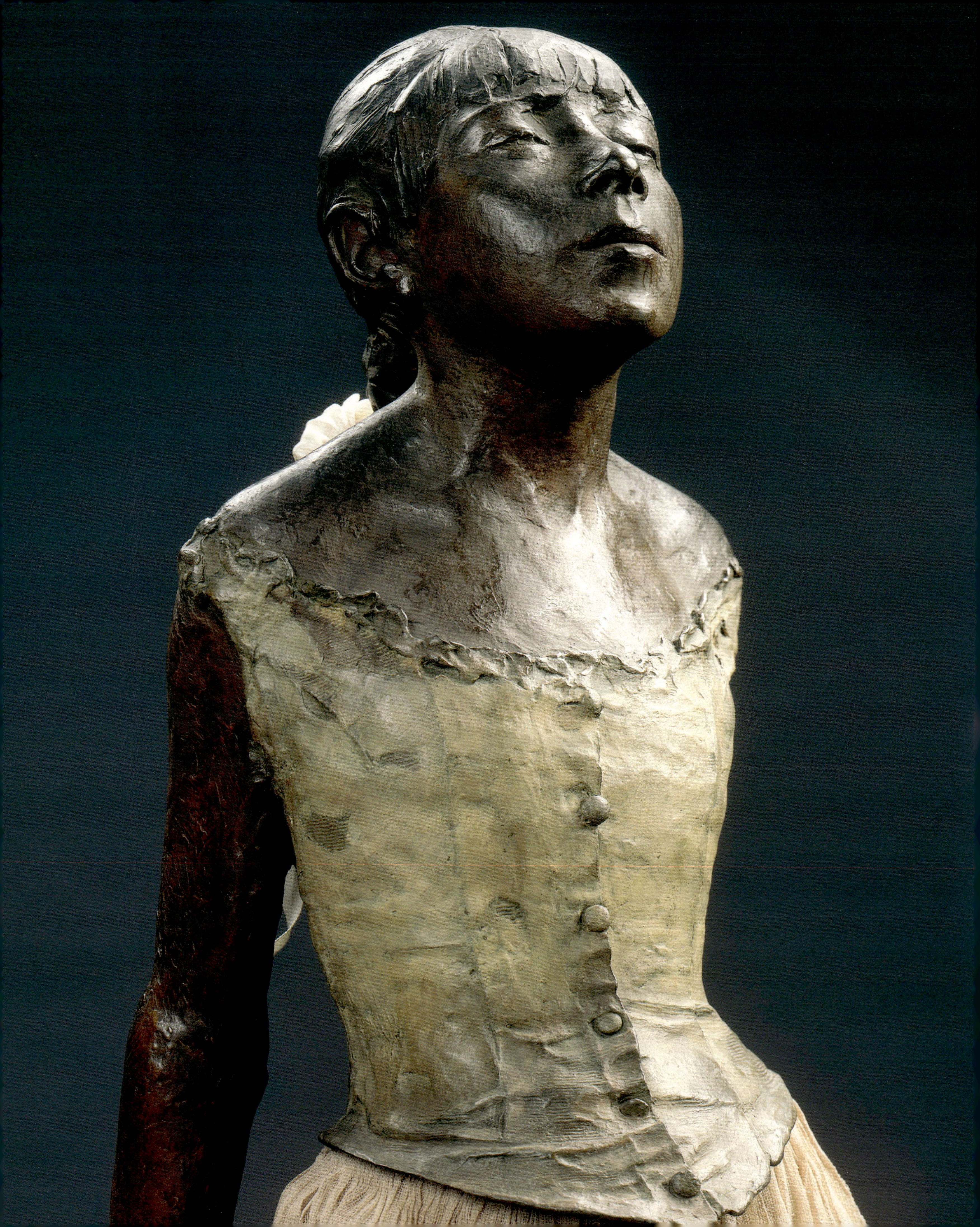

'Little flower of the gutter'

In the 1881 exhibition, Degas caused a sensation with one of his works—an almost life-sized figure of a little dancer, the only sculpture he was ever to exhibit in his career. As mentioned, at the opening of this sixth exhibition on 2 April, just as in 1880, an empty glass case was installed in the space. The absence of the work within it provoked a sense of eager anticipation, as noted by Jules Claretie in *Le Temps*:

> Monsieur Degas was supposed to exhibit a dancer made of wax. But at the moment, all we have is the glass case that is destined to contain and protect the statuette, which is said to be charming. He *has* sent some interesting drawings, but what we are all *really* waiting to see is his sculpture. But he's such a tease that he hasn't sent it.[70]

After an intriguing interlude, the wax figure of the *Little dancer aged fourteen* dramatically appeared. The art world was astonished. Degas had produced a sculpture, both steeped in tradition and thoroughly modern in its form and use of materials—prefiguring the idea of assemblage found in modern sculptural practice. Claretie grasped the modern nature of the work, while noting its debt to traditional forms:

> Besides some very interesting drawings—profiles of murderers and some riveting studies of the low life prey of the courts, [Degas] has on display a dancer sculpted in wax whose naturalism is at once both strangely seductive and peculiarly disturbing. It reminds me of those polychromatic Spanish sculptures but with something very pointedly modern, very Parisian about it. The lecherous little snout on this barely pubescent young girl, this little flower of the gutter, is unforgettable.[71]

Degas had been interested in physiognomical studies for some years, encouraged by his good friend Ludovic Lepic. In a notebook dated 1877 he depicted the head of a café-concert singer with the features of a monkey.[72] This interest drew him in 1880 to attend a trial for murder; and in his pursuit of a criminal physiognomy he produced pastel profiles of charged murderers, visually linking Parisian low life with the animal world.[73] This 'frightening' realism was applied to the *Little dancer aged fourteen*, when Degas fashioned in wax the 'Neanderthal-like' features of his model, the humble dancer Marie van Goethem.[74] (Marie was one of the many young dancers at the Opéra who came to be known as 'little rats'—a suggestion of their low-life origins and the fact they were often seen scurrying behind the scenes.)

Those who didn't understand Degas' new aspiration for realism viewed his sculpture with distaste. Henry Trianon admonished the artist for exhibiting a subject he considered more suited to a scientific institution:

> If he wants to show us a statuette of a dancer, he chooses her from among the most odiously ugly; he makes it the standard of horror and bestiality. And, yes, certainly among the dregs of the dance schools are poor girls who look like this young monster … she is sturdy and carefully studied, but what is the use of these things in the art of sculpture? Put them in a museum of zoology, anthropology, or physiology, fine; but, in a museum of art, forget it.[75]

In a perceptive analysis published in *Le Temps*, Paul Mantz recognised the radical nature of the sculpture, and acknowledged Degas' intellectual pursuit:

> The only true sculptor of the Intransigent academy is Degas. With a few pastels that will not increase his renown, he shows the *Little dancer aged fourteen*, the wax statuette which has been promised for so long … The piece is finished and let us acknowledge right away that the result is nearly terrifying … The unhappy child is standing, wearing a cheap gauze dress, a blue ribbon at the waist, her feet in supple shoes which make the first exercises of elementary choreography easier. She is working. Back arched and already a little tired, she stretches her arms behind her. Formidable because she is thoughtless, with bestial effrontery she moves her face forward, or rather her little muzzle—and this word is completely correct because this poor little girl is the beginning of a rat. Why is she so ugly? Why is her forehead, half-covered by her hair, marked already, like her lips, with a profoundly vicious character?
>
> Degas is no doubt a moralist: he perhaps knows things about the dancers of the future that we do not. He gathered from the espaliers of the theater a precociously depraved flower, and he shows her to us withered before her time. The intellectual result has been reached.[76]

'Chasing away the gods'

The conflict concerning participation, and the artistic direction of the group-shows, continued after the 1881 exhibition. Gauguin in particular was highly critical of Raffaëlli's work. In a letter to Pissarro on 14 December 1881, he complained:

> Last night Degas told me in anger that he would hand in his resignation rather than send Raffaëlli away. If I examine calmly your situation after ten years during which you undertook to organize these exhibitions, I immediately perceive that the number of impressionists has progressed, their talent increased, their influence too. Yet on Degas' side—and thanks only to his volition—the tendency has been getting worse: each year another impressionist has left and been replaced by nullities and pupils of the Ecole [des Beaux-Arts].

(opposite)
Little dancer aged fourteen
(*La petite danseuse de quatorze ans*)
modelled 1880–81; cast 1920–21
(detail)
bronze, gauze and satin
cast P of 29
98 x 35.2 x 24.5 cm
Musée d'Orsay, Paris
Czestochowski and Pingeot 73

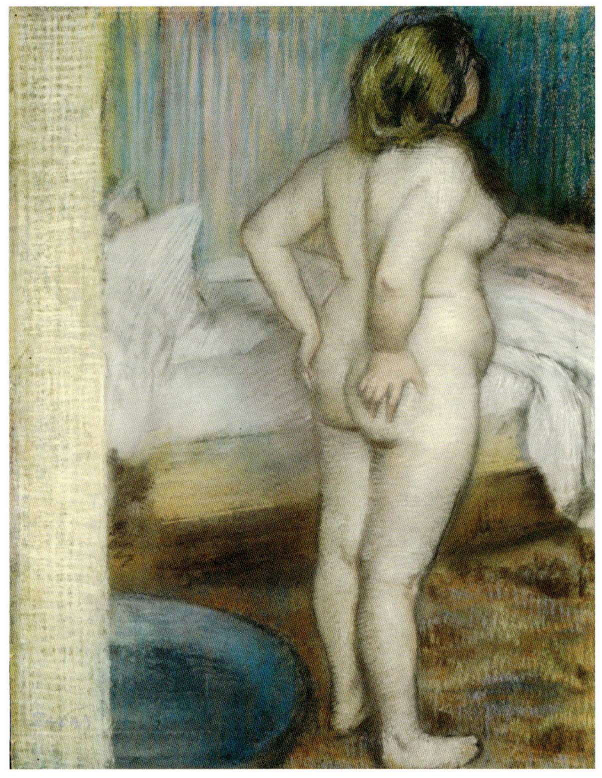

The morning bath (Etude de nu (Femme à son lever) (La Boulangère)) c 1886
pastel on buff wove paper, affixed to original pulpboard mount 67 x 52.1 cm
The Henry and Rose Pearlman Foundation; on long-term loan to the Princeton University Art Museum
Lemoisne 877

Gauguin commented that, as far as his own participation was concerned, he could not continue to 'serve as a buffoon for M. Raffaëlli and Company'.[77]

With Gauguin's threat of possible withdrawal, Caillebotte's absence in the 1881 exhibition, and with others of the Impressionist fold no longer active within the group, Pissarro sought to reorganise affairs without Degas' followers. For this reason Degas, while he had remained a staunch supporter of the six exhibitions held since 1874, chose not to show his work at the seventh exhibition in 1882, though he continued to remain a financial member of the group.[78]

When he did return—to take part in the eighth and final exhibition, in 1886—Degas failed to display all the works that were listed against his name in the catalogue. His contribution of a group of nudes in pastel drew close attention. (Degas listed 10, but he may have shown less.[79])

Pissarro's protégés Georges Seurat and Paul Signac were both major contributors to this final event, and Pissarro's own work was greatly influenced by these two young artists. The very radical nature of Seurat's *Sunday afternoon on the island of la Grande Jatte*[80] was clearly evident in terms of scale, the application of pure colour and use of complementary colours, and the frieze-like forms of the figures. Despite this, it was not Seurat's work or that of his stylistic colleagues Signac and Pissarro that achieved critical notoriety. Instead, much of the criticism was levelled at Degas for his images of the nude women. Many of the visitors who flocked to see the exhibition were highly amused by what they saw. George Moore described the reaction at the opening as 'boisterous laughter, exaggerated in the hope of giving as much pain as possible'.[81]

Degas' pastels of women bathing, drying themselves and barely clothed, were exquisitely rendered, but purposefully devoid of any allusion to a classical or romanticised past—his women were contemporary, without beautification. Some commentators condemned his approach as an aesthetic of ugliness and viewed the subjects as examples of coarse low life. JM Michel, writing in *La petite Gazette*, observed that the Realist school had 'noisily chased away the gods', and that 'one really must not ask it to pluck Amphitrite out of the ocean or to dry the hair of Venus Astarte'; and he linked the portrayal of the nudes to Zola's tragic heroine of the demimonde, in his novel *Nana*: 'No! Nana bathing, washing herself with a sponge … arming herself for battle—this is the Impressionist ideal.'[82]

Maurice Hermel, in *La France libre*, provided a sensitive appraisal of Degas' *Nude drying herself*:

> In a corner of some broadly sketched greenery is a large bather in the open air who slides over her upraised elbows, the white line that will cover her ample nudity … Consider the delicious harmony of all the elements. The visual joy of the whiteness of the slip, shot through with tender green and lilac; consider the flesh, pink in the light, brown in the shadow, infinitely shaded by the ambient atmosphere, that has substance and its own quivering life, and is all truth embellished by the rarest colours.

But Hermel acknowledged that admirers of classical delicacy and beauty would be blind to those qualities: 'You will understand then, that what lovers of porcelain nymphs see in this beautiful piece is nothing but a vulgar slattern.'[83]

Joris-Karl Huysmans dwelt on extensive physical detail in his analysis of the nudes:

> [Degas] chooses someone short, fat and pot-bellied; in other words, someone whose graceful curves have been drowned under rolls and rolls of fat; who from a sculptural point of view, seems to have lost all sense of any inner supporting structure, all sense of line; who has become in life, independently of whatever social class she may have actually belonged to, a sausage maker, a butcher's wife; a creature, in a word, whose vulgarity of form and coarseness of features suggests the virtues of abstinence; who is, indeed, utterly repulsive.

> There's a redhead, stuffed and fed to the gills, bending her back in such a way that her pelvis arches against the tensed flesh of her buttocks. It's almost as if she's about to break into two as she tries to bring her arm up to her shoulder to sponge her back … Another, having finished her household chores, is shown leaning with her hands on her ample rump, stretching in an almost masculine way, like a man who stands in front of a fire and lifts his coat-tails in order to warm himself … But in addition to that particular note of scorn and loathing which it has to be acknowledged is present in his work, there is also this unforgettable truth in the way in which his drawing strips his subjects bare. His drawing is both unrestrained and self-assured, and is born as much out of a fiery, controlled lucidity, as a cool, measured intensity.[84]

Paul Adam, in *La Revue contemporaine*, also found the subjects unsightly, but like Huysmans recognised the quality of Degas' draughtsmanship, commenting that his nudes were 'consummate exercises in foreshortening':

> These nude women who are in the process of washing themselves or sponging themselves down, with their froglike poses, their thighs, their backs, their hips twisted, bulged through constant squatting, are consummate exercises in foreshortening. And in the way Degas draws the fat bourgeois woman getting ready for bed one can see the exquisitely pure and self-assured line of Ingres, whose student Degas once was.[85]

'An Ingres, and a Delacroix'

After the entrenched conservatism of much French art of the mid nineteenth century, a new, contemporary art had emerged and developed in several directions—notably along the path pursued by Monet and the Impressionists. Degas, however, was to move in another direction. Such a duality had been astutely observed as early as the mid 1870s by Paul Mantz, who saw both Monet and Degas as inheritors of France's masters from the Neoclassical and Romantic ages:

> One of the methods that Degas loves to use is to carve up the canvas arbitrarily—to cut off the arms or legs, for example. A painting is supposed to have the feeling that it hasn't been composed. I don't want to predict what the future might hold for the artists of the rue le Peletier. Will they be regarded as masters? I think they will. So Degas will occupy the place that Ingres occupies for us now, while Monet, who is the brilliant colourist of the group, will take over from Delacroix.[86]

Looking back, it was during the series of eight Impressionist exhibitions between 1874 and 1886 that French art came of age. In spite of factional schisms and individual difficulties, by presenting their work in an independent forum the contributing artists were able to showcase a new art, which in turn had a profound impact on later generations of artists, into the twentieth century.

Over the years of his participation in these public events, Degas evolved as an artist, developing his unique modern style and his thoroughly modern subject matter. This was recognised by many of the critics who viewed and commented on his work. Degas' art became more exploratory in composition and in execution as he matured; at the same time his subjects took on the appearance of greater intimacy and informality.

Unlike other artists associated with the Impressionist exhibitions, Degas did not set out to capture the fleeting surface appearance, or to work *en plein air*. Despite the spontaneous appearance of his subjects, his art was carefully considered and composed, with a sense of liveliness achieved through thoughtful distillation of favourite motifs. Of all the artists associated with the group-exhibitions, Degas successfully absorbed the rich lessons of the old masters and applied these in his modern day subjects, leading him to his own singular style.

Notes

Unless otherwise specified, all translations are by Mark Henshaw, Curator, International Art, National Gallery of Australia, Canberra—drawn from the original French texts republished in Ruth Berson (ed), *The new painting: Impressionism, 1874–1886: documentation*, 2 vols, Fine Arts Museum of San Francisco, San Francisco, 1996.

1 Jules-Antoine Castagnary, 'Exposition du boulevard des Capucines: Les Impressionnistes', *Le Siècle*, 29 April 1874, p 3.

2 Société anonyme – a term in French law to do with limited public companies. Degas, Monet, Pissarro, Sisley, Morisot and Cézanne formed the Société Anonyme (coopérative à capital variable)—of artists, painters, sculptors, printmakers etc—on 27 December 1873. See 'Degas: chronology of the artist's life', online at metmuseum.org/explore/Degas, viewed August 2008.

3 For information on the Salon, see Gérard Georges Lemaire, *Histoire du Salon de peintre*, Klincksieck, Paris, 2004, ch 2; and William Hauptman, 'Juries, protests and counter-exhibitions before 1850', *The Art Bulletin*, March 1985, vol 67, no 1, pp 95–109. See also Albert Boime, *The Academy and French painting in the nineteenth century*, Phaidon, London, 1971; Jean-François Heim et al, *Les Salons de peinture de la révolution française 1779–1799*, CAC Sarl, Paris, 1989; Dominique Lobstein, *Les Salons au XIXe siècle: Paris, capitale des arts*, Editions de la Martinière, Paris, 2006.

4 EC, 'Chronique: Beaux-arts: expositions de peintres modernes', *Revue de France*, vol 10, April 1874, pp 254–55.

5 Castagnary, *Le Siècle*, p 3.

6 See Stephen F Eisenman, 'The intransigent artist or how the Impressionists got their name', in Charles S Moffett, Ruth Berson and Barbara Lee Williams et al, *The new painting: Impressionism 1874–1886*, National Gallery of Art, Washington, 1986, pp 51–59.

7 Degas to James Tissot, 1874, in Marcel Guérin (ed), *Edgar Germain Hilaire Degas: letters*, Bruno Cassirer, Oxford, 1947, p 39.

8 Théophile Thoré, *Salons de W Bürger 1861 à 1868*, Paris, 1870, 2 vols, p 369. See also Gary Tinterow, 'Raphael replaced: the triumph of Spanish painting in France', in Gary Tinterow and Geneviève Lacambre (eds), *Manet/Velázquez: the French taste for Spanish painting*, The Metropolitan Museum of Art, New York, 2003, pp 49–50, n 124.

9 Edouard Manet, *Luncheon on the grass* (*Déjeuner sur l'herbe*) 1863 (listed as *Le bain* in the 1863 Salon catalogue), Musée d'Orsay, Paris.

10 Duranty was co-founder of the monthly journal *Le Réalisme*, published between July 1856 and May 1857.

11 Edmond Duranty, *La nouvelle peinture: à propos du groupe d'artistes qui expose dans les galeries Durand-Ruel*, E Dentu, Paris, 1876.

12 Claude Monet, *Le Temps*, November 1900, republished in Michael Howard (ed), *The Impressionists by themselves*, The Chancellor Press, London, 1992, p 28.

13 On 19 July 1870, the French government declared war on Prussia and hostilities commenced, with the confederation of German states coming to the aid of William I of Prussia. Degas enlisted in the National Guard in September. In the fighting he lost a friend, Joseph Cuvelier, and he suffered permanent damage to his own eyesight, which plagued him in later years. The siege of Paris by the German armies resulted in the capitulation of the city in January 1871, and the surrender of the French in February; peace was negotiated by the French National Assembly at Versailles, but in March rebellious Parisians organised a revolutionary government, the Paris Commune. The Communards were defeated by the French army in May 1871—the last week in May became known as *La semaine sanglante* (the blood-soaked week).

14 Painted by Pierre Puvis de Chavannes, 1874–78.

15 Noted by Paul Tucker, 'The first Impressionist exhibition in context', in Moffett et al, p 101, with further details, p 115, n 35.

16 Paul Tucker, 'The first Impressionist exhibition and Monet's Impression, sunrise: a tale of timing, commerce and patriotism', *Art History*, vol 7, no 4, December 1984, p 466.

17 Degas submitted works to the Salon between 1865 and 1870; his open letter suggesting improvements was published in *Paris Journal*, 12 April 1870, see Richard Kendall (ed), *Degas by himself: drawings, prints, paintings, writings*, Little, Brown & Co, Boston ,1987, pp 99–100.

18 In Moffett et al, many of the exhibits for the Impressionist exhibitions are identified and noted next to reproductions of the exhibition catalogues. Degas did not always show all the works he listed in the catalogues.

19 The term was coined by Leroy in relation to Monet's painting *Impression: sunrise* 1873, which Leroy believed to be unfinished and sketchy, an 'impression' only: Louis Leroy, *Le Charivari*, 25 April 1874, pp 79–80.

20 Degas to Félix Braquemond, 1874, in Guérin (ed), p 38.

21 Tucker, in Moffett et al, p 105.

22 Paul-Armand Silvestre, 'Chronique des beaux-arts: physiologie du refuse—l'exposition des révoltés', *L'Opinion nationale*, 22 April 1874, pp 2–3.

23 Villiers de l'Isle-Adam, writing under the nom de plume C de Malte, 'Exposition de la société anonyme des artistes peintres, sculpteurs, graveurs et lithographes', *Paris à l'eaux-fortes*, 19 April 1874, pp 12–13.

24 Philippe Burty, 'Exposition de la société anonyme des artistes', *La Republique française*, 25 April 1874, p 2.

25 Emile Cardon, 'Avant le Salon', *La Presse*, 28 April 1874, p 2.

26 Emile Cardon, 'Avant le Salon: l'exposition des révoltés', *La Presse*, 29 April 1874, p 3.

27 Published in *Le Siècle*, 29 April 1874.

28 Castagnary, *Le Siècle*, p 3.

29 Etienne Carjat, 'L'Exposition du boulevard des Capucines', *Le Patriote français*, 27 April 1874, p 3.

30 Marc de Montifaud (Emile de Montifaud), 'Exposition du boulevard des Capucines', *L'Artiste*, 1 May 1874, pp 307–13.

31 '*Ah! Giotto! Laisse-moi voir Paris, et toi, Paris laisse-moi voir Giotto!*': notebook 22, p 5, reprinted in Theodore Reff, *The notebooks of Edgar Degas: a catalogue of the thirty-eight notebooks in the Bibliothèque nationale and other collections*, 2 vols, Hacker Art Books, New York ,1985, vol 1, p 111. This notebook, which Degas used in Paris and in Normandy, is dated by Reff to 1867–74.

32 Carjat, *Le Patriote français*, p 3.

33 The Société Anonyme was dissolved on 15 May 1874 following the poor response to the first exhibition. See 'Degas: chronology of the artist's life', online at metmuseum.org/explore/Degas, viewed August 2008.

34 Degas to Félix Bracquemond, 1876, in Guérin (ed), p 44.

35 Stéphane Mallarmé, 'The Impressionists and Edouard Manet', *Art Monthly Review and Photographic Portfolio*, 30 September 1876 (the original French text now lost), pp 117–22.

36 Bertall, 'Les Impressionnalistes', *Les Beaux-arts*, 1876, pp 44–45; *Le Soir*, 15 April 1876, p 3.

37 Charles Bigot, 'Causerie artistique: l'exposition des "intransigeants"', *La Revue politique et littéraire*, 8 April 1876, pp 349–52.

38 *Portrait of Eugène Manet* 1874, collection of Sir Joseph E Hotung, Lemoisne 339.

39 Emile Zola, 'Deux expositions d'art au moins de Mai', *Le Messager de l'Europe*, Saint Petersburg, June 1876, quoted in Marilyn Brown, *Degas and the business of art: a cotton office in New Orleans*, Penn State Press, Pennsylvania ,1994, p 70.

40 Emile Zola, quoted in Moffett et al, p 171.

41 Marius Chaumelin, *La Gazette [des étrangers]*, 8 April 1876, quoted in Moffett et al, p 171.

42 Richard R Brettel, 'The "first" exhibition of Impressionist painters', in Moffett et al, p 189, describes the occasion as 'arguably the most important dinner party of painters held in the nineteenth century', which, according to Brettel, took place in either January or February 1877.

43 Gustave Caillebotte, *Paris street: rainy day* 1877 (212.2 x 276.2 cm), Art Institute of Chicago, Chicago; Pierre-Auguste Renoir, *Ball at the Moulin de la Galette* 1876 (78.7 x 113 cm), Musée d'Orsay, Paris; Claude Monet, *Interior view of the Gare Saint-Lazare* 1877 (75.5 x 104 cm), Musée d'Orsay, Paris.

44 *Portrait of Monsieur HR*, also known as *Henri Rouart in front of his factory* c 1875, Museum of Art, Carnegie Institute, Pittsburgh, Lemoisne 373.

45 See Jane Kinsman, 'Painterly prints: the monotypes', this publication, pp 85–89.

46 Jules Claretie, 'La mouvement parisien: L'exposition des impressionistes', *L'Indépendance belge*, 15 April 1877, p 1.

47 *Portrait*, also known as *Portrait of a young woman* 1867, Musée d'Orsay, Paris, Lemoisne 163.

48 Paul Mantz, *Le Temps*, 22 April, 1877, quoted in Moffett et al, p 219.

49 See Ronald Pickvance, 'Contemporary popularity and posthumous neglect', in Moffett et al, p 250; Degas' notebook no 31, p 5, reprinted in Reff, vol 1, pp 135–38, also includes plans of the venue.

50 Paul Gauguin in Victor Merlès, *Correspondance de Paul Gauguin: documents; témoignages*, vol 1, Fondation Singer-Polignac, Paris, 1984, p 12.

51 Mary Mathews Gedo, 'Retreat from an artistic breakthrough: Gauguin's nude study (Suzanne sewing)', *Zeitschrift für kunstgeschichte*, vol 58, no 3, 1995, p 407, n 4, mentions that two pictures by Gauguin were included in this exhibition; Gedo cites Pickvance, but the latter simply lists the sculpture *hors catalogue*: Pickvance, in Moffett et al, note on p 271.

52 '[Caillebotte] is excited about the idea of an exhibition, since his visit to the International Exhibition has persuaded him that ours could only gain from the comparison … I believe that the moment has never been more propitious': Camille Pissarro to Eugène Murer, dated as early as May 1878, quoted in Pickvance, in Moffett et al, p 246 and n 17.

53 Claude Monet to George de Bellio, 10 March 1879, in Richard Kendall (ed), *Monet by himself: paintings, drawings, pastels, letters*, Macdonald Orbis, London, 1989, p 29.

54 For Monet's correspondence on the subject, see Virginia Spate, *Claude Monet: the colour of time*, Thames & Hudson, London ,1992, p 136 and n 10.

55 Mary Cassatt to Louisine W Havemeyer, quoted in Adelyn D Breeskin, *The graphic work of Mary Cassatt: a catalogue raisonné*, H Bittner & Co, New York, 1948, p 12.

56 Quoted in Roy McMullen, *Degas: his life, times and work*, Secker & Warburg, London, 1985, p 325.

57 *Miss La La at the Cirque Fernando* 1879, National Gallery, London, Lemoisne 522.

58 F-C de Sèyne, *L'Artiste*, May 1879, quoted in Moffett et al, p 279.

59 *Laundresses carrying linen in town* c 1876–78, Christies' London, 28 March 1988, lot 16, Lemoisne 410.

60 Paul-Armand Sylvestre, 'Le monde des arts : les Indépendants', *La Vie moderne*, 24 April 1879, p 38.

61 Claude Monet, quoted in Moffett et al, p 293, and n 3.

62 Henry Harvard, *Le Siécle*, 2 April 1880, quoted in Charles Moffett, 'Disarray and disappointment', in Moffett et al, p 293.

63 Joris-Karl Huysmans, 'L'Exposition des Indépendants en 1881', *L'Art moderne*, G Charpentier, Paris, 1883, pp 225–57.

64 *Young Spartans exercising* c 1860–62, reworked 1880, National Gallery, London, Lemoisne 70; *Little dancer aged fourteen*; modelled 1880–81; cast 1919–21, various institutions, Czestochowski and Pingeot 73.

65 Degas disliked obvious ostentation. A case in point being his dismissive comments to Whistler, recalled by William Rothenstein: 'Degas was the only man of whom Whistler was a little afraid. "Whistler, you behave as though you have no talent," Degas had once said to him; and again when Whistler, chin high, monocle in his eye, frock-coated, top-hatted, and carrying a tall cane, walked triumphantly into a restaurant where Degas was dining: "Whistler, you have forgotten your muff"', William Rothenstein, *Men and memories: recollections 1872 –1938* (ed and abridged by Mary Lago), Chatto & Windus, London ,1978, pp 54–55.

66 Degas to Félix Bracquemond, 1880, in Guérin (ed), pp 55–56.

67 Gustave Caillebotte to Camille Pissarro, 24 January 1881, quoted in McMullen, pp 330–31.

68 John Rewald, 'Degas and his family in New Orleans', *Gazette des Beaux-Arts*, vol 30, August 1946, p 122.

69 Caillebotte, quoted in McMullen, p 331. Degas had invited Jean-François Raffaëlli to exhibit with the group in 1880, when the young artist showed a large and diverse range of work. He included Raffaëlli again in 1881, although this was more to do with friendship and Degas' loyalty than his proselytising in the cause of Realism. At best Raffaëlli could be described as 'the poet of the humble' (Albert Wolff, *Le Figaro*, 10 April, 1881, quoted in Moffett et al, p 368).

70 Jules Claretie, 'La vie à Paris: les artistes indépendants', *Le Temps*, 5 April 1881, p 3.

71 Jules Claretie, *La Vie à Paris: 1881*, Victor Harvard, Paris, 1881, pp 148–51.

72 Michael Pantazzi, in Jean Sutherland Boggs, Henri Loyrette, Michael Pantazzi et al, *Degas*, The Metropolitan Museum of Art and National Gallery of Canada, New York, 1988, pp 205–6; fig 101.

73 Pantazzi, in Boggs et al, p 209 and fig 104. See also Douglas Druick, 'Framing the little dancer aged fourteen', in Richard Kendall, *Degas and the little dancer*, Yale University Press, New Haven and London in association with Joslyn Art Museum, 1998, ch 4.

74 Druick, p 91.

75 Henry Trianon, *Le Constitutionnel*, 24 April 1881, quoted in Fronia E Wissman, 'Realists among the Impressionists', in Moffett et al, p 362.

76 Paul Mantz, *Le Temps*, 23 April 1881, quoted in Wissman, in Moffett et al, p 262.

77 Quoted in John Rewald, *The history of Impressionism*, The Museum of Modern Art, New York, 1961, p 465.

78 For an account of the ructions, see Rewald, pp 464–72.

79 Martha Ward, 'The rhetoric of independence and innovation; 1886: the eighth exhibition', in Moffett et al, p 452. Ward notes: 'The catalogue lists ten works but apparently fewer were shown', and that Huysmans describes four works, and a revue in *L'Art moderne* (Brussels) refers to six poses.

80 Georges Seurat, *Sunday afternoon on the island of La Grande Jatte* 1884–86, Art Institute of Chicago, Chicago.

81 Quoted in Rewald, p 526.

82 JM Michel, *La Petite Gazette*, 18 May 1886, quoted in Ward, in Moffett et al, p 453.

83 Maurice Hermel, *La France Libre*, 27 March 1886, quoted in Ward, in Moffett et al, p 452, translation slightly modified by Mark Henshaw.

84 Joris-Karl Huysmans, *Oeuvres complètes*, vol 10, Les Editions G Crès & Cie, Paris, 1929, pp 20–25.

85 Paul Adam, 'Peintres impressionnistes', *La Revue contemporaine: littéraire, politique et philosophique*, vol 4, April 1886, pp 541–51.

86 Arthur Baignères, 'Exposition de peinture par un groupe d'artistes, rue le Peletier, II', *L'Echo universel*, 13 April 1876, p 3.

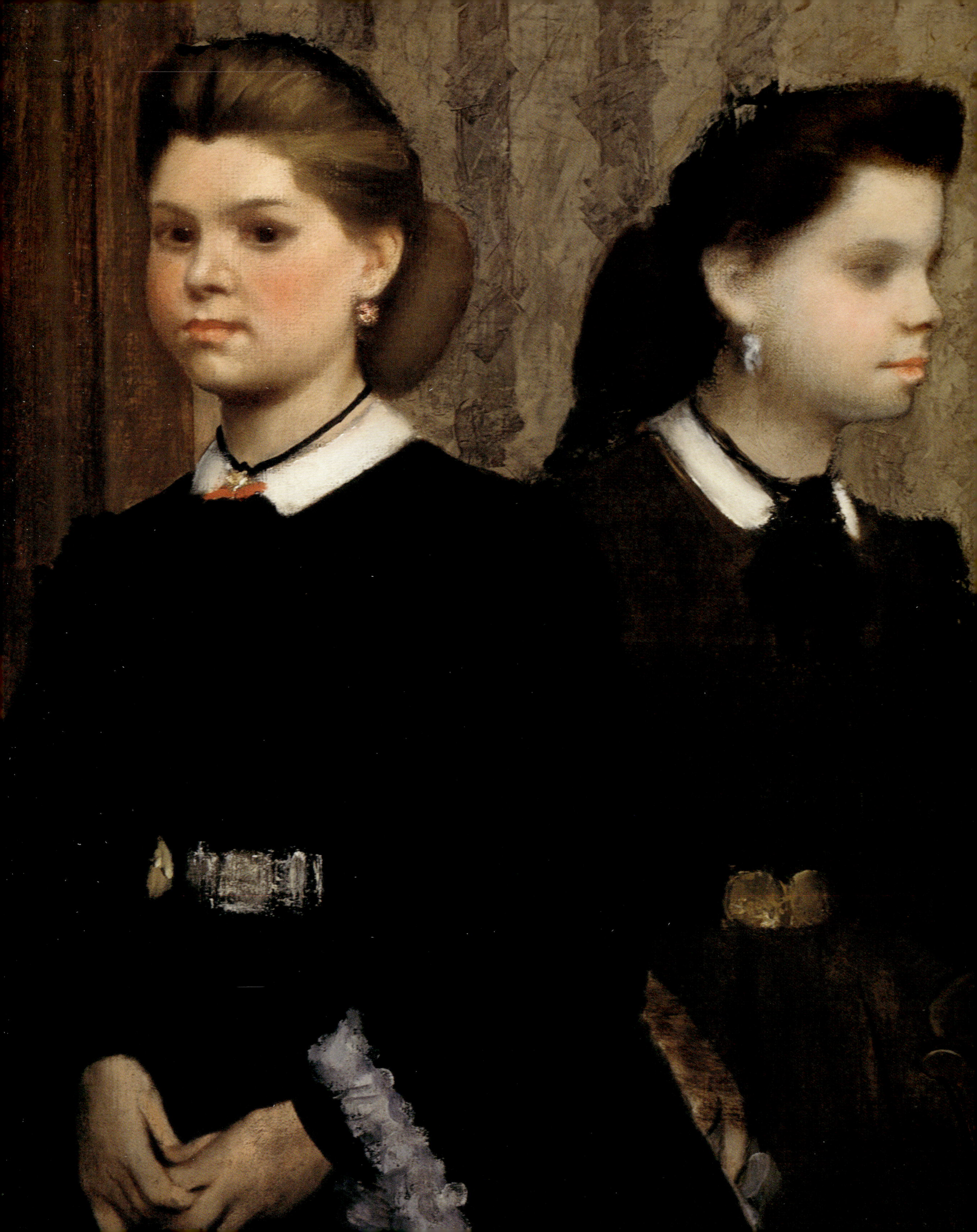

THE EARLY YEARS

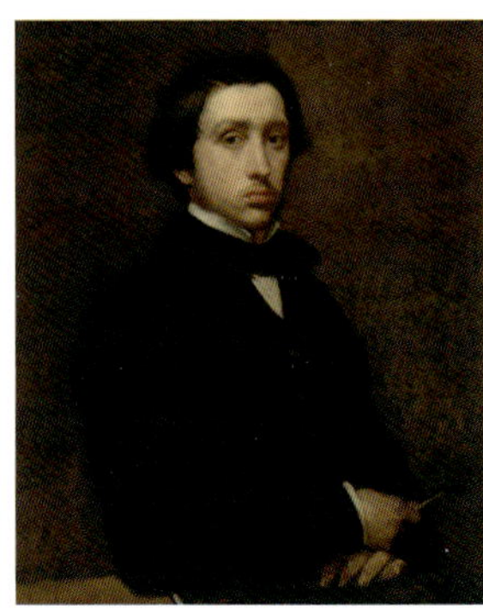

(above)
Degas with charcoal holder (Degas au porte-fusain) 1855
oil on paper, laid down on canvas
81 x 64.5 cm
Musée d'Orsay, Paris
Lemoisne 5

(previous page)
The Bellelli sisters (Giovanna and Giulia Bellelli)
1865–66 (detail cat 9)

FROM VERY EARLY in his artistic career Edgar Degas made careful copies of the work of other artists, absorbing the lessons of the past. In his student years he was a prolific copyist from casts of the Parthenon friezes and other Classical Greek and Hellenic sculptures—as well as of engravings and paintings, most significantly the paintings of Jean-Auguste-Dominique Ingres and others of the French Neoclassical school. He continued the practice while living and travelling in Italy during 1856–59, spending time in Naples, Rome and Florence, copying in the Museo Nazionale in Naples and the Capitoline in Rome, and from works by Italian Renaissance masters. In Rome he met the French Symbolist artist Gustave Moreau, who encouraged him to embrace a wider range, including Venetian art. Moreau urged Degas to value the art he saw in Italy for its colour, technique and texture, as well as line—a focus of Neoclassicism. Degas also broadened his interest by copying the illustrations in volumes of expeditions to the South Pacific—plates from *Description géographique, historique et commerciale de Java* by Thomas Stamford Raffles and John Crawfurd (1824), and Louis de Freycinet's *Voyage autour du monde* (1824–44)[1] —paving the way for the incorporation, without romanticising, of non-Western elements in his art. In his recognition of the intrinsic value of this material as art Degas was ahead of his time.

It should not be supposed that Degas, the keen copyist, was without direction or certainty until he found his subjects in modern life. Edouard Manet is reported to have expressed such a view, noting that while he was painting contemporary Paris Degas was still creating *Semiramis building Babylon* c 1860–62.[2] Yet Degas' painting of the Queen of Assyria is not a conventional rendering of a subject from Greek mythology—it is a radical interpretation, and suggests a distillation of elements drawn from the old masters such as Piero della Francesca (c 1410/20–1492), as well as Assyrian reliefs. Figures and costumes are simplified and treated as areas of colour, and the composition is arranged in an asymmetrical manner—an approach that was to become characteristic of Degas' art.

Degas' interest in classical or historical subjects cannot be viewed simply as dressing figures in period costumes, to act out irrelevant themes of the past—which was frequently the practice of artists of the day. The pejorative term *pompiers* (literally the French word for firemen) was applied to such artists, whose subjects were regularly helmeted for battle (just as firemen wore helmets). *Pompiers* became a disparaging epithet for backward-looking artists known for their ostentation, and whose art was dull and uninspiring. Edmond Duranty was one of several writers who were critical of the preoccupation with historical subjects championed at the annual Salon exhibitions. In a pamphlet published in 1876, he wrote: 'It is in the way that the public rewards *laziness* in artists, and encourages imitation. They willingly praise pastiches of the great masters. They distance themselves from anything that represents a new or daring interpretation of nature. All of that is a closed book to them.'[3]

In contrast, Degas' embrace of the old masters was forward looking. His copying of their works constituted a process of absorption and refinement that informed his stylistic development over many years. He had a thoroughly modern attitude to the work that he copied: he chose all kinds of art, often from unfamiliar quarters, art that appealed to him and from which he could adopt methods and motifs in a process of compositional and pictorial problem solving. In a discussion with his friend the illustrator Georges Jeanniot, Degas spoke of the experience of copying and how it affected his own work:

> It is very good to copy what one sees: it is much better to draw what you can't see any more but in your memory. It is a transformation in which imagination and memory work together. You only reproduce what struck you, that is to say the necessary. That way, your memories and your fantasy are freed from the tyranny of nature. This is why pictures made in such a way, by a man who has a cultured memory and knows the old masters and his craft, are almost always remarkable works—look at Delacroix.[4]

On 7 April 1853, as a young student of the academic history painter and illustrator Félix Barrias, Degas registered to be permitted to copy art at the Louvre. Two days later he registered with the Cabinet des Estampes at the Bibliothèque Nationale. Degas' early copies from the Louvre include portraits of young men painted in the sixteenth century by the Italian masters Franciabigio (1482–1525)[5] and Parmigianino (1503–1540), works that would subsequently influence his own ideas of portraiture, particularly self-portraits.[6] From that time Degas continued to hone his skills as an artist, while absorbing lessons from master paintings, sculptures and drawings from the Classical period through to the nineteenth century.

Degas, however, was not simply a copyist. Rather, from his studies he would adopt and transform. In his early years, one great influence was Eugène Delacroix, whose rich palette and bold application of paint contributed to Degas' style. Degas also would adopt a favourite figure derived from Delacroix and include this motif in his own new subject matter. (See p 45 and cat 4.)

Ingres was another towering figure in Degas' artistic development—an interest first encouraged by his teacher at the Ecole des Beaux-Arts, Louis Lamothe, a former pupil of Ingres. Degas' meeting with Ingres, then aged 75, took place after Degas had arranged for the loan of an Ingres painting, *The bather* 1808, to be shown at a retrospective of the artist's work at the *Exposition Universelle* of 1855. The painting belonged to Edouard Valpinçon, father of Degas' friend Paul, and at first Valpinçon senior had declined to lend the work. Degas was instrumental in the reversal of Valpinçon's decision and he asked that Ingres be advised of this. Subsequently the meeting with Ingres took place. This was a momentous occasion in the life of the young Degas and he gave several accounts of it, including the advice offered by the Neoclassical master: 'Study line … draw lots of lines.'[8] Degas echoed Ingres' sentiments in his own statements on the importance of drawing: 'Make a drawing, do it again, make a tracing of it, start again, and do another tracing';[9] and '[D]rawing is not the same as form, it is a way of seeing form …'[10]

At the *Exposition Universelle* and other exhibitions held concurrently in Paris, Degas concentrated his attention almost entirely on the art of Ingres. This was despite major collections of Gustave Courbet and Delacroix also on display at the same time.[11] Degas was profoundly inspired by Ingres' emphasis on line and contour, the careful use of gesture, and the play of space and form in his compositions. This influence is evident in Degas' early portraits, including self-portraits, portraits of his family, of the Bellelli sisters, and of his friends. His great admiration of Ingres continued throughout his life, leading George Moore to reflect in 1890: 'Degas was a pupil of Ingres, and any mention of this always pleases him, for he looks upon Ingres as the first star in the firmament of French art.'[12]

Diego Velázquez (1599–1660) has a prominent position among the old masters studied by Degas. This major figure in the Spanish Baroque style had become increasingly popular with French artists of the nineteenth century, notably Manet. Both Manet and Degas had developed Velázquez-inspired compositions before they first met in the Louvre in 1862, in front of his *Portrait of the Infanta Maria Margarita* c 1659—now attributed to Velázquez and his studio.[13] Degas was making a copy of this painting directly onto a copper plate when Manet approached him. Manet then followed suit and etched his own copy of the *Infanta*. Their encounter marked the beginning of a complex relationship of admiration, frustration and rivalry. Degas went on to make several portraits of Manet, including an etching produced at about the time of their first meeting, titled *Manet seated— right profile.*[14]

Pictorial devices employed by Velázquez were adopted by Degas to develop a rich play of illusion and allusion,

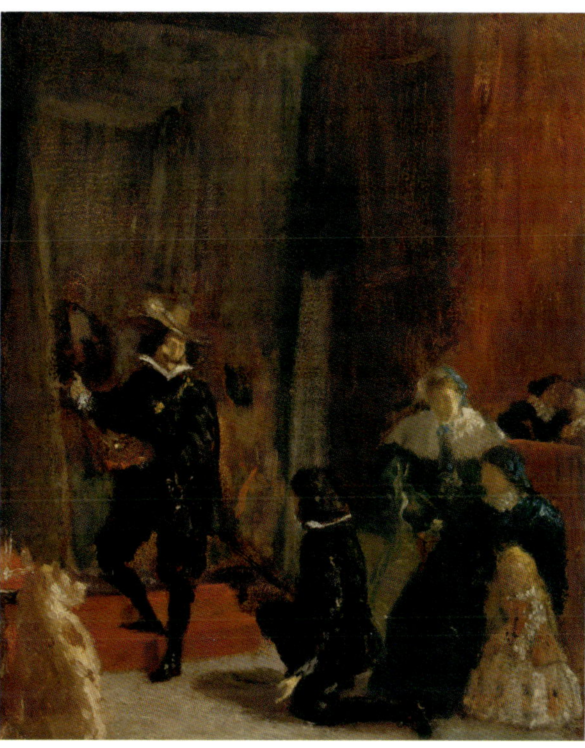

Homage to Velázquez (*Homage à Velázquez*) 1858
oil on canvas, 31 x 25 cm
Neue Pinakothek, Munich
Brame and Reff 12
© Artothek

reminiscent of the *bodegónes* of the Spanish School, where scenes are shown within scenes, and reality is unclear and ambiguous. In an early painting, *Homage to Velázquez*,[15] which was probably executed during his visit to Rome in 1857–58, Degas composed his own variation of Velázquez's masterpiece *Las Meninas* from about 1656—it likely that Degas came across a reproduction of this work in illustrated books of notable paintings.[16] In the original composition, Velázquez depicted himself at the easel next to his subject, the Infanta, surrounded by her maids of honour. The Red Cross of the Order of Santiago is prominent on the artist's breast. He gazes out, most likely at the Spanish King Philip IV and Queen Mariana, whose reflections in the mirror on the wall behind the artist indicate their presence beyond the picture plane. In his *Homage,* Degas places the king within the painting, standing at the easel, and to represent him he borrows the courtier shown in the background of the original work. He depicts Velázquez kneeling at the king's feet to receive the Cross of Santiago. Degas may have been reinterpreting an anecdote that after the death of Velázquez the king himself made an addition to the original canvas by painting in the Cross on the artist's breast[17] —Velázquez actually received the honour in 1659, three years after he'd painted *Las Meninas.* It is remarkable that as a young man Degas had the confidence to create his own intriguing interpretation of *Las Meninas.* The pictorial device of images within images would reappear in his later work as he embraced contemporary subject matter.

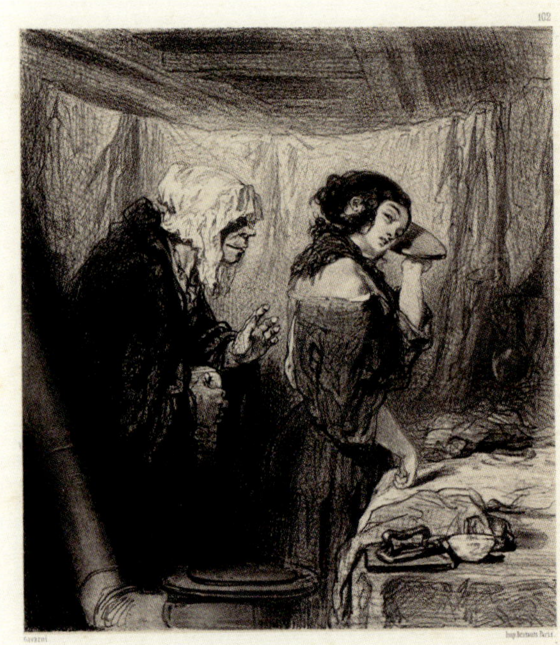

(above)
Paul Gavarni
Satan from *Les artistes anciens et modernes*, no 102 1847
lithograph
20.4 x 18 cm (comp),
43.6 x 30.4 cm (sheet)
National Gallery of Australia, Canberra
Felix Man Collection, Special Government Grant 1972

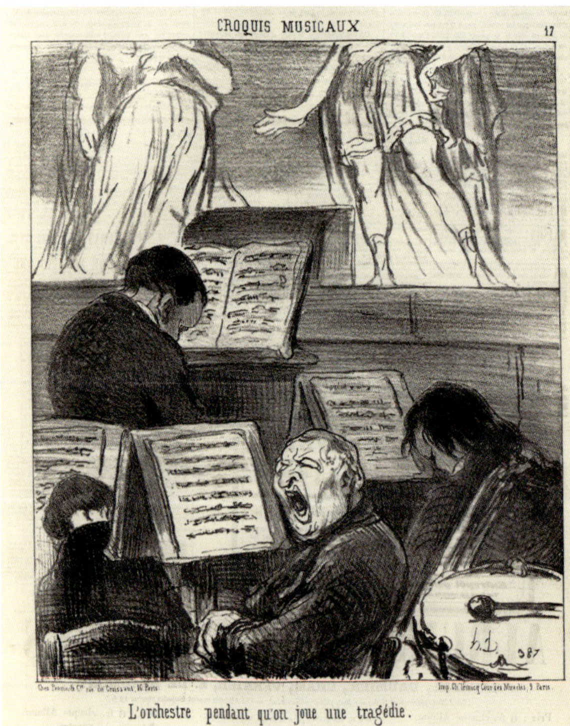

(below)
Honoré Daumier
The orchestra while the tragedy plays out (L'orchestre pendant qu'on joue une tragédie), from the series *Croquis musicaux (Musical sketches)*, published in *Le Charivari* 5 and 7 April 1852
lithograph, 34.6 x 26.4 cm (sheet)
National Gallery of Australia, Canberra
Purchased 1980

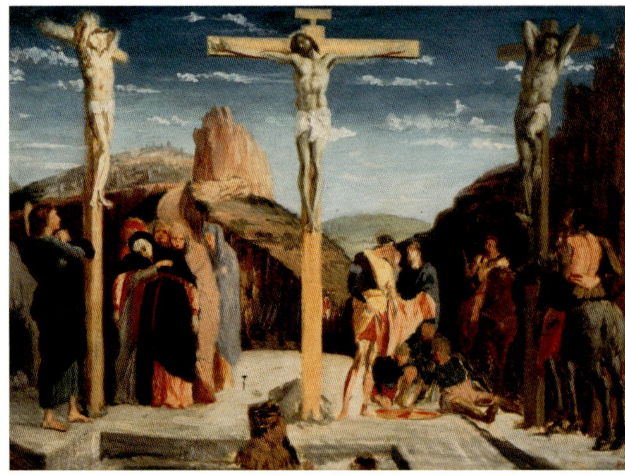

(right)
The crucifixion, after Mantegna (Le calvaire, après Mantegna) 1861
oil on canvas, 69 x 92.5 cm
Musée des Beaux-Arts, Tours
Don de la Compagnie générale du gaz pour la France et l'étranger, 1934
Lemoisne 194

Degas became noted for his play of space within his compositions and, again, it was a case of lessons learned from the old masters, whose works were recycled and reinterpreted in his modern subject matter. In 1861 he made a copy after a painting in the Louvre by the fifteenth-century Italian master Andrea Mantegna (1431–1506), *The crucifixion* 1456–59. Degas first copied a detail of this work in a pencil drawing of about 1855 and then, in 1861, as a painting of comparable size to the original work.[18] Mantegna's painting is a masterpiece of foreshortening, with the cropping of the foreground figures creating an impression of movement and a sense of viewing the 'plateau' composition from below. These compositional devices became Degas' signature style as he matured as an artist. His highly developed spatial sense allowed an appreciation of the advent of Cubism—although he observed: 'it's harder to do than painting'.[19]

Degas' extensive collection of caricatures drawn by Honoré Daumier and Paul Gavarni provided him with an almost limitless repertoire of subjects. Gavarni's work inspired him with a wealth of themes from the everyday, as well as introducing visual devices such as figures viewed from behind or close together tête-à-tête. However Gavarni lacked the radical approach to composition that distinguished the work of Daumier, whose inventive spatial arrangements with differing viewpoints were adopted by Degas in many of his own compositions relating to the theatre, performances at the opera, or representations of laundresses. Daumier's sense of classical majesty, his facility with line, and the noble presence of his figures led Degas to comment that 'there were three great draughtsmen in the nineteenth century, Ingres, Delacroix and Daumier'[20] —the three artistic companions of his career.

New Orleans

In 1872 Degas accompanied his younger brother René on his return to New Orleans after a visit to Paris. René de Gas (his preferred form of the name) had married his first cousin Estelle and, with other relatives, operated a business in Louisiana as cotton merchants. Edgar and René left Liverpool for New York on 12 October. In a letter to his friend, the Danish artist Lorentz Frölich, Degas told of their voyage on the *Scotia*, 'an English boat, swift and sure', in a journey that took 10 days.[21] The two brothers then travelled by train to New Orleans.

Degas' work in New Orleans was focused on the family. He worked on several paintings, including *Children on a doorstep (New Orleans)* 1872, outside the house of his uncle Michel Musson; *The song rehearsal* 1872–73, depicting two of Musson's daughters singing while accompanied at the piano by René de Gas; and his early masterpiece of group portraiture, *A cotton office in New Orleans* 1873 (cat 11), a view of the family business in which Musson, René, and another of Degas' brothers, Achille, are shown at work.[22]

In a letter to James Tissot, written early in his stay, Degas seems to have been overtaken by homesickness: 'Everything is beautiful in this world of the people, but one Paris laundry girl, with bare arms, is worth it all for such a pronounced Parisian as I am.'[23] His initial fascination with the foreign location had already turned to disenchantment, and in his letter to Frölich he expressed a concern that he might be overwhelmed by too many different experiences:

> How many new places I have seen, what plans that put into my head, my dear Frölich! Already I am giving them up, I want nothing but my own little corner where I shall dig assiduously. Art does not expand, it repeats itself …
>
> In this way I am accumulating plans which would take me ten lifetimes to carry out. I will abandon them in six weeks, without regret, to return to and never again leave *my home*.[24]

Degas would return to France to consolidate his work: to develop his art from the lessons he had continually learned since his early years, the images that he had accumulated in his memory bank, and to establish his own style—an art of Paris relevant to his time; an art of modern life.

Notes

1 Theodore Reff, 'Further thoughts on Degas's copies', *The Burlington Magazine*, vol 113, no 822, September 1971, pp 534–43. Reff published several articles listing the copies made by Degas, see 'Degas's copies of older art', *The Burlington Magazine*, vol 105, no 723, June 1963, pp 241–52; 'New light on Degas's copies', *The Burlington Magazine*, vol 106, no 735, June 1964, pp 250–60; 'Addenda on Degas's copies', *The Burlington Magazine*, vol 107, no 747, June 1965, pp 320–23.

2 Related by George Moore, 1870s, re-published in Julie Wilson Bareau (ed and trans), *Manet by himself*, Little, Brown & Co, Boston, 1991, p 303. *Semiramis building Babylon* 1860–62, Musée d'Orsay, Paris, Lemoisne 82.

3 Edmond Duranty, *La nouvelle peinture: à propos du groupe d'artistes qui expose dans les galeries Durand-Ruel*, E Dentu, Paris ,1876, p 2.

4 Quoted in 'Memories of Degas by Georges Jeanniot', in Richard Kendall (ed), *Degas by himself*, Little, Brown & Co, Boston, 1987, p 299.

5 Franciabigio's *Portrait of a man* was originally attributed to Raphael.

6 Henri Loyrette, 'What is fermenting in that head is frightening', in Jean Sutherland Boggs, Henri Loyrette, Michael Pantazzi et al, *Degas*, The Metropolitan Museum of Art and National Gallery of Canada, New York and Ottawa, 1988, p 36. See also Theodore Reff, 'Copyists in the Louvre, 1850–1870', *The Art Bulletin*, vol 46, no 4, December 1964, p 555.

7 *Copy after Delacroix's, 'The entry of the crusaders into Constantinople'* c 1859–60, Kunsthaus, Zurich, Brame and Reff 35.

8 For the various accounts of the Degas' meeting with Ingres and the lending of Valpinçon's *The bather*, see Henri Loyrette, *Degas*, Librarie Arthème Fayard, Paris, 1991, pp 55–56. For an extensive account, see Paul Valéry (David Paul trans), *Degas, Manet, Morisot*, Pantheon Books, London, 1960, pp 34–35.

9 Degas, quoted in Kendall (ed), p 319.

10 Degas, quoted in Theodore Reff, 'Three great draftsmen', in *Degas: the artist's mind*, Thames & Hudson, London, 1976, p 53. This essay is reprinted as 'Three great draftsmen: Ingres, Delacroix and Daumier', in Ann Dumas et al, *The private collection of Edgar Degas*, The Metropolitan Museum of Art, New York, 1997, pp 137–75.

11 Reff, 1976, p 43.

12 Reff, 1976, p 53.

13 See Véronique Gerard Powell and Claudie Ressort, *Musée du Louvre: Départment des peintures: Ecole espagnoles et portugaise*, Réunion des Musées nationaux, Paris, 2002, inv 9411, pp 247–51.

14 Jean Adhémar and Françoise Cachin, *Degas: the complete etchings, lithographs and monotypes*, Thames & Hudson, London, 1974, cats 16–20; the dating could not have occurred before 1862.

15 *Homage to Velázquez* 1857–58, Neue Pinakothek, Munich, Brame and Reff 12.

16 *The family of Felipe IV*, or *Las Meninas* c 1656, Museo del Prado, Madrid, López-Rey 124; Gary Tinterow and Geneviève Lacambre, *Manet/Velázquez: the French taste for Spanish painting*, The Metropolitan Museum of Art and Yale University Press, New York and New Haven, 2003, p 473.

17 The incident was related by Antonio Palomino (1724) based on a biographical account (lost) written by an artist in Velázquez's studio, Juan de Alfaro, in Jonathan Brown, *Velázquez: painter and courtier*, Yale University Press, New Haven, 1986, reviewed by Sir Lawrence Gowing, *New York Times*, 10 August 1986, online at times.com/books/98/12/06/specials/brown-velasquez, viewed August 2008; also recorded by Charles Blanc in *Histoire des peintres de toutes les écoles: Ecole espagnole*, Jules Renouard, Paris, 1869. See Gisela Hopp catalogue entry for Degas' work, *'Erinnerung an Velázquez'*, in *Neue Pinakothek: Katalog der Gemälde und Skulpturen*, Pinakothek-DuMont, Munich, 2003, p 80.

18 *The crucifixion, after Mantegna* 1861, Musée de Beaux-Arts, Tours, Lemoisne 194.

19 René Gimpel, *Diary of an art dealer*, Farrar, Straus & Giroux, New York, 1966, p 416.

20 Degas, quoted in 'Memories of Degas by Georges Jeanniot', in Kendall (ed), p 299.

21 Degas to Lorenz Frölich, 27 November 1872, in Marcel Guérin (ed), *Edgar Germain Hilaire Degas: letters*, Bruno Cassirer, Oxford, 1947, p 20.

22 *Children on a doorstep (New Orleans)* 1872, Ordrupgaardsamlingen, Copenhagen, Lemoisne 309; *The song rehearsal* 1872–73, Dumbarton Oaks Research Library and Collection, Washington DC, Lemoisne 331; *A cotton office in New Orleans* 1873, Musée des Beaux-Arts, Pau, Lemoisne 320.

23 Degas to James Tissot, in Guérin (ed), p 18.

24 Degas to Frölich, in Guérin (ed), pp 20–21.

1 *Self-portrait*
c 1857–58
oil on paper, laid down on canvas
20.6 x 15.9 cm
The J Paul Getty Museum, Los Angeles
95.GG.43

Self-portraiture gives aspiring young artists the convenience of having a ready, willing and always available subject. Degas was no exception, and during the 1850s and early 1860s he painted no less than 18 self-portraits. At the age of 21, he portrayed himself in the large formal self-portrait of 1855. This painting was in the manner of his idol, Jean-Auguste Dominique Ingres' *Self-portrait at 24 years* 1805.[1] Degas also painted more contrived poetic interpretations, which followed the fashion of his older contemporary Gustave Courbet, the French Realist painter.

Degas painted this portrait of himself in a fedora when he was about 23 years old—on paper, which was then laid onto canvas. It is an understated and casual self-portrait revealing a youthful ingenuity and vivacity. The boldness of the gaze, combined with the relaxed outward appearance and casual wispy beard makes for an assured self-portrait, showing both skill and freshness. Degas depicts himself as a young man of growing confidence, his hat adding a jaunty air to the composition. The artist was also sketched in this much-prized hat by his friends—the sculptor Stefano Galetti, and painter Gustave Moreau. Having arrived in Rome in October 1857, it is probable that Degas met Moreau in January 1858, when Moreau was making studies of nudes at the Villa Medici.[2] This painting is probably dated around this time.

A slightly earlier pencil drawing in red chalk by Degas, made when he was about 21, reveals his gift as a draughtsman, and the pronounced influence of Ingres on the young artist (cat 2).

Notes

1 Musée d'Orsay, Paris, Lemoisne 5. The self-portrait by Ingres is in the Musée Condé, Chantilly. The other painted early self-portraits are listed in Lemoisne, vol 2, cat nos 2–5, 11–14, 31–32, 37, 51, 103–105, Brame and Reff 28–30.

2 Gustave Moreau's letter to his parents in Paris, dated 14 January 1858, Musée national Gustave-Moreau, cited in Boggs et al, 1962, p 50.

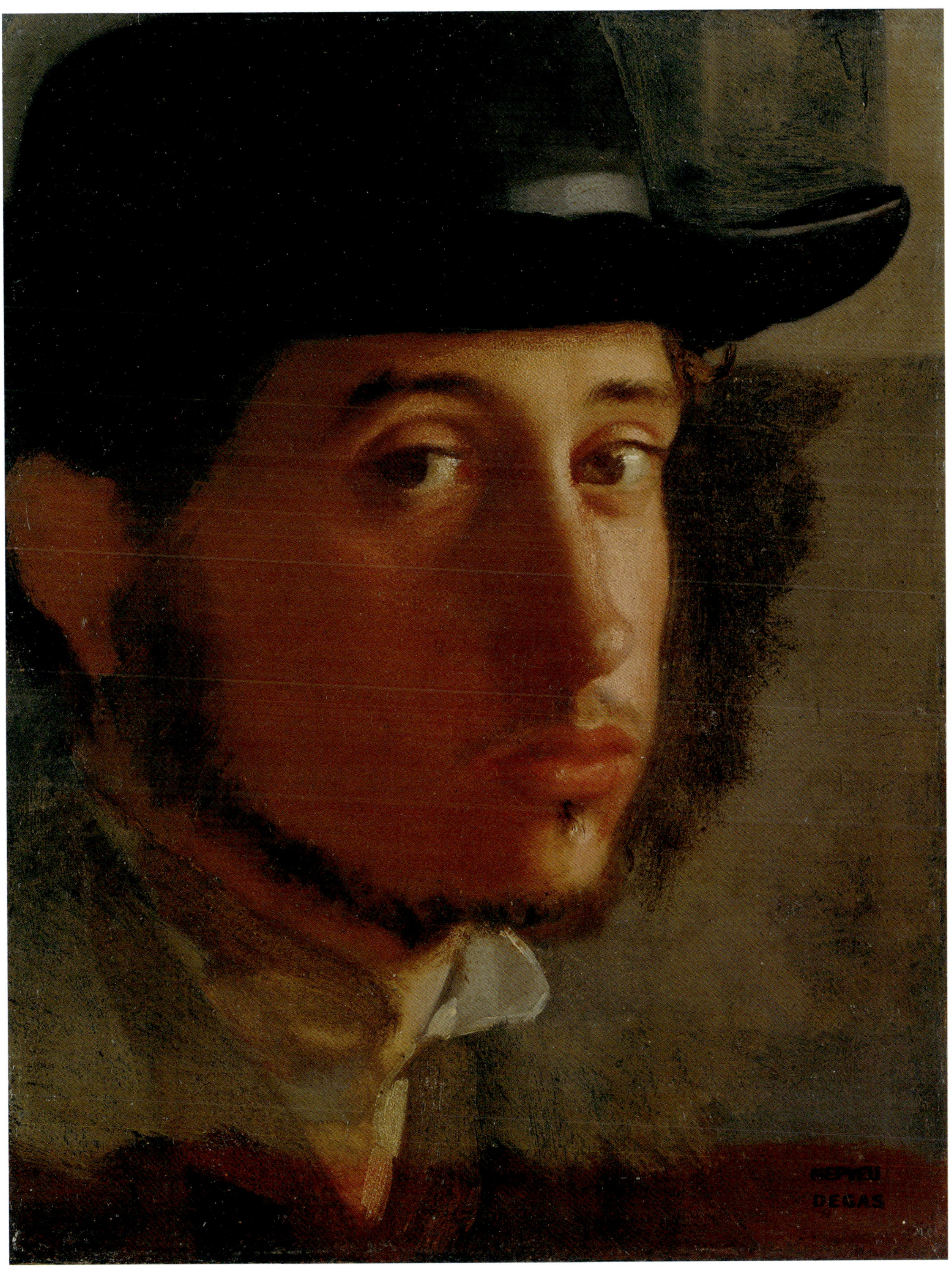
DEGAS

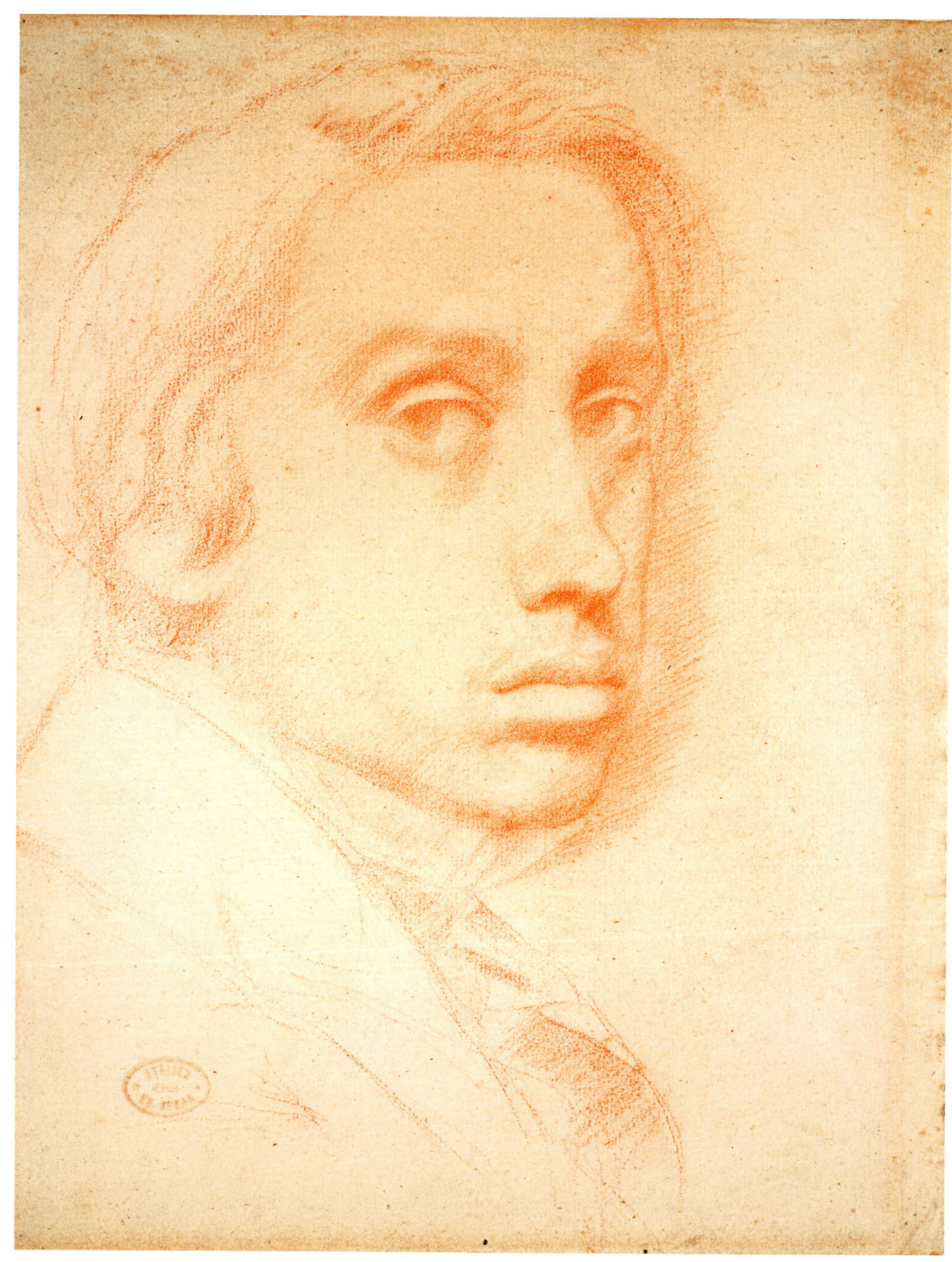

2 *Self-portrait* (*Autoportrait*)
c 1855
red chalk on laid paper
31 x 23.3 cm
National Gallery of Art, Washington DC
1991.182.23
Woodner Collection

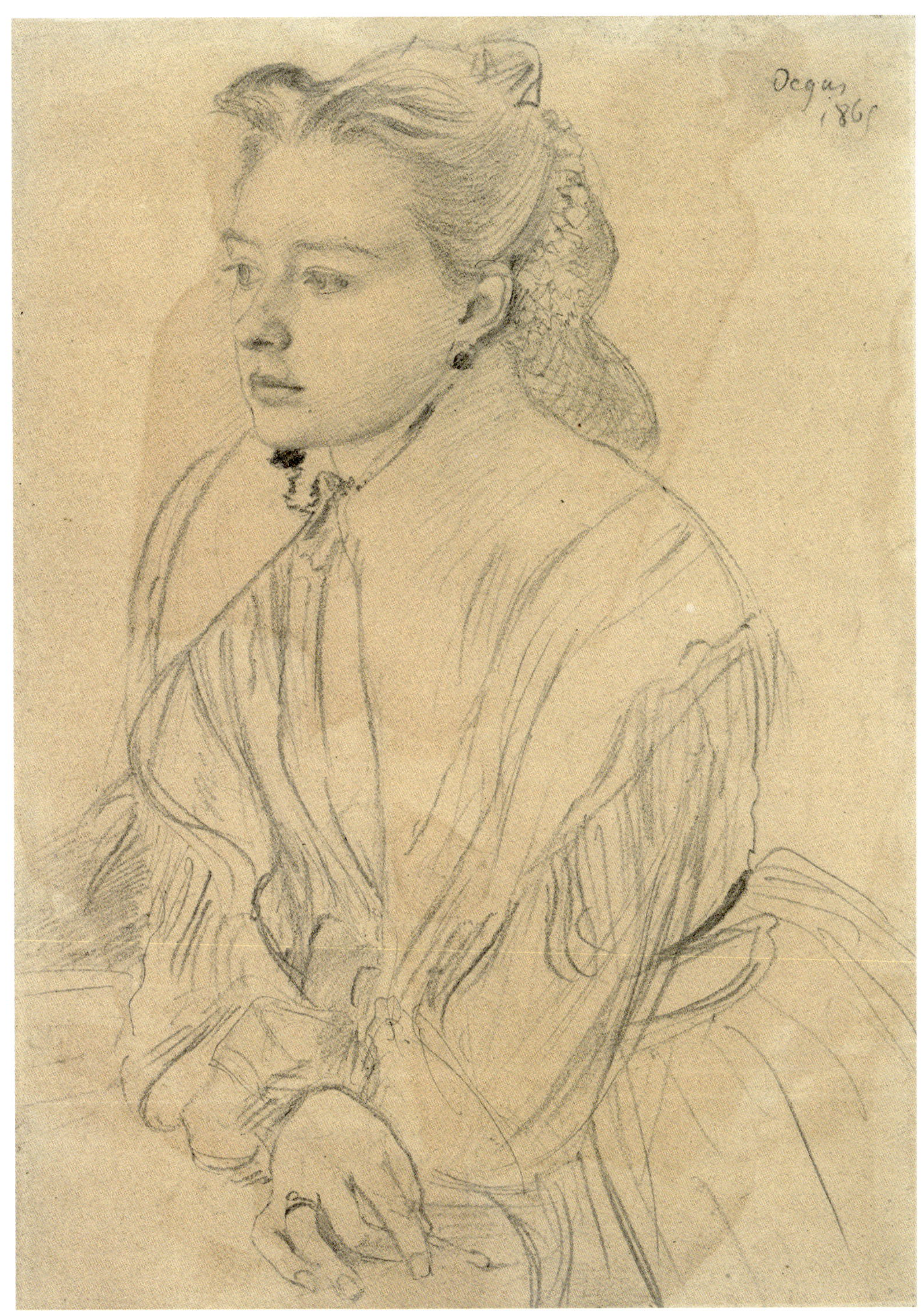

3 *Portrait of Hélène Hertel*
(*Portrait de Mademoiselle Hélène Hertel*)
1865
pencil on light brown paper
27.5 x 19.2 cm
Musée d'Orsay, Paris
Housed at the Département des arts graphiques,
Musée du Louvre
RF 5604
Legacy Lucien Marcel Bing, 1922
Vente I: 313

4 *Copy after Delacroix's 'Entry of the crusaders into Constantinople'*
(*Copie d'après Delacroix, La prise de Constantinople*)
c 1860
oil on cardboard
35 x 38 cm
Kunsthaus Zürich
2006/19
Gift of René Wehrli, 2005
Brame and Reff 35

In his quest to learn from the masters, Degas did not seek to strictly reproduce the original, but to discover the wonderful secrets of gifted artists and keep before him elements that could be reformulated in his own work—'a transformation in which imagination and memory work together'.[1]

It should be no surprise that Degas chose to copy Eugène Delacroix's masterpiece of 1840, which hung in the Louvre. The sense of drama and the complex original composition were bound to attract the younger artist. His studies after Delacroix are characterised by a youthful exuberance and accomplished manner. He worked in small colour sketches, as Delacroix himself had done in his preliminary studies, using loose brushwork and a brilliant palette.

A motif from his *Copy after Delacroix's 'Entry of the crusaders into Constantinople'* c 1860—the semi-naked woman crouching in the right foreground, with her back to the viewer and her long hair falling over her face in profile—reappears in the preparatory drawings and the painting by Degas, *Semiramis building Babylon*[2]. The figure then reappears in various guises in Degas' later paintings, drawings, prints, sculptures, monotypes and pastels.

Notes

1 In Georges Jeanniot, 'Souvenirs sur Degas,' *La revue universelle*, vol LV (15 October 1933), p 158; quote translated by Michael Pantazzi.

2 Musée d'Orsay, Paris, Lemoisne 82.

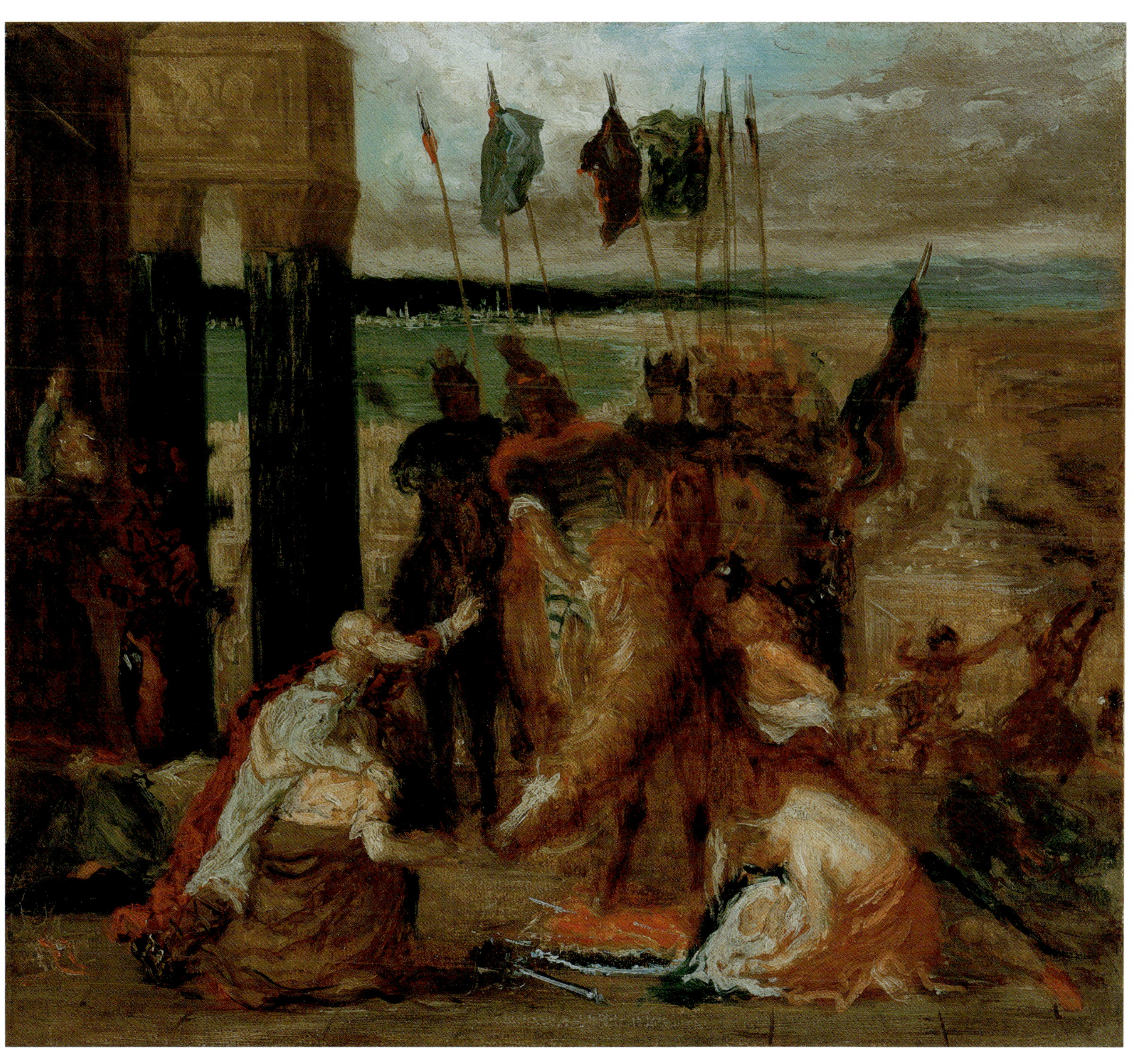

5 *Roman beggar woman* (*Mendiante romaine*)
1857
oil on canvas
100.3 x 75.2 cm
Birmingham Museums and Art Gallery, Birmingham
1960P44
Lemoisne 28

For much of his early career Degas copied older artists' work, honing his skills and absorbing lessons from the master painters. During the years 1856 and 1857, when he was in Italy, Degas made a series of sketches and pen-and-wash drawings which included local figures in contemporary dress.[1]

In *Roman beggar woman*, he has created a portrait of a woman in Italian traditional dress—the kind of subject favoured at the Villa Medici in Rome, where he attended evening classes from late 1856. The painting indicates that, despite his youth, Degas had already developed a clear sense of originality. He has avoided the sentimental or Arcadian view of poverty of the time, characterised by picturesque scenes of Italian folk. Rather, the work reveals a more contemporary interpretation of an old and impoverished woman dressed in ragged clothes and a shawl, her drawn face and bony hand in profile, and her meagre victuals nearby. In *Roman beggar woman* Degas has achieved a degree of veracity that avoids any romanticism. It is painted with small delicate brushstrokes, in a dark palette of browns and blacks.

Roman beggar woman has significance in heralding Degas' long-time interest in portraiture, and his innovations in this field.

Note

1 Theodore Reff, *The notebooks of Edgar Degas*, vol 1, Hacker Art Books, New York, 1985, notebook 11, pp 67–73.

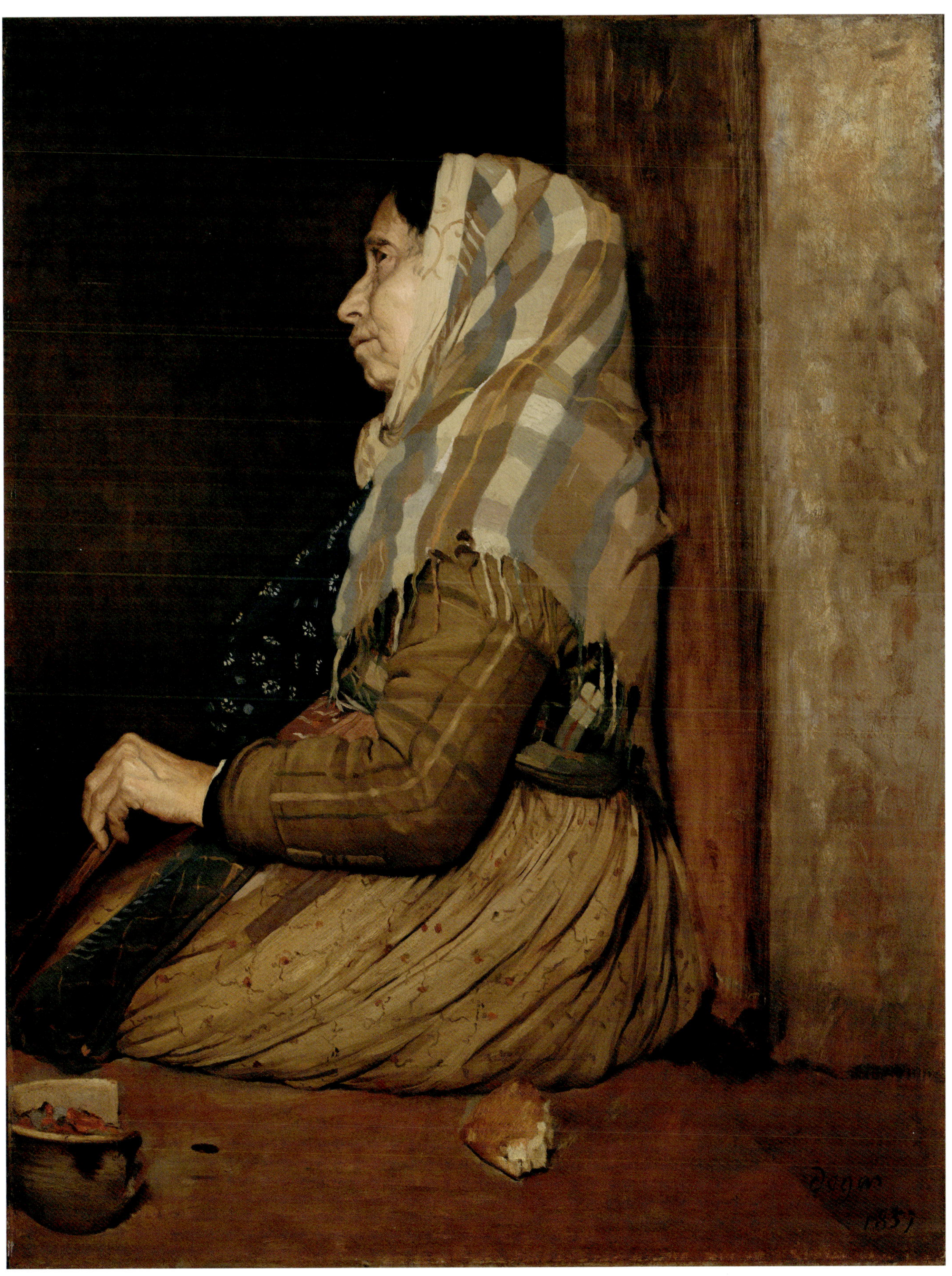

6 ***Self-portrait*** (***Autoportrait***)
late 1857
second state of five
edition of three
etching
23 x 14.4 cm (plate), 26.3 x 17.2 cm (sheet)
Bibliothèque nationale de France, Paris
res Dc 327dh fol, boîte 2, Rc A 27729
Reed and Shapiro 8 / Adhémar 13

From the 1850s to the 1890s, Degas is thought to have made about 66 intaglio and lithographic prints. He began his career in printmaking in Paris, and shortly afterwards when he travelled to Italy learned traditional etching[1] and engraving techniques from the printer, Joseph Tourny.

As with his painting at this time, Degas copied the prints of the old masters, and Rembrandt van Rijn was a particular favourite with the young artist, just as he was with Tourny. This early self-portrait is reminiscent of the seventeenth-century Dutch master in terms of the pose, and also in the technique of close cross-hatching and the dramatic contrasts in light and dark.

Another work, Degas' portrait of his younger sister, Marguerite (cat 7), was inspired by Rembrandt's portrait of his wife Saskia, in terms of the pose and the gesture of the hand held to her face[2], and confirms Degas' early talent for etching.

After the embrace of lithography by artists in the first half of the nineteenth century, the technique had acquired a bad reputation among those making original prints as it came to be associated with poor-quality colour reproductions (known as 'chromolithographs') used for commercial purposes. In response to this, in the early 1860s the French publisher Alfred Cadart and the printer Auguste Delâtre promoted a revival of the etching technique amongst artists, and established the Society of Etchers.

Both Manet and Degas were part of this revival, and both took up etching. The former became the subject of Degas' *Manet seated, right profile* (cat 8), made some time after the two men first met at the Louvre in 1862; it is one of several etchings which Degas made of his fellow artist. This work is the most accomplished in terms of technique, and the most resolved as a composition. The unusual pose, with Manet sitting sideways on a chair with the details of a modern room as a backdrop, and the careful rendering of the details of the face and clothing, make this one of the first modern etchings made by Degas.

Notes

1 In etching, a copper plate is covered with an acid-resistant waxy coating (resist), and the image is scratched into it with a metal needle. The copper plate is then immersed in acid, which eats away at the exposed areas of the plate. Thick buttery ink is then rubbed into these incisions, and the plate is run through a printing press to create the impression on paper.

2 Rembrandt van Rijn, *Portrait of Saskia* 1633, Kupferstichkabinett, Staatliche Museen, Berlin.

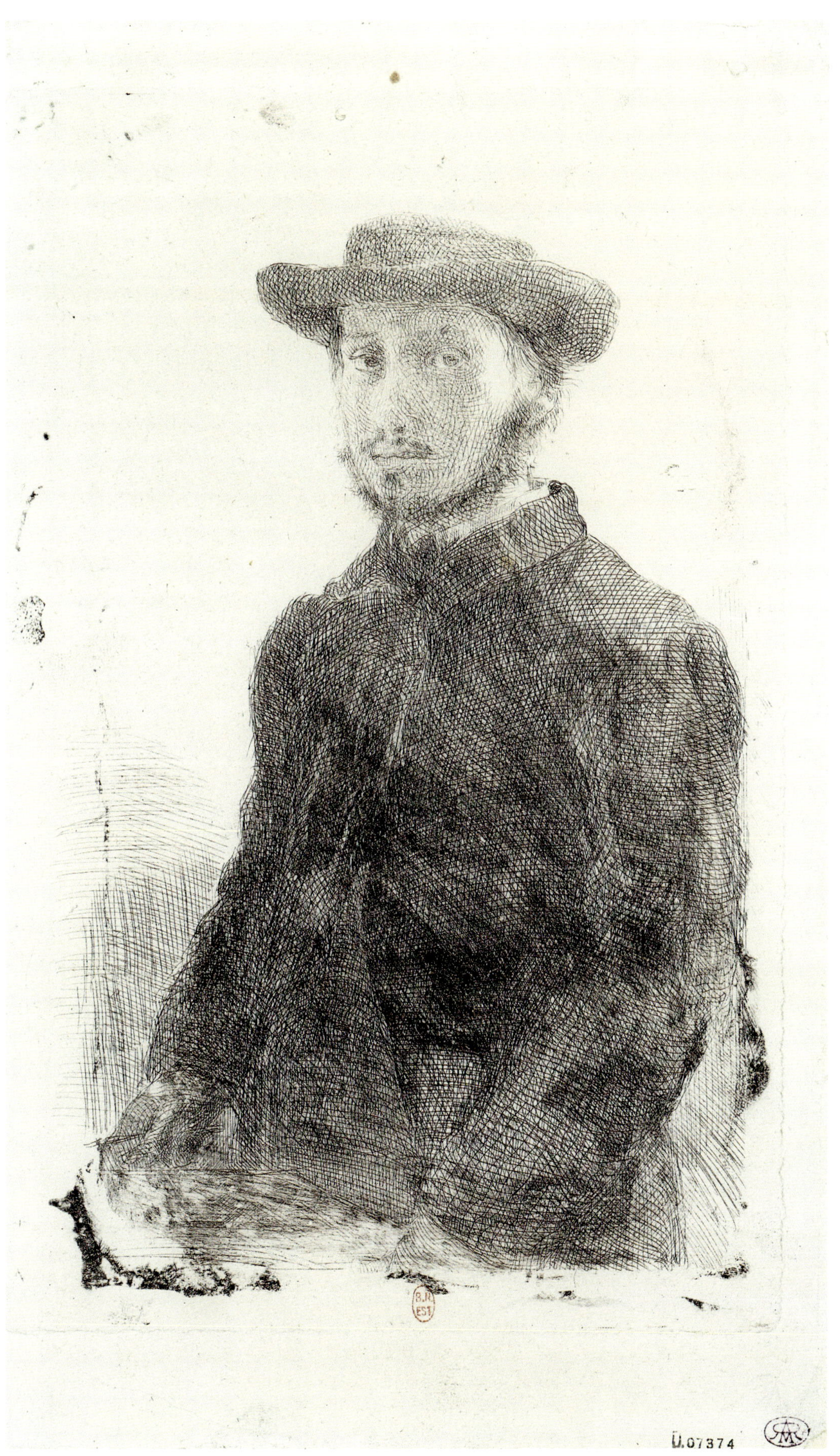

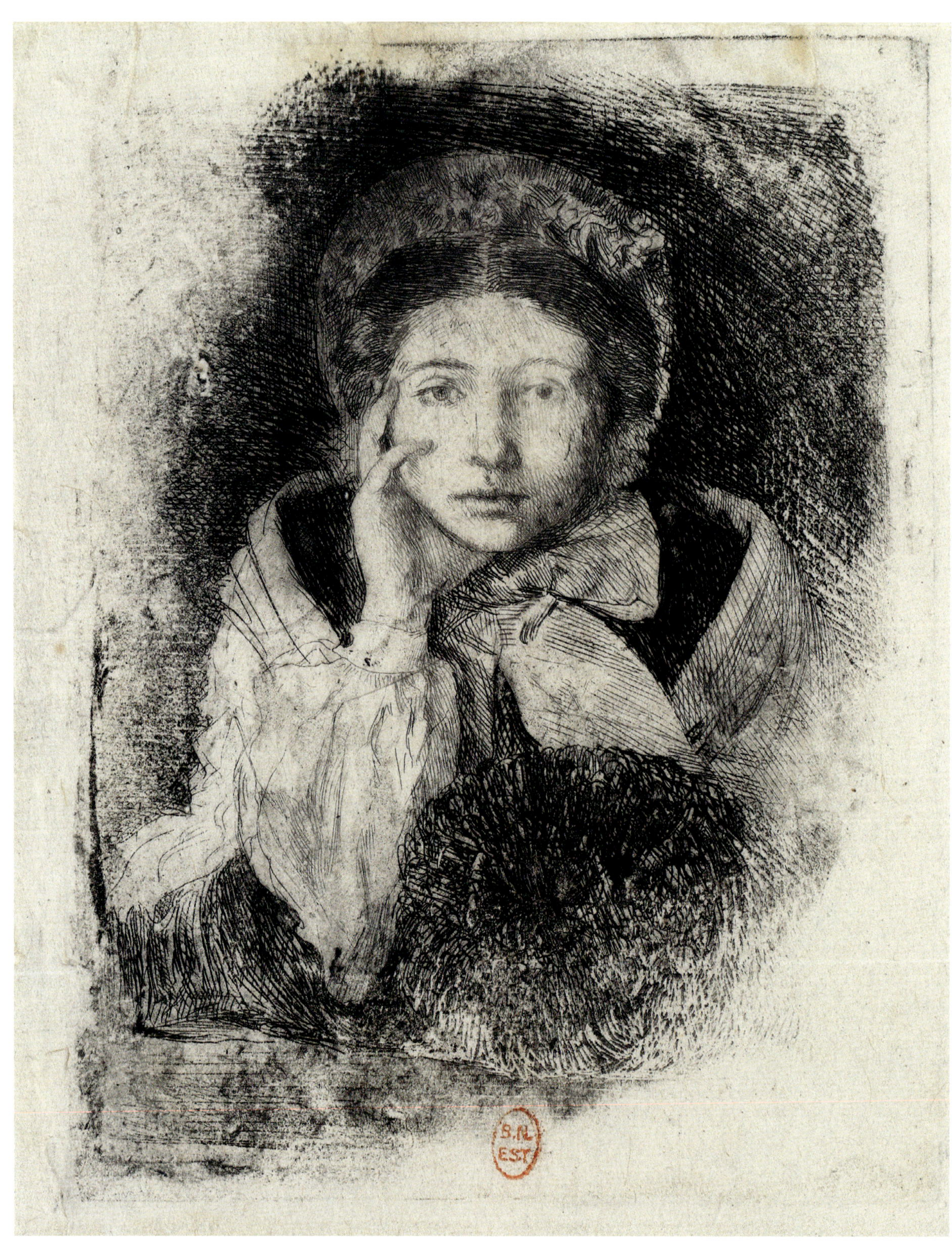

7 *Marguerite de Gas, the artist's sister* (*Marguerite de Gas, soeur de l'artiste*)
1860–62
third state of six
etching
11.6 x 8.8 cm (plate), 11.7 x 8.8 cm (sheet)
Bibliothèque nationale de France, Paris
res Dc 327dh fol, boîte 2
Reed and Shapiro 14 / Adhémar 23

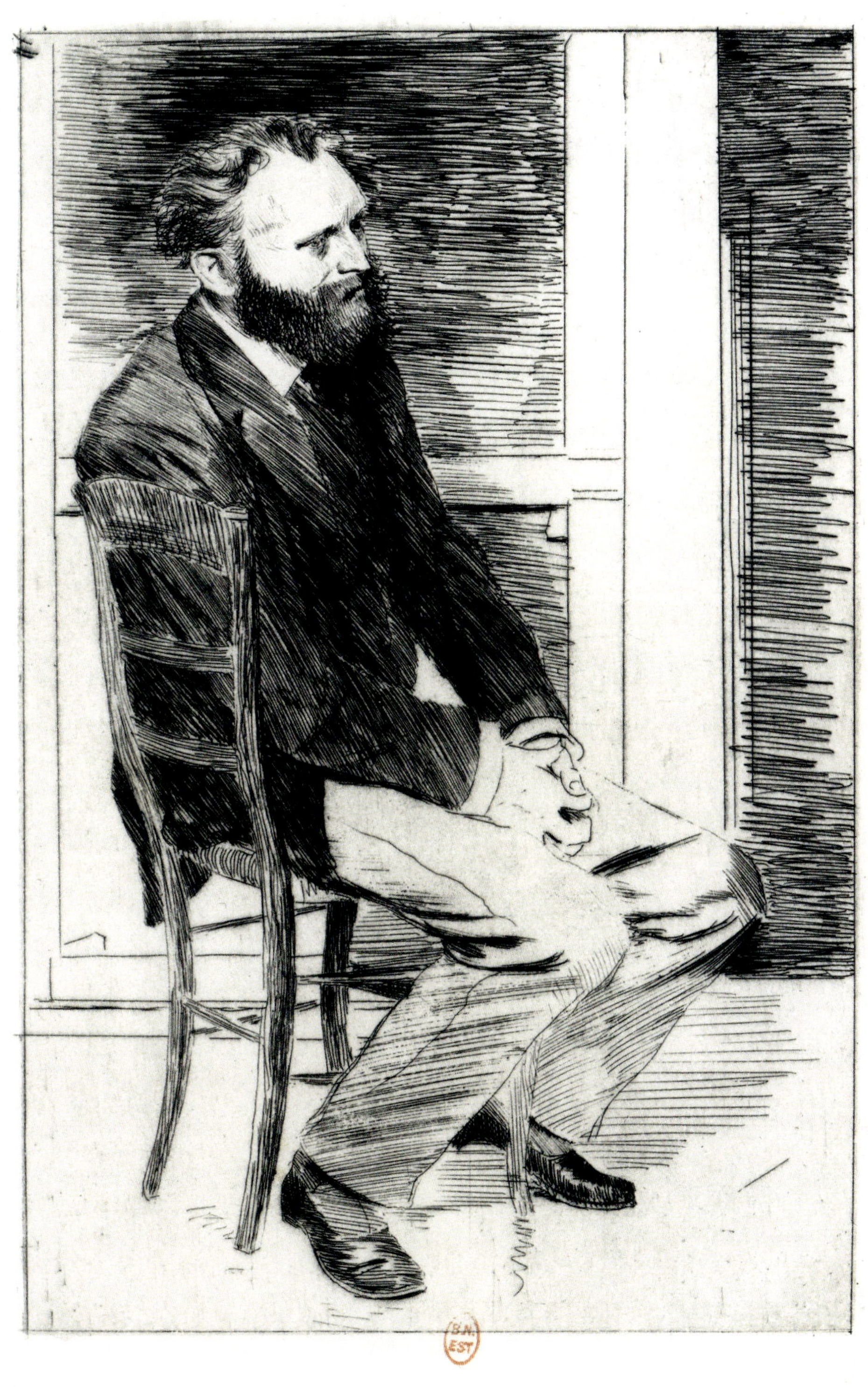

8 *Manet seated, right profile* (*Manet assis, tourné à droite*)
1864–65
first state of four
edition of five
etching
19.5 x 13.3 cm (plate), 31.4 x 22.6 (sheet)
Bibliothèque nationale de France, Paris
res Dc 327dh fol, boîte 2, Rc A 27729
Reed and Shapiro 18 / Adhémar 19

9 *The Bellelli sisters (Giovanna and Giulia Bellelli)* (*Giovanna et Giulia Bellelli*)
1865–66
oil on canvas
92 x 73 cm
Los Angeles County Museum of Art, Los Angeles
M.46.3.3
Mr and Mrs George Gard De Sylva Collection
Lemoisne 126

Throughout his life, Degas displayed a remarkable talent for portraiture. As he matured as an artist this was to manifest itself in radical compositions, and his ability to express with great subtlety the character of his sitters—as seen in this portrait of Giovanna and Giulia Bellelli.

While travelling as a young man in Italy in the summer of 1858, Degas stayed in Florence at the apartment of his mother's sister Laura Bellelli, her husband Gennaro and their children Giovanna (known as Nini) and Giulia (known as Julie), on the Piazza Maria Antonia. This was an unhappy marriage, exacerbated by the fact that Gennaro had been banished from Naples in 1849 for his political beliefs and now languished in Florence, directionless. The entire family was the subject of a major Degas painting, *The Bellelli family* 1858–67, which the artist intended for the Salon of 1867.[1]

Degas' cousins Giovanna and Giulia also became the subject of this double portrait which has been dated by Lemoisne around 1865, and by Loyrette as c 1865–1866,[2] at a time when the sisters were on the verge of becoming young women. In this work, the silhouetted forms, the emphasis on line, and the sombre colouring indicate the important influence that Ingres had on the young artist. Ingres' influence is also clearly evident in a fine pencil drawing of about the same time: *Portrait of Hélène Hertel* (Comtesse Falzacappa) (cat 3), which is remarkable for the beautifully rendered facial features. The three-quarter view and the more cursory and sketchy depiction is also characteristic of many drawings by Ingres. *Portrait of Hélène Hertel* is a sensitive and accomplished drawing of a young woman in Parisian society, and provides reason for Degas' growing reputation as a talented portraitist and draughtsman.

Notes

1 Musée d'Orsay, Paris, Lemoisne 79.
2 Boggs et al, *Degas*,1988, p 120.

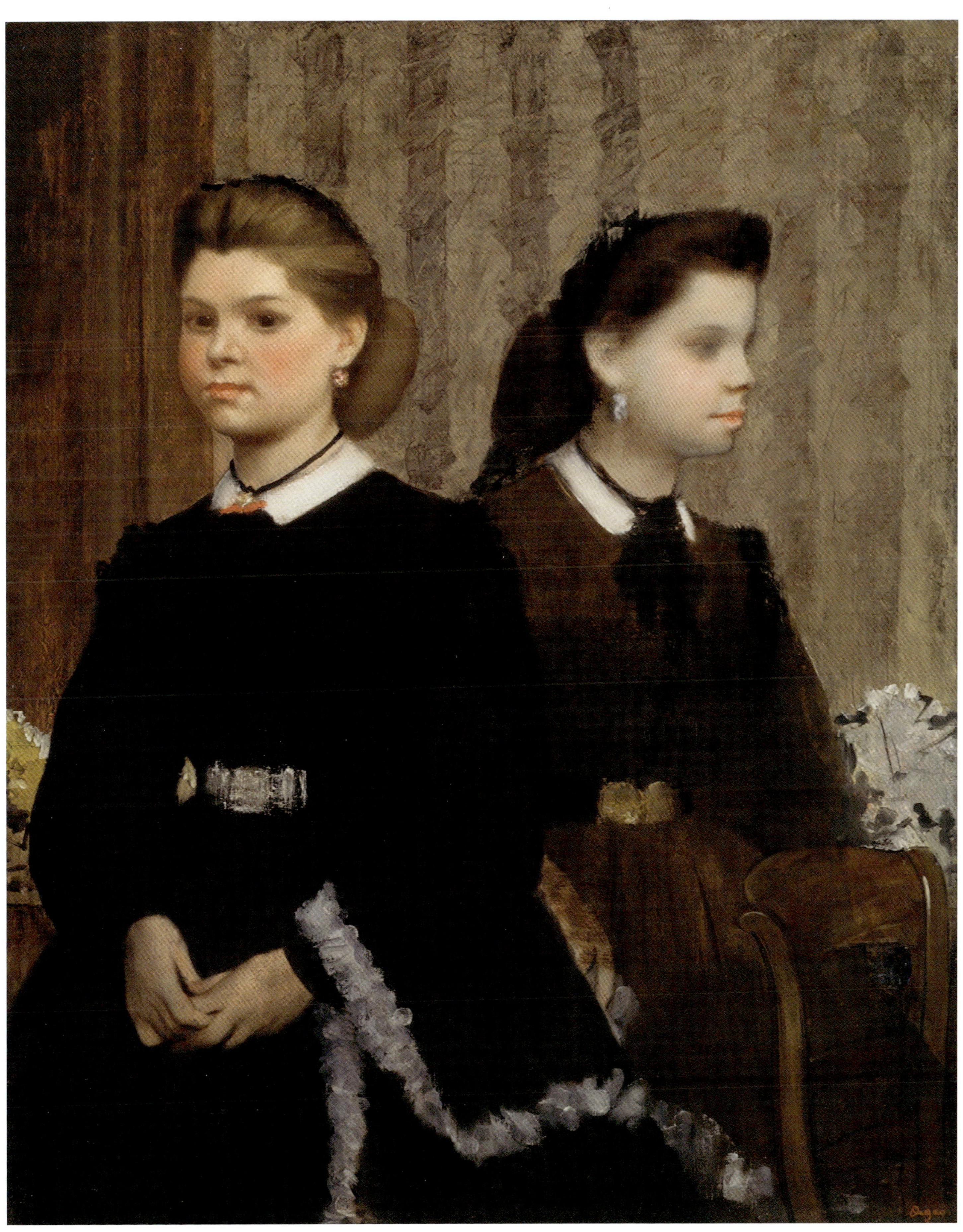

10 *Portrait of a woman* (*Portrait de femme*)
c 1876–80
oil on canvas
46.3 x 38.2 cm
National Gallery of Victoria, Melbourne
409-4
Felton Bequest, 1937
Lemoisne 415

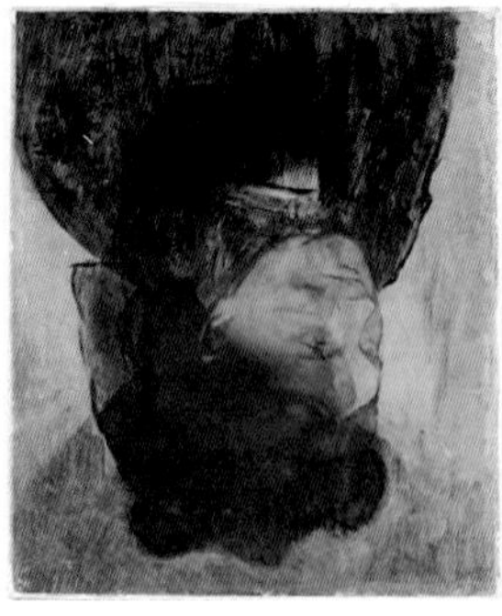

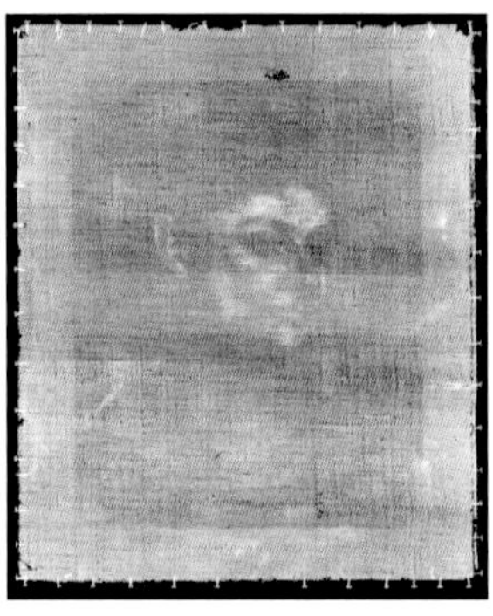

(above)
Infra-red scan of *Portrait of a woman* c 1876–80
National Gallery of Victoria, Melbourne

(below)
X-ray of *Portrait of a woman*
c 1876–80
National Gallery of Victoria, Melbourne

The intrinsic merits of *Portrait of a woman* are difficult to appreciate, due to the unfortunate fact that the ghostly impressions of another composition are showing through as a dark stain across the sitter's face, disfiguring this engaging portrait. On the surface of this double-layered work we see a thinly and freely painted image of a plumpish woman in a black dress and bonnet. The unidentified sitter leans forward, poised on the brink of conversation, her eyes alive with interest. The concentration with which she listens to an off-stage interlocutor has been captured with deft, quickly applied brushstrokes that accord with Degas' painting style of the late 1870s.[1]

Beneath the portrait, and running in the opposite direction, lies a second portrait which Degas abandoned at some stage, recycling the canvas to create the present work. The shoulders of this underlying figure show through the top layer of paint to form the strong diagonal lines radiating out from the present sitter's black bonnet to the top corners of the canvas. X-radiography reveals that the subject of the earlier portrait was 'a young woman in three-quarter view to the right, her hair pulled back in a bun'.[2]

Infrared photography of the canvas further shows that this first portrait was finely and delicately modelled—reminiscent of Degas' classical style of around 1860, when he was working in veneration of the old masters. While the slightly elongated ear and general features of the over-painted subject are reminiscent of a female portrait Degas executed in Rome towards the end of the 1850s, exact identification of the earlier sitter still eludes us.[3]

Ted Gott

Notes

1 The date of 1876–80 was first proposed by Lemoisne 415.

2 Sonia Dean, *European painting of the 19th and early 20th centuries in the National Gallery of Victoria*, National Gallery of Victoria, Melbourne, 1995, p 45.

3 *Portrait de jeune femme (Mme Millaudon)* 1857–59, Lemoisne 44.

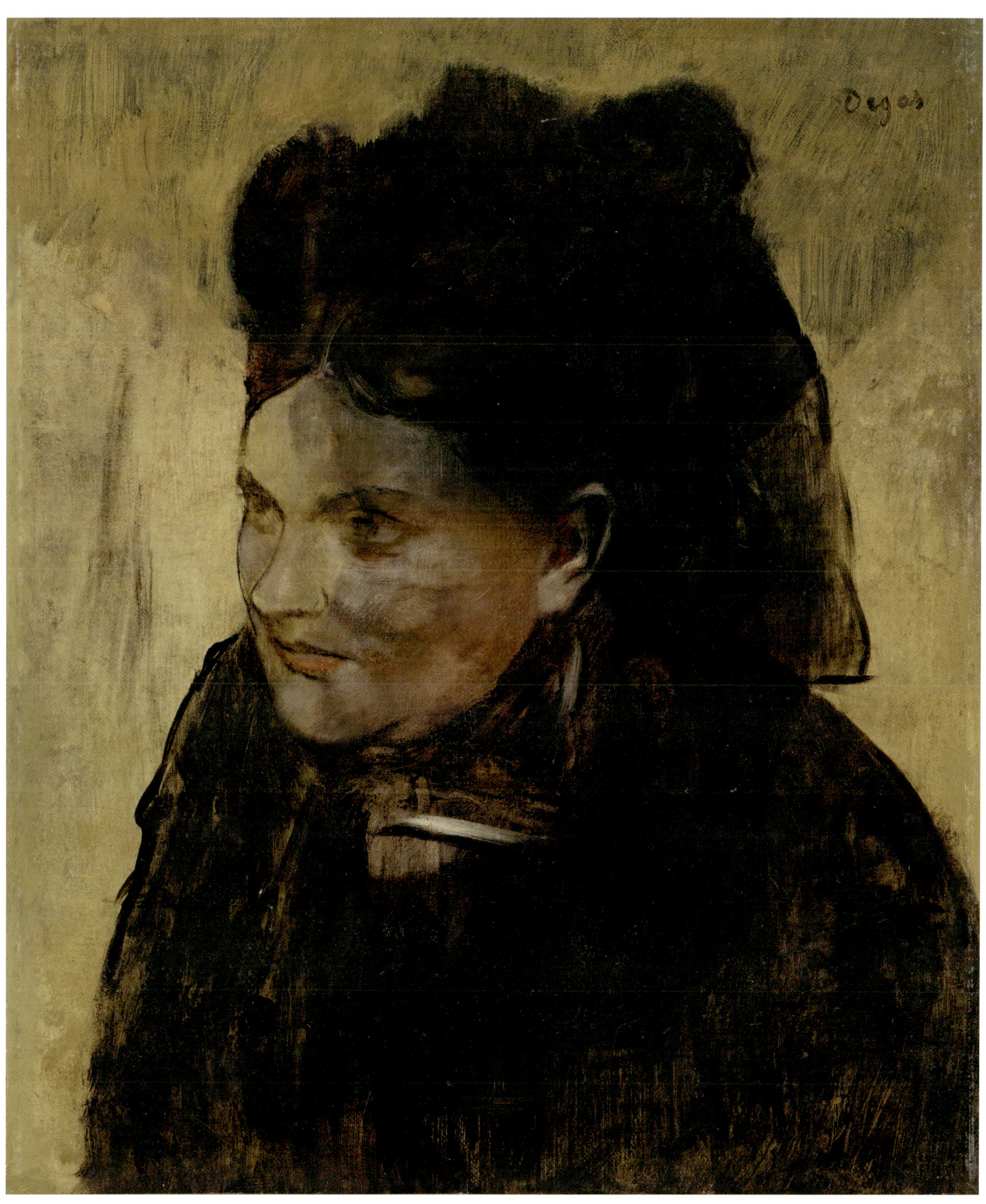
Degas

11 *A cotton office in New Orleans* (*Un bureau de coton à la Nouvelle-Orléans*)
1873
oil on canvas
73 x 92 cm
Musée des Beaux-Arts, Pau
878.1.2
Lemoisne 320

A cotton office in New Orleans was displayed at the second Impressionist exhibition in 1876, to mixed reviews. It was then shown two years later at the Société Béarnaise des Amis des Arts in the French provincial city of Pau. The Musée des Beaux-Arts in Pau acquired the painting in the same year, through the auspices of Degas' friend, Alphonse Cherfils, who originally hailed from Pau. This work was the first Degas painting acquired by any public museum.

Made during Degas' sojourn in New Orleans between October 1872 and early 1873, *A cotton office…* is outstanding for its modern interpretation of a group portrait. It is a composition of extraordinary innovation, where the figures do not pose in front of the artist in a formal arrangement before some velvet backdrop (which was often the case at this time). Rather, Degas depicts his relatives and associates at work in the family's cotton office and prefigures the casual snapshot which would appear in portrait photography in the 1890s. The artist has included his uncle Michel Musson seated in the foreground quietly contemplating a ball of cotton. One brother, René, is shown reclining on a seat reading a newspaper, and the other, Achille, lounging to the side with his legs crossed. Musson's business partner, James Prestidge, is seated on a high stool behind René, while the clerk is seriously engaged with the book of accounts.

Degas' composition conveys both action and inaction. The office is full of activity and the scene is enlivened by the cropping of the figures, the interior and its furniture. Even the waste paper basket has been cropped, reinforcing the sensation of viewing a busy environment. At the same time, there is a casual air and stillness in some of the figures, notably Degas' relatives. Each figure in the group has been portrayed sensitively, and the various personalities revealed through their individual poses, countenances, and gestures. In a letter to James Tissot dated 18 February 1873, Degas expressed his modest view that it was 'A raw picture if ever there was one, and I think from a better hand than many another.'[1]

Notes

1 Edgar Degas to James Tissot, 18 February 1873, quoted in Marcel Guerin (ed), *Edgar Germain Hilaire Degas: letters*, Bruno Cassirer, Oxford, 1947, p 29.

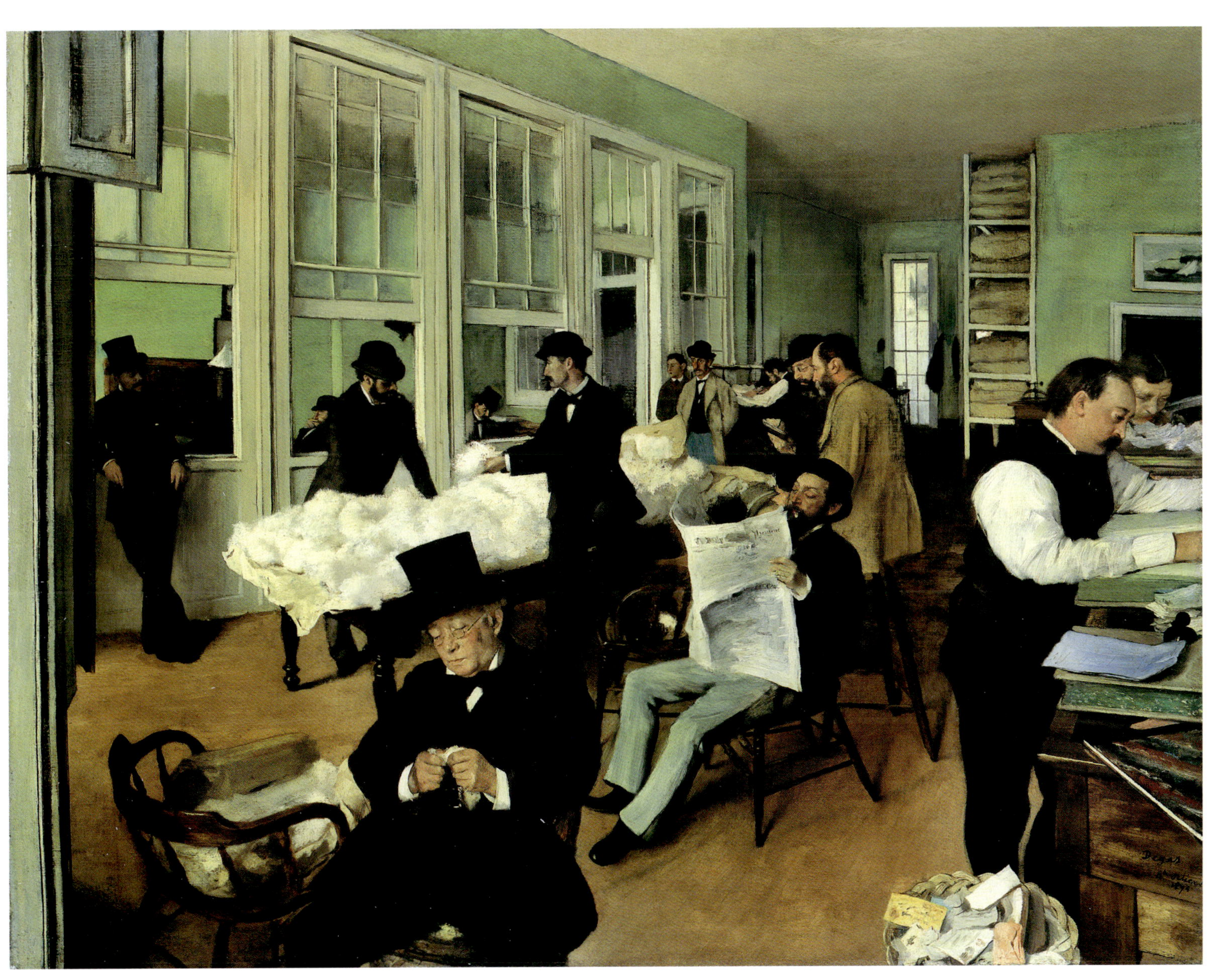

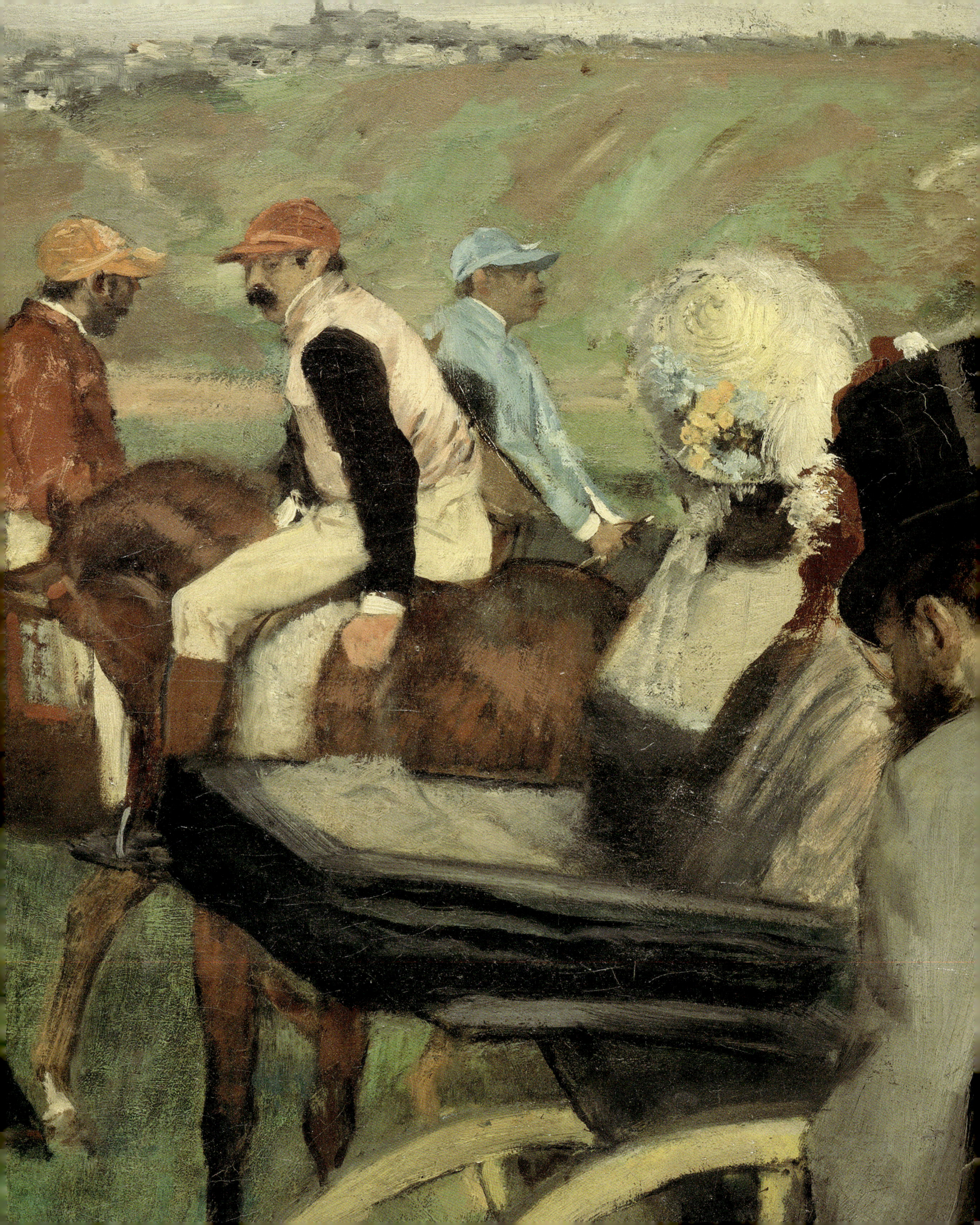

THE RACES

DEGAS SUCCESSFULLY SUBMITTED *Scene from the steeplechase*[1] for exhibition at the Salon of 1866. While painted on the grand scale of history paintings destined for Salon exposure, the dramatic incident depicted by Degas is clearly modern—and probably located near Paris on the steeplechase course at Vincennes. A jockey has been thrown from his horse and lies inert in the foreground. Two riderless horses gallop alongside, indicating that another has fallen in this hazardous pastime for gentlemen jockeys. The sense of drama and movement is heightened by the cropping of the horses and riders who continue with the race—it is as if all the figures are leaping out of the picture plane, except for the luckless fallen jockey.

At the time he painted this work, Degas already had a considerable knowledge of horse breeding—and also of the horse's anatomy; yet he was later to lament in a declaration of harsh self-criticism that he was 'completely ignorant of the mechanism of its movements': 'I knew infinitely less than any non commissioned officer, who, because of his years of meticulous practice, could imagine from a distance the way a certain horse would jump and respond.'[2]

Degas' investigation of the horse in motion was a career-long obsession, and he produced copious studies, drawings and pastels as well as wax sculptures and paintings of the subject. His fascination with figures in movement was stimulated by the discovery of Eadweard Muybridge's photographic studies involving a man riding a galloping horse, amongst other investigations. It would appear that Degas' initial interest in Muybridge developed after he came across an article by Jules Marey on the photographer. This was published in *La Nature* and provided information on Muybridge's

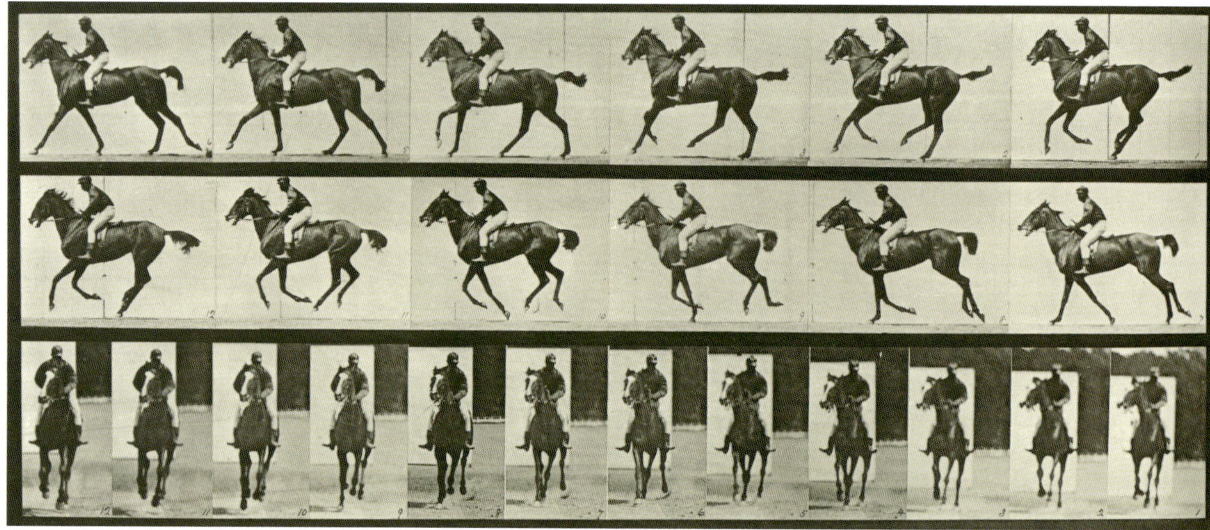

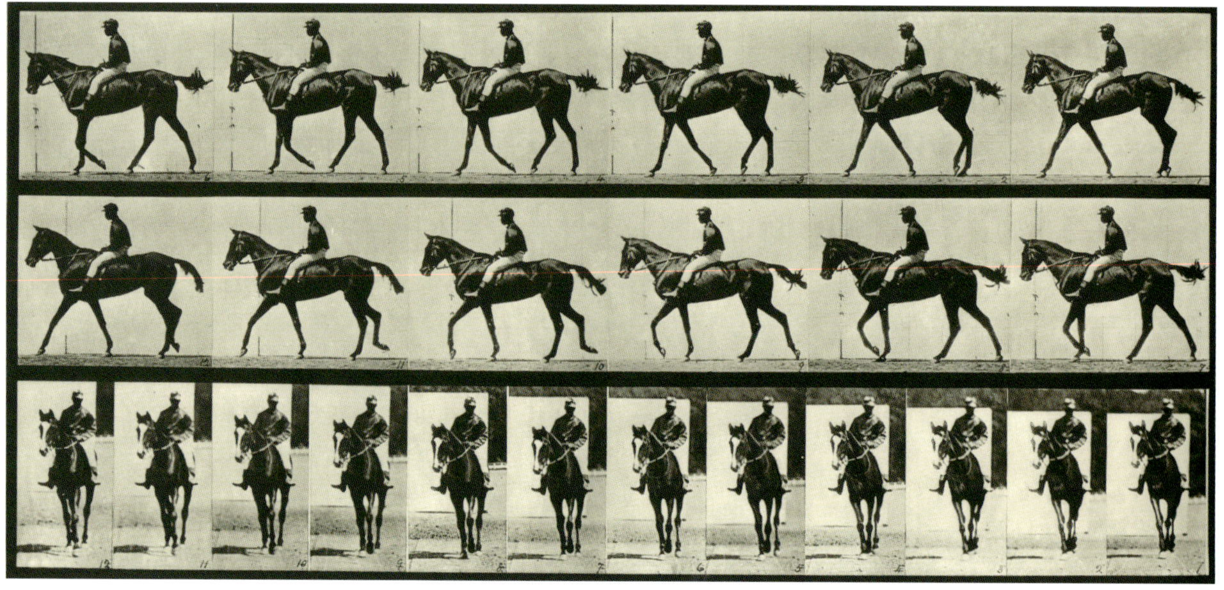

(previous page)
The racecourse (Amateur jockeys close to a carriage)
1876–87 (detail cat 15)

(above right)
Eadweard Muybridge
Animal locomotion, plate 621, motion study photograph: animals and movements, horses, canter; thoroughbred bay mare, Annie G
1887
collotype photograph, 18 x 41 cm
Collections of the University of Pennsylvania Archives

(below right)
Eadweard Muybridge
Animal locomotion, plate 580, motion study photograph: animals and movements, horses, walking; saddle; thoroughbred bay mare, Annie G 1887
collotype photograph, 19 x 39 cm
Collections of the University of Pennsylvania Archives

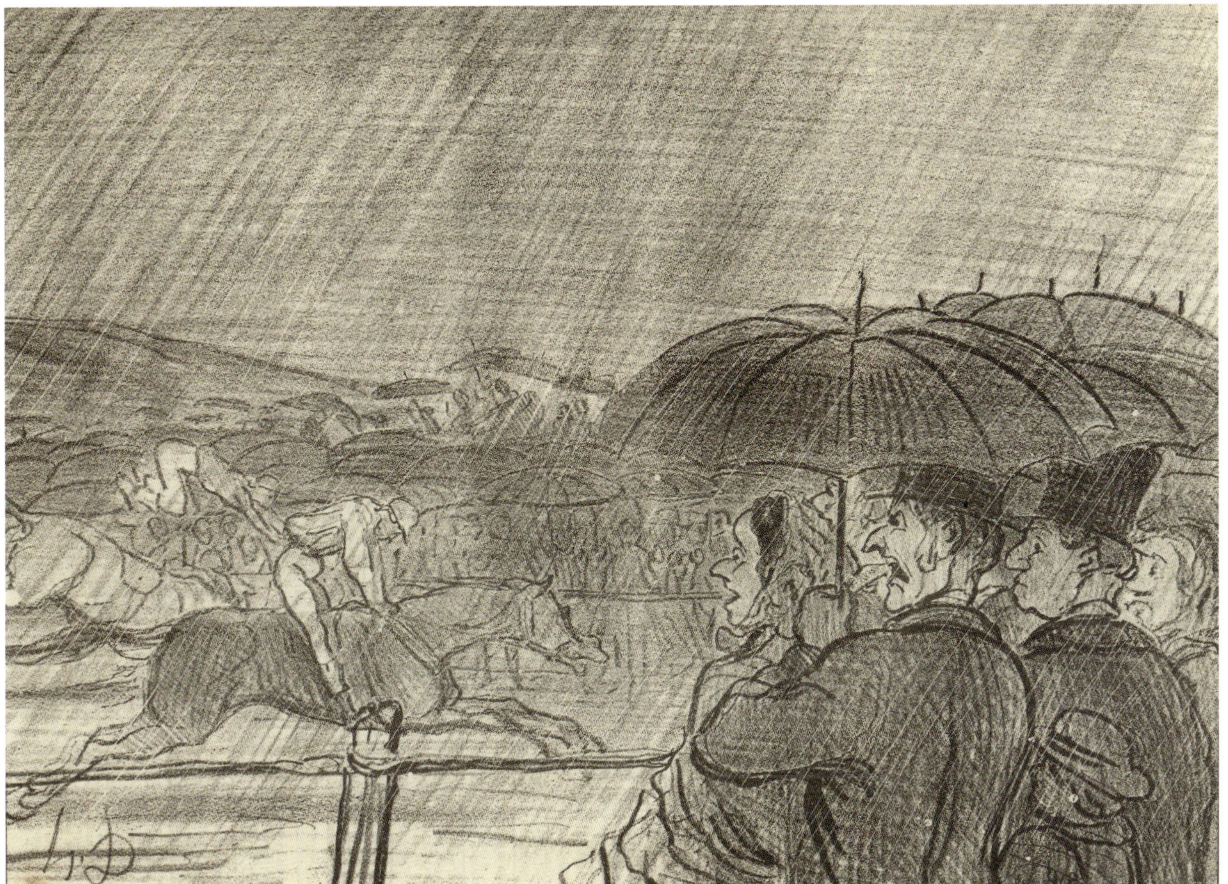

Honoré Daumier
Nautical sports of 1856: Oh! it's amazing how fast they can go ... and without oars (Courses nautiques de 1856: Oh! c'est admirable comme ils vont vite ... et sans avirons!), from the series *What's on (Actualités)*, published in *Le Charivari* 14 May 1856
lithograph, 26.4 x 34.6 cm (sheet)
National Gallery of Australia, Canberra
Purchased 1980

instantaneous photography of horses in motion.[3] Muybridge's studies were to assist Degas.

Early sketches of horses from his student days, his copies from casts of the Parthenon frieze and depictions of horses in the paintings of such diverse artists as Théodore Géricault (1791–1824), Alfred de Dreux (1810–1860) and Gustave Moreau (1826–1898), were all source material for Degas' own horse compositions.[4]

Horseracing became a key focus for Degas from the early 1860s. The spectacle of the race itself, the speed of the horses, the jockeys' colours and the glamorous racegoers, all became subject matter for his art. While it was Edouard Manet's boast that he painted modern Paris before Degas, it has been argued that it was Degas rather than Manet who was the first of the two to depict the horse in the context of the modern horserace.[5] Such a comparison exposes a certain rivalry between the two artists in their early years; one which dissipated however in their maturity. Degas continued to maintain his interest in horseracing throughout his artistic career.

The public racing of horses in France was a relatively modern phenomenon adopted from the British racing scene, which had its beginnings at Newmarket in 1750. The Derby at Epsom was first run in 1780 and became the prototype for flat-track racing. There was prize money to be won, and the opportunity to wager on an outcome. The first French racetrack, L'hippodrome, was established at Fontainebleau in 1776, followed by the course at Vincennes outside Paris. While the 'sport of kings' was frowned upon during the French Revolution, horseracing reappeared during the reign of Emperor Napoléon Bonaparte (1804–14/15) and prospered from the time of the July Monarchy (1830–48). As with many subjects relating to French society, horseracing became the butt of jokes by French caricaturist Honoré Daumier.

In 1833, the Société d'Encouragement pour l'Amélioration des Races de Chevaux en France[6] was established to promote and administer all aspects of horseracing, and to oversee thoroughbred breeding. The Société successfully lobbied for the establishment of the Hippodrome de Longchamp in the Bois de Boulogne on the outskirts of Paris. The new racecourse, with its elegant grandstands, opened on 26 April 1857, and its spring racing season became an important event in the calendar of Parisian high society, accompanied by balls and other festive occasions. These associated activities were

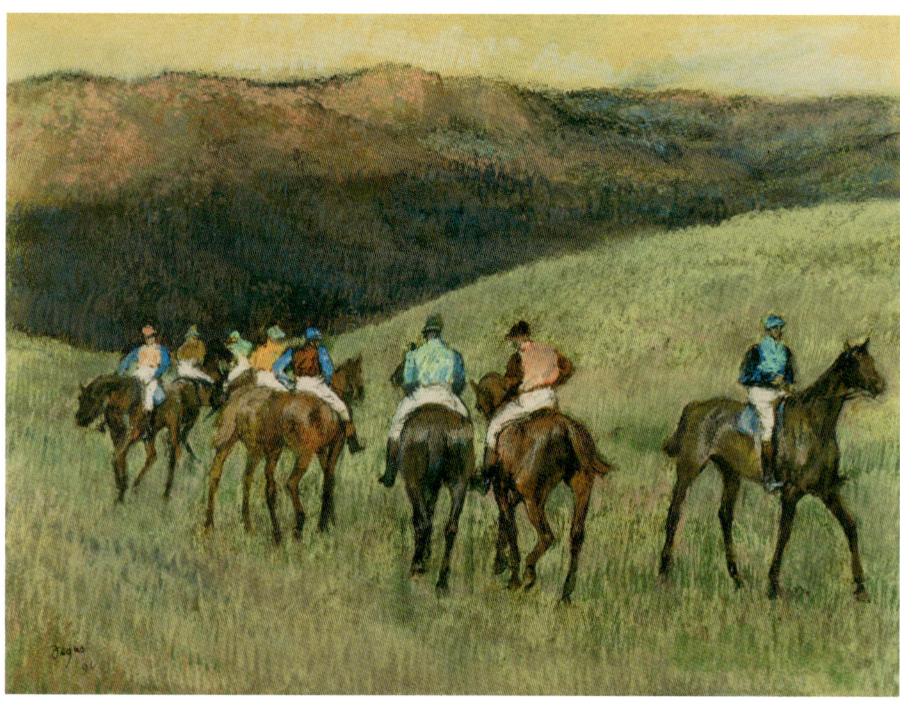

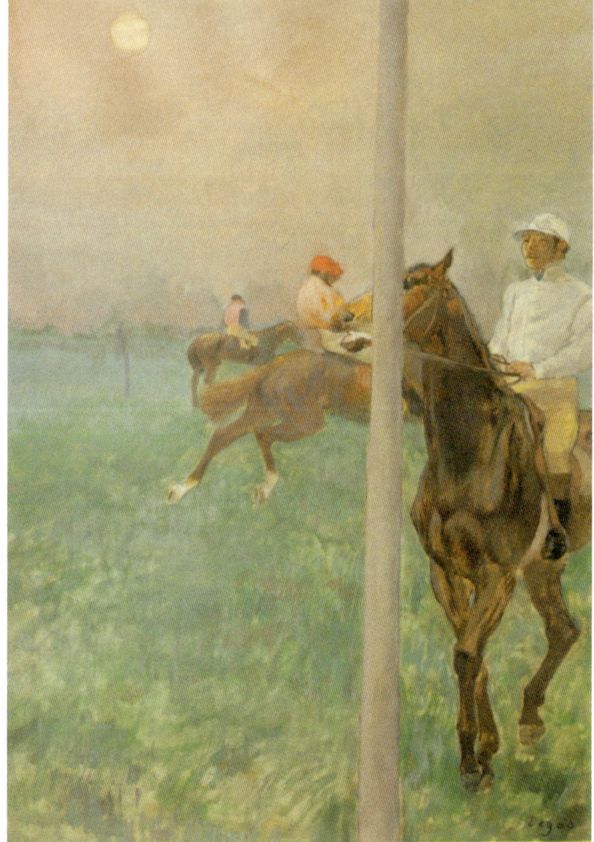

Race horses in a landscape 1894
pastel on paper, 47.9 x 62.9 cm
Museo Thyssen-Bornemisza, Madrid
Carmen Thyssen-Bornemisza Collection
Lemoisne 1145

Jockeys before the start (Jockeys avant la course) 1878–79
oil, peinture à l'essence, gouache and pastel on paper
107.3 x 73.7 cm
The Barber Institute of Fine Arts, University of Birmingham, Birmingham
Lemoisne 649

organised by the Cercle de la Société, otherwise known as the Le Jockey Club, whose members were renowned for their wealth and social status. The new cultural milieu spawned a new subject for French art and literature.

Degas' keen interest in horses broadened through his friendship with Paul Valpinçon, whom he had known since their schooldays. He made frequent visits to Valpinçon's estate, Ménil-Hubert, in the Normandy countryside, spending six weeks there on his initial visit during September and October 1861. He regularly returned to this oasis of domestic life and continued to make the journey into his seventies.[7] It was at Valpinçon's estate and the surrounds in Normandy that Degas made a series of sketches and descriptions in his notebooks, in which he observed the similarity of the Normandy landscape to the English countryside.[8] At this time he was reading Henry Fielding's *The history of Tom Jones: a foundling* (1749),[9] and he was taken with Fielding's portrayal of the lush green countryside of Somerset, which may have influenced his own sketches.

While staying at the Ménil-Hubert chateau, Degas was able to visit the nearby racetrack at Argentan and the Haras National du Pin stud farm—the oldest stud farm in France, established in the early eighteenth century on the order of Louis XIV. Sketches in the artist's notebooks dating from 1867 to 1874 (though mostly in the notebooks dated between 1867 and 1869 that he took to Normandy) reveal Degas' sustained interest in horses, racing, and racegoers.[10] He combined the subject of the racecourse with an identifiable group portrait in *At the races in the countryside* 1869—his depiction of the Valpinçon family (cat 13).

It was in his equestrian scenes that Degas became involved in creating modern landscapes populated with contemporary figures. While he depicted Longchamp in some of his early racecourse compositions, from the 1870s the location became less specific and the riders appear as anonymous figures distinguished by their colours. Gentlemen amateurs are often dressed in top hats with red coats and tails in the English manner, denoting their higher social status, while the professional jockeys clad in their racing colours usually appear more agile.

While Degas did not make a name for himself as a landscape painter, his horseracing compositions reveal a particular interest in the depiction of landscape, influenced in part by Japanese woodblock prints, *ukiyo-e*. In the Japanese tradition the landscape is not organised in the Western manner of mathematical perspective sweeping back to a single point; rather there are high horizon lines and an emphasis on linearity. Just when Degas began acquiring Japanese prints is uncertain, but by the time of his death he had amassed a significant collection, including landscapes by Kitagawa Utamaro, Ando Hiroshige and Katsushika Hokusai.[11] In Degas' racecourse scenes, particularly the later work, the influence of Japanese art, notably the colour woodblock prints, is evident in the sinuous outlines, the flat colour and the high horizon line, as in *At the races: before the start* c 1880 (cat 22).[12]

The inclusion of horseracing in his artistic repertoire did not mean that Degas worked *en plein air*. Despite sketching horses in various locations and at various times, his finished horse paintings were composed in the studio. 'Painting is not a sport,' he declared to Ambroise Vollard, and he revealed that he used small wooden models of horses, positioning them to determine lighting for his compositions. Vollard responded: 'What would the Impressionists say to that, Monsieur Degas?', to which the artist rejoined: 'You know what I think of people who work out in the open. If I were the government I would have a special brigade of gendarmes to keep an eye on artists who paint landscapes from nature. Oh, I don't mean to kill anyone; just a little dose of bird shot now and then as a warning.'[13]

Notes

1 *Scene from the steeplechase: the fallen jockey* 1866, reworked 1880–81 and c 1897, collection of Mr and Mrs Paul Mellon, National Gallery of Art, Washington DC, Lemoisne 140.

2 Degas in François Thiébault Sisson, 'Degas sculpture par lui-même', *Le Temps*, 23 May 1921, p 3, quoted by Henri Loyrette, in Jean Sutherland Boggs, Henri Loyrette, Michael Pantazzi et al, *Degas*, The Metropolitan Museum of Art and National Gallery of Canada, New York and Ottawa, 1988, p 123.

3 A reference to the essay in the journal *La Nature* (*revue des sciences et de leurs applications aux arts et à l'industrie: journal hebdomaire illustré*) which was published 5 October 1878, pp 289–95, was made by Degas in his notebook 31, p 81. See Reff 1985, p 137. See also Reff 1970, pp 293–94; Jean Sutherland Boggs, *Degas at the races*, National Gallery of Art, Washington DC, 1998, p 137.

4 On Degas' early studies of horses, see Jean Sutherland Boggs, 'The horse and art in legend', in Boggs, pp 16–35. Henri Loyrette considers that the role of the three artists mentioned is much overlooked, in Boggs et al, *Degas*, p 101, cat 42.

5 Richard Kendall, *Degas landscapes*, Yale University Press, New Haven, pp 70–71.

6 The Society for the Enhancement of Horse-racing in France.

7 Degas wrote to Paul Valpinçon's daughter Hortense, 3 August 1904, that he was planning to stay despite his ill health. In subsequent correspondence, in January 1906 and in 1907, he complains of his poor eyesight and begs her now to visit him in Paris, in Marcel Guérin (ed), *Edgar Germain Hilaire Degas: letters*, Bruno Cassirer, Oxford, 1947, pp 220, 224, 225.

8 Theodore Reff, *The notebooks of Edgar Degas: a catalogue of the thirty-eight notebooks in the Bibliothèque nationale and other collections*, 2 vols, Hacker Art Books, New York 1985, vol 1, pp 160–161.

9 Fielding's novel, translated into French in 1841 by Léon de Wailly, is most likely the version read by Degas.

10 Reff, vol 1, pp 110–16, Boggs et al, *Degas*, p 103, n 5, notes the predominant dates of the notebooks is 1867 to 1869.

11 *Catalogue des estampes anciennes et modernes: collection Edgar Degas vente à Paris à l'Hotel Drouot*, 6–7 November 1918, under the listing 'Japon'.

12 *At the races: before the start* c 1880, Virginia Museum of Fine Arts, Richmond, Lemoisne 502.

13 Ambroise Vollard, *Degas: an intimate portrait* (Randolph T Weaver trans), Crown Publishers, New York, 1937, p 56.

13 ***At the races in the countryside** (**Carriage at the races**)*
*(**Aux courses en province** (**La voiture aux courses**))*
1869
oil on canvas
36.5 x 55.9 cm
Museum of Fine Arts, Boston
26.790
1931 Purchase Fund
Lemoisne 281

This is an early example of Degas' paintings of the races, and its brilliant green colouring suggests the influence of English horseracing scenes on the artist. The composition is a transitionary one, as it combines the artist's growing interest in depicting horses and the racetrack with painting a family portrait. The family seated in their carriage has been identified as Degas' close friends, the Valpinçons.[1] Their son Henri is seated on the knee of a wet nurse, and the group is accompanied by the family pet. The Valpinçons lived at their château, Ménil-Hubert, in Normandy, which had a racecourse nearby.

The family, horses and carriage have all been placed in the foreground to one side of the painting, which provides a strong sense of movement. This sense is reinforced by the cropping of figures. In the background, the horses are seen racing. As yet, Degas has not adequately rendered the horse in motion—this was a pictorial problem he continued to try to resolve during his artistic life. The painting is notable for its clear colours and fine brushwork, reminiscent of the seventeenth-century Dutch masters.

At the races in the countryside (*Carriage at the races*) was sold to the Paris art dealer Paul Durand-Ruel, who in turn sold the painting via Charles Deschamps to the noted baritone and art collector of the day, Jean-Baptiste Faure. The singer collected French nineteenth-century art, including works by Delacroix, Corot, and Manet. Faure ultimately acquired 11 significant paintings by Degas, becoming the largest collector of his work during the artist's lifetime.

Note
1 Henri Loyette, Boggs et al, *Degas*, 1988, p 157.

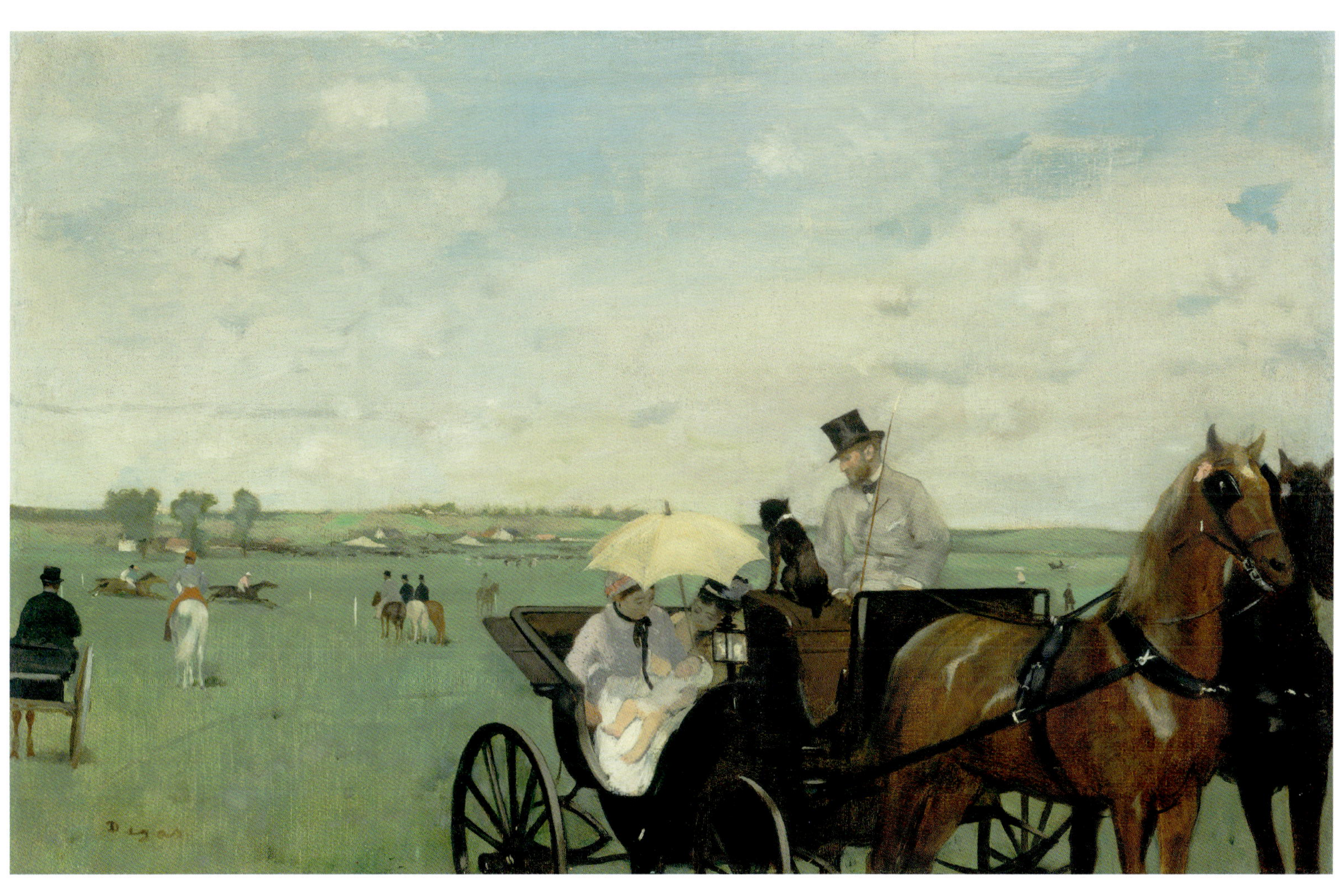
Degas

14 *Woman with field glasses* (*Femme à la lorgnette* (*La dame aux jumelles*))
1875–76
peinture à l'essence on cardboard
48 x 32 cm
Galerie Neue Meister, Staatliche Kunstsammlungen Dresden
2601
Lemoisne 431

With the advent of the Jockey Club, the social scene surrounding the racetrack became a subject of both French literature and art. (In *Remembrance of things past*, for instance, Marcel Proust refers to the social kudos relating to the racing scene, the renown of the Jockey Club and its sometimes caddish members.) In his earlier years, the Jockey Club was another aspect of the races which Degas pursued in his work. The single figure of a woman viewing the races through a set of field glasses was a motif Degas had explored on several occasions from the mid 1860s, when he made sketches as a *peinture à l'essence*—de-oiling his colours by placing his paint on blotting paper, leaving the pigment on the surface of the paper and mixing with turpentine.[1]

This single figure of a woman painted in oil on cardboard about a decade later, continued such an interest. The young racegoer is fashionably dressed for the occasion in a dark cream outfit with light cream lace collar and cuffs with flounces at the hems. Degas reveals his competence as a painter by this time, especially through his use of scumbling to indicate the ornate lace borders. Using this technique in a masterful way, Degas thinned creamy white paint which he applied over the darker coloured fabric of the dress, providing a rich texture and a decorative note to the woman's ensemble.

What is also notable about this composition is the subject's gaze. She looks directly at the viewer in quite an independent fashion, albeit through binoculars. This direct gaze is unusual for Degas outside the field of portraiture. Along with other earlier and later depictions of a woman with field glasses, another early painting is notable for Degas' mastery of scumbling—in *Woman ironing* c 1869 (see p 198) he uses the technique to depict the rich fabrics in the laundry.[2]

Notes

1 Burrell Collection, Glasgow, Lemoisne 268. British Museum, London, Lemoisne 179. For a description of Degas' technique, see Denis Rouart, *Degas: in search of his technique*, translated from the French by Pia C DeSantis, Sarah L Fisher and Shelley Fisher, Skira, Geneva, 1988, pp 26–35.

2 Neue Pinakothek, Munich, Lemoisne 216.

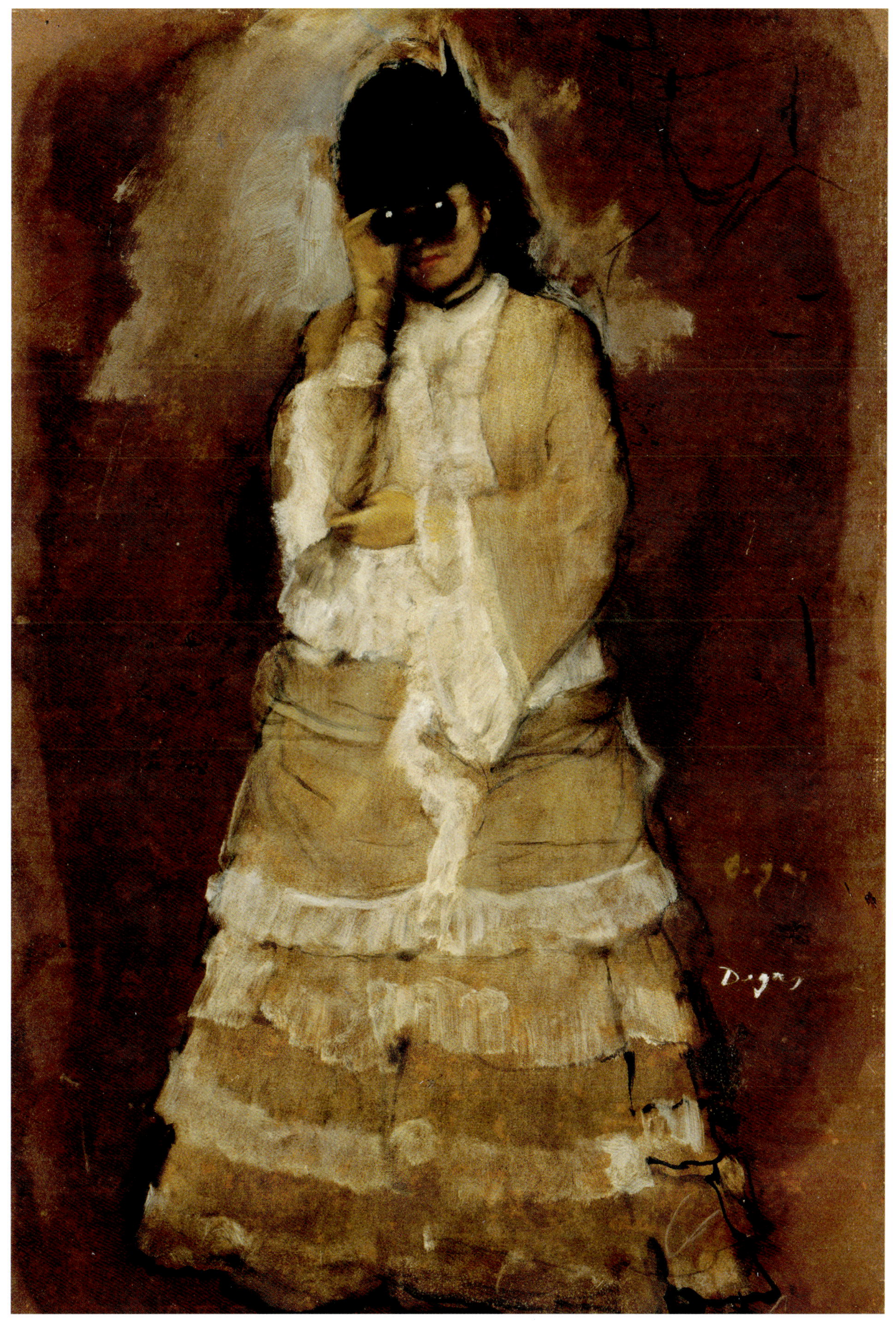

15 *The racecourse (Amateur jockeys close to a carriage)*
(Le champ de courses (Jockeys amateurs près d'une voiture))
begun 1876, completed 1887
oil on canvas
66 x 81 cm
Musée d'Orsay, Paris
RF 1980
Legacy of Count Isaac de Camondo, 1911
Lemoisne 461

This completed composition has all the hallmarks of Degas' signature style. It is decidedly asymmetrical, with the group of racegoers and the carriage placed to the forefront and cropped, to emphasise movement. One significant male figure with a top hat in the foreground is not only dramatically cropped, but has his back to the viewer—another characteristic motif favoured by the artist. The painting's structure, with cropped figures in the foreground and races continuing in the background, is reminiscent of Daumier's racing imagery—such as his caricature *Nautical sports* published in *Le Charivari* in 1856, where a crowd of racegoers watches jockeys racing in the rain (see p 61).

The racecourse (Amateur jockeys close to a carriage) was begun by Degas in 1876, and he agreed to complete the painting for delivery to the singer Jean-Baptiste Faure within the year. He failed to deliver however, and wrote apologetically in March the following year that he was unable to concentrate on the task because of his financial woes: 'Your pictures would have been finished a long time ago if I were not forced every day to do something to earn money.'[1]

The painting then underwent an excruciating gestation of 11 years before finally being handed over to Faure. Though Faure was a keen collector of Degas' work, the relationship between the artist and his major patron grew increasingly fraught. On 10 June 1886, after having received a 'friendly summons' regarding the painting, Degas invited Faure to view the work's progress. Still, almost a month later, on 2 July, Degas was begging for a 'few more days to finish your big picture of the Races'.[2] It was only after the threat of court action and a suit filed against the artist that Degas finally relinquished *The racecourse* … in the following year.

Notes

1 Marcel Guerin, 1947, p 45
2 Guerin, pp120 and 121. See also cat 53, p130.

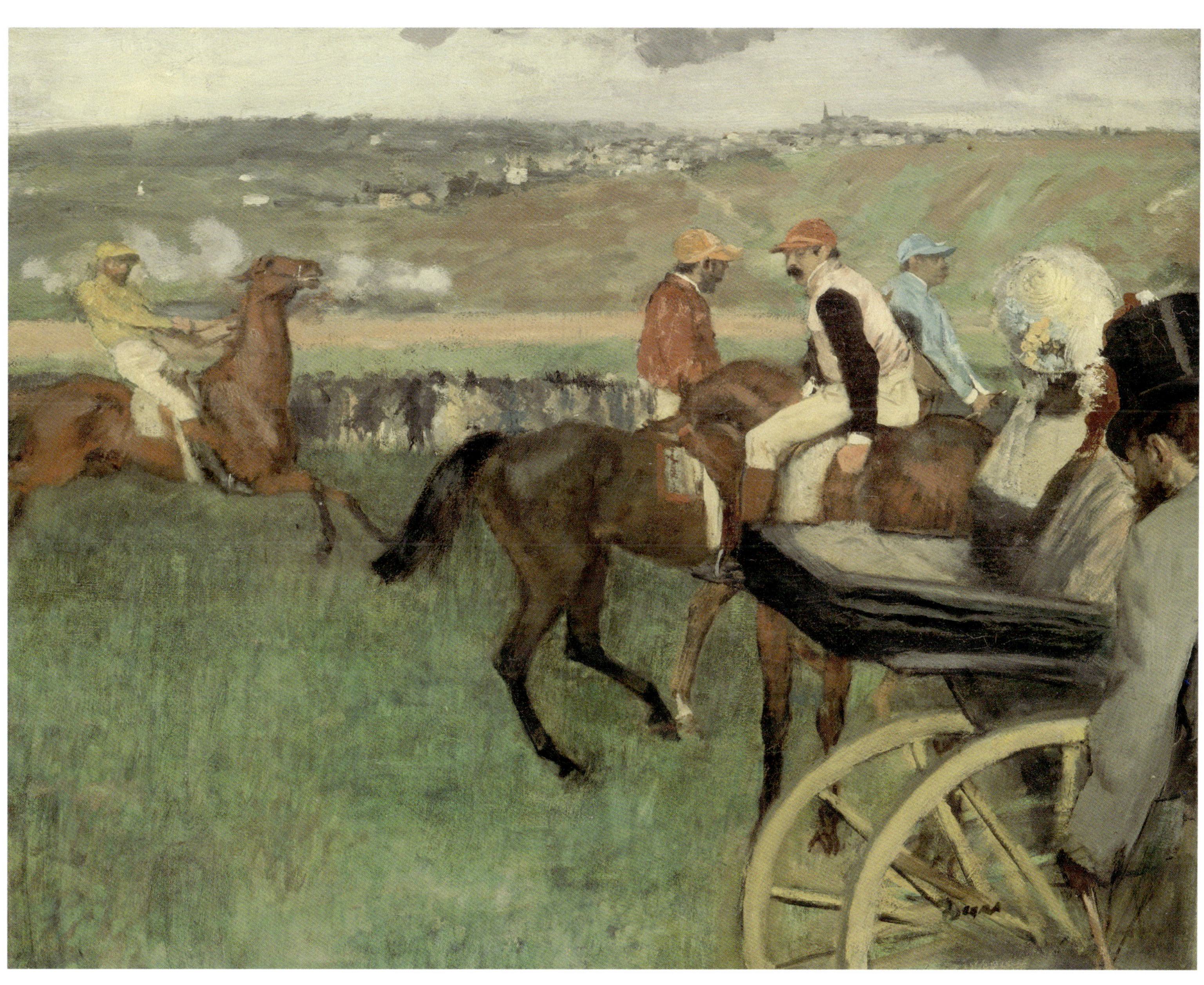

16 *Rider in a red coat, taking off his top hat*
(*Cavalier en habit rouge, enlevant son chapeau haut-de-forme*)
c 1868–70
peinture à l'essence on pink paper
43.5 x 27.6 cm
Musée d'Orsay, Paris
Housed at the Département des arts graphiques, Musée du Louvre
RF 12276
Brame and Reff 66

In this work a gentleman rider in full British riding gear—a red coat with tails and top hat—is viewed from behind. The vividly coloured coat of the distinctly plump figure has been painted in *peinture à l'essence* (see p 66), with gouache highlights on a pink sheet of paper. (It was common for Degas to choose such coloured papers to provide a strong contrast to his outline and his additions of colour.)

Rider in a red coat directly relates to Degas' painting, *The departure of the hunt* [1], which depicts a group of huntsmen in full British riding regalia preparing for a countryside chase. *The departure of the hunt* is now believed to have been painted in two stages, and transformed from a French hunting scene to an English one—with the riders now dressed in their red coats and top hats. This drawing is thought to be in response to Degas' visit to England in 1872, and the painting was perhaps intended for the English market. [2]

Degas often depicted jockeys in their racing colours. Between 1868 and 1870 he made a series of drawings of jockeys seated on their horses, seen from various viewpoints. In *A jockey on his horse* (cat 18) the rider is shown in three-quarter view, looking out determinedly as if preparing for a race. Such exercises provided Degas with a repertoire of poses he could adopt in later compositions.

One of these later compositions shows a slender young man in oversized racing apparel, drawn in charcoal on brown coloured paper (cat 17). This work can probably be dated c 1884, as it relates to other charcoal drawings of that time.[3] The jockey is shown in three-quarter view, with his facial features delicately drawn beneath a riding cap. The remaining costume is cursorily sketched, creating a composition reminiscent of an Ingres-style portrait combining the delicate lines of the sitter's face with the looser, freer renderings of their clothing.

Degas had a great fascination for horses, and nowhere is this more evident than in his 'portrait', *Head of a horse* (cat 21). This spirited characterisation—with the animal's lively expression, its open mouth, and its eyes and ears alert—was probably a preparatory drawing for the related painting, *Jockeys before the start* c 1878 (see p 62).[4]

Notes

1 Private collection, Lemoisne 119.
2 Boggs et al, *Degas*, 1998, pp 75–76.
3 For example, *Study of a jockey*, c 1884, Collection Mr and Mrs Paul Mellon, III, 105, 4; which in turn relates to the pastel, Kunsthaus, Zürich, c 1885–87, Lemoisne 850.
4 Barber Institute of Fine Arts Gallery, Birmingham, Lemoisne 649.

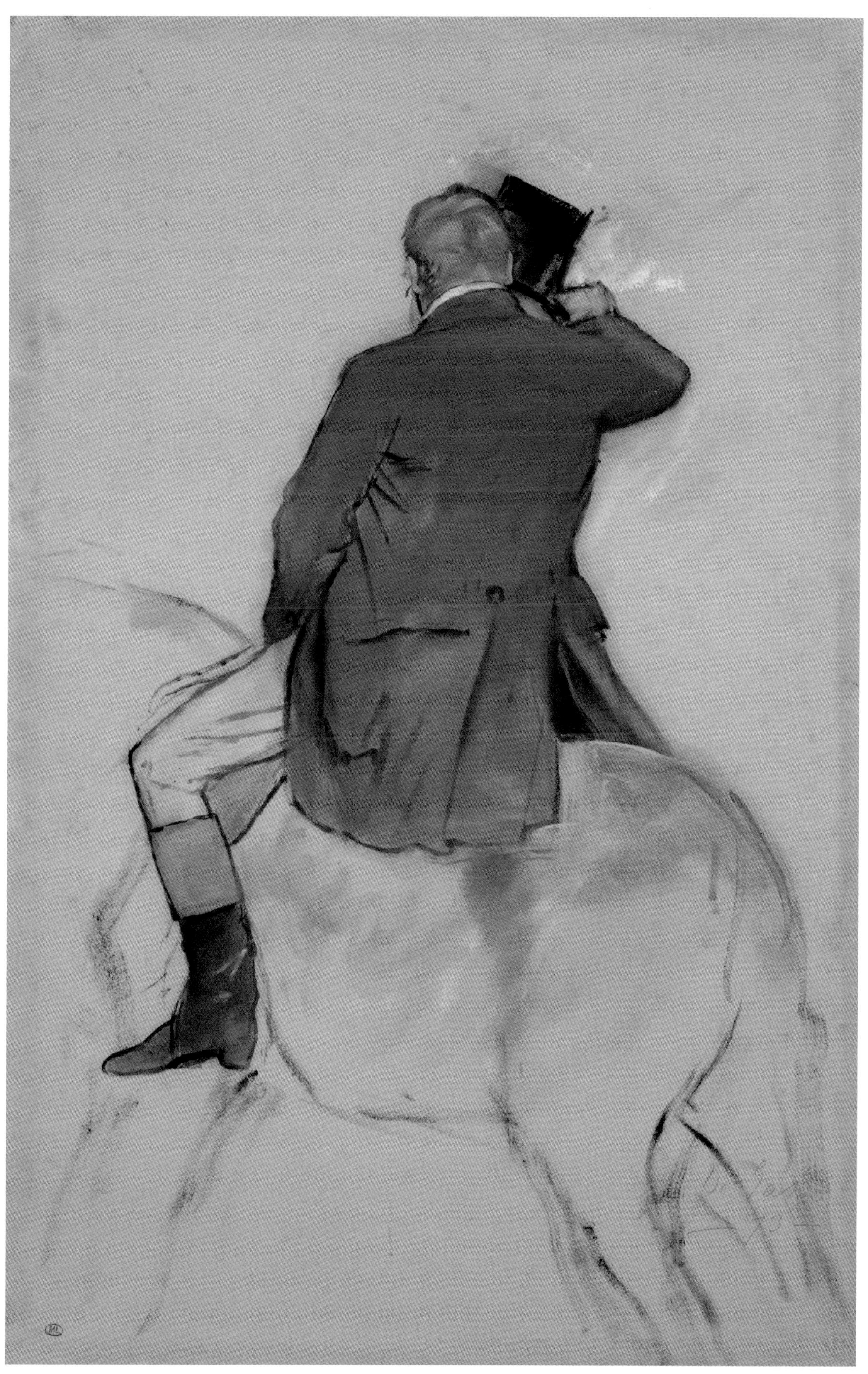

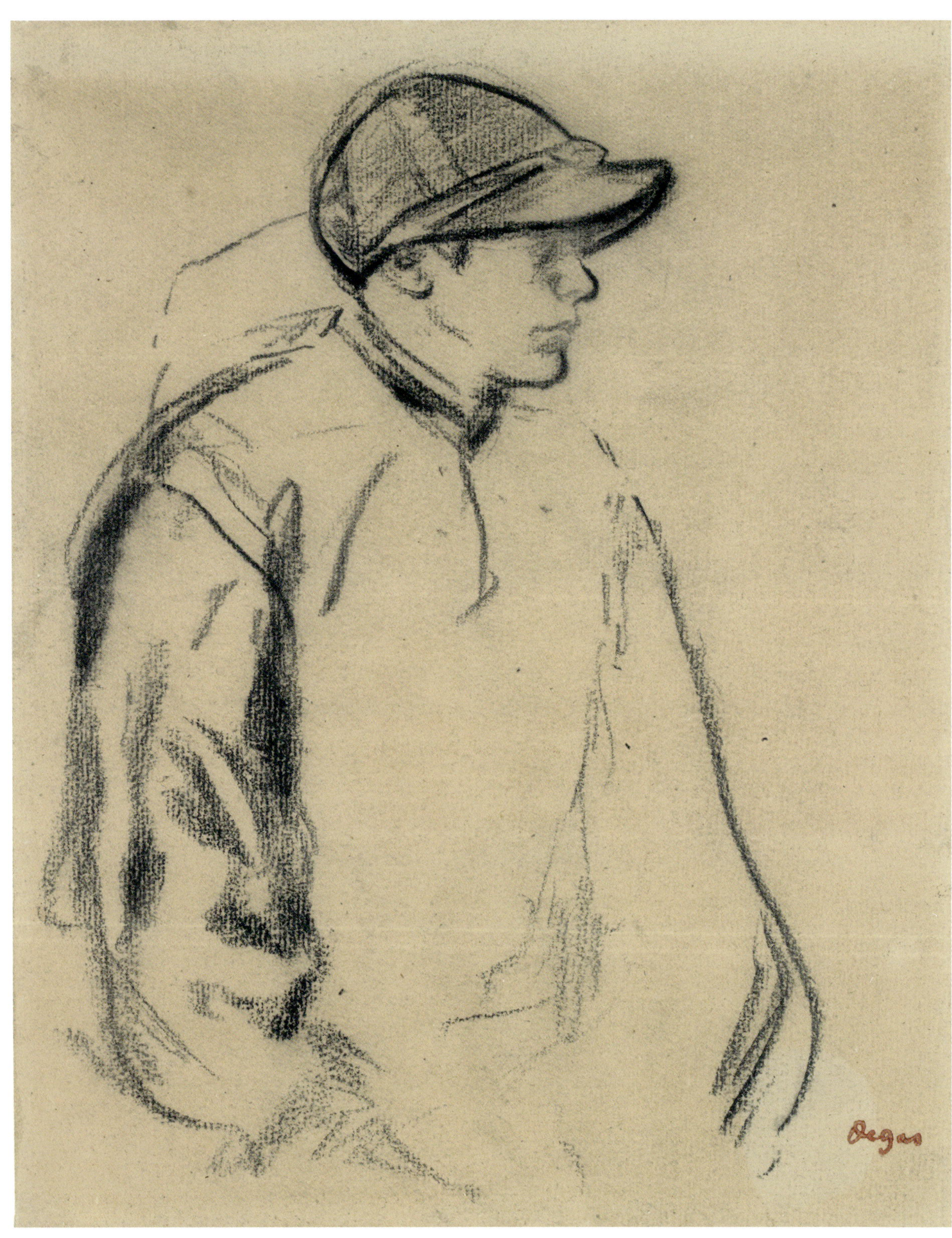

17 *Study of a jockey* (*Etude d'un jockey*)
c 1884
charcoal on brown paper
31 x 23.8 cm
The British Museum, London
1920,0420.14
Vente III: 105.4

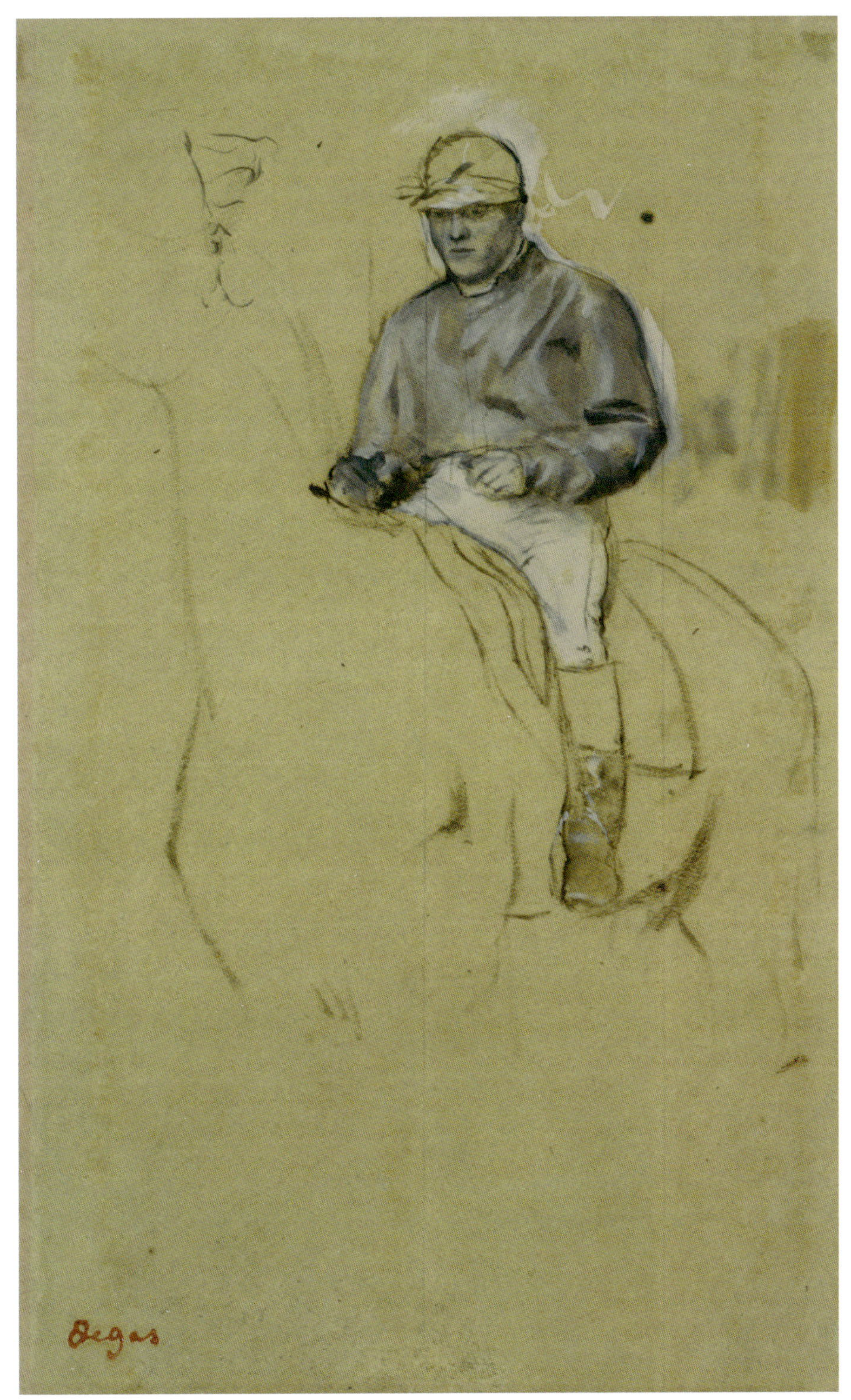

18 *A jockey on his horse*
(*Un jockey sur son cheval*)
c 1868–70
oil and graphite on faded pink paper
32.7 x 18.3 cm
The Metropolitan Museum of Art, New York
1972.118.206
Bequest of Walter C Baker, 1971
Vente III: 128.2

19 *Horse galloping on right foot* (*Cheval au galop sur le pied droit*)
modelled c 1890; cast c 1926
bronze
cast O of 25
30.5 x 47 x 21.3 cm
Minneapolis Institute of Art, Minneapolis
55.15
The David Draper Dayton Fund
Czestochowski and Pingeot 47

At the time of Degas' death in 1917, there were about 150 sculptured pieces in the artist's studio, which formed about 80 wax models. Under direction of the artist's friend, the sculptor Paul Albert Bartholomé, the foundryman Albino Palazzolo made 73 bronze sculptures from the wax models.

To retain Degas' original wax models during the process of making the bronzes, Palazzolo ingeniously devised an alternative to the lost-wax method. He made a series of unique bronze *modèles* which protected the pliable wax; these in turn were used to make the moulds from which the bronze sculptures were editioned.[1]

Over his career, Degas had made wax figurines to solve pictorial problems, such as depicting a horse in motion, which he had then incorporated into his paintings and drawings. *Horse walking* (cat 20), for example, appears in a painting from the 1870s (see p 62, top), and a painting from the 1880s *Jockeys on horseback before distant hills* (cat 23) was recycled as a pastel in the 1890s (see p 62).

This remarkable later bronze, *Horse galloping on right foot*, is a most accomplished study, capturing all the excitement of a horse in motion, with its feet barely touching the ground.

Note

1 For a further discussion of the complexities of the making of the bronzes, see Arthur Beale, 'Little Dancer aged fourteen: the search for the lost modèle', in Richard Kendall, *Degas and the little dancer*, 1998, pp 97–108; reprinted in Czestochowski and Pingeot, pp 86–95.

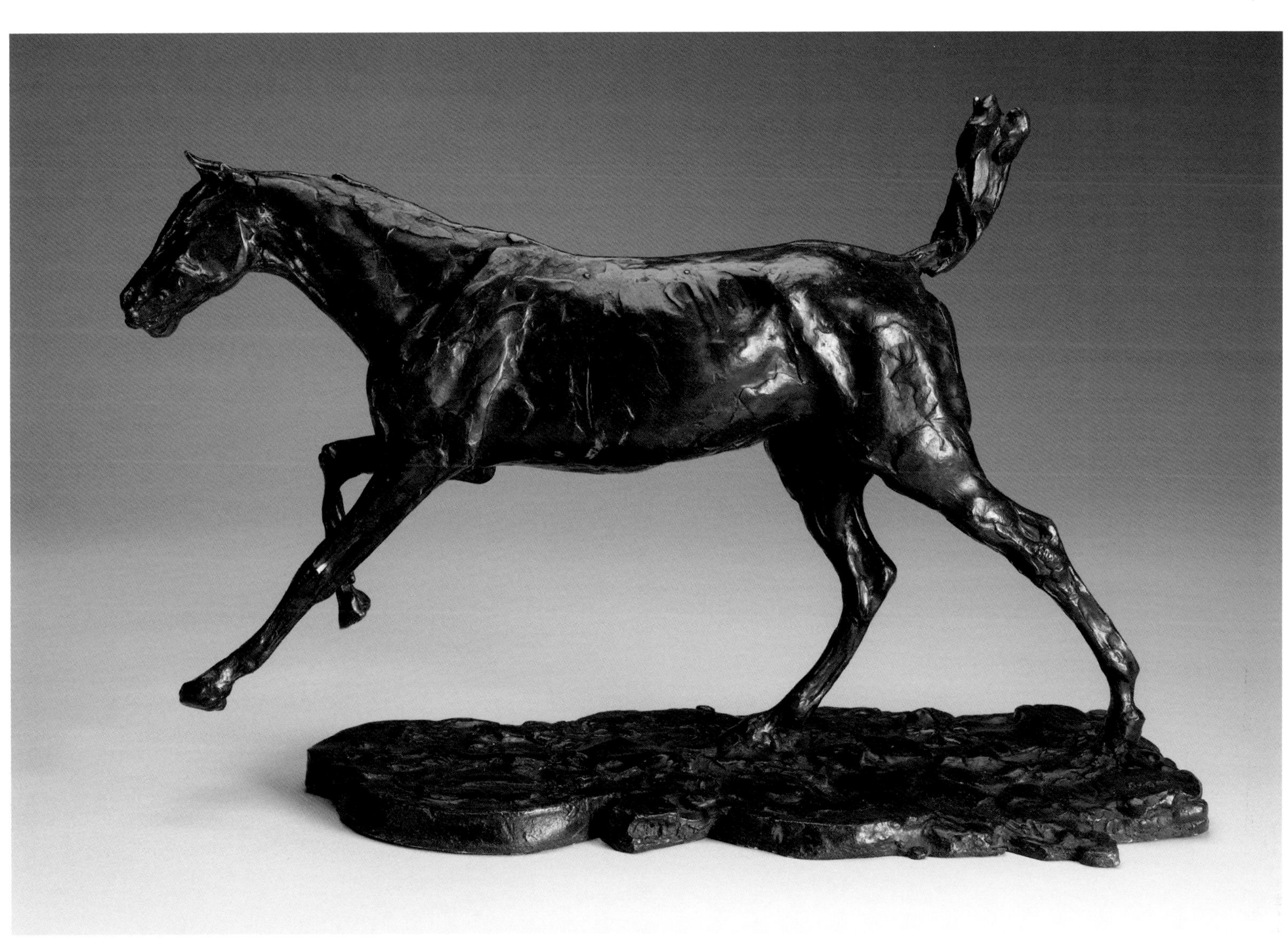

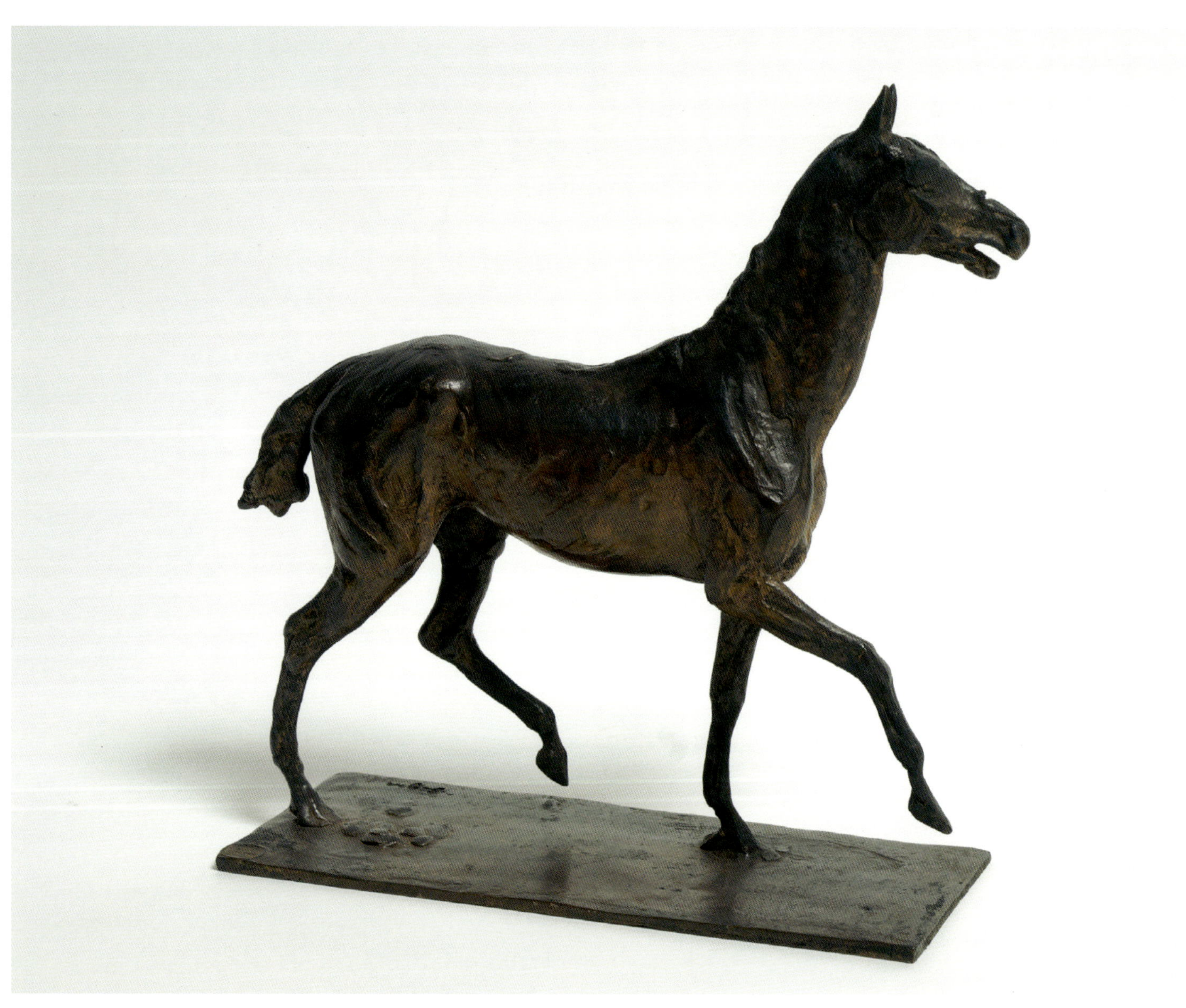

20 *Horse walking* (*Cheval marchant au pas relevé*)
modelled c 1881; cast 1919–30
cast T of 21
bronze
23.1 x 22.8 x 9.3 cm
The Trustees of the Barber Institute of Fine Arts,
University of Birmingham, Birmingham
50.3
Czestochowski and Pingeot 11

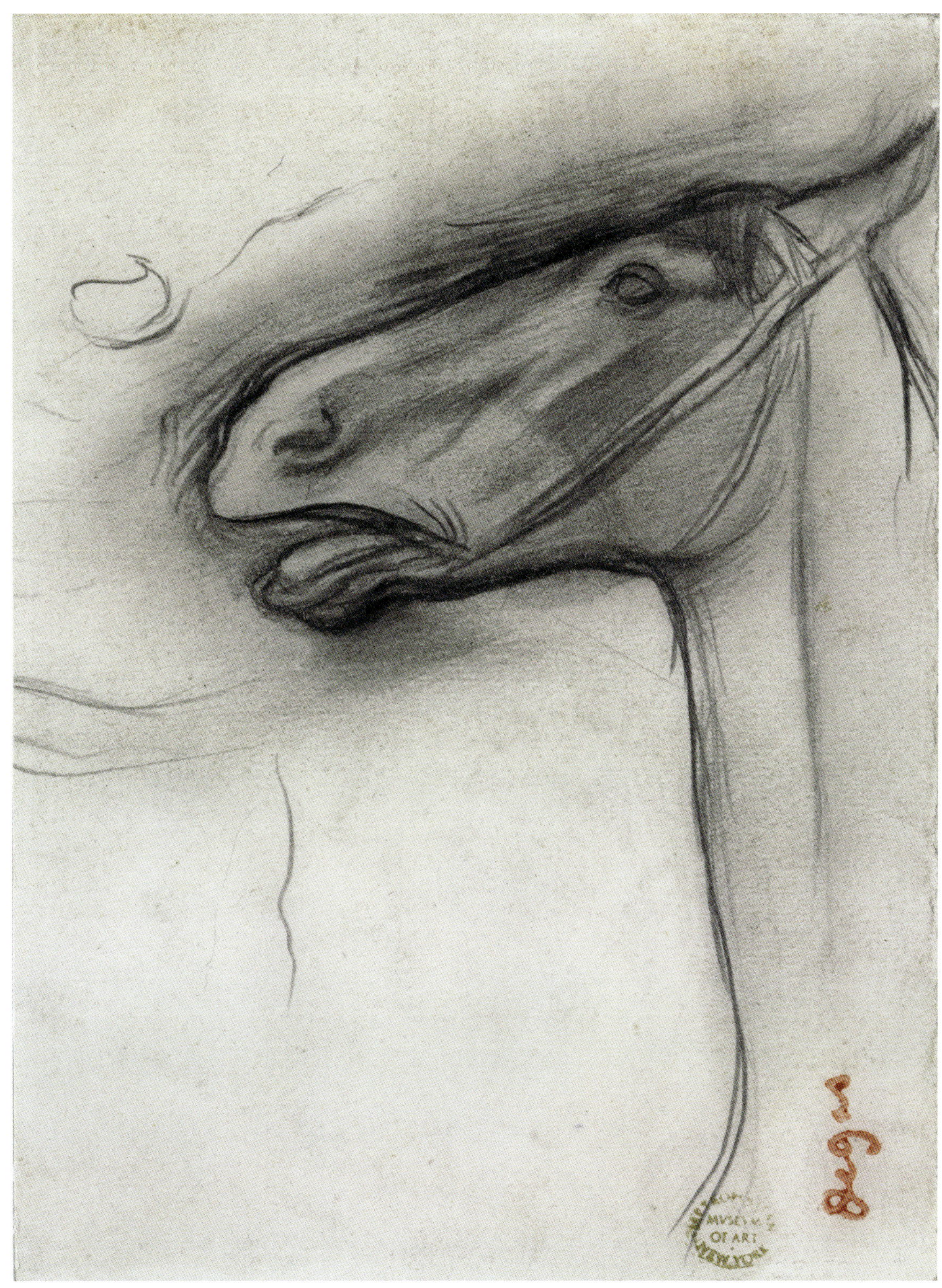

21 *Head of a horse* (*Tête d'un cheval*)
c 1878
graphite on paper
16.7 x 12.1 cm
The Metropolitan Museum of Art, New York
23.230.13
Gift of AE Gallatin, 1923
Vente IV: 233.f

22 *At the races: before the start* (*Aux courses: avant le départ*)
c 1885–92
oil on canvas
40 x 89.9 cm
Virginia Museum of Fine Arts, Richmond, Virginia
85.496
Collection of Mr and Mrs Paul Mellon
Lemoisne 502
Photograph: Katherine Wetzel

At the races: before the start—a work which was created over an extensive period of time—reveals Degas as an accomplished artist in his exploration of the theme of horses and horseracing. This painting is quintessentially Degas, with his creation and reinforcement of a feeling of motion achieved through careful placement of the figures of horses and riders, and the strong asymmetry adding to the painting's sense of movement.

Degas used wax models to perfect the positions of his figures and explore the forms and space around them. In tandem with this and other related canvases, he explored the idea of movement with several wax sculptures which were subsequently cast in bronze—including *Horse rearing* and *Horse galloping on right foot* (cat 19). Degas then incorporated these as motifs on the canvases. Also in evidence is the influence of Eadweard Muybridge's photographic essays of horses in motion (see p 60). In his search for how to depict horses walking, trotting, galloping and cantering, Degas made careful examination of Muybridge's photographs.

At the races: before the start is one of the last in an important series of horizontal canvases Degas began in the early 1880s. The work is characterised by the depiction of horses and jockeys in a variety of positions, in a horizontal frieze-like composition, a format he favoured for many of his works both of the ballet and of horses during this period. This radical format allowed Degas to stretch the horses across the picture plane—from cropped figures falling off the edge of the canvas in the foreground, to tiny figures disappearing into the hills in the background.

The high horizon line, flattened sense of space, and brilliant colours, suggest the influence of Japanese *ukiyo-e* woodcuts. Degas had become interested in Japanese art early in his career, in the 1860s, and the style was to permeate his compositions as he matured as an artist over later years.

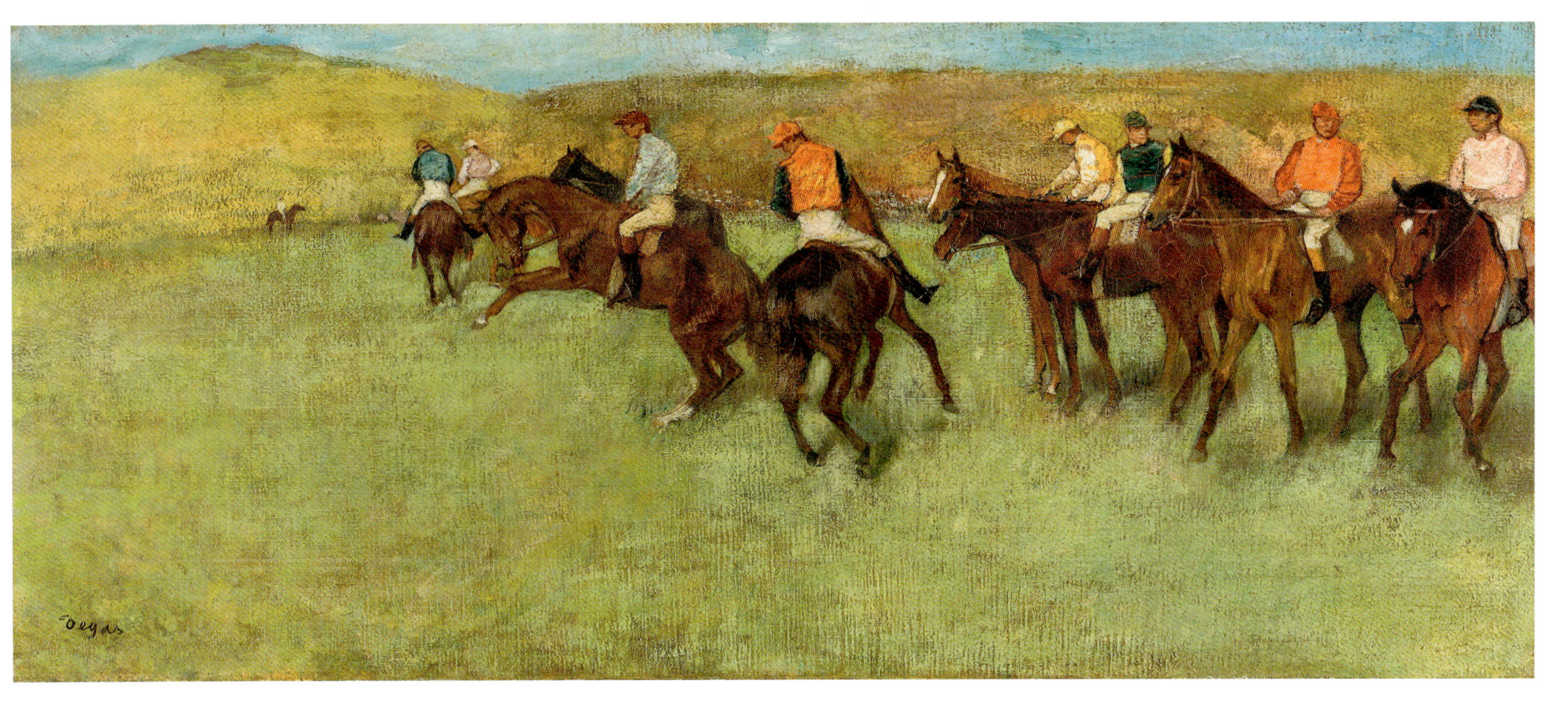

23 *Jockeys on horseback before distant hills (Riders before hilly country)*
c 1884
oil on canvas
44.9 x 54.9 cm
Detroit Institute of Arts, Detroit
1998.65
Gift of W Warren and Virginia Shelden, in memory of Mrs Allan Shelden
Lemoisne 767

During the 1880s, Degas turned his attention to the theme of horses on a regular basis. He became more interested in the subject of horses and riders in a landscape, and *Jockeys on horseback before distant hills (Riders before hilly country)* is remarkable in this respect. The informal grouping of horses and jockeys depicted with delicate brushwork, contrasts with the background of a loosely painted landscape of mountainous terrain and almost abstract forms.

In the course of his association with the Impressionists, Degas was vocal about their method of creating landscapes *en plein air*—rejecting the method of Monet and others who painted out-of-doors with the aim of capturing the changing seasons, times of day and weather conditions.

Degas did, however, include landscape scenes in his compositions of horses and races. These evolved in the 1870s to include significant renderings of paddocks, hillsides and skies, and in some instances identifiable locations, though lacking the Impressionist concentration on surface appearance, which Degas considered superficial. During the late 1870s, Degas explored landscapes in his monotypes, and by the 1880s the landscape element in the artist's composition of horseracing came to the fore.

Degas was to replicate the figures of the jockeys, horses and mountains a decade later in the medium of pastel (see p 62, top), using bold strokes of greens, blues and violets to create imaginary landscapes rich in colour and atmospherics.

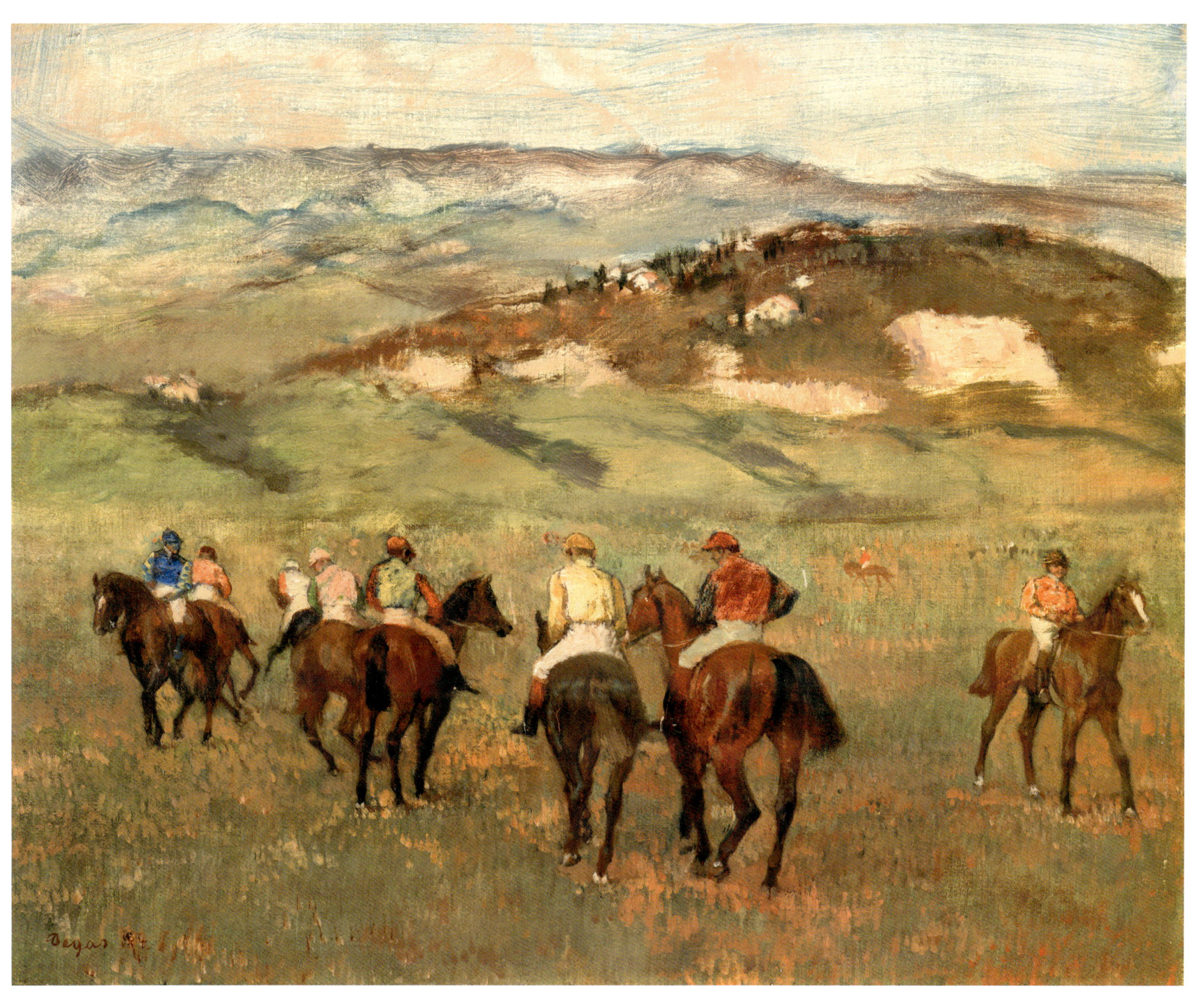

24 *The return of the herd* (*La rentrée du troupeau*)
c 1898
oil on canvas
71 x 92 cm
New Walk Museum and Art Gallery, Leicester
IIA1969
Lemoisne 1213

Moving away from the theme of horses and horseracing, but still exploring the subject of animals within the landscape is Degas' painting *The return of the herd*. This late powerful work, a pinnacle of daring by Degas, anticipates modernism in terms of its composition, palette and technique. It reveals the change in Degas' art practice when he adopted a warmer-hued palette; the colours are applied with thick paint, incorporating shapes as building blocks to form the composition.

Degas' brother René rented a holiday cottage at Saint-Valéry-sur-Somme by the English Channel in northern France, and Degas made a series of moody landscapes of the township there, usually bereft of figures. The exception is *The return of the herd,* where he depicts cattle winding their way through a little seaside village.

The return of the herd highlights the influence Paul Gauguin had on Degas in his later years. Degas had met Gauguin through Camille Pissarro, when Gauguin was about 30 years old. On Pissarro's recommendation, Degas had supported Gauguin's inclusion in the 1879 Impressionist exhibition. Despite their argument over who should participate in the subsequent group-exhibition of 1882 (particularly the inclusion of Jean-François Raffaëlli), Degas and Gauguin admired each other's work. Gauguin was impressed with Degas' 'aesthetic distortions', and Degas became an enthusiastic collector of Gauguin's work during the 1890s, acquiring a significant group of paintings, sculptures and prints. The vivid palette of warm browns, pinks and oranges, and the other-worldliness of *The return of the herd,* are testimony to the effect Gauguin had on the older artist.

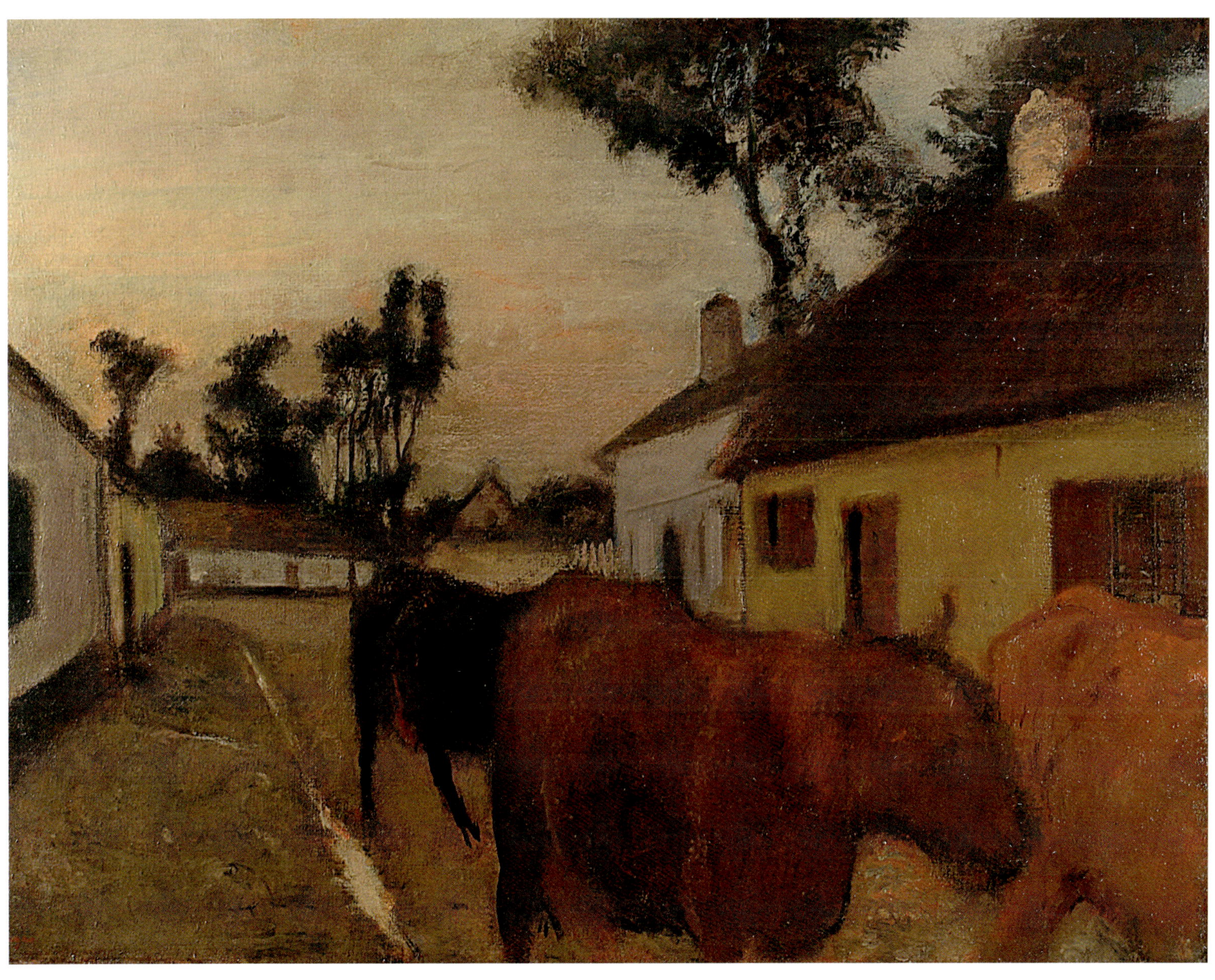

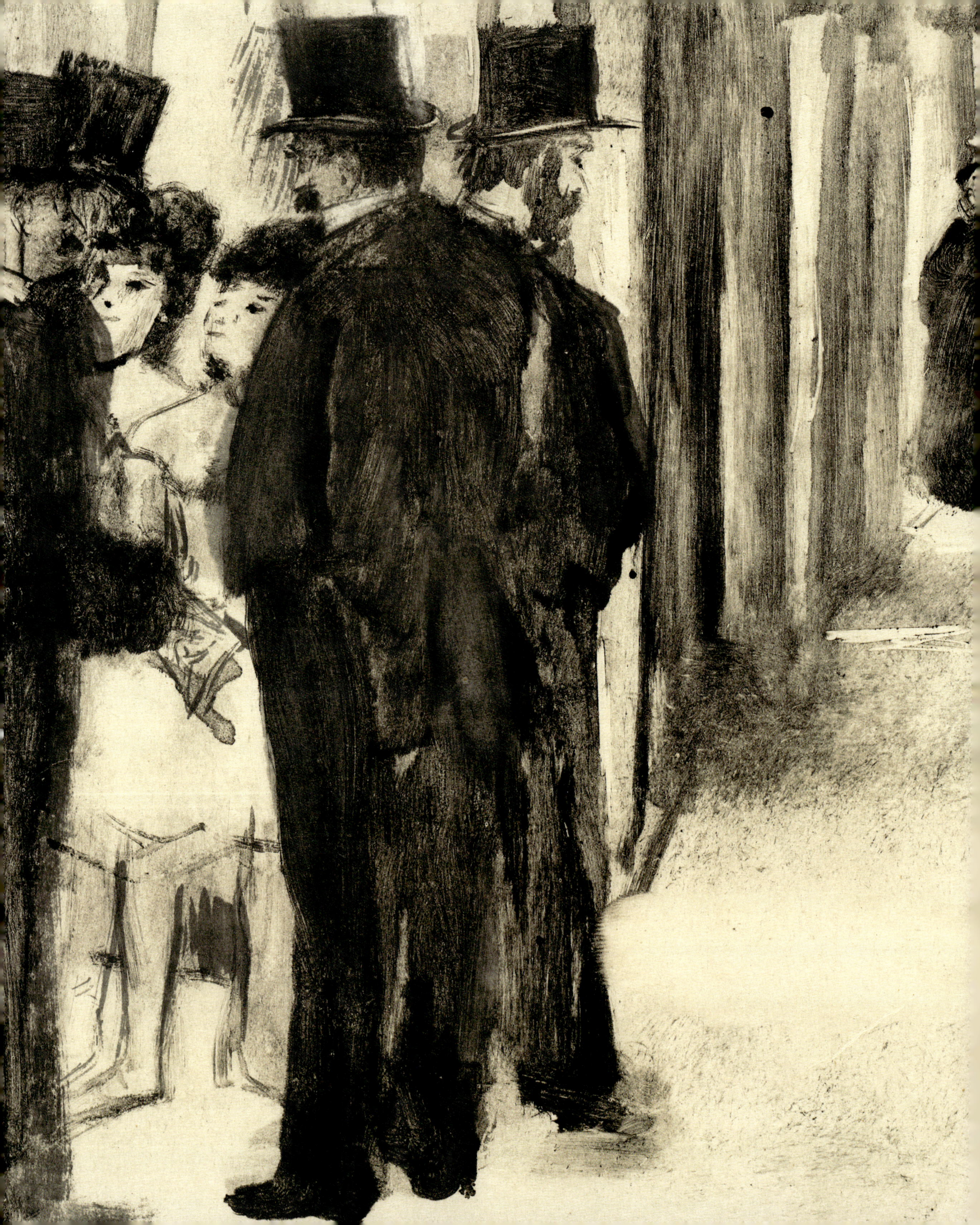

PAINTERLY PRINTS:
THE MONOTYPES

A SERIES OF SHORT STORIES by Degas' friend Ludovic Halévy, a popular librettist and writer about life in contemporary Paris, inspired a group of monotypes made by the artist in the second half of the 1870s.

Halévy's satirical essays, which lampoon the upper and lower echelons of French society, were originally written for *La vie Parisienne.* They appeared between 1870 and 1875 in separate publications: *Madame Cardinal* (1870) and *Monsieur Cardinal* (1871), which were republished jointly in 1872. A further essay, 'Les petites Cardinal' (1875), relates the adventures of the Cardinals' two daughters, Pauline and Virginie, who were ballet dancers at the Paris Opéra. Collections of these stories were published in 1880 and 1883.

Monsieur Cardinal, a government official banished to the provinces, serves his constituents 'with all his strength and power'. His office is his 'temple', where a bust of Voltaire has pride of place on the mantelpiece. In the manner of Jean-Jacques Rousseau and the Enlightenment, Cardinal admires the country yokels; he sees the nobility of man in nature, despite the true reality of life in backwater Ribeaumont. Halévy keeps Madame Cardinal in a permanent state of angst—a hurrying bundle of floating flounces, bouncing glasses and puffy features. She attends to the needs of her husband, yet considers herself a 'failed mother', made distraught by the antics of her daughters as they are pursued by predatory rich men—the 'Lions'—who frequent the Paris Opéra. Pauline adopts the grand title of 'Pauline de Giraldas' and has many suitors; Virginie runs away with the Marquis Cavalcanti to live in a palace in Florence.

(previous page)
Pauline and Virginie Cardinal chatting with some admirers
1876–77 (detail cat 31)

(below)
Place de la Concorde (Viscount Lepic and his daughters crossing Place de la Concorde) (Vicomte Lepic et ses dérivés croisant la Place de la Concorde) 1875
oil on canvas, 78.4 x 117.5 cm
The State Hermitage Museum, St Petersburg
Lemoisne 368
Photograph © The State Hermitage Museum

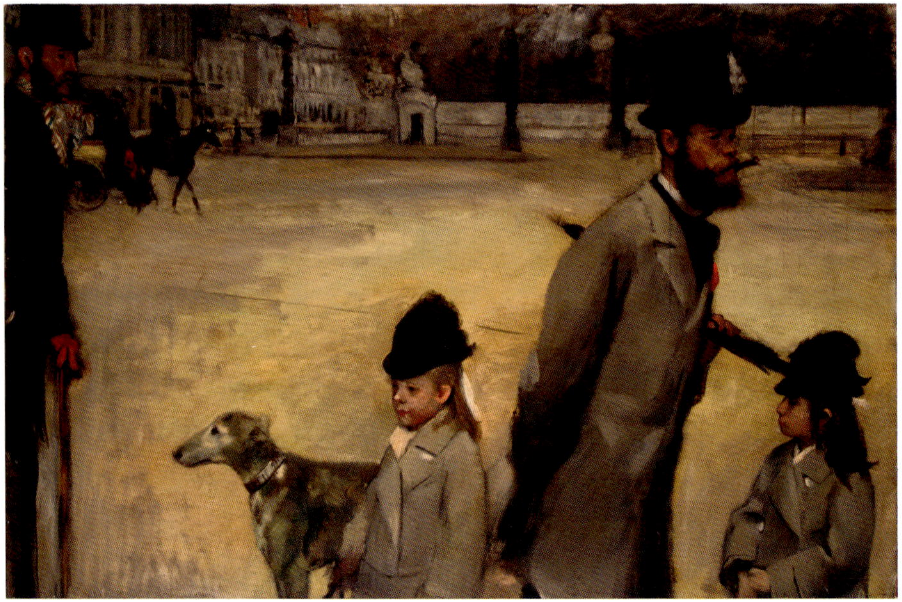

In his Cardinal series of monotypes Degas is the visual narrator of these stories of assignation and intrigue behind the scenes at the Opéra. He showed several of the monotypes at the third Impressionist exhibition in 1877, leading the critic Jules Claretie to comment:

> His drawings have an extraordinary quality. They are life itself. Both Goya and Gavarni are present in such an artist … M. Degas has created images out of Paris and its everyday life, its various guises, its surfaces and its depths, which many a person would find astonishing if ever it crossed a publisher's mind to put them together in the form of an album. If that day ever comes, people will see what insight this man has into life.[1]

It was once believed that Degas had prepared his monotypes of the Cardinal family to illustrate the 1883 compilation of Halévy's stories, but that the author had rejected them. The art dealer René Gimpel reflected: 'Halévy never did understand Degas' talent, but Mme Halévy, who admired him, asked him to make sketches, assuring him that she would convince her husband. But she failed.'[2] More recently, it has been argued that Degas responded to the stories earlier than in the years 1880–83, the dates previously given for his Cardinal monotypes. Not only had some of these monotypes appeared on public display in 1877, but the subject matter already existed in three publications of the Cardinal stories when Degas became captivated by the monotype process.[3]

In early studies of his monotypes, it was generally thought that Degas began experimenting with the process around 1874, guided by his friend Ludovic Lepic, who he painted a year later with his daughters in a work titled *Place de la Concorde.* Lepic had been making a type of painterly print (*eau-forte mobile*) and Degas extended this idea by manipulating ink applied to an unmarked plate—claiming the method as his own.[4] The first monotype, *The ballet master,*[5] was signed by both Lepic and Degas; but Degas soon became besotted with the new technique, and committed himself to the production of monotypes. In his discussion of Degas' figurative monotypes (not the later landscapes[6]), Michael Pantazzi proposed compressing the period of their production, based on evidence that would have Degas beginning around 1876 and ending his initial obsession with the technique earlier than previously thought.[7]

Degas was intrigued with process, and keen to adopt innovative techniques. He readily embraced the production of monotypes, calling them his *plats du jour,* and pursued two ways of making them—his *cuisine.* One method, the black field or subtractive method, involves covering a copper plate with ink or paint, then creating the image in the ink by wiping with a rag, brush or other implement (even the fingers). The paper support is moistened and placed over the plate, then pressure is applied in a printing press. The other production approach, known as the light field method, is an additive process where the image is created by drawing or brushing ink or paint directly onto a clean plate. Again wet paper is placed over the plate, and pressure applied in a printing press. For an artist who took pride in his lack of spontaneity, the process of making monotypes allowed Degas to develop his powers of observation and provided an almost instantaneous means of experimentation in line, form, brushwork and composition. Making monotypes was an important outlet for Degas' ideas, and enhanced and influenced his future art practice.

The behind-the-scenes world of the Opéra attracted Degas' fascinated gaze. Along the corridors, on the stairs, behind the stage scenery and in the practice rooms, rich men generally of a mature age pursued the young dancers in the hope of sexual assignations. In *Pauline and Virginie Cardinal chatting with some admirers* c 1876–77 (cat 31), the two sisters are flirting with a pack of Opéra 'Lions'. One of the men turns to look behind, only to see Madame Cardinal approaching down the corridor. Like so many of Degas' monotypes the composition is radical and inventive—a huddle of figures on one side, an empty corridor on the other, with just a whisper of the figure of the mother in the distance. The flattened space, cropped figures and views from behind are all characteristic of his style at the time.

In another of his Cardinal monotypes Degas introduced the predatory figure of the Italian Marquis Cavalcanti, who was pursuing Virginie to her parents' consternation. Matters came to a head at a dinner with the Marquis and the Cardinals at the Café Anglais, near the Opéra on the boulevard des Italiens. The restaurant was noted for its 'three emperors dinner', featuring creamed chicken soufflés, fillets of sole, escallops of turbot, chicken à la portugaise, lobster à la Parisienne, ducklings à la Rouennaise, ortolans, and a selection of eight wines to complement the food. In his monotype *The famous Good Friday dinner* c 1876–77 (cat 30), Degas shows no interest in the sumptuous food on offer; instead the dining table appears bare. The focus is on Monsieur Cardinal, seen from behind. He is engaged in heated argument with the balding Marquis. Madame Cardinal looks askance, her profiled face caught in the light. Another figure rushing out of the composition on the right adds to the sense of commotion. The turbulence of the occasion is evoked by Degas within the sweeping lines of the composition, where the light illuminating the table seems to be swinging from one side to the other. The father's anger appears to rise up through his massive body—about to lunge forward from his chair, which is pushed out from the table in a gesture of rage.

Aside from the Cardinal series, Degas' figurative monotypes are of an intensely intimate nature—depicting nudes, reclining or bathing, as well as scenes in the brothels of Paris. The obvious sexual nature of his brothel scenes was the aspect of Degas' monotypes that Pablo Picasso came to admire.[8]

Prostitution in nineteenth-century Paris became a prominent theme in Naturalist literature, as well as a subject for art—notably in the case of Edouard Manet's *Olympia* 1863.[9] As an habitué of the artistic and literary gatherings in Paris's cafés, Degas had first-hand contact with the key proponents of Naturalism—Emile Zola and Joris-Karl Huysmans—both of who wrote about the tragic life of prostitutes. Edmond de Goncourt's *La fille Eliza* (1877) also explores the subject, and Degas made sketches that relate to this novel.[10] It has been argued that with his direct exposure to the literary world, Degas should be considered a key figure in consideration of the 'troubled yet fruitful marriage' of art and literature at this time.[11]

While Manet and Degas maintained a competitive friendship over the years, Zola and Degas were rivals in their pursuit of modern day subjects—each contesting the adequacy of the other's chosen field to deal with contemporary subject matter. Their relationship was an uneasy one. Degas was critical of Naturalism's careful, scientific descriptions of modern life; he likened Zola's approach to 'a giant studying a telephone book', claiming that the writer was 'cramming everything about a subject into a book'. In contrast, his monotypes are indicative of a simple, yet penetrating approach; for Degas, art had the advantage: 'In a single brushstroke we can say more than a writer in a whole volume.'[12] For his part, Zola while acknowledging Degas' interest in contemporary themes, was dismissive of his ability to convey them given the sheltered nature of his art practice: 'I cannot accept a man who shuts himself up all his life to draw a ballet-girl as ranking co-equal in dignity and power with Flaubert, Daudet and Goncourt.'[13]

In 1878, Zola began the 'scientific' and careful documentation of prostitution in Paris, while developing an outline for a story of a demimondaine, Nana—a compilation

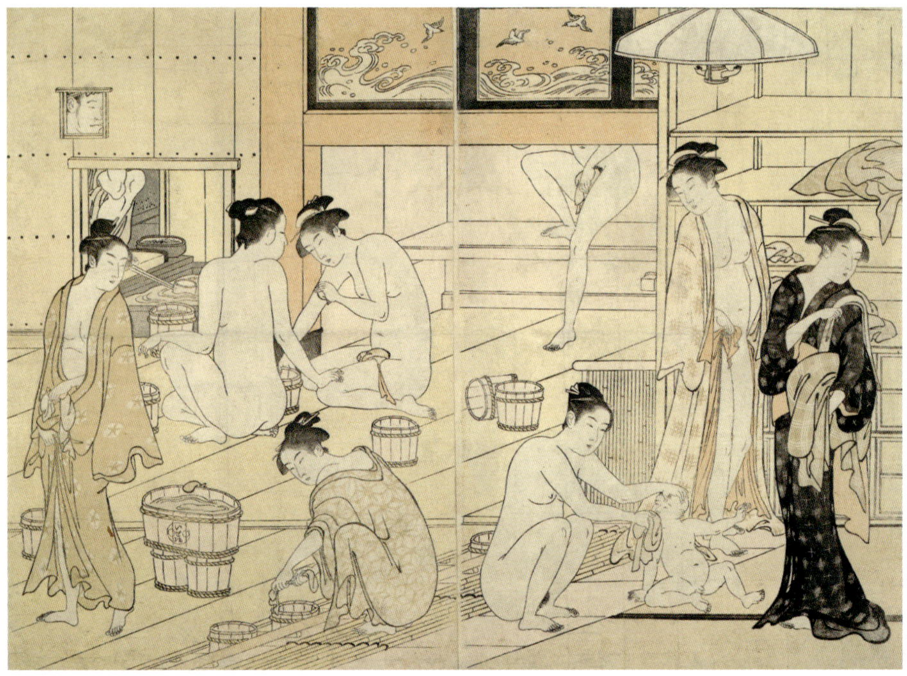

(above)
Torii Kiyonaga
Interior of a bathhouse c 1787
nishiki-e (woodblock print); ink and colour on paper
26.3 x 38.8 cm
Museum of Fine Arts, Boston
William Sturgis Bigelow Collection, 1930
Photograph © 2008 Museum of Fine Arts, Boston

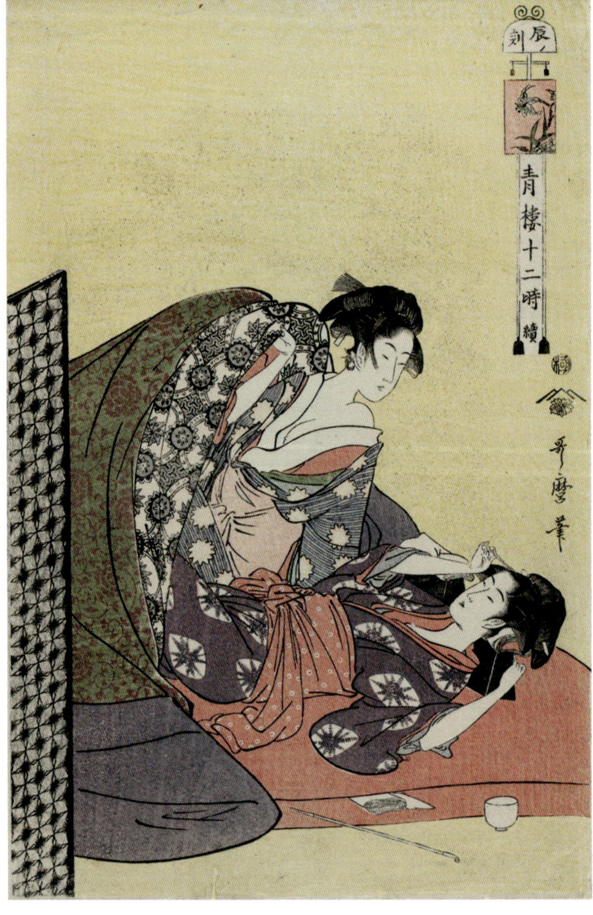

(right)
Kitagawa Utamaro
The hour of the dragon (Tatsu no koku), from the series *The twelve hours in the Yoshiwara* (*Seirō jūni toki tsuzuki*) c 1794
nishiki-e (woodblock print); ink and colour on paper
38.2 x 25.2 cm
Museum of Fine Arts, Boston
William Sturgis Bigelow Collection, 1911
Photograph © 2008 Museum of Fine Arts, Boston

of cocottes known to Zola and his followers, who provided him with notes. Nana was the daughter of the unfortunate Gervaise Macquart, the principal character in Zola's 1876 novel, *L'Assommoir* (*The dram shop*). From her initial impoverished state, Nana was embraced by Parisian high society and became a woman for whom 'tomorrow never exists'. Yet, she was 'the product of Gervaise and an alcoholic, Coupeau', and with that inheritance Nana was destined to fall back into destitution and an early death.[14]

Nana was published in 1880; Degas' monotypes of prostitutes were produced earlier (probably 1876–77), so there is no direct relationship other than the topical subject matter. Huysmans' first published novel, *Marthe: histoire d'une fille* (1876), appears to have preceded Degas' efforts. Huysmans tells the poignant tale of a young woman blessed with good looks, but orphaned at 15. An affair with her first true love, Leo, fails and she becomes 'a hired labourer of passion' in the brothels and dance halls of Paris. For his bleak account of the demimonde, Huysmans drew on personal experience, and the character of Leo, a journalist and poet, was loosely autobiographical.

Though contemporary writers explored similar subject matter, Degas' monotypes of prostitutes do not have an obvious link with literature. They were neither overly romantic in nature, nor a means of titillation. Nor were they depicted in the autobiographic manner of Huysmans' tragic tale. In more than 50 brilliantly observed extant compositions, Degas explored the humour and sadness, vulgarity and boredom within the confines of the brothels—known in the parlance of the day as *maisons de tolérance* or *maisons closes* (cats 33–38).

If Degas borrowed from Honoré Daumier's caricatures for his scenes at the Opéra, Paul Gavarni would have provided themes of a more sexual nature. Japanese woodblock prints, *ukiyo-e*, also offered ideas on the subject of prostitution. Degas had in his own collection Torii Kiyonaga's *Interior of a bath house* 1787;[15] and he would have been aware of Kitagawa Utamaro's series, *The twelve hours in the Yoshiwara* c 1794,[16] which depicts the relaxed figures of Japanese prostitutes acting out their daily lives. Paris's prostitutes and Degas' work later inspired Henri de Toulouse-Lautrec's suite of lithographs, *Elles*, of 1896.

René de Gas destroyed about 70 possibly sexually charged 'sketches' which he found at the time of his brother Edgar's death. According to the publisher Ambroise Vollard, these were not brothel scenes, but Vollard may have said this to suggest the completeness of his publications of the 1930s, when he produced a series of photogravures of Degas' original monotypes to illustrate Guy de Maupassant's *La Maison Tellier* and Lucian of Samostata's *Mimes de courtesans*.[17]

Sumptuous couches, brilliant lights and reflecting mirrors provide the background for Degas' naked or lightly clad women with hardened features—lolling, joking together and sometimes overwhelming their timid clients with their matter-of-fact approach to sexual encounters. Françoise Cachin has commented that the artist's 'peeps through the keyhole of a brothel door teach us much about him, his art and his age.'[18]

Degas' exploration of the monotype process from the mid 1870s had a dramatic effect on his entire art practice—his paintings, pastels (many of which were made over monotypes), drawings and prints. It was the one field in which he could develop imagery without careful draughtsmanship and the squaring up of compositions, and where he was required to take risks. One wrong step or mistake could mean that his work might be lost—another aspect of the monotypes that Picasso subsequently appreciated. The informality of the compositions echoed his subject matter, which was now thoroughly Parisian and modern: the ballet, and behind-scenes activity at the Opéra, the café-concert, nude women bathing, and scenes of prostitution.

As a consummate technician, the monotype allowed Degas the freedom to experiment, and as a result his art became increasingly informal and radical in its composition and execution. These qualities characterised his painting and printmaking for the next 20 years, and set him apart from his fellow Impressionists.

Notes

1 Jules Claretie, 'La mouvement parisien: l'exposition de impressionistes', *L'Indépendant belge*, 15 April 1877, p 1.

2 Gallimard, quoted in René Gimpel, *Diary of an art dealer*, Farrar, Straus & Giroux, New York, 1966, p 23.

3 Michael Pantazzi, 'Degas, Halévy, and the Cardinals', in Jean Sutherland Boggs, Henri Loyrette, Michael Pantazzi et al, *Degas*, The Metropolitan Museum of Art and National Gallery of Canada, New York and Ottawa, 1988, pp 280–81; whence bibliography on earlier scholarship. In his discussion, Pantazzi quotes from Halévy's diary entry of 3 June 1880, that the author already intended the drawings would be done by Henry Maigrot, and these duly appeared in the compilation *Les petites Cardinal*, Calmann-Lévy, Paris, 1880.

4 Henri Loyrette, *Degas the man and his art*, Harry N Abrams, New York, 1993, p 76; see also Denis Rouart (trans Pia C DeSantis, Sarah L Fisher and Shelley Fletcher), *Degas: in search of his technique*, Rizzoli and Skira, New York and Geneva, 1988, 'Monotypes', pp 96–106.

5 *The ballet master* c 1874, National Gallery of Art, Washington DC.

6 See Jane Kinsman 'The ballet, the theatre and the café-concert', this publication, pp 111–115.

7 Michael Pantazzi, 'The first monotypes', in Boggs et al, *Degas*, pp 257–60. Pantazzi provides details of previous scholarship on the subject.

8 Aldo Crommelynck, conversation with Jane Kinsman, Paris, 22 March 2006.

9 Edouard Manet, *Olympia* 1863, Musée d'Orsay, Paris.

10 A bound album of Degas' sketches, which includes images inspired by Edmond de Goncourt's novel, originally owned by Ludovic Halévy, is in the Getty collection, Los Angeles. See also Theodore Reff, *The notebooks of Edgar Degas: a catalogue of the thirty-eight notebooks in the Bibliothèque nationale and other collections*, 2 vols, Hacker Art Books, New York, 1985, notebook 28, vol 1, pp 128–31. See also Carol Armstrong, with a postscript by David Hockney, *A Degas sketchbook*, the J Paul Getty Museum, Los Angeles, 2000.

11 Theodore Reff, *Degas: the artist's mind*, Thames & Hudson, London, 1971, p 147.

12 Degas, quoted in Reff, p 165, nn 77, 78.

13 Zola, quoted in Reff, p 166; originally referred to in George Moore, *Impressions and opinions*, Walter Scott, London, 1893, pp 298–99.

14 Zola's notes on *Nana*, in George Holden (trans and introduction), *Nana*, Penguin Books, Harmondsworth, 1972, pp 11–13.

15 Colta Ives, 'Degas, Japanese prints and Japonisme', in Ann Dumas, Colta Ives, Susan Alyson Stein et al, *The private collection of Edgar Degas: a summary catalogue*, The Metropolitan Museum of Art, New York, 1997, pp 247–48.

16 Shûgō Asano and John Clark, *The passionate art of Kitagawa Utamaro*, 2 vols, The British Museum, London, 1995, cats 150–61.

17 Ambroise Vollard, *Recollections of a picture dealer*, Dover Publications, New York, 1978, p 258. Vollard kept a group of these monotypes, which then appeared in his publications, Guy de Maupassant, *La Maison Tellier*, Ambroise Vollard, Paris, 1934 and Lucian of Samostata, *Mimes de courtesans*, Ambroise Vollard, Paris, 1935. Eugenia Parry Janis, *Degas: a critical study of the monotypes*, Fogg Art Museum, Harvard, 1968, p xx, has argued that given the absence of prostitutes in Degas' notebooks in the Bibliothèque nationale, it is likely that René de Gas had censored his brother's work.

18 Françoise Cachin, 'The monotypes', in Jean Adhémar and Françoise Cachin, *Degas: the complete etchings, lithographs and monotypes*, Thames & Hudson, London, 1973, pp 76–77.

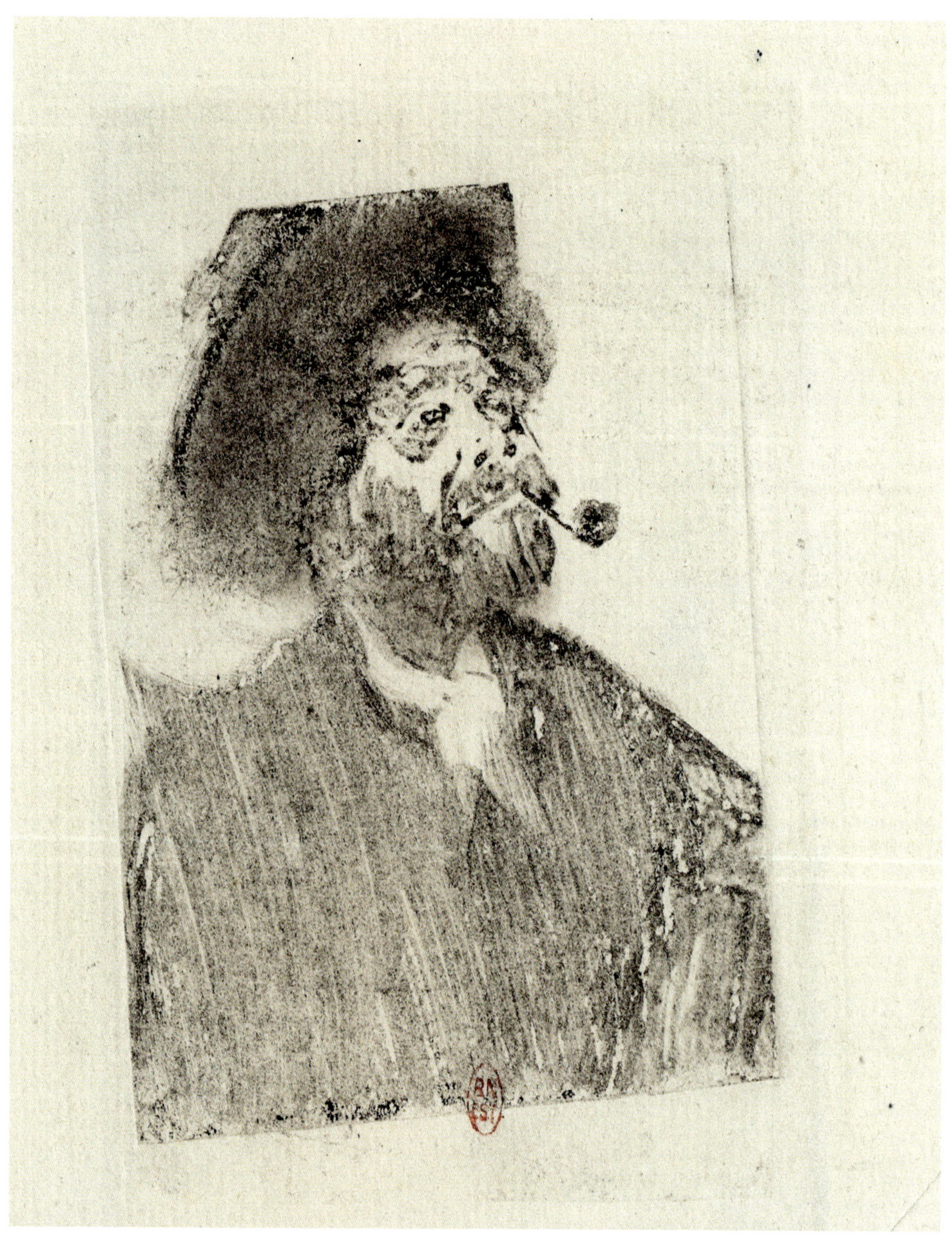

25 *Man smoking a pipe (Desboutin)*
(*L'homme à la pipe (Desboutin)*)
c 1876
monotype in black ink on grey-brown paper
8 x 7.1 cm (plate), 18.1 x 16.3 cm (sheet)
Bibliothèque nationale de France, Paris
Janis 233 / Cachin 35

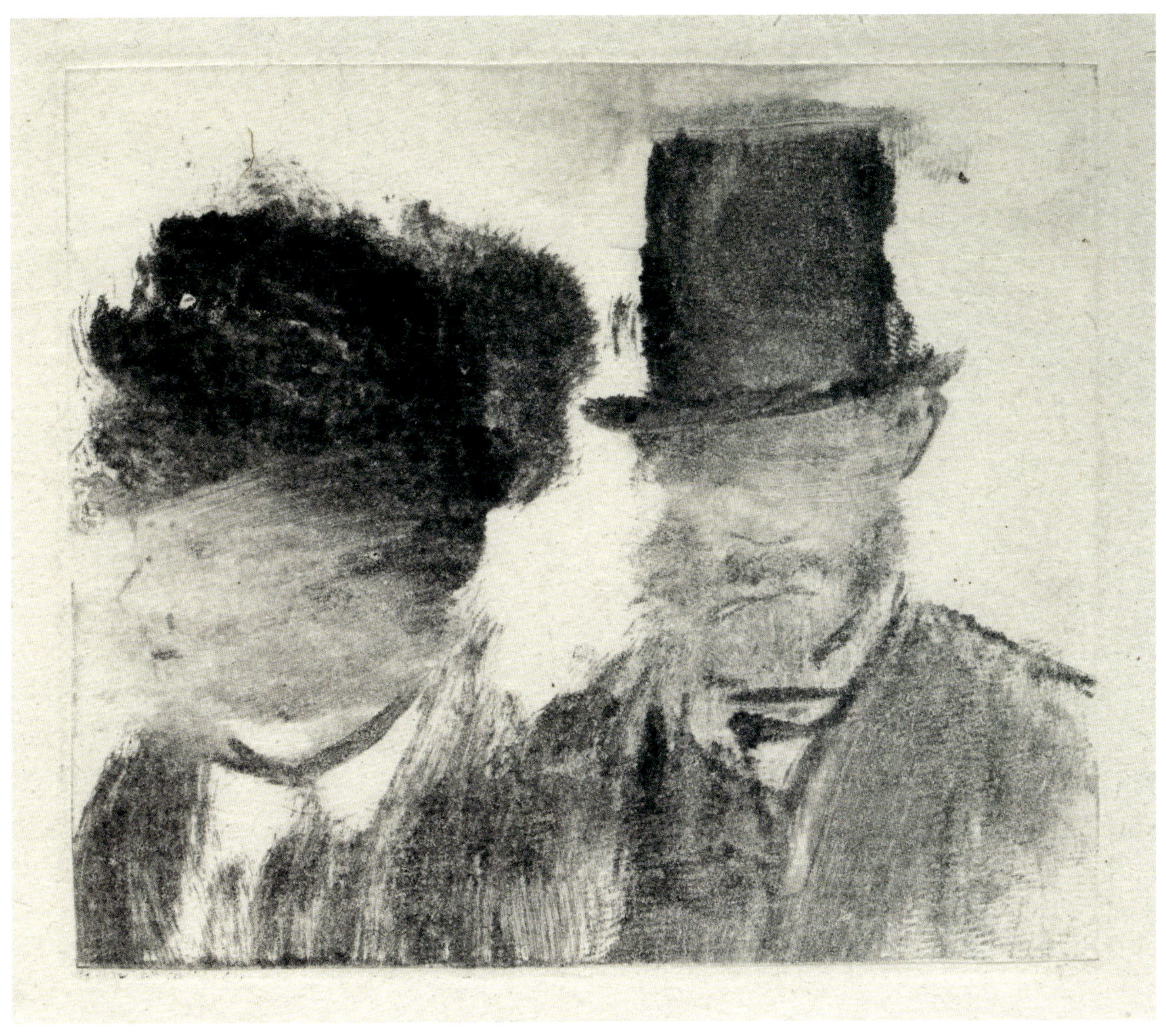

26 *Heads of a man and a woman*
(*Têtes d'un homme et d'une femme*)
c 1877–80
one of two impressions
monotype
7.2 x 8.1 cm (plate), 13.5 x 15.5 cm (sheet)
The British Museum, London
1949,0411.2422
Janis 235 / Cachin 47

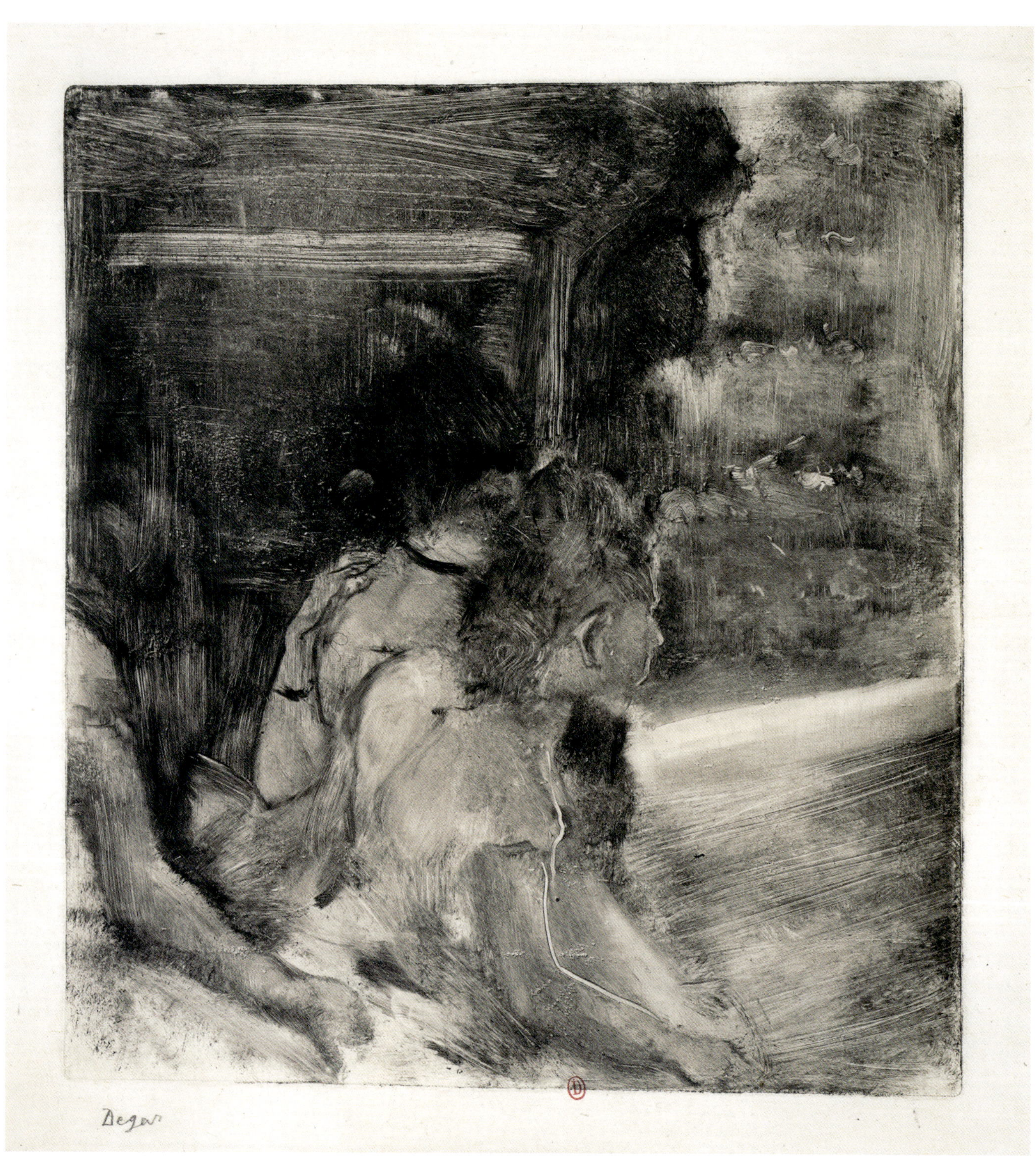

27 ***At the theatre*** (***Au théâtre***)
c 1878
monotype in black ink on china paper
30.9 x 27.5 cm (plate), 37.4 x 34.4 cm (sheet)
Bibliothèque de l'institut national d'histoire de l'art, Paris
EM DEGAS 8
Collections Jacques Doucet
Janis 15 / Cachin 16

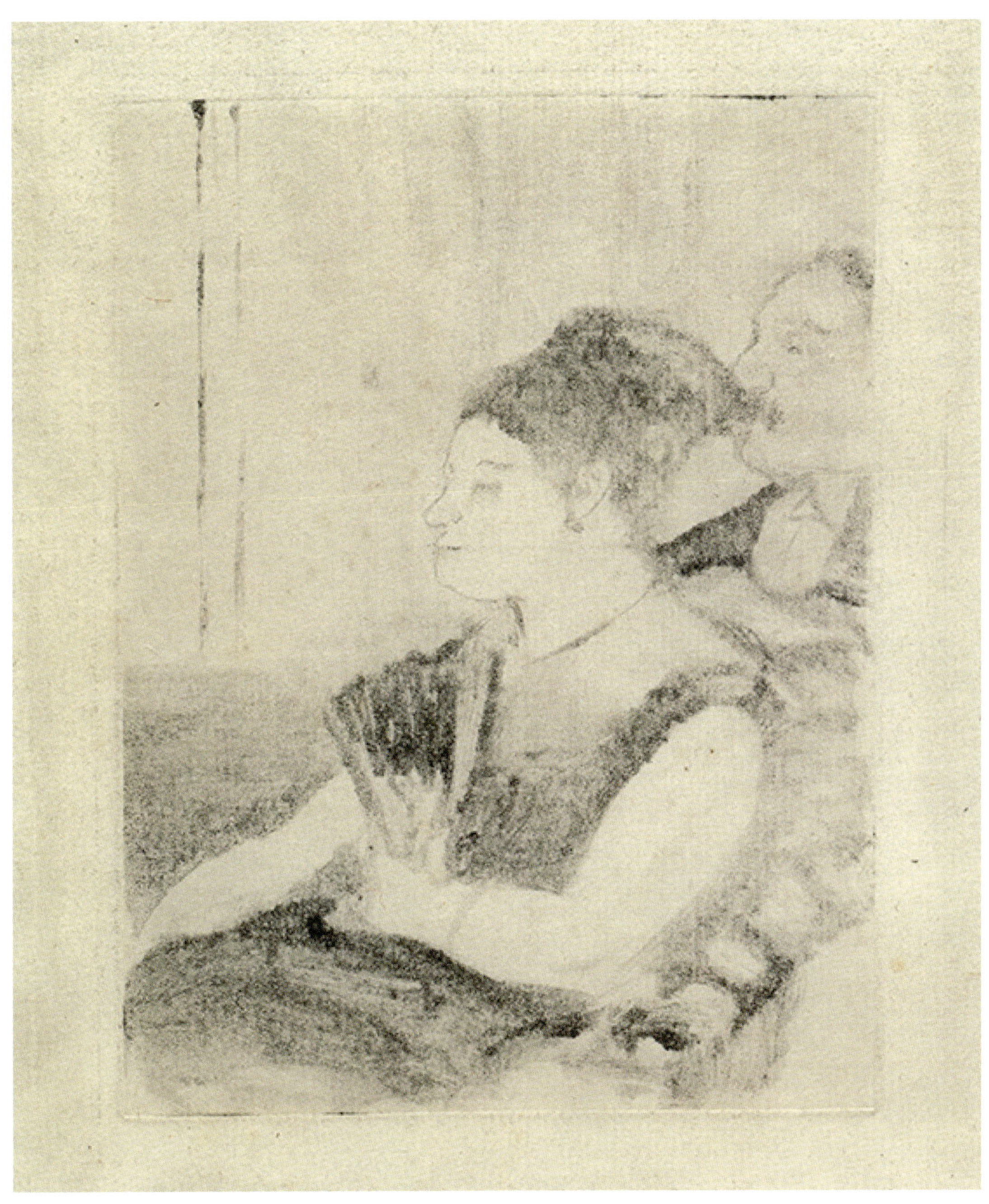

28 *The loge* (*La loge*)
c 1877
monotype in black ink on china paper
12.1 x 15.9 cm (plate), 25 x 18.6 cm (sheet)
Private collection
Janis 55 / Cachin 18

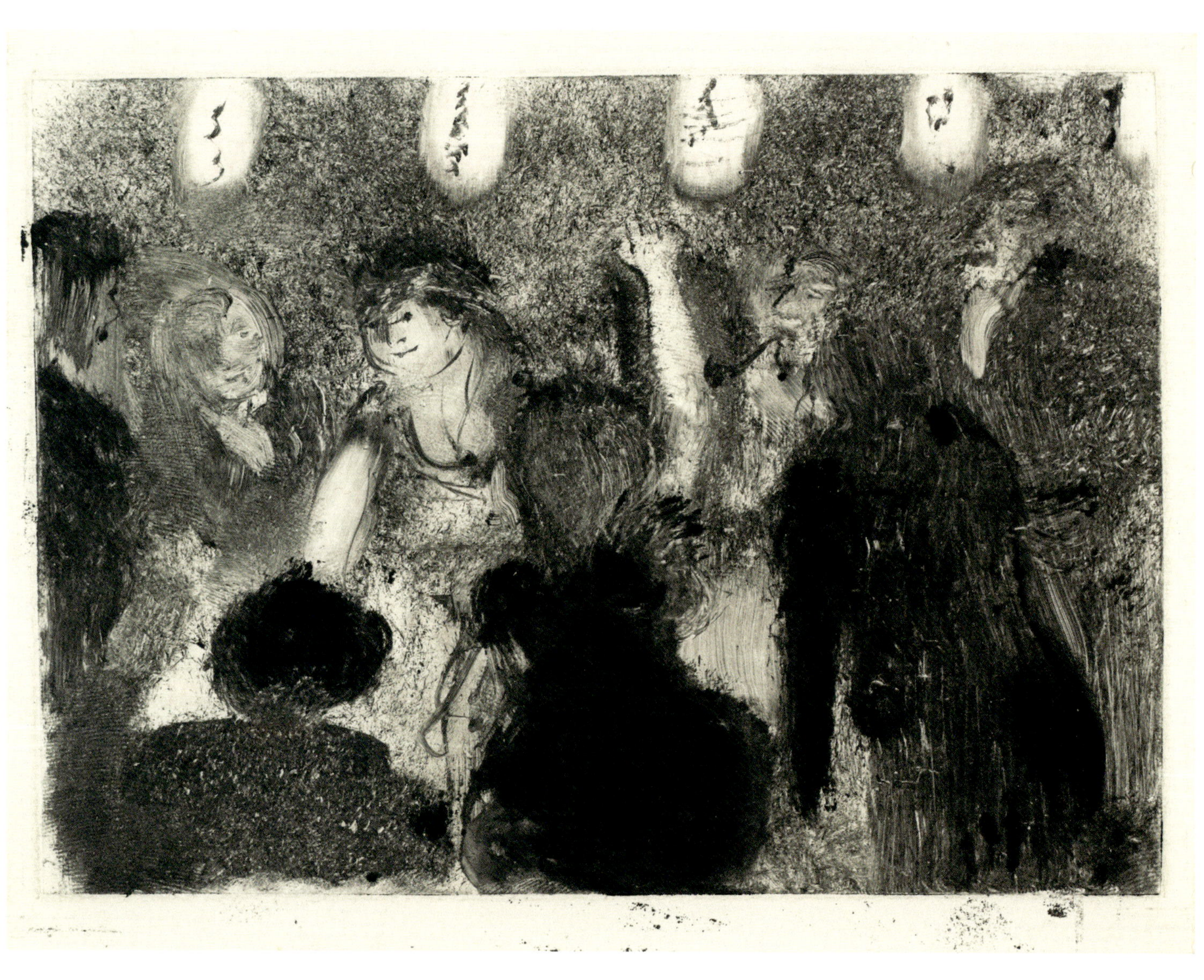

29 *A party in the waiting room*
c 1879–80
monotype in black ink on white wove paper, heightened with brush and ink
11.8 x 16.2 cm (plate), 14.4 x 17.3 cm (sheet)
National Gallery of Australia, Canberra
80.468

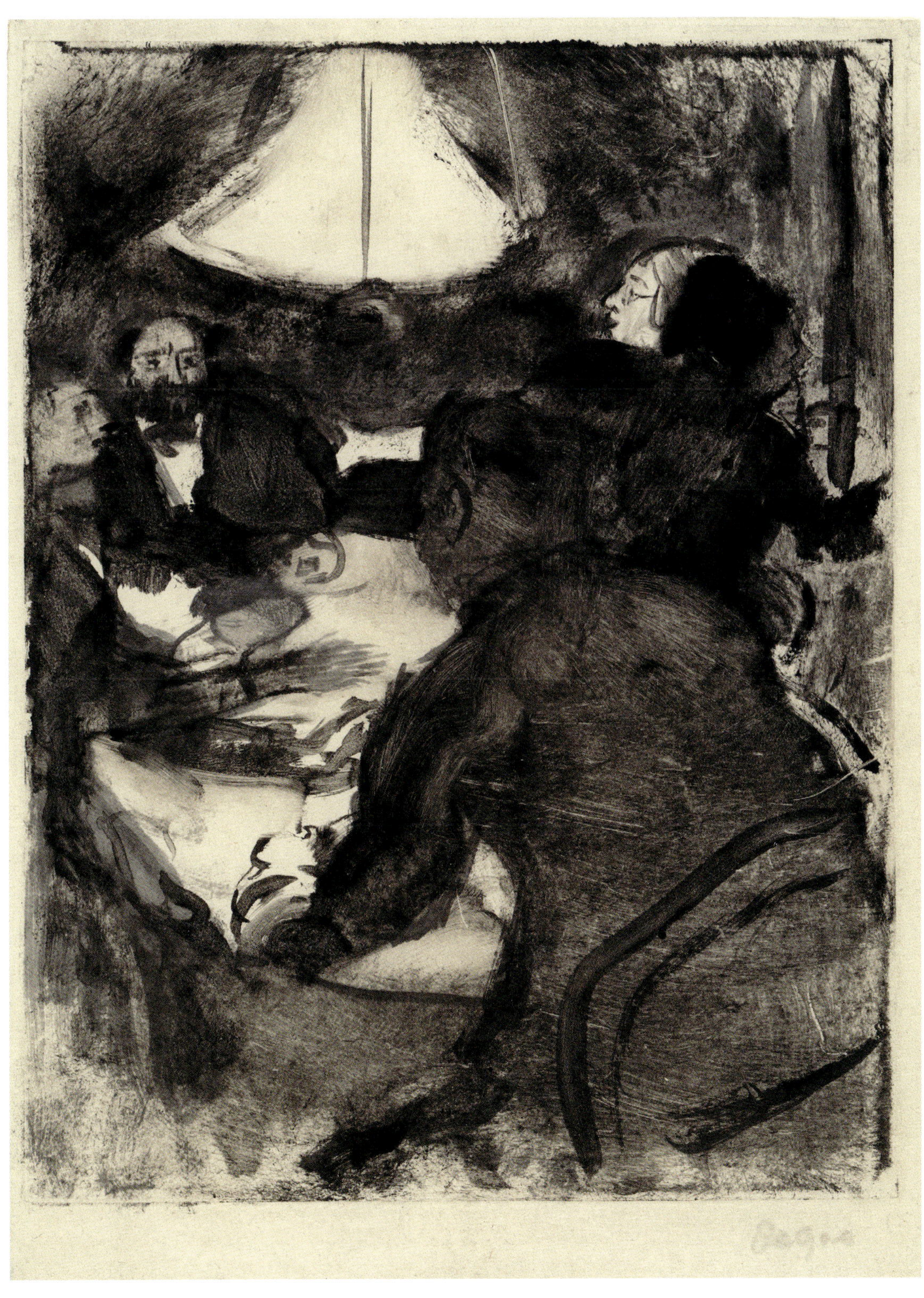

30 *The famous Good Friday dinner* (*Le fameux dîner du Vendredi*)
1876–77
monotype in black ink on china paper, tipped onto light-weight cardboard
21.5 x 16 cm (plate), 27 x 17 cm (sheet)
National Gallery of Australia, Canberra
2006.734
The Poynton Bequest 2006
Janis 205 / Cachin 82

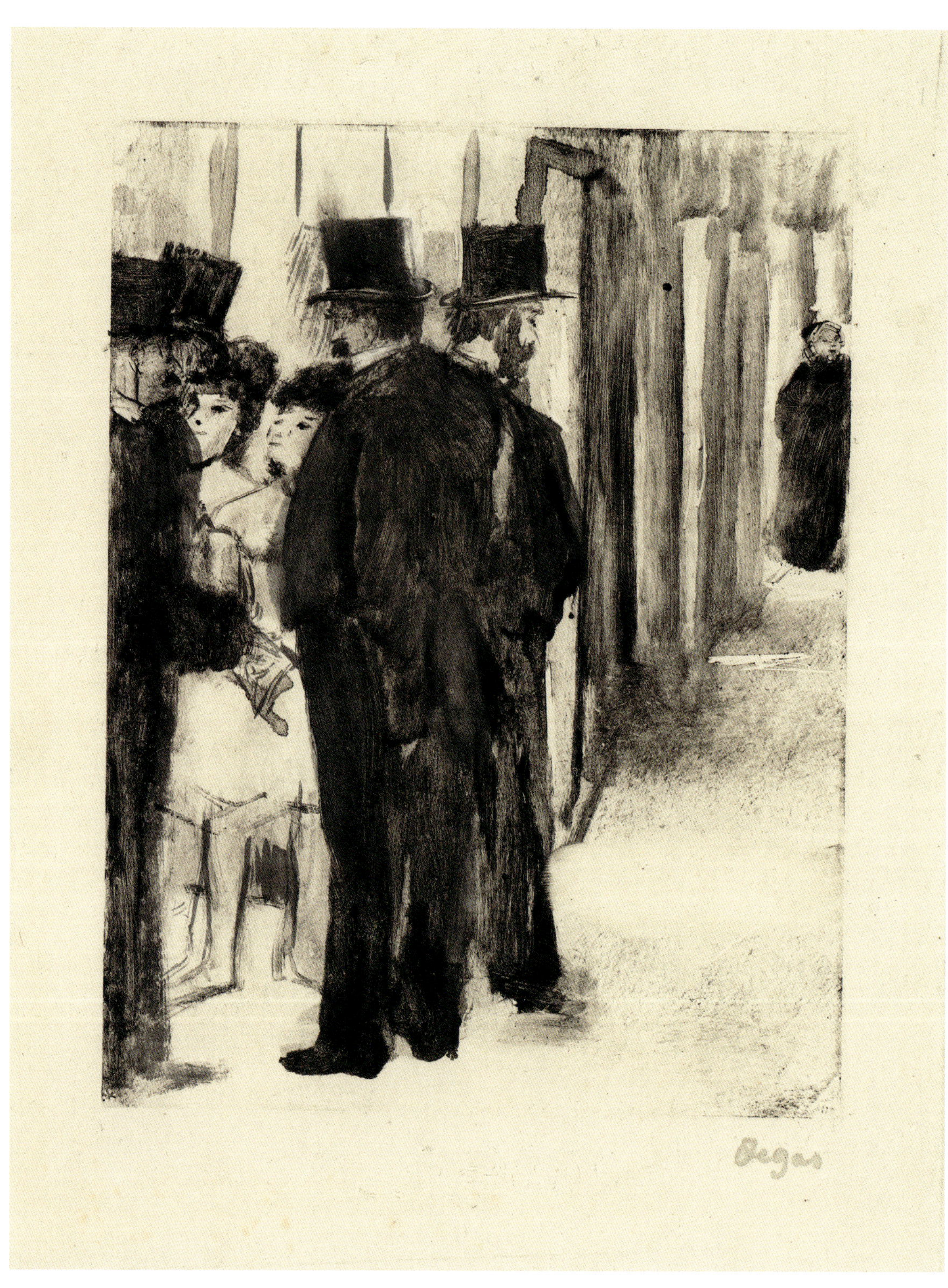

31 ***Pauline and Virginie Cardinal chatting with some admirers***
(***Pauline et Virginie Cardinal bavardant avec des admirateurs***)
1876–77
monotype in black ink on china paper, heightened with white and grey gouache
21.8 x 16.2 cm (plate), 33.4 x 22 cm (sheet)
National Gallery of Australia, Canberra
2006.1060
The Poynton Bequest 2006

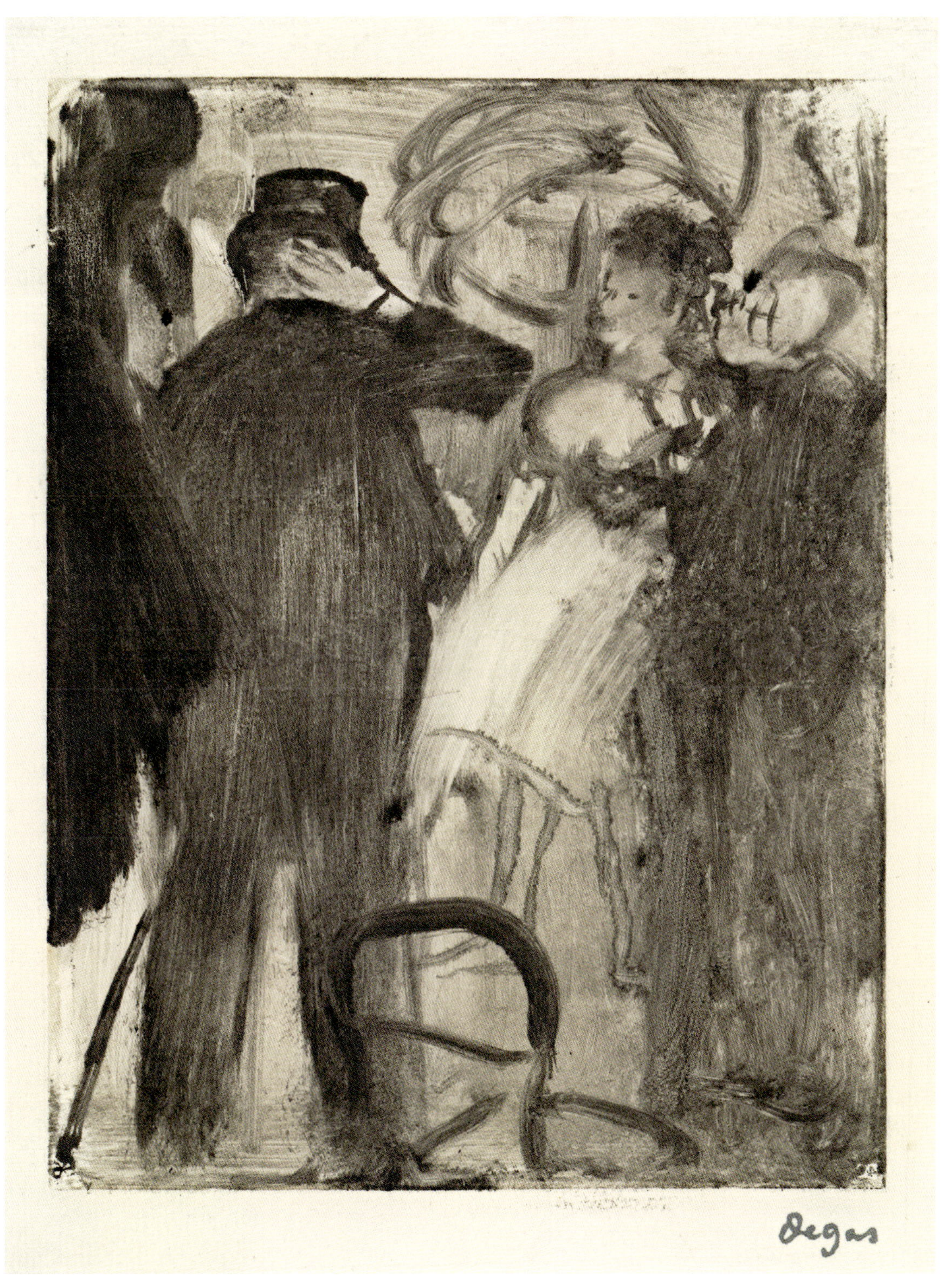

32 *The one that looked around most avidly was the Marquis Cavalcanti*
(*Celui qui tournait le plus c'était le marquis Cavalcanti*)
1876–77
monotype in black ink heightened with grey on cream laid paper
21.3 x 16 cm (plate), 27.3 x 19.6 cm irreg (sheet)
National Gallery of Victoria, Melbourne
P2-1974
Felton Bequest, 1974
Janis 222 / Cachin 68

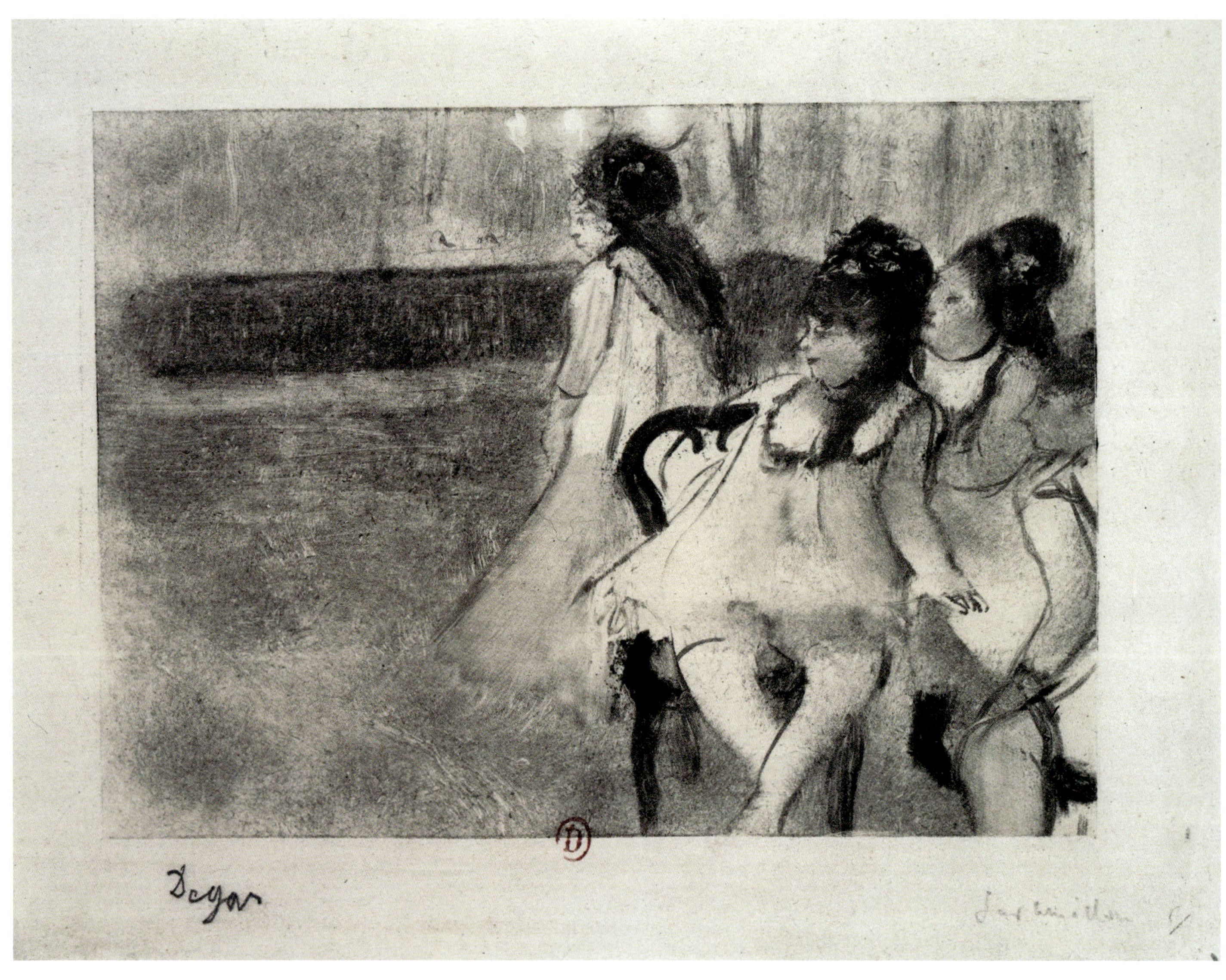

33 *Prostitutes in their camisoles* (*Pensionnaires en chemise*)
1876–77
first of two impressions
monotype in black ink on china paper
11.9 x 16.2 cm (plate), 16 x 21 cm (sheet)
Bibliothèque de l'institut national d'histoire de l'art, Paris
EM DEGAS 12
Collections Jacques Doucet
Janis 69 / Cachin 92

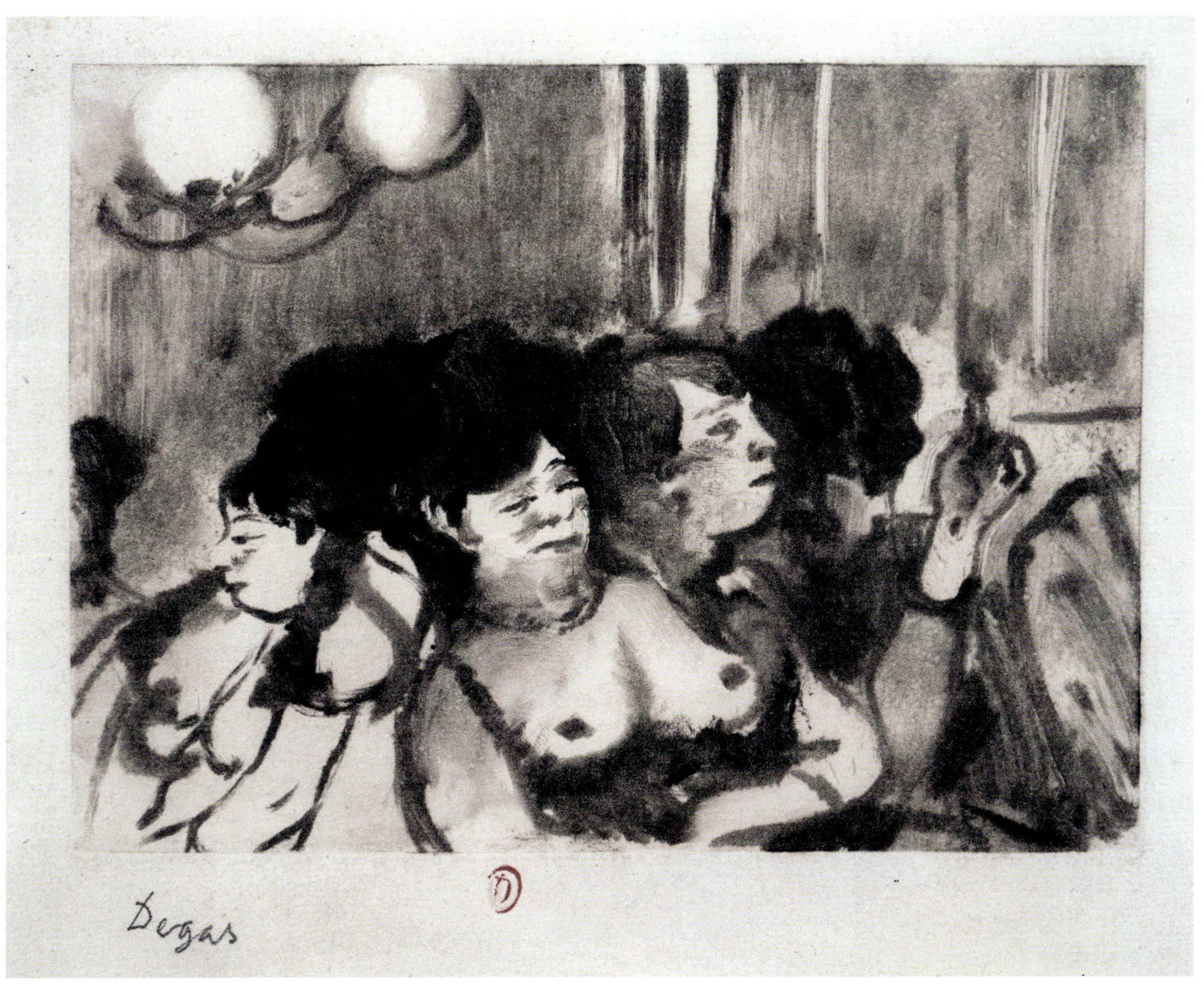

34 *In the salon* (*Au salon*)
1876–77
first of two impressions
monotype in black ink on white paper
12 x 16 cm (plate), 19.7 x 25.5 cm (sheet)
Bibliothèque de l'institut national d'histoire de l'art, Paris
EM DEGAS 11
Collections Jacques Doucet
Janis 79 / Cachin 88

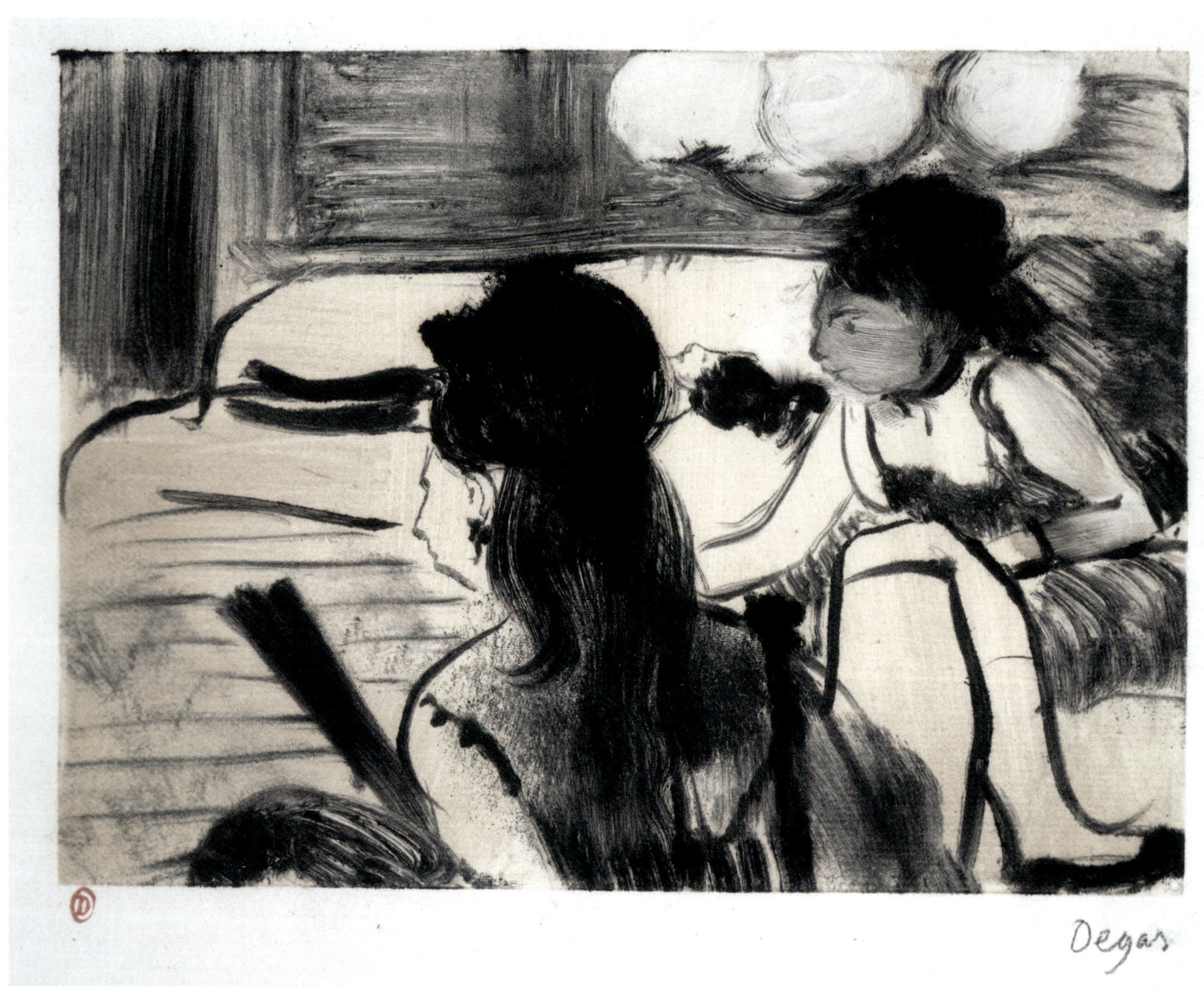

35 *Brothel scene* (*Scène de maison close*)
1876–77
monotype in black ink on cream paper, with pale ochre watercolour
16.1 x 21.4 cm (plate), 21 x 26.1 cm (sheet)
Bibliothèque de l'institut national d'histoire de l'art, Paris
EM DEGAS 9
Collections Jacques Doucet
Janis 68 / Cachin 83

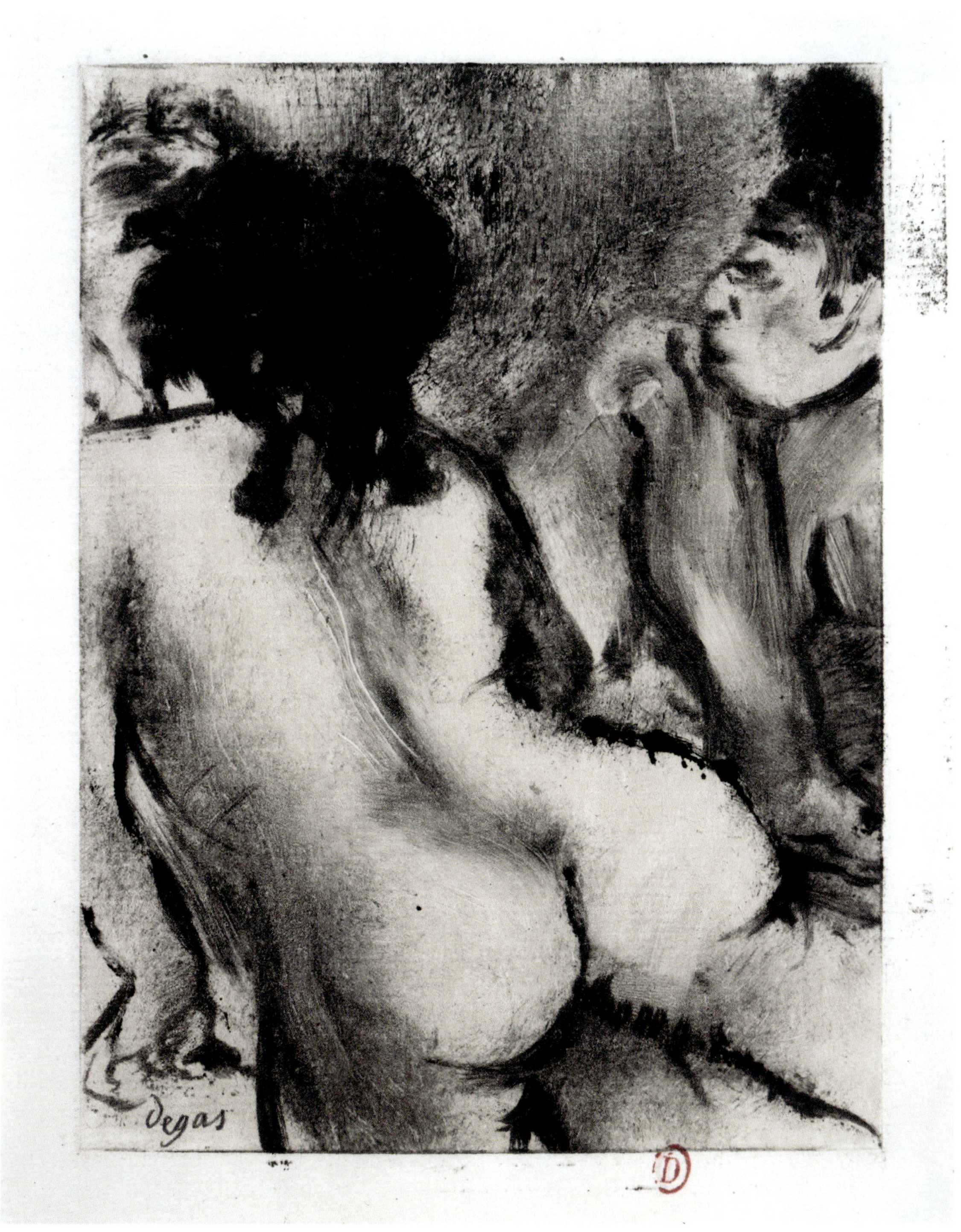

36 *The go-between* (*L'entremetteuse*)
1876–77
monotype in black ink on paper
16.1 x 11.8 cm (plate), 24.3 x 14.4 cm (sheet)
Bibliothèque de l'institut national d'histoire de l'art, Paris
EM DEGAS 6
Collections Jacques Doucet
Janis 107 / Cachin 108

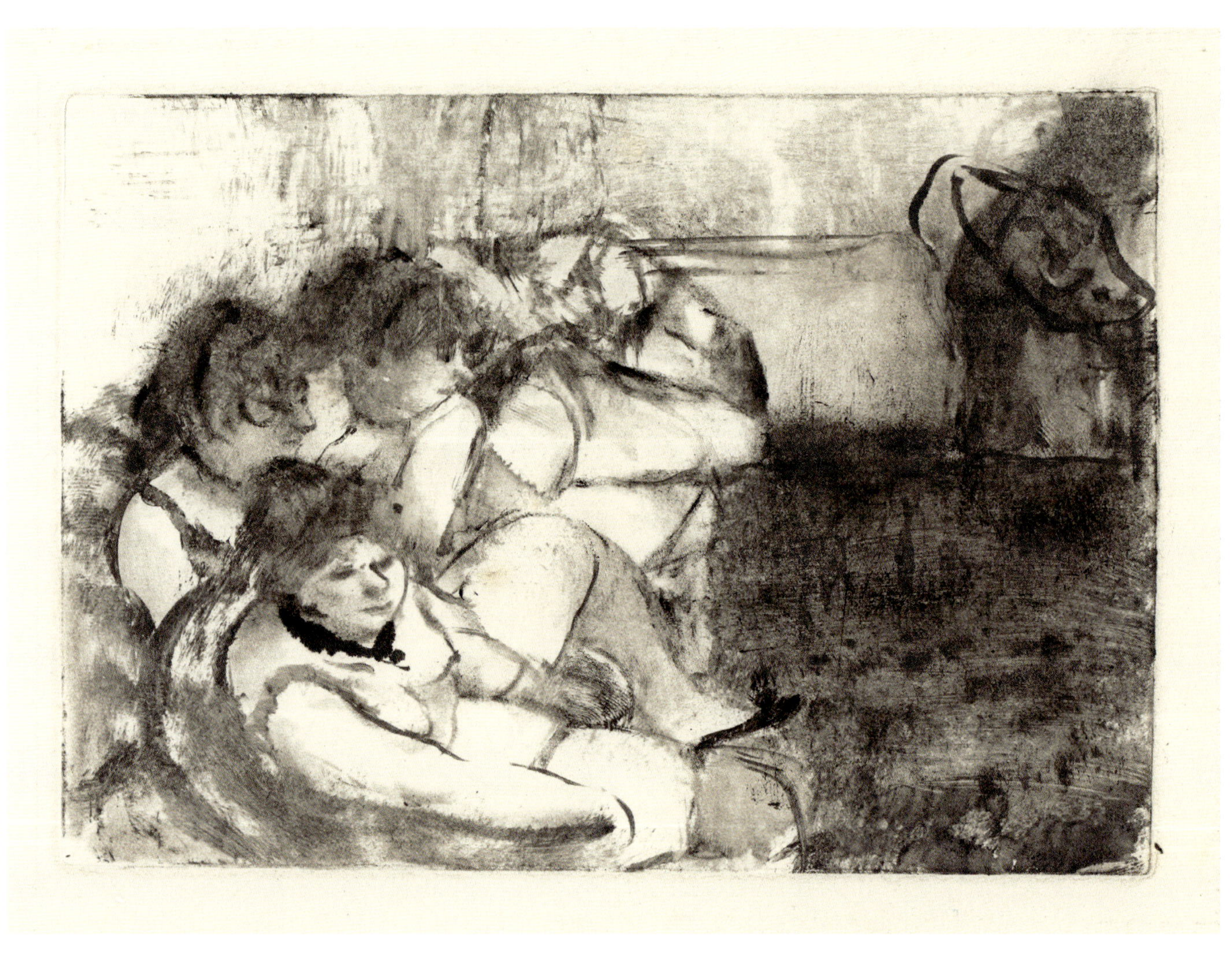

37 *In the salon* (*Au salon*)
1876–77
monotype in black ink on white wove paper
12.2 x 17.2 cm (plate), 20 x 24 cm (sheet)
National Gallery of Australia, Canberra
82.1272
Purchased 1982
Janis 66 / Cachin 93

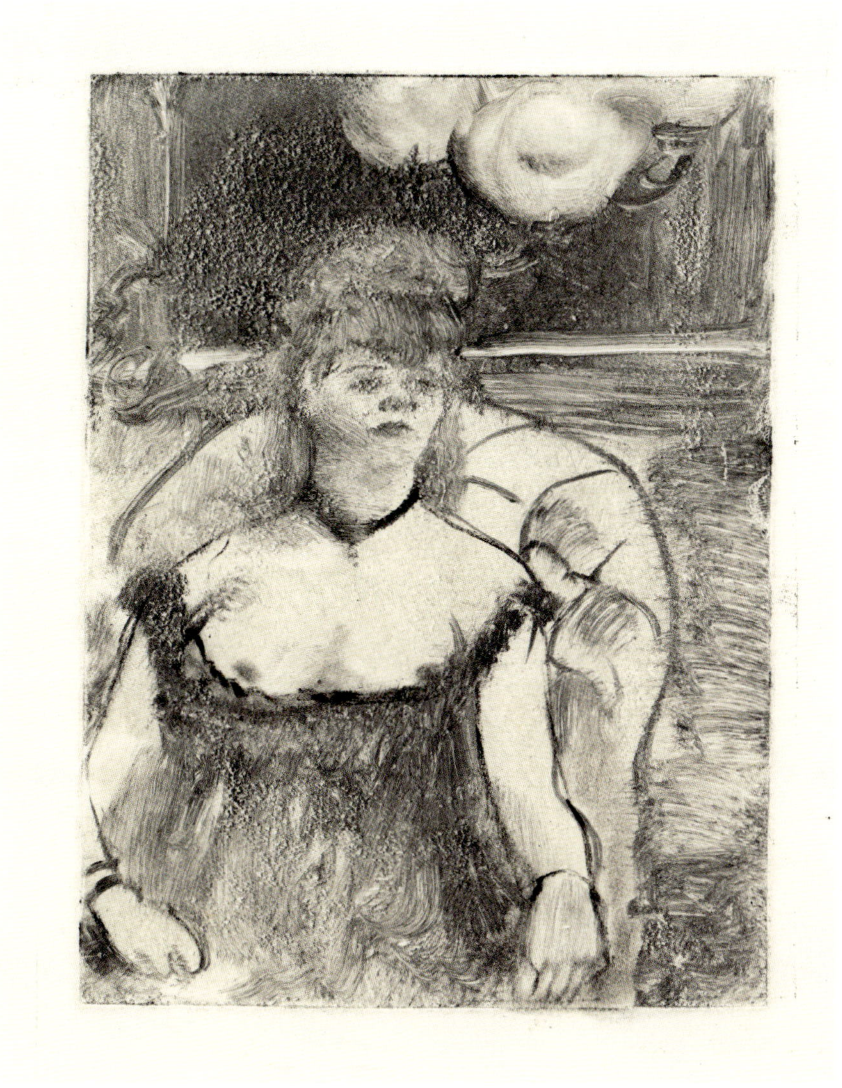

38 *Prostitute seated in an armchair* (*Pensionnaire assise dans un fauteuil*)
1876–77
monotype in black ink on white wove paper, heightened with brush and ink
15.8 x 11.4 cm (plate), 23.8 x 17.5 cm (sheet)
National Gallery of Australia, Canberra
80.467
Purchased 1980
Janis 78 / Cachin 89

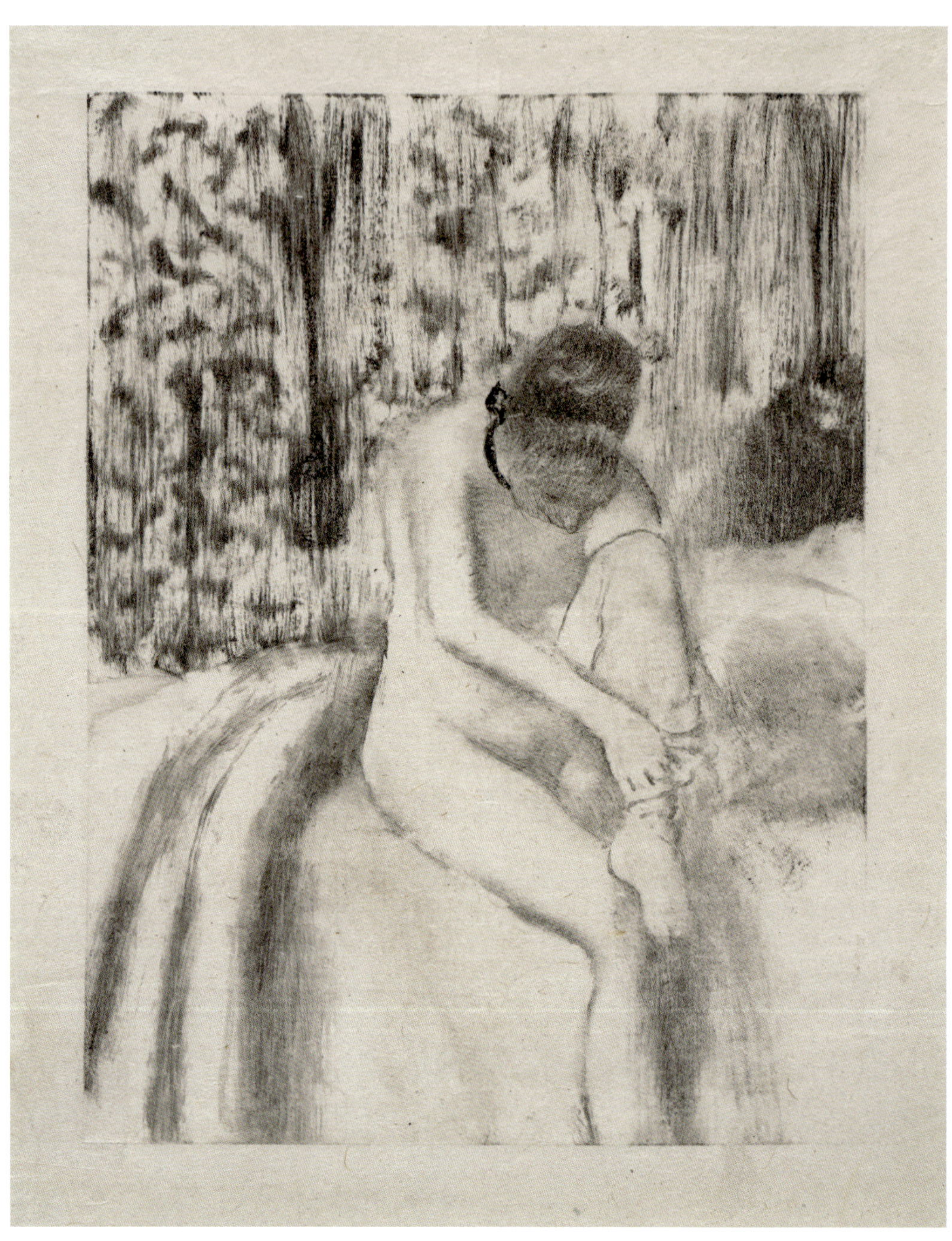

39 *Girl putting on her stockings* (*Fille mettant ses bas*)
1876–77
monotype in black ink on china paper, mounted on cardboard
15.9 x 11.8 cm (plate), 19.7 x 15.7 cm (sheet)
The Metropolitan Museum of Art, New York
29.107.54
HO Havemeyer Collection, Bequest of Mrs HO Havemeyer, 1929
Janis 169 / Cachin 125

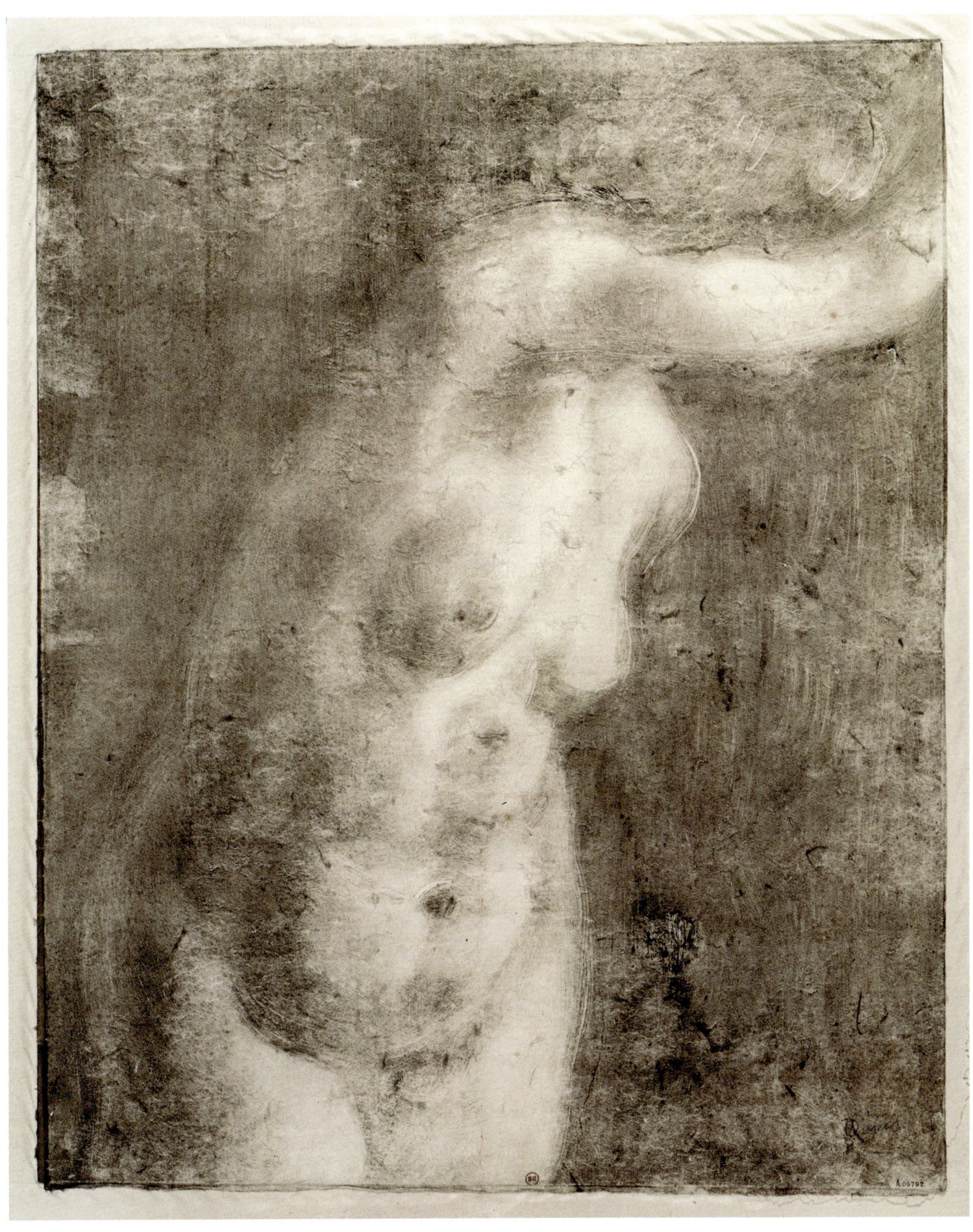

40 *Female torso* (*Torse de femme*)
c 1885
first of three impressions
monotype in brown ink on Japanese rice paper, mounted on cardboard
50 x 39.3 cm (plate), no margins (sheet)
Bibliothèque nationale de France, Paris
EF 100 a Res.2
Janis 158 / Cachin 162

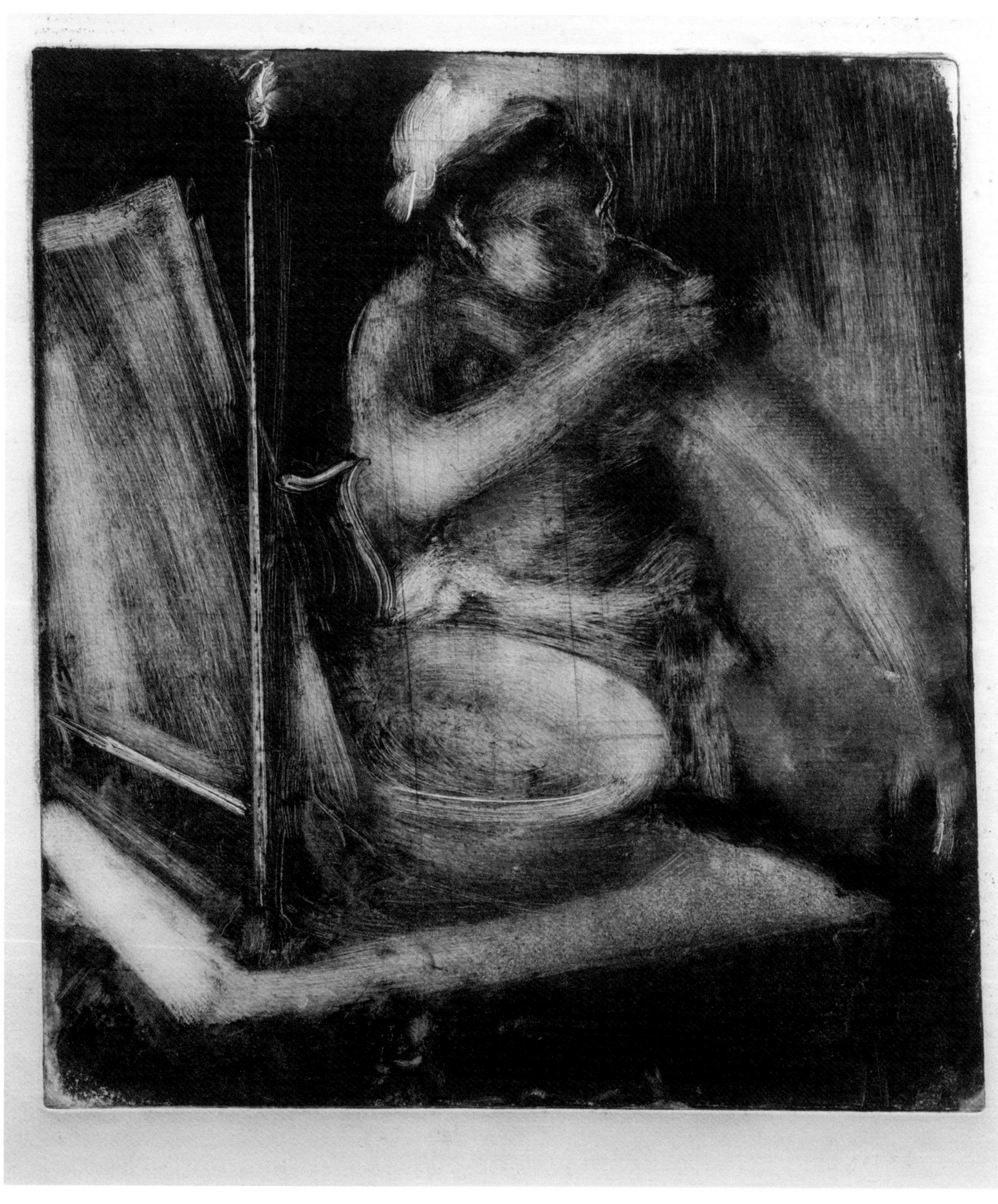

41 *Washing* (*Arms*) (*La toilette* (*Les bras*))
c 1882
monotype in black ink on white paper
31.1 x 27.3 cm (plate), 50.5 x 35.3 cm (sheet)
UCLA Grunwald Center for Graphic Arts,
Hammer Museum, Los Angeles
1964.25.1
Given through the UCLA Arts Council by B Gerald Cantor
Janis 146 / Cachin 152

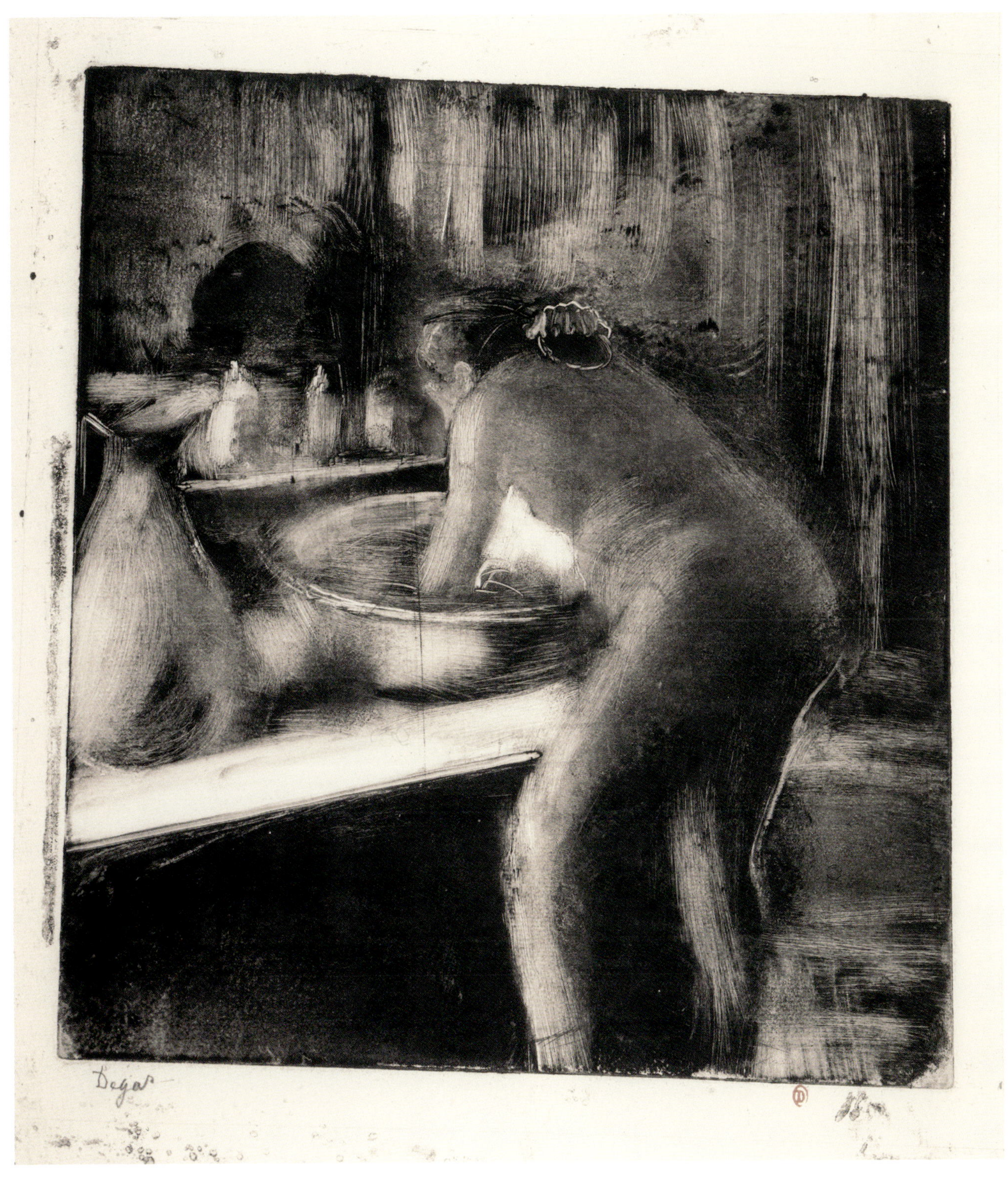

42 *Woman washing* (*A sa toilette*)
1882–85
first of two impressions
monotype in black ink on white paper
31.3 x 28 cm (plate), 51.5 x 35.4 cm (sheet)
Bibliothèque de l'institut national d'histoire de l'art, Paris
EM DEGAS 5
Collections Jacques Doucet
Janis 149 / Cachin 154

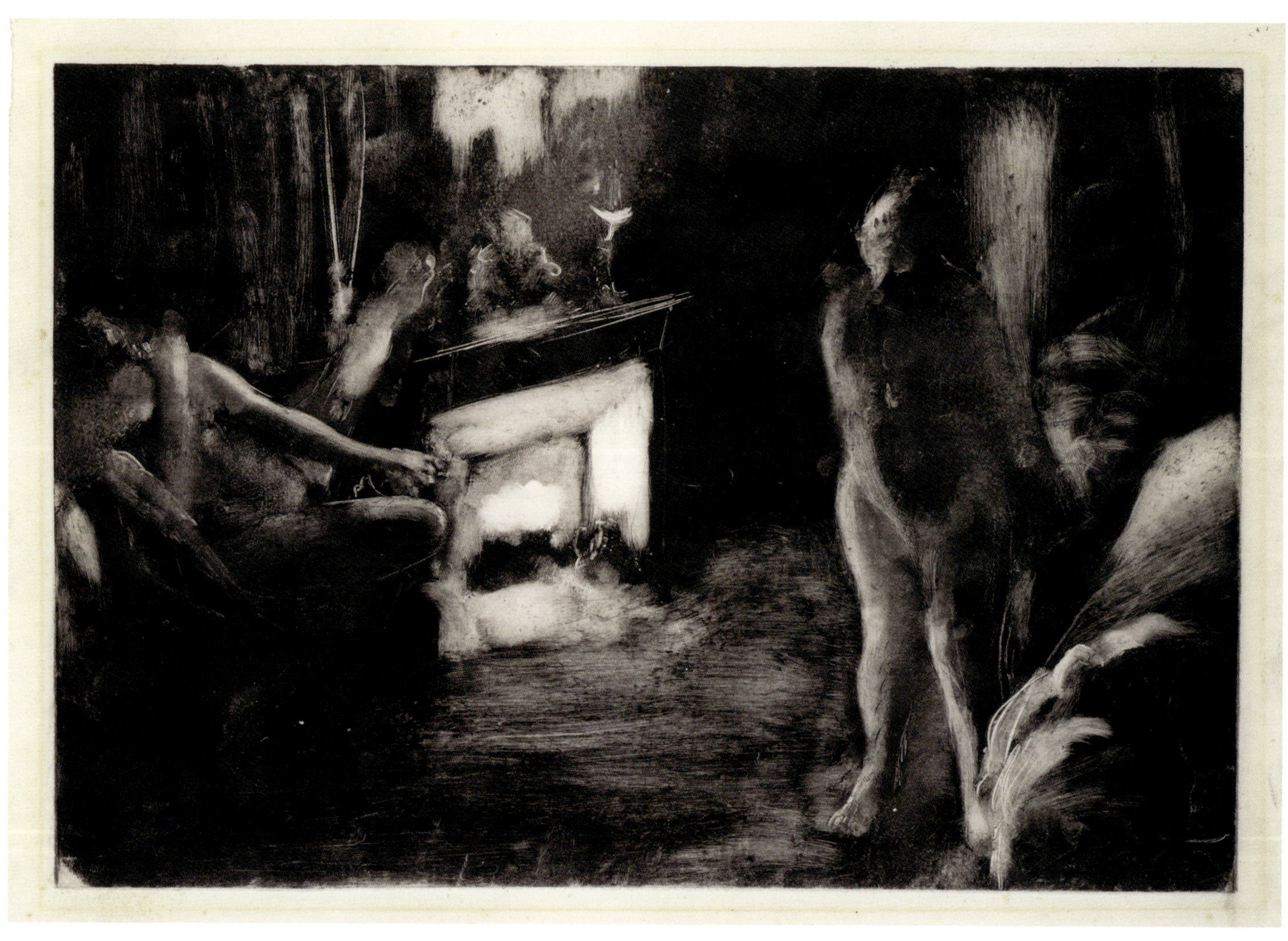

43 *The fireside* (*Le foyer, la cheminée*)
c 1880–85
monotype in black ink on white heavy laid paper
42.5 x 58.6 cm (plate), 50.2 x 64.8 cm (sheet)
The Metropolitan Museum of Art, New York
68.670
Harris Brisbane Dick Fund, Elisha Whittelsey Collection,
The Elisha Whittelsey Fund, and C Douglas Dillon Gift, 1968
Janis 159 / Cachin 167

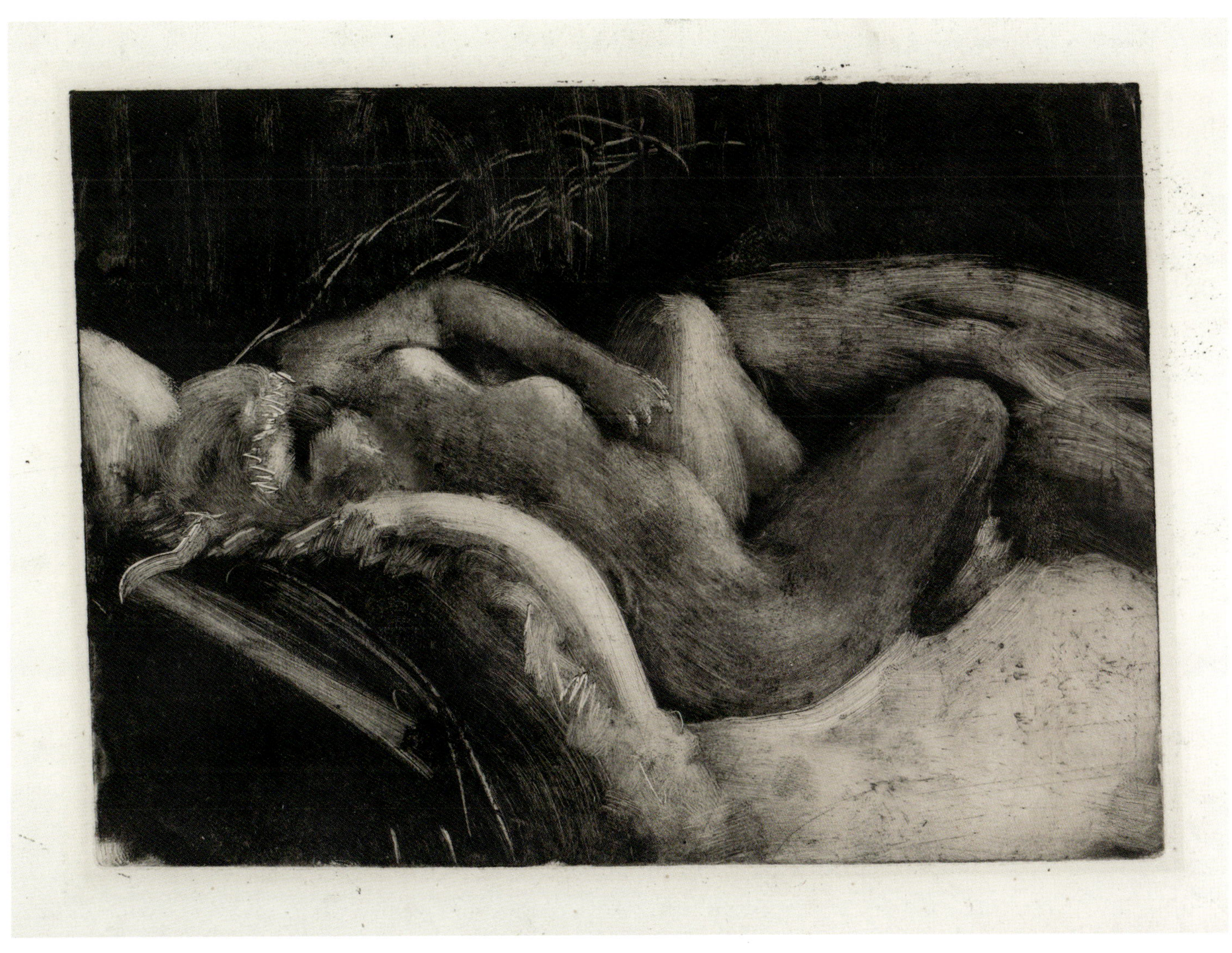

44 *Sleep* (*Le sommeil*)
c 1883–85
first of two impressions
monotype in black ink on cream-coloured vellum, pasted on museum mount
27.6 x 37.8 cm (plate), 35.5 x 51 cm (sheet)
The British Museum, London
PD 1949-4-11-2425
Bequeathed by Campbell Dodgson
Janis 135 / Cachin 164

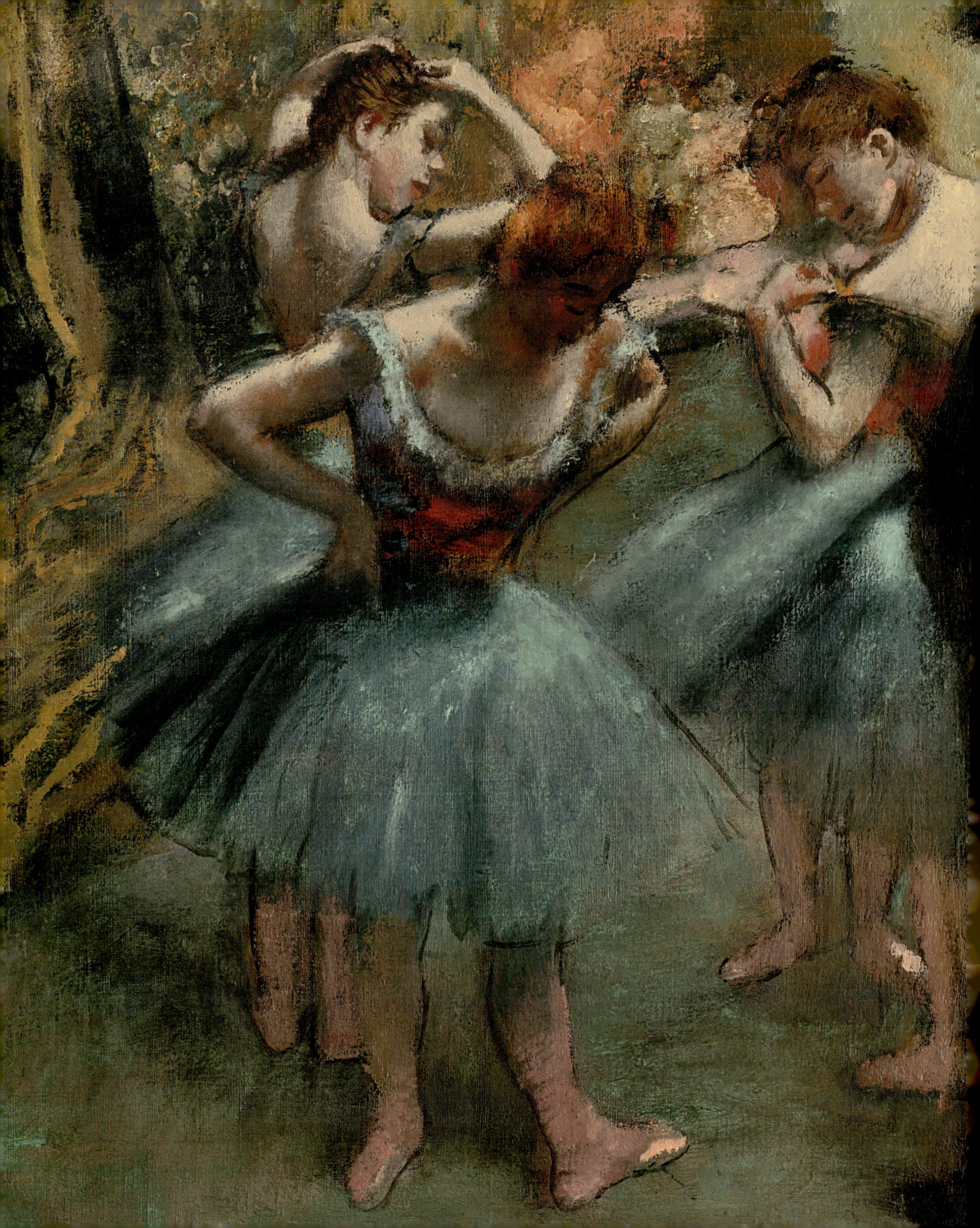

THE BALLET, THE THEATRE AND THE CAFÉ-CONCERT

FOR MORE THAN 30 YEARS from the 1870s—in painting, drawing, pastel, sculpture and print—Degas returned again and again to the subject of the ballet at the Paris Opéra. Initially his ballet compositions in oil were arranged as a performance on stage, viewed from the orchestra pit. Then the artist approached his subject more directly, as if opening a door to discover the dancers in class—practising alone, dancing together, resting or chatting, and with the ballet master occasionally included in the composition. Degas' beautiful apparitions—magic spirits flitting across the stage—were also at times caught in ungainly poses.

As a young man, Degas attended performances at the opera house on the rue le Peletier, Paris, which was destroyed by fire in 1873. From that time he frequented the new opera house designed by the architect Charles Garnier, which opened to the public in January 1875. The Opéra Garnier came to be a celebration of the new Paris after the horrors of the Franco–Prussian war and the uprising of the Communards. Garnier had exhibited a model for his opera house at the 1863 Salon, and stylistically it would have been in keeping with other Salon exhibits, including his own watercolours. The Opéra Garnier was the embodiment of the aesthetics of the Second Empire, nurtured and promoted by Napoléon III during his reign until 1870. The critic and poet Théophile Gautier likened the design to those for Venetian palaces, admiring the 'graciously curving ramp' of the staircase and the way 'the well of the staircase is supported by coupled Ionic columns in Seracolin marble upon which are posed immense arches and which unite, from floor to floor, the balconies with their richly ornamented balustrades', upon which 'the curious can lean over as in a painting by Paolo Veronese, simultaneously spectators and spectacle, to watch at their leisure the marvel of modern civilisation …' Overwhelmed by this imagined spectacle, Gautier continued to describe the interior of the Opéra Garnier and its inhabitants as: 'this cascade of diamonds, of pearls, of feathers, of flowers, of white shoulders, of satins, of velvets, of moirés, of gauzes, of laces, which here foams on the white marble steps, to the sparkling of vivid lights, framed by a fairy architecture.'

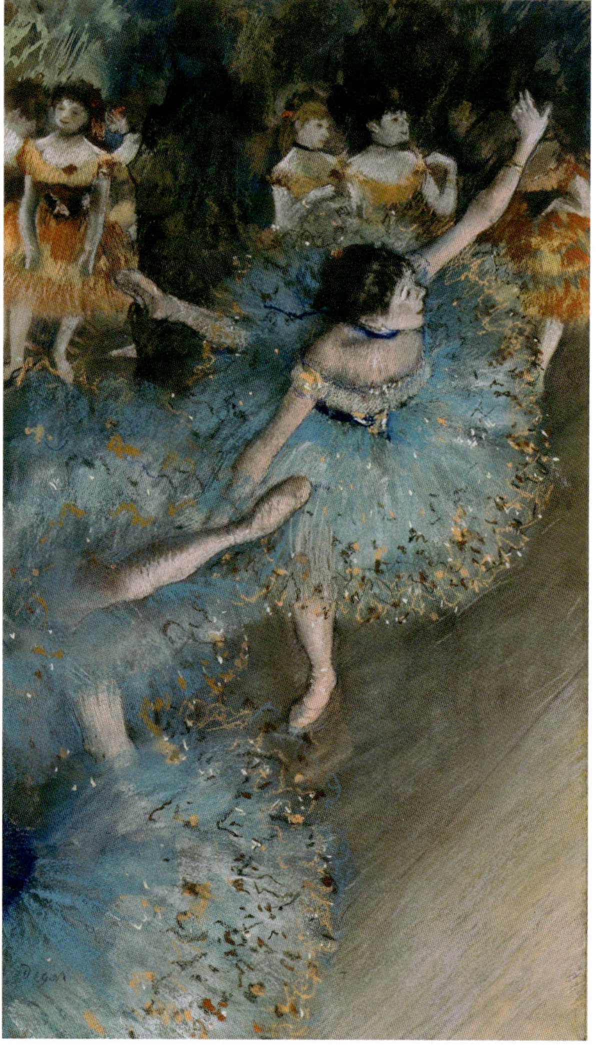

(previous page)
Dancers, pink and green
c 1890 (detail cat 75)

(right)
Swaying dancer (Dancer in green) (Danseuse basculant (Danseuse verte)) 1877–79
pastel and gouache on paper,
64 x 36 cm
Museo Thyssen-Bornemisza, Madrid
Lemoisne 572

(opposite)
Mlle Bécat at the Café des Ambassadeurs (Mlle Bécat au Café des Ambassadeurs)
1877–78 (detail cat 80)

There were grand public spaces and an auditorium that held four tiers of boxes and seating for 2156 patrons. The decoration included oil paintings by Gustave Boulanger and a sculpture by Jean-Baptise Carpeaux, both working with classically inspired themes executed in a rich neo Baroque, overly elaborate style—in Gautier's words, 'The temple of modern civilisation.'[1]

Research has provided details of Degas' frequent attendance at the Opéra Garnier as a subscriber in the years between 1885 and 1892.[2] In 1885, for instance, he attended 56 times, including many repeat visits to performances. Given his sustained interest in the subject of the ballet, it is likely that there were numerous solo visits, as well as occasions when he was in the company of friends, the ballet enthusiasts Ludovic Halévy, Paul Valpinçon and Ludovic Lepic.

As well as full-scale productions, a ballet performance would often be presented between the acts of an opera, or between excerpts of several operas, or within the opera itself. In 1831 Marie Taglioni danced in the 'ballet of the nuns' in the third act of Meyerbeer's opera *Robert le Diable*—she was the first to dance *en pointe*, instead of wearing high-heeled shoes.[3] The principal dancers were fêted by the citizens of Paris; but the critics could be unmoved. A jaded Hippolyte Prévost found the première performance of *La Source* in 1866 to be 'two hours of *ballonnées*, of *jetés-battus*, of gracious poses …

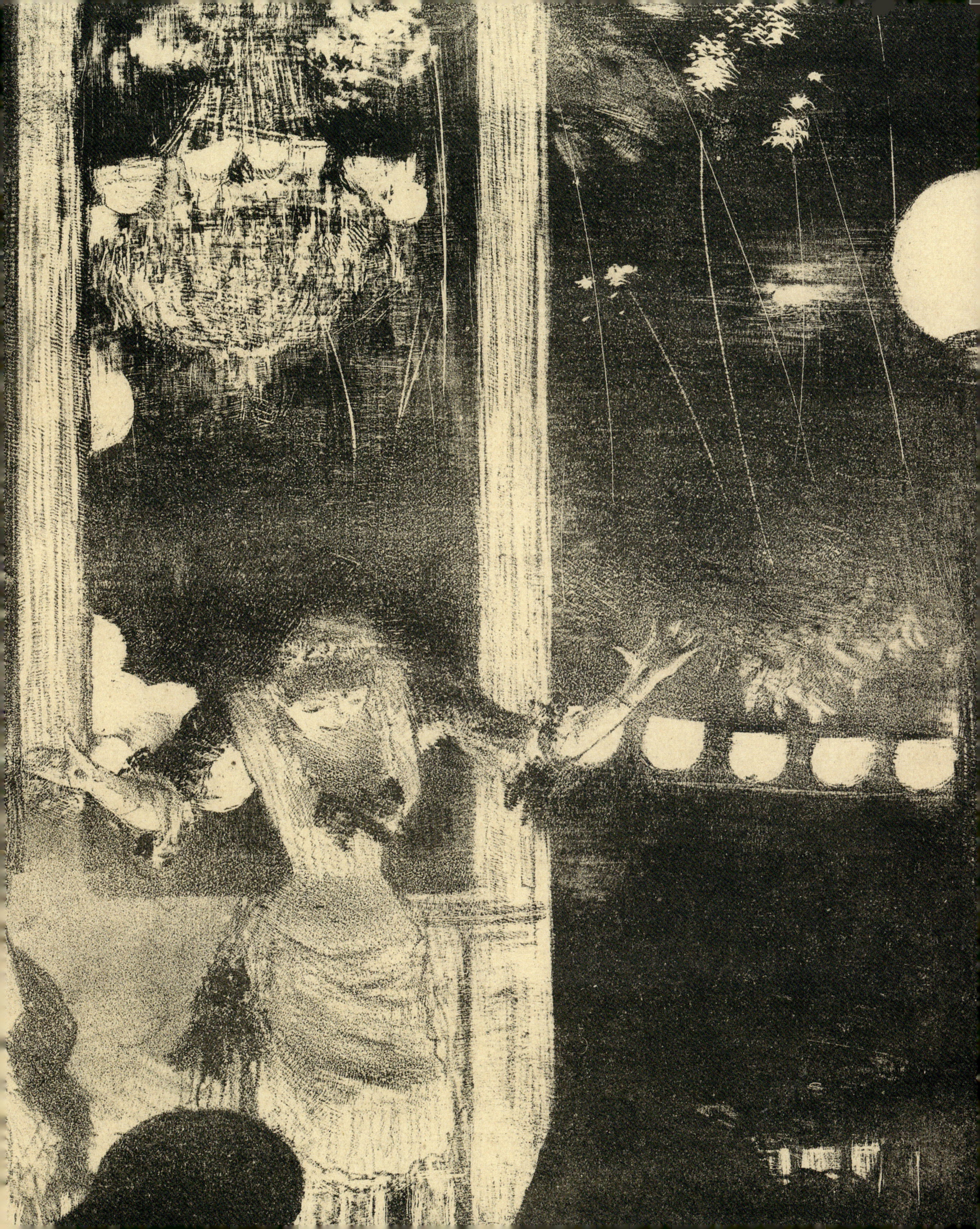

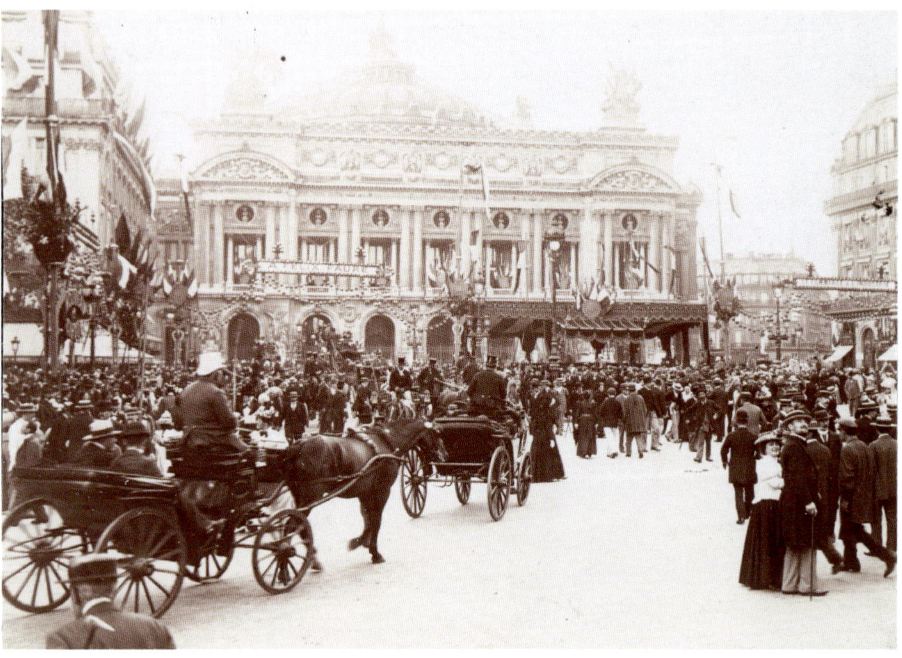

Henri Lemoine
The Opera, Paris (*L'Opéra, Paris*)
c 1900
aristotype photograph,
7.5 × 10 cm
Musée d'Orsay, Paris

enough to satisfy anyone'.[4] Generous intervals allowed time for the male patrons of Le Jockey Club, the 'Lions', to return from supper in a leisurely fashion, often with young companions from the ballet corps.

Stage sets rich in detail and grand in scale delighted Parisian audiences. A fascination with discoveries of new lands and peoples, and the increasing popularity of travel abroad inspired the Opéra designers to create visual extravaganzas: 'We see horses on the stage, interminable processions, entire regiments parading with superb equipment, immense perspectives, crowds, swarms of dancers, shipwrecks, burning towns. Soon we will be present at a battle, a naval engagement …'[5] The wondrous stage effects incorporated machinery that could propel dancers over and under the stage—all lit by gas, or the new electric light.

The excesses and artifice of stage design did not capture Degas' imagination; and details of architectural motifs, or a focus on the audience, were rarely included in his compositions. He found inspiration in the dancers themselves—on stage or behind the scenes, in the maze of corridors, in foyers and alcoves, and on the stairs. It was in these spaces that subscribing patrons could mingle with the dancers.

Ballet dancers feature in several of the eight sonnets written by Edgar Degas in 1888–89, a further demonstration of his fascination with the transformation through dance of these humble young girls. Masked in theatrical makeup and dressed in ethereal costumes, they are transported to another realm, the common ugliness of their features and their lives forgotten—the ballerina becomes a 'winged spirit', dancing on 'a grass of floor boards'.[6]

Degas' painting of 1868, *Mlle Fiocre in the ballet 'La Source'* (cat 45) (shown at the Salon that year, with the artist listed under the more aristocratic surname, de Gas[7]), may be seen as a bridge between his early portraits and later depictions of the ballet. Following his portrait likenesses of the dancers in *La Source*—where the background appears more of a landscape than a stage set—Degas went on to combine portraits of musicians in the orchestra pit with scenes of a performance. In *The ballet of 'Robert le Diable'* 1871 (cat 48) he also includes a portrait likeness of a man in the front row of the audience. In terms of his compositional schema—the prospect from the orchestra pit, or figures seen behind stage sets, or performances viewed from the wings—a major influence was Honoré Daumier, who Degas admired and whose caricatures he collected. While Daumier depicted a multitude of types of live performances, Degas concentrated mostly on the dance, or the occasional café-concert.

The device of the view from the orchestra pit was applied by Degas in a series of scenes at café-concerts, including *Mlle Bécat at the Café des Ambassadeurs* and *The song of the dog*, both of 1876–77 (cats 80 and 81), depicting popular singers at these lowly establishments. The café-concert was a particularly French institution.[8] These venues were frequented by a cash-strapped, often destitute audience, the type Huysmans described in dark detail in his account of the demoralised demimonde, and where his prostitute Marthe performed on occasions. Café-concerts, such as at the Alcazar and the Ambassadeurs in the centre of Paris, specialised in performances with a repertoire 'almost entirely composed of those concerns which arise below the belt'.[9] In contrast to the extravagance of the Opéra Garnier, the actual physical nature of the café-concert was unpretentious, often with facades fashioned out of cardboard.

The generally held view that Degas' ballet compositions were artificial constructions has been tempered in recent times. It is argued that his direct exposure to performances had an immediate effect on his art, and that frequently in his work there is a specificity of detail in the costumes, choreography and set design that can be linked to particular ballets. The observation is made that these details correspond to contemporary images of performances at the Opéra found in photographs, drawings and prints, as well as the original set designs.[10]

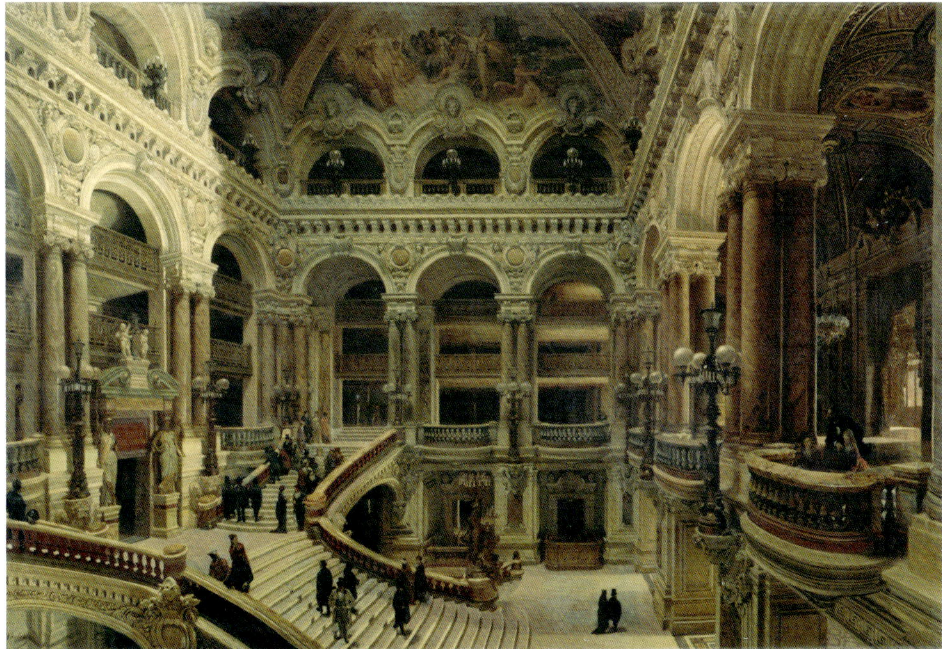

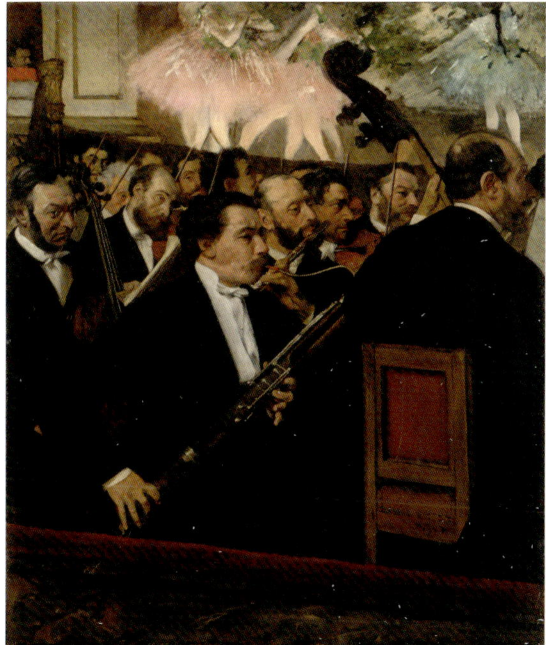

Victor Navlet
Staircase at the Paris Opera
(Escalier de l'Opéra à Paris) c 1880
oil on canvas, 131 x 196 cm
Musée d'Orsay, Paris

Edgar Degas
The orchestra of the opera
(L'orchestre de l'opéra) c 1870
oil on canvas, 56.5 x 46.2 cm
Musée d'Orsay, Paris
Lemoisne 186

As he progressed as an artist, Degas' ballet images were less about an actual performance. Rather, he concentrated on activity off-stage, in the rehearsal rooms, or in ante chambers where dancers are grouped together watching, exercising, adjusting, resting—as in *The dance class* c 1873, and *Before the ballet* 1890–92[11] (cats 51 and 70). Here Degas evokes a sense of movement with asymmetrical compositions, the inclusion of empty spaces, high horizon lines, and the cropping of figures, architectural forms and furniture.

By the end of the 1880s, Degas was moving towards more simplified compositions. His constant battle with failing eyesight was a factor in this change of style. In a letter dated 15 August 1895 to his sister Marguerite Fevre, Degas complained: 'I can hardly read now, even with a magnifying glass. I work all the same but on a large scale …'[12]

In these later years his subjects were governed by an interest in form and the application of paint. He moved to a more abstract style, a more brilliant palette and a looser handling of paint, as seen in *A group of dancers* 1890s (cat 76), where wispy evanescent dancers are set against a dramatic backdrop, and in the vividly coloured grand scale painting, *Dancer with bouquets* 1895–1900 (cat 77).[13]

Notes

1 Théophile Gautier, *Moniteur universel*, 5 August 1867, quoted in David van Zanten, *Designing Paris: the architecture of Duban, Labrouste, Duc and Vaudoyer*, MIT Press, Cambridge, 1987, p 230.

2 Henri Loyrette, 'Degas à la Opéra', in *Degas inédit: Actes du Colloque Degas, Musée d'Orsay 18–21 Avril, 1988*, La documentation française, Paris,1989, pp 46–63, which includes a list of the operas he attended over these years.

3 'Paris Opera ballet: a brief history', online at cmi.univ- mrs.fr/~esouche/dance/POBhis, viewed August 2008.

4 Hippolyte Prévost, 'La revue musicale', in *La France politique, scientifique et litteraire*, 18 November 1866, p 1, quoted in Jill DeVonyar and Richard Kendall, *Degas and the dance*, Harry N Abrams in association with the American Federation of the Arts, New York, 2003, p 23.

5 Charles Bauquier, *Le Monde illustré*, 3 March 1860, p 192, quoted in DeVonyar and Kendall, p 27.

6 'Danse, gamin ailé, sur les garzons de bois': the first line of the eighth sonnet, 'Petite danseuse', by Degas. His sonnets were published in their entirety in *Huit sonnets d'Edgar Degas*, Wittenborn & Co, New York, 1946, p 37.

7 Pierre Sanchez and Xavier Seydoux, *Les catalogues des Salons*, vol 9 (1868–70), L'Echelle de Jacob, Dijon, 2005, p 85.

8 Gustave Coquiot, *Les cafés-concerts*, Librairie de l'art, Paris, 1896. For further accounts, see Jane Kinsman, 'Paris intense', in *Paris in the late 19th century*, National Gallery of Australia, Canberra, 1996, pp 24–28, which includes description by André Chadourne, *Les cafés-concerts*, E Dentu, Paris, 1889, p 2.

9 Coquiot, p 33.

10 DeVonyar and Kendall, pp 157–93.

11 The Corcoran Gallery of Art, Washington DC, Lemoisne 398; National Gallery of Art, Washington DC, Lemoisne 941.

12 Richard Kendall (ed), *Degas by himself: drawings, prints, paintings, writings*, Little, Brown & Co, Boston, 1987, p 233.

13 National Gallery of Scotland, Edinburgh, Lemoisne 770; Chrysler Museum of Art, Norfolk, Lemoisne 1264.

45 *Mlle Fiocre in the ballet 'La Source'* (*Mlle Fiocre dans le ballet de 'La Source'*)
1867–68
oil on canvas
130.8 x 145.1 cm
The Brooklyn Museum, New York
21.111
Gift of James H Post, A Augustus Healy, and John T Underwood
Lemoisne 146

This painting is a significant stepping stone in Degas' development, as it traverses conventions of style and genre. In this single work, the artist can be seen to be shifting from an art with overtly historical references to one that is more modern in style. Taken from a spectacular ballet that opened to the public on 12 November 1866 at the Paris Opéra, the subject signals Degas' early interest in dance. *Mlle Fiocre in the ballet 'La Source'* was painted on a grand scale, and in brilliant colour, for the Salon of 1868. In his review of the Salon that year, published in *L'Evénement illustré* on 9 June, the critic Emile Zola praised Degas' use of colour, which reminded him of Japanese woodblock prints, *ukiyo-e*.

The painting features the dancer Eugénie Fiocre, who was then the toast of Paris. In *La Source* (The Spring), Fiocre starred as the exotic and malevolent Nouredda, from faraway Georgia, who is pursued by the hunter Djémil. The male lead is assisted in his efforts by the tragic nymph of the spring, Naïla (danced by Guglielmina Salvioni), who is sacrificed for her troubles. The theme, choreography and music of the ballet itself were rich in Romanticism and enhanced by the elaborate oriental costumes of Nouredda and the richly coloured robes of Naïla. Degas has depicted the dancers in costume, but at no time is there a concession to the actual performance—except for their ballet shoes. In the actual performance of this rather idiosyncratic and unintelligible ballet, Mlle Fiocre was accompanied by a real horse, which is shown here drinking at the spring.

This composition is not of a ballet performance per se, and the scene is not a theatrical set. Rather it is a painting of figures in a landscape—Nouredda and her two female companions beside a flowing river. The group of craggy rocks behind them is reminiscent of the grottoes of Gustave Courbet. The evident influence of Courbet and Realism represents a move towards modern subjects by Degas.

Mlle Fiocre in the ballet 'La Source' reveals Degas' range of influences in his formative years, and is proof that at this time he had both the confidence and skill to work on a large scale.

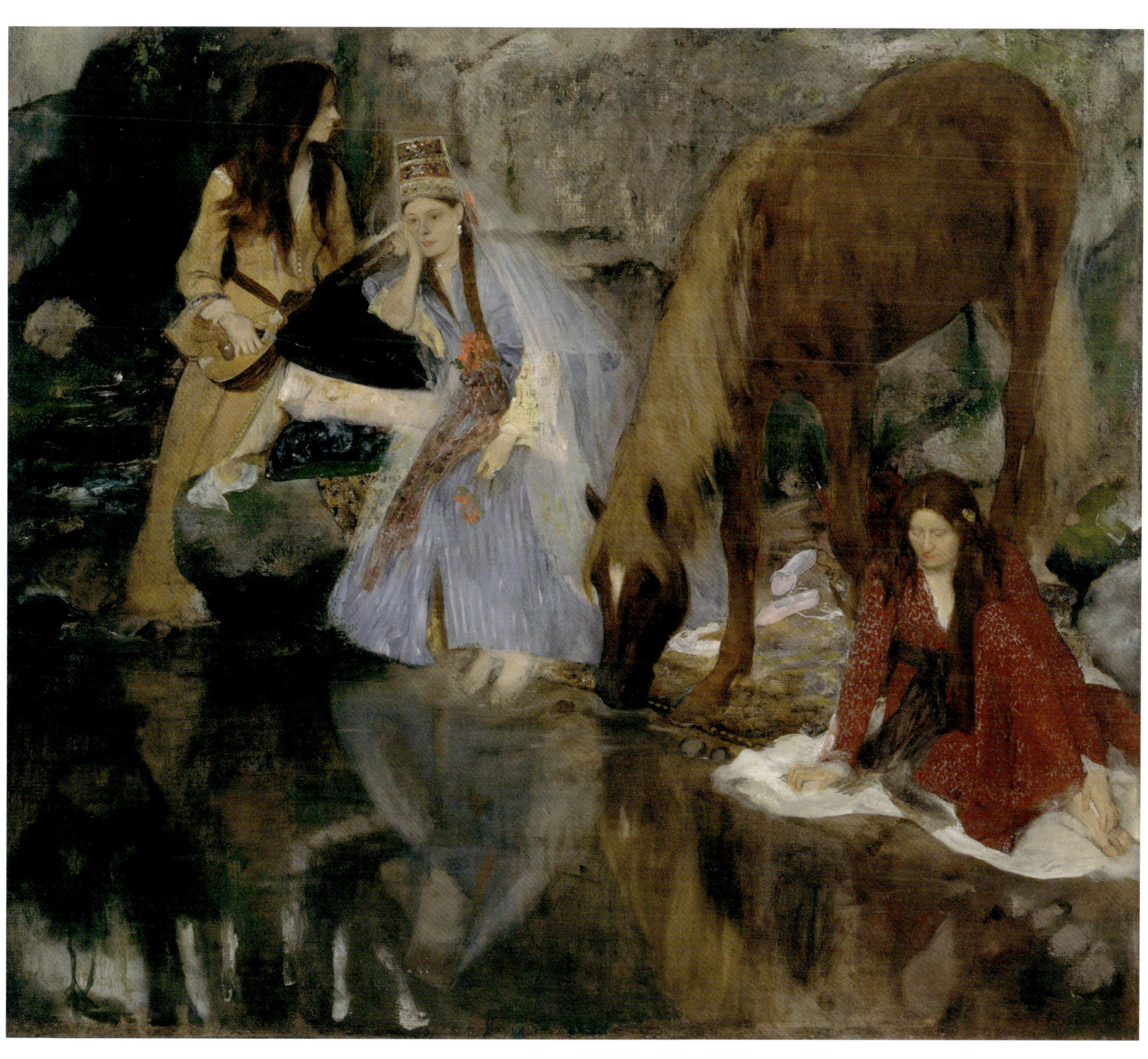

46 *Horse at a trough* (*Cheval à l'abreuvoir*)
modelled 1866–68; cast 1920
cast A of 24
bronze
16.5 x 22.5 x 13.5 cm
The Metropolitan Museum of Art, New York
29.100.433
HO Havemeyer Collection, Bequest of Mrs HO Havemeyer, 1929
Czestochowski and Pingeot 13

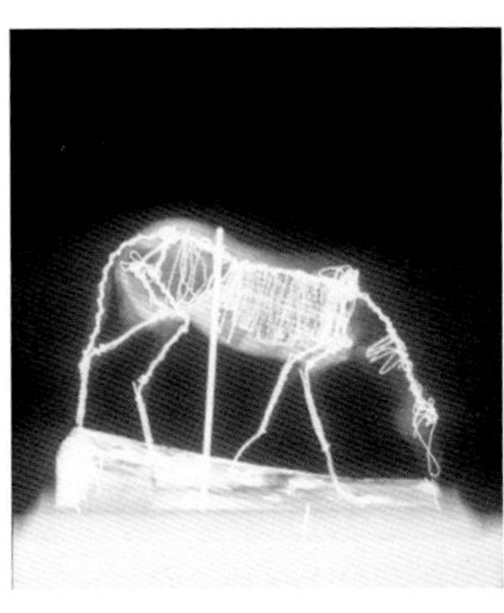

X-ray of *Horse at a trough*
1866–68
Virginia Museum of Fine Arts, Richmond
Collection of Mr and Mrs Paul Mellon
Image courtesy of the Board of Trustees, National Gallery of Art, Washington DC

Hand-in-hand with his compositions in painting and drawing over a considerable period of time, Degas made three-dimensional wax figures. In this way he was able to explore the form and movement of his subjects—whether a horse, a dancer or a woman bathing. Many of these wax figures were found in his studio at the time of his death and were subsequently cast in bronze. The practice of modelling sculpture in wax was not unusual at this time; Degas' friend Joseph Cuvelier also composed wax horse statuettes.

A modern X-ray of *Horse at a trough* (left) demonstrates Degas' early methodology, where he has attached a skeletal wire figure to an armature. The tightly wound wire creates a three-dimensional cage. The artist then applied wax to this structure, to create the form of his subject.

It is likely that this sculpture was made prior to the completion of Degas' painting *Mlle Fiocre in the ballet 'La Source'* (cat 45), shown at the Salon of 1868. The horse in both instances is standing on sloping ground, and drinking. As Degas once recounted to Ambroise Vollard, he was in the habit of using wooden models of horses in his studio to help in his compositions. Given its relatively small size, this figure of a horse probably assisted Degas in his preparation of the Salon painting.

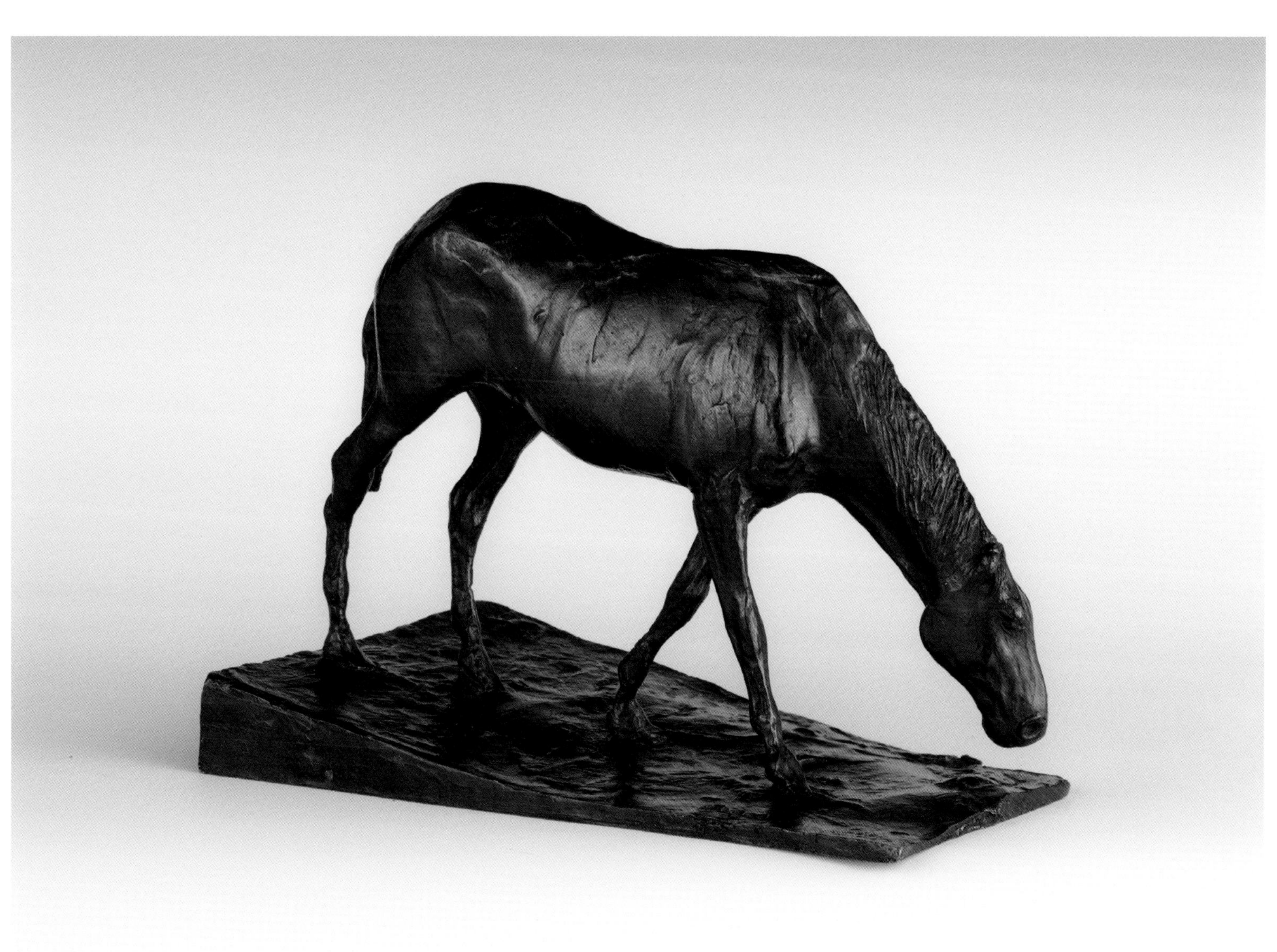

47 *Nude study for Mlle Fiocre in the ballet 'La Source'*
(*Nus, étude pour Mlle Fiocre dans le ballet de 'La Source'*)
1867–68
oil on canvas
81.3 x 64.5 cm
Collection Albright-Knox Gallery, Buffalo, New York
58:2
Gift of Paul Rosenberg and Co, 1958
Lemoisne 148

In preparation for his major painting *Mlle Fiocre in the ballet 'La Source'* (cat 45), Degas made sketches in his notebooks (21 and 22) and preparatory drawings of the dancer Eugénie Fiocre. Two of these were head studies from photographs (c 1866 and dated August 1867) and one was a full-length study of the dancer dressed in her elaborate costume and headdress (dated 3 August 1867). In the manner of a finely drawn Ingres sketch with an emphasis on outline, Degas also prepared this smaller preliminary oil before embarking on his large painting.

For this preparatory work, Degas used a single nude model twice, to place the forms of Fiocre and her seated companion, who are closer together than in the final Salon painting. He also experimented with the depiction of water, with the reflections of the figures more clearly outlined than in the final work. Around this time Degas made a drawing after Whistler's painting *Symphony in white no 3* 1866, and this study may have contributed to his arrangement of two of the female figures in the final composition.

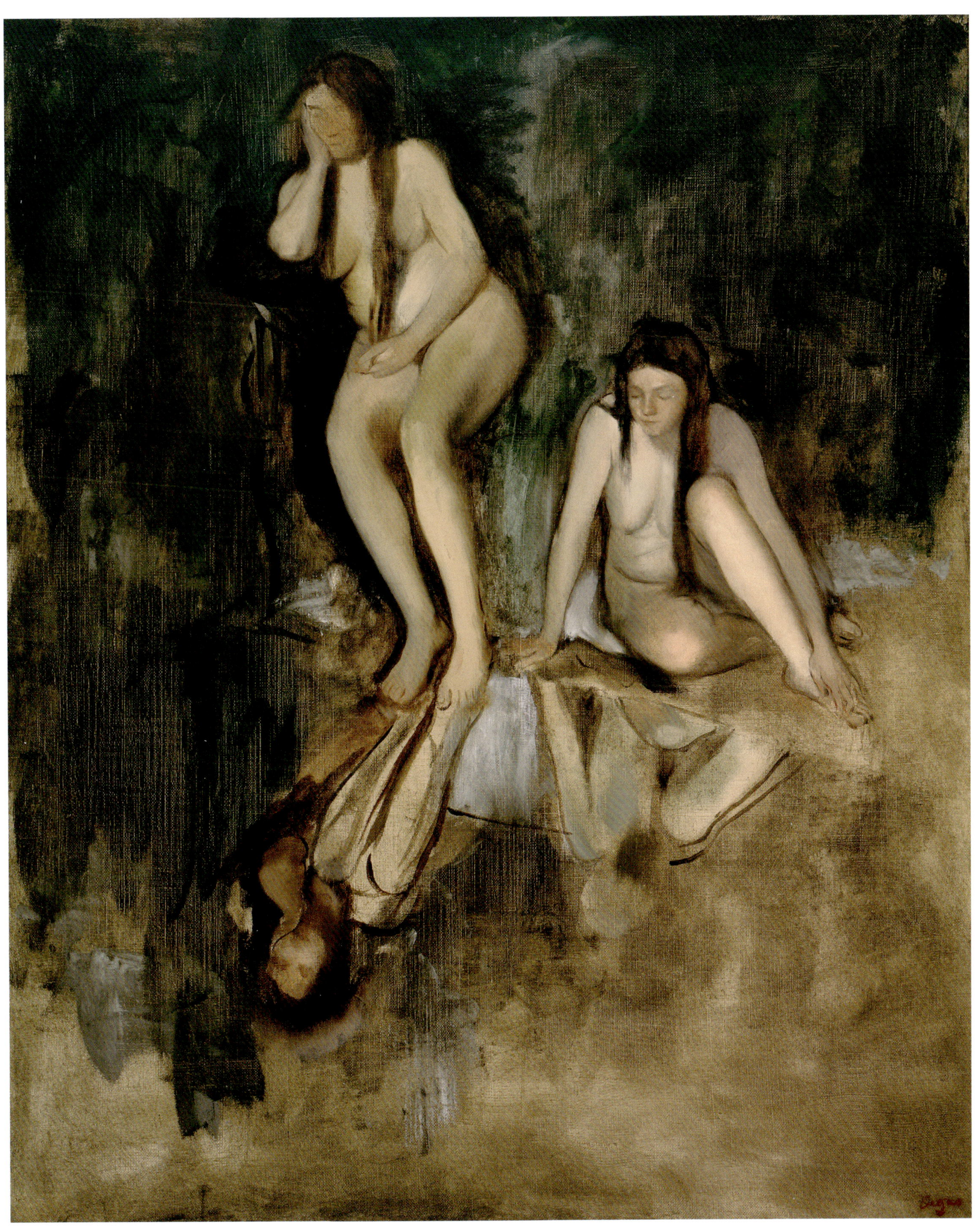

48 *The ballet of 'Robert le Diable'* (*Ballet de 'Robert le Diable'*)
1871 (although dated by the artist 1872)
oil on canvas
66 x 54.3 cm
The Metropolitan Museum of Art, New York
29.100.552
HO Havemeyer Collection, Bequest of Mrs HO Havemeyer, 1929
Lemoisne 294

Degas was a keen opera-goer, and was particularly fond of Meyerbeer's *Robert le Diable*, which he first saw in performance in the early 1870s. He continued his enthusiasm for this opera later in life, his subscription details revealing that he attended performances from 1885 to 1892.

Now comparatively unknown, Giacomo Meyerbeer was a dominant force in the French opera world of the nineteenth century and *Robert le Diable* was his most popular production. It opened in Paris on 21 November 1831 and was admired for its new style of 'grand' opera. *Robert le Diable* continued its popularity, even during the disastrous days between 1870 and 1872, when Paris was being ravaged: a program of 23 performances was scheduled around the months of the Franco–Prussian war and the Communards' uprising. Attending the opera during this period, Degas made sketches of the orchestra, the opera loges, the audience, the stage sets and of nuns dancing.[1]

The ballet of 'Robert le Diable' captures all the excitement of the performance, as well as being an innovative group portrait of musicians. Behind the musicians is the first row of the audience, including a man eyeing an opera box through his opera glasses. Degas has placed his 'portraits' of the musicians and the opera-goers as large figures in the foreground. On the stage, the ballet dancers dressed in nun's habits remain ethereal and ghost-like, flitting about the space, having escaped from their coffins. Degas has made dramatic use of contrasts of light and dark amongst the medieval colonnades of the stage set.

That Degas has chosen to view the scene from the orchestra reveals his debt to Honoré Daumier. This was a regular pictorial device used by the French caricaturist, and one which Degas adopted. He greatly admired Daumier, and was an avid collector of the satirist's work.

The composition of the ballet scene viewed from the orchestra pit was one that Degas repeated in subsequent paintings and in a series of etchings he made of the subject titled *On the stage* (cats 49 and 50).

Notes

1 Reff, notebook 24 for the orchestra and audience; two studies of the nuns dancing are now in the collection of the Victoria and Albert Museum, Vente III, 364, i and ii. The later 1876 version of *Robert le Diable* is also housed at the Victoria and Albert Museum, London, Lemoisne 391.

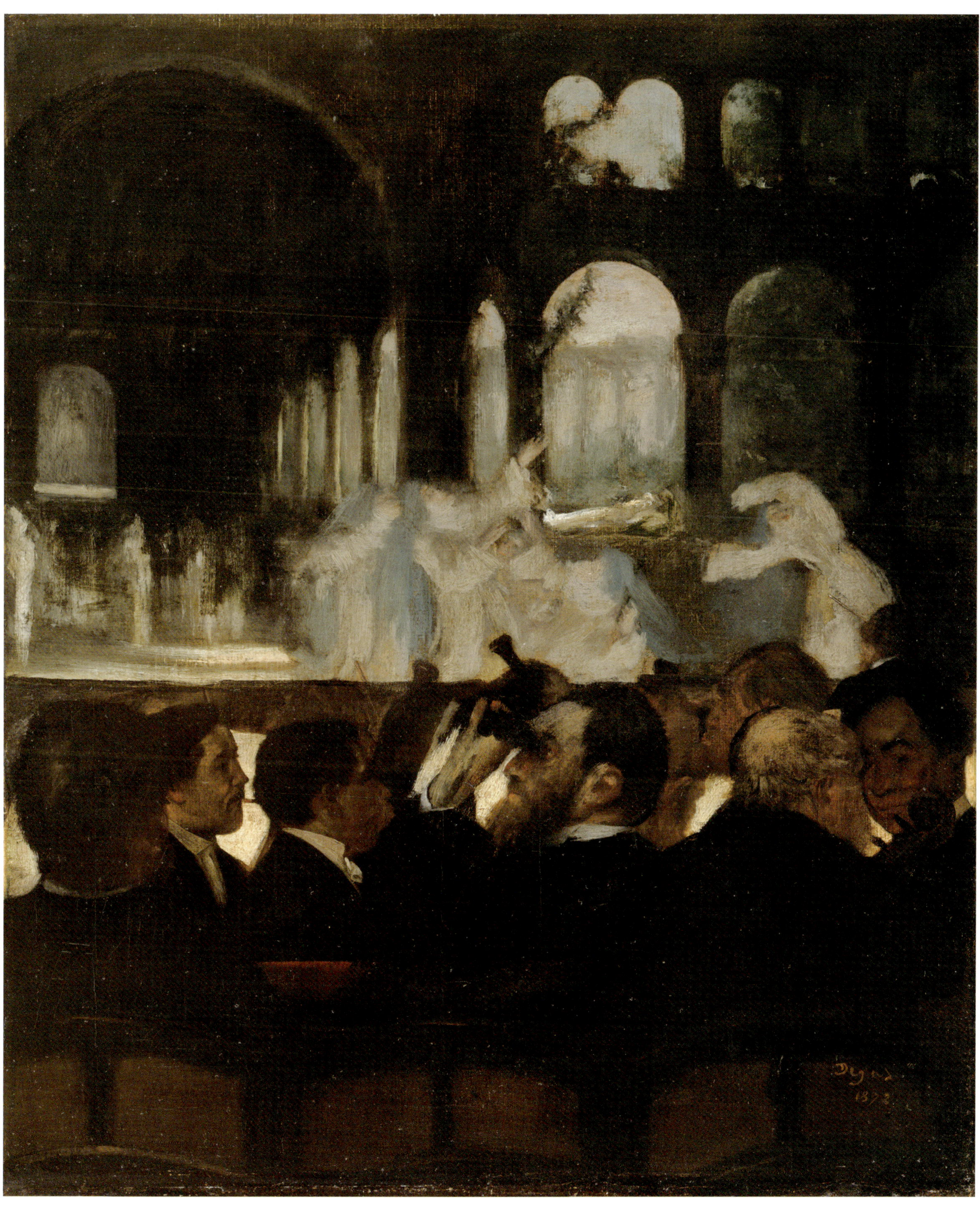

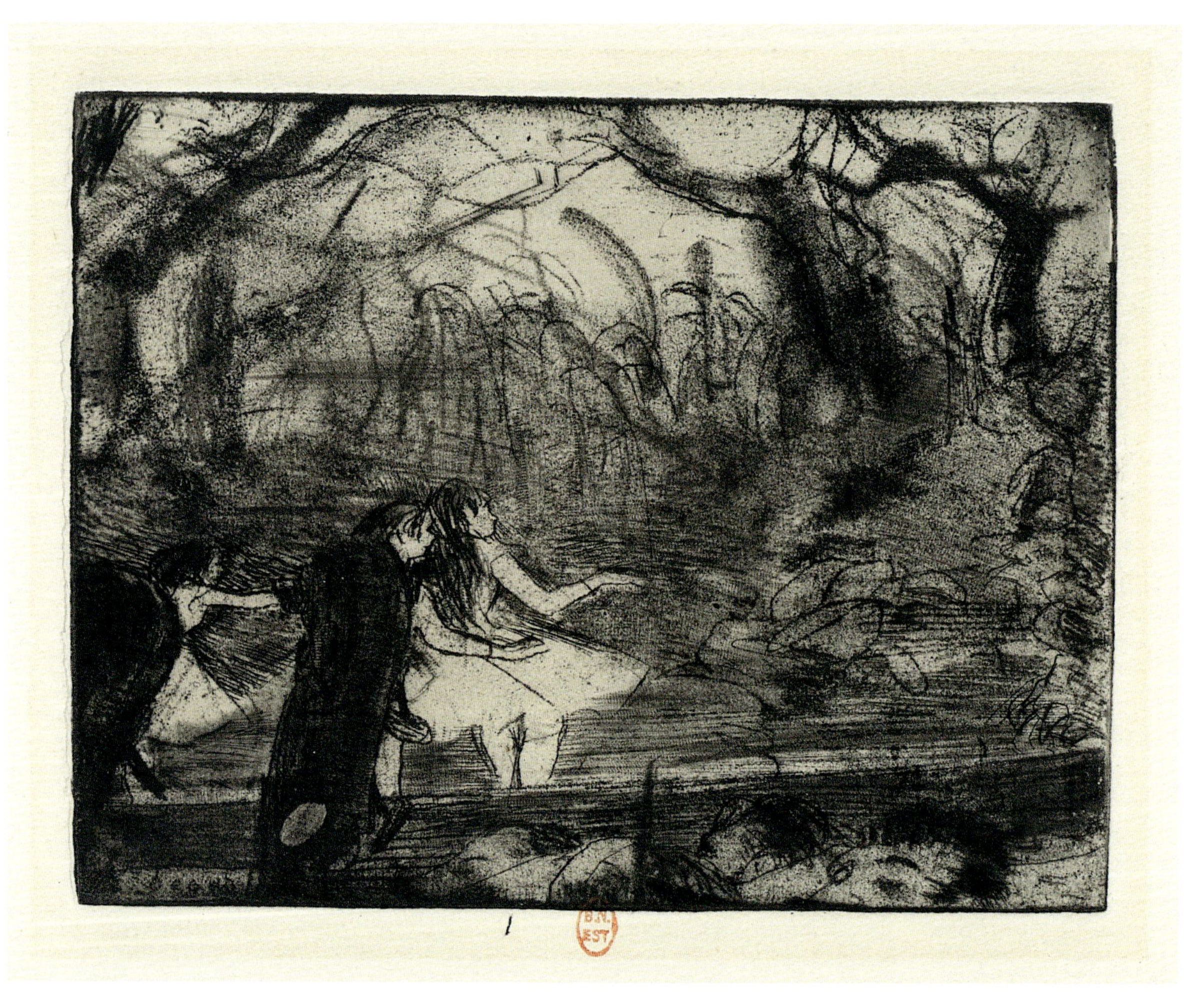

49 *On the stage* (*Sur la scène*)
1876–77
second plate, third state of five (or possibly six)
edition of two
soft-ground etching
9.9 x 12.7 cm (plate), 12.8 X 15.6 cm (sheet)
Bibliothèque nationale de France, Paris
res Dc 327dh fol, boîte
Reed and Shapiro 24 / Adhémar 26

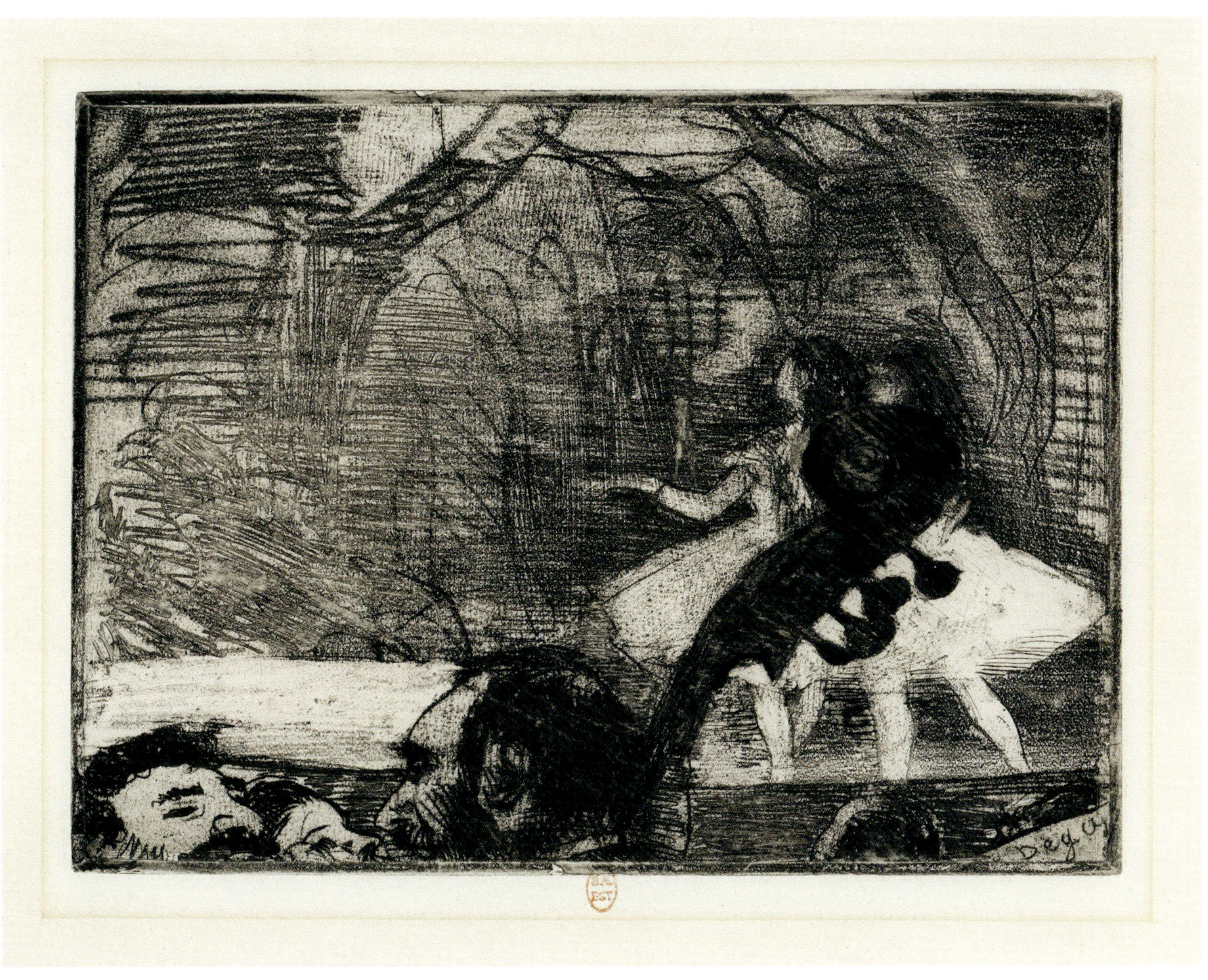

50 *On the stage* (*Sur la scène*)
1876
third plate, fourth state of five
edition of two
soft-ground etching
12 x 16 cm (plate), 15.9 x 24.4 cm (sheet)
Bibliothèque nationale de France, Paris
res Dc 327dh fol, boîte
Reed and Shapiro 22 / Adhémar 27

51 *The dance class* (*Ecole de danse*)
c 1873
oil on canvas
47.6 x 62.2 cm
Corcoran Gallery of Art, Washington DC
26.74
William A Clark Collection, 1926
Lemoisne 398

Degas painted *The dance class*, an ambitious and complex interpretation of the dance subject, on his return to Paris from New Orleans in 1873.

This is not a glamorous portrayal of the life of the dancer. By clever design and the clustering of figures, Degas manages to evoke a real sense of what it was like to be in the midst of a class. The painting evokes the pitter-patter of the dancers' feet as they make their way down a spiral staircase to the left of the composition. In the right foreground are several ungainly figures—one dancer is bending down tying her slippers, with her bottom facing the viewer; another is seated with her legs inelegantly apart, her hand to her chin and chatting away obliviously; a third dancer has her foot raised resting on a chair, responding in conversation while tying her sash behind her. Behind this group we see further clusters of dancers on points or practising at the barre. Combined, these motifs convey a vivid sense of the sights and sounds of a class.

The radical cropping of the ballerinas on the stairs, with only their legs and tutus to be seen, the informality of the dancers in the foreground, and the key compositional component of the empty floor lit from behind, all contribute to making this an extraordinary early Degas painting of the ballet.

Degas' fine painting style, his slashes of pink, red and orange, his innovative use of light and dark—where natural light flows through the openings and windows—all add a vitality to *The dance class*. The painting represents a crucial stage in his development toward more radical compositions with empty centres and cropped figures.

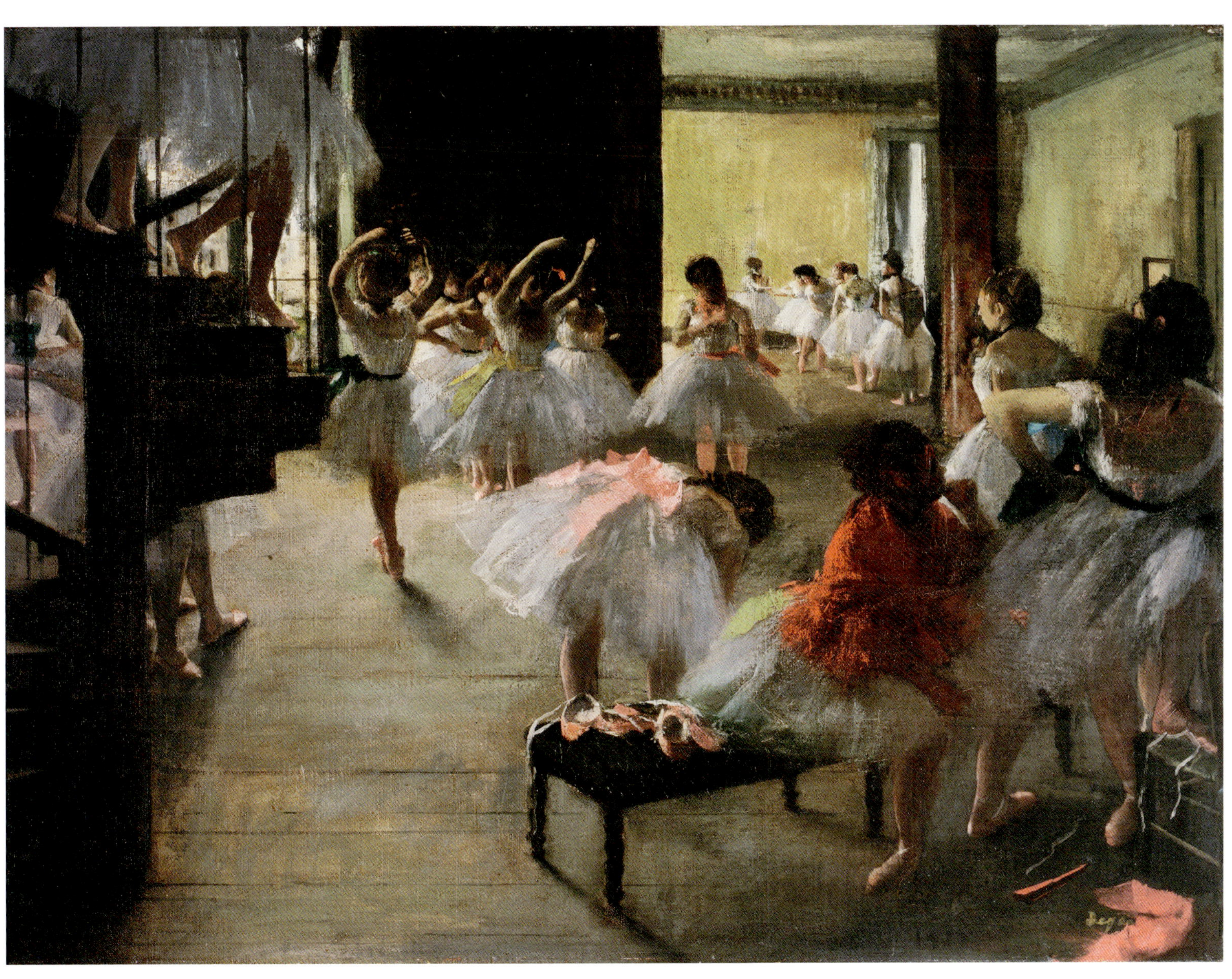

52 *Ballet dancer with arms crossed* (*Danseuse à mi-corps*)
c 1872
oil on canvas
61.3 x 50.5 cm
Museum of Fine Arts, Boston
48.534
Bequest of John T Spaulding, 1948
Lemoisne 1025

This is an unusual ballet painting by Degas, as he has concentrated on just one figure, a dancer in repose with her arms crossed in quiet contemplation. It is an astonishingly bold painting, if the proposed date of about 1872 is correct. Because of the scale of the figure, the dramatic use of red, the sketchiness of the painting, and the unfinished appearance, the work was previously considered to be made about 1890.[1]

Recent research has revealed the existence of a similar composition of a ballet dancer with arms folded, painted in 1872 by Degas' friend Evariste de Valernes. This impoverished artist inscribed on his canvas that he made this in Degas' studio. Given the close resemblance of the subject—Degas' canvas shows the dancer in a three-quarter view—it was deduced that both artists were working on their canvases at that time. Further comparable motifs of a dancer with folded arms appear in other Degas paintings of the mid 1870s, including the pendant for *The dance class* (cat 51).[2] In these paintings, the dancer is either shown resting during a ballet class, or backstage waiting in the wings during a performance. The dancer in *Ballet dancer with arms crossed*, similarly may be waiting backstage or resting in class.

Notes

1 Lemoisne, volume 3, pp 596–97.

2 Richard Thomson, *The private Degas*, Arts Council of Great Britain, London, 1987, pp 60–65. The two paintings which include a comparable ballerina are The Metropolitan Museum of Art, New York, Lemoisne 397, where the dancer can be barely seen behind the figure of Jules Perrot, and the National Gallery of Art, Washington DC, Lemoisne 1024.

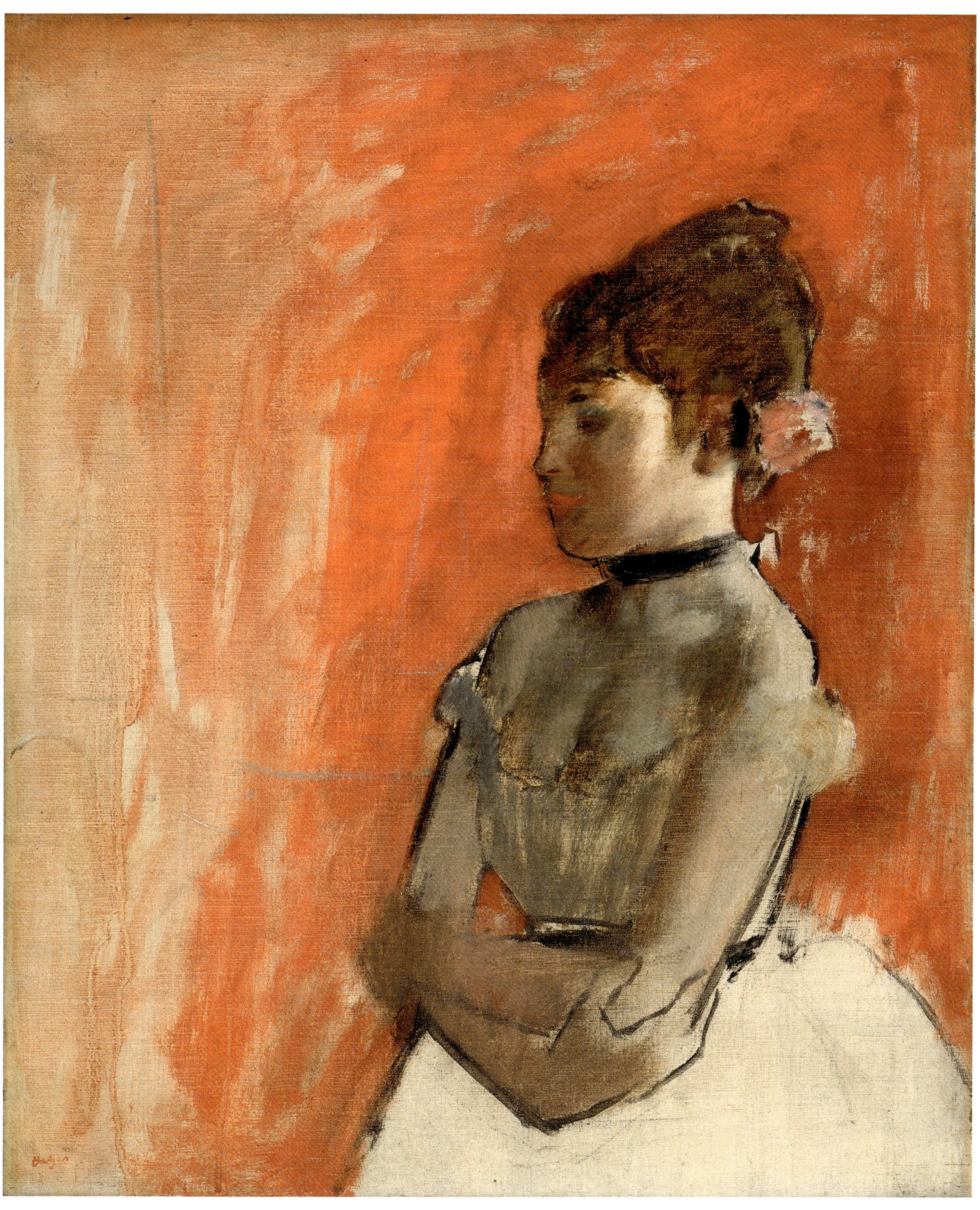

53 *The dance class* (*La classe de danse*)
begun 1873, completed 1875–76
oil on canvas
85 x 75 cm
Musée d'Orsay, Paris
RF 1976
Legacy of Count Isaac Camondo, 1911
Lemoisne 341

Like many of Degas' ballet paintings, *The dance class* 1873–76 does not depict a performance; rather, the artist chose to explore behind-the-scenes. Degas began the painting in 1873, though it took several years and some editing to realise this early masterpiece. The work is a particularly complex arrangement of figures—dancers attending a class taken by the ballet master Jules Perrot.

At this stage of his artistic development, Degas had a singular and mature sense of colour, applying rich greens and flashes of reds, yellows, blues and pinks and, in the case of the dancers' tutus, delicate highlights of white.

For this composition, Degas has combined a range of individualised figures, in a variety of poses. This could potentially have been a discordant grouping, but he has moulded them into an organic whole. The ebb and flow of dancers, their gestures and their stances, echo through the assembled troupe.

This apparent seamlessness did not come easily to Degas. *The dance class* was one of six paintings commissioned for Jean-Baptiste Faure in 1873; Degas abandoned working on this painting and developed an alternate version which he completed in 1874, which was then delivered to Faure in the following year.[1] Degas then returned to this earlier painting, making some dramatic changes such as fitting new figures into the composition, like a jig-saw puzzle. He had originally planned that the standing dancer in the foreground would be based on the drawing *Dancer adjusting her slipper* (cat 58). He later revised this twice, ending with a figure dressed with a green sash and holding a fan, with her back turned to the viewer.

Note

1 The Metropolitan Museum of Art, New York, Lemoisne 397.

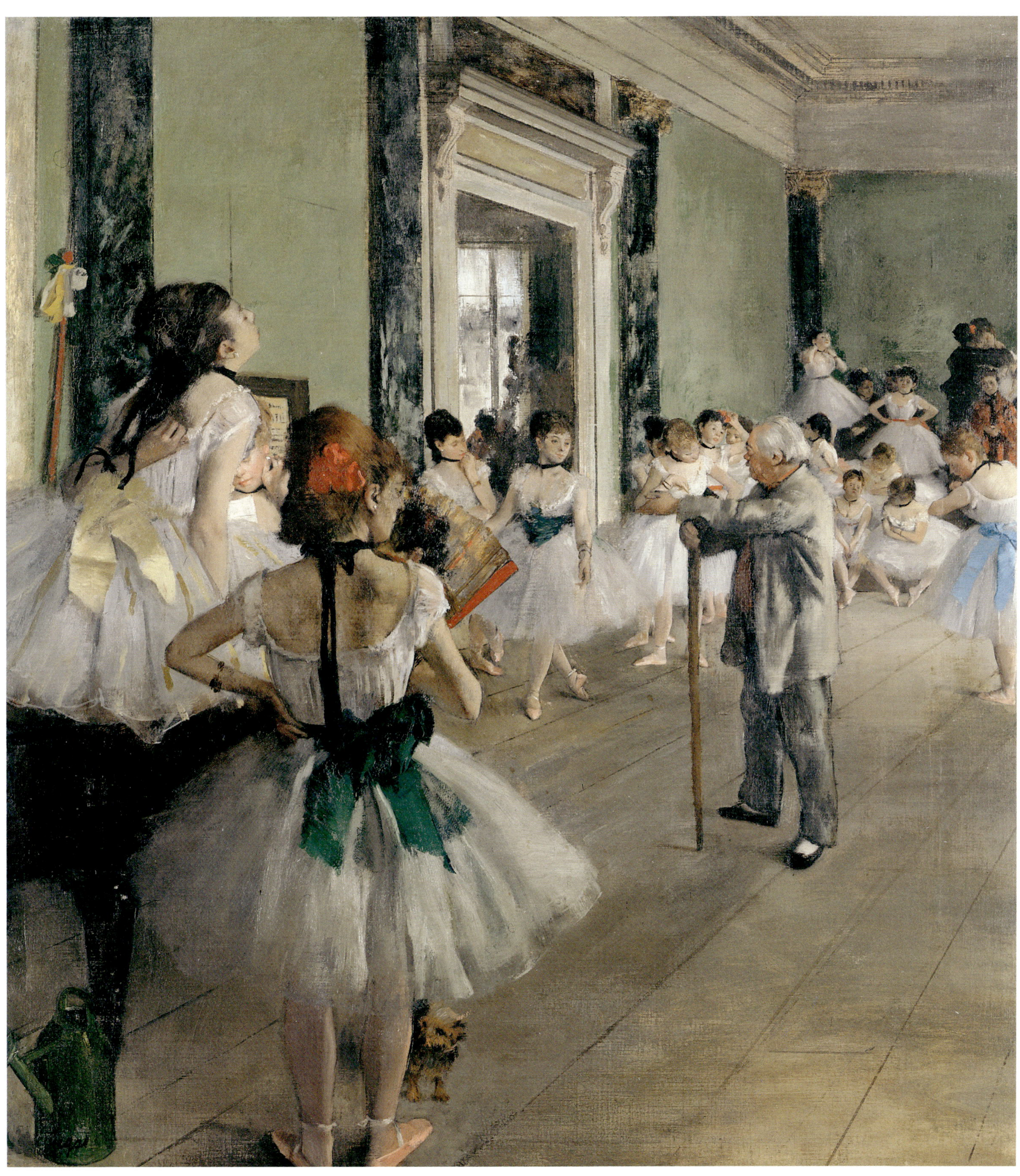

Drawing the dance

Degas made several drawings in preparation for his major painting, *The dance class* 1873–76 (cat 53).

The skilfully rendered *Dancer scratching her back* (cat 54) is the preliminary drawing for the figure seated on the piano in the foreground of the painting.

Degas also made two studies of the key figure in the painting, the ballet master Jules Perrot. A black chalk drawing (cat 55) is an accomplished work, projecting a sense of liveliness and of the ballet master's character. Though Jules Perrot has his head turned away from the viewer, Degas has created an insightful portrait through his rendering of Perrot's profile, the gesture of his hands, and his overall stance. This drawing is notable for the strong simple outline of the ballet master, seen holding a staff, which reinforces the vertical lines. The outline is coupled with vigorous cross-hatching, using a combination of chalk, crayon and charcoal.

A far more formal rendering of Perrot is found in a later *peinture à l'essence* drawing on brown paper, made in 1875 (cat 56). Perrot had created a name for himself in Paris as both a dancer and choreographer—particularly for Romantic ballets—at the Paris Opéra. After falling out with management he moved abroad, first to London and then to St Petersburg. He returned to Paris in 1861. Degas conveys the immense stature of the figure. With long white hair, dressed in a flamboyant red Russian shirt and loosely cut suit, he stands authoritatively gesturing with his left arm. The strong white highlighting, the careful outline and the rich red shirt on the coloured paper, suggest that this may not be a preliminary drawing for *The dance class* (cat 53), but rather that Degas may have produced the oil on paper after the painting.[1]

Degas made use of his drawings of figures to assist him with compositions as he developed his theme. He also recycled certain favourite images of his dancers in a variety of compositions. The finely drawn figure of the dancer *en pointe* (cat 57) reappeared in reverse, and as a more sketchy figure, in a painting of about 1877.

Degas also made drawings which are more like exercises in researching movement than delicate renditions of drawings, to assist him to place figures in his compositions. Two figures of dancers practising (cats 59 and 60) capture the dynamism of the dancers' movements, twirling and whirling or stretching and pointing across a page. The lines demonstrate Degas' constant search for ways to depict movement.

He also produced wax models of dancers, subsequently made into bronzes (cats 61–64).

Note

1 For a discussion on the dating and the order, and of whether the drawing was made before or after the painting, see Michael Pantazzi in Boggs et al, *Degas*, 1988, p 239.

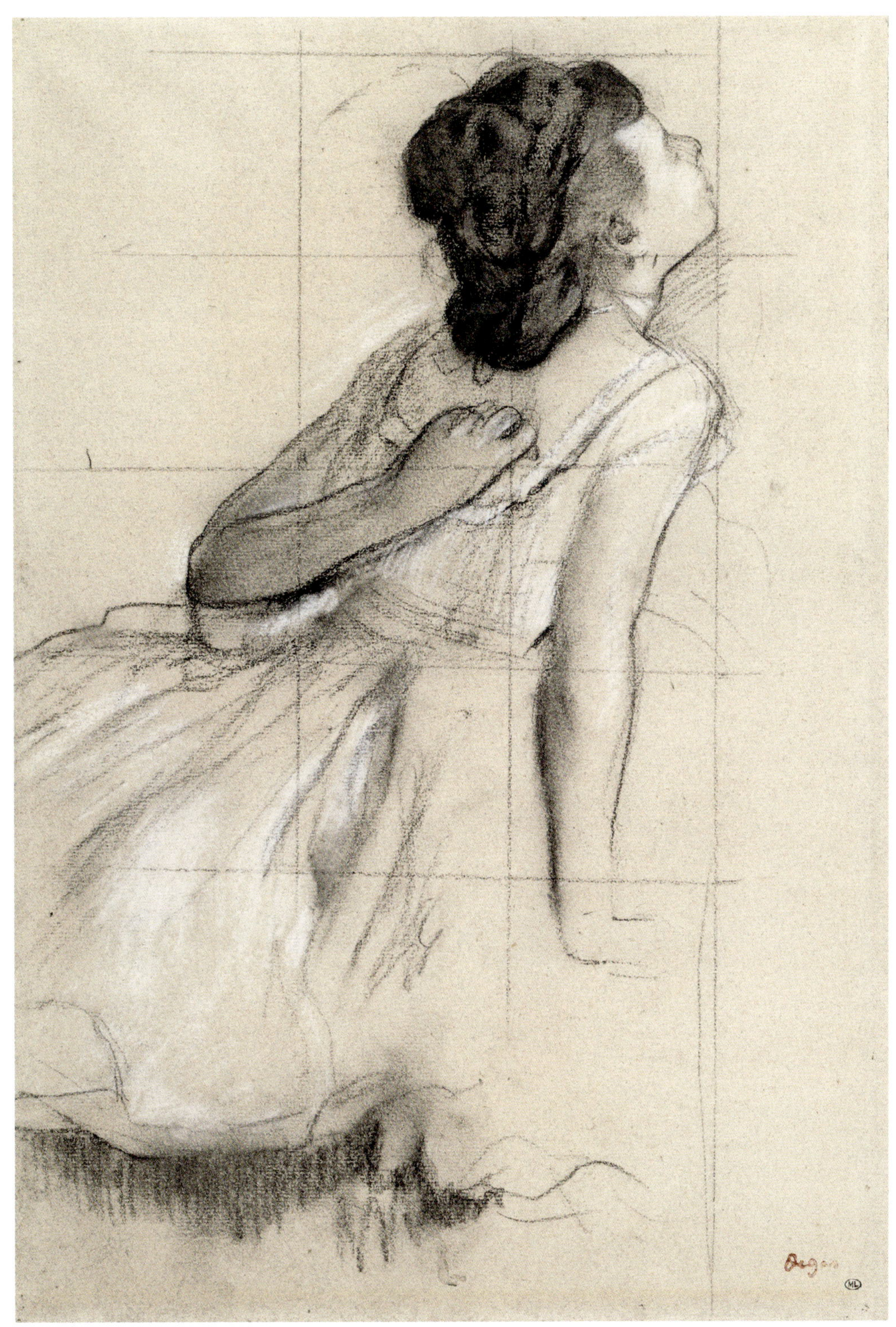

54 *Dancer scratching her back* (*Danseuse se grattant le dos*)
c 1873–74
charcoal and pastel on pink paper
46.5 x 30.8 cm
Musée d'Orsay, Paris
Housed at the Département des arts graphiques, Musée du Louvre
RF 4645
Acquis en 1919
Vente III: 341.1

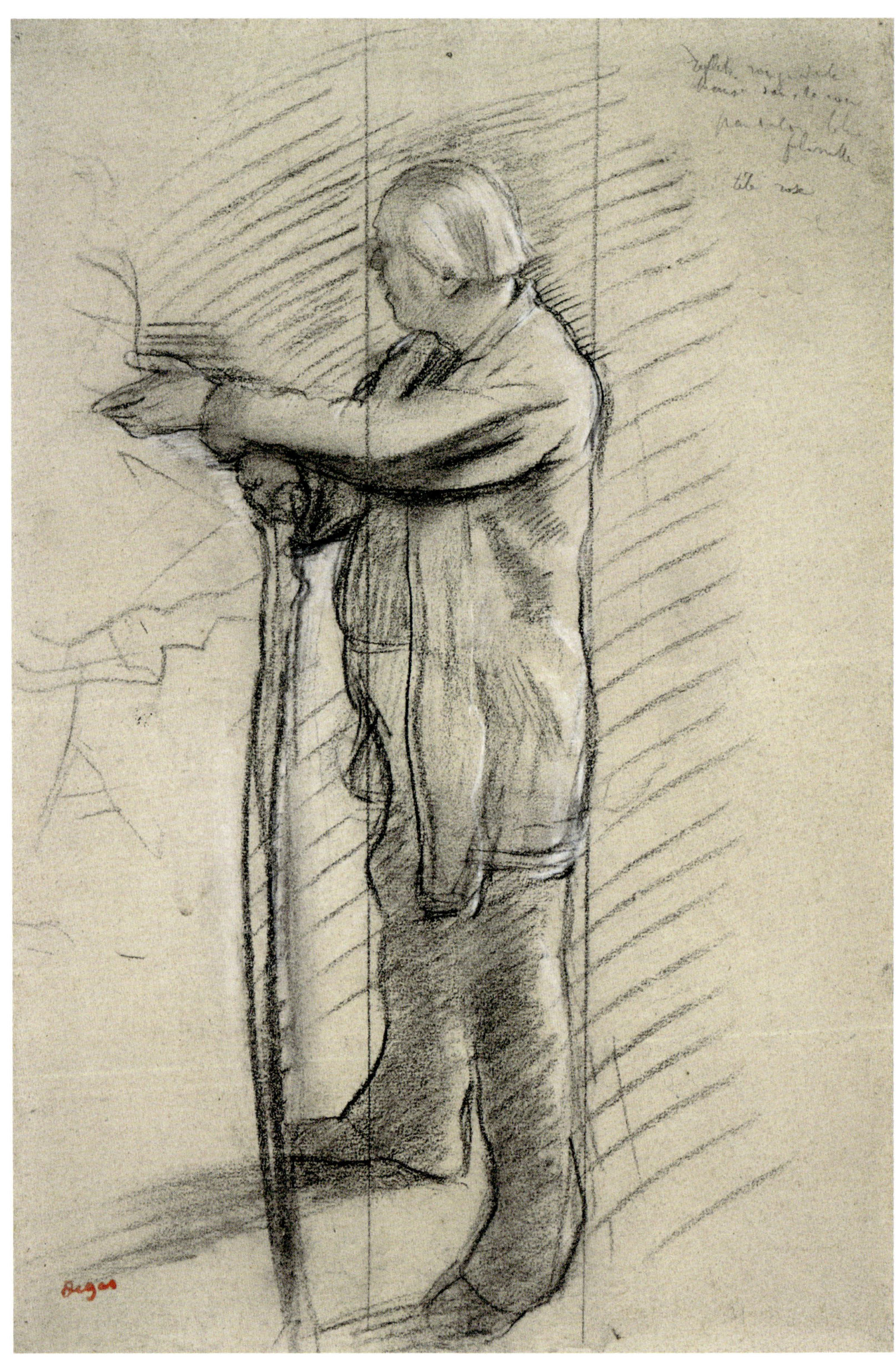

55 *The ballet master, Jules Perrot*
c 1875
black chalk, conté crayon and charcoal on paper
47 x 31.2 cm
The Fitzwilliam Museum, Cambridge
PD.25.1978
Vente III: 157.2
Bequeathed by ASF Gow through the National Arts Collection Fund

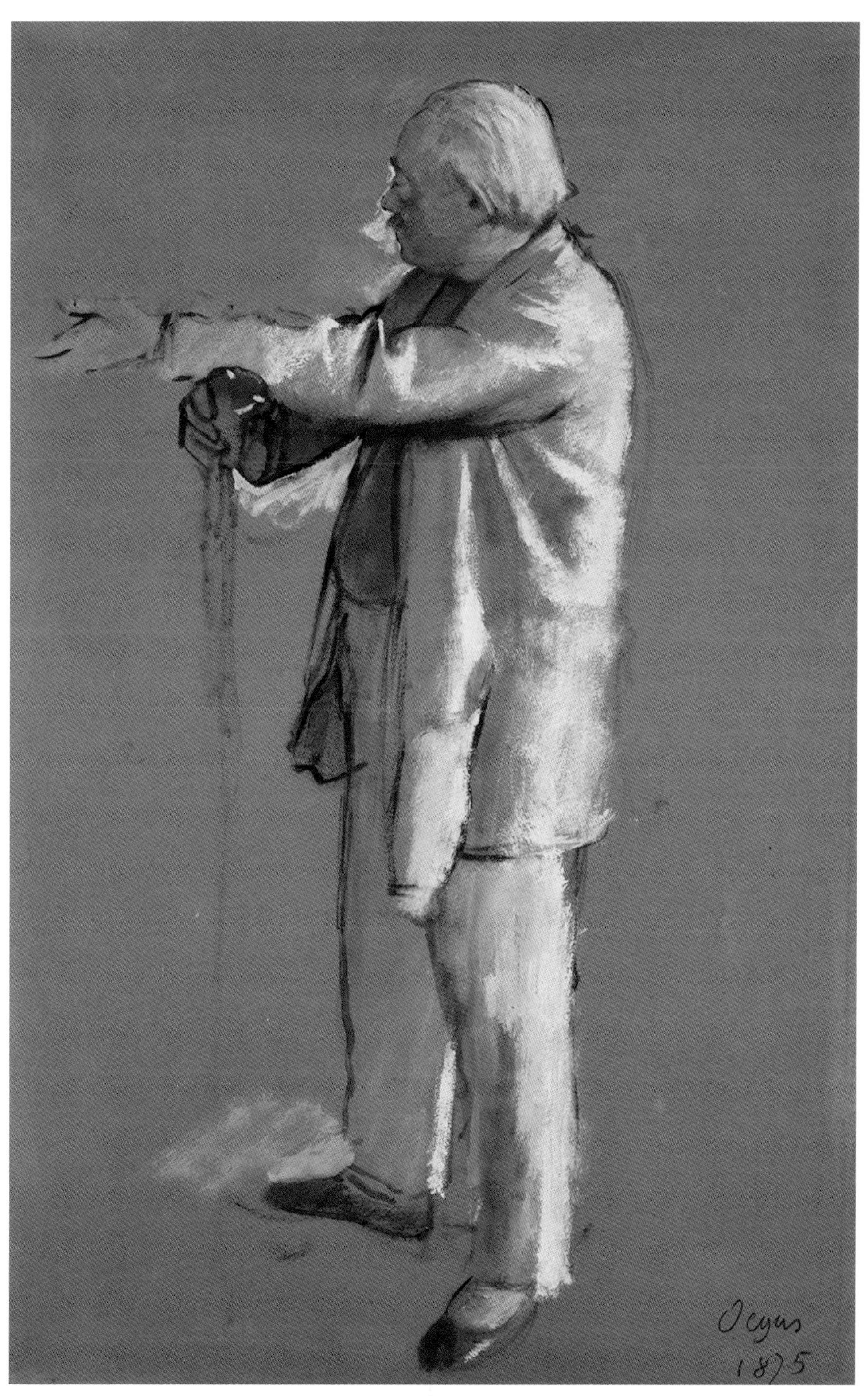

56 *The ballet master, Jules Perrot*
c 1875
oil on brown woven paper
47.9 x 29.8 cm
Philadelphia Museum of Art, Philadelphia
1986-26-15
The Henry P McIlhenny Collection in memory of Frances P McIlhenny, 1986
Lemoisne 364

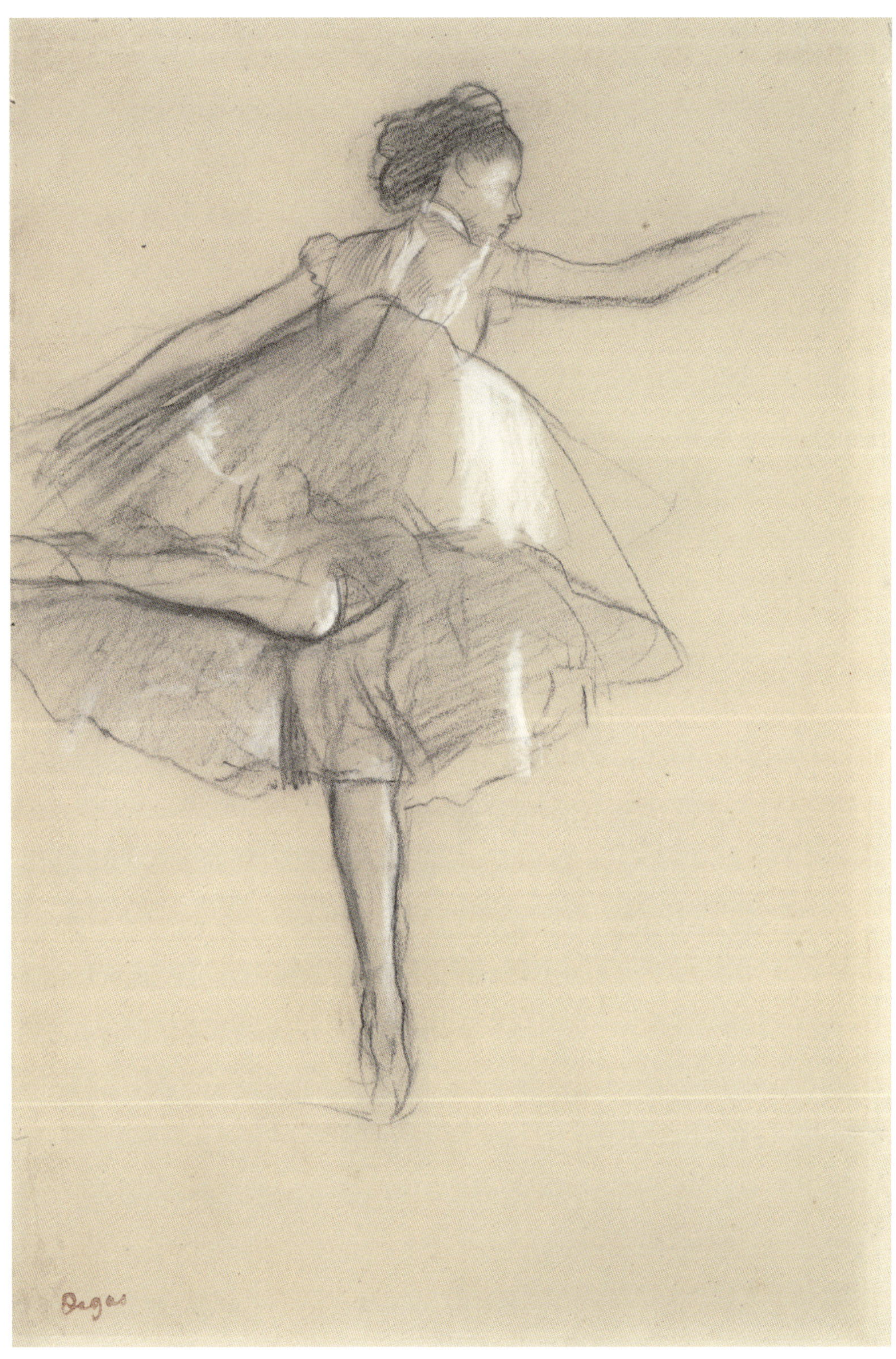

57 *Dancer on pointe* (*Les pointes*)
c 1880
charcoal on light brown paper, heightened with white
45.4 x 29.8 cm
The Metropolitan Museum of Art, New York
1974.356.43
Bequest of Emma A Sheafer, 1974, The Lesley and Emma Sheafer Collection
Vente III: 181

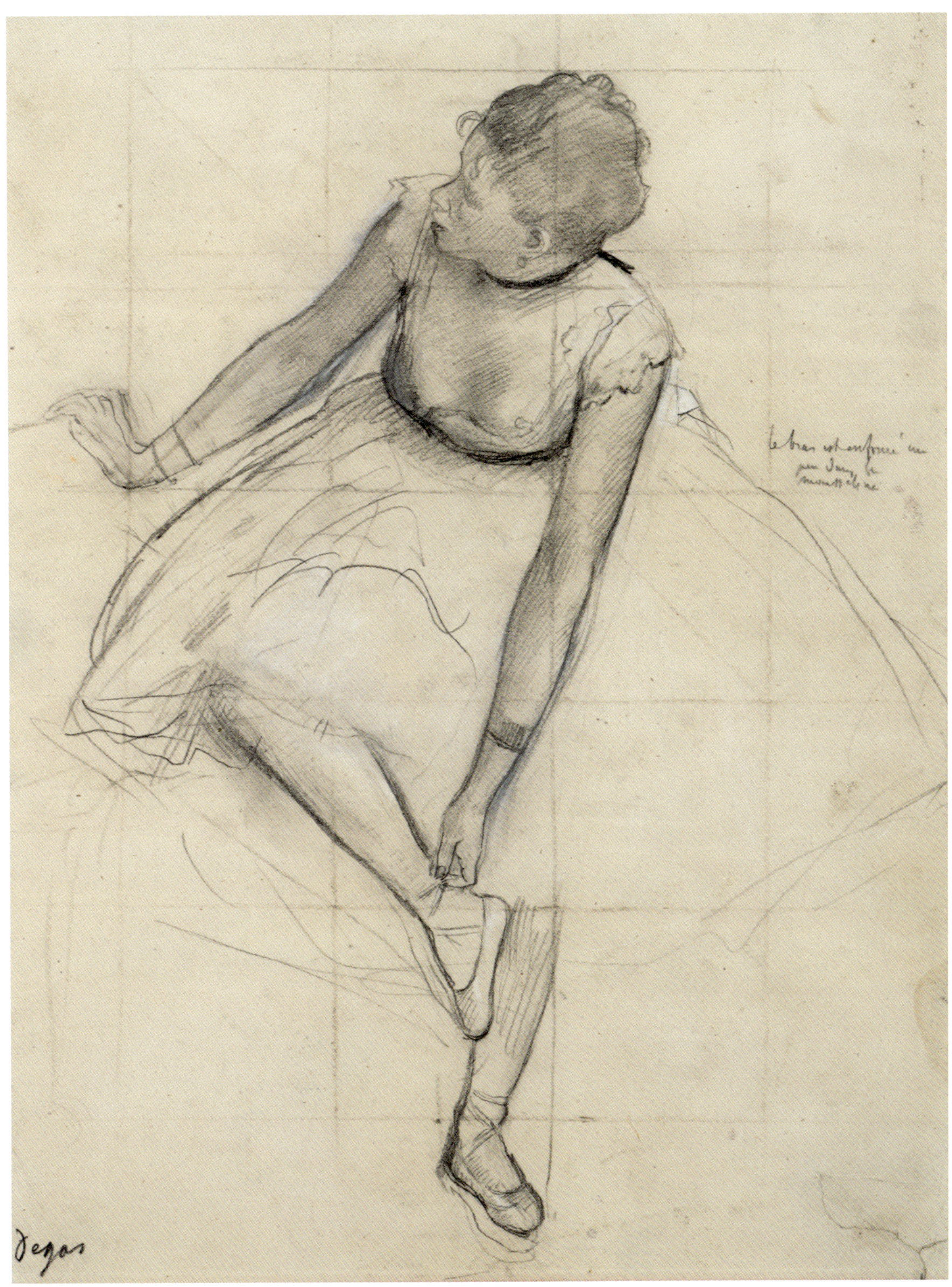

58 *Dancer adjusting her slipper*
1873
graphite heightened with white chalk on (faded) pink woven paper, squared for transfer
33 x 24.4 cm
The Metropolitan Museum of Art, New York
29.100.941
HO Havemeyer Collection, Bequest of Mrs HO Havemeyer, 1929

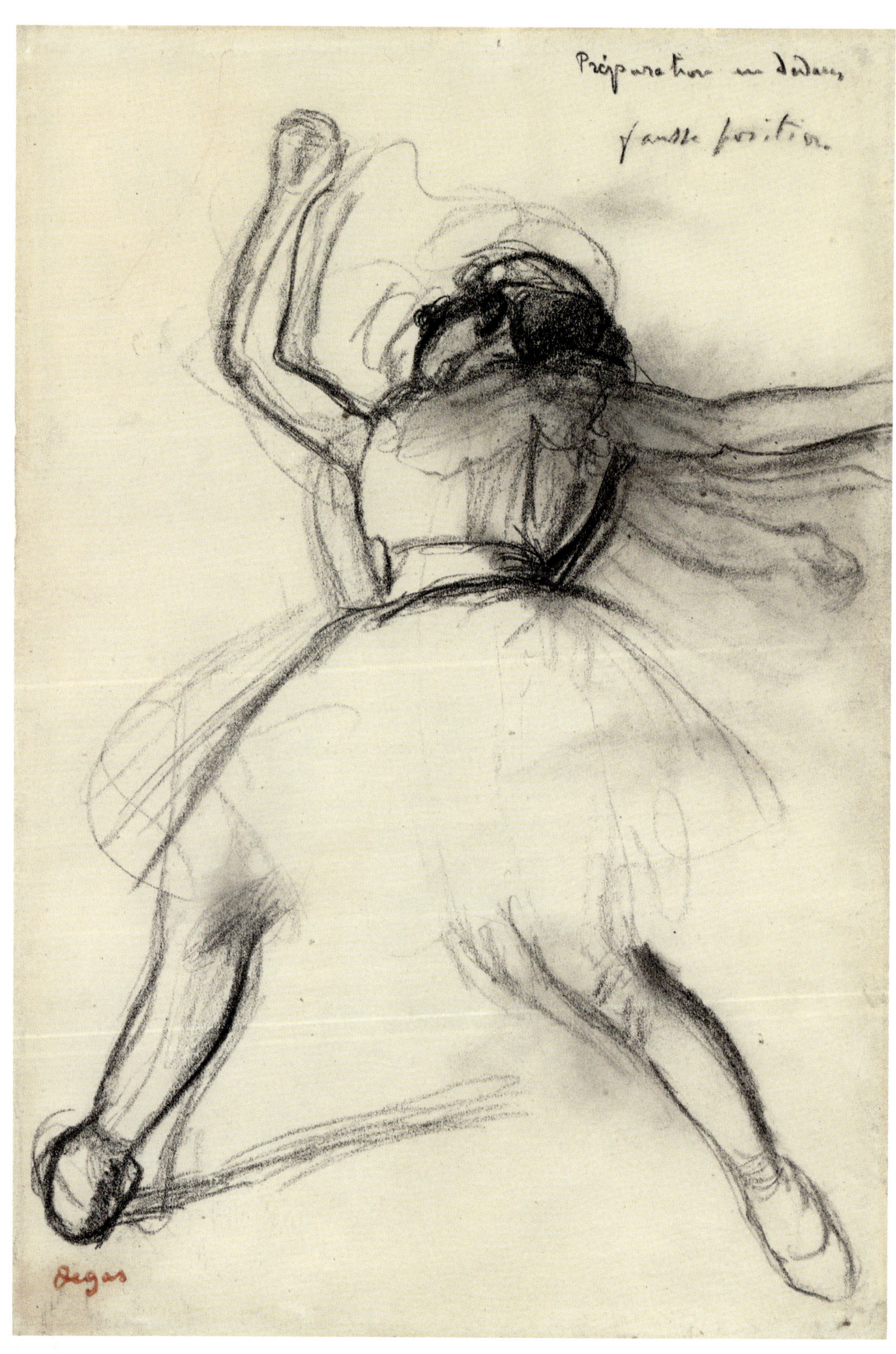

59 *Dancer in preparation*
(*Danseuse préparation en dedans*)
c 1885
charcoal, with stumping, on buff paper
33.6 x 22.7 cm
Stephen Ongpin, London
Vente III: 136.2

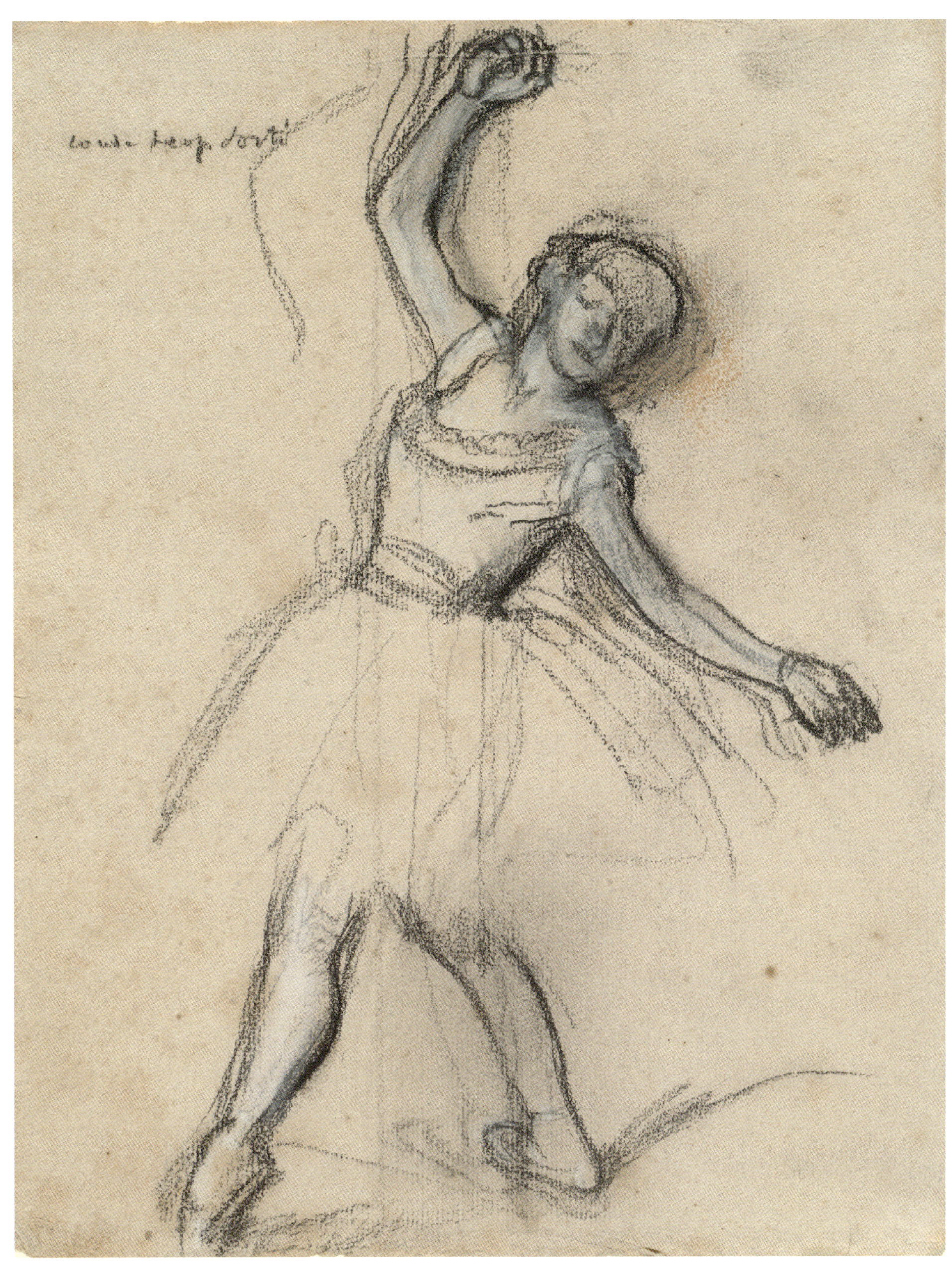

60 *Dancer in fourth position*
(*Danseuse en quatrième devant*)
c 1885
black chalk and pastel on buff handmade laid paper
30 x 23.8 cm
National Gallery of Australia, Canberra 2008.924
Gift of Margaret Hannah Olley, AC, 2008

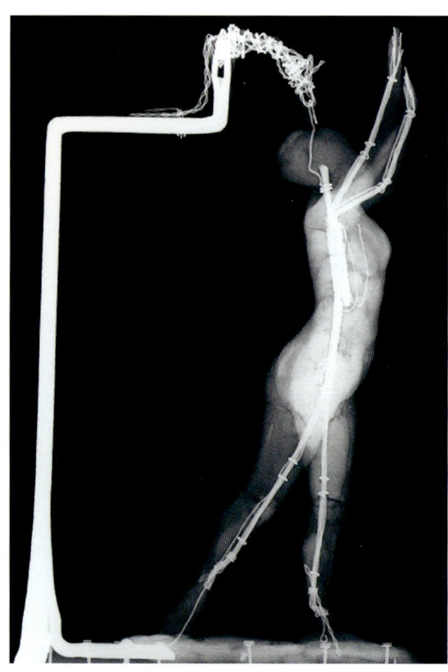

(above)
X-ray of *Dancer moving forward, arms raised* c 1885–90
National Gallery of Art, Washington DC

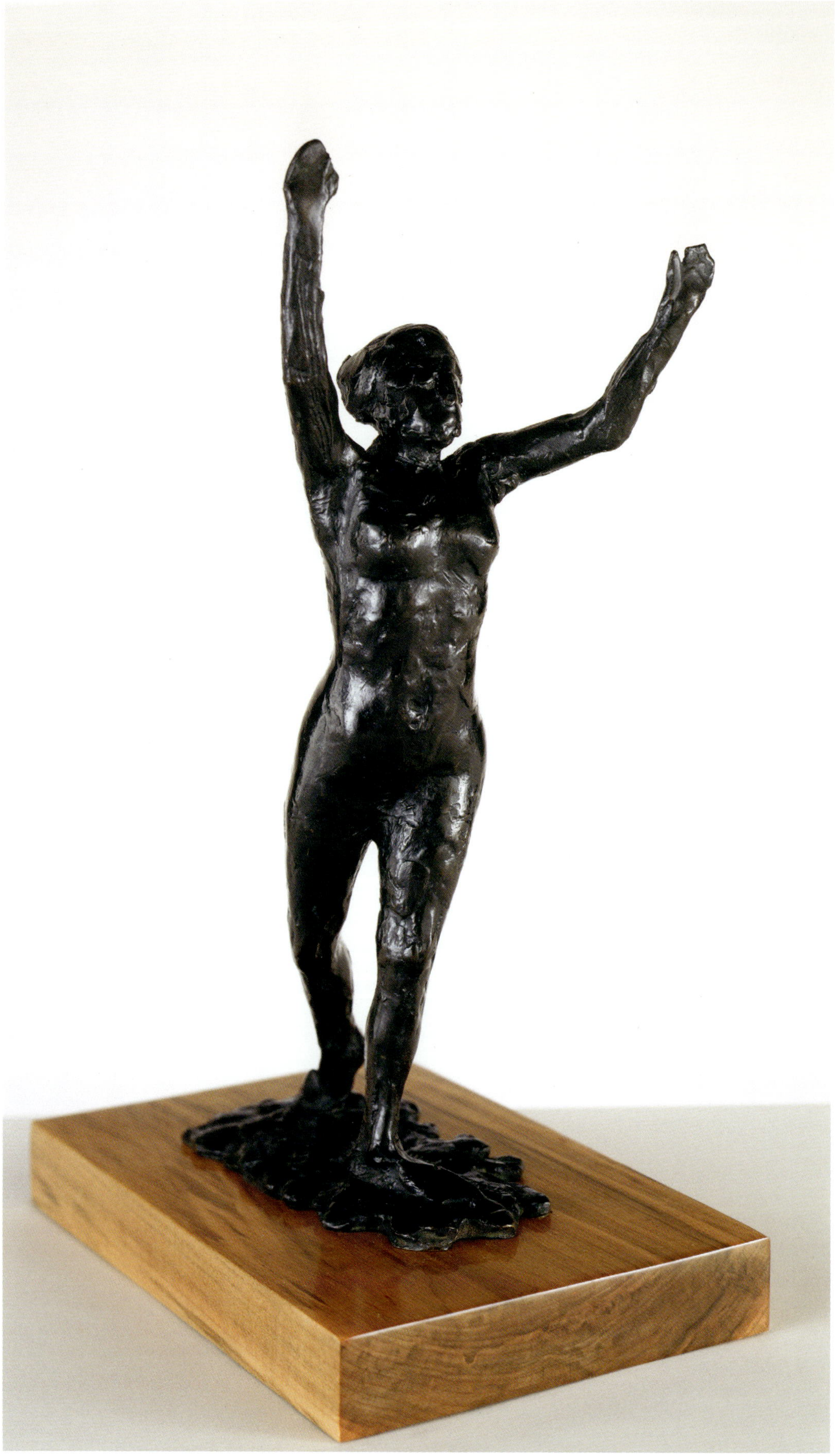

61 ***Dancer moving forward, arms raised, first study** (**Danseuse s'avançant les bras levés, première étude**)*
modelled c 1885–90; cast c 1919–31
cast F of 14
bronze
35 x 17.5 x 15.1 cm
Hirshhorn Museum and Sculpture Garden, Smithsonian Institution, Washington DC
HMSG66.1291
Gift of Joseph H Hirshhorn, 1966
Czestochowski and Pingeot 19

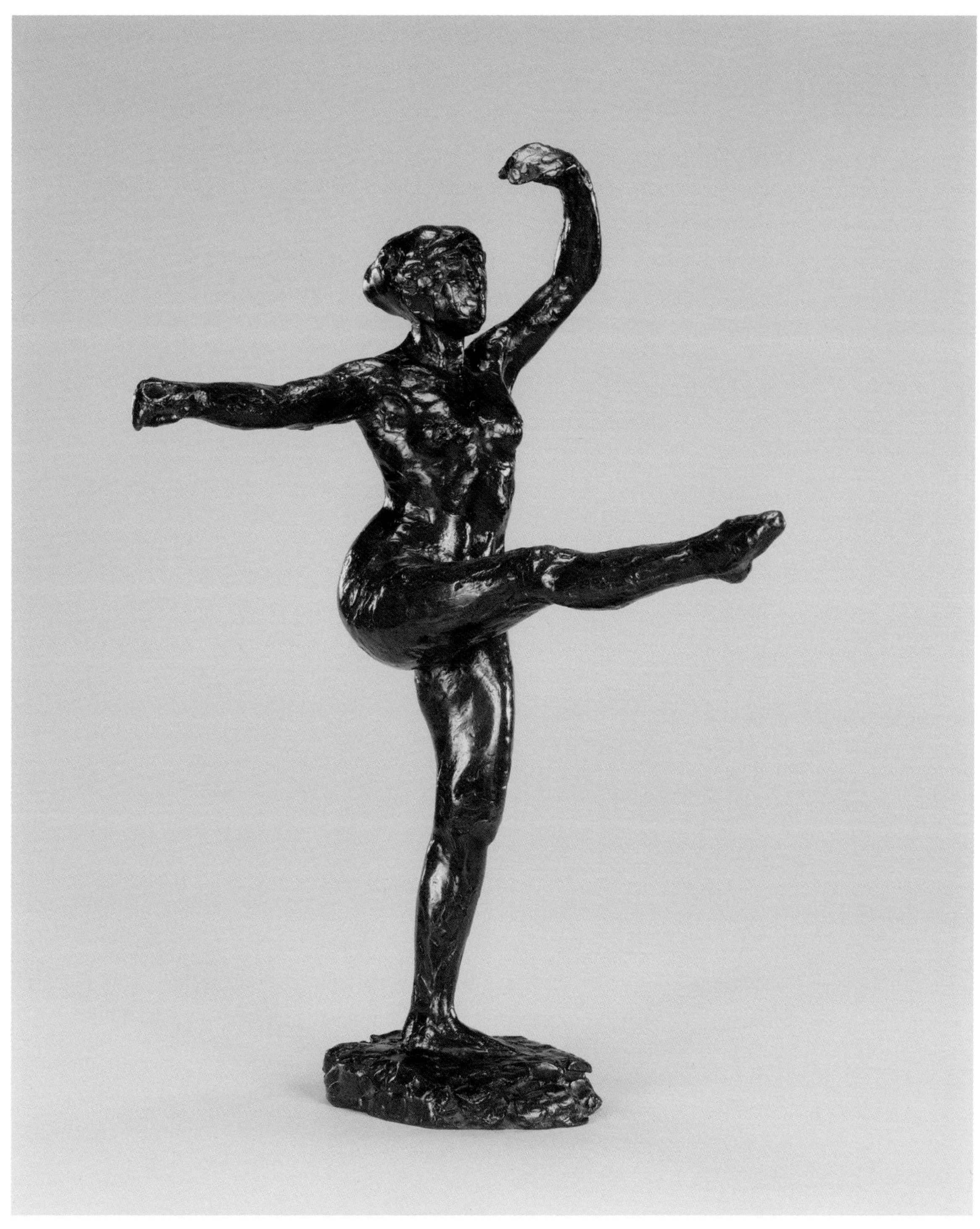

62 *Dancer, fourth position, standing on her left leg, third study*
(*Danseuse, position de quatrième devant sur la jambe, troisième étude*)
modelled 1882–85; cast 1919–21
cast F of 13
bronze
57.5 x 33.3 x 38.5 cm
The Baltimore Museum of Art, Baltimore
BMA.1950.413
The Cone Collection, formed by Dr Claribel Cone and Miss Etta Cone
of Baltimore, Maryland
Czestochowski and Pingeot 5

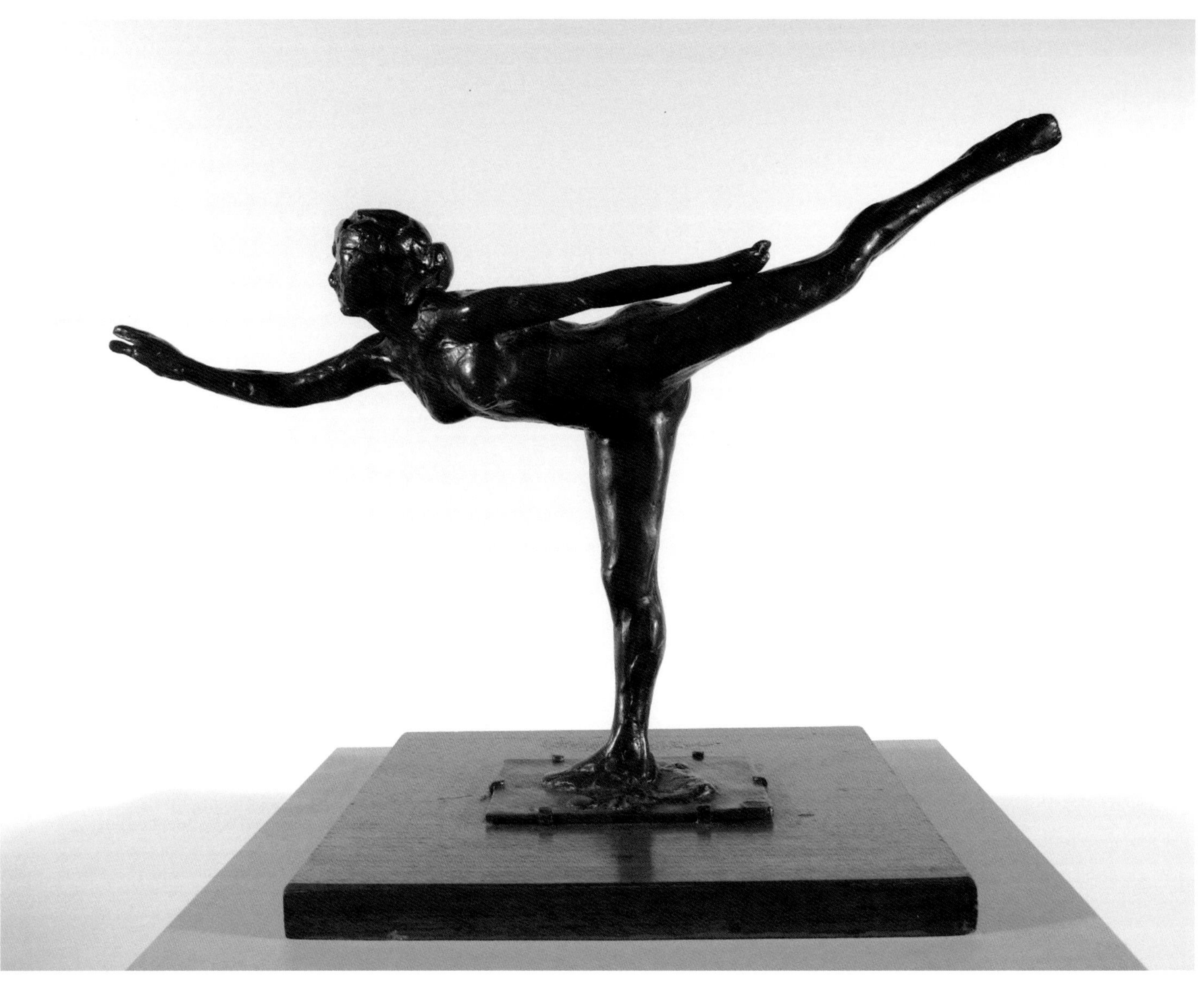

63 *Dancer, open arabesque on her right leg, left arm aligned* (*Danseuse, arabesque ouverte sur la jambe droite, bras gauche dans la ligne*)
modelled 1883–95; cast 1919–30
cast D of 23
bronze
28.8 x 43.7 x 10.9 cm
New Walk Museum and Art Gallery, Leicester
Purchase 7A 1950
Czestochowski and Pingeot 3

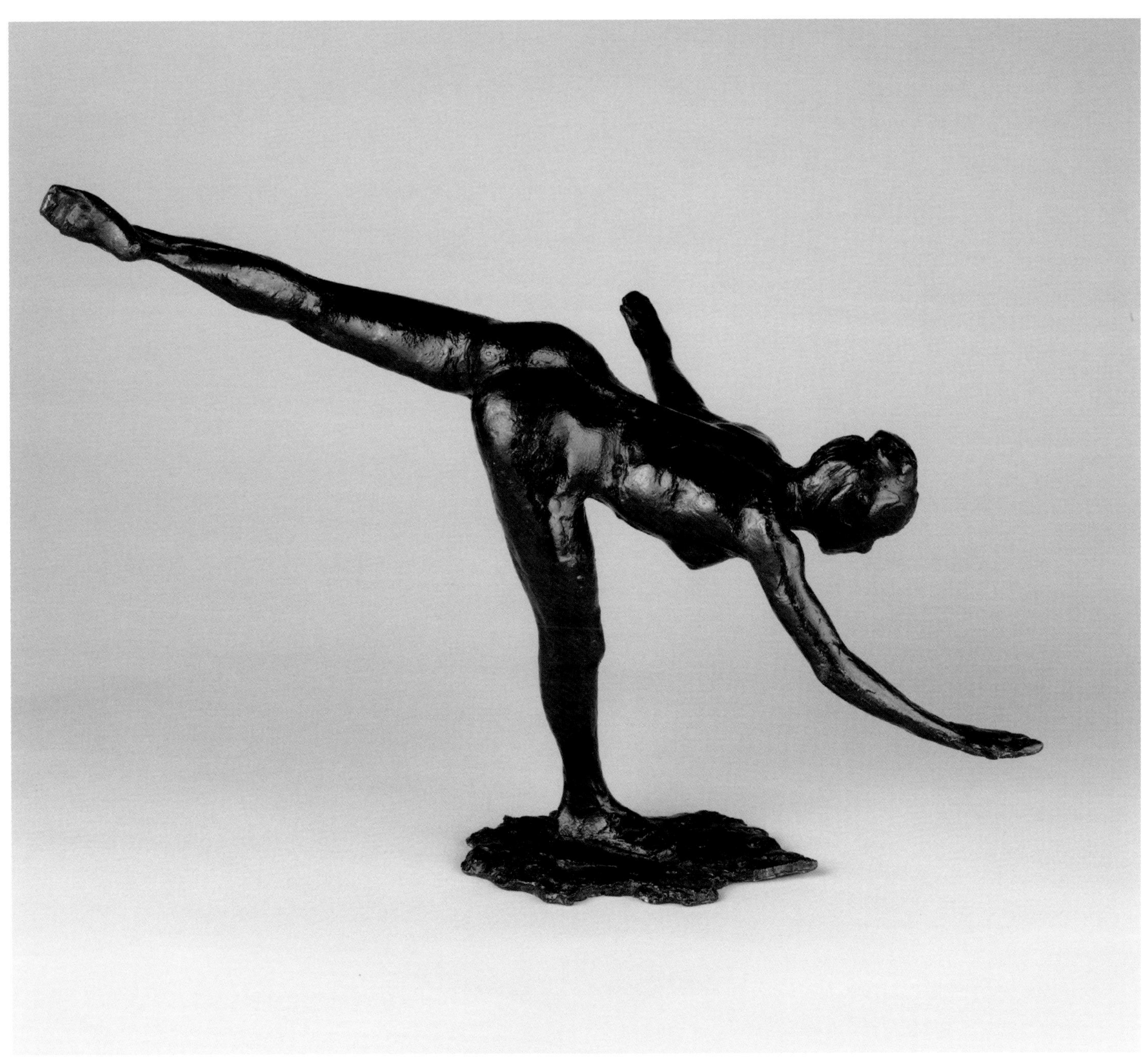

64 ***Dancer, grande arabesque, third study*** (previously known as ***second study***)
(***Danseuse, grande arabesque, troisième étude*** (autrefois appelée ***deuxième étude***))
modelled c 1892–96; cast 1920
cast A of 24
bronze
40.3 x 54.3 x 33 cm
The Metropolitan Museum of Art, New York
29.100.397
HO Havemeyer Collection, Bequest of Mrs HO Havemeyer, 1929
Czestochowski and Pingeot 16

65 *Study for 'Little dancer aged fourteen'* (*Etude pour 'La petite danseuse de quatorze ans'*)
modelled c 1878–81; cast 1919–21
cast D of 26
bronze
72.4 x 34.9 x 31 cm
Toledo Museum of Art, Toledo
1950.246
Purchased with funds from the Libbey Endowment, Gift of Edward Drummond Libbey
Czestochowski and Pingeot 56

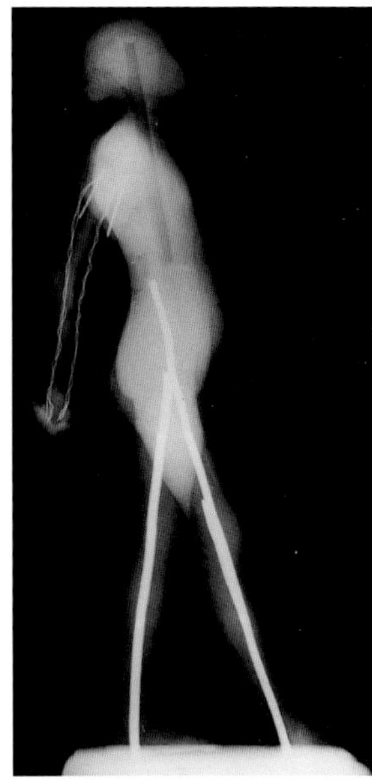

(above)
X-ray of *Study for 'Little dancer aged fourteen'* c 1878–81
National Gallery of Art, Washington DC

This is a remarkable sculpture. A prelude to the *Little dancer aged fourteen* (cat 67), this one is smaller but has a far greater sense of liveliness. As its title suggests, the nude sculpture was originally thought to be a study for the larger work with a tutu. Yet recent research by Daphne Barbour suggests otherwise—that the method of its fabrication indicates an undertaking 'too ambitious to be dismissed as a studio model'.[1]

Unlike other wax sculptures by Degas, this figure was cast rather than modelled by hand. Made of beeswax mixed with red iron-oxide pigments, applied over a plaster core and armature, it was 'largely cast in a two-part mould … [with] its arms … modelled separately and attached to the body at each shoulder using nails'. Barbour argues that the size of this work—larger than all other known sculptures by Degas, except the dressed *Little Dancer*—the complexity of its fabrication, and the 'absence of spontaneity that typifies many of [his] sculptures', suggests that the work was 'premeditated and that [t]his nude version of the little dancer was not his first attempt at this subject matter in three dimensions because not only does it seem to have been cast from a now lost model, but the inflexibility of the inner plaster core allowed for little manipulation of the pose once cast.'[2]

The model for this sculpture was the dancer Marie van Goethem—easily recognisable by her facial features and short fringe—who was also the model for *Little dancer aged fourteen*. Despite her pug-like looks, this work is a wonderful exploration of a ballerina standing in fourth position while at the same time possessing a great sense of animation. Degas achieves this through the nude dancer's upright posture, a combination of a slim body, long limbs on large feet and the placement of arms well behind the body. It is this finessed positioning by Degas that provides the work with its extraordinary sense of vitality.

Notes

1 Daphne Barbour has provided a detailed account of her research in 'Degas's little dancer: not just a study in the nude', *Art Journal*, vol 54, no 2, Conservation and Art History, Summer 1995, pp 28–32.

2 Barbour, p 30.

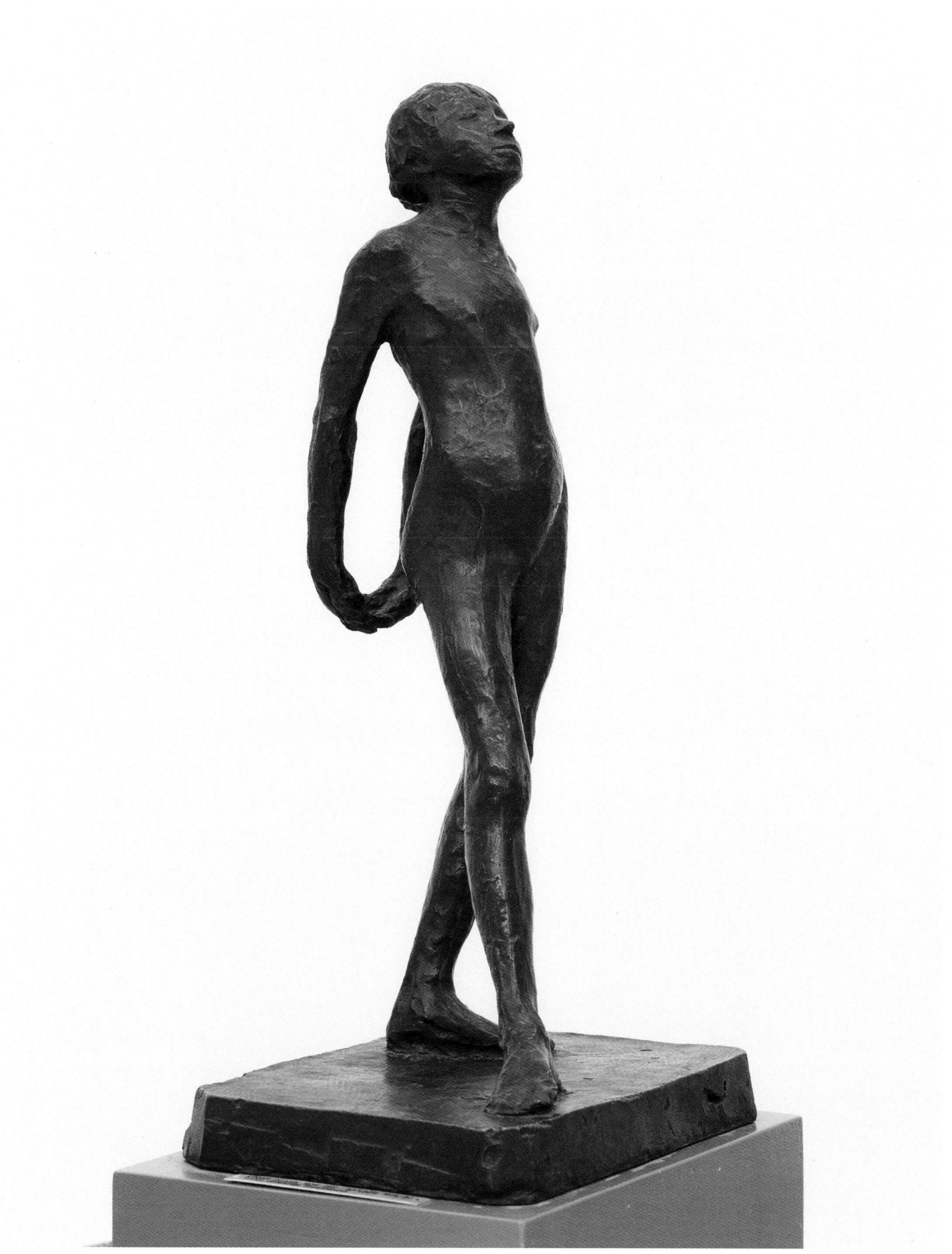

66 *Four studies of young dancers* (*Quatres études de jeunes danseuses*)
1878–79
chalk and charcoal heightened with grey wash and white on white paper
49 x 32.1 cm
Musée d'Orsay, Paris
Housed at the Département des arts graphiques, Musée du Louvre
RF 4646
Acquis en 1919
Vente III: 341.2

In preparation for both his sculptures of the 14-year-old dancer (cats 65 and 67), Degas made several chalk and charcoal studies of Marie van Goethem, both nude and in her ballet costume .[1]

Four studies of young dancers is an important study in chalk and charcoal, showing different views of the young dancer. Two focus on the face: one almost in profile, the other frontally, with Marie's characteristic bobbed fringe. The other two figures of the dancer are back views, one at an angle, and these studies show how Degas intended to place the ballerina's shoulders and the location of her arms as she stands in a rigid pose. Marie's plait of long dark hair falls down her back between her shoulder blades.

Note

1 For example: private collection, Vente III no 386; Nasjonalgalleriet, Oslo, Vente IV no 287 (for nude studies); The Art Institute of Chicago, Lemoisne 586 ter; private collection, Lemoisne 586 bis. See Richard Kendall, *Degas and the little dancer*, 1998, cat nos 36, 38, 40, 41 and this work cat 43.

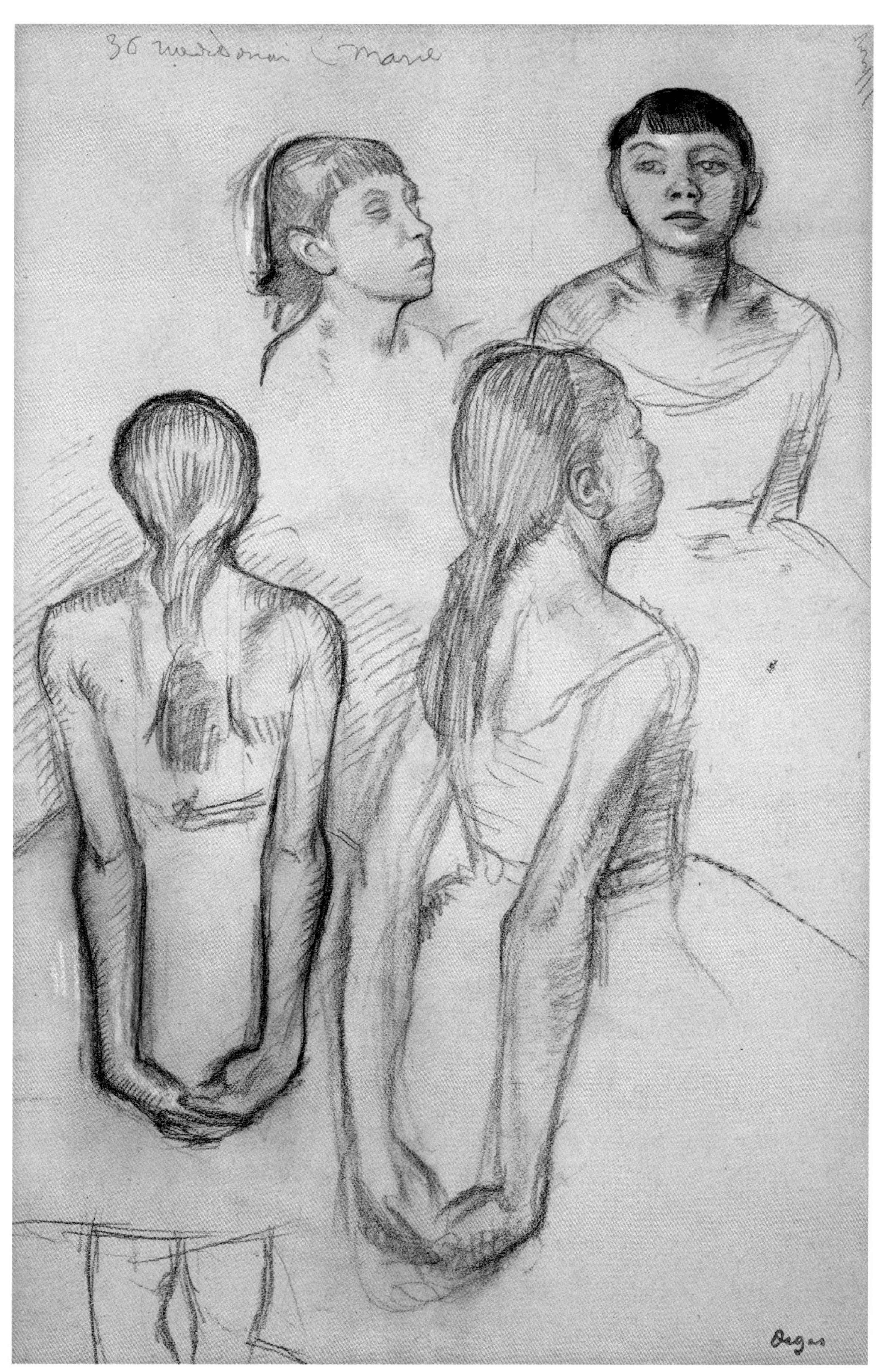

67 *Little dancer aged fourteen (La petite danseuse de quatorze ans)*
modelled 1880–81; cast 1920–21
bronze, gauze and satin
cast M of 29
97.8 x 41.3 x 34.9 cm
Saint Louis Art Museum, Saint Louis
inv 135.1956
Funds given by Mrs Mark C Steinberg
Czestochowski and Pingeot 73

The appearance of *Little dancer aged fourteen* in the Impressionist exhibition of 1881 caused a sensational stir in the art world (see discussion p 29). This 'Little flower of the gutter', as one commentator described it at the time, was a radical statement regarding the possibilities of sculpture. It was as if Degas was throwing down the gauntlet to the art world and the accepted conventions of sculpture of his day. The original model was built of wax, tinted a skin colour. Degas added to this the fabric of her tutu, real hair bound by a silky ribbon, and ballet shoes.

What was also astonishing was that the sculpture was almost life-size, and was far from idealised. Degas' contemporary, the noted sculptor Auguste Rodin, had caused a sensation five years earlier with the display of his life-size realistic figure in plaster, *The age of bronze* (also known as *The vanquished one*), when he first exhibited this work in Brussels in 1876. The sculpture led to accusations it was so lifelike that it may have been cast from a live model.

The crude features of the *Little dancer*'s physiognomy, based on those of his model, the young ballerina Marie van Goethem, also caused controversy. Critics complained that Degas had chosen his model 'from among the most odiously ugly', and achieved a 'standard of horror and bestiality' not suitable for an exhibition of art. Rather, they claimed, it belonged to one of 'zoology, anthropology, or physiology.'[1]

As a self-taught sculptor, in this one provocative work Degas pushed the boundaries of scale, technique, use of materials, subject matter, genre and style. *Little dancer aged fourteen* both tantalised and unsettled contemporary audiences. It goaded and intrigued. Subsequently, it has continued to do so in the form of a bronze cast, which also has the additions of a tutu in fabric, and a ribbon to bind her hair.

Though the *Little dancer* … made a sensational debut in the 1881 Impressionist exhibition because of her radical appearance, the sculpture should also be viewed as the product of many years of relentless exploration by Degas of a favourite theme.

Note

1 Henry Trianon, *Le Constitutionnel*, 24 April 1881, quoted in Fronia E Wissman, 'Realists among the Impressionists', in Moffett et al, *The new painting*, 1986, p 362. See p 29 for the complete quote and other commentary.

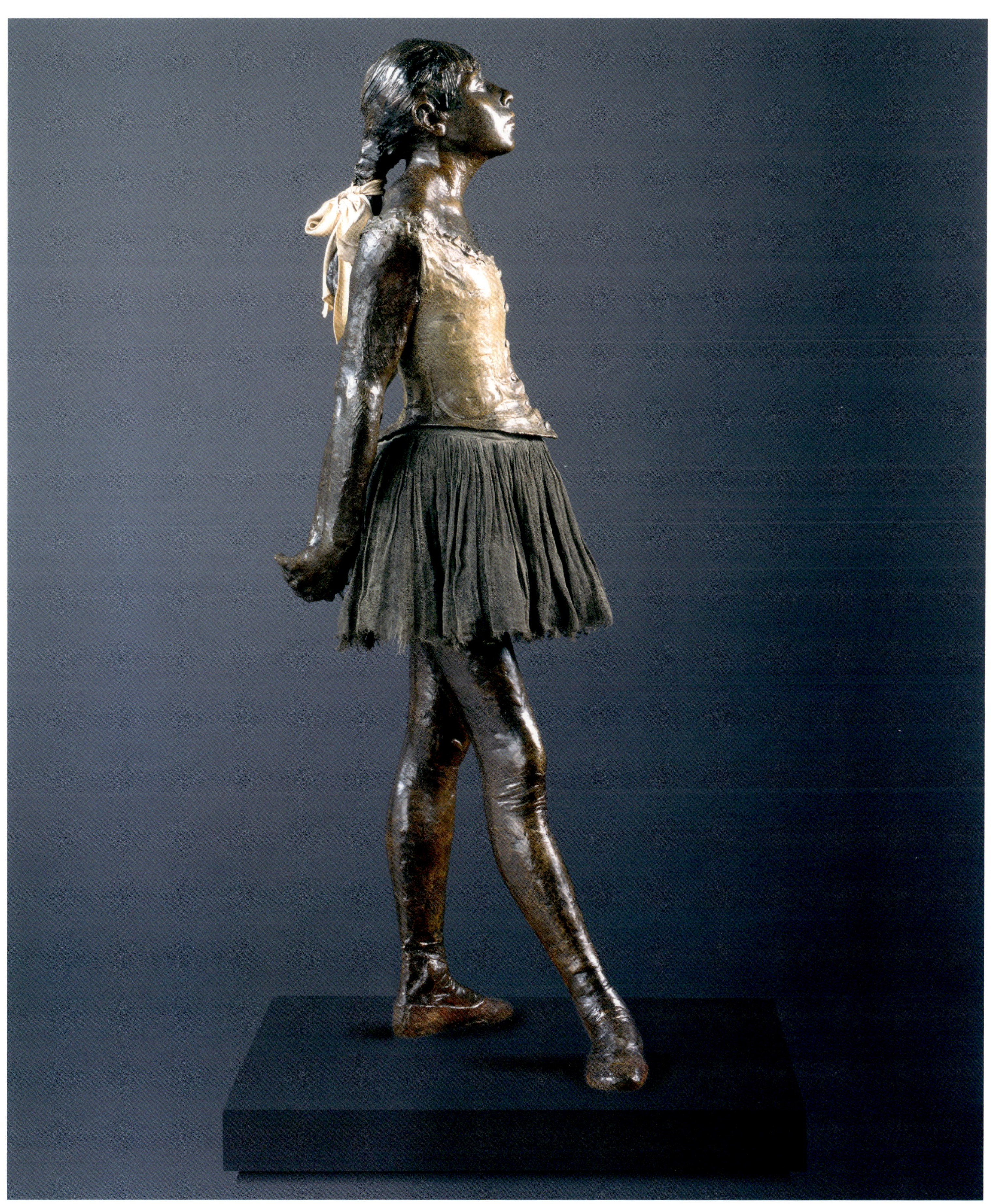

68 *Rehearsal before the ballet*
1877
oil on canvas
50.8 x 61.6 cm
Museum of Fine Arts, Springfield, Massachusetts
41.01
The James Philip Gray Collection
Lemoisne 844
Photograph: David Stansbury

Degas developed a great skill in using pastel. His natural affinity with this difficult medium allowed him to embrace a complicated range of applications, including combining pastel with gouache, tempera and *peinture à l'essence*, blowing water over the pastel to make paste-like colours, and retouching applied pastel with a brush.[1]

The rich range of effects he developed in pastel influenced the look of his work in other media, in this case oil painting. In *Rehearsal before the ballet*, Degas applied layers of colour, building up a rich surface, and adopted feathery brushwork replicating the look of a pastel. He also adopted an exuberant palette of vivid pinks and golds.

Rehearsal before the ballet is a composite painting, in which Degas has combined some of his favourite motifs of dancers. He has also combined dancers performing on stage, with a view behind-the-scenes. On stage, we see a ballet troupe performing in the background; closer to the viewer, dancers are swaying with their arms raised and *en pointe* in an arabesque. In the foreground, behind the stage scenery, a dancer rests with her hands on her hips. As with many of Degas' ballet scenes, the artist has cropped the figures to emphasise the movement and suggest that the dancers are advancing into the viewer's space.

Note

1 For the complex nature of Degas' techniques, see: Denis Rouart, 1988, pp 39–67; Shelley Fletcher and Pia Desantis, 'The search for his technique continues', *The Burlington Magazine*, vol 131, no 1033, April 1989, pp 256–65; Jean Suttherland Boggs and Anne Maheux, *Degas pastels*, Thames & Hudson, London, 1992; Richard Kendall, *Degas: beyond Impressionism*, National Gallery Publications, London, 1996, chapter 4.

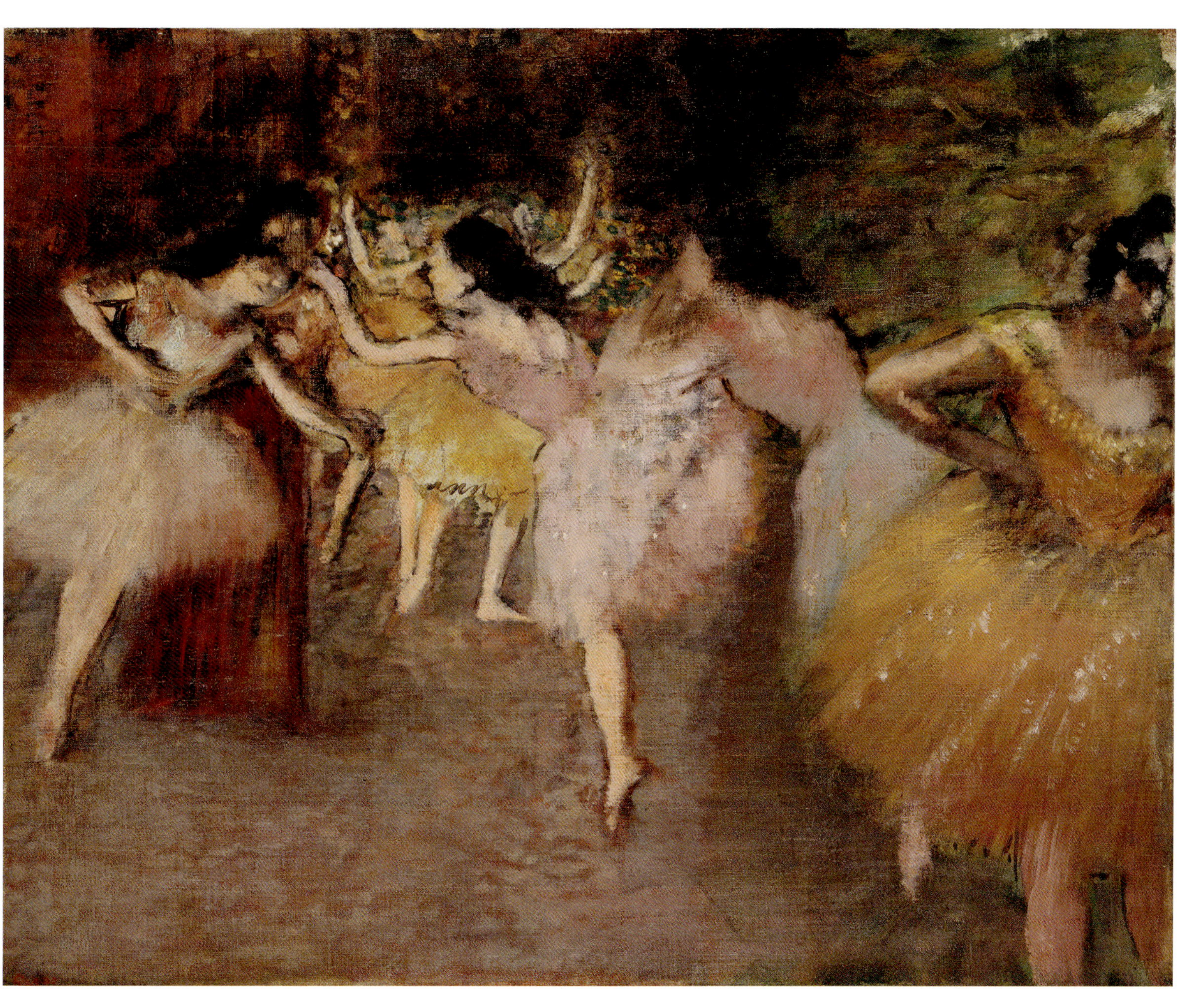

69 *Three dancers at a dance class* (*Trois danseuses à la classe de danse*)
1890s
oil on cardboard
50.5 x 60.6 cm
Queensland Art Gallery, Brisbane
1:0784
Purchased 1959 with funds donated by Major Harold de Vahl Rubin
Lemoisne 1308

By the 1890s Degas became interested in devising close-up images of ballet dancers. They are no longer viewed from afar, whether on the stage or in the rehearsal room. He would repeat over and over again certain compositions with particular figures, in favourite poses and in various combinations. This composition of three dancers represents three poses to which Degas was particularly partial—a dancer with a fan, a dancer tying her ballet slipper ribbon, and a dancer seated on a bench and bending over from exhaustion.

Although the figures are pictured in the foreground, there is a lack of specificity to their faces, the arrangement of their hair and their ballet costumes. Behind these figures we see the rehearsal room, which is also shown in a cursory manner—the windows, walls and the floor are all painted in light feathering strokes, reminiscent of Degas' technique in pastel drawing in his mature years.

It has been noted that from the 1890s and into the 1900s, about three-quarters of Degas' art was concerned with the ballet. In 1903, when the noted American Degas collector, Mrs Louisine Havemeyer, questioned the artist about such concentration, he responded that, 'it is all that is left us of the combined movements of the Greeks.' Discussing this conversation, the authors Jill DeVonyar and Richard Kendall explained Degas' slightly mystifying response at this time by arguing that 'Degas insisted on the association of his ballet subjects with the serene timeless values of classical civilization.'[1]

In *Three dancers at a dance class* the figures have a quiet air to them, with no real suggestion of place or occasion, and thus suggest the influence of Antiquity on the artist in this and other works of his later years.

Note

1 Jill DeVonyar and Richard Kendall, *Degas and the dance*, Harry N Abrams in association with the American Federation of Arts, New York, 2003, pp 234–35

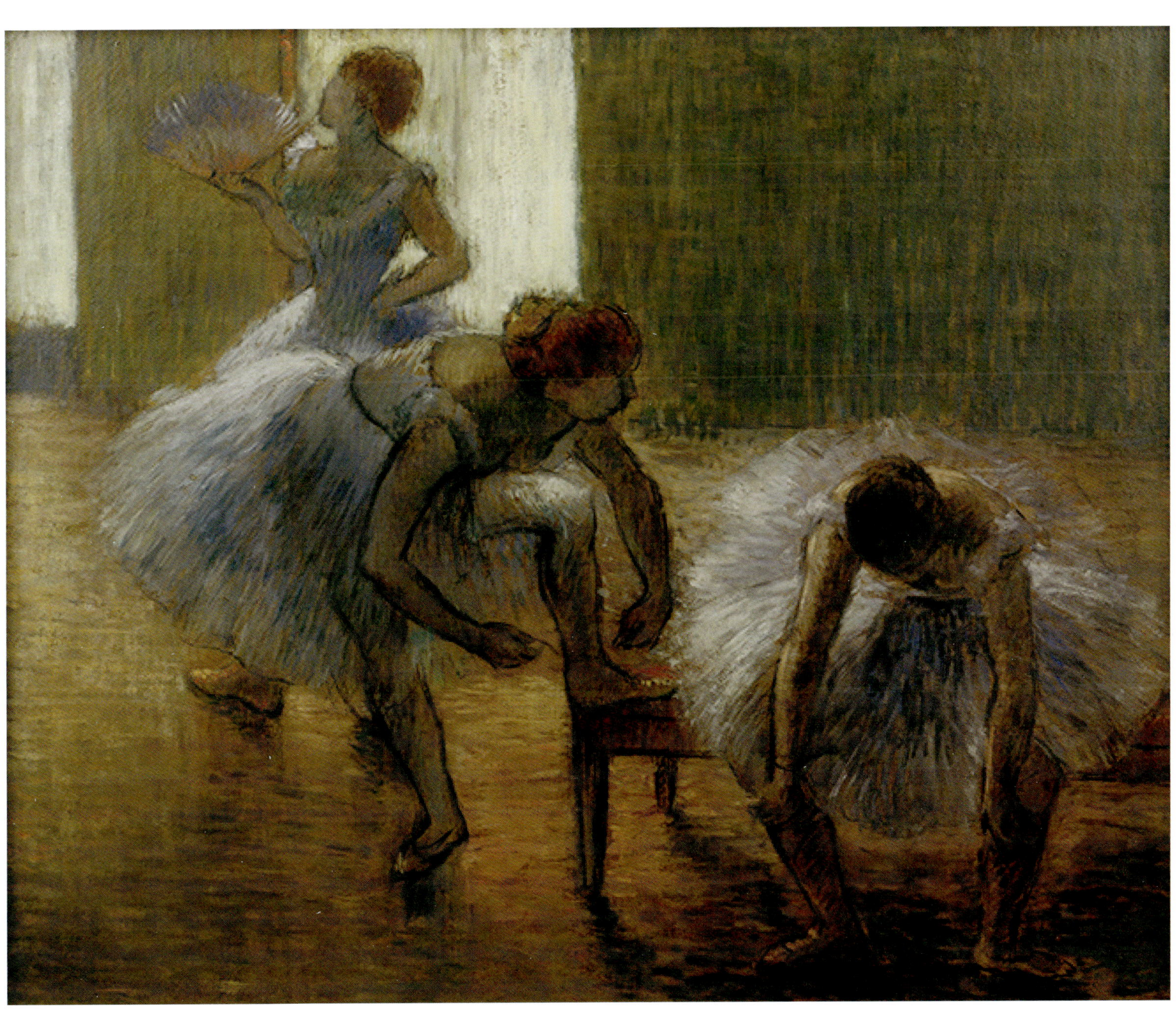

70 ***Before the ballet*** (***Le foyer de la danse***)
1890–92
oil on canvas
40 x 89.9 cm
National Gallery of Art, Washington DC
1942.9.19
Weidener Collection
Lemoisne 941

This ballet scene is composed in the horizontal format adopted by Degas for his frieze-like compositions of dancers and horses. In this late version of this particular format, as with other works by Degas of this period, the figures have taken on the appearance of isolated sculptures in static poses.

Degas has carefully arranged two groups of figures. On the left, the distant dancers are at the barre, although they appear almost motionless, belying any real suggestion of carrying out their routine exercises. On the right-hand side, in the foreground two figures are seated: one dancer adjusts her tights, the other the ribbons of her ballet shoes. Like many of Degas' compositions at this time, the painting consists of an arrangement of his favourite poses. It is as if Degas has taken a leaf out of the Neo-Impressionist's book, where monumentality of form was sought over a fleeting appearance.

Despite the strong asymmetry of *Before the ballet*, Degas has perfected a beautifully balanced composition, weighing the vast expanse of floor and the tight cluster of dancers in the distance and foreground. Unlike his early pictures, which evoke the sounds of a busy rehearsal room, this painting has a quietness, and the dancers possess an other-worldliness to them. The emphasis on the interior—painted in greens and pinks, with drawn translucent curtains, dim lighting and the vast emptiness of much of the room—strongly conveys the closed nature of this world of ballet.

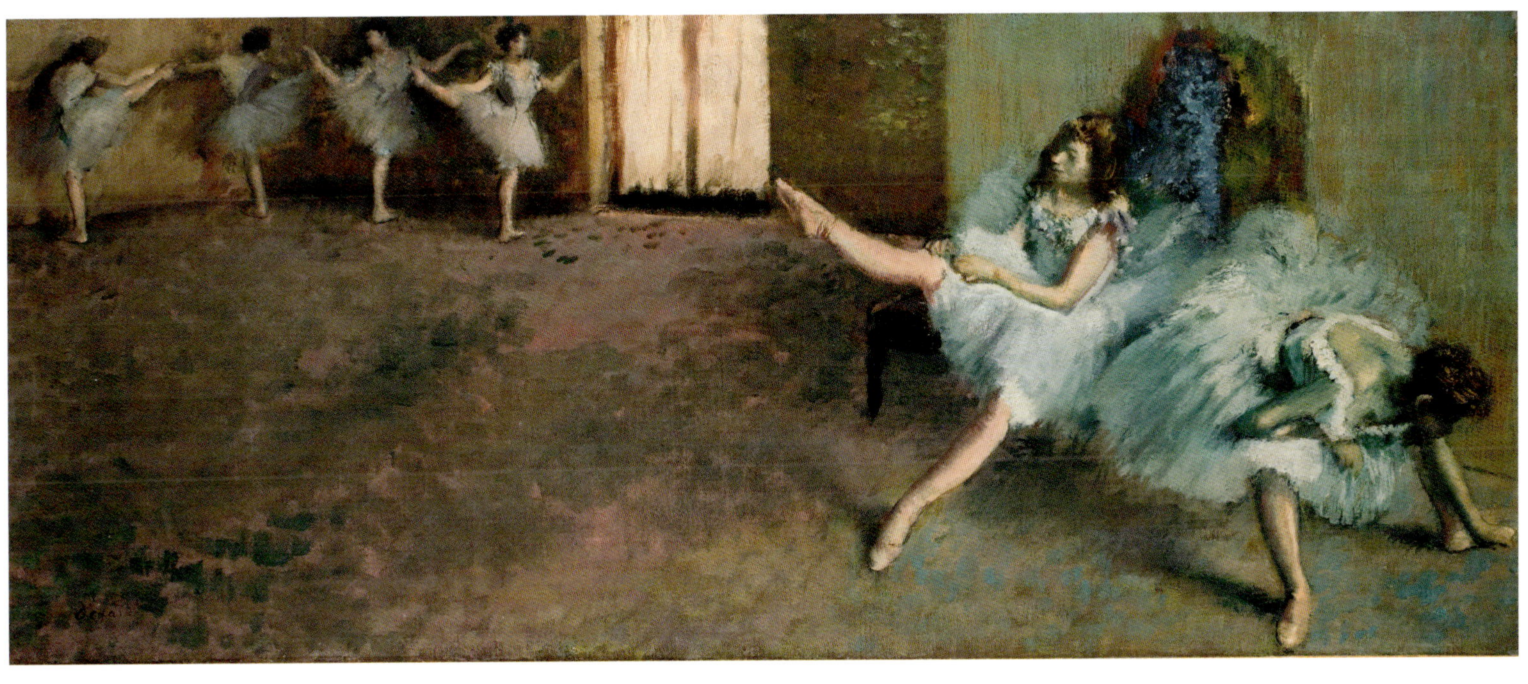

71 *Dancer at rest, hands on her hips, right leg forward, first study*
(*Danseuse au repos, les mains sur les hanches, jambe droite en avant, première étude*)
modelled 1882–95; cast 1919–37 or later
cast Q of 20
bronze
46 x 14.2 x 23.6 cm
Queensland Art Gallery, Brisbane
1951:202
Purchased 1955 with bequest funds of Beatrice Ethel Mallalieu
Czestochowski and Pingeot 41

Degas made sculpture throughout much of his artistic career, and there is a clear interplay between his wax figures (which were subsequently cast in bronze), and his drawing and painting. The wax models could be turned around to provide new angles from which to view a particular pose or gesture. Figures in two dimensions could be traced and then drawn in reverse. In this way Degas developed a method where he could build a rich repertoire of favourite figures from a range of viewpoints in both his three-dimensional and two-dimensional work.

There was no set order for how this interrelationship between two-dimensional and three-dimensional work took place. As we have seen earlier (cat 46), the model of the horse drinking was made to assist Degas realise his ambitious painting *Mademoiselle Fiocre in the ballet 'La Source'* (cat 45). A further replication in two- and three-dimensions is visibly evident in *Dancer at rest …* (opposite) and a charcoal drawing *Study of a nude* (cat 72), where Degas explored the possibilities of depicting a nude figure of a dancer with her right foot placed in front of her left, holding her head up and resting her hands on her hips. This nude figure then reappears in compositions of two or three dancers as nudes or in tutus, and in charcoal or pastel.[1] In this way Degas introduced an element of seriality to his work.

In another drawing of this period, *Two dancers with a fan* (cat 73), Degas composed a study of two nude dancers; the figure with the fan regularly appeared in other drawings of this period, as either an individual figure or in combination with others.

Unlike the delicate pencil drawings of ballet dancers from the 1870s (cats 54, 57 and 58), these drawings of nude dancers from the period 1895–1900 are large-scale figures, with certain Amazonian qualities—drawn with dynamic strokes of charcoal, one of Degas' favourite mediums of this time.

Note

1 See Richard Kendall, *Beyond Impressionism*, cat no 75, private collection, Vente II, no 284; cat no 77, The Art Institute of Chicago, Lemoisne 1017; cat no 78, private collection, Brame and Reff 161; cat no 79, private collection, Lemoisne 1252.

THE PAINTER–PHOTOGRAPHER

MANY YEARS AFTER DEGAS made most of his *plats du jour*, as he called his monotypes, he became obsessed, albeit briefly, with another process of making art—photography. This episode began during the summer of 1895 and continued into the following year. Degas' photographic subjects range from portraits, interiors and women bathing, to the occasional landscape. As with many of his monotypes, this was an excursus in black and white, and despite his keen interest in colour Degas found the experience a welcome one. He reflected in 1906: 'If I could live my life over again I should do nothing but black and white.'[1] The limited palette allowed him to concentrate on form and to experiment with light and shade; he also turned his attention to such issues as exposure, enlarging, cropping and the use of different papers.

In 1885 Degas was obviously intrigued by what was still the relatively new process of photography. While staying in Dieppe that year he choreographed a photograph, *The apotheosis of Degas* (cat 85), as a light-hearted homage to Jean-Auguste-Dominique Ingres— the arrangement of the group in the photograph mimics Ingres' monumental painting, *The apotheosis of Homer* 1827. Degas is seated at the centre, as the figure of Homer is posed in the Ingres composition and, like the blind Homer, Degas' facial expression is blank. He holds his walking stick in the same way as Homer holds a staff, and has taken off his hat as if to be crowned with the laurel branches held by the three 'muses' who stand behind him—Catherine, Rose and Yoyo (Marie) Lemoinne, daughters of the artist's friend, the journalist John Lemoinne. On either side, the sons of Ludovic Halévy—Elie and Daniel—kneel as if in prayer, in contrary attitudes to the personifications of *The Iliad* and *The Odyssey* in Ingres' painting. Photographed by the English artist Walter Barnes, a protégé of Degas, the tableau was set on the steps of the house of Dr Emile Blanche while Degas was staying nearby with the Halévys. Aside from these close associations, *The apotheosis of Degas* demonstrates the artist's dry humour, while at the same time referencing his great Neoclassical idol, Ingres.

About a decade later, in the mid 1890s, Degas embarked upon making his own photographs. According to the correspondence of Frederico Zandomeneghi, in 1895 Degas photographed a series of small portraits of this Italian artist, including one in the manner of a portrait by Diego Velázquez and another of Zandomeneghi with the sculptor Albert Bartholomé posing as river gods (neither of which is extant).[2] At this time Degas also made photographic portraits of Louise Halévy and her son Daniel, taken at the Halévys' home at 22 rue de Douai, Paris (cats 87 and 88).

Degas was assisted in the technical side of the photographic process by Guillaume Tasset, a partner in the local art-supplies firm, Tasset and Lhote at 31 rue Fontaine. Tasset had studied art under Jean-Léon Gérôme and had exhibited at the Salon before he began his photographic business. Degas was also helped by Tasset's daughter Delphine, a highly skilled technician who worked in a darkroom next to the shop.

Also included in Degas' photographic oeuvre of 1895 are three self-portraits. Two were taken in front of a bookcase in his library and portray him as a thoughtful man of letters with his hand to his chin. A third was set in front of a plaster by Bartholomé, *Crouching* (or *Weeping*) *girl: study for the monument to the dead* 1889–95, a work in Degas' collection.[3] While there has been some discussion as to whether Degas actually took the photographs in which he appears, the compositions have the hallmarks of Degas' style.[4] The gesture of a hand to the face recalls many of his earlier painted portraits, including *Portrait of the artist with Evariste de Valernes* and *Woman leaning near a vase of flowers (Mme Paul Valpinçon)* of 1865, and *Mme Edmondo Morbilli* 1869.[5] This type of gesture, which appears in portraits by Ingres, derives from Pompeian frescoes and Classical sculpture and signifies modesty (*pudicitia*).

Another self-portrait taken at this time is of the artist in his studio (cat 96). Degas, in silhouette, is dressed in a painter's smock and seated before some carefully arranged draperies. With his hands placed firmly on his knees and his head in profile he stares out to the left of the composition. Degas' brother René de Gas was also photographed in the artist's studio with similar props (cat 95), but looks directly at the viewer—the photographer—with a rather quizzical expression.

During this period of intense interest in photography, Degas' compositions became more complex. He would photograph friends and associates in rooms, taking particular care with their placement, adjusting the stance and gestures and the relationship of the sitters, rearranging furniture and works of art, and setting up reflections of figures in mirrors—a motif he adopted from the art of Ingres and Velázquez.

In many of his paintings Degas delighted in creating images within images by including in the composition other artists' paintings, prints or tapestries.[6] With his photographs he continued this practice, using the work of other artists

(previous page) *Paul Poujaud, Marie Fontaine and Degas* probably autumn 1895 (detail cat 91)

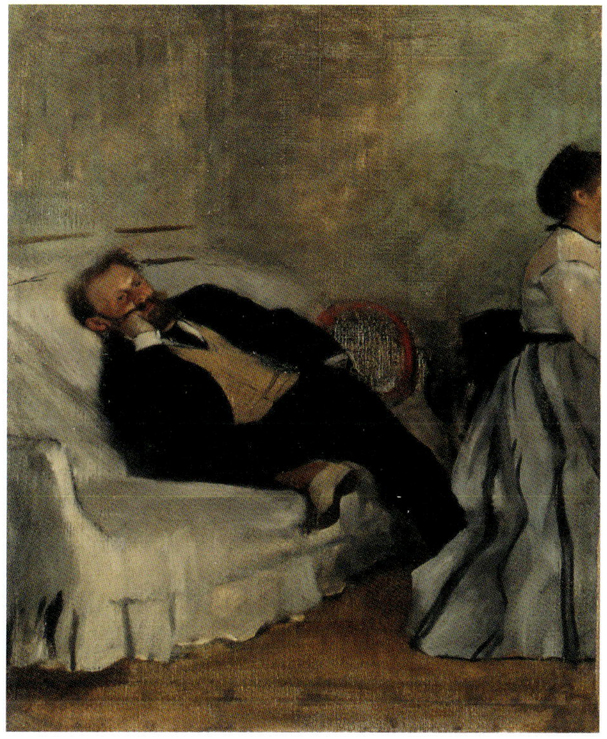

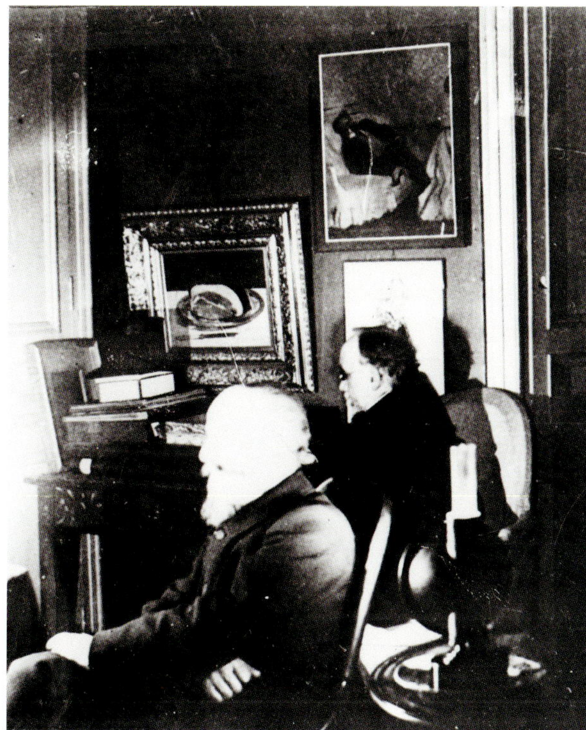

(far left)
Monsieur and Madame Edouard Manet c 1868–69
oil on canvas, 65 × 71 cm
Kitakyushu Municipal Museum of Art, Japan
Lemoisne 127

(left)
Self-portrait with Bartholomé
probably late 1895
(detail cat 89)

as well as his own. This is evident in a double photographic portrait of Degas and Bartholomé (cat 89). The sculptor's face is brilliantly lit from a source outside the composition, while the other side of the image disappears into blackness. Behind Bartholomé, Degas sits at his desk. Above him is a painting by Manet, *The ham* c 1875–78, a work in Degas' collection.[7] Another painting on the wall is by Degas himself, the double portrait *Monsieur and Madame Edouard Manet* c 1868–69 (above).[8] Degas had given this painting as a gift to the Manets, only to discover when visiting their home that Manet had sliced off a strip of the canvas to remove the profile of Mme Manet playing the piano, which displeased him. Degas spoke of his reaction to Ambroise Vollard: 'I had a fearful shock when I saw it like that at his house. I picked it up and walked off without even saying good-bye.'[9] Many years after the event, and more than a decade after Manet's death, the slight was apparently forgiven. By including the cropped work in his photographic portrait (cat 89) Degas was perhaps alluding, in a gently ironic way, to the occasionally fraught relationship of these two artists.

In a double portrait of Louise Halévy and her elder son Elie (cat 90), taken in his own sitting room, Degas included a painting by Mary Cassatt, *Girl arranging her hair* 1886.[10] The American-born Cassatt was a protégé and good friend of Degas and had long admired his pastels. In exchange for this painting by Cassatt, Degas gave her one of his pastels, *Woman bathing in a shallow tub* 1885. Degas also included in the photograph a Manet pastel in his collection, *Madame Manet on a blue sofa* c 1874. In this work Mme Manet is shown with her feet up and her bonnet untied. Manet's rather homely depiction of his wife is a distinct contrast to Degas' more formal portrayal of Mme Manet seated at the piano.[11]

Degas preferred to stage his photographic sessions in the evenings, using artificial light rather than natural daylight. Lamps, wall lights and chandeliers were placed to serve as props and as a means of diffusing or spotlighting his scenes, or to augment reflections in mirrors. In much the same way as he had arranged wooden models of horses to work out his racetrack compositions,[12] Degas carefully composed his photographic portrait subjects. Daniel Halévy parodied the regimented nature of these 'sittings', which would often occur after dinner: 'Degas raised his voice, became dictatorial, gave orders that a lamp be brought into the little salon and that anyone who wasn't going to pose should leave. The *duty* of the evening began. We had to obey Degas' fierce will, his artist's ferocity.'[13]

As well as using his own home as a backdrop, Degas orchestrated similar sessions at the homes of others. A group photograph (cat 92) shows Julie Manet (daughter of Berthe Morisot and Eugène Manet) and her cousins Paule and Jeannie Gobillard at their home with Geneviève Mallarmé (daughter of the Symbolist poet Stéphane Mallarmé). The artist Henry Lerolle and his daughters Christine and Yvonne

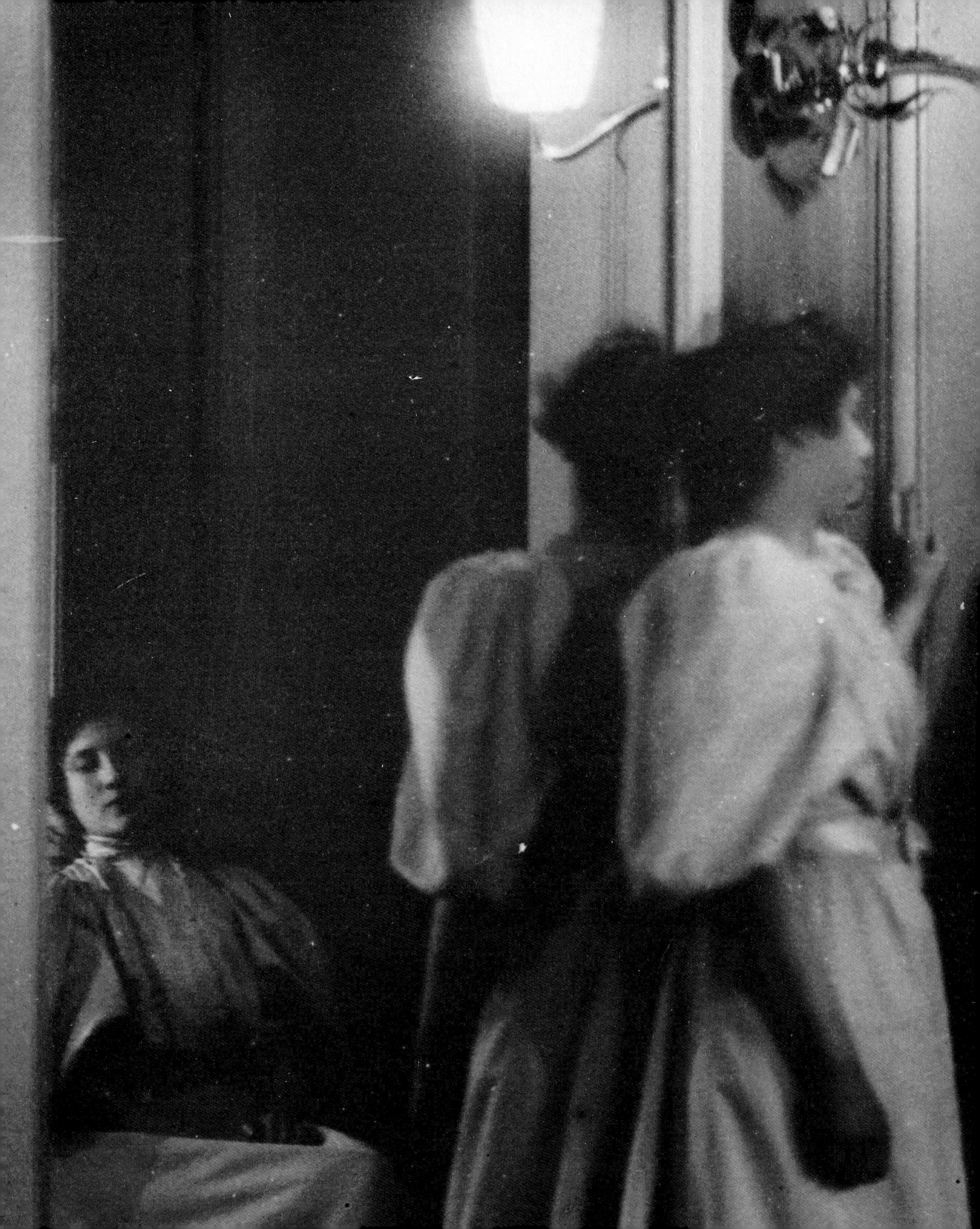

also seem to have been commandeered at their home for portraits (cat 93). The photographs of Lerolle and his daughters, and a self-portrait of Degas with the two girls (cat 94), are notable for the dramatic arrangement of the figures, beautifully lit by artificial lamplight and set before rich swathes of drapery and elegant mirrors.

If Degas embraced photography as a new means of portraiture, he also created compositions that often reappeared in his drawings or paintings, such as his photograph *Nude (drying herself)* (cat 98). Another, *Nude (putting on stockings)* (cat 97), is a rather tender study of a young woman dressing in his studio, and reveals Degas as an accomplished photographer.

But photography remained a relatively brief interlude. Degas' explorations into photographic portraiture ceased at around the time his longstanding and affectionate relationship with the Halévys also ended. The lighthearted occasions he spent with his camera and the partly Jewish Halévy family came to a halt with the political scandal of the Dreyfus Affair—a scandal that spawned French anti-Jewish hysteria and tested many friendships. In 1894, a Jewish officer in the French army, Captain Alfred Dreyfus, was convicted of treason. It was later discovered that documents implicating him had been forged, yet this fact was concealed by the army, and the government refused to reopen the case. It was then that Emile Zola wrote his 4000-word open letter to the French President, under the title *J'accuse*, published in January 1898. Shortly after this, Degas attended what was to be his last dinner with the Halévys. The topic that the artist and the family had desperately tried to avoid for so long was raised by some youthful guests. In his account of the occasion Daniel Halévy, wishing to present their old friend in the best light, described Degas' reaction:

> His lips were closed; he looked upwards almost constantly, as though cutting himself off from the company that surrounded him. Had he spoken it would no doubt have been in defence of the army, the army whose traditions and virtues he held so high, and which was being insulted by our intellectual theorizing. Not a word came from those lips, and at the end of dinner Degas disappeared.[14]

Notes

1 Françoise Cachin, 'The monotypes', in Jean Adhémar and Françoise Cachin, *Degas: the complete etchings, lithographs and monotypes*, Thames & Hudson, London, 1973, p 76.

2 Malcom Daniel, *Edgar Degas, photographer*, The Metropolitan Museum of Art, New York, 1998, p 20.

3 Colta Ives, Susan Alyson Stein, Julie A Steiner et al, *The private collection of Edgar Degas: a summary catalogue*, The Metropolitan Museum of Art, New York, 1997, p 3, cat 9.

4 Daniel, p 131. Daniel correctly argues: 'Whether or not someone other than Degas operated the camera, the framing, pose, and lighting [of these works] are wholly consistent with Degas' photographic style.'

5 *Portrait of the artist with Evariste de Valernes* 1865, Musée d'Orsay, Paris, Lemoisne 116; *Woman leaning near a vase of flowers (Mme Paul Valpinçon)* 1865, The Metropolitan Museum of Art, New York, Lemoisne 125; *Mme Edmondo Morbilli* 1869, private collection, New York, Lemoisne 255.

6 Theodore Reff devoted a chapter to this topic, titled 'Pictures within pictures', in *Degas: the artist's mind*, Thames & Hudson, London, 1976, pp 90–146.

7 Dumas, Ives, Stein et al, cat 797. This painting is now in the Burrell Collection, Glasgow Museums.

8 *Monsieur and Madame Edouard Manet* c 1868–69, Kitakyushu Municipal Museum of Art, Kitakyushu, Japan, Lemoisne 127.

9 Ambroise Vollard, *Degas: an intimate portrait* (Randolph T Weaver trans), Greenberg, New York, 1927, p 72. The painting is shown in the photograph with a canvas strip that had been added by Degas with a view to repainting the portrait.

10 Ives, Stein, Steiner et al, cat 46. The painting is now in the National Gallery of Art, Washington DC.

11 Mary Cassatt, *Girl arranging her hair* 1886, National Gallery of Art, Washington DC; *Woman bathing in a shallow tub* 1885, The Metropolitan Museum of Art, New York, Lemoisne 816; Edouard Manet, *Madame Manet on a blue sofa* c 1874, Musée du Louvre, Paris, Départment des arts graphiques, Fonds du Musée d'Orsay, Musée du Louvre, Paris. Ives, Stein, Steiner et al, cat 806.

12 See Jane Kinsman, 'The races', this publication pp 59–83

13 Daniel Halévy, in his journal dated 29 December 1895, describing events a fortnight previously, quoted in Daniel, p 31.

14 Daniel Halévy, quoted in Jean Sutherland Boggs, 'The late years: 1890–1912', in Jean Sutherland Boggs, Henri Loyrette, Michael Pantazzi et al, *Degas*, The Metropolitan Museum of Art and National Gallery of Canada, New York and Ottawa, 1988, p 493.

(opposite)
(Portrait in front of a mirror of the artist Henry Lerolle and his two daughters, Yvonne and Christine 1895–96
(detail cat 93)

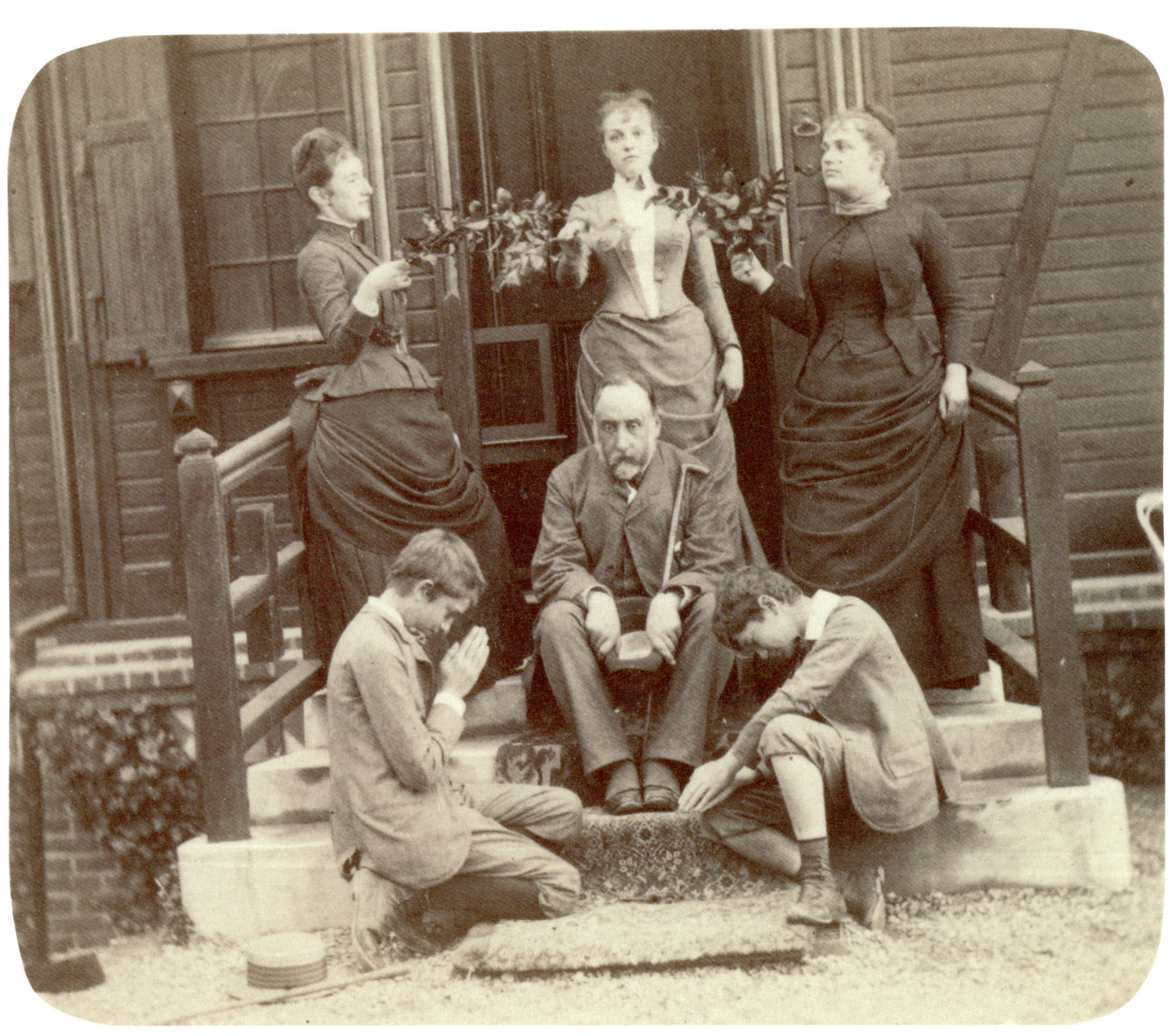

85 **Edgar Degas** (arrangement)
France 1834–1917
Walter Barnes (collaborator)
England 1844–1911
Apotheosis of Degas (After Ingres' Apotheosis of Homer)
(*L'apothéose de Degas (D'après Ingres L'apothéose d'Homère)*)
1885
albumen silver photograph
8.3 x 9.5 cm (image), 9.7 x 13.9 cm (sheet)
The J Paul Getty Museum, Los Angeles
86.XM.690.4
Terrasse 2

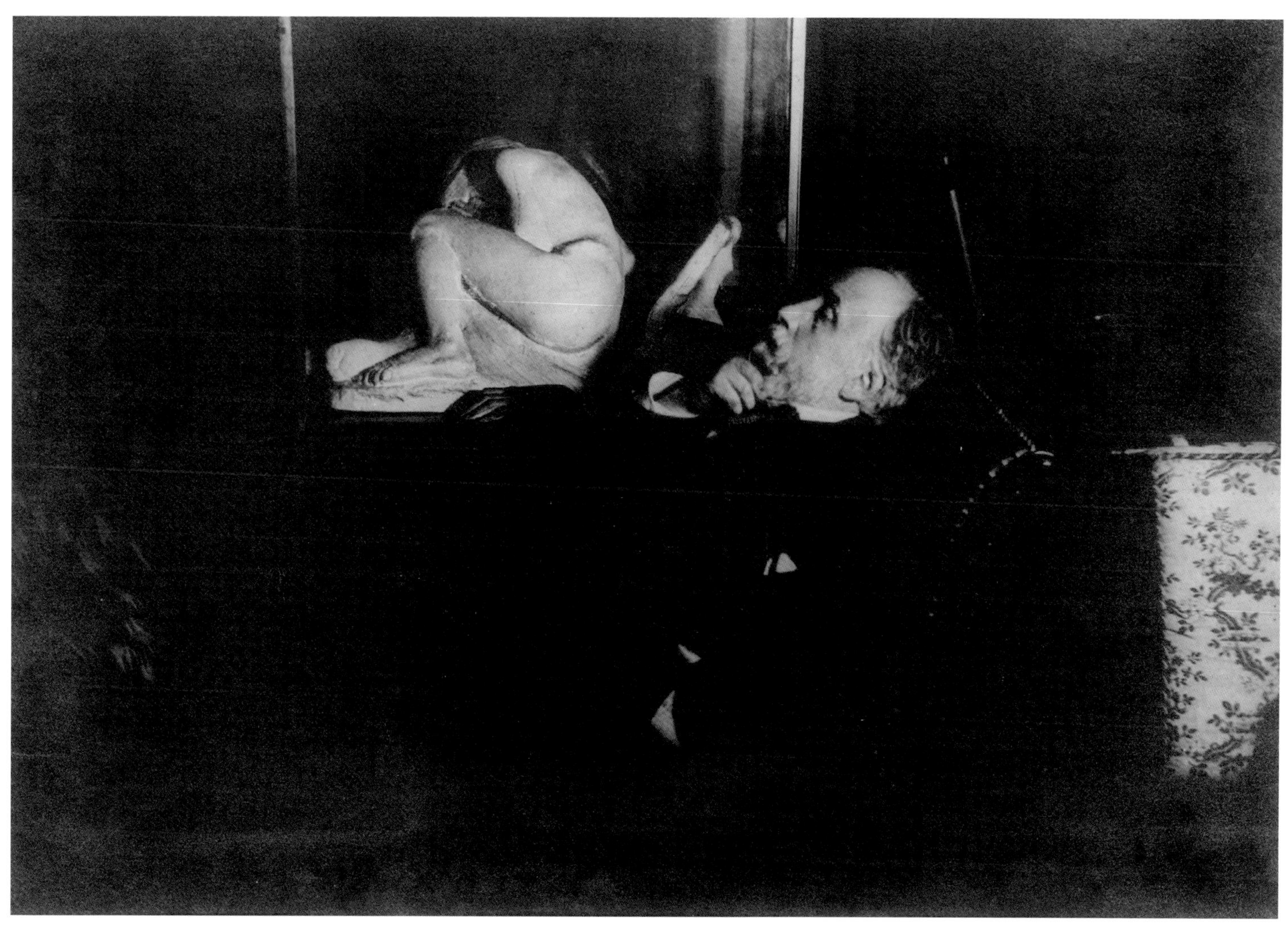

86 *Self-portrait with Bartholomé's 'Weeping girl'*
(*Autoportrait à la statue de Bartholomé*)
probably late 1895
Degas' home, 23 rue Ballu Paris
gelatin silver photograph
28.5 x 39.3 cm
Musée d'Orsay, Paris
RF 2430
Gift of the Society of Friends of the Musée d'Orsay, 1992
Daniel 23

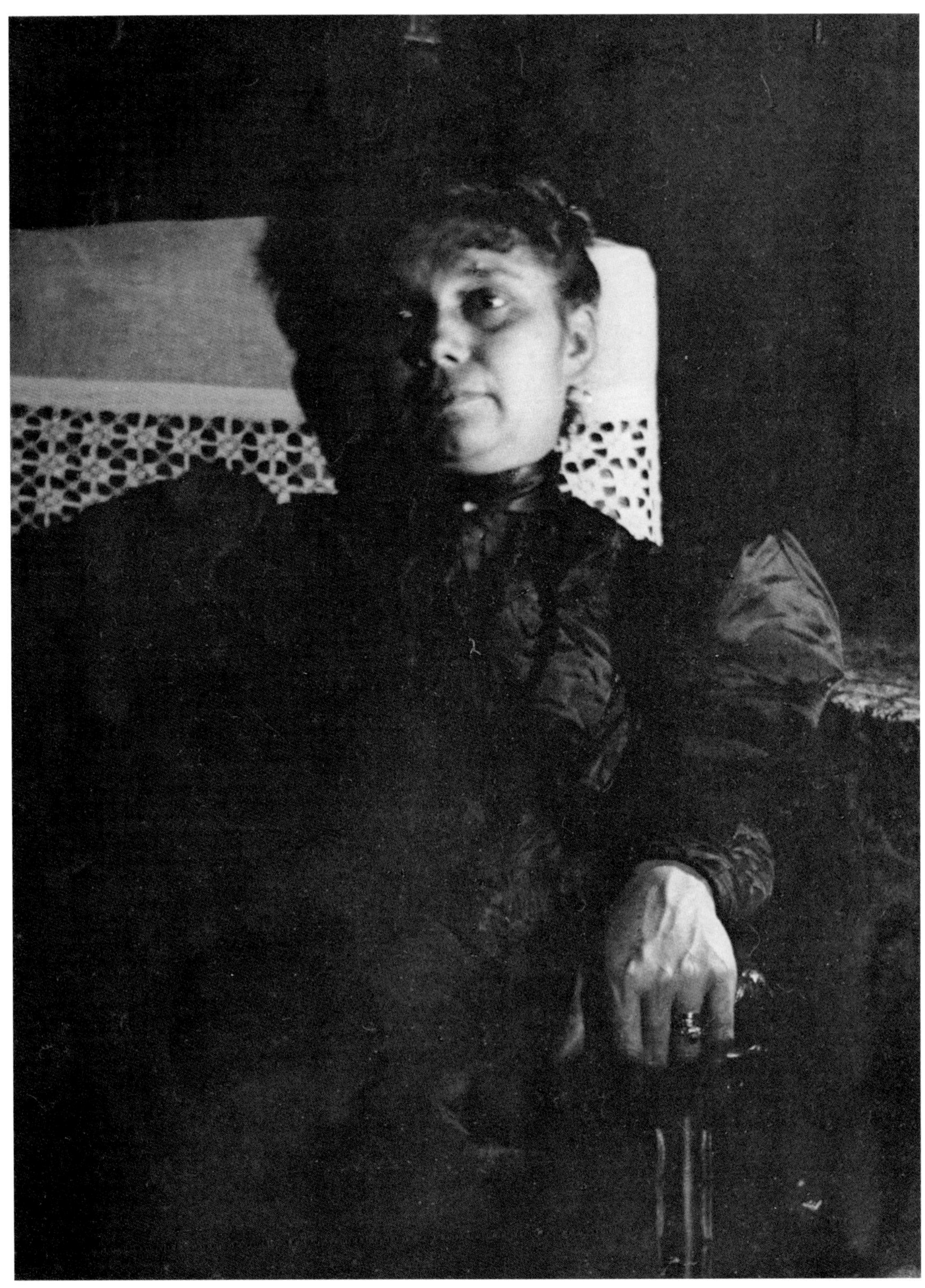

87 *Louise Halévy*
14 October 1895
Halévys' home, 22 rue de Douai Paris
gelatin silver photograph
40.6 x 30 cm
Musée d'Orsay, Paris
PHO 1994-1-1
Gift of Mme Françoise Joxe-Halévy's children, 1994
Daniel 4

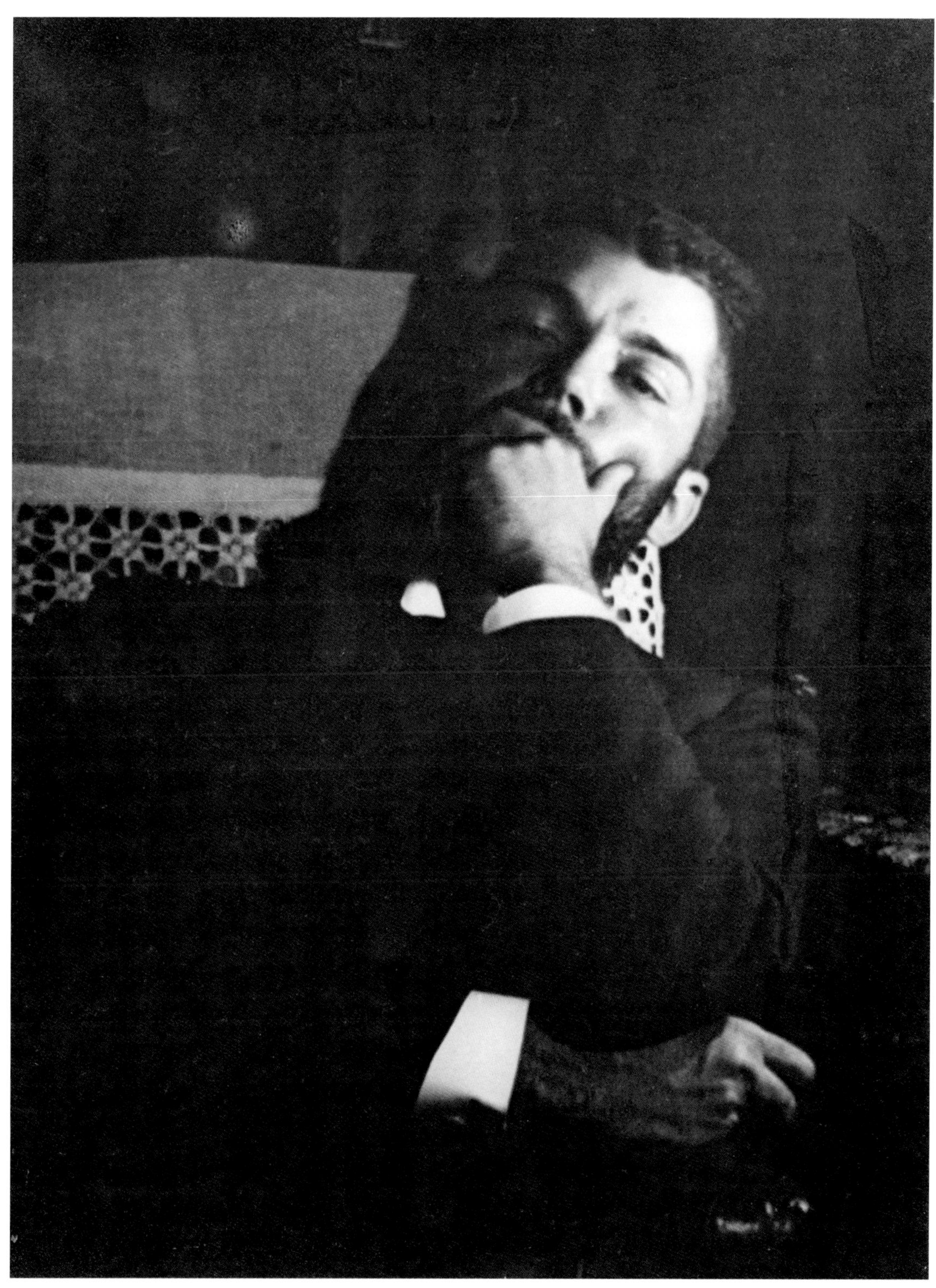

88 *Daniel Halévy*
14 October 1895
Halévys' home, 22 rue de Douai Paris
gelatin silver photograph
40.7 x 29.7 cm
Musée d'Orsay, Paris
PHO 1994 1 2
Gift of Mme Françoise Joxe-Halévy's children, 1994
Daniel 5

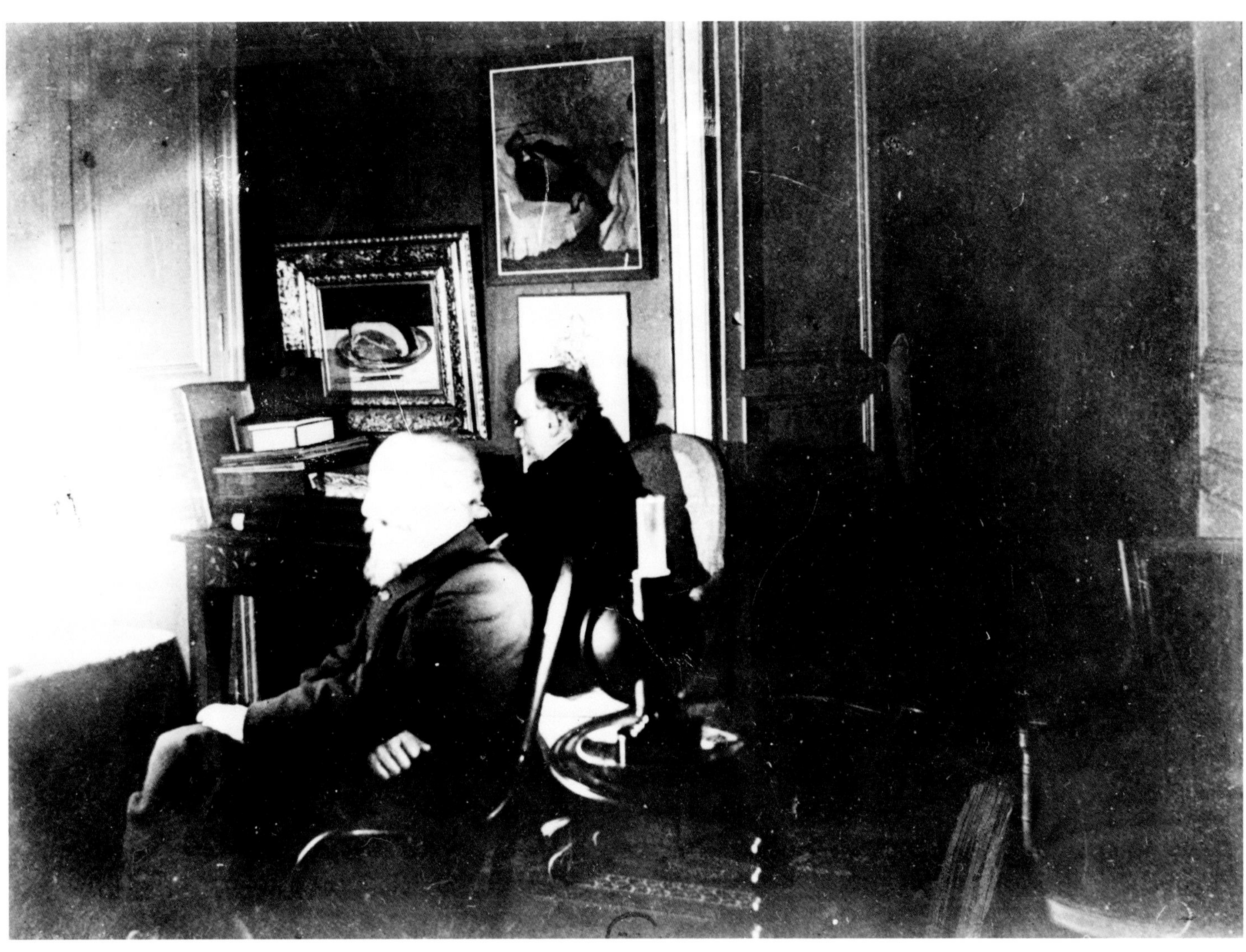

89 *Self-portrait with Bartholomé*
(*Autoportrait avec Bartholomé*)
probably late 1895
Degas' home, 23 rue Ballu Paris
gelatin silver photograph
modern copy of original print
Bibliothèque nationale de France, Paris
N2 Degas, 78 C 87493
Daniel 24 / Terrasse 59

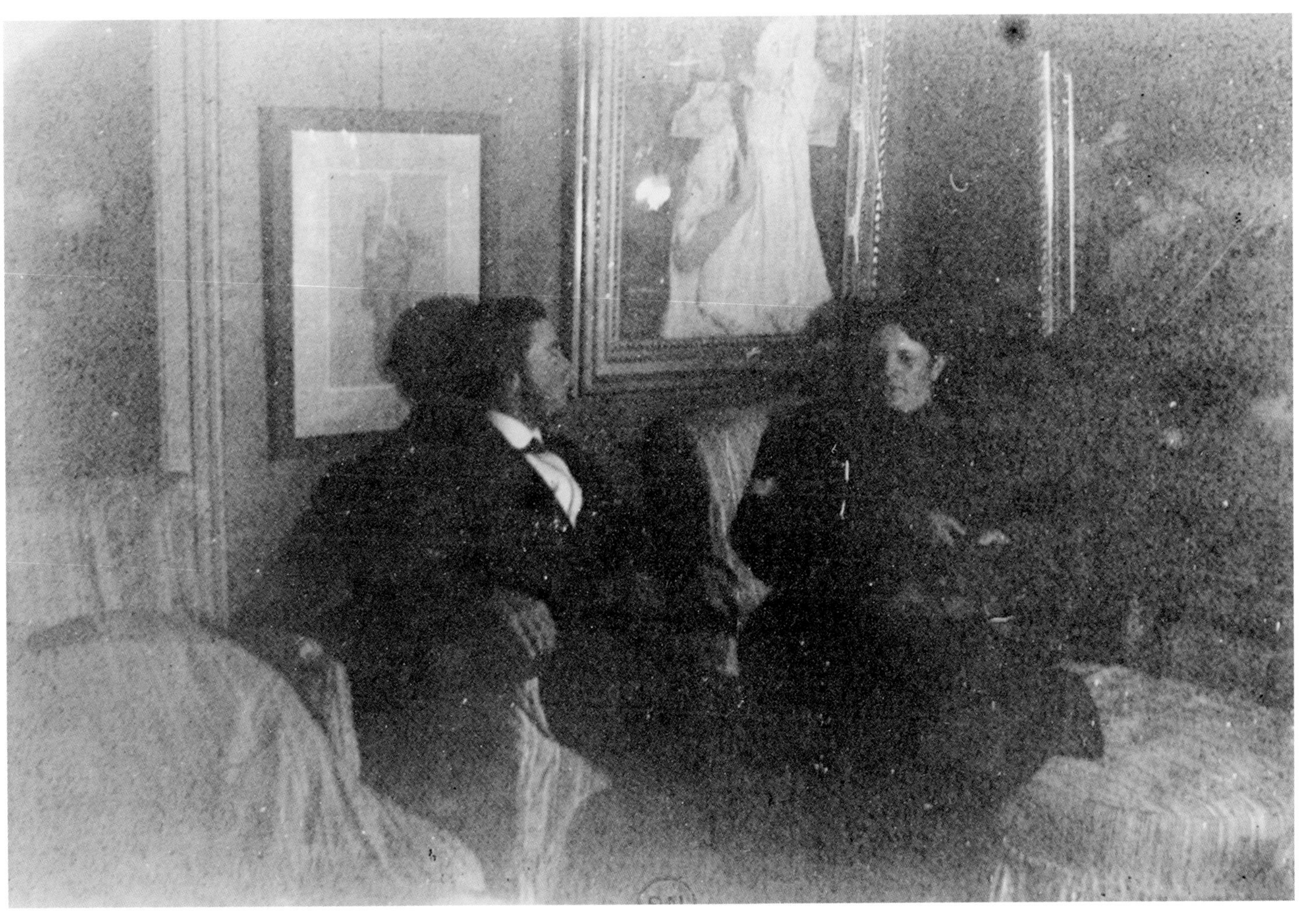

90 ***Elie and Louise Halévy in Degas' living room***
(***Elie et Louise Halévy dans le salon de Degas***)
probably late 1895
Degas' home, 23 rue Ballu Paris
gelatin silver photograph
modern copy of original print
Bibliothèque nationale de France, Paris
N2 Halévy, 64 B 33362
Daniel 27 / Terrasse 51

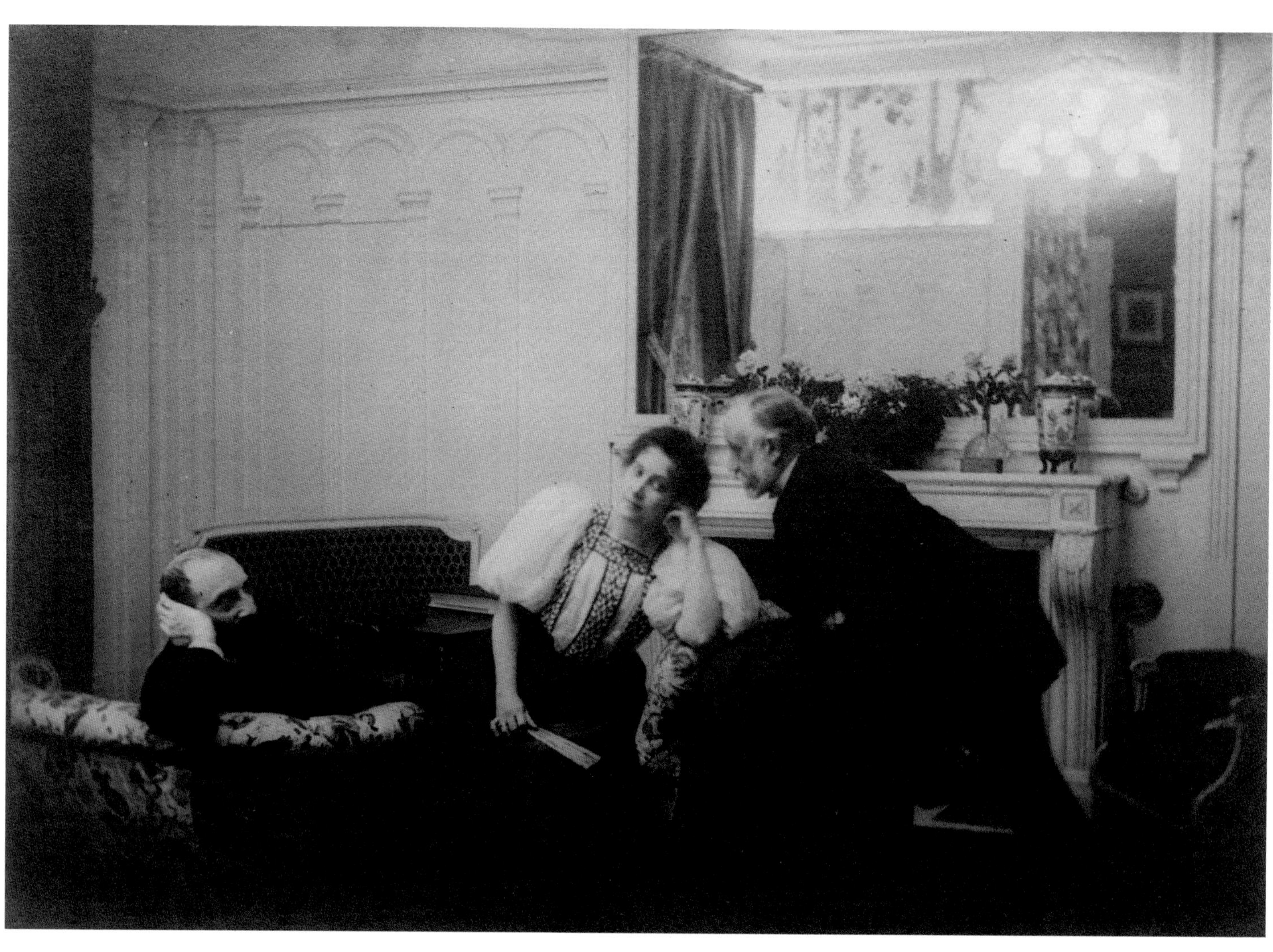

91 *Paul Poujaud, Marie Fontaine and Degas*
(*Paul Poujaud, Marie Fontain, et Degas*)
probably late 1895
Salon of Ernest Chausson, 13 rue Solférino Paris
gelatin silver photograph, mounted on board
29.4 x 40.5 cm
The Metropolitan Museum of Art, New York
1983.1092
The Elisha Whittelsey Collection, The Elisha Whittelsey Fund, 1983
Daniel 30 / Terrasse 9

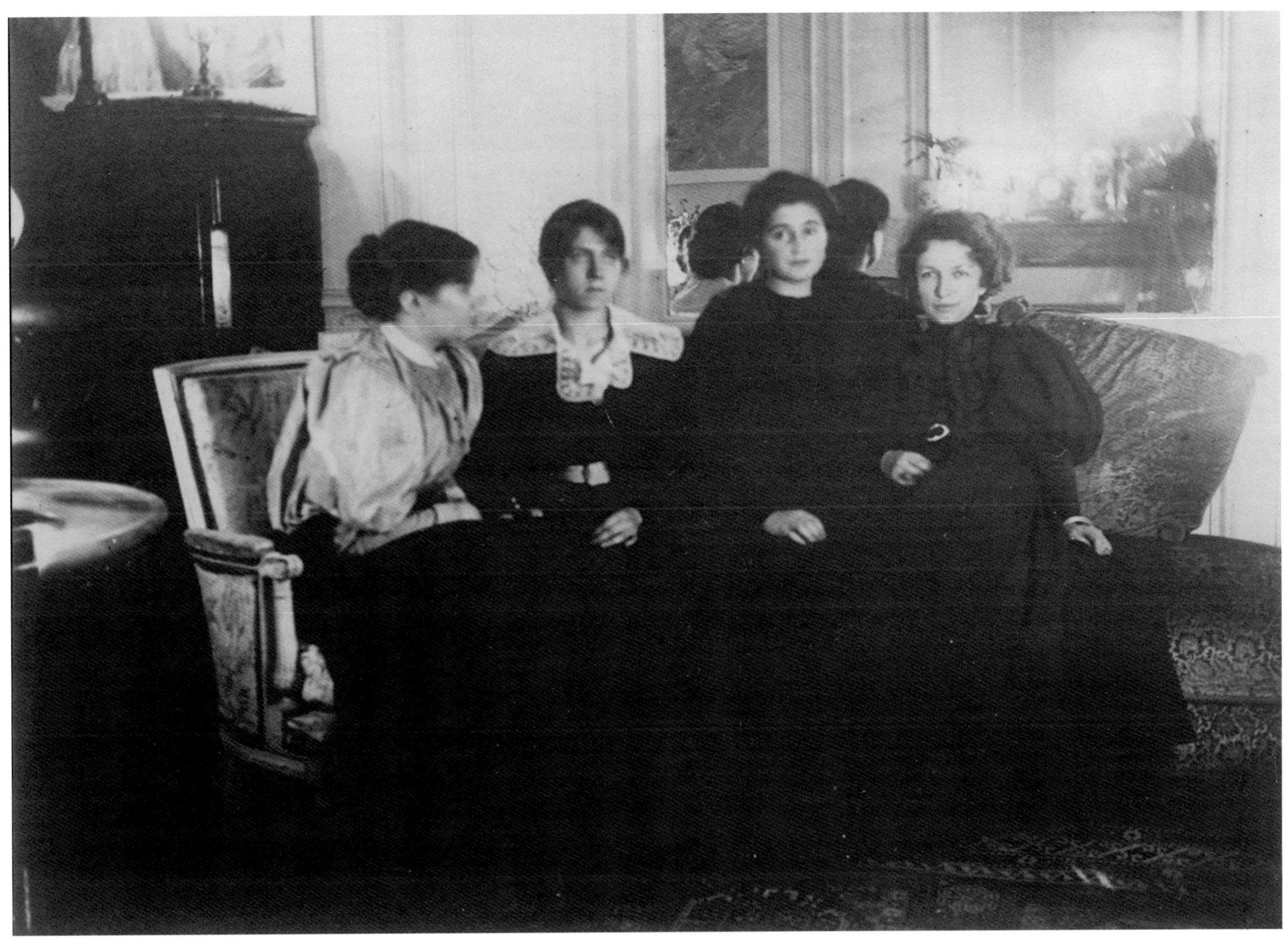

92 *Paule Gobillard, Jeannie Gobillard, Julie Manet and Geneviève Mallarmé*
(*Paule Gobillard, Jeannie Gobillard, Julie Manet et Geneviève Mallarmé*)
16 December 1895
Salon of Julie Manet and Paule and Jeannie Gobillard, 40 rue de Villejust Paris
gelatin silver photograph, mounted on board
28.4 x 38.9 cm
The Metropolitan Museum of Art, New York
2000.655.1
Gift of Paul F Walter, 2000
Daniel 17

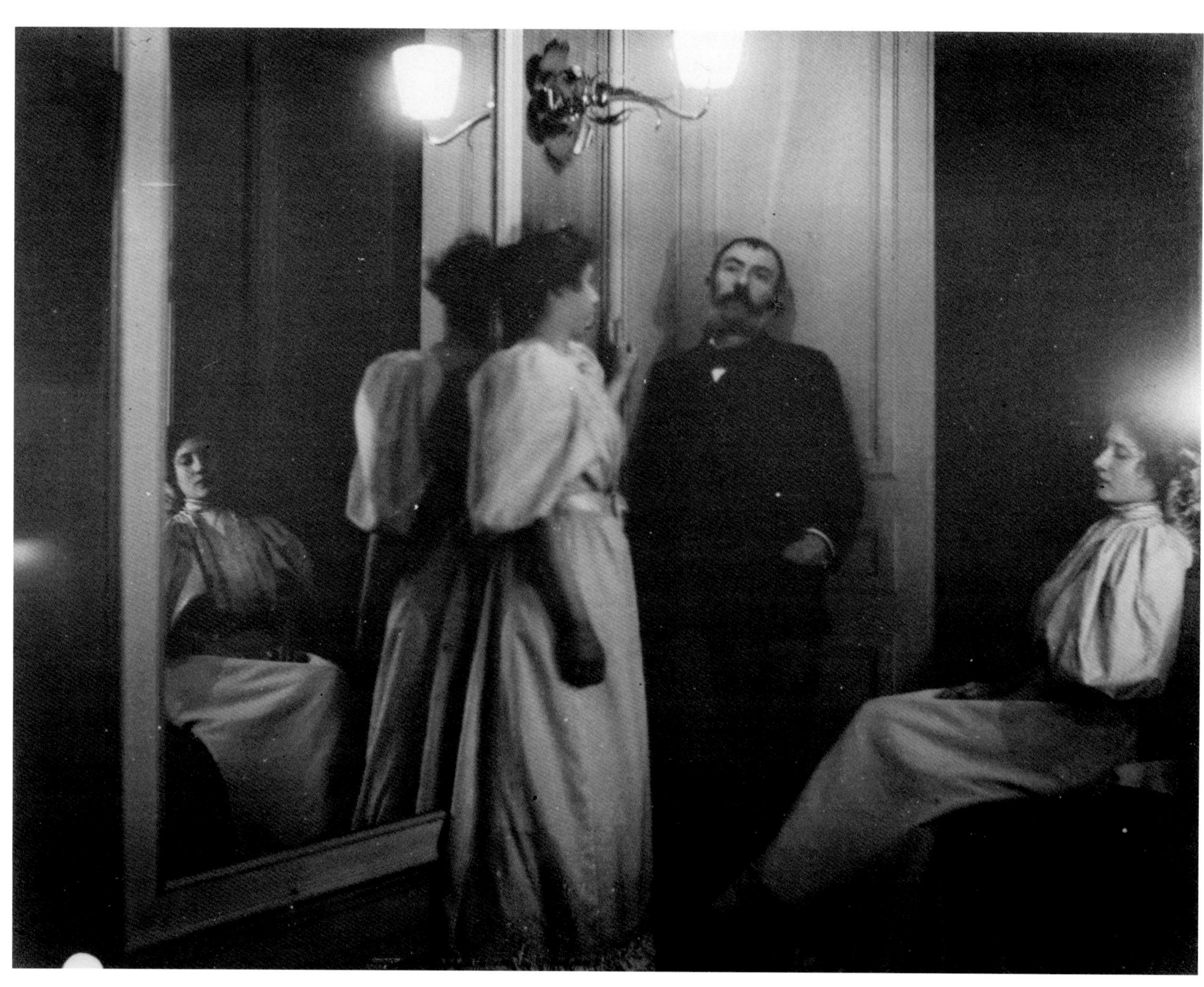

93 *Portrait in front of a mirror of the artist Henry Lerolle and his two daughters, Yvonne and Christine*
(*Portrait au miroir du peintre Henry Lerolle et de ses deux filles, Yvonne et Christine*)
c1895–96
gelatin silver photograph taken from a glass negative and enlarged
29 x 36.2 cm
Musée d'Orsay, Paris
PHO 2004 4

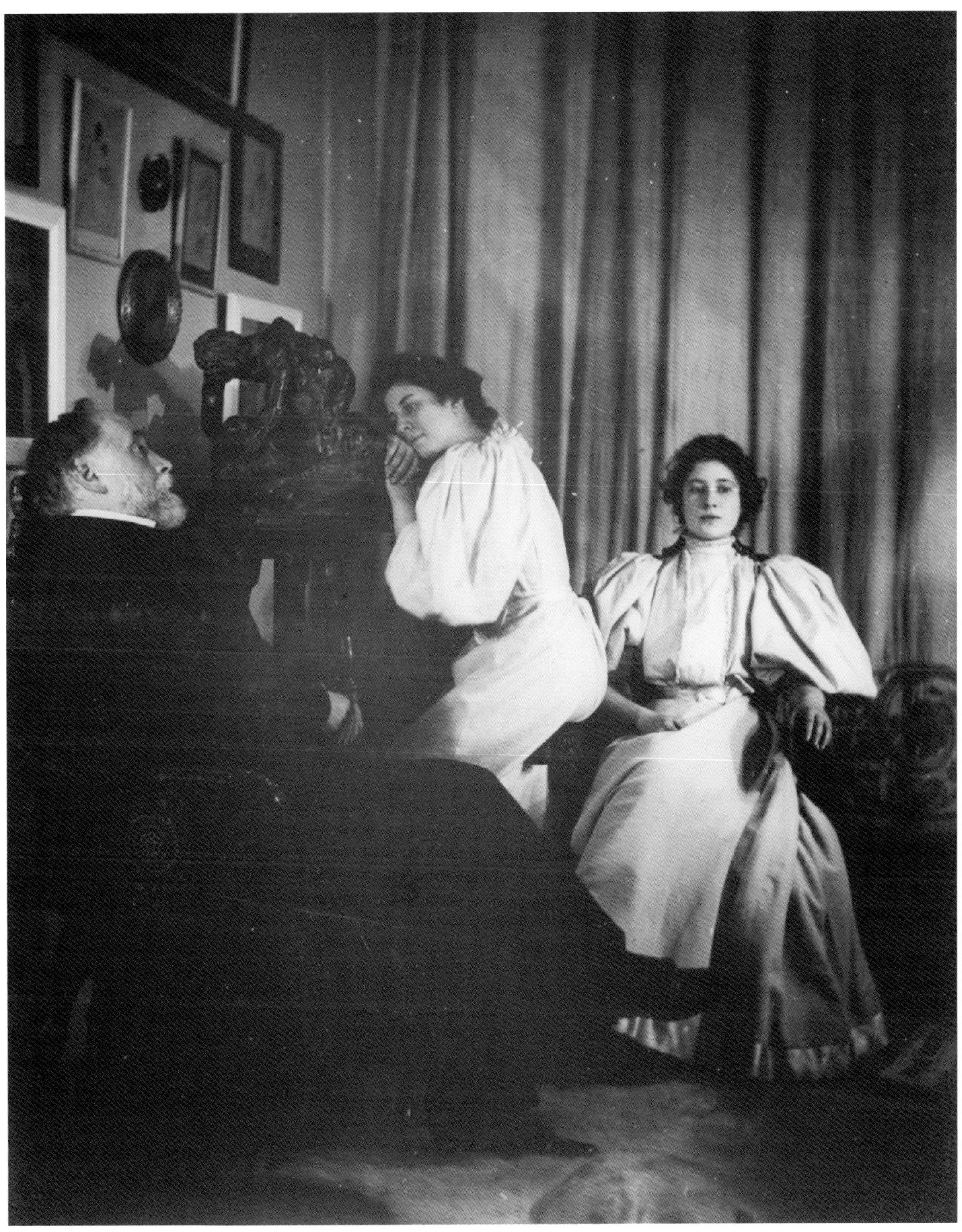

94 *Self-portrait with Christine and Yvonne Lerolle*
(*Autoportrait avec Christine et Yvonne Lerolle*)
probably 1895 or 1896
Henry Lerolle's home, Paris
gelatin silver photograph, mounted on board
37.1 x 29.3 cm (image), 55.4 x 45.5 cm (mount)
The Metropolitan Museum of Art, New York
2004.335
Purchase, The Horace W Goldsmith Foundation Gift
through Joyce and Robert Menschel and Rogers Fund, 2004
Daniel 32 / Terrasse 57

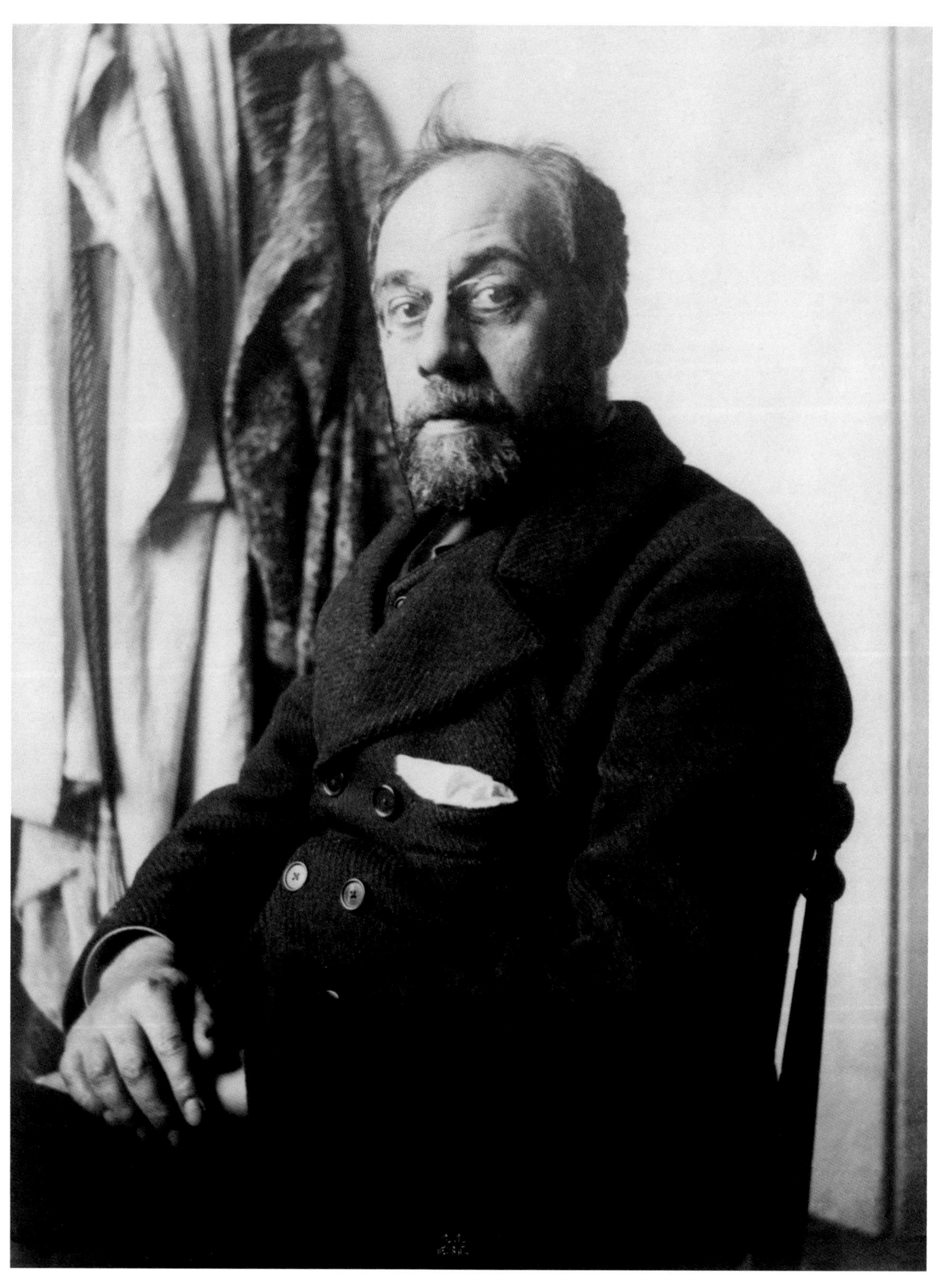

95 *René Degas in the artist's studio* (*René Degas dans l'atelier du peintre*)
probably late 1895 or 1896
Degas' studio, 37 rue Victor Massé Paris
gelatin silver photograph
35.8 x 26.6 cm
Bibliothèque nationale de France, Paris
N2 Degas, 70 C 42 940
Daniel 26 / Terrasse 52

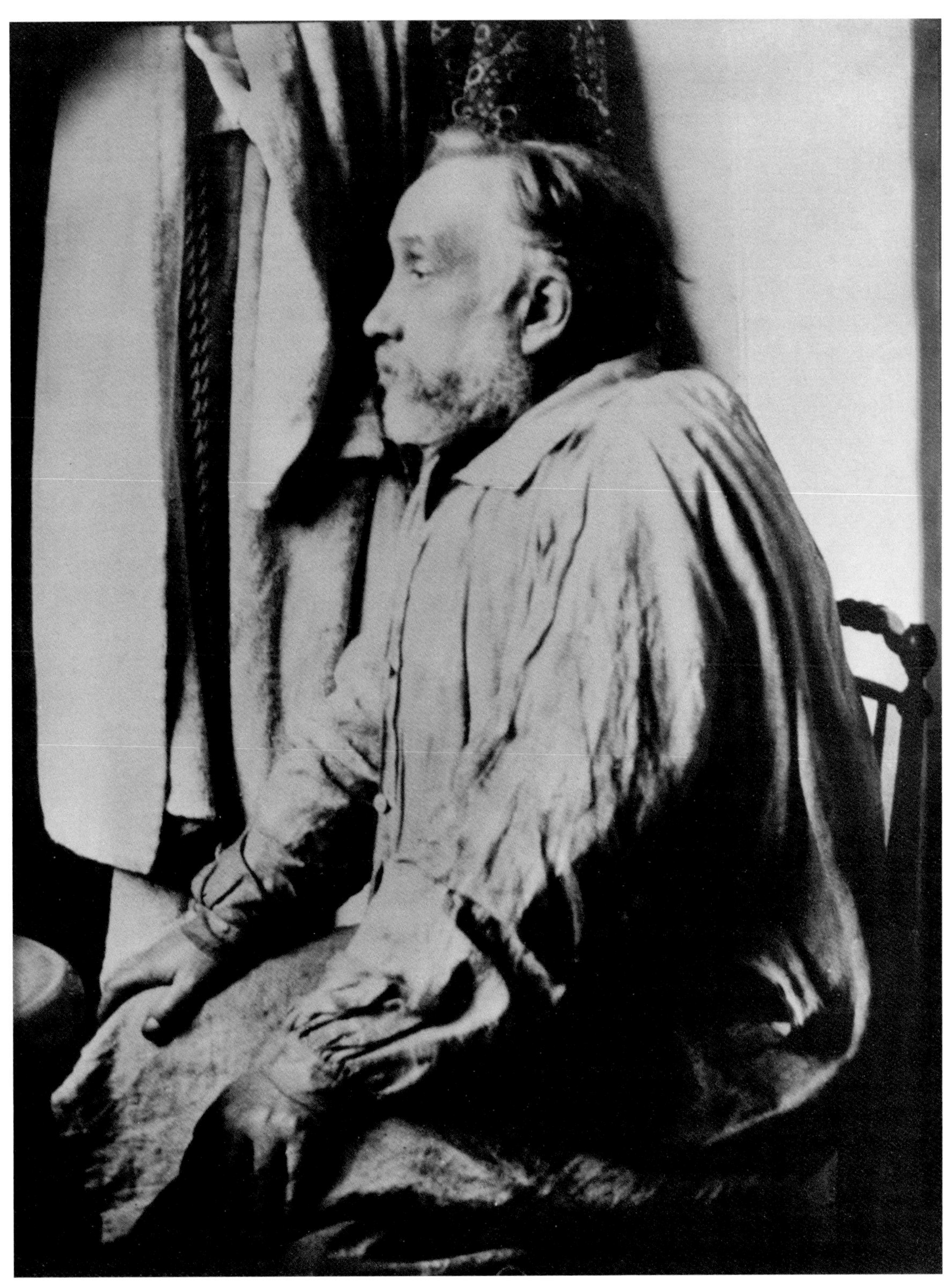

96 ***Self-portrait in the studio*** (***Autoportrait dans l'atelier***)
probably late 1895 or 1896
Degas' studio, 37 rue Victor Massé Paris
gelatin silver photograph
dimensions unknown
Bibliothèque nationale de France, Paris
N2 Degas, 78 C 87480
Daniel 25 / Terrasse 23

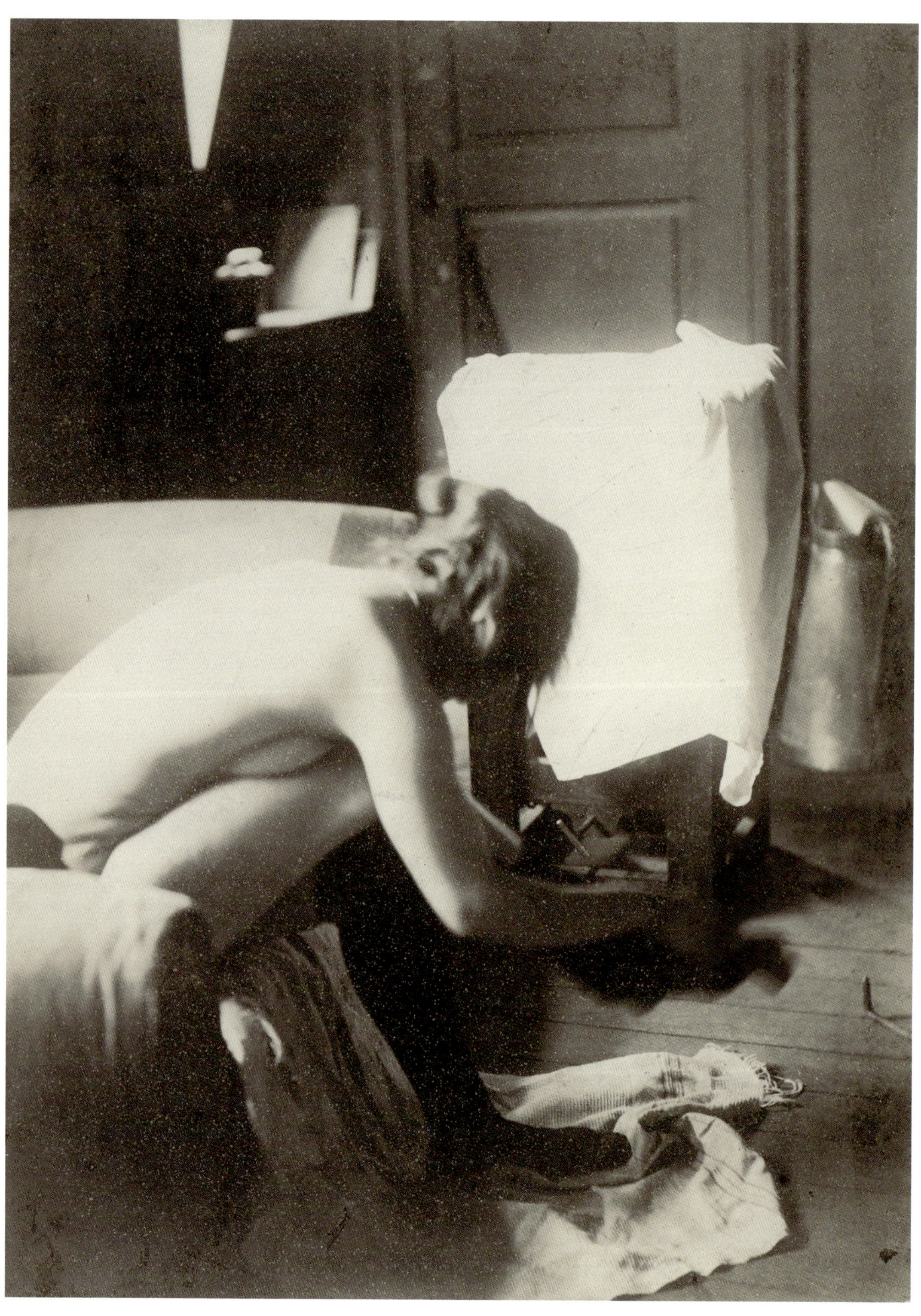

97 *Nude (putting on stockings)* (*Nu (mettant ses bas)*)
late 1895 or 1896
gelatin silver photograph
17 x 12.1 cm (image), 18.9 x 14 cm (mount)
The J Paul Getty Museum, Los Angeles
84.XM.495.1
Daniel 41

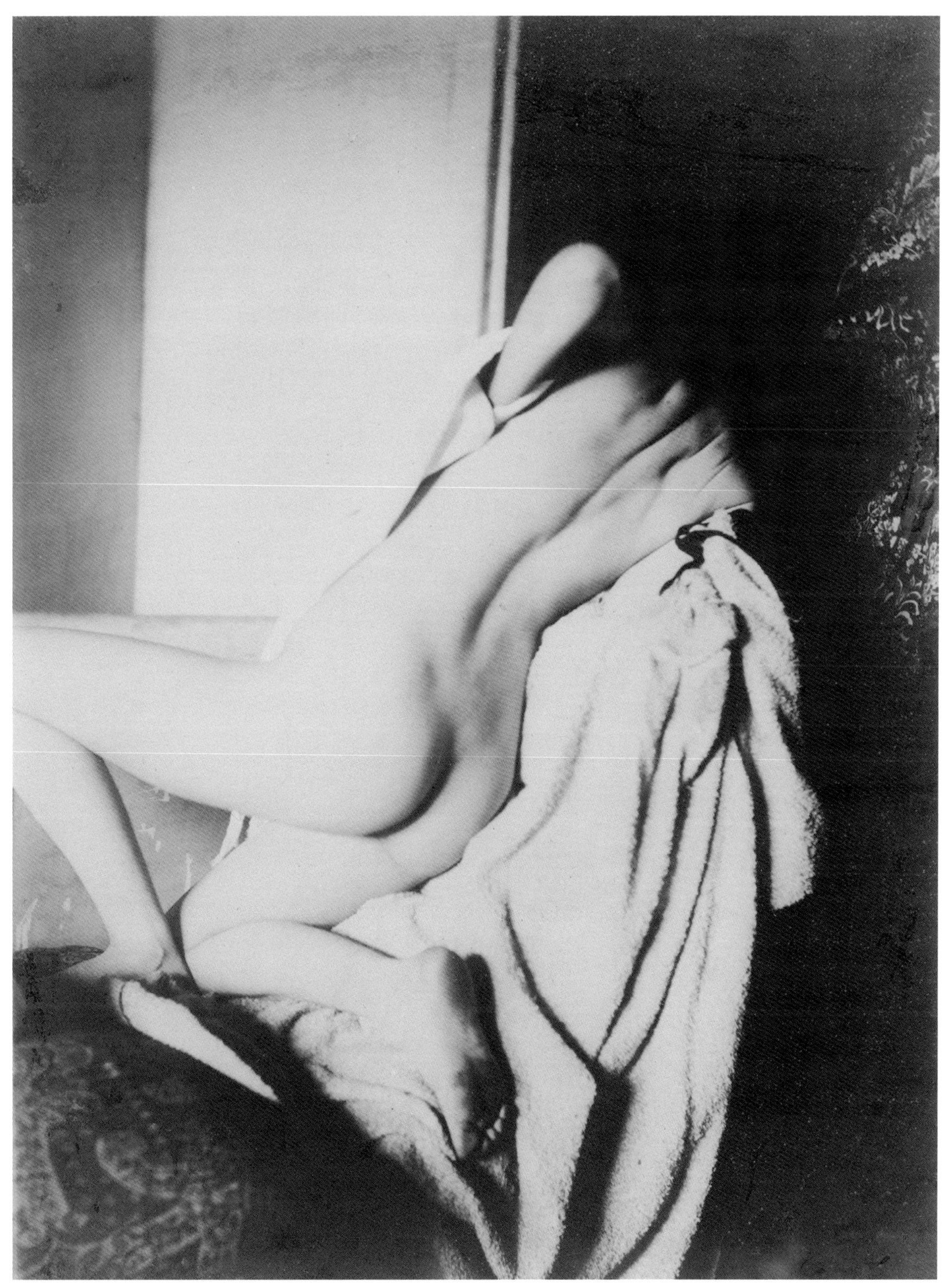

98 *Nude (drying herself)* (*Nu (séchage)*)
late 1895 or 1896
Degas' studio, 37 rue Victor Massé Paris
gelatin silver photograph
16.5 x 12 cm (image), 46.4 x 36.8 cm (mount)
The J Paul Getty Museum, Los Angeles
84.XM.495.2
Daniel 40 / Terrasse 25

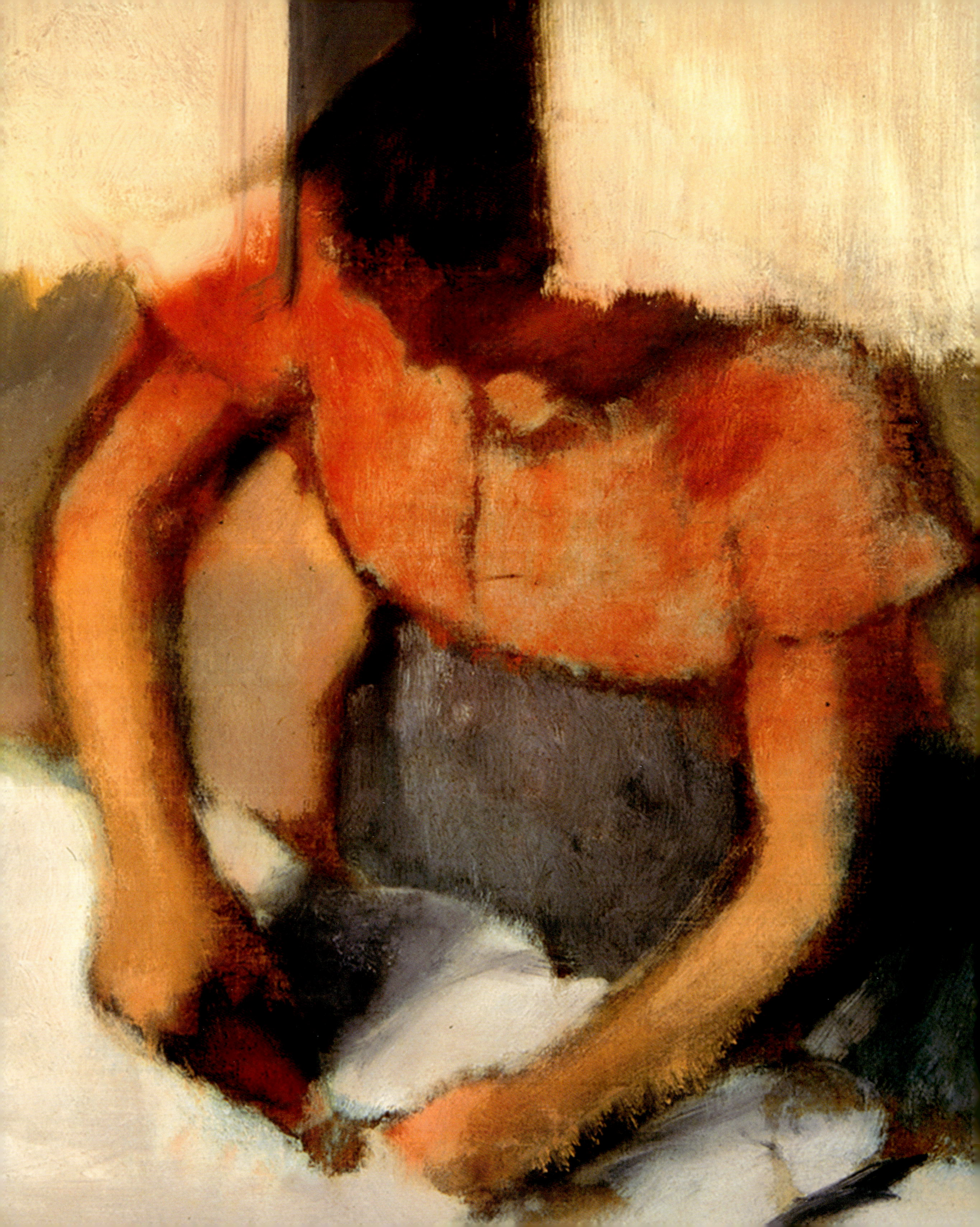

WORKING WOMEN

ANALYSIS OF THE VARIOUS catalogues raisonné of Degas' work reveals his fascination, even obsession, with the depiction of women and the female form.[1] He began his career with portraits of his relatives, particularly his aunts and female cousins, and with genre paintings of classical myths in which women are powerful and strong, an unusual evocation at that time.[2] His career-long observation of ballet dancers commenced in the early 1870s, when he also began various series focusing on the working women of Paris—laundresses, cabaret singers and milliners. His later abstract works were even more closely focused on women, depicting nudes at their toilette.

In addressing so much of his art to the study of women Degas stood apart from many of his Impressionist colleagues. Their preoccupation, the genre of landscape, was of less interest to him.[3] But like his fellow Impressionists, Degas was a keen observer of contemporary life and he spent much time documenting the leisure activities of the French, focusing primarily on women's roles within these pursuits—dancers at the ballet, women peering through their binoculars at the races, cabaret singers performing at café-concerts, and prostitutes entertaining clients at brothels. Other painters, Edouard Manet for example, addressed the role of women in the realm of men's activities, such as barmaids and prostitutes. However Degas' representation of women who were not directly involved in pleasure pursuits—laundresses and milliners—was less conventional.[4] He brought a hitherto unseen realism to his female subjects, particularly to those working women.

It was this realism that shocked and appalled many contemporary viewers of Degas' art. The critic Joris-Karl Huysmans described the artist's female subjects, shown at the eighth Impressionist exhibition in 1886, as having been deliberately humiliated and debased. In his treatise *Certains*, first published in 1889, Huysmans commented that Degas 'brought an attentive cruelty and a patient hatred to bear upon his studies of nudes'.[5] This type of contemporary interpretation of the artist's approach to the representation of women, coupled with Degas' mother's early death when he was 13 and his failure to marry, has led to a longstanding belief in Degas' misogyny.[6]

Contradicting this notion of misogyny, Degas appears to have been quite revolutionary in his attitude towards women. There were many intellectual and artistic women within his circle of friends, and he was instrumental in assisting the few women who showed their work in the Impressionist exhibitions, especially the American artist Mary Cassatt.[7] Cassatt, who became his closest female friend, helped to promote his work in America. Degas used her several times as a model in a series of prints, as well as for paintings and pastels.[8] His prints of Cassatt examining works in the paintings and antiquities galleries in the Louvre around 1879–80 (cats 104, 105, 106 and 107) show her facing away from the viewer and leaning on a furled umbrella in a confident and assured pose. The seated figure reading a guidebook is Cassatt's sister Lydia. In this series, and the pastel that followed,[9] Degas experiments with composition. For the paintings gallery print he uses a mirror image of Cassatt as she appears in the antiquities gallery, and he condenses the space between the standing figure and the seated one. Cassatt is presented by Degas as a connoisseur and an intellectually engaged woman, studying Classical works of art as part of her creative process.

Degas used Cassatt as a model again, in two of his milliners series of about 1882.[10] He accompanied her on several visits to millinery shops in Paris, and through this engagement developed a keen interest in the subject. Although he often complained to some of his male companions that he was 'dragged' to these shops, Paul Gauguin paints a very different picture, recalling: '[Degas] went into ecstasies before the milliner's shop in the rue de la Paix, the charming laces, those famous touches by which our Parisian women drive you into buying an extravagant hat.'[11]

In his portrayal of millinery shops, Degas links his own social circle, with its consumer interests in elite fashion, to his personal investigations into lower-class working women and their environs. His exploration of this theme can be understood in light of Charles Baudelaire's seminal essay of 1863, 'The painter of modern life'. Baudelaire encourages young emerging artists to use contemporary fashion, particularly women's fashion, in their art, to project the atmosphere of reality and the modern era.[12] By setting his series in hat shops, Degas was addressing the current fashions of the time, while slyly acknowledging the social hierarchies that feed the fashionable world.

In his novel of 1883 devoted to the same theme, *Au bonheur des dames* (*The ladies' delight* or *The ladies' paradise*), Emile Zola creates an atmosphere of pandemonium within a new Parisian department store where there are large cluttered spaces for clients to lose themselves in, and mirrors that confuse and dazzle. Degas and Zola were both interested in analysing the underbelly of Parisian culture, and in their works there are several correlations; but the vast shopping 'paradise'

(previous page)
Woman ironing
c 1882–86
(detail cat 100)

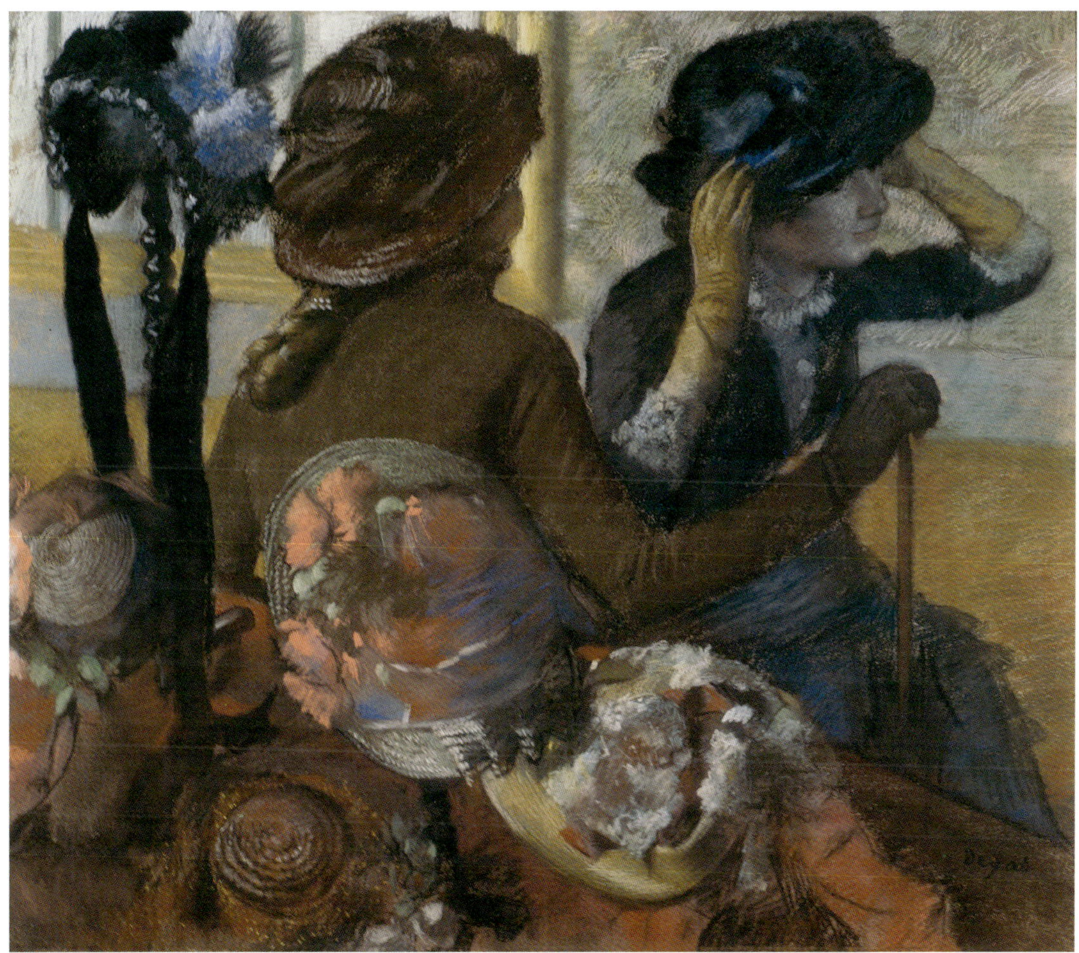

described by the author is a far cry from the millinery shops depicted by the artist. The spaces created by Degas in his milliners' images are quite ambiguous. He suggests intimate spaces that focus on the relationships between the customer and the salesgirl, or the milliner and her apprentice. Although he uses mirrors in this series, they are not the reflective devices that serve his ballet dancer compositions. Rather, Degas positions the mirrors to obscure the figures of the sales assistants and apprentices, hence demonstrating their lower status in relation to the milliners (the *modistes*), and their wealthy clients.

As in his prints of Cassatt at the Louvre, Degas plays with spatial arrangements. He uses radical cropping, often cutting the faces of the sales assistants in half with the edge of the canvas or through the placement of long mirrors and hats on stands.

In nineteenth-century Paris, there was an understanding that *modistes* performed the dual role of hat-maker and prostitute, but Degas deliberately eschewed this aspect in his portrayal of milliners. Unlike his images of ballet dancers, where the black top-hats of the predatory males, the 'Lions', are often glimpsed mingling amongst the young girls backstage, Degas ignored the sexual role of the *modiste*. In the entire milliners series, including his sketchbook drawings of the subject, not a single male appears. Instead of the sexualised male gaze, Degas focuses on the female perspective of women, intently studying their reflections in the shop mirrors and admiring the merchandise.

Another group of women who became the focus of Degas' observations were the laundresses—both the washerwomen and the ironers. Like the milliners, these women were forced by dint of poor economic circumstance to perform sexual favours in addition to their arduous work in the laundries. In Degas' time the laundress was quite a popular subject for artists and cartoonists. Typically these women were scantily dressed due to the torrid conditions of their working environment, and artists often portrayed them in a flirtatious and sexually suggestive manner. The laundress also featured prominently in pornographic images.[13] Zola's novel of 1877, *L'Assommoir* (*The dram shop*), illustrates the harsh reality of the life of a laundress, as the protagonist spirals down into alcoholism and prostitution.

At the milliner's (*Chez la modiste*)
1882
pastel on paper, 75.5 x 85.5 cm
Museo Thyssen-Bornemisza, Madrid
Lemoisne 729

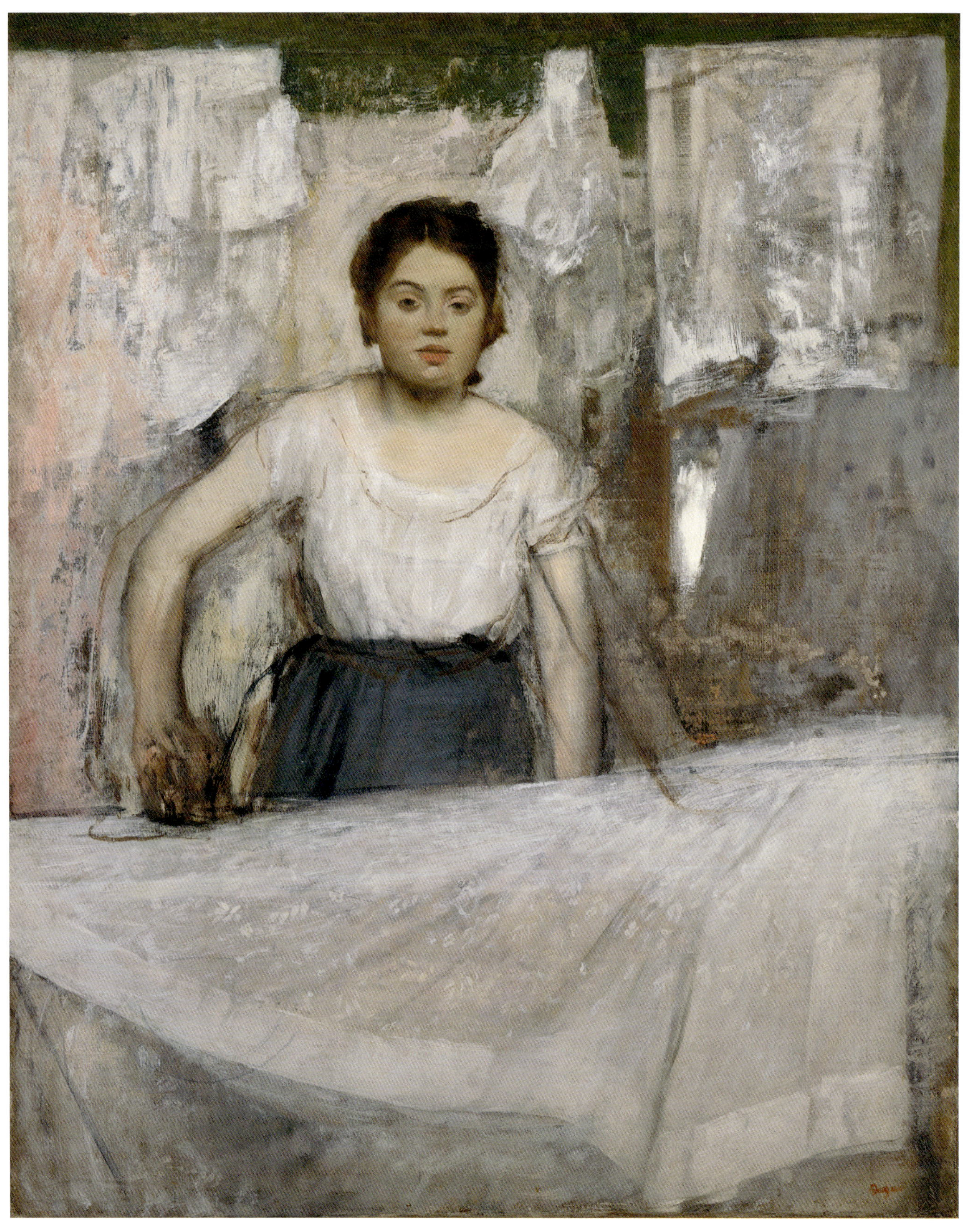

Woman ironing (*Repasseuse*) c 1869
oil on canvas, 92.5 x 74.0 cm
Neue Pinakothek, Munich
Lemoisne 216

Again Degas has countered convention by avoiding all evidence of a male presence in his laundress images. In some of his preliminary sketches men appear, idling in the corners of the laundries, watching the women at work, but Degas never transferred those figures to his final paintings or pastels; and in only two early examples of this theme does Degas show the women acknowledging the presence of the viewer (opposite).[14]

Degas' laundresses confront the prevailing nineteenth-century stereotype in another important way—they are presented as women hard at work. Their working conditions were exceedingly difficult: airborne diseases, such as tuberculosis, were rampant; the laundry space was often makeshift and cramped; and, due to boredom, alcoholism was prevalent. Degas captures the arduous nature of these women's lives with a realism not seen before in French art, and his understanding of their hardship is clear. In *Laundresses carrying linen* c 1876–78 (see p 26)[15], two washerwomen bend in opposite directions under the weight of the loads of laundry balanced on their hips. Similarly, in paintings of ironers such as *Woman ironing* c 1882–86 (cat 100)[16], Degas evokes the oppressive conditions, depicting the washing draped to dry over clotheslines that run above the table, partially obscuring the woman's head as she bends to her task.

Throughout this series, Degas exploited the cramped working environments and the abundance of hanging washing to create interesting spatial arrangements, with the bright colours of the laundry items used as clever visual devices to splice the canvas. *Woman ironing* also alludes to the dark and misty atmosphere in which the women worked, seen in Degas' blurred brushstrokes and muted background tones.

The comments of critics such as Huysmans stemmed from Degas' flouting of contemporary conventions for the representation of women.[17] Although some critics and fellow artists applauded his move away from 'the smooth and slippery flesh of ever nude goddesses'[18] towards the depiction of real women, the transition was fraught with controversy. Nevertheless Degas paved the way for a new appreciation of the female form, with all its faults and flaws.

Notes

1 See Paul-André Lemoisne, *Degas et son oeuvre*, 4 vols, Paul Brame and CM de Hauke, Paris, 1946; Philippe Brame and Theodore Reff, *Degas et son œuvre: a supplement*, Garland Publishing, New York, 1984; Eugenia Parry Janis, *Degas monotypes: essay, catalogue and checklist*, Fogg Art Museum, Cambridge, 1968; Sue Welsh Reed and Barbara Stern Shapiro, *Edgar Degas: the painter as printmaker*, Museum of Fine Arts, Boston, 1984; and Joseph S Czestochowski and Anne Pingeot, *Degas sculptures: catalogue raisonné of the bronzes*, International Arts and Torch Press, Memphis, 2002.

2 For detailed analyses of Degas' innovation in several early genre paintings, see Norma Broude, 'Degas's "misogyny"', *The Art Bulletin*, vol 59, no 1, March 1977, pp 95–107.

3 Degas did produce a group of landscape images. See Richard Kendall, *Degas landscapes*, Yale University Press, New Haven, 1993. Also some art historians, such as Eunice Lipton, have suggested that Degas' racing images can be read within that genre of painting. See Eunice Lipton, *Looking into Degas: uneasy images of women and modern life*, University of California Press, Berkley, 1986, pp 17–72.

4 As well as some visual artists, such as Honoré Daumier, many nineteenth-century authors, such as Emile Zola and the Goncourt brothers (Edmond and Jules de Goncourt), focused on the plight of lower-class women in Paris. See Rachel Bowlby, *Just looking: consumer culture in Dreiser, Grissing and Zola*, Methuen, New York, 1985.

5 Quoted in Broude, in *The Art Bulletin*, March 1977, p 95. For an analysis of Huysmans' criticism, see Carol Armstrong, *Odd man out: readings of the work and reputation of Edgar Degas*, The University of Chicago Press, Chicago, 1991.

6 Art historians, such as Norma Broude, only began looking beyond this idea in the 1970s. See Broude, in *The Art Bulletin*, March 1977, pp 95–107.

7 Norma Broude notes that Degas' encouragement of female artists was seen as a sign of his senility or a love affair, rather that an appreciation of the women's talents. See Broude, in *The Art Bulletin*, March 1977, p 102.

8 For a further analysis of the two artists' relationship, see Jeffrey Meyers, *Impressionist quartet: the intimate genius of Manet and Morisot, Degas and Cassatt*, Harcourt, Orlando, 2005, pp 267–87.

9 *Miss Cassatt at the Louvre*, c 1880 , private collection, Lemoisne 581.

10 *At the milliner's*, 1882, The Metropolitan Museum of Art, New York, Lemoisne 682, and *At the milliner's*, c 1882, The Metropolitan Museum of Art, New York, Lemoisne 693.

11 Quoted in Ruth E Iskin, *Modern women and Parisian consumer culture in Impressionist painting*, Cambridge University Press, New York, 2007, p 87.

12 For more information on Baudelaire's influence on Impressionism and fashion, see Ruth E Iskin, 2007, pp 62–68.

13 For more information on the conditions of laundresses in nineteenth-century Paris, see Eunice Lipton, 'The laundress in late nineteenth-century French culture: imagery, ideology and Edgar Degas', *Art History*, vol 3, no 3, September 1980, pp 295–313; and Eunice Lipton, *Looking into Degas: uneasy images of women and modern life*, University of California Press, Berkley, 1986, pp 116–50.

14 Eunice Lipton suggests that the small number of images where the laundress is looking at the viewer have overt sexual overtones linked to the dual role of ironer and prostitute. See Lipton, in *Art History*, September 1980, pp 304–10.

15 *Laundresses carrying linen in town* c 1876–78, Christie's London, 28 March 1988, lot 16, Lemoisne 410.

16 *Woman ironing*, c 1882–86, Reading Public Museums and Art Gallery, Reading, Pennsylvania, Lemoisne 276.

17 Although often critical of Degas' work, Huysmans was not always so. In his 1880 review published in *L'Art moderne* (Paris, 1883), he describes some of Degas' laundresses as 'ravishing'. See Lipton, 1986, p 140.

18 Huysmans, quoted in Broude, in *Art Bulletin*, March 1977, p 95.

99 *Woman ironing, set against the light* (*Repasseuse à contre-jour*)
begun c 1876, completed c 1887
oil on canvas
81.3 x 66 cm
National Gallery of Art, Washington DC
1972.74.1
Collection of Mr and Mrs Paul Mellon
Lemoisne 685
Image courtesy of the Board of Trustees, National Gallery of Art, Washington

Woman ironing, set against the light reveals the artist's debt to Honoré Daumier's Realist paintings of the working classes, such as *Laundress on the Quai D'Anjou* c 1860.[1] Degas was also influenced by Realist engraver and caricaturist, Paul Gavarni, as well as the generalised 'types' found in French caricature, which he avidly collected. Like these artists, Degas embraced everyday themes in a true-to-life manner that did not glorify or sexualise the subject. For artists, as well as writers, the idea that the laundress was a theme worth exploring gained currency in the later half of the nineteenth century. It was part of a concerted search for modern subject matter and a growing interest in Realism.

Following a visit to the artist's studio, writer Edmond de Goncourt described how Degas, 'places before our eyes, in their poses and their graceful outlines, laundresses, laundresses … speaking their language and explaining to us, by … [his] technique, the pressure of the iron, its circular movement'.[2]

In *Woman ironing…*, Degas demonstrates his interest in the movements, postures and rhythms of the woman at work. The laundress bends over the table seemingly oblivious to the world around her. The painting's viewer watches over the woman's shoulder, looking down on her, the table and the work spread out before her, with previously pressed garments and a bowl of water set on one side.

Unlike many of his contemporaries, Degas' interest focused intently on these women's characteristic gestures rather than their social situation. In *Woman ironing…*, the laundress leans down hard into her work, leaving a trail of steam and pressed cloth behind the iron. This scene, painted with Degas' usual oblique angles, is theatrically framed with a curtain of coloured garments above and behind the figure.

Notes

1 Albright-Knox Art Gallery, Buffalo. New York. Henri Loyrette et al, *Daumier*, 1808–1879, Musee des Beaux-Arts du Canada, Ottawa, 1999, cat no 162.

2 Letter to Henry Lerolle, 1887, quoted in Linda Nochlin and Joelle Bolloch, *Women in the 19th century: categories and contradictions*, The New Press, New York, 1997, p 32.

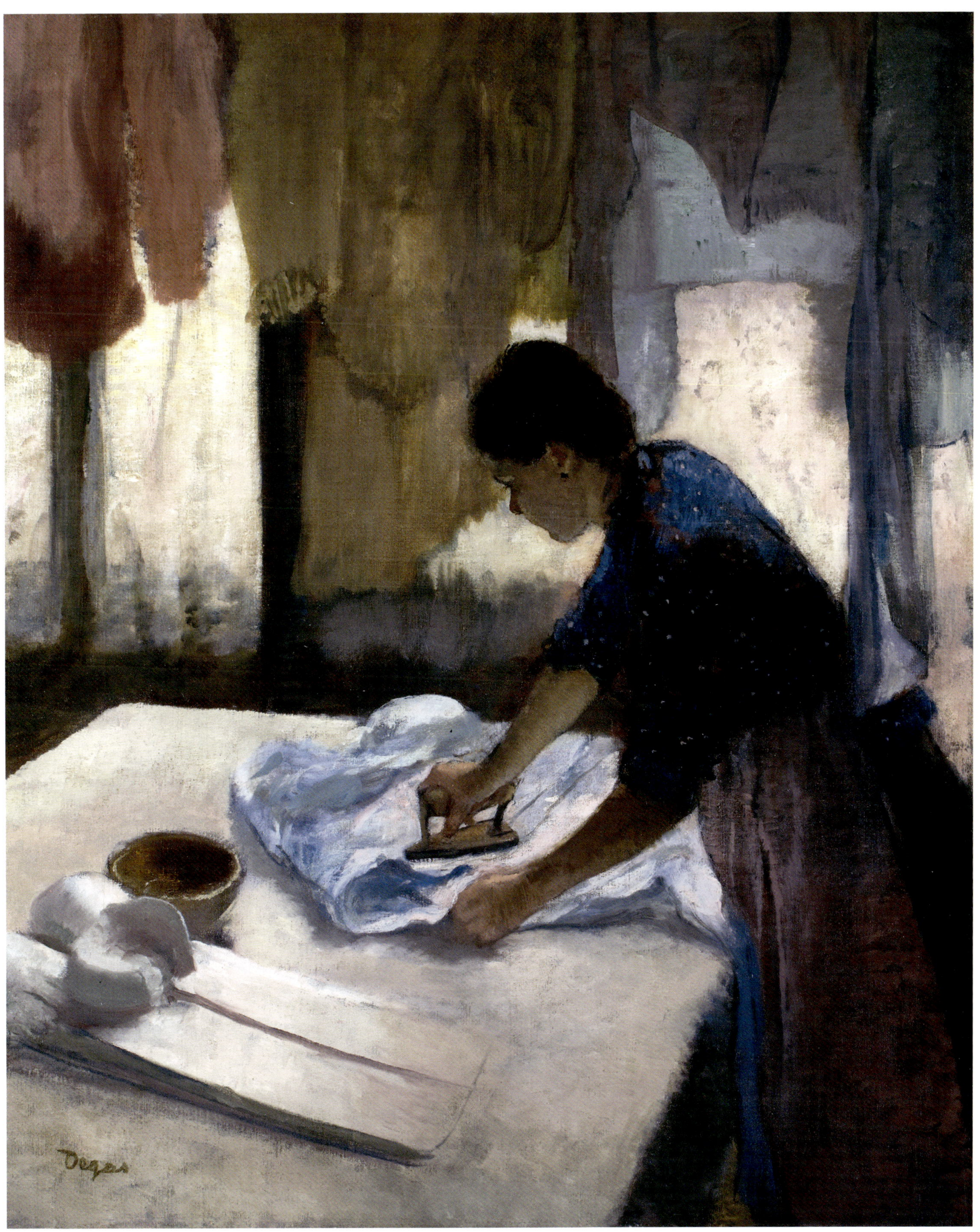
Degas

100 *Woman ironing* (*Blanchisseuse repassant*)
c 1882–86
oil on canvas
64.8 x 66.7 cm
Reading Public Museum and Art Gallery, Reading, Pennsylvania
76.45.1
Gift, Martha Elizabeth Dick Estate
Lemoisne 276

The image of the laundress was an accepted theme in Japanese *ukiyo-e* colour woodblock prints, which gained popularity in Europe during the nineteenth century. In this painting, Degas incorporates many pictorial devices evident in the *ukiyo-e* woodblocks, such as the oval shape created by the woman's arms and the use of a curtaining veil across her face. These devices directly correlate to Kitagawa Utamaro's *Suited to the dyed stripes stocked by Shimaya, from summer outfits* c 1795–96, in which a seated woman faces the viewer with both her rounded arms in a bucket, and her face almost blocked by a hanging textile.[1] Authors Richard Kendall and Jill DeVonyar contend that Degas had access to this print prior to painting *Woman ironing*.[2]

In comparison with the earlier example (cat 99), this *Woman ironing* is far more claustrophobic. Degas has shortened the space in which the laundress works, with the table radically cropped, cutting across the lower edge of the canvas on a sharp diagonal. Again the artist uses a curtain of fabric, this time hanging in front of the laundress's face, impressing upon the viewer her confined surroundings. The vibrant colours and loose brushstrokes which Degas uses in this painting provide an intensity which echoes the hot and steamy atmosphere in which these women worked.

The amount of flesh shown by laundresses, with their loose, flimsy clothing, was a strong taboo in nineteenth-century France and is one of the reasons why the profession was seen as harbouring loose morals. However, this image is far from being a sexual image of a woman. Instead, Degas presents her bare arms as rather scrawny, and she has her shirt buttoned up to her throat, with no hint of the voluptuous curves typical of many nineteenth-century depictions of laundresses. The screen of drying clothing also produces a feeling of anonymity, with the laundry blocking the viewer from clearly seeing the woman's face. This painting exemplifies Degas' move away from his early detailed works to his later style, which is more boldly painterly.

Notes

1 The New York Public Library, New York, catalogue raisonné no 446.

2 Jill DeVonyar and Richard Kendall, *Degas and the art of Japan*, Reading Public Museum, Reading, 2007, p 54

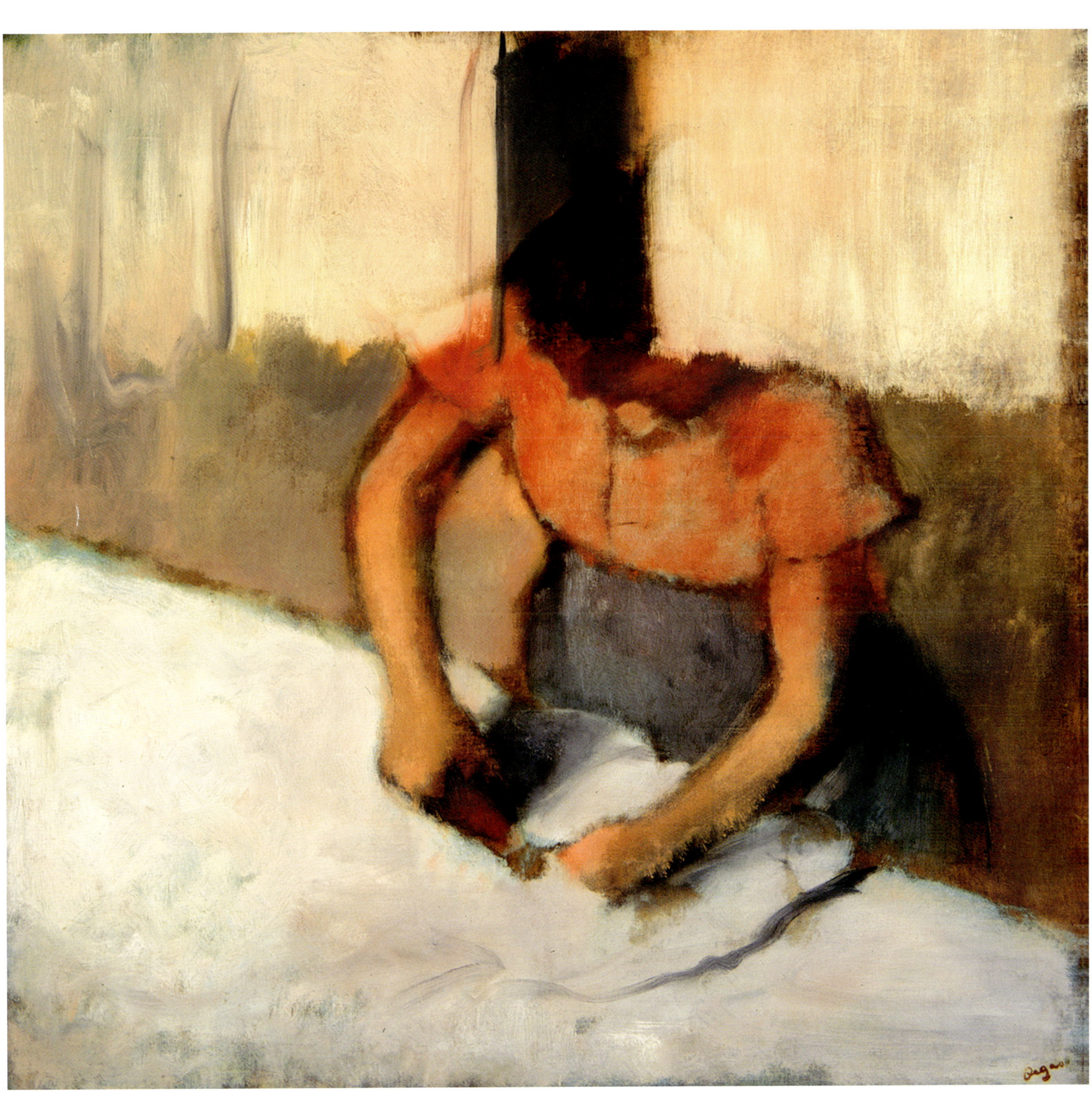

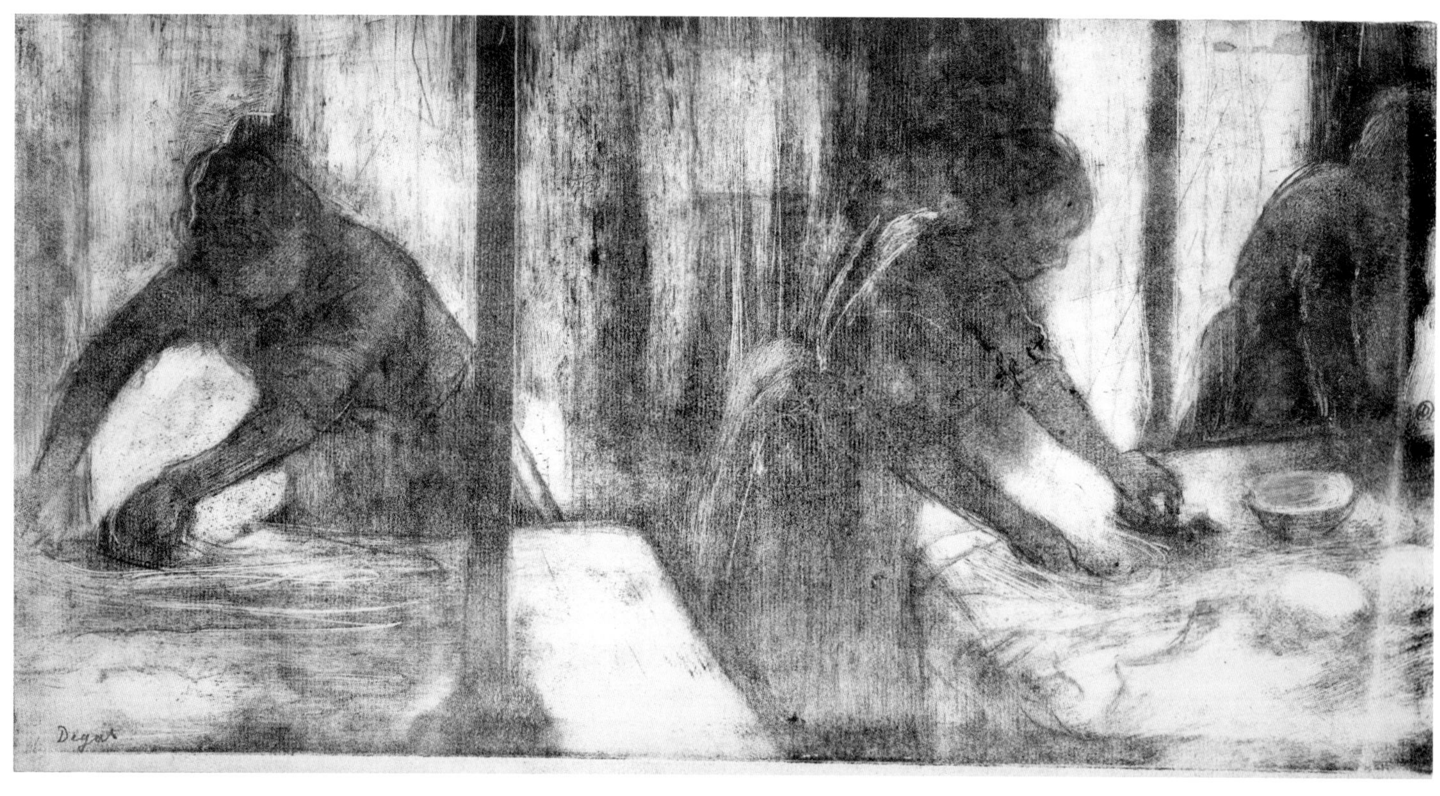

101 *Women ironing* (*Les repasseuses*)
c 1878
second impression of two
monotype in black ink on paper, touched up with charcoal
22.5 x 42.8 cm (plate), 23.5 x 42.8 cm (sheet)
Bibliothèque de l'institut national d'histoire de l'art, Paris
EM DEGAS 13
Collections Jacques Doucet
Janis 259 / Cachin 55

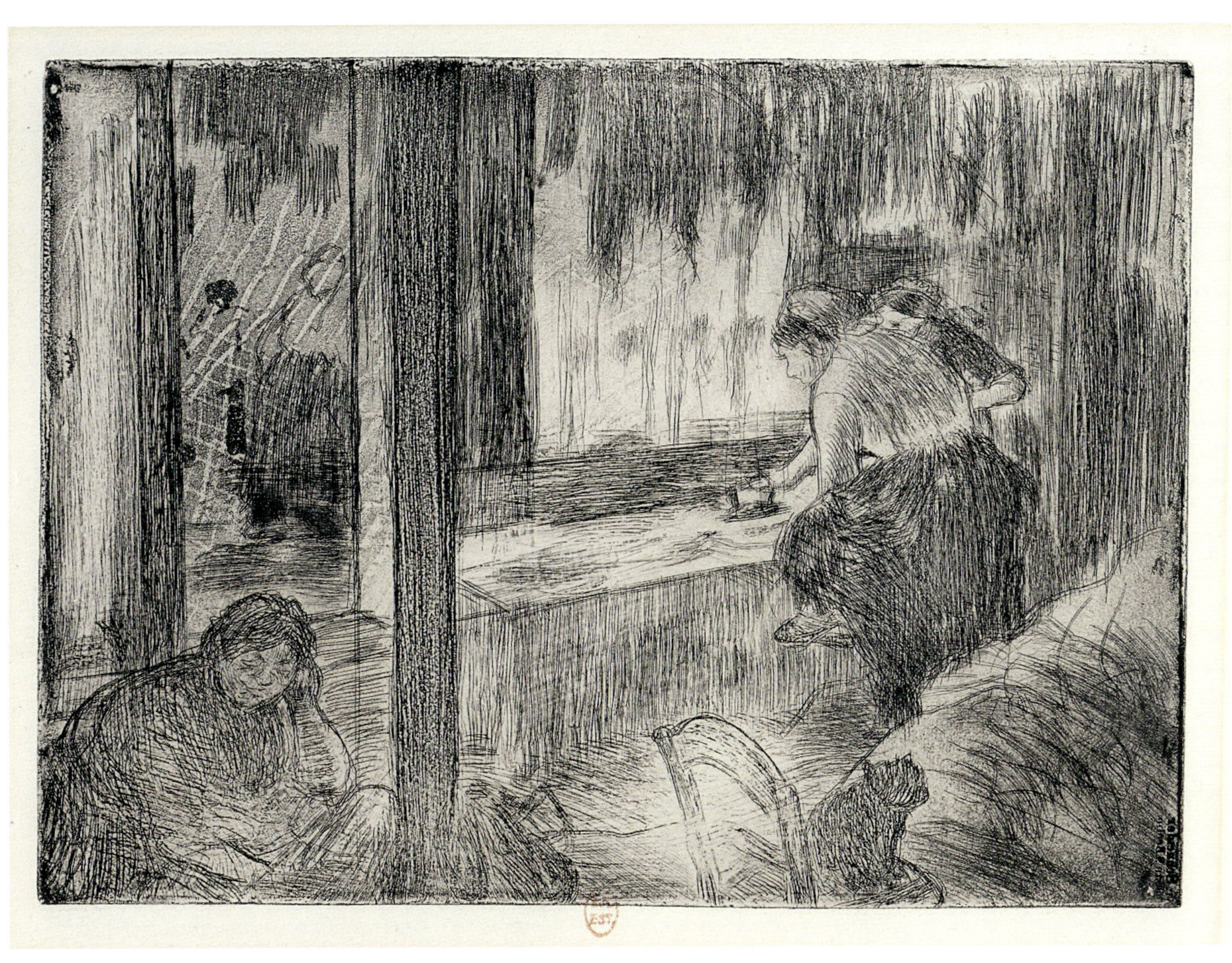

102 *Washerwomen* (*Les blanchisseuses*)
1879–80
fourth state of four
edition of eight
etching and aquatint
11.8 x 16 cm (plate)
Bibliothèque nationale de France, Paris
res Dc 327dh fol, boîte 5
Reed and Shapiro 48 / Adhémar 32

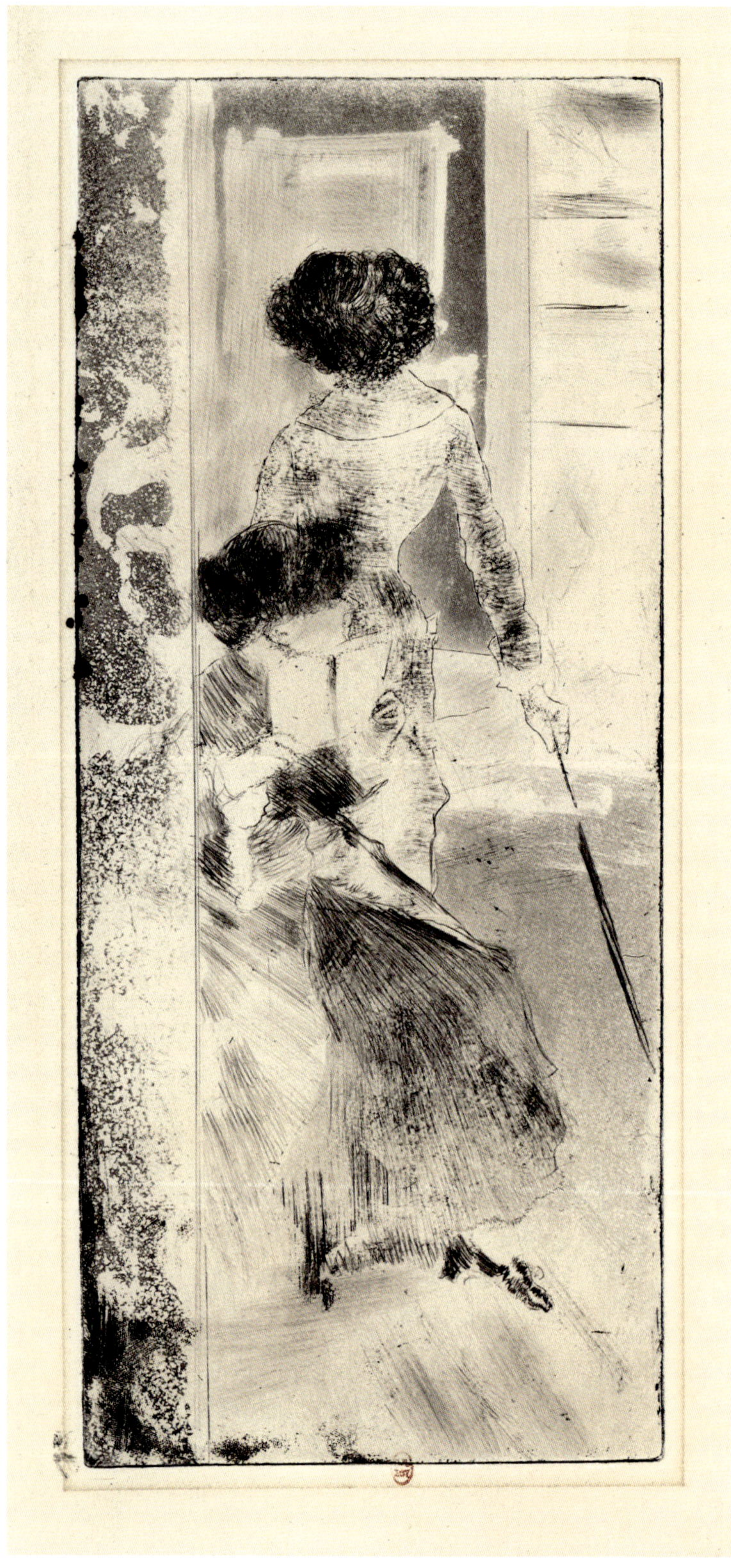

104

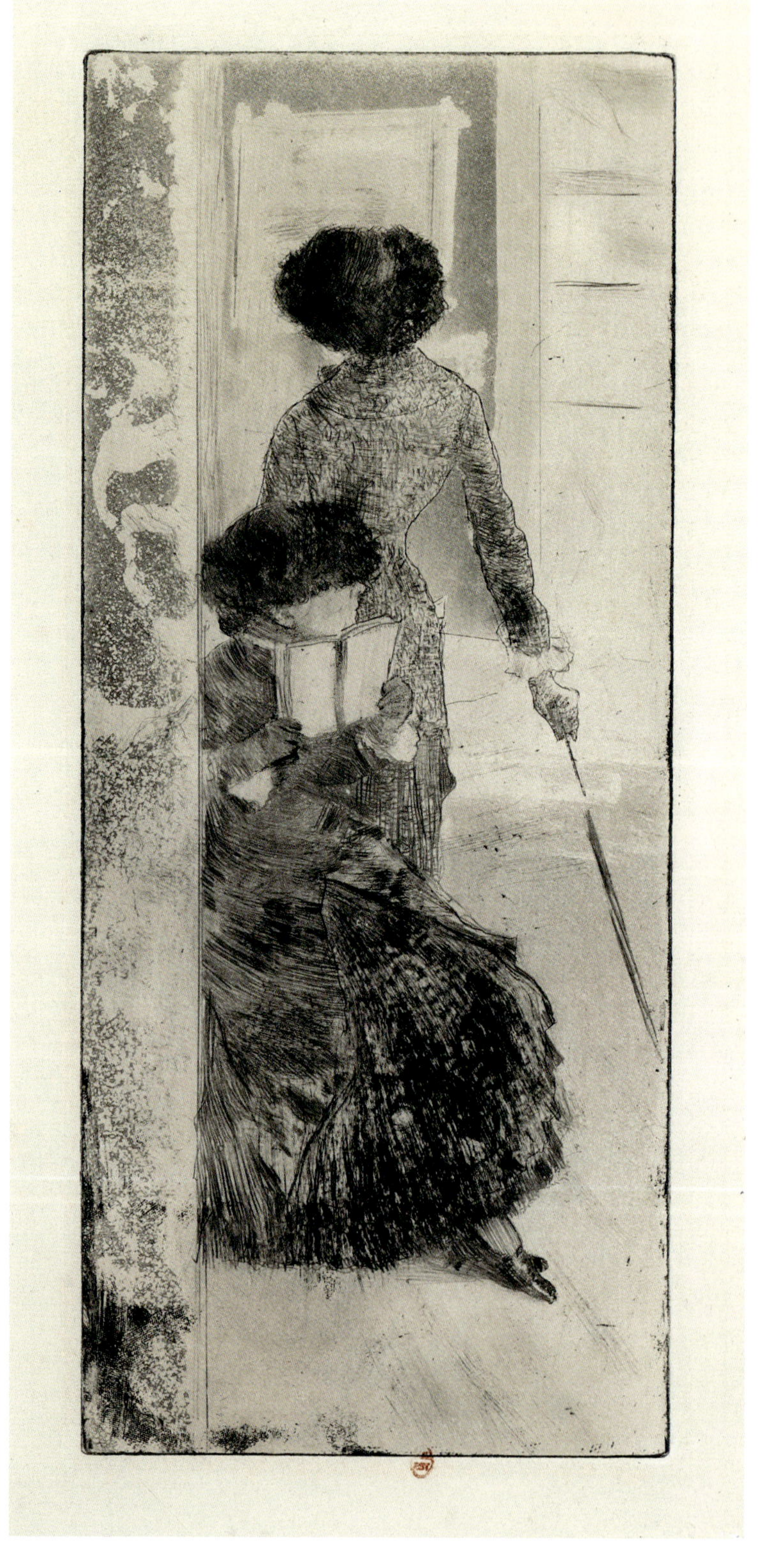

105

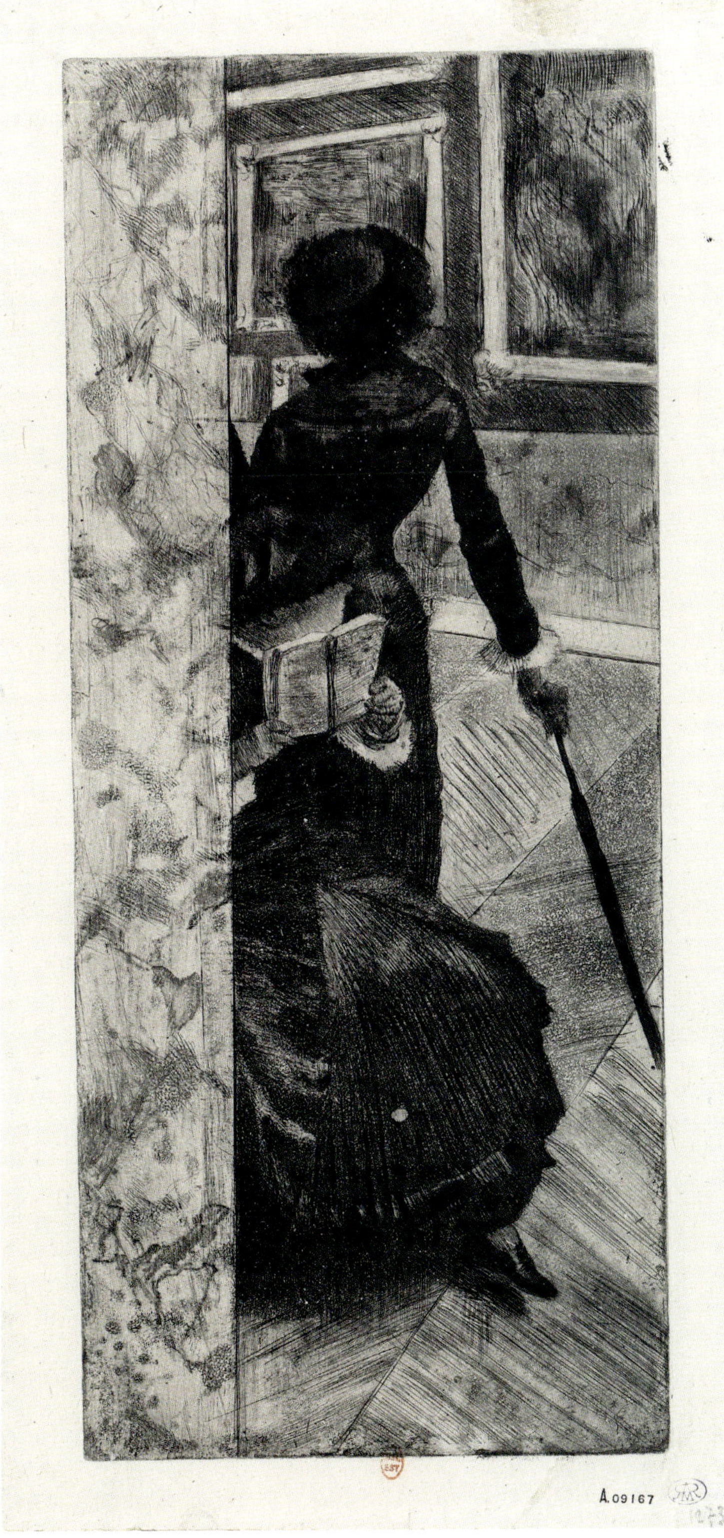

106

104 *Mary Cassatt in the Louvre, looking at paintings*
1879–80
first state of twenty
edition of one
etching, aquatint, drypoint and electric crayon
30.5 x 12.6 cm (plate), 41 x 24.8 cm (sheet)
Bibliothèque nationale de France, Paris
res Dc 327dh fol, boîte 6
Reed and Shapiro 52 / Adhémar 54

105 *Mary Cassatt in the Louvre, looking at paintings*
1879–80
second state of twenty
edition of one
etching, aquatint, drypoint and electric crayon
30.5 x 12.6 cm (plate), 41x 24cm (sheet)
Bibliothèque nationale de France, Paris
res Dc 327dh fol, boîte 6
Reed and Shapiro 52 / Adhémar 54

106 *Mary Cassatt in the Louvre, looking at paintings*
1879–80
tenth state of twenty
edition of two
etching, aquatint, drypoint and electric crayon
30.5 x 12.6 cm (plate), 39.2 x 27.7 cm (sheet)
Bibliothèque nationale de France, Paris
res Dc 327dh fol, boîte 6
Reed and Shapiro 52 / Adhémar 54

107 *Mary Cassatt in the Louvre, Museum of Antiquities*
1879–80
sixth state of nine
edition of one
etching, aquatint, drypoint and electric crayon
26.7 x 23 cm (plate), 43 x 30.6 cm (sheet)
Bibliothèque nationale de France, Paris
res Dc 327dh fol, boîte 5
Reed and Shapiro 51 / Adhémar 53

Mary Cassatt in the Louvre, looking at paintings (cats 104–106) and *Mary Cassatt in the Louvre, Museum of Antiquities* are clearly related prints, both showing the artist Mary Cassatt admiring work at the Musée du Louvre in Paris, with her sister Lydia seated behind her. Both works were traced onto their plates from the same drawing of the two figures (see p 249).[1] An established analysis of the preparatory sketch demonstrates that *Looking at paintings* came after *Museum of Antiquities*, although this has not been conclusively proven.[2]

Museum of Antiquities began as a print centred solely on the two figures, and it was not until the third state of the etching that Degas decided to place them in the setting of the Etruscan gallery. In the following states, the artist plays with the intensity of the print rather than changing the detail of the background. Similarly, the first two states of *Looking at paintings* have little background detail. However, throughout the 20 states of the print, the level and type of patterning on the pillar, floor and walls fluctuates considerably.

Both prints were undertaken as part of a journal that Degas proposed, following a small windfall produced from the fourth Impressionist exhibition in 1879. The planned journal, 'Le Jour et la nuit (Day and night)' was intended to comprise original prints by the artist and several of his Impressionist friends, including Mary Cassatt, Camille Pissarro and Marcellin Desboutin. Degas was characteristically late with his contribution—he made 20 states of *Looking at paintings*, more than most of his other prints. Consequently the publication never eventuated, much to the annoyance of the other artists. (Cassatt's mother noted that 'Degas is never ready for anything—this time he has thrown away an excellent chance for all of them'.[3]) The prints made by Cassatt, Pissarro and Degas were exhibited at the fifth Impressionist exhibition instead.[4]

Degas' admiration for Japanese prints has been well documented. At his death he had a large number of well-known *ukiyo-e* artists in his private collection. The series *Looking at paintings* has long been held to be Degas' most conscious work based on *hashira-e* prints, a form of *ukiyo-e* prints known as the 'pillar-picture format'. These were prints laid out in a scroll-like design which were hung on interior pillars as decoration. Although Degas' two prints are very similar in appearance, in *Looking at paintings* he has shortened the space between the two figures, overlapping them substantially, and elongated the image.

Notes

1 *Study for 'Mary Cassatt at the Louvre: the Etruscan Gallery'* c 1879, National Gallery of Art, Washington DC.
2 Sue Welsh Reed and Barbara Stern Shapiro, *Edgar Degas: the painter as printmaker*, Museum of Fine Arts, Boston, 1984, p 170; and Ronald Pickvance, 'Degas at the Hayward Gallery', *The Burlington Magazine*, vol 127, no 988, July 1985, p 476.
3 Quoted in Reed and Shapiro, p 169.
4 Reed and Shapiro, p 169.

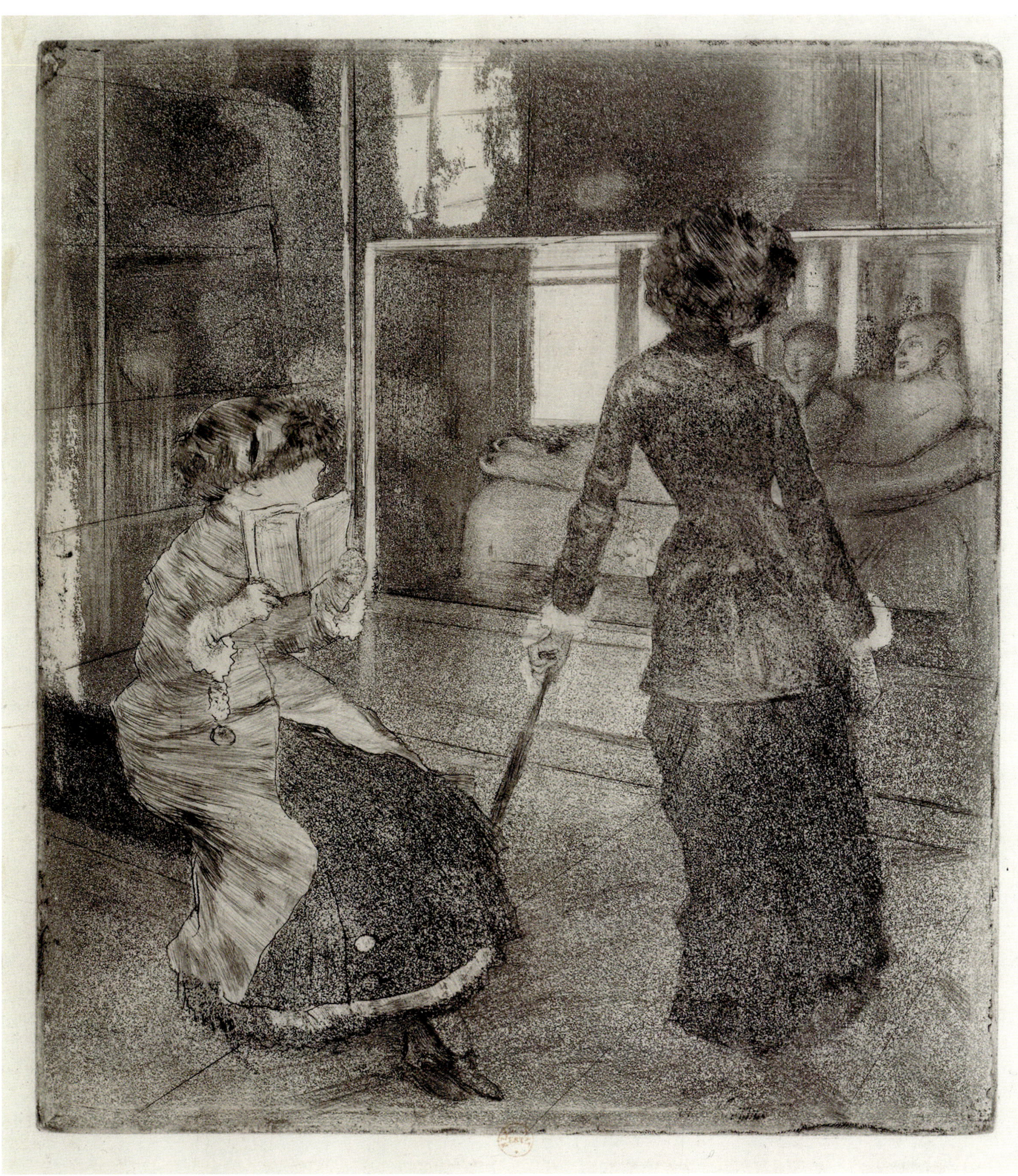

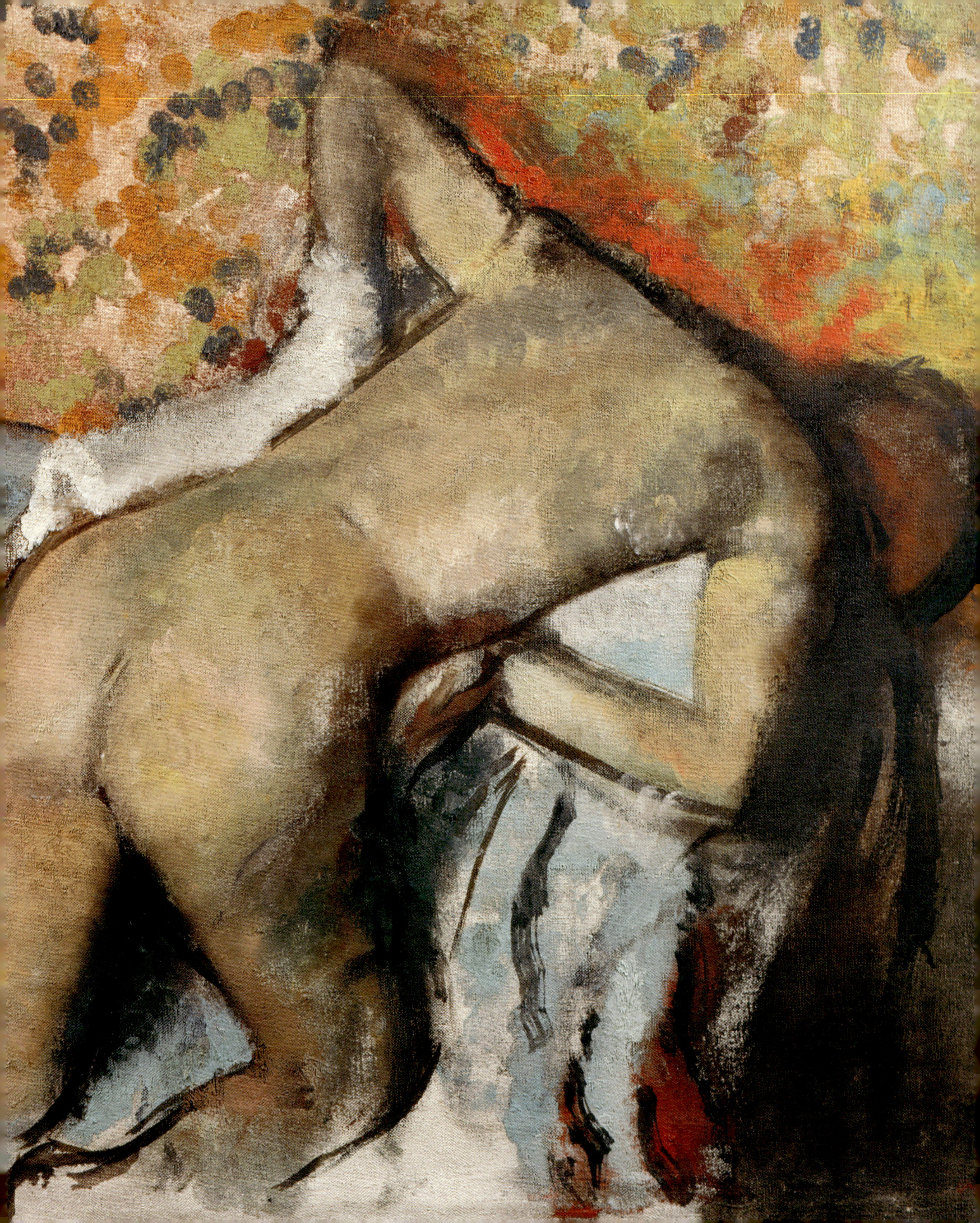

TOWARDS ABSTRACTION

IN HIS LAST YEARS, Degas was still actively making art, continuing the process of refining and distilling which had been his practice throughout his career; composing and recomposing; tracing and fusing the elements in his images. He continued to draw inspiration from the repertoire of images he had developed over the years, and to pursue variations and permutations of these images. One of his favourite subjects was the female bather—rendered from different viewpoints, with different backdrops, and with different attitudes of the body in a series of compositions; in etchings, lithographs and drawings, as well as the three-dimensional form of wax models. Here we have women washing or drying themselves, or having their hair combed, or getting in and out of the tub.

In a series of lithographs of the nude figure produced in the early 1890s, Degas shows a woman washing or drying herself, sometimes accompanied by an attendant. He depicts her in a simplified, unadorned manner, without drapery or jewellery, concentrating on mass and on silhouette. A particular prompt for this group of works was Eugène Delacroix's painting *Entry of the crusaders into Constantinople* 1840. As a young man, Degas had made a study in oil of this work in about 1859–60 (cat 4).[1] The semi-nude crouching female figure in Delacroix's composition, viewed from behind and with her hair cascading over her head, reappeared three decades later in these lithographs. In an earlier, beautifully finished pastel of c 1886 a woman with flowing hair is seated on a plump chaise longue, while her hair is combed by an attendant—this work may have been shown at the eighth Impressionist exhibition in 1886.[2]

(previous page)
After the bath, woman drying herself
1895
(detail cat 125)

(right)
Kitagawa Utamaro
Girl dressing a companion's hair
from the series *Twelve types of women's handicraft* c 1797–98
nishiki-e (woodblock print);
ink and colour on paper
38 x 27.6 cm (image and sheet)
Art Gallery of South Australia, Adelaide
South Australian Government Grant 1983

Degas revisited this motif with skill and apparent effortlessness in the late 1880s and early 1890s, in a variety of mediums, inspired in part by Japanese woodblock prints, *ukiyo-e*—particularly Kitagawa Utamaro's *Girl dressing a companion's hair* c 1800, which was in his collection.[3] In a lithograph made around 1891, Degas transforms the motif by using lithographic tusche vigorously brushed directly onto celluloid, which he then transferred onto the stone (cat 120). The presence of the woman is indicated by an elegant, minimal flourish signifying a tress of her hair.

In these later years, Degas embraced the use of charcoal, sometimes highlighted with pastel or crayon, and he traced and retraced his work. While he may have abandoned the strict approach of the great master of the nude figure, Jean-Auguste-Dominique Ingres, he continued to pursue his drawing, taking it to another level. These later drawings were no longer the careful, delicate studies that were sometimes preliminary works for a larger painting—such as his charcoal and pastel drawing *Dancer scratching her back* c 1873–74 (cat 54).[4] Rather, Degas produced some monumental, almost Amazonian figures with broad sweeps of his charcoal, rejecting an obvious display of dexterity for a powerful and spirited approach—such as we have in the robust figure of the nude seated on the rim of the bath tub, drying her toes against a backdrop of blue, in *The bath* 1895 (or before) (cat 123).

As indicated, Degas was an artist of great practical virtuosity, whose natural bent was to explore technical advances as well as seeking to understand traditional methods of making art. Denis Rouart—who was both a painter and a collector, and the grandson of Degas' friend Henri Rouart—devoted a book to this aspect of Degas' practice: *Degas in search of his technique* (first published in 1945). In his introduction, Rouart wrote of the testing time for the nineteenth-century artist, with academic teaching replacing the traditional apprenticeship where artists were introduced to the painter's craft—and he laid the blame 'in part' at the feet of the French Neoclassical artist Jacques-Louis David:

> One must remember that at that time the painter's craft was passing though a critical period. The tradition of

> apprenticeship had already been much compromised during the course of the eighteenth century and ended by disappearing completely at the century's close. David only aggravated this condition by his desire to make a tabula rasa of all that had been produced previously. He did not limit his reformist's ardor to choice and composition of subject, nor to a style of drawing and painting, but expanded it to encompass technique. Claiming to scorn his masters' teaching in this area even though he had used it so successfully himself, he did not believe it his duty to transmit this baggage to his students. He is in part responsible for the academicism which during the nineteenth century came to replace the teaching of craft in the studio-workshops.[5]

In his own discussion of the parlous state of French art, Degas exclaimed to the young artist Georges Rouault: 'We paint like pigs.'[6]

Artists such as Delacroix, Manet and Cézanne, all sought to discover the painter's craft as practised by the old masters. This was also an important mission for Degas, and throughout his life he searched for ways to perfect his techniques and to innovate, embarking on various forays—at times using tempera, gouache, pastel, painting with essence on oiled papers, and making monotypes. Towards the end of his life, his study of the working methods of the Venetian artists, Paolo Veronese and Titian, became an obsession.[7]

From around 1890, Degas began to change his method of underpainting—exchanging the application of tints in black and brown, which he had employed earlier, for rich greens, reds, purples oranges and yellows—colours that he also used for his late monotypes and pastels. The change in colour affected a change in his technique. Richard Kendall has made the observation that: 'This eruption of colour had similarly radical implications for his painting in oil, challenging the precedence of drawing, subverting form with hue and compromising a lifetime's fidelity to Degas' solemn idol, Jean-Dominique Ingres.'[8]

The later oil paintings and pastels—such as *A group of dancers* 1890s (cat 76), and *Dancer with bouquets* 1895–1900 (cat 77) —are characterised by the adoption of a new shimmering colour: brilliant greens, Titian reds, sulphuric yellows and moody purples, found in his luminous paintings of dancers, where colour and line are fused. In these works the application of paint is more summary.

Degas also began to apply paint with his hands, in the manner of Titian. In Rouart's essay on Degas' painting techniques the author notes that in the case of Titian,

> [w]hen there were large surfaces to glaze, he worked with all fingers or with the flat of his hand … But if Titian occasionally uses his fingers, and he isn't the only one, it certainly appears that Degas was the first to make a much more systematic use of them to execute the underpainting on his canvas.[9]

What may have begun as underpainting also came to be a means of creating texture on the surface, along with the use of broad brushstrokes. Degas would apply dabs of colour on the surface of a painting—as in *After the bath, woman drying herself* c 1895 (cat 125), with the effect of rendering the bather almost as an abstract form.

Over many years, Degas had acquired a collection of other artists' works. As his failing eyesight deteriorated, he became less and less an active practitioner and more a serious collector of the efforts of others. He amassed an extraordinary collection, including important works by Ingres and Delacroix, as well as some of his contemporaries.[10] One of these, Paul Gauguin, had been helped in his development by Degas. In his later years, Degas came to admire Gauguin's work, marvelling at his application of colour, moody atmosphere and the evocation of exotic worlds. Before Gauguin left for Tahiti in 1891, Degas began to acquire an extensive collection of his paintings, woodcuts and monotypes. Gauguin's influence becomes apparent in Degas' vividly coloured and simplified compositions, such as *The return of the herd* c 1898 (cat 24).[11] This scene of cattle ambling through a village lane at twilight is painted with a brilliant palette of mauves and yellows tempered by the evening light, so that the animals and the village buildings coalesce into simplified shapes.

As Degas matured as an artist, his art revealed a greater intimacy and informality and, in the case of his paintings, a more brilliant palette and looser brushwork. His astonishing landscape monotypes of the 1890s, shown in his exhibition at the Durand-Ruel Gallery in 1892, consist of almost abstract elements rendered in unusual acid colours of greens and yellows. As in the case of his earlier forays into making figurative monotypes (which had an influence on his art more generally), so too the monotypes of landscapes impacted on his art in the 1890s in terms of technique and palette (only to take a brief respite with his interest in black and white photography). Degas' nudes, in their simplified shapes and limited palette, took on an abstract form, though in this regard Degas has been overlooked in some art histories. This later work can now be considered as prescient of subsequent developments in twentieth-century art. Unlike Monet, he cannot necessarily be viewed as an obvious stepping-stone

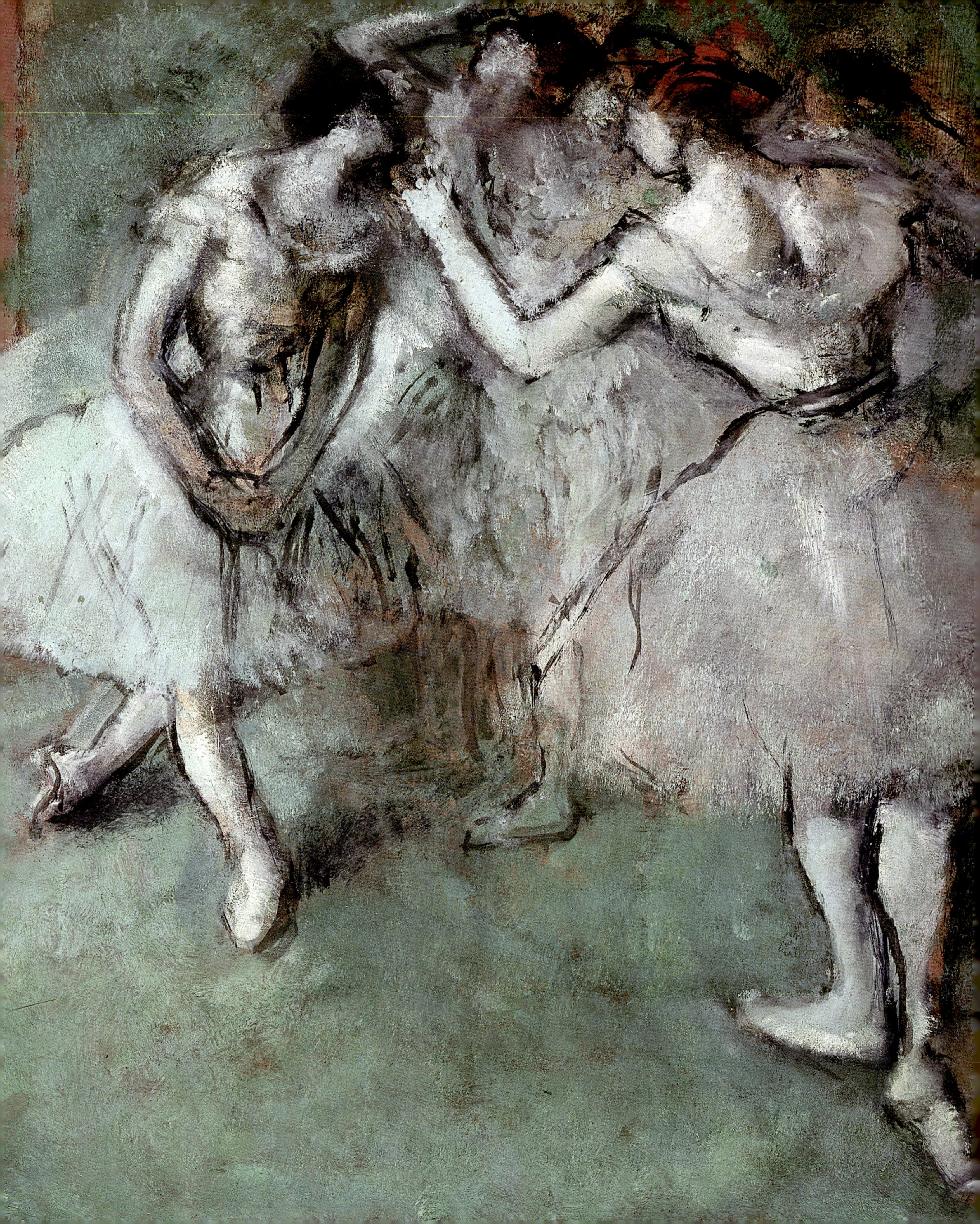

towards the new major style of Abstract Expressionism. Yet his work was admired and collected by Picasso and Matisse; and his body of work, with its range and inventiveness, and his openness to other artists' work from whatever tradition he studied, ranks him as a key contributor in the evolution of modern art in the twentieth century.

As Paul Valéry astutely observed, Degas was:

> An uneasy participant in the tragicomedy of Modern Art, mad about drawing, divided against himself; on the one hand driven by an acute preoccupation with *Truth*, eager for all the newly introduced and more or less felicitous ways of seeing things and of painting them; on the other hand possessed by a rigorous spirit of classicism, to whose principles of elegance, simplicity and style he devoted a lifetime of analysis … Degas seemed to me the epitome of the pure artist … [12]

Notes

1 *Copy after Delacroix's 'Entry of the crusaders into Constantinople'* c 1860 (cat 4); Kunsthaus, Zurich, Brame and Reff 35. See Richard Thomson, *The private Degas*, Arts Council of Great Britain, London, 1987, for this observation and many other proposed sources which Degas drew upon. Degas continued with this motif in the later painting. Nude women with tumbling hair were featured in Degas' early painting, *Scene of war in the middle ages* c 1863–65, Musée d'Orsay, Paris, Lemoisne 124.

2 *Nude woman having her hair combed*, c 1886–88, Metropolitan Museum of Art, New York, Lemoisne 847. For the discussion whether this was included, see Garry Tinterow in Joan Sutherland Boggs et al, *Degas*, Metropolitan Museum of Art and National Gallery of Canada, New York and Ottawa, 1988, p 453, n 1.

3 Jill DeVonyar and Richard Kendall, *Degas and the art of Japan*, Reading Public Museum and Yale University Press, Reading, New Haven and London, 2007, pp 82–83, fig 82.

4 Musée du Louvre, Département des Arts Graphiques, Fonds du Musée Orsay, Paris. This drawing was preparatory for the oil painting *The dance class*, begun 1873, finished 1875–76, Musée d'Orsay, Paris, Lemoisne 341.

5 Denis Rouart, *Degas in search of his technique*, Pia C DeSantis, Sarah L Fisher and Shelley Fletcher (trans), Rizzoli, New York, 1988, p 9.

6 They met after the museum had opened in January 1903, where Rouault was a curator. Edgar Degas, quoted in Richard Kendall, *Degas: beyond Impressionism*, National Gallery Publications, London, 1996, p 65. Kendall devotes a chapter on the subject, 'The metaphor of craft', at pp 57–87. See also Georges Rouault, *Degas: souvenirs intimes, L'Intransgeant*, 9 March 1937, p 37.

7 Kendall 1996, pp 113–123 outlines the important changes that took place.

8 Kendall 1996, p 114.

9 Rouart 1988, p 80.

10 For an analysis of Degas as a collector, see Ann Dumas, Colta Ives, Susan Alyson Stein et al, *The private collection of Edgar Degas*, The Metropolitan Museum of Art, New York, 1998.

11 Leicestershire Museums and Art Galleries, Leicester; Lemoisne 1213. For Degas' collection of works by Gauguin, see Colta Ives, Susan Alyson Stein and Julie A Steiner et al, cat nos 480–503.

12 Paul Valéry, *Degas: Manet: Morisot*, David Paul (trans), Pantheon Books, New York, 1960, p 64.

(opposite)
A group of dancers 1890s
(detail cat 76)

108 *The little dressing room*
(*Le petit cabinet de toilette*)
1879–80
fifth state of five
edition of four
drypoint
11.9 x 7.9 cm (plate), 30 x 21.5 cm (sheet)
The British Museum, London
1949,0411.2420
Reed and Shapiro 41

This composition is unusual, as it combines the theme of the brothel and the bather. The first version or state of this etching has a young woman, nude and in profile, washing herself at a basin. By this fifth and final state, the subject has undergone a metamorphosis—the young woman wears nothing but a choker and a bracelet. She gazes into a mirror which reflects the elaborate floral wallpaper of the boudoir. In the earlier states, what was just a hint of a patron has been converted into a dark figure lurking in the corner of the room in the foreground. He is dressed in a top hat and coat and seated on a plump divan. In this work Degas has used the technique of drypoint, in which a hard metal needle is used to scratch into the plate, throwing up a burr which holds ink and adds richness to the printed line.

At the same time as his return to printmaking, Degas began experimenting with monotypes. If this experimentation with monotypes (or 'painterly prints') affected his painting, it also influenced his methods of printmaking. Degas became more interested in creating richly worked impressions, rather than the carefully inked and wiped uniform editions which had been promoted in the reference book *Etching revival* by Alfred Cadart a decade previously.

Degas gave *The little dressing room* drypoint to the artist Camille Pissarro: the two men had worked together making experimental etchings which were rich in texture and inking. Pissarro's son Lucien subsequently sold the impression to the noted print collector Campbell Dodgson, of the Department of Prints and Drawings at the British Museum.[1]

Note

1 Dodgson went on to become Keeper, a role he held from 1912 until 1932.

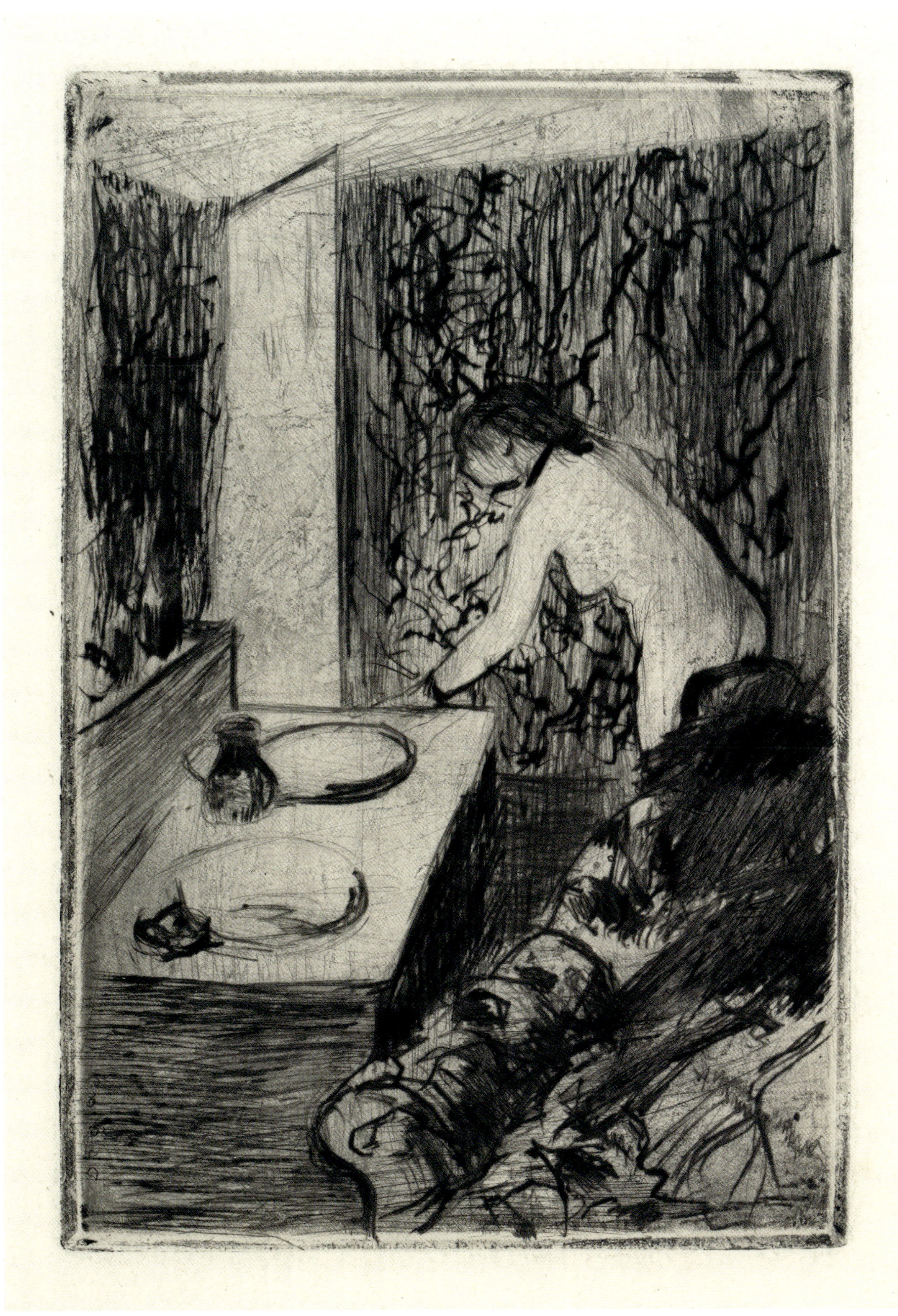

Degas and variations on a theme

Degas made an astonishing 22 versions of *Getting out of the bath*. He developed the compositions from relatively simple ones, to ones that were thoroughly complex; he then returned to a more simplified version for the last and twenty-second state. The process signals Degas' interest in exploring, almost endlessly, variations of his imagery.

The outline for this work was drawn using drypoint, and the various changes in texture and details were made using aquatint. Unlike some other compositions, Degas did not draw this bather from a nude model; rather it was a product of his mind, as he imagined rather wickedly how a certain woman of Parisian society might look: 'Our friend Mme X must look like this when she gets out of the bath.'[1]

The sequence of the multiple versions began simply as a woman getting out of her bath while her maid holds up a large towel to wrap her mistress in. As the states changed, elements of furniture, walls, floors, mirrors, vases and flowers were added and then taken away. Lines and tones were altered. Textures were embellished and then refined. The second state is a simple version of the subject. The eighth state has more emphasis on the decorative design of the vases, which now hold floral arrangements; the chairs, the walls, the doors and the tufts of the carpet are provided with more detail. The ninth state further embellishes the walls, now covered with rich floral wallpaper, and the decorative elements of the chairs and the vases.

Denis Rouart provides an account of how Degas came to make this print, when visiting the home of Rouart's grandfather: 'One evening a heavy frost had prevented Degas from returning home after dinner with Alexis Rouart, and the artist had to stay overnight with his friend. In the morning [he] expressed the desire to make a print; his host lived next door to his factory [and] found the gas carbon rod there which enabled Degas to etch the copper he had been given.'[2]

The adoption of new tools was something that appealed to Degas, and in a letter to Alexis Rouart he expressed his delight in discovering new techniques such as scratching the copper plate with emery pencils and applying a carbon rod to achieve a pretty grey. This correspondence, dated by Guerin to 1882, has more recently been dated to the time of the making of this print.[3]

Two of these works have an interesting provenance. Cat 109 was owned by Alexis Rouart and cat 111 by Campbell Dodgson.

Notes

1 Quoted in Richard Thomson, *Degas: the nudes*, Thames & Hudson, London, 1988, p 82.

2 Denis Rouart, *Degas in search of his techniques*, Rizzoli International Publications, New York, 1988, p 115.

3 Sue Welsh Reed and Barbara Stern Shapiro, *Edgar Degas: the painter as printmaker*, Museum of Fine Arts, Boston, 1984, pp 125–26.

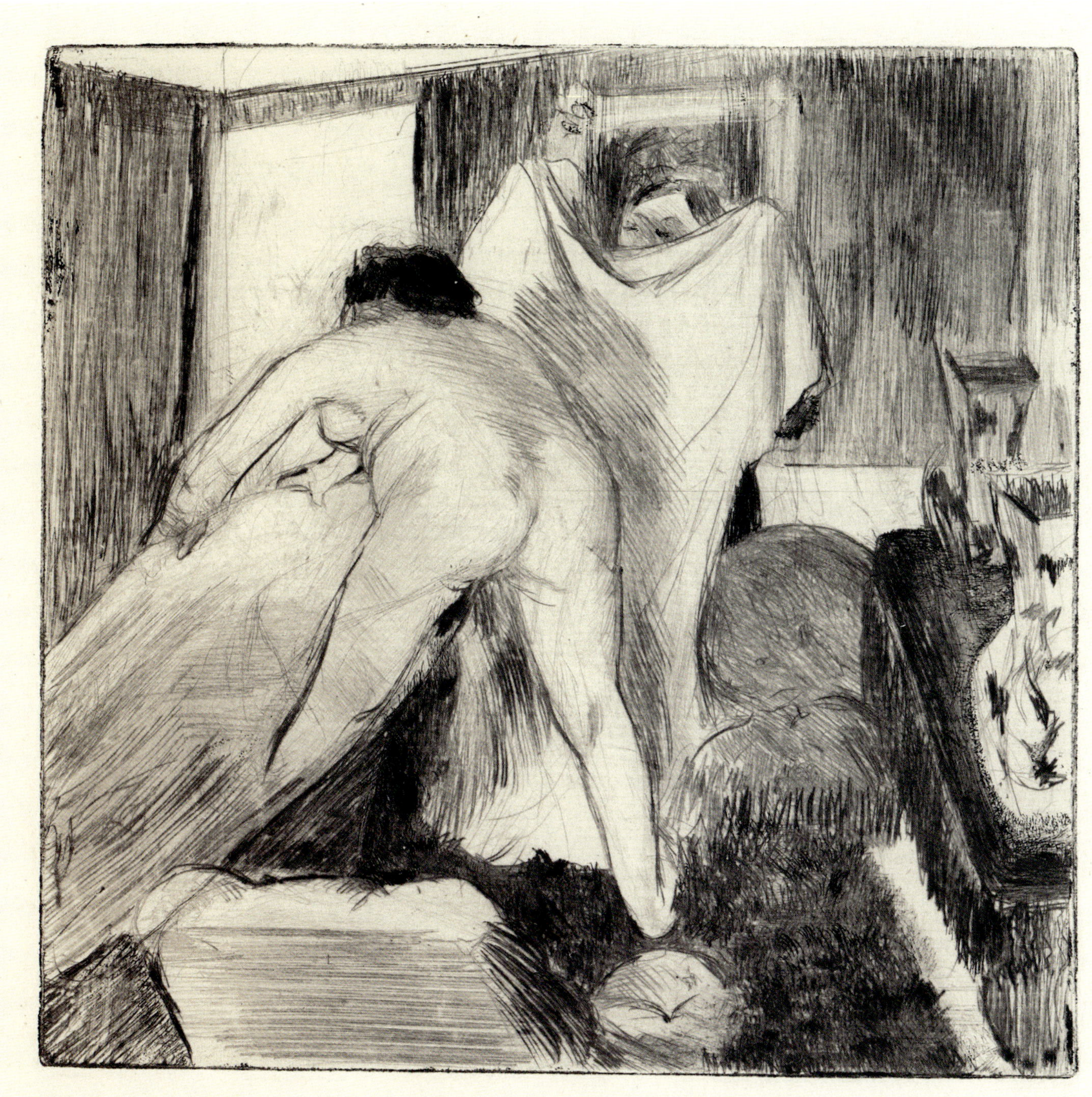

109 *Getting out of the bath* (*La sortie du bain*)
1879–80
third state of twenty two
edition of three
drypoint and aquatint
12.7 x 12.7 cm (plate), 29.7 x 21.6 cm (sheet)
National Gallery of Australia, Canberra
2008.182
The Poynton Bequest, 2008
Reed and Shapiro 42

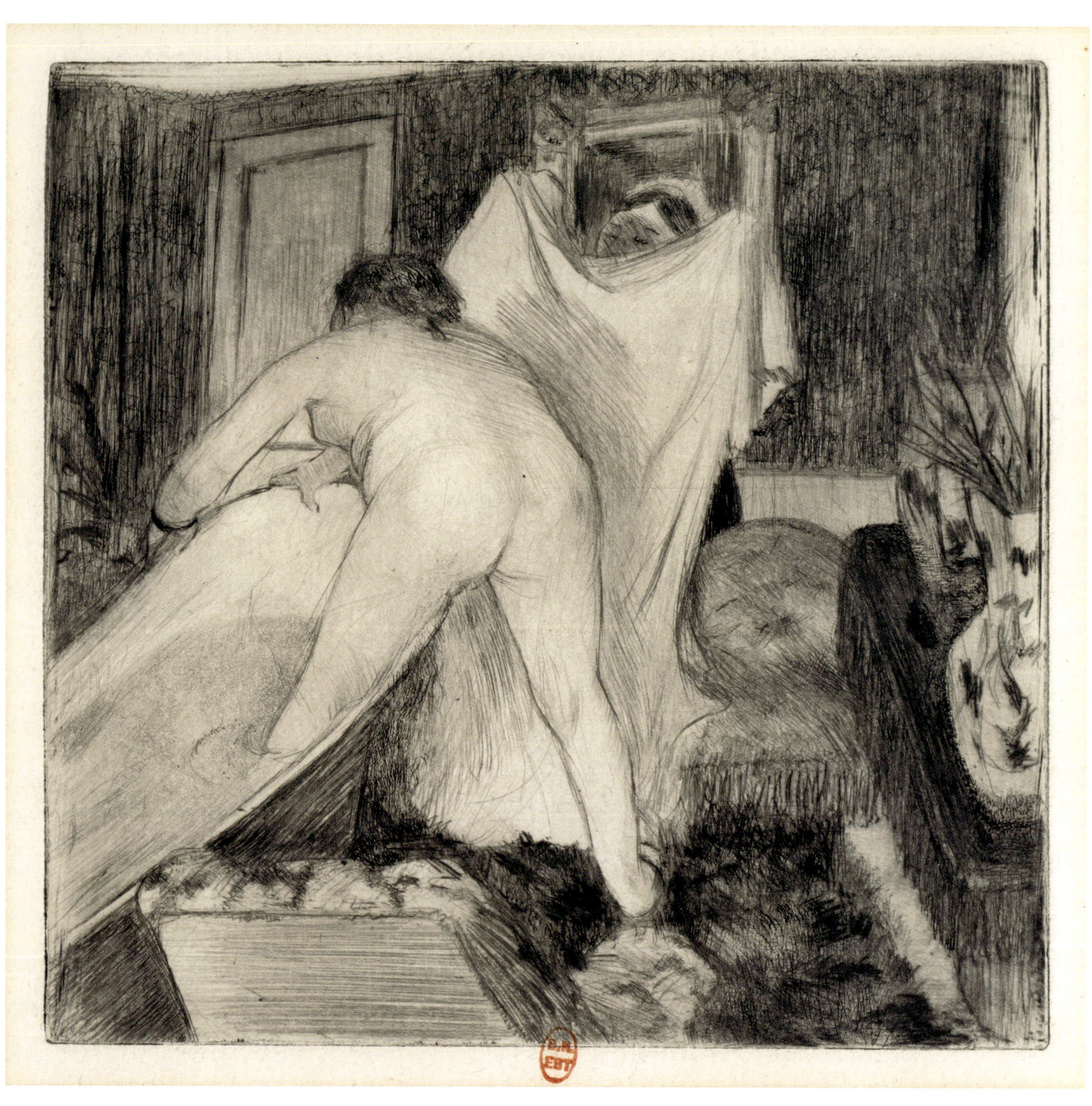

110 *Getting out of the bath* (*La sortie du bain*)
1879–80
eighth state of twenty two
edition of one
drypoint and aquatint
12.7 x 12.9 cm (plate), 29.7 x 21.6 cm (sheet)
Bibliothèque nationale de France, Paris
Reed and Shapiro 42

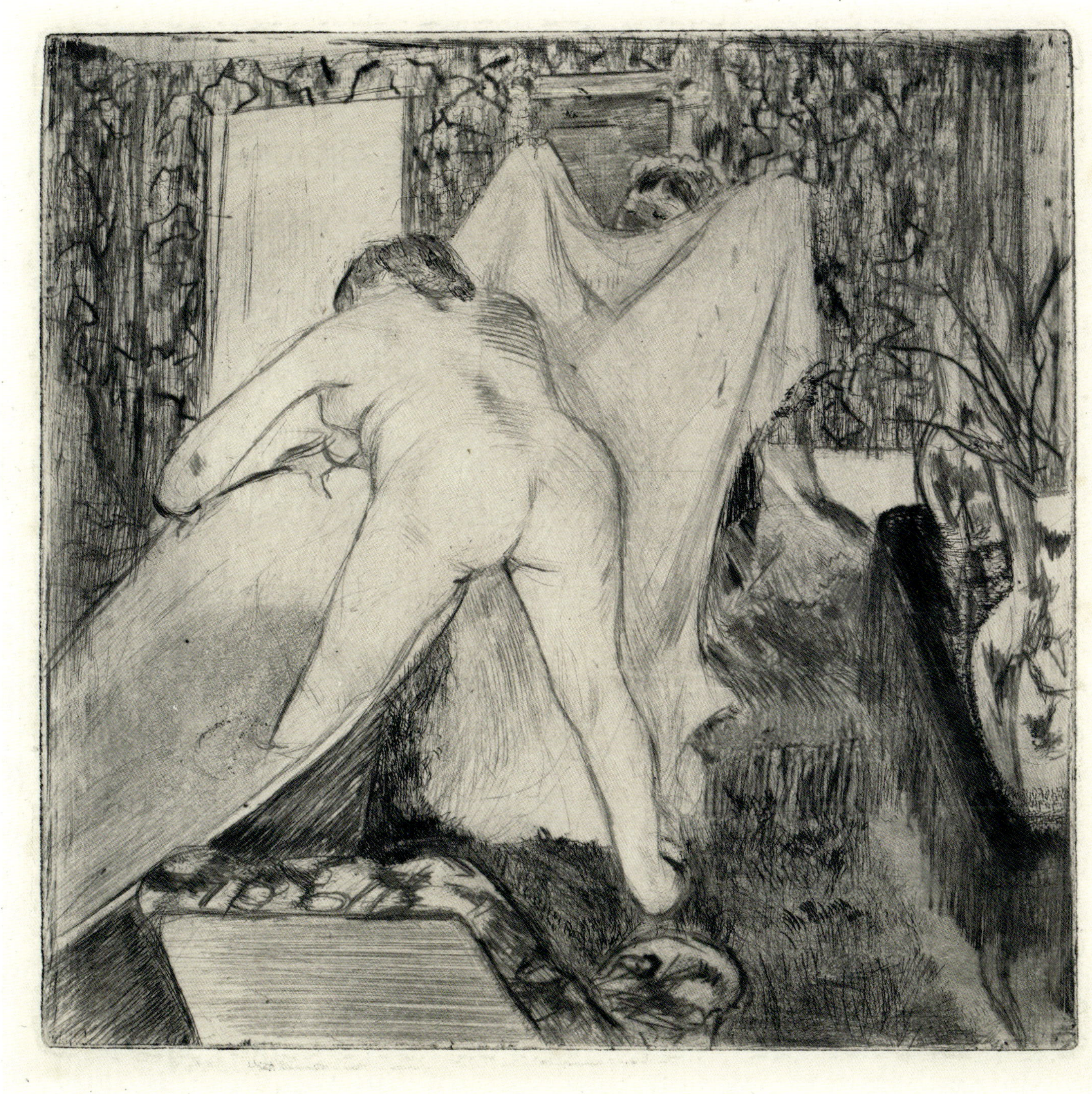

111 *Getting out of the bath* (*La sortie du bain*)
1879–80
ninth state of twenty two
edition of two
drypoint and aquatint
12.7 x 12.9 cm (plate), 29.7 x 21.6 cm (sheet)
The British Museum, London
1949, 0411.2421
Reed and Shapiro 42

Degas and lithography

Lithography is a printing process where the artist draws directly onto a stone, or onto transfer paper from which an image is transferred to a stone. The drawing medium is a greasy substance called tusche, in the form of a crayon or a liquid applied with a brush. To print the image, the stone's surface is dampened with water, which remains only on the unmarked areas, since water is repelled by the greasy tusche. Printing ink is rolled over the surface, and adheres only to the drawn marks. Paper is placed face down onto the stone and substantial pressure is applied using a lithographic press.

The technique of lithography has had a chequered career with artists. Invented in 1796, it was promoted in the first half of the nineteenth century as an art form. By mid-century, however, lithography, particularly colour lithography, had fallen into disrepute. It had come to be associated with cheap, poor-quality, mass-produced prints, and many artists shunned the technique and turned to etching for their original prints.

In the 1870s, perhaps inspired by Honoré Daumier, Degas had explored the use of lithography in such works as his portrait of Mademoiselle Bécat (cat 80). Lithography underwent a revival as an artist's medium in the 1890s, and Degas was one of many who embraced the process, as it allowed for the immediacy of drawing directly onto the stone or onto transfer paper. In 1891 the artist planned to make a suite of lithographs of nude dancers, and of nudes at their toilette.

Degas made six states of *Nude woman at her toilette, standing*, experimenting with techniques, inkings and croppings, and with details of his motifs. In the fourth state, the woman's long hair tumbles over her face (an element originally derived from Delacroix's drawings—see p 255). In this state Degas has cropped the background of floral wallpaper and the chaise longue (with hairpieces) in the foreground. In the sixth and final state, Degas concentrates on the figure of the woman, rather than the room she is in, and has removed details of the wallpaper and the chaise, including the background and the hairpieces.

In *After the bath III* (cats 114 and 115), Degas has reversed the image. In the first state the artist has added the detail of the maid about to wrap her mistress in a bathrobe, which appeared in his earlier drypoint of the subject *Getting out of the bath* (cat 109). For the second and final state, Degas' focus is solely on the bather. He has cropped the composition, and the maid and anything else which he thought extraneous. He was sufficiently pleased with this version to have it printed in an edition of 11.

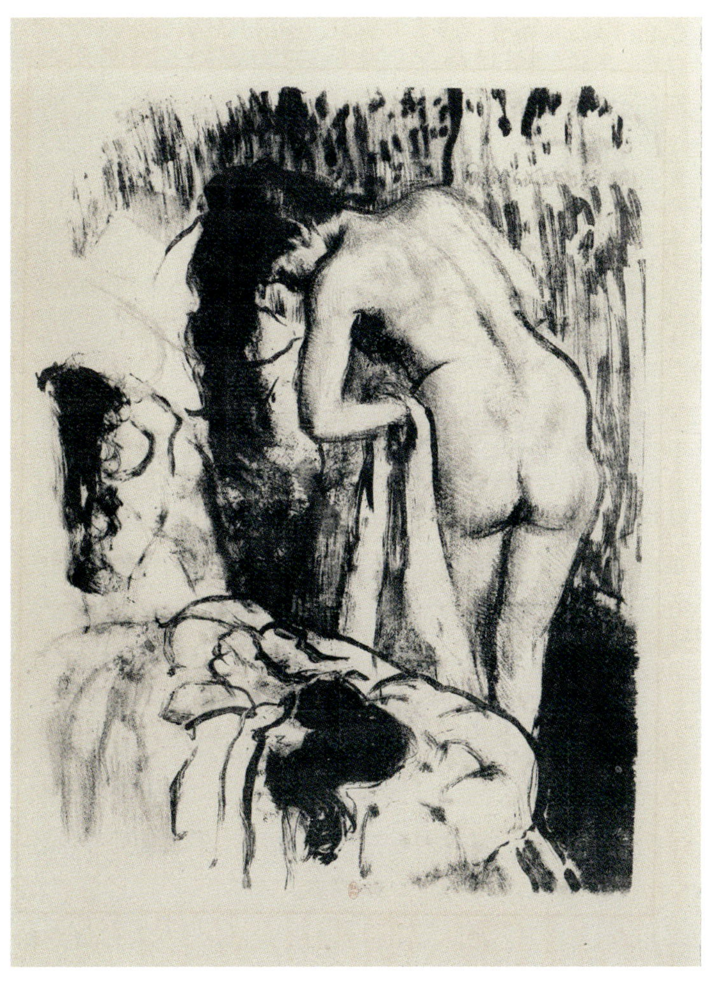

112 *Nude woman at her toilette, standing*
(*Femme nue debout à sa toilette*)
1891–92
fourth state of six
edition of twenty
lithograph
33 x 24.5 cm (stone), 45.5 x 29.3 cm (sheet)
Bibliothèque nationale de France, Paris
Reed and Shapiro 61

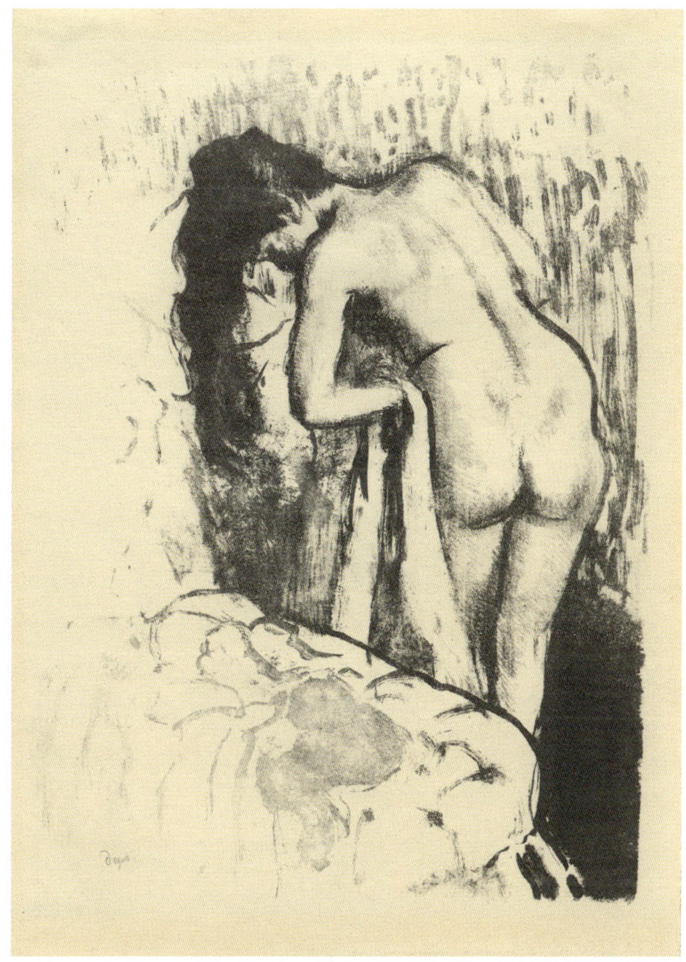

113 *Nude woman at her toilette, standing*
(Femme nue debout à sa toilette)
c 1890
sixth state of six
lithograph
33.3 x 24.5 cm (stone)
Tony and Carol Berg
Reed and Shapiro 61

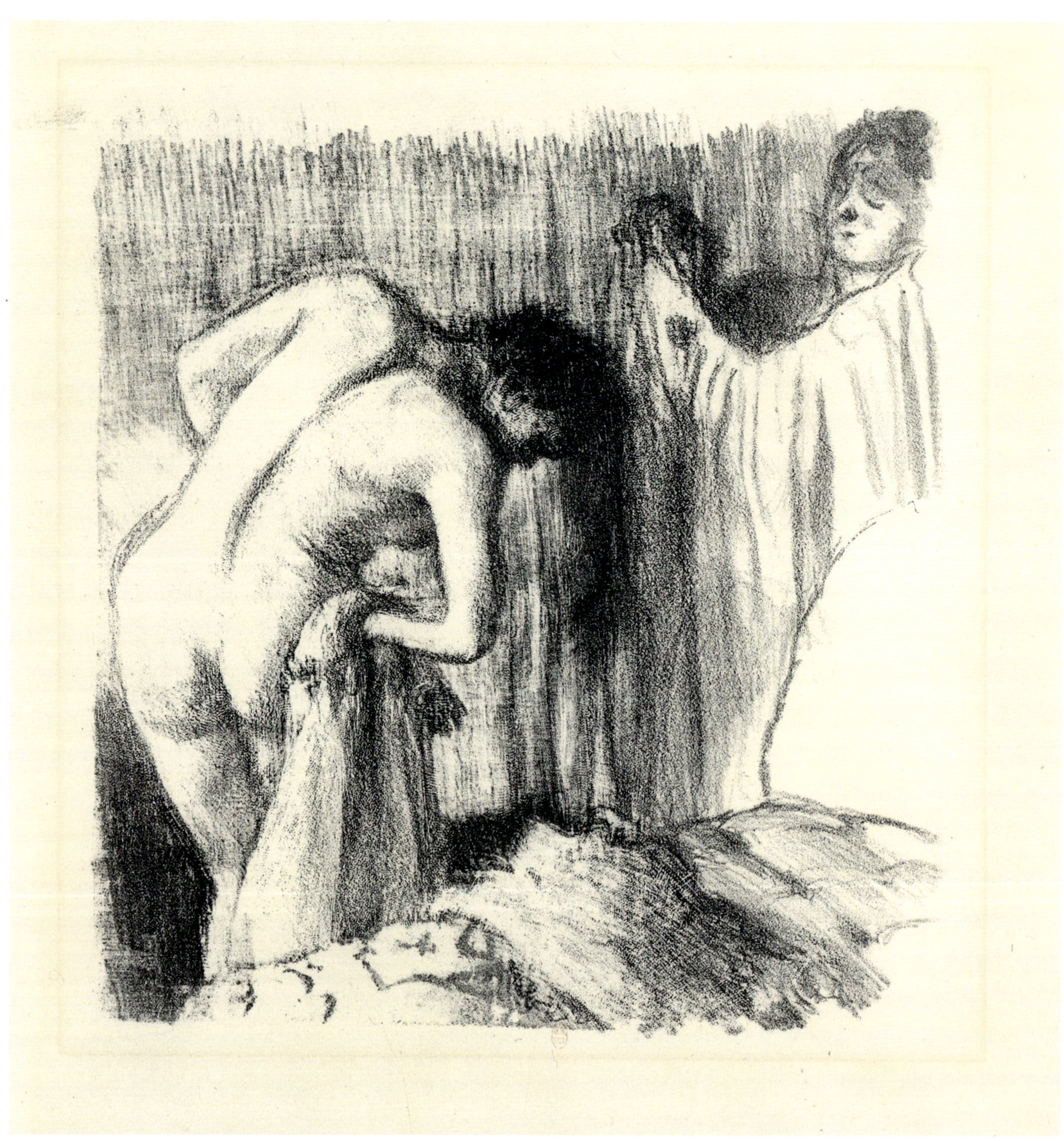

114 *After the bath III* (*Après le bain III*)
1891–92
first state of two
edition of twenty
lithograph on textured cream laid paper
25 x 23 cm (image), 29 x 23.5 cm (stone), 34.4 x 26.7 cm (sheet)
Bibliothèque nationale de France, Paris
Reed and Shapiro 65

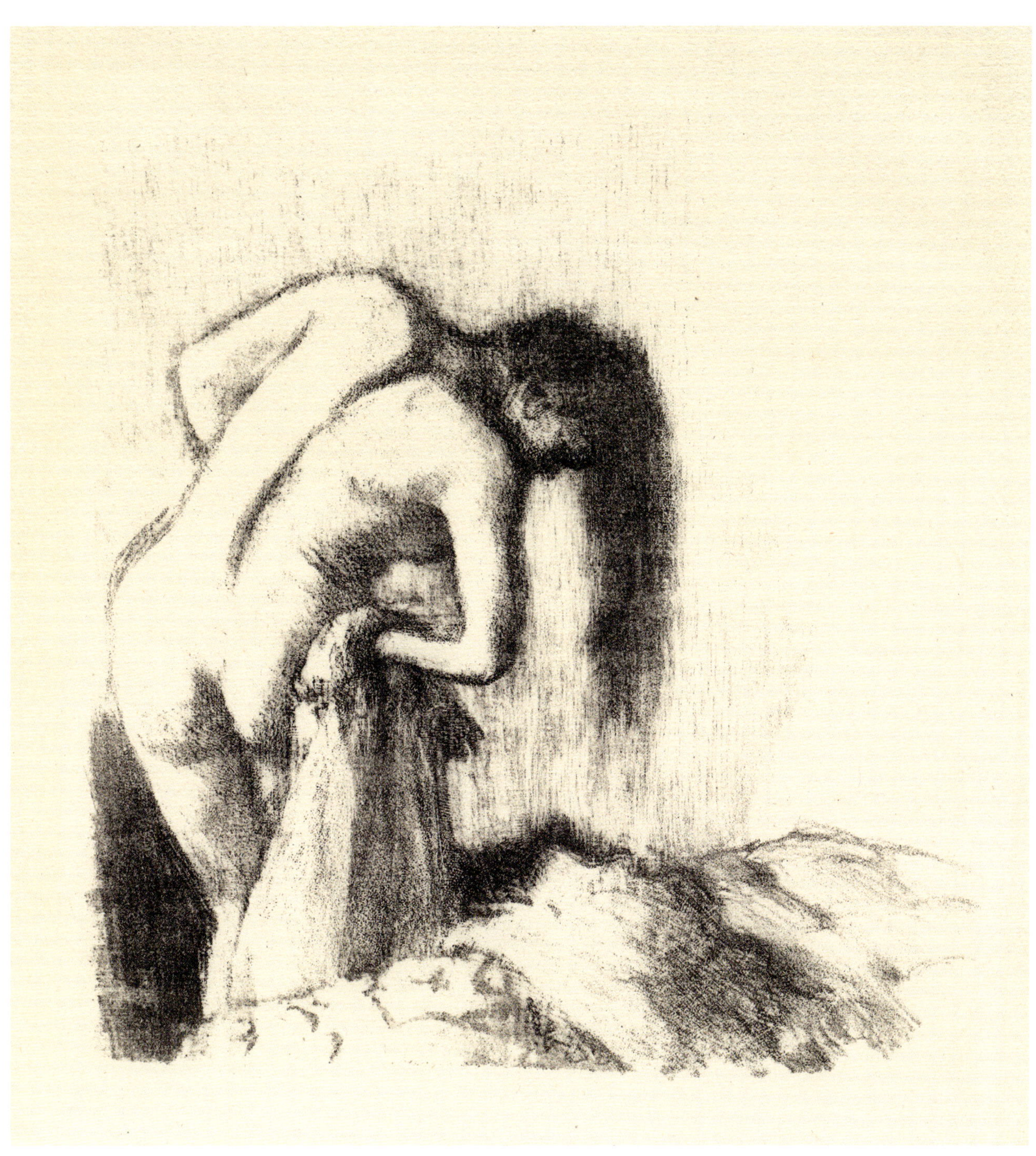

115 *After the bath III* (*Après le bain III*)
1891–92
second state of two
edition of twelve
lithograph on textured cream laid paper
25 x 23 cm (image), 29 x 23.5 cm (stone), 34.4 x 26.7 cm (sheet)
National Gallery of Australia, Canberra
2007.8
The Poynton Bequest 2007
Reed and Shapiro 65

Women at their toilette

'I have not done enough horses. The women must wait in their tubs.'[1]

Degas was an artist who turned his mind to many different arts and became thoroughly accomplished in several fields. He was a noted sculptor, though a self taught one. Degas, it has been remarked, worked in the tradition of the 'Sculptor/Painter' beginning with Michelangelo and which included 'Honoré Daumier, Paul Gauguin and Henri Matisse.'[2]

Degas' facility in making three-dimensional forms was clearly evident in many of his sculptures. It is apparent in the timeless, classically inspired *Woman rubbing her back with a sponge, torso* (cat 117), in which the absence of the left arm and head mimics ancient Greek sculpture such as the Aphrodite torso from Kyrene.[3] This work is reminiscent of Degas' earlier monotype of a torso (cat 40).

Echoes of Antiquity can also be found in *Dancer putting on her stocking* (cat 118), whose visual ancestry can be found in the west side of the Parthenon frieze. A copy of this frieze was held at the Ecole des Beaux-Arts, and Degas made a drawing of the figure of a man tying his sandal (from slab xv, section 29) in his notebook between September 1854 and June 1855.[4] Now, around 50 years later, Degas has reformulated this figure. No longer distinct entities, Degas' dancers and bathers became indistinguishable in his last years. There is a variation of this figure as a bather in a drawing from this period (cat 123).

As a sculptor, Degas was capable of great innovation, as is clearly evident in *The tub*. His above-stated determination to resist making sculptures of women bathers in favour of making horses did not last very long. *The tub* is a radical composition of a monumental figure of a woman lying in a tub. Set on a large base as part of the sculpture, *The tub* was intended to be viewed from above. Degas' original plan for this work is evident in a model made of wax, lead, wood, plaster with the addition of a real sponge. This, like his model of *Little dancer aged fourteen* (cat 67), was intended as a polychrome sculpture, and an early example of assemblage. Such intent, however, was not translated when the figure was cast into bronze. Because of the careful attention to detail and the unusually realistic pose, *The tub* is one of the more sensual examples of Degas' bathers.

A further example of the radical adoption of assemblage is evident in *Woman washing her left leg* cat (124), in which a polychrome model was successfully converted into a coloured bronze sculpture with a green inkpot. With such ventures this Sculptor/Painter heralded new approaches to sculpture for the next century.

Notes

1 Revised translation; Degas letter to Bartholomé, 1888, Guerin (ed), 1947, p 124; quoted in Boggs et al, *Degas,* 1988, p 469.

2 Ann Dumas, 'Degas: painter/sculptor', in Czestochowski and Pingeot, p 39.

3 Museo Nazionale delle Terme, Rome.

4 Reff, 1976, vol 1, notebook 2, p 78.

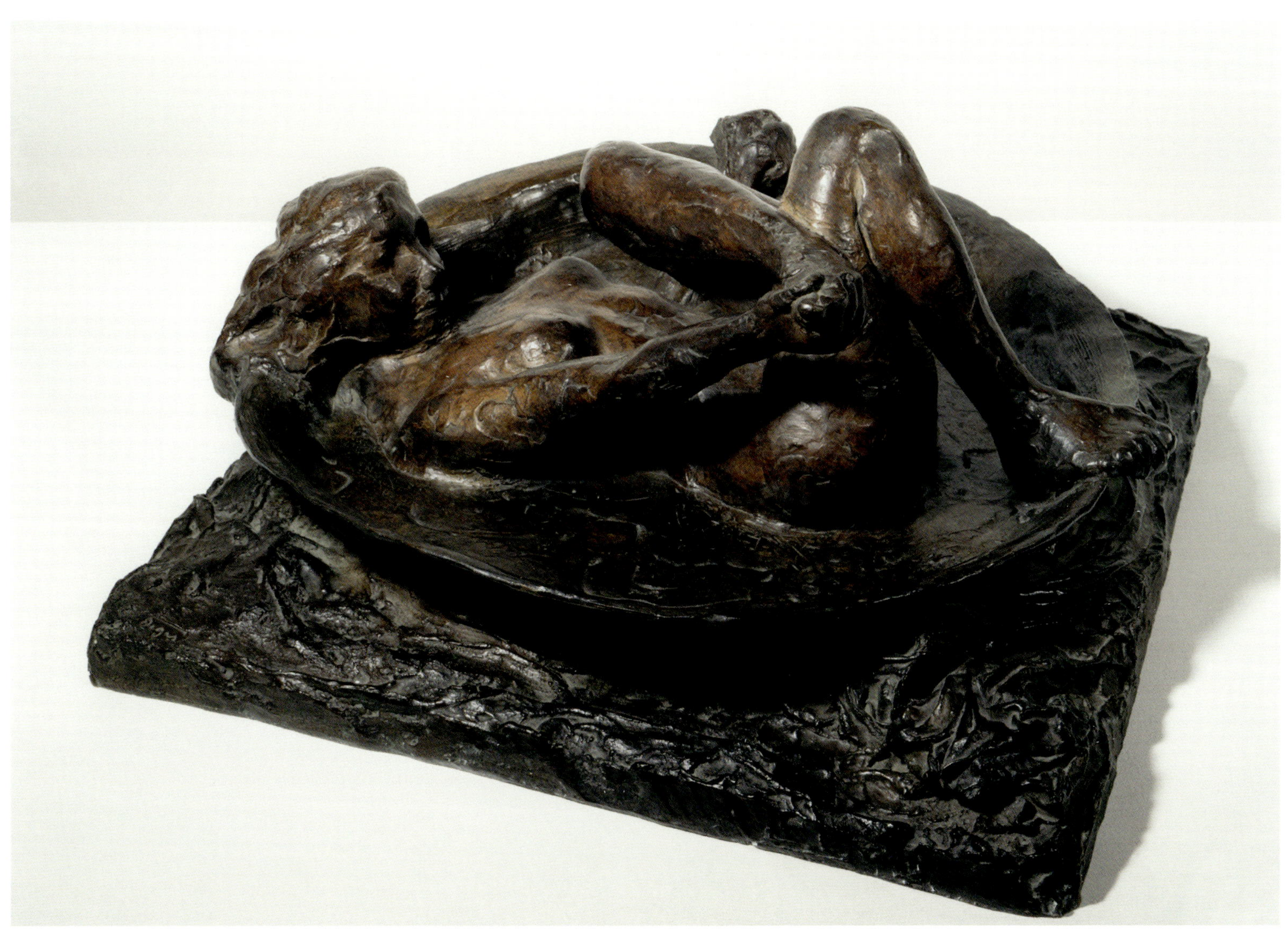

116 *The tub* (*Le tub*)
modelled 1888–89; cast 1919–30
cast P of 22
bronze
25.5 x 43.8 x 45.8 cm
Musée d'Orsay, Paris
RF 2120
Czestochowski and Pingeot 26

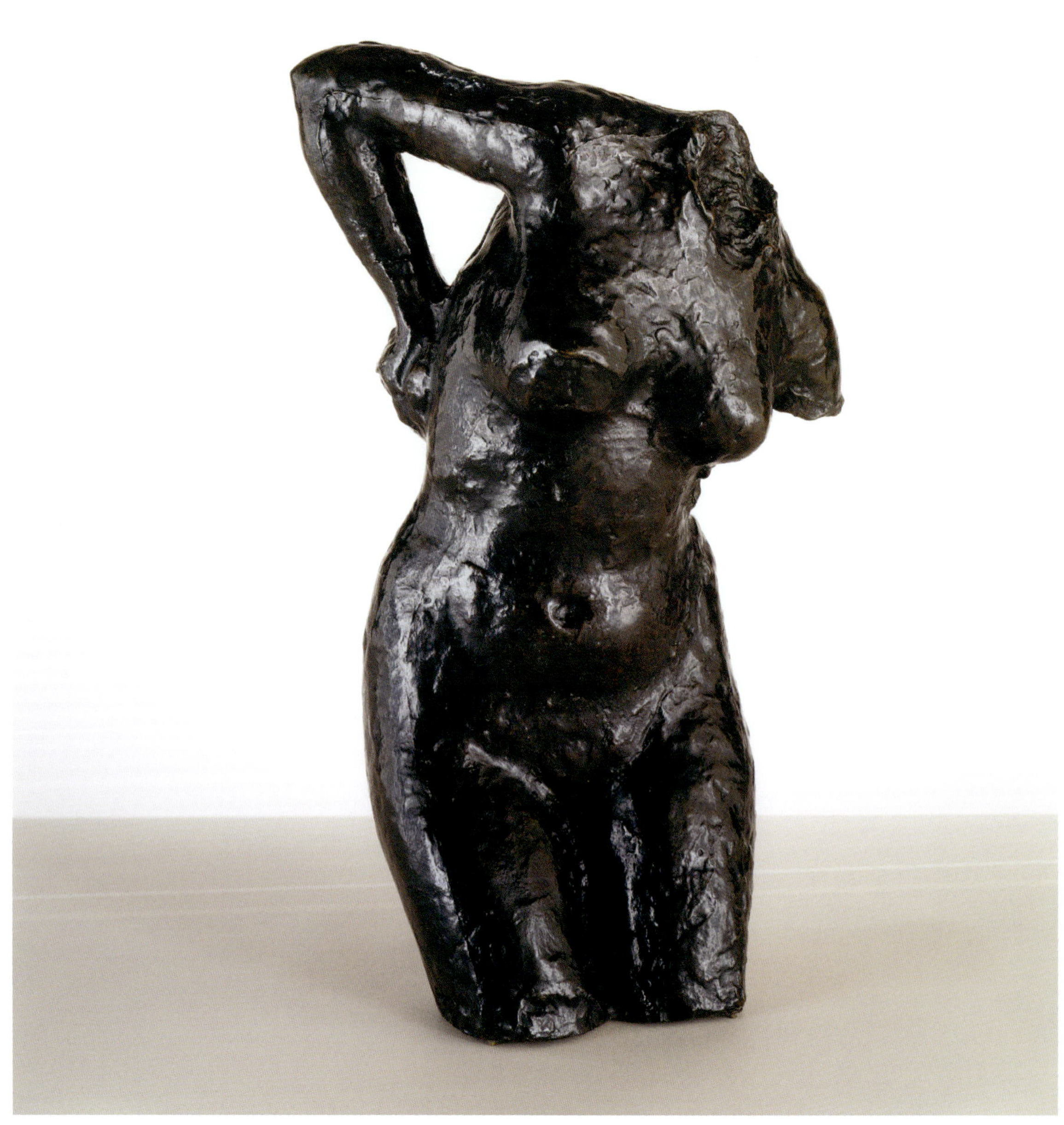

117 *Woman rubbing her back with a sponge, torso*
(*Femme se frottant le dos avec une éponge, torse*)
modelled 1888–92; cast 1919–21
cast D of 23
bronze
43.1 x 26.5 x 17.7 cm
Hirshhorn Museum and Sculpture Garden, Smithsonian Institution, Washington DC
HMSG66.1304
Gift of Joseph H Hirshhorn, 1966
Czestochowski and Pingeot 28

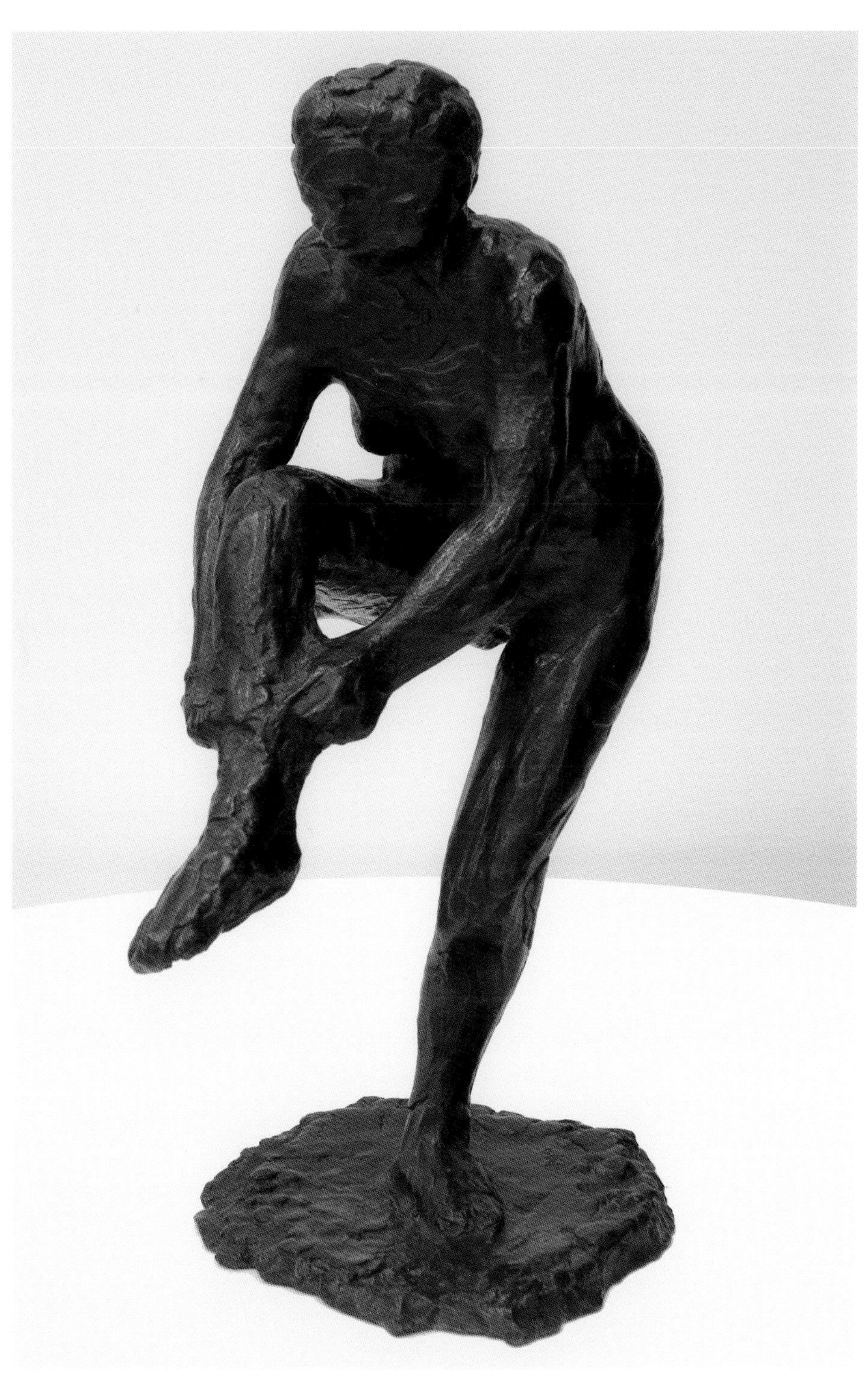

118 *Dancer putting on her stocking, first study,* previously known as *third study*
(*Danseuse mettant son bas, première étude* autrefois appelée *troisième étude*)
modelled 1896–1911; cast 1919–37 or later
cast H of 15
bronze
47.6 x 20 x 31.4 cm
Auckland Art Gallery Toi o Tamaki, Auckland
1956/29
Purchased 1956
Czestochowski and Pingeot 29

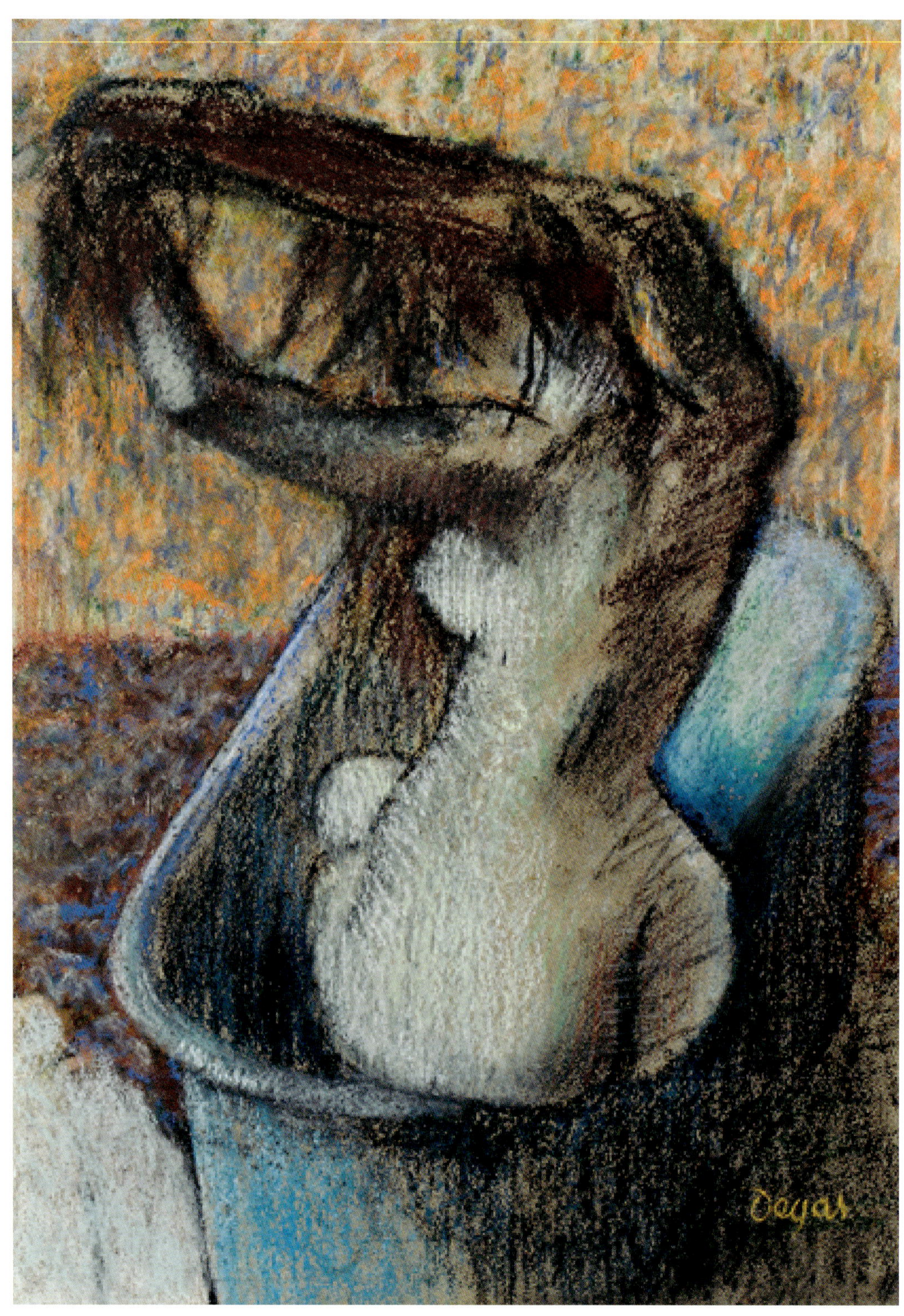

119 *Woman combing her hair at the bath* (*Femme à la baignoire se coiffant*)
1887–90
pastel on paper
66 x 46 cm
Mildura Arts Centre Collection, Mildura
M51
Senator RD Elliott Bequest, presented to the City of Mildura, by Mrs Hilda Elliot, 1956
Lemoisne 1173

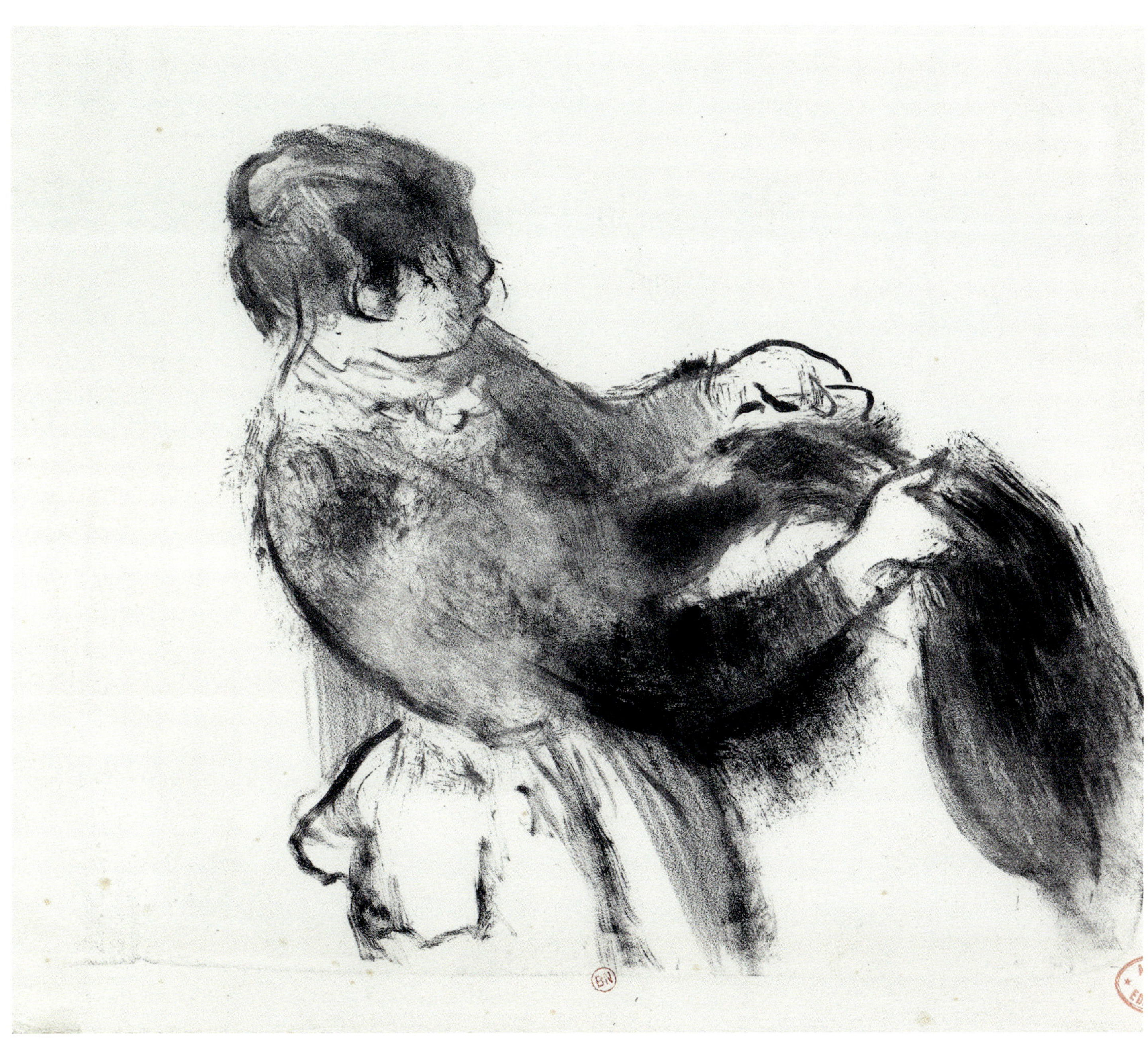

120 *Maid untangling hair* (*Suivante démêlant des cheveux*)
c 1891
first state of two
edition of one
lithograph touched with ink
21.5 x 23 (image), 25.1 x 29.9 cm (sheet)
Bibliothèque nationale de France, Paris
res Dc 327dh fol, boîte 6
Reed and Shapiro 60 / Adhémar 47

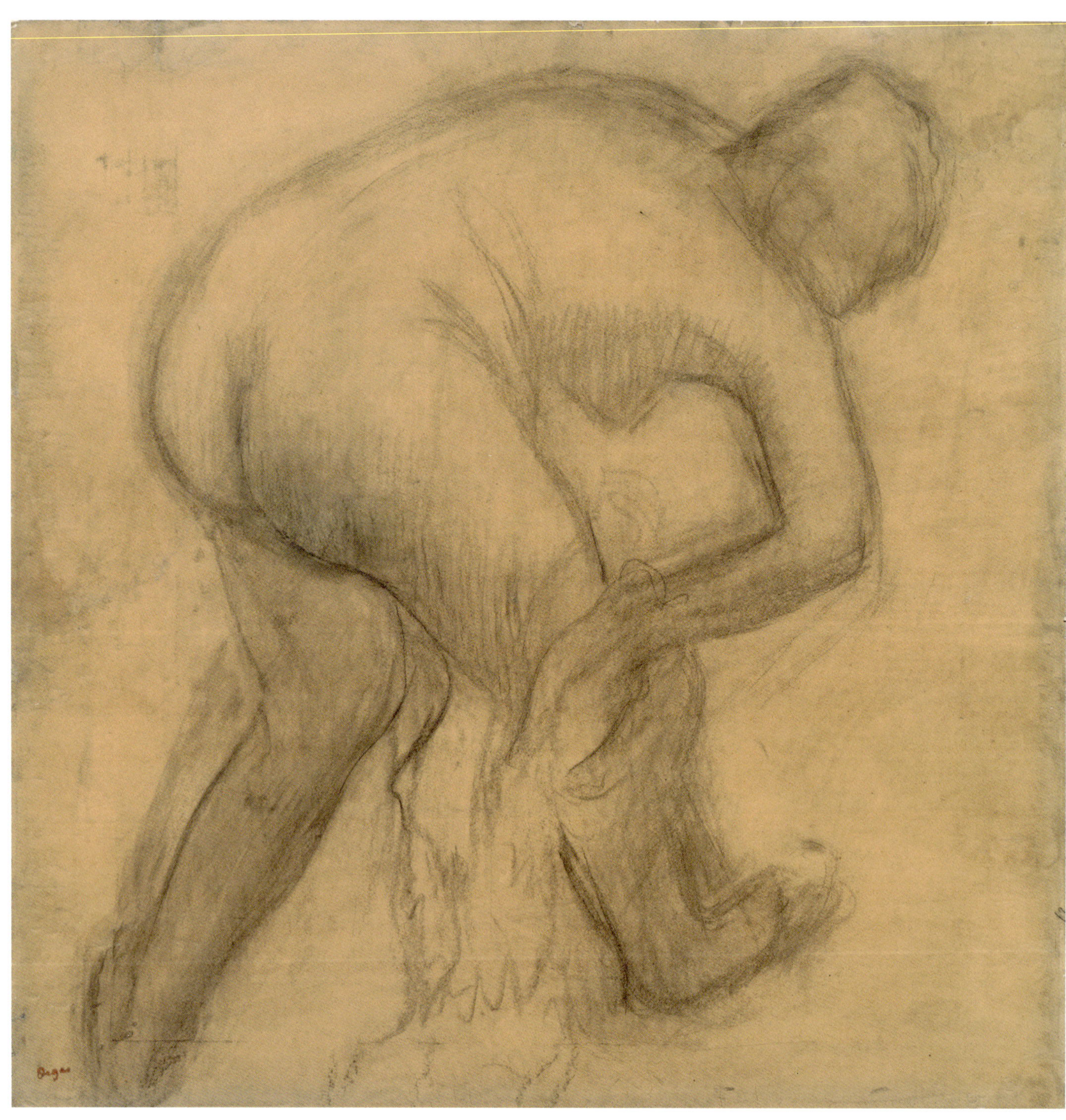

121 *Woman drying herself (Femme s'essuyant)*
c 1890–95
charcoal
73.3 x 70.6 cm
National Gallery of Victoria, Melbourne
1801–04
Felton Bequest, 1947
Vente III: 312

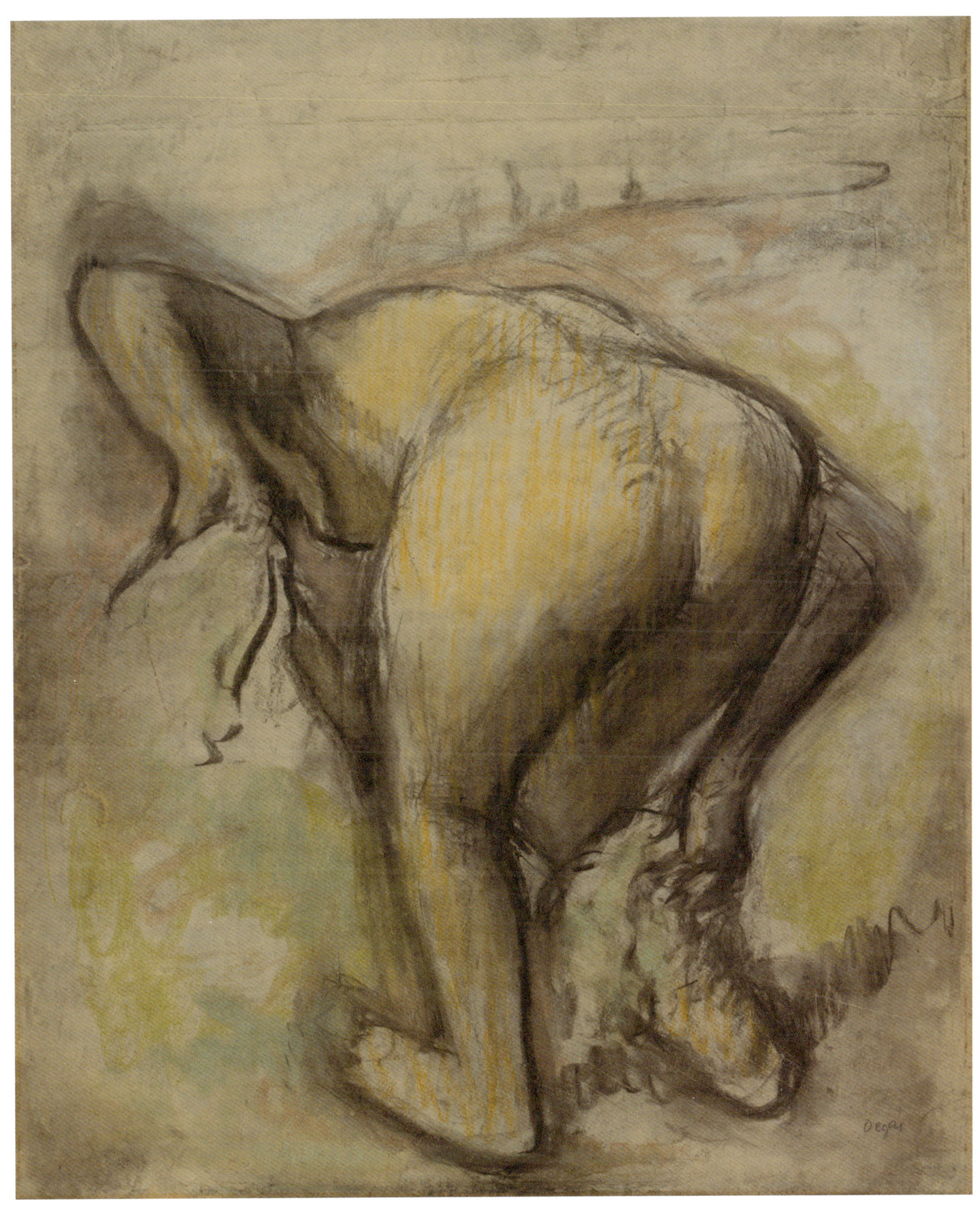

122 *Woman bending over, viewed from behind (Femme nue baissée, de dos)*
1900
charcoal and pastel on wove paper laid on card
73.6 x 60.4 cm
Richard Owens, Sydney

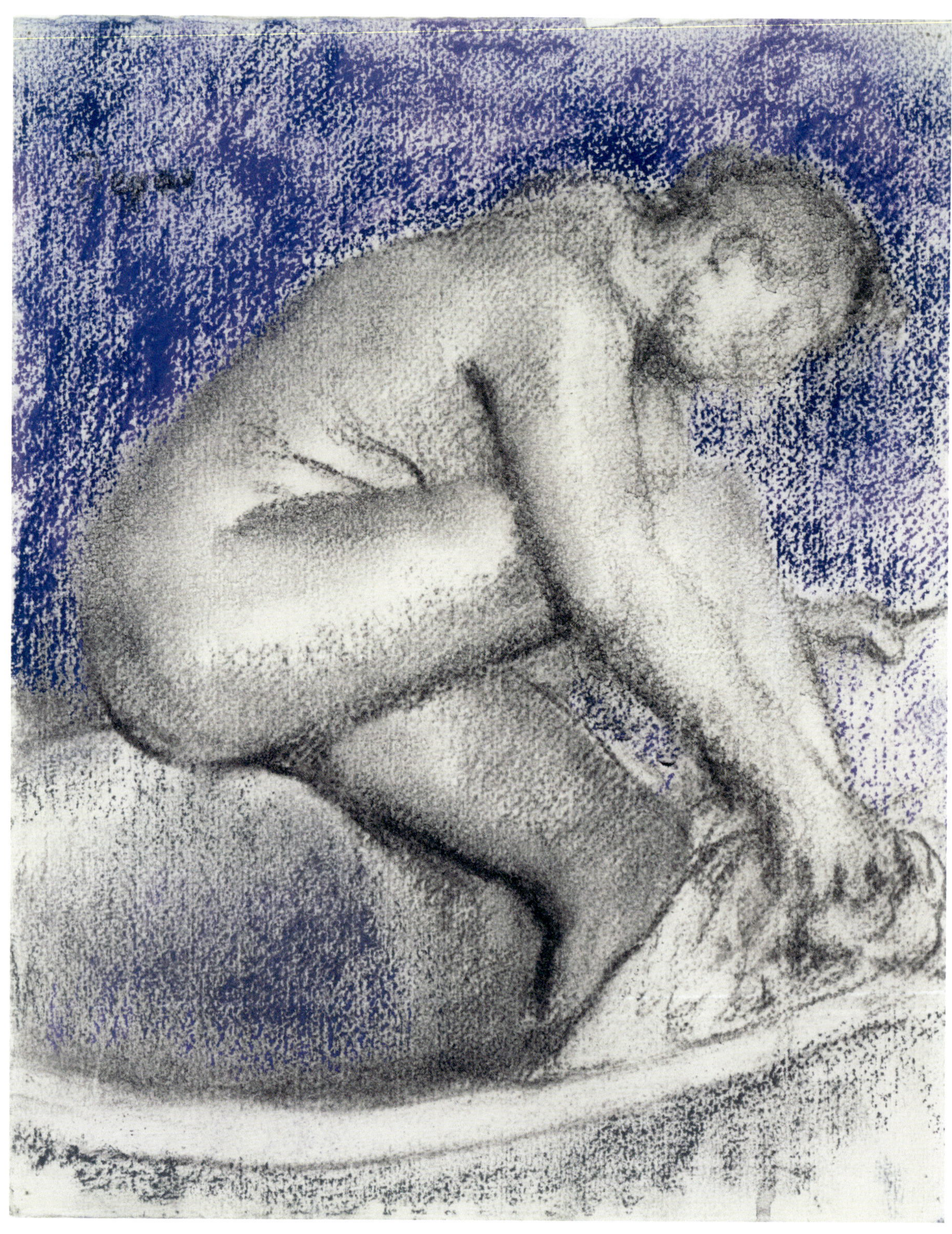

123 ***The bath*** *(**Le bain**)*
1895 or before
charcoal and pastel on paper
32.1 x 25.7 cm
The Metropolitan Museum of Art, New York
29.100.186
HO Havemeyer Collection, Bequest of Mrs HO Havemeyer, 1929
Vente III: 312 / Lemoisne 1406

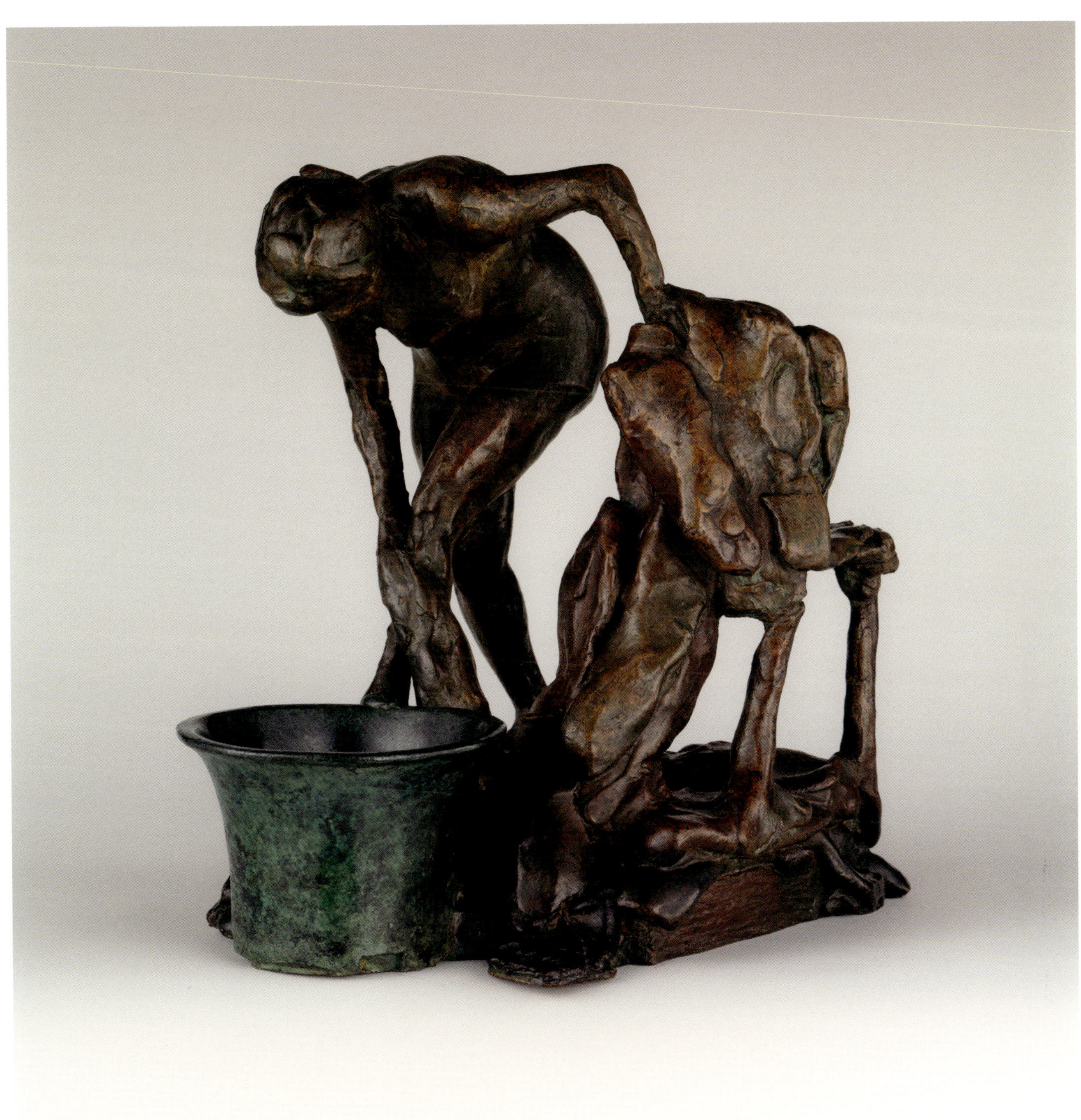

124 ***Woman washing her left leg, second study***
(***Femme se lavant la jambe gauche, deuxième étude***)
modelled c 1883–86; cast 1920
cast B of 16
bronze, ochre, red and light green patinas for the bather, dark green for the pot
20 x 18.7 x 14.9 cm
The Metropolitan Museum of Art, New York
29.100.416
HO Havemeyer Collection, Bequest of Mrs HO Havemeyer, 1929
Czestochowski and Pingeot 61

125 *After the bath, woman drying herself* (*Après le bain, femme s'essuyant*)
c 1895
oil on canvas
75.5 x 86 cm
The Henry and Rose Pearlman Foundation, on long term loan to the Princeton University of Art Museum, Princeton, New Jersey
L.1988.62.10
Lemoisne 1117
Photographer: Bruce M White

Degas made a significant group of paintings of nude bathers in the 1890s. These works were startling in their abstracted forms, as well as being notable for their dramatic colouring and their radical application of paint. As he matured as an artist, Degas' work also acquired greater intimacy and informality. This is clearly evident in *After the bath, woman drying herself*.

This work is a remarkable exercise in the power of experimentation—something that evolved when Degas began making monotypes. Degas depicts an almost contorted figure of a nude woman drying herself as she kneels on, and leans over the back of, a chaise longue. Her head is shown in only a cursory manner, with the addition of just wisps of hair. This, combined with the strange pose, creates a dramatic sense of abstracted forms. Only a few features of the woman's limbs and hair, the towel she is drying herself with, and the bath behind her, have been indicated by the artist using strong outlines. The simplicity of forms and the shorthand method of showing certain details are evident in Degas' drawings in pastel and charcoal and in his lithographs of the 1890s.

Degas' choice of colours is characteristic of his art at this time, consisting of rich oranges and browns, icy blue-greens and startling yellow-greens. The application of paint is also worth noting, as it heightens his apparent move towards more abstract forms. For this painting, he resorted to techniques ranging from thickly applied impasto paint, to applying dabs of paint with a brush or with his fingers. This latter method is used to suggest the decoration of the wall of the room, without detailing it.

After the bath, woman drying herself displays all the daring of Degas' art in his later years. His scenes of women bathing anticipate modernism, and contribute to the rich artistic tradition of nudes, which was carried through into the twentieth century by artists such as Pablo Picasso and Henri Matisse.

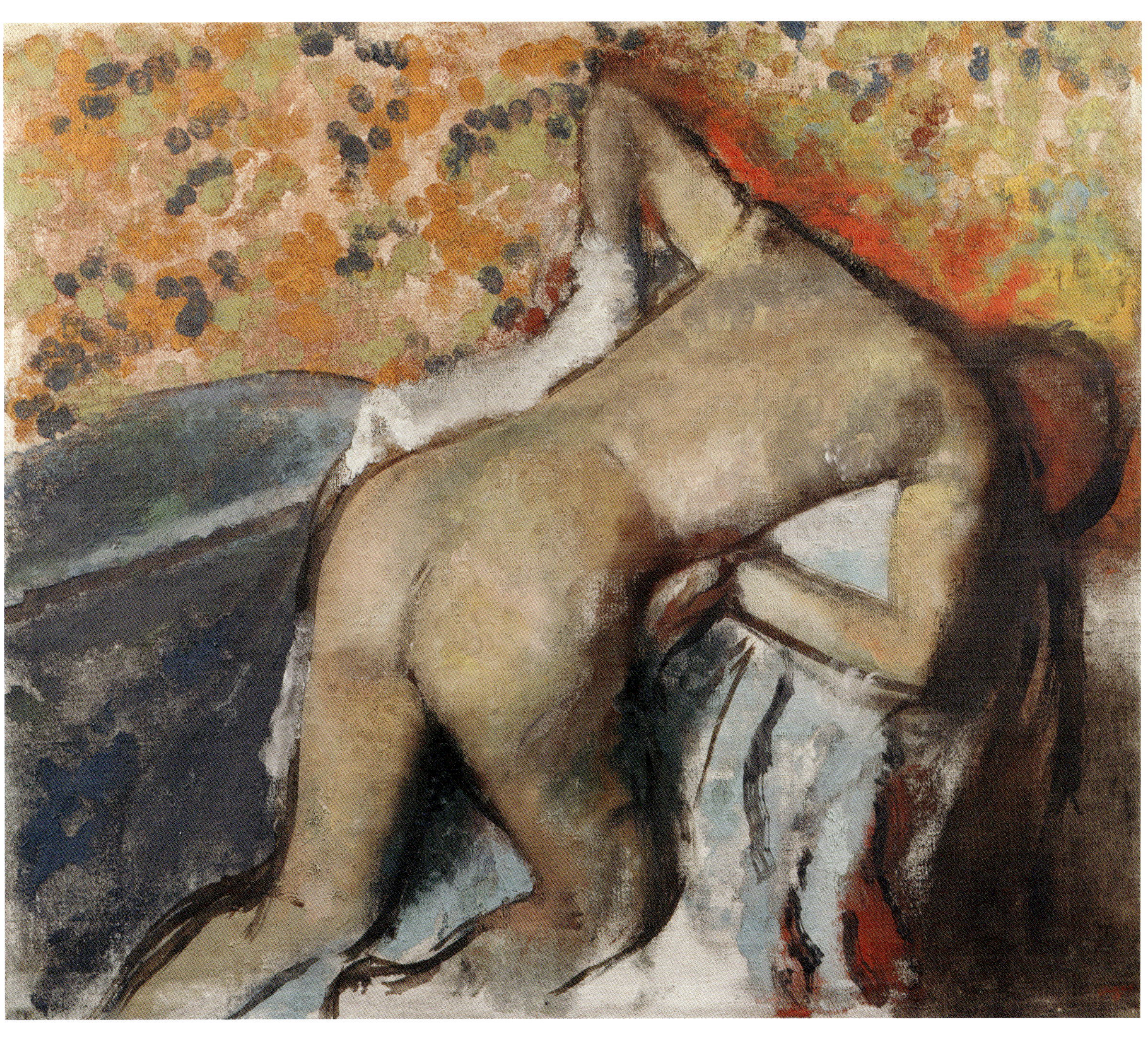

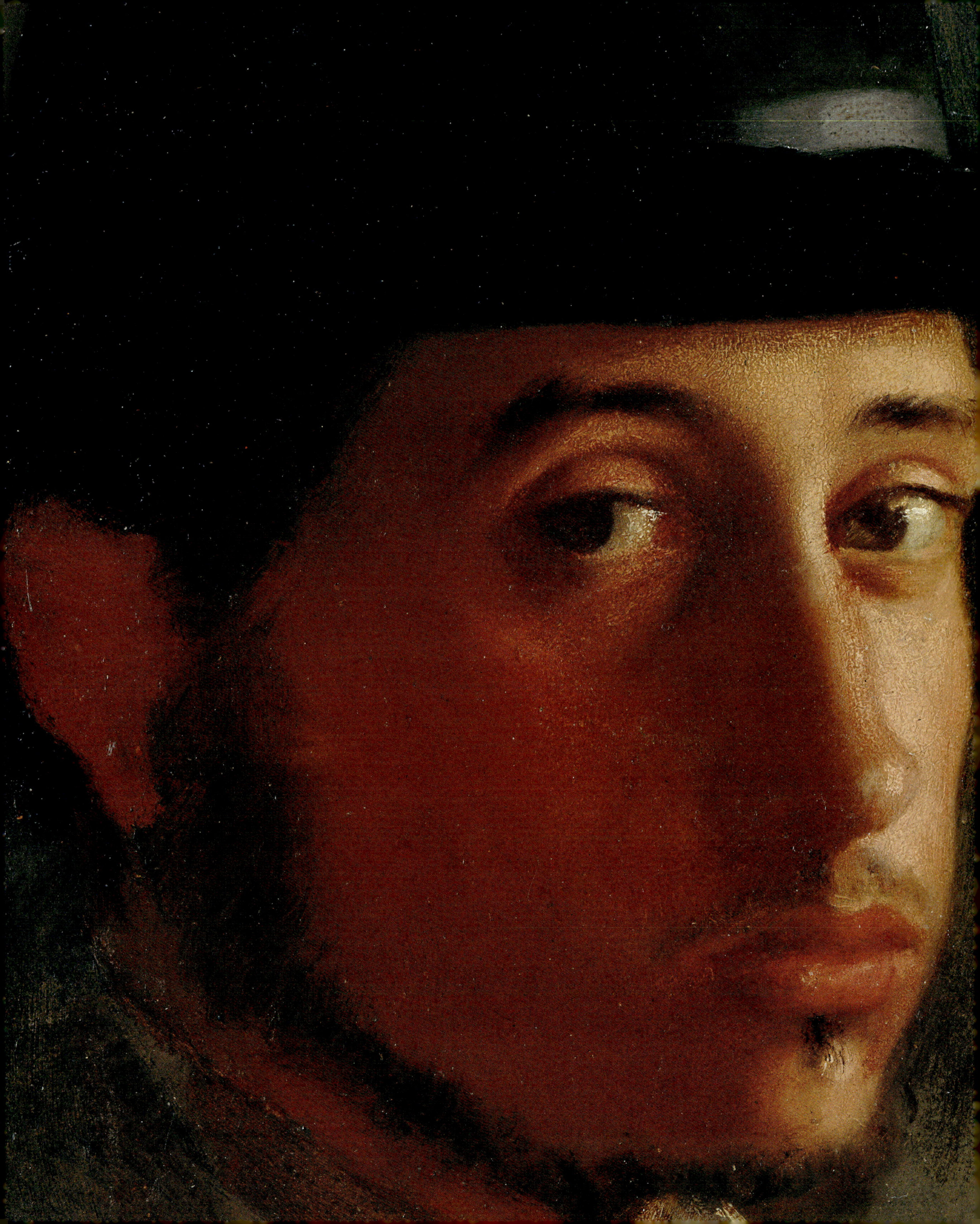

DEGAS: THE ARTIST'S LIFE

Michael Pantazzi

M. Degas remains the incontestable and uncontested master. With his truly admirable sense of movement in his drawing and his harmonious use of colour, M. Degas could not help but leave an indelible mark…

Armand Silvestre, in *La Vie moderne*, 24 April 1880

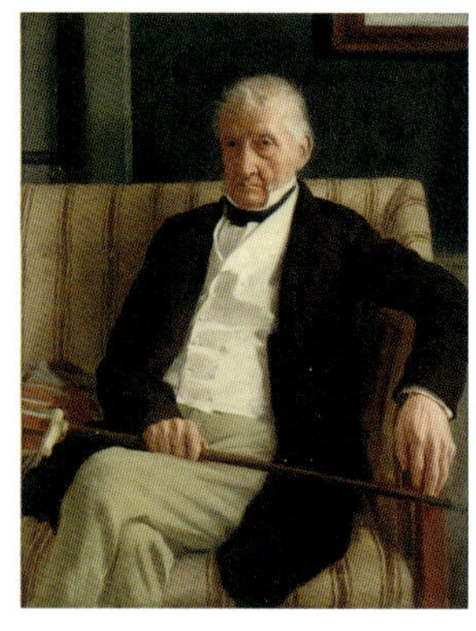

Hilaire De Gas 1857
oil on canvas, 53 x 41 cm
Musée d'Orsay, Paris
Lemoisne 27

(previous page)
Self-portrait
1857–58
(detail cat 1)

EDGAR DEGAS WAS BORN IN PARIS on 19 July 1834, first child of Auguste De Gas, a banker, and Célestine Musson. Both parents were of French ancestry but were born abroad. His mother belonged to a merchant family in New Orleans which still kept connections and a residence in Paris. His father, born in Italy, came from a family of bankers established in Naples. The duality of the name—originally Degas but recently recast as De Gas by the socially ambitious family—requires explanation. Judging by letters received by the artist, or references in the press, in which the name was misspelled as 'Degaze' or 'Degaz' or 'Degasse', it was pronounced with emphasis on the final 's'.

In spite of an embellished genealogy, the artist's grandfather, Hilaire Degas, was the son of a baker, himself the son of a butcher. The family was from the Orléans region in central northern France. In 1793, at the time of the French Revolution, Hilaire had fled to Naples where he'd worked his way into the finance business. In 1804 he'd married Aurora Freppa, the daughter of his employer, from a family of Genoese origin. By 1809 he was a broker and as affairs prospered he established, in 1836, a bank with his sons Henri, Edouard and Achille. The eldest son, Auguste—the artist's father—was already in Paris at the time, setting himself up as a banker of distinctly indifferent talents. Auguste, who was an intensely musical man—a trait inherited by the artist—had a solid visual culture and was given to introspection. (Into his old age Degas kept a portrait of his father, shown listening to the guitarist Lorenzo Pagans.)

The progress of the De Gas family in Naples advanced with some speed. Hilaire had purchased, section by section, the splendid seventeenth-century Palazzo Pignatelli, one of the grandest in the city. It became his family home; he also had a villa above the city at Capodimonte. Hilaire Degas still owned a portion of the palazzo at the time of his death. In accordance with his new-found social status, Hilaire arranged suitable marriages for his three daughters. The elder child, Rosa, married Giuseppe Morbilli, Duke of San Angelo a Frosolone; Laura married Baron Gennaro Bellelli (from a recently ennobled family); and Stefanina married Gioacchino Primicile Carafa, Duke of Montejasi. Gioacchino's sister, Candida Primicile Carafa, married in turn Edouard De Gas, her brother-in-law. Henri and Achille De Gas remained bachelors. There were to be marriages among cousins at the next generation,[1] and Degas drew or painted most of these people.

After Edgar's birth, Auguste De Gas' family increased with alarming regularity: two sons in a row, of which only Achille, born in 1838, survived; then a still-born child followed by Thérèse, born in 1840; then came Marguerite (cat 7), in 1842, and René in 1845: these last two being Edgar's favourites. Judging by the only known portrait of the painter's mother, Célestine, Edgar and Thérèse inherited her eyes. There are reasons to believe that Célestine was unhappy; her letters to her De Gas sisters-in-law in Naples show her life was far from social. Célestine died in 1847 and her husband never remarried. There has been a degree of speculation on the effect her death had on the painter.[2] Edgar was sent as a boarder in 1845 to the Lycée Louis-le-Grand, reputed to be the best in Paris. There he found a friend in Henri Rouart, his senior by one year; Paul Valpinçon and Ludovic Halévy arrived in his class a month later. The younger Rouart, Alexis, also subsequently came to the school. They all became Degas' friends for life—with the exception of Halévy, from whom he was separated by the Dreyfus Affair in the later 1890s. Degas certainly received a solid education, superior to that of many an artist, and likely drew at school—the headmaster for the art classes was Léon Cogniet, at the time already an Academician.

On leaving the lycée in 1853, Degas enrolled in the studio of Felix Barrias (a student of Cogniet's), made copies at the Louvre and, to please his father, entered in the autumn of 1853 the Faculté de Droit of the University of Paris, to study law. It was to be the only semester he spent there. His father's disappointment was apparently not long-lived. He insisted, however, that if his son studied art, he must do it properly. Thus Degas successfully competed for a place at Paris's Ecole des Beaux-Arts, and was admitted on 6 April 1855. Henri Fantin-Latour, also in the competition, was one of his class-mates. Degas spent only one year at the Beaux-Arts, as a student of the history painter Louis Lamothe (a pupil of Jean-Auguste-Dominique Ingres). He lived at home with his father during this time, rather comfortably, since his younger brothers and sisters were mostly at boarding schools—though he used them as models when they came home. During this period he was particularly under the spell of the Italian masters seen at the Louvre; among the moderns he worshipped Ingres above all—a passion he retained to his death. He even contrived to meet the painter, when he stepped in to arrange the loan of Ingres' *Valpinçon bather*—now in the Louvre, but then owned by Paul Valpinçon's father—for the Paris Universal Exposition of 1855. He made a copy of the painting in a notebook.

First mentor: Grégoire Soutzo

Degas' few notebooks of this period are unremarkable, though interesting, with sketches from the antique and the old masters—even Hogarth. From travels made in summer 1856 to the south of France, sketchy notes survive for two historical compositions—*Saint John the Baptist and the angel*, and *Candaules' wife*, along with names and addresses of models he used, and reference books to be consulted. In the absence of a model, Degas drew his own legs or hand. He also painted a few self-portraits, which show him with a serious, searching face—culminating in the *Self-portrait* (Musée d'Orsay, Paris; Lemoisne 5) and the portrait of his young brother René (Smith College Museum of Art, Northampton, Mass.; Lemoisne 6). Both painted in 1855, these are Degas' first masterpieces. In 1856 his mentor of the moment was the Greco-Romanian prince Soutzo—a family friend who was an artist and collector of prints.[3] Among several notes about the prince, Degas—who ranked him with Corot—wrote on 18 January 1856: 'I had a great conversation with Mr Soutzo today. What

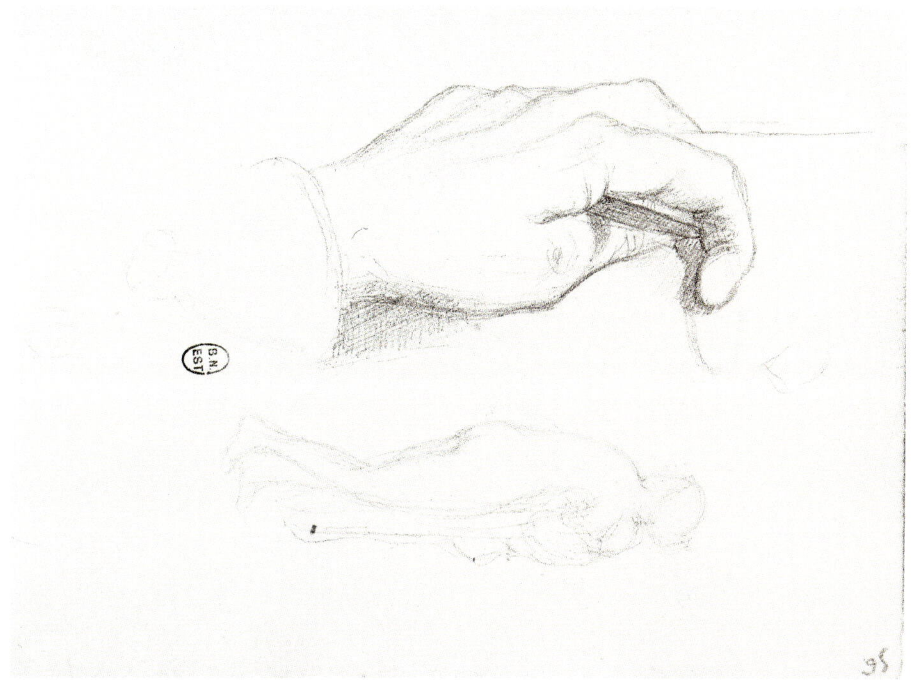

courage there is in his studies. It is essential—never bargain with nature. One certainly needs courage if one is to approach nature head-on in its grand planes and lines and it is cowardly to do it by means of facets and details. It is a war.'[4] The phrase 'It is a war' could have been Degas' motto.

Soutzo's influence on Degas' formative years—one may even say a moral influence relating to the nature of art—has been discussed by Richard Kendall in as much depth as the evidence allows.[5] In passing, it is necessary to clarify the conundrum of Soutzo's identity, not least because he is credited with having directed Degas' first experiments in printmaking; there is as well some confusion with the Soutzo collector's marks noted by Frits Lugt and the sales of the three, rather than two, Soutzo collections.[6] Degas' friend was identified by Jean Adhémar as Nicolas J Soutzo, known to have been collecting in Paris.[7] But further research established him to be Grégoire Soutzo—the identity generally accepted today.[8] Nicolas J Soutzo was only a child when Degas undertook his first print.

Grégoire Soutzo was the second child of Prince Michel Soutzo and Roxane Caradja, the daughter of the prince of Wallachia. Michel was installed as prince of Moldavia in 1819.[9] His suite included the French artist Louis Dupré, who left sketches of the travels and portraits of Michel and Roxane in an album of lithographs, *Voyage à Athènes et à Constantinople, ou Collection de portraits, de vues et de costumes grecs et ottomans* (*Travels to Athens and to Constantinople, or Collection of portraits, views and Greek and Ottoman costumes*), published in 1825. Degas would

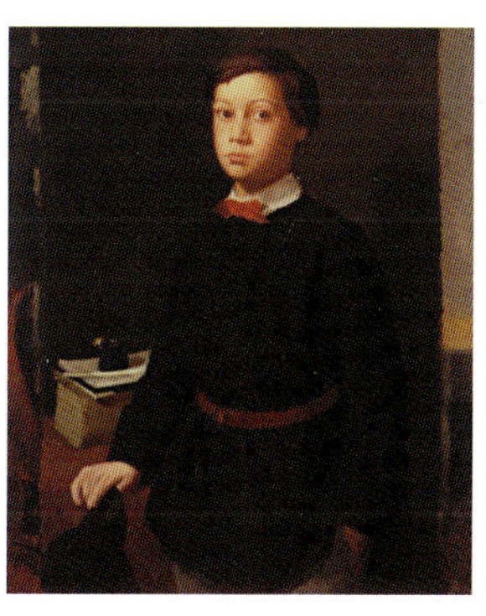

(above)
The artist's left hand, with a study for 'Candaules' wife' (La main gauche de l'artiste, avec une étude pour 'La femme de Candaules') 1856
graphite on paper, 10.5 x 13.7 cm
Bibliothèque nationale de France, Paris

(below)
René de Gas 1855
oil on canvas, 92 x 74.9 cm
Smith College Museum of Art, Northampton, Massachusetts
Lemoisne 6

copy details from the album in 1860–62, when he worked on *Semiramis building Babylon* (Musée d'Orsay, Paris; Lemoisne 82) and included a figure from the album in his painting.[10] In 1821, the beginnings of the armed insurrection that led to the Greek War of Independence forced Michel Soutzo and his family to flee, eventually to exile in Pisa.[11] In 1828, Michel placed his three eldest sons, including Grégoire, in the progressive school run in Geneva by the artist Rodolphe Töpffer. Subsequently, in the early 1830s, Michel was Greek minister plenipotentiary to Paris and met up again with Louis Dupré, who exhibited Michel's portrait at the Salon of 1833. He also exhibited a portrait of Michel's daughter, Hélène, at the Salon of 1835 (his last), and drew a group portrait of the family, in which Grégoire is shown holding a drawing. [12] Such art training as Grégoire had, was likely received from Töpffer and Dupré. The Soutzos returned to Paris in 1839–40, and were evidently musical—perhaps the basis of the connection with Auguste De Gas.[13]

The matter of Degas' artistic debt to Grégoire Soutzo is complicated by the fact that Soutzo's oeuvre has vanished, save for a landscape inscribed to Degas' uncle, Henri Musson, which was formerly owned by Degas and is now in the Musée d'Orsay in Paris (inventory no RF 1992.6).[14] A second Soutzo landscape was copied by Degas into a notebook on 15 February 1856.[15] Soutzo never exhibited, and no etchings by him are known, but he was a substantial collector of prints—largely northern European—to which Degas doubtlessly had access; as Henri Loyrette suggests, the prints may well have broadened the young artist's horizons. Fifty years after Degas had etched his brother Rene's portrait (Adhémar 21 / Reed and Shapiro 15), René told Paul-Andre Lemoisne that he could still recall the smell of acid filling the apartment when his brother, under Soutzo's guidance, had prepared the copper plate in the kitchen.[16] (As the portrait of René dates later, he evidently remembered the smell from an earlier experiment: the preparation of Degas' first etching, *Greek landscape*, or *The anchorage* of 1856 (Adémar 1 / Reed and Shapiro 1).) The allegation however that Soutzo suggested to Degas the term 'monotype' (from the Greek *monos-typo*s, meaning single type or proof) is certainly false, as the term came into use only after Soutzo's death.[17] On his return from Rome in 1857, Degas gave Soutzo a second state of his etched *Self-portrait* (National Gallery of Canada, Ottawa ; Adhémar 13 / Reed and Shapiro 8)—one of only two self-portraits known to have left the artist's studio.[18]

Degas in Italy

In 1856, Auguste De Gas decided that it was time for his eldest son to visit his family in Naples. Somewhat unexpectedly, Degas would stay in Italy for over three years, and the visit would leave an indelible mark on his artistic education. He arrived in Naples in July of that year, and lived with his grandfather, Hilaire. Here he drew family members, and spent time drawing in the museums. In early October Degas left for Rome, where he remained for nine months. In July 1857, he was asked by his grandfather to return to Naples and during that summer, in the villa at Capodimonte, he painted the dated portrait of Hilaire De Gas (Musée d'Orsay, Paris; Lemoisne 27) (see p 240), in a direct but formal manner which was intended for posterity. He returned to Rome in October 1857, for another nine months, followed by an extended stay in Florence from July 1858 to March 1859. Degas, always very open with his father, informed him of his progress and received advice in return. Throughout this period he made a large number of studies and painted several self-portraits in which one detects a sharper self-awareness (cat 1).

In Rome, Degas also found the French engraver Joseph Tourny (a friend of Auguste De Gas), to whom the artist always remained devoted. Degas has left portraits of Tourny, and it is surely this encounter that pushed Degas to experiment further with etching. Indeed, he borrowed Tourny's fine profile for the head of Dante in a history painting, *Dante and Virgil* (private collection; Lemoisne 34). Degas met other students in Rome—Léon Bonnat, whose portrait he painted twice after they returned to Paris; Edouard Brandon, who years later was to lend two works by Degas to the first Impressionist exhibition;[19] Elie Delaunay and others. However, his single most significant encounter was with Gustave Moreau, who he probably met in early 1858.[20] Six years older than Degas, Moreau was on a second study tour. He had worked with the much-admired Théodore Chassériau, was familiar with the work of Eugène Delacroix, and was much more sophisticated in his views on art than Degas. Differences in their views separated the men in later life, but for the time being Moreau was the most interesting and articulate artist Degas had met. He was an outstanding pedagogue who later taught both Henri Matisse and Georges Rouault. While in Rome, Degas and Moreau went in the evenings to the Villa Medici—the French Academy, where the director, Victor Schnetz, Ingres' successor, allowed external students to join the classes and draw from the model. Moreau opened Degas' eyes beyond Ingres and gave him a sense of focus. The two met in Florence again, and travelled together, sometimes copying the same works of art. Moreau left several sketches of Degas, none more revealing than one showing him still very young, looking in awe at a painting in the Uffizi Gallery. In another sketch, prefiguring a mock apotheosis photographed by Walter Barnes in Dieppe half a century later (cat 85), Moreau depicts Degas crowned with laurels.

In Florence, Degas lived in an apartment lent him by his relatives, the Bellellis. He felt lonely, and certain character traits that would become evident in his later life are already in evidence. He wrote to Moreau, 'I remember conversations we had in Florence on the sadness which is part of him who occupies himself with art,' and added some lines later, 'I read with interest the Provincial Letters [by Blaise Pascal] where the I is admonished as detestable.'[21] That 'I' gave Degas some trouble, and he had difficulty finishing the paintings he undertook. He met another Frenchman then living in Florence, Marcellin Desboutin, who would later play a significant role in his art in the 1870s (cats 25 and 82, and p 252) and, at the Caffe Michelangiolo, he met the young Florentine modernist painters, dubbed 'The Macchiaioli'. Telemaco Signorini was his own age, and they would meet again later in Paris.[22]

While in Florence at the end of December 1858, Degas began his most ambitious work to date, the very large group portrait of his Bellelli relatives—his unhappy aunt Laura (to whom he was close, and who was at the time on the verge of nervous breakdown), her two charming daughters, Giulia and Giovanna (whom he very much loved; cat 9), and Laura's embittered and difficult husband, Gennaro. A letter of this time from Auguste De Gas, is revealing of the relationship between father and son, and of the young painter's already pronounced difficulty in calculating the time it took to bring a work to completion:

> You start such a large painting on 29 December and think you will finish it by 28 February. That's extremely doubtful. If I can give you a piece of advice, it's to do it calmly and patiently; otherwise you run the risk of not finishing it and giving your uncle Bellelli good reason to complain. Since you decided to undertake this picture, you must finish it and finish it properly. I dare to hope that your habits have changed, but I admit that I have so little faith in your resolutions that it will be a great weight off my mind when your uncle writes to tell me that you have completed the picture and completed it well.[23]

Indeed, there was no time to complete the picture in two months—Degas reworked and finished it later in Paris—but the painting was an extraordinary performance, and an act of semi-dissimulation: a family drama in the guise of a state portrait. Degas probably exhibited it at the Salon of 1867, at which time he retouched it.[24]

Degas was extremely interested in portraits, and painted a great many during his career, the greater part remaining in his

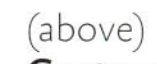

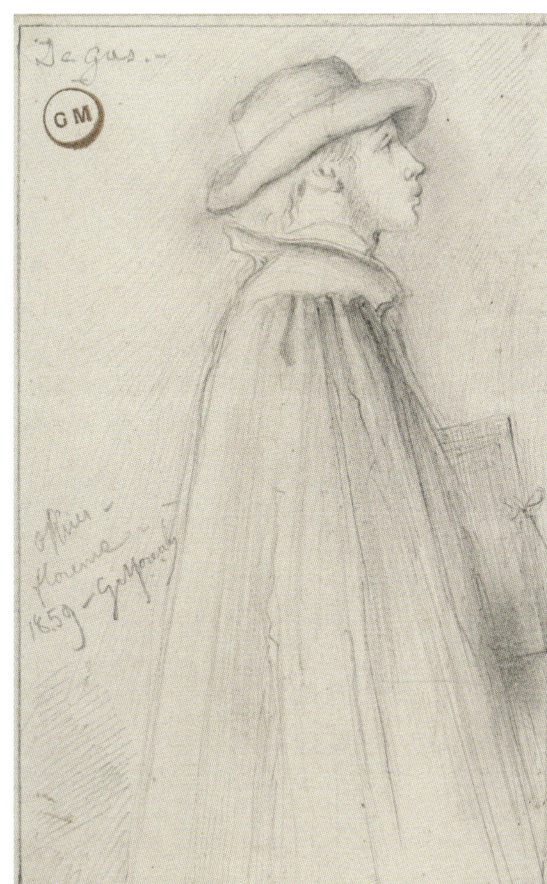

(above)
Gustave Moreau
Degas in the Uffizi (Portrait de Degas aux offices) 1859
charcoal on paper, 15.3 x 9.4 cm
Musée national Gustave-Moreau, Paris

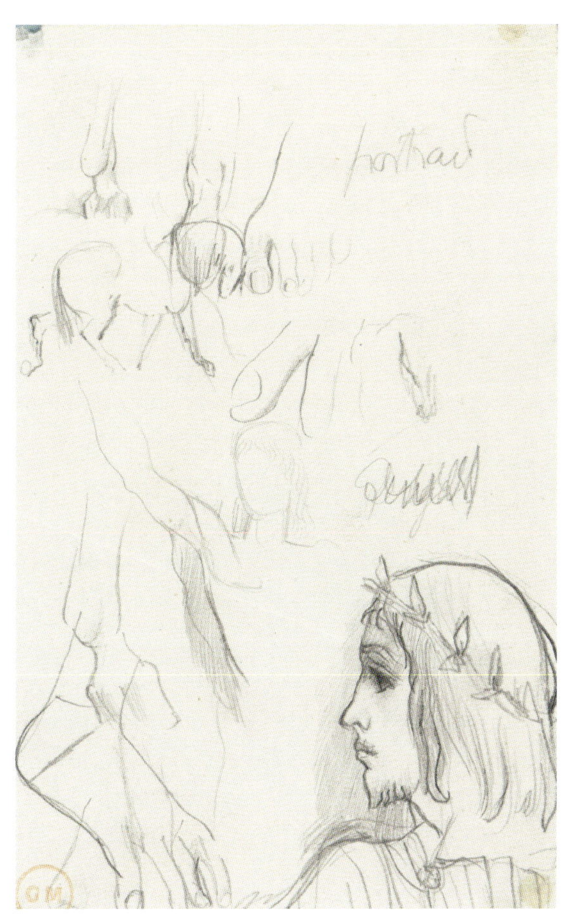

(below)
Gustave Moreau
Sheet of studies with a portrait of Degas, in profile, crowned with laurels (Feuille d'études diverses avec portrait de Degas de profil couronné de lauriers) 1859
graphite on white paper, mounted on blue paper, 15.9 x 10 cm
Musée national Gustave-Moreau, Paris

Unknown photographer
Edgar Degas on the front steps (Edgar Degas sur les marches d'un perron) c 1860
albumen silver photograph, 9 x 5.7 cm
Musée d'Orsay, Paris

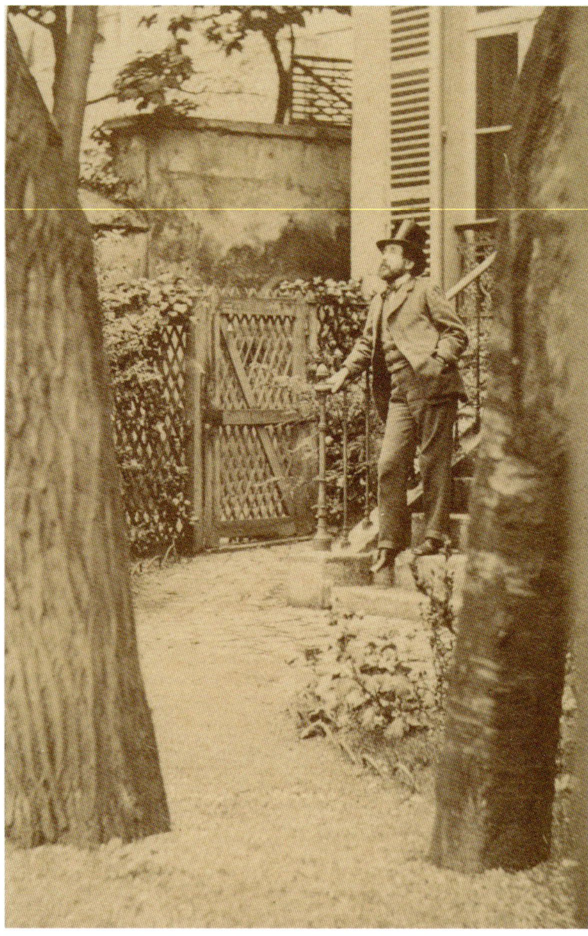

studio. Indeed, over one-fifth of his work is portraiture.[25] *The Bellelli family* (Musée d'Orsay, Paris; Lemoisne 79) was to be the first of Degas' works in which the psychology of the sitters and the social ambience they belonged to took priority. This approach would evolve, in 1867, into the splendid but only slightly less angst-ridden double portrait of Thérèse De Gas and her husband, Edmondo Morbilli (Museum of Fine Arts, Boston; Lemoisne 164). The style recalls the late Renaissance, particularly the work of Bronzino. The elegant appearance is undercut, however, by our knowing the circumstances: Thérèse's loss of her only child, and Edmondo's wretched health, not yet showing beneath the splendid, even arrogant looks.

In the later 1860s and in the 1870s, Degas adopted a brisker, unconventional manner—increasingly more daring, with a more subjective interpretation which disconcerted some. He painted almost exclusively his family and friends, who were willing and trusted sitters. So far as is known, he seldom undertook commissions—the portrait of Ernest May, known as *Portraits at the Stock Exchange* (Musée d'Orsay, Paris; Lemoisne 499), and that of Madame May seem to be among the few. May's portrait could hardly pass for one in the conventional sense, and is practically a genre scene. Degas intended to show it at the fourth Impressionist exhibition of 1879—it is listed in the catalogue, but apparently wasn't exhibited.

Degas exchanged portraits with fellow artists, and painted friends and their children—in some cases several times. In addition to etched portraits of Manet (cat 8), he also painted the artist with Mme Manet (Kitakyushu Municipal Museum of Art; Lemoisne 127; p 177). The picture inaugurated the not always happy reception of his work: Manet cut out the section showing his wife, and inevitably Degas was angry.[26] Degas' portrait of Adèle Dietz-Monnin in fancy-dress, happily waving at an unseen interlocutor—possibly also a commission—also provoked a rift. The lady—the wife of a senator, and the mother-in-law of Degas' friend Hermann de Clermont—was unhappy with the result. Degas famously replied to her in a letter (which he didn't, however, send):

> Let us leave the portrait alone, I beg of you. I was so surprised by your letter suggesting I reduce it to a boa and hat that I shall not answer you [...] Must I tell you that I regret having started something in my own manner only to find myself transforming it completely into yours? [27]

This picture, too, was destined for the fourth Impressionist exhibition of 1879 but there is no record that it was shown. Degas learned that portraiture was the art of compromise, and the least likely activity to permit pictorial freedom, but he remained unbending, to his own cost. The earlier portrait of a friend's wife, Berthe Jeantaud, was swiftly disposed of by her, though her insipid portrait by Jean-Jacques Henner was bequeathed to a museum.[28] Mary Cassatt was shown in several works by Degas with great effect, as a bold silhouette viewed from behind (cats 104–107). However, when it came to a portrait (National Portrait Gallery, Washington, DC; Lemoisne 796), she concealed it then sold it, writing bluntly to Durand-Ruel in 1912: 'I do not want to leave it to my family as being [a picture] of me. It has some qualities as art, but it is so painful and represents me as such a repugnant person that I would not want it known that I posed for it.'[29] (Discretion did not prevail, however, as it was exhibited in Berlin in 1913, identified by her name.) Of his sitters, Ernest May alone willed his portrait to the Louvre, where he was the head of the Society of Friends.

The Parisian circle

When Degas left Italy in March 1859, he was a changed man, with a new sense of his artistic future. He had a number of paintings in his luggage, ranging from a few historical subjects prepared in Rome, to portraits and even genre pictures such as the

Roman beggar woman (cat 5). He had assimilated everything Italy had to offer and his notebooks were already full of projects. He also wanted to make his mark with a grand composition, but that had to wait until a studio and apartment could be found at a suitable price. The belief that, because of his father, Degas was rich and had no need to make a living, was untrue: Auguste's financial circumstances were relatively precarious. Grégoire Soutzo, who had by now married, offered the artist his modest former bachelor premises but instead a studio and apartment was found at 13 rue de Laval (now rue Victor-Massé) in Montmartre. Degas was now set up on his own.

His friends' correspondence indicates that the artist did not see his prospects as being very good at this time. His father was not altogether certain where things were going. As he wrote of his son to his brother-in-law, Michel Musson: 'Our Raphael still works but has produced so far nothing finished.'[30] A self-portrait of about 1862 shows the artist in an uncommonly romantic mood (private collection; Lemoisne 104) but a photograph (opposite) of about the same period restores the idea of a rather withdrawn person. It was nevertheless at this time that Degas was absorbed—one might say obsessed—by the thought of historical subjects with a dramatic content, but recast in fundamentally new ways—an exercise later described by his friend Edmond Duranty as efforts to 'throw light on these antique subjects in the blaze of contemporary life.'[31] He applied himself to painting increasingly larger and more ambitious works filled with many figures. If in Italy he had explored Dante and the Bible, leading to a sketchy but novel *David and Goliath*, now he was searching for other subjects, from Antiquity and even modern literature. In the event, his energies were consumed by four compositions: *Alexander and Bucephalus* (National Gallery of Art, Washington, DC; Lemoisne 99), the vast, biblical *Daughter of Jephthah* (Smith College Museum of Art, Northampton, Mass; Lemoisne 94), *Semiramis building Babylon* (Musée d'Orsay, Paris; Lemoisne 82), and *Young Spartans* (National Gallery, London; Lemoisne 70). From 1859, he worked simultaneously on several compositions which gestated over several years, some undergoing several transformations or remaining unfinished. He was doubtlessly counting on *Alexander* for his Salon debut, but eventually completed only one of these four projected works: *Semiramis.* It does not seem without significance that three of the narratives Degas chose for his paintings were about victorious youngsters who, by an act of faith, prove to the world their worth.

A number of these compositions cast a horse in the principal part, and at this time—the early 1860s—Degas began painting racing scenes. Géricault provided him with an invaluable impetus for the study of horses, which Degas now observed at the race track, just as he had earlier copied them from casts of the Parthenon friezes at the Ecole des Beaux-Arts. At this time he also formed a friendship with the sculptor Joseph Cuvelier, under whose direction he seems to have made his first essays in sculpture. Degas was certainly forming a large group of friends and acquaintances—his notebooks of the period list numerous names and addresses. As the young artists he'd met in Rome receded into the background, new artists took their place: Henri Fantin-Latour (known from his student days), James Whistler (from whom he learned the art of displaying a work), James Tissot, and the Stevens brothers, two of whom were painters. Legend has it that Degas first met Edouard Manet at the Louvre in 1862, though as mentioned Manet's parents already knew Auguste De Gas. Degas certainly saw more of him at the Café Guerbois in the Grande-Rue-des Batignolles (now Avenue de Clichy). Before the Franco–Prussian War, this café was Manet's habitual haunt—he lived next door. As an artist, Manet was generally considered to be above all others in Paris, and the divinity of the young generation.

The relationship with Manet, mixing admiration and the occasional contretemps on both sides, was beneficial for both men. Auguste Renoir also frequented the Café Guerbois; Claude Monet was there only rarely, and Camille Pissarro was often out of Paris. In the years to follow, Degas would be closer to Pissarro, and somewhat less so to Renoir. Paul Cézanne, whose work Degas collected in later life, worked at some distance. Degas' relationship with Monet was polite—no more; Degas observed his extraordinary evolution, but never owned a single Monet work. Round this time, Degas' old school-friends, Henri Rouart and Ludovic Halévy were married or soon-to-be married. In 1869 Degas painted Paul Valpinçon with his wife and newborn child at their country retreat (cat 13). Degas also had musician friends: Désiré Dihau, a bassoonist at the Paris Opéra, and Georges Bizet, the future composer of *Carmen*, and who in 1869 married Halévy's cousin Geneviève Halévy. (Geneviève was the first of a number of women whose hair was to fascinate Degas; he asked her to allow him to watch her comb it.) His friendship with the Morisot family and their talented daughter Berthe dates from this period; Berthe was to marry Edouard Manet's brother, Eugène, in 1874.

In 1865, Degas did what was expected of him, and sent the Salon his *Scene of war in the Middle Ages* (Musée d'Orsay, Paris; Lemoisne 124). The work was accepted. He followed in 1866 with a modern work, *The steeplechase* (National Gallery of Art, Washington, DC; Lemoisne 140). For the next four years he sent only portraits: in 1868, the extremely novel portrait of Mademoiselle Fiocre (cats 45 and 47), the star from the Opéra (for Degas, a social success); in 1869 the portrait of another dancer, *Joséphine Gaujelin* (Isabella Stewart Gardner Museum, Boston; Lemoisne 165); and finally, in 1870, the subtle portrait of Berthe Morisot's sister, Yves Gobillard (Metropolitan Museum of Art, New York; Lemoisne 213) and the strange effigy of Madame Camus (National Gallery of Art, Washington, DC; Lemoisne 271). The history paintings, of which he preferred *Semiramis*, were shelved with the exception of *Young Spartans*, which was retouched in anticipation of the fifth Impressionist exhibition of 1880, but failed to be exhibited. In the later part of the decade Degas' name was becoming well known, and he began making his first sales.

In 1870–71, the Franco-Prussian war and the Paris Commune brought the Second Empire to an end, and disrupted Degas' artistic progress. He enlisted, as did the Manet brothers, as a volunteer in the artillery defending Paris, and found himself under the command of his old friend Henri Rouart. While serving, he suddenly noticed his eyesight was impaired—a subject of increasing worry over coming years. He was also much perturbed by the death in battle of Joseph Cuvelier, and of Henri Regnault, a painter friend. (For more detail on the war, see footnote 13, p 32.)

In 1872, Degas and his brother René (who had been in Paris) undertook a five-month journey to the United States to visit their Musson relatives and brother Achille in New Orleans.[32] René, who was married to a widowed cousin, Estelle Musson, lived there with a house full of children, only two of whom were René's. Degas wrote to Désire Dihau from New Orleans, 'Ah! my dear friend, what a good thing a family is,' and manifestly enjoyed himself.[33] The contact with the charming and courageous Estelle, who was blind, and of whom Degas grew fond, was inevitably a reminder of his own failing eyesight. Perhaps surprisingly, there is next to nothing of this New Orleans trip in Degas' surviving notebooks except for a few quick sketches of passengers on the ship that took him there, and of some relatives in New Orleans itself. His letters from America are lively, however. He wrote that he saw many things, admired them, made mental notes, but would leave the place without regret. From America he brought back to Paris a number of paintings, notably *A cotton office in New Orleans* (cat 11). An astute viewer might have observed that all was not well with René and the New Orleans family: in the painting, everyone is at work except René, who is reading a newspaper, with a cigarette dangling between his lips, and Achille, at far left, watching him from a distance.

The year 1874 was indelibly marked in the annals of modern art by the appearance in Paris of the group of painters subsequently known as the Impressionists. Their first exhibition organised that year was largely due to the efforts of Degas, who, in an uncharacteristic bout of energy, rallied the artists, looked for an exhibition space and generally believed in an artistic revolution. As it happened, beginning in 1874, a series of events of a personal nature completely changed Degas' relatively worry-free life. His father, Auguste, had sold his Italian assets in 1873 to his brothers Henri and Achille, retaining only the bank in Paris, which subsisted on credit. A year earlier, Auguste had advanced a large loan to René for his business investments in New Orleans.

In February 1874, Auguste died during a visit to Naples. While Degas was recruiting artists for the first Impressionist exhibition, the distribution of Auguste's modest Paris estate between his children was taking place. Henri Musson, the artist's uncle, was meanwhile trying to settle the debts of the De Gas bank. In the midst of this financial drama—total ruin was not yet anticipated—young Achille De Gas, the artist's brother, injected a note of passion into matters by shooting and wounding the husband of a former mistress. He went briefly to prison, where Degas dutifully visited him. In February 1875, Achille De Gas, Auguste's brother, also died in Naples, leaving the artist as one of his heirs. By 10 December 1875, it became evident that René had to pay back his father's loan in order to settle the bank's creditors. René defaulted. Such hopes as Degas entertained of settling his father's debts were soon dispelled when he learned that his share of the Palazzo Degas would be available only when his co-heir, Lucie Degas, then aged nine, attained her majority. The situation was desperate. In June 1876, Degas returned to Naples with his brother Achille in a last attempt to raise credit on his frozen assets, but failed.

Auguste's main creditor, the Banque d'Anvers, took the matter to court. In January 1877, the judgment compelled Degas and his impecunious architect brother-in-law, Henri Fevre —Marguerite's husband—to pay 40 000 francs in monthly instalments. Degas, who was ready to do everything to protect his father's good name, agreed. The payments lasted over 10 years and transformed the painter's existence. The facade however was preserved, and nobody outside the family knew, except for a few friends. Henri Rouart, by now an industrialist, helped, and apparently another friend, Hermann de Clermont, also assisted financially; Degas and Henri Rouart were very close and the Rouart family became the only true family Degas had. But René De Gas, the most loved of his brothers, and partly the cause of the catastrophe, still had a surprise in store. In 1878, he eloped with a woman named America Olivier, leaving Estelle and the children permanently stranded. Degas, who had had enough of matters, now showed it. (Oddly, both his cousin Edmondo Morbilli and Mary Cassatt were to accuse the artist of uncharitableness towards René, with whom he did eventually become reconciled.)

From the late 1860s, Degas had already made efforts to sell his paintings both in France and abroad. Paul Durand-Ruel, a dealer interested in new painters, had a branch in Brussels, but it soon closed; Degas was also in contact with an associate gallery in London known as the Society of French Artists, run by Charles Deschamps, an enthusiastic if reckless young man and the nephew of the famous international dealer Ernest Gambart.[34] Degas travelled to London in October 1871 and his early concentration on racing scenes is at least partly explained by the British interest in such pictures. The artist sent pictures to London, where Deschamps exhibited for the first time *The ballet of 'Robert le Diable'* (cat 48), one of two works which Degas sent him in 1872, and *At the races in the countryside (Carriage at the races)* (cat 13), again one of two paintings, in 1873. By 1874, Degas' relationship with Deschamps intensified, all the more as Paul Durand-Ruel was experiencing serious financial difficulties (he was only to resume his relationship with the Impressionists in 1880, when he found a solid financial backer).

Degas' reluctance to exhibit his paintings was a matter of some consequence. His experience at the Salon had left him with revulsion for the selection process, and for the manner in which pictures were shown. In 1867, after sending to the Salon two paintings, he asked for permission to retouch them. There was still a month to do it, but the administration indicated it was impossible. Degas explained himself in a letter to the Superintendent of Fine Arts on 13 March and was eventually allowed three days to do the work.[35] In 1868 he contributed to the Salon—apparently without conflict—*Mlle Fiocre in the ballet 'La Source'* (cat 45) and seemed not unhappy the following year. In 1870, however, he published in the *Paris Journal* of 12 April an open letter to the Salon Jury, proposing radical improvements: to reduce the display to only two rows of paintings, to preserve a distance of at least 20 or 30 centimetres between each work, to amalgamate paintings with drawings, and to give artists the right to withdraw their works from exhibition after a few days.[36] The suggestions were of course not adopted, and thereafter Degas returned to the Salon only as a visitor. Intransigent about the 'Salon style' of hanging, Degas was also ready to break an old relationship when the same hanging philosophy was applied in the private exhibition of a common friend who he admired: we can note that Degas' estrangement from Monet grew after the latter had opposed the idea of showing many more drawings by Berthe Morisot at her posthumous exhibition of 1896.

After 1870, Degas exhibited his work only rarely—a point to which we will return, as it concerns his ideas in general about art and society. This related to his disdain for all forms of official recognition, and his intense sense of privacy. Somewhat similarly, Berthe Morisot prevented her name from being placed on the posters of the Impressionist exhibitions, and Auguste Renoir felt apologetic about accepting late in life the Legion of Honour.[37] The monthly payments ordered by the court for repaying his father's loans meant that Degas had to work a good deal more than before, and paint faster, something he was temperamentally unable to do. Large pictures were thus out of the question, and he turned to pastel as an apparently more expedient method, and executed more small works. His new-found passion for monotypes in the summer of 1876 was to an extent a short-cut to provide him with a base for his pastels, some of which appeared in the third Impressionist exhibition of 1877.

Degas exhibited in seven of the eight Impressionist exhibitions held between 1874 and 1886. In the early years he also sent pictures to the annual Salon of the Société Bearnaise des Amis des Arts, at Pau, which somewhat adventurously held three 'Impressionist' exhibitions in 1876, 1877 and 1878 (Degas' friends Alphonse Cherfils and Paul Lafond were involved).[38] In 1876, Degas exhibited there his *Orchestra musicians* (Städtische Galerie im Städelschen Kunstmuseum, Frankfurt; Lemoisne 295), which created a lively debate, and was purchased by Cherfils himself. The same year, Degas had included in the second Impressionist exhibition in Paris his *A cotton office in New Orleans* (cat 11), but it found no buyer. In 1878, the work was shown in Pau with a tag price of 5000 francs. It was purchased after some hesitation by the Société for the Pau Museum—the first and only of his paintings to be bought in his lifetime by a French institution.

Degas' technique

Degas' contribution to the Impressionist exhibitions was at first of a catalytic nature, and he remained a drawcard to the end. From his point of view, the exhibitions had a number of advantages. For one, because there was no selection jury, he could exhibit what and when he pleased. For someone as uncertain as Degas on the question of when he would finish a work, this system had distinct advantages. The works announced in the catalogues did not always coincide with those actually shown and some works only appeared on the walls days or weeks after the exhibition had opened.[39] The best known such case is that of the sculpture *Little dancer aged fourteen* (cat 67), which was announced but not seen in 1880, and only made a late appearance in 1881. Degas' remark that no one else's painting was less spontaneous than his was certainly true: his complex technique, and quasi-artisanal approach to preparing a work, were against it. He was quite open about what he considered his ineptness and was apt to tell his friends about it. To Albert Bartholomé, he wrote in 1892, 'I thought I knew a little about perspective, I know nothing at all, I thought that one could replace it by a process of perpendiculars and horizontals, measure angles in space by means of good will alone. I dug myself into it …'[40] And to Henry Lerolle, in 1897, he surprisingly added as a coda to a refusal for a dinner invitation: 'It is in vain that I repeat to myself every morning, tell myself again, that one must draw from the bottom upwards, begin with the feet, that the form is far better drawn upwards than downwards, [yet] mechanically I begin with the head.'[41]

The manner in which Degas built up a composition can be observed in work dating as early as the mid 1860s—in *Scene of war in the Middle Ages* (Musée d'Orsay, Paris; Lemoisne 124), shown at the Salon of 1865. In essence the work is painted on paper mounted on canvas. It is obvious however that at a late stage of design Degas painted out a female figure at the centre and added two strips of paper at the far right to accommodate a rider with his captive. Degas was his own severest critic, and if dissatisfied with the result, even after works were sold, his first instinct was to retouch them or perhaps paint a second version. In the case of *The dance class* (cat 53) he did both: he painted a second version (Metropolitan Museum of Art, New York; Lemoisne 397), then changed the principal foreground figure in the first version. The discarded figure—based on the squared drawing *Dancer adjusting her slipper* (cat 58)—he used again, for a pastel. Still dissatisfied, he gradually enlarged the pastel on all sides with the addition of nine strips of paper, some no more than a centimetre wide. The resulting work is the *Dancers in the wings* (Norton Simon Museum, Pasadena; Lemoisne 585).[42]

This complicated process inevitably proved difficult when applied to works on canvas. *The dancing lesson* (Sterling and Francine Clark Art Institute, Williamstown, Mass; Lemoisne 820) from about 1880 had to be re-stretched just to give Degas another centimetre at the top and two more at the bottom. On other occasions he substantially enlarged a painting, repositioning the subject in a different manner: the *Portrait of Mme René De Gas, née Estelle Musson* (New Orleans Museum of Art; Lemoisne 306) was expanded at the top and bottom after the artist brought it back from New Orleans, but remained unfinished in his studio; after his death, the canvas was reduced to its earlier dimensions. The Havemayers in New York had to wait between 1891 and 1894 for Degas to finish retouching an early work they purchased, *The collector of prints* (Metropolitan Museum of Art, New York; Lemoisne 138).[43] If Degas could not retouch a painting, as was often the case with works he had sold, all that remained was for him to take them back and replace them. This happened with the six paintings sold to the singer–collector Jean-Baptiste Faure, including *The ballet of 'Robert le Diable'* (cat 48), which he withdrew and eventually replaced—but not before a court case arose.[44]

Works on paper were constantly added to or otherwise recomposed, and a good number of Degas' preparatory works have, at the top or on the back, instructions to his *colleur* (the artisan who enlarged and mounted them) indicating the dimensions of the additions. A pastel, *At the Louvre* (private collection; Lemoisne 582) required elaborate preparation: the figures, removed from a drawing, were repositioned and fleshed out with strips of paper which filled gaps and enlarged the composition at the top, bottom and left.[45] A study showing the scheme for the composition (Vente IV: 250b; National Gallery Of Art, Washington, DC) served for the etching of the same design, *Mary Cassatt at the Louvre: the Etruscan Gallery* (see opposite). Degas inscribed helpful notations to jog his memory on some studies of dancers, such as the *Dancer in fourth position* (cat 60), but also remarks of a critical nature. On one version of *Preparation for a 'Pirouette en dehors'* (private collection; Vente III: 119b) he notes: 'bras mauvais' (the arms are bad), and that the space between the feet is 'trop large' (too wide);[46] on another, a version of *Dancer practising at the barre* (private collection; Vente II: 215b), he notes 'bad/too twisted/left leg less stretched out on the barre.'[47]

Of course, an etching plate can be worked and reworked, which was the case with *Mary Cassatt in the Louvre: looking at paintings* (cats 104–106). The monotype process does not permit several states. However, when a project was public—as in the rare case of the monotype illustrations for *La famille Cardinal*, intended for publication but turned down by the author—Degas executed several versions for the same episode, to achieve the desired effect. The designs for *The famous Good Friday dinner* (cat 30), *Pauline and Virginie Cardinal chatting with some admirers* (cat 31) and *The most embarrassed was the Marquis Cavalcanti* (cat 32) each required a second version distinguished by small (but to Degas, important) modifications. In only one case do we know which variant Degas thought most successful among three attempts: it was *Ludovic Halévy finds Mme Cardinal in the dressing room* (André Bromberg collection, Paris; Brame and Reff 96), of which he gave the first impression to Ludovic Halévy.

Degas never threw away a sketch, indeed he kept everything for reference or future use—a great advantage for art historians, but in retrospect, some friends thought, a mistake. In later life for instance, studies for *Scene of war in the Middle Ages* (Musée d'Orsay, Paris; Lemoisne 124) which was exhibited at the 1865

Salon, inspired new designs for bathers, which Picasso admired and included in his tributes to Degas (p 255, bottom). Drawings could also be run through the press for the production of counterproofs, a procedure that intensified in the later part of the century: *The bath* (cat 123), for instance, has a reverse twin (private collection; Lemoisne 1047). The original and the mirror image of a design may lead to quite different compositions and further variations. Degas used the monotype process (which by definition yields only one proof) to the last drop of ink: very often taking two proofs, knowing full well that the second would be imperfectly inked but could serve as the basis for a pastel—a necessity in the years 1876–77 when he was forced to sell some small, quickly executed pastels for urgently needed funds. On one known occasion a wet first proof of a monotype was run through the press to produce a counterproof. Similarly, the negative of a photograph could be used to give a number of differently cropped prints. The artist was certainly thrifty with canvas—as many artists are—and did not hesitate to recycle failures. In the background of *Portrait of a woman* (cat 10) we can detect the covered traces of another head, while the portrait of Mme Jeantaud, *Woman with an umbrella (Berthe Jeantaud)* (National Gallery of Canada, Ottawa; Lemoisne 463) was painted on top of a half-length woman: what looks like Mme Jeantaud's scarf, down her bosom, is in fact the sleeve, cuff and hand of the woman painted underneath.

In addition to there being no selection jury, the second great advantage offered Degas by the Impressionist exhibitions was the way his work was displayed. He could avoid the clutter of the Salon, could mix paintings with works on paper, could frame works as he wished, and could place them on walls with colours of his own choosing. James Whistler had launched the idea of harmonised exhibition interiors, drawing a law suit when his exhibition at the Flemish Gallery in London in 1874 was hung on pink-grey and white walls with a brown ceiling, and in an additional small room coloured in yellow.[48] Whistler followed with other aesthetic arrangements in exhibitions at the Fine Art Society in London in 1880, 1881 and 1883, the last being the notorious installation *Arrangement in white and yellow* in February 1883. There are few references to Degas' installations, but according to Gustave Goetschy, the small room Degas devised in 1881 for presenting the *Little dancer aged fourteen* (cat 67) had walls covered with yellow fabric.[49]

Degas was also particularly careful about his frames, favouring modern ones painted in orchestrated colours—whether for a painting, pastel or drawing.[50] (Pissarro and Mary Cassatt also did this.) For his early work, he preferred frames of the period. Referring to one such picture, he wrote to Durand-Ruel: 'an old frame of 30 years ago would be suitable.'[51] For his modern works however, he explored a variety of profiles and had frames specially made, very few of which have survived. A coxcomb design for a moulding of Whistlerian derivation was used for a frame, tinted apple green, on his *Portrait of friends in the wings* (Musée d'Orsay, Paris; Lemoisne 526), which was shown at the fourth Impressionist exhibition of 1879. Almost 20 years later he chose a variation on the type, in brown, for the unusual square-shaped *After the bath, woman drying her neck* (Musée d'Orsay, Paris; Lemoisne 1306). Count Isaac de Camondo, who purchased the work and retained the frame, had mouldings designed for his other Degas works, made very much in keeping with the artist's wishes. Degas subsequently favoured a simpler frame design—eventually a flat strip surrounding the painting with a raised narrow strip on the outer perimeter, influenced by the type of frames used by the pre-Raphaelites and George Frederic Watts. Degas' mouldings could be gilt, or white—as for *Dancer resting* (private collection; Lemoisne 560).[52] Also white and of great simplicity was the frame, now lost, for the large *Dancers tying their ballet slippers* (Cleveland Museum of Art; Lemoisne 1144).[53] His *At the races: before the start* (cat 22) was almost certainly originally framed in white: he wrote to Durand-Ruel on August 1885 from Paramé, 'For the simple white frame destined to replace that of the long horizontal horses, there are several at home, 21 rue Pigalle. Sabine [Neyt] will show them to you. Send Prosper [Garny] with the measurements.'[54]

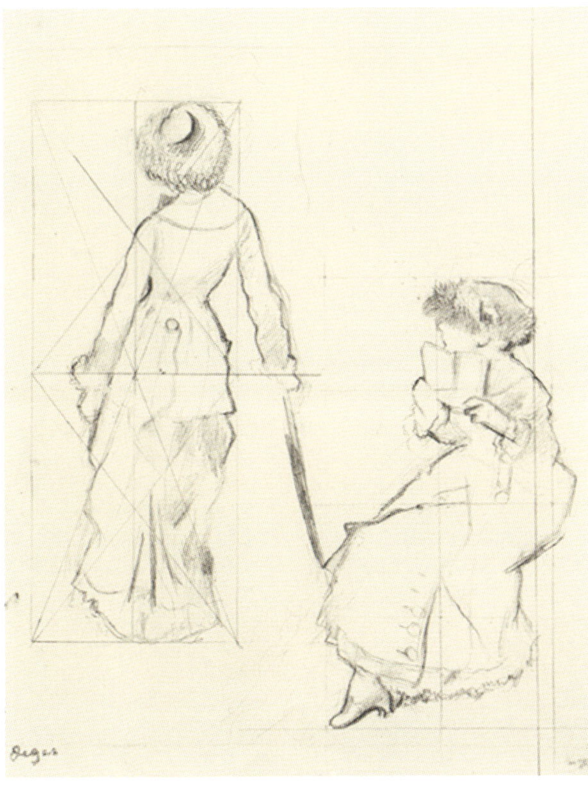

Study for *Mary Cassatt at the Louvre: the Etruscan Gallery* (Etude pour *Mary Cassatt au Louvre: Musée des Antiques*) c 1879
graphite on wove paper, 32.3 x 24.5 cm
National Gallery of Art, Washington DC
Collection of Mr and Mrs Paul Mellon
Image courtesy of the Board of Trustees, National Gallery of Art, Washington DC

After the last Impressionist exhibition, in 1886, Degas ceased (with one exception) to show his work. In 1886, when Octave Maus organised a showing of the Belgian avant-garde group *Les XX*, Monet contributed nine works and Renoir eight, but Degas refused to participate. (The painter Theo Van Rysselberghe had written to Maus, with the words underlined: 'We could even go grovelling to Degas to try and get the latter to exhibit.'[55]) In 1898, Degas was asked to participate in the first exhibition of one of Whistler's creations—the International Society of Sculptors, Painters and Gravers. He was not a member of the Society, and failed to reply; the Society borrowed from other sources instead. The following year, Degas was invited again. His reply of 26 March 1899 is worth quoting, as it sums up the artist's philosophy:

> I do not wish to exhibit and am taking the precaution of replying to your second invitation so that the *sans gene* ['do-as-you-please' situation] of last year is not repeated. I thought that my silence would be enough and that by not accepting in writing I was quite simply refusing. So I beg you, Monsieur, not to think that you have any claim on my independence, to refuse all offers of loans whether they come from a dealer or amateur [collector] … [56]

Degas' philosophy went further, anticipating by a century the issue of artists' exhibition rights which are so sensitive in today's galleries and museums. In 1900, when the Paris Universal Exposition was organised, Degas wrote to his friend Paul Lafond, the new curator of the museum at Pau, regarding *A cotton office in New Orleans* (cat 11) held in the collection there:

> I would like to know, Lafond, if the Museum at Pau was approached for the loan of my painting for this gathering. The point is to stop it from travelling, a matter about which I was not consulted. Would you have the kindness to look into it and to give the protection of my independence priority over and above any other arrangement that might seem convenient or useful (to you with respect to this loan). I believe you are honourable enough to do so.[57]

When it proved too late to change the matter, Degas threatened to sue the state. As the incident unfolded, Degas' friend Albert Bartholomé wrote to Lafond: 'Conclusion: I refuse to get involved […] I won't discuss the question of the right of the State in this matter, I know nothing about it. The trial would be a curious event, so let Degas sue.'[58] In the end, the painting *did* travel to Paris, and was exhibited, and Degas held no grudge against Lafond.

Regarding Degas' control of exhibiting his work, his swan song had taken place earlier, back in 1892, with the only one-man show of his works held in France during his lifetime. He had prepared the works in the style he liked, and had them shown at Durand-Ruel's gallery. Uncharacteristically, it was an exhibition of small landscapes in pastel over monotype. An American painter, Philip Hale, reported that all were framed in identical shadow boxes (framed mats), each being 'tinted the dominant colour of the picture.'[59] None of the frames seem to have survived, but five appear in a photograph of a Degas exhibition at Durand-Ruel's New York gallery in 1901.[60] The exhibition in Paris likely opened on 7 November 1892, when it was attended by the American dealer George Lucas.[61] Accounts of the number of works exhibited vary, but Degas, who was precise in such matters, stated that 26 landscapes were shown and that he was pleased with the result.[62] As Durand-Ruel purchased 24 of the landscapes *en bloc*, the suggestion is that two additional works were loans.[63] A rumour (not unjustified in Degas' case) that the exhibition could not be visited must have circulated, because Mme Hermann de Clermont, his friend's wife, asked how she could be admitted to see it. Degas replied on Tuesday 15 November: 'There is no trick, Dear Lady, for opening the door of 16 rue Laffitte. Walk in without knocking. It closes at the end of the week.'[64] The letter shows the exhibition closed on Saturday 19 November. However, it was not taken down immediately, because on the following Monday the American painter Theodore Robinson saw it. His diary entry for 21 November reads: 'Degas show on—it is very curious—*paysages de fantaisie* [imaginary landscapes], some charming things, but disquieting—too enigmatical. A curious feeling in some of the refined drawing—tho[ugh] one doesn't know quite what it is.'[65]

The 1890s: greater recognition

Through the 1880s and the 1890s, Degas' reputation grew enormously. His every word was repeated and his pictures were exhibited from New York to Berlin to St Petersburg. This was largely the doing of his principal dealer, Durand-Ruel, who had a branch in New York and contacts everywhere. With time he became, so to speak, Degas' financial manager: he paid the artist's rent, insurance and other expenses. More importantly, from the 1880s Degas was no longer plagued by his father's old debt and could indulge his passions for collecting works by Ingres and Delacroix and contemporaries, or the younger generation—even Vincent van Gogh. When he couldn't buy, he offered pastels in exchange. He felt he was forced to work for dealers in order to pay his bills, and wrote to Henri Rouart on 8 August 1887: 'I have never done with the finishing of my pictures and pastels etc. … How long it is and how my last good years are passing in mediocrity!'[66] Among his Delacroix drawings was a study for one of the figures in a painting he saw often, the *Barque de Dante* (1822) (Musée du Louvre, Paris) (see opposite), which echoed his own preoccupations with the nude. Degas' collection was hung on the second floor of his house. He occasionally sold through other dealers, notably Theo van Gogh (Vincent's brother), but never defected to Georges Petit, Durand-Ruel's rival, as Monet, Renoir and Pissarro had done. Around 1895, however, a new figure emerged on the art market scene—Ambroise Vollard. Young, ambitious, irreverent and persuasive, Vollard was to handle Cézanne and Renoir, and took an interest in Degas. He was particularly interested in the artist's later works, which Durand-Ruel had some difficulty in selling.

Degas may well have been strict about exhibiting only on his own terms, but he benefited from all this activity—to an extent of which he was perhaps not always fully aware. In 1893, he could well scoff at Albert Bartholomé and Mary Cassatt preparing works for the World's Columbian Exhibition in Chicago, and have no idea that his own would also be on display (courtesy of Alexander J Cassatt and Mr Albert Spencer). Exhibition catalogues record some 1000 titles of works by Degas which were shown in his lifetime, mostly outside France, in some 200 exhibitions—dealers' shows, international shows, secessions, biennials, or exhibitions organised by the state. It must be said, however, that many of these exhibitions circulated the same works. Any pretext was welcome to a dealer, be it showing Degas' racing scenes at the *Sports in art* exhibition at the Galerie Georges Petit in 1884, or some works for the *Childhood* exhibition at the Petit Palais in 1901.

Sometimes the Degas representation could be outstanding, with Durand-Ruel or Vollard contributing vast numbers from stock: 24 works to the Cassirer Gallery in Berlin for the exhibition *Max Liebermann, HGE Degas, Constantin Meunier* in 1898; 36 works for an Impressionist show at the Grafton Gallery in London in 1905; and 29 works for a Degas/Cézanne exhibition at the Cassirer Gallery in 1913. When originals could not be obtained, photographs (black and white, and later colour) of his works were used—something that took place as early as 1876. In 1887, the dealer Alfred Beugniet, in an act of consecration of sorts, even included one of Degas' palettes in an exhibition of artist's tools. Collectors readily supplied loans, but few people closer to Degas would have ever obliged, for fear of antagonising him.

The first Degas exhibition held abroad was not, as often stated, the 1911 survey at the Fogg Art Museum at Harvard University (Cambridge, Massachussetts), where 12 works were shown, supplemented with reproductions. Indeed, the Durand-Ruel gallery had held two exhibitions in New York, in 1901 and 1909 (photographs of the latter display exist).[67] Degas had become very famous—to some the most important painter of the times. His mere appearance raised the artistic temperature, as observed on 30 June 1906 by the theatre director Jacques Copeau (then an assistant at the Georges Petit Gallery), in a letter to his friend André Gide: 'The day before yesterday *great emotion*: M. Degas was in the gallery. I had never met him and observed him for a long time. Do you know him? That gave me an immense feeling of moral and almost physical well-being.'[68]

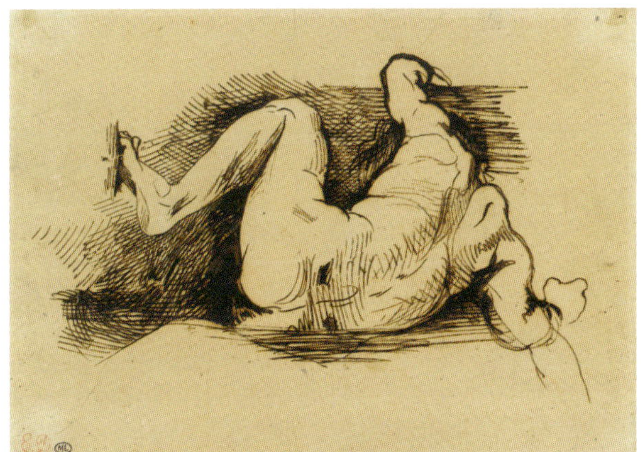

Eugène Delacroix
Study of a man seen from behind (for the 'Barque de Dante') (Etude d'homme vu de dos (pour 'La barque de Dante')) c 1820–21
pen and brown ink on paper, 15 x 21 cm
Musée du Louvre, Département des arts graphiques, Paris
© RMN / Thierry Le Mage

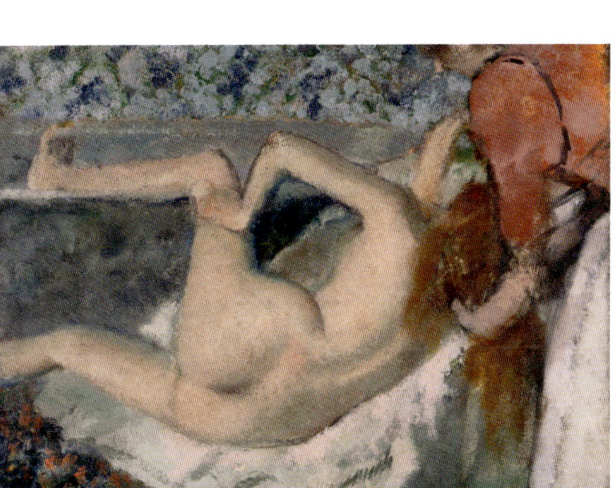

Edgar Degas
After the bath (Après le bain)
c 1895
oil on canvas, 65.1 x 81 cm
The J Paul Getty Museum, Los Angeles
Lemoisne 1104

Over these later decades, Degas' eyesight was a source of constant worry. The question, which has a bearing on his late style, has formed the object of scholarly interest.[69] As noted earlier, his sight deteriorated after 1870. He complained constantly of seeing poorly and his portrait by Marcellin Desboutin of around 1876 (see p 252) shows him already aged and wearing glasses. He was looked after by various physicians, including Dr Edmond Landolt, an eminent and erudite ophthalmologist of independent opinions. (Landolt experimented with different lenses, and also attended to Mary Cassatt.) In a letter to his sister Thérèse Morbilli, Degas wrote in 1892: 'You cannot imagine the gaps I have in my vision, I see through a strainer.'[70] Judging by his correspondence, the condition seemed to vary in intensity: in 1896, for instance, his handwriting in letters written 10 days apart shows enormous variations in the firmness of his hand.[71]

In a sense, he could compensate through his remarkable visual memory. In a conversation about the later work of Paul Renouard (a newspaper and magazine artist and writer, in whose

Marcellin Desboutin
Edgar Degas 1876
oil on canvas, 46 x 31 cm
Châteaux de Versailles et de Trianon, Versailles
© RMN / Gérard Blot

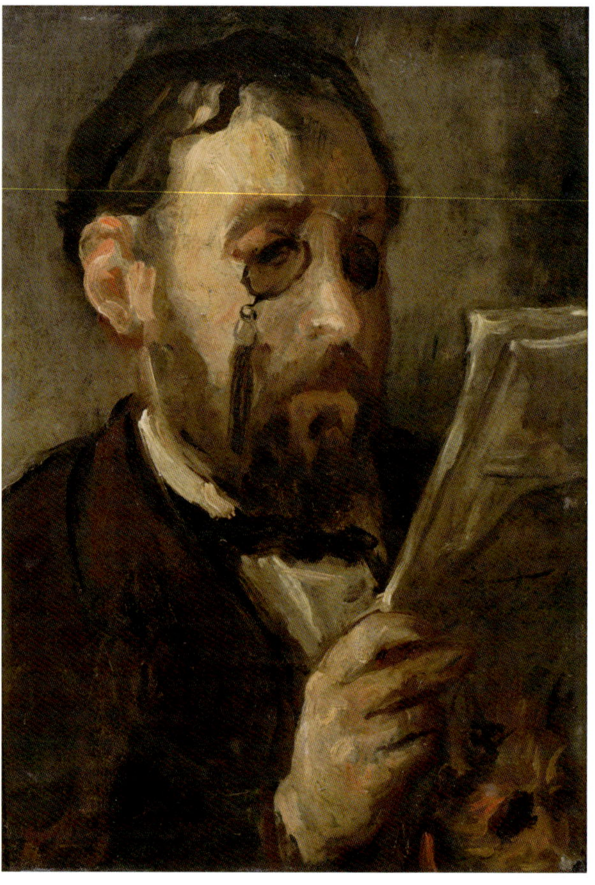

published work Degas was interested, in the 1870s), Degas said to his friend, the painter Georges Jeanniot: 'It is all very well to copy from what one sees. But it is much better to draw from what one sees only in one's memory. It is a transformation during which the imagination collaborates with memory.'[72] The principles of Horace Lecoq de Boisbaudran concerning drawing from memory were familiar to him, as they were to Corot and others, but Degas' memory was prodigious. A model was necessary to confirm the truth of that which the mind had imagined (ie, remember first, verify later), but Degas could still visualise persons or scenes years after seeing them, as his correspondence demonstrates. At the mention of the name of an acquaintance, he wrote to Albert Bartholomé, 'I hear him, I see him, all red with anger.' In a condolence letter to Dr Paul Paulin regarding the latter's mother, who he hadn't met in a long time, Degas commented, 'I see your old mother before me, with her square shoulders, her lively and happy eyes, small and stout.' Regarding Evariste de Valernes' studio in 1890, he recalled: 'I see it again, as if it were in front of me,' or again, in 1892, writing to his sister Thérèse in Naples about friends there and their mother, he said: 'I see [her] from here, with her bright eyes like in her portrait.'[73]

Degas' notoriously caustic spirit and an unsuspected interest in politics led him into a socially disastrous position in the Dreyfus Affair which divided France in the later 1890s. The artist was anti-Dreyfus, and showed it. His much-discussed anti-Semitism during the Dreyfus case led to a sad break with his long-time friends the Halévy family, and with Pissarro, who, however, sublimely rose above it and kept his admiration for Degas' art intact. Before the Dreyfus trial, Degas would appear to have entertained no specific anti-Semitic views—he had several Jewish friends—though a case has been made that his portrait of the Jewish businessman–collector Ernest May is manifestly anti-Semitic.[74] During the Dreyfus trial, and later, Degas was very public in voicing his opinions, virtually shouting them. He certainly held an almost abstract view of the issue, which he saw as a question of patriotism rather than of Dreyfus' alleged guilt. As he told André Gide: 'Dreyfus innocent? Dreyfus guilty? I don't care. France matters to me more than an individual. If saving an innocent Dreyfus must compromise a guilty France, it is imperative that Dreyfus *become* guilty in order for France to be declared innocent.'[75] Degas remained passionately anti-Dreyfus long after Dreyfus' acquittal: as late as January 1907, Maurice Denis found him attending an anniversary meeting of the Dreyfus' verdict held at the Action Française.[76]

Women, and solitude

In his later years, Degas' complained of loneliness, and the only constant in his life was his old maid Zoé Clozier. Degas' representation of women is discussed elsewhere in this catalogue, but his relations with women deserves some attention here. Anyone familiar with the body of his correspondence knows that he was constitutionally unable to lie, and incapable of subterfuge—a serious drawback in society. No open book was more open, hence Degas' well-known sense of privacy. His life was dependent on acceptance by others of his shortcomings, which were considerable. He was the first to know that he was a difficult friend and would have made an intolerable husband or partner, even by nineteenth-century standards. How many people end a letter with 'believe in my unbearable friendship'?[77] As early as 1858, his friend Tourny wrote affectionately to say how he and his wife 'still think of the De Gas who grumbles and the Edgar who growls, but we will miss even more these growlings and grumblings next winter.'[78] In time the grumbles became epic. Over half a century later, at the time of Degas' triumph at the Rouart sale, Renoir wrote: 'Degas must still growl out of principle, without that he would not longer be Degas.'[79]

On the other hand, Degas could be enchanting, touching and extremely funny. There are hints in his notes about love, but unlike Delacroix—another bachelor consumed by his art—Degas did not keep notes specifically on the subject. Various names turn up in his youth—a Mlle Bréguet, or a Pauline (who James Tissot knew in September 1862). Afterwards Degas drew a veil over the subject. He said nothing, and his artist friends knew nothing. Manet was consumed with curiosity on the subject. There was a rumour in the 1870s that Degas had conceived a passion for Mme Camus, a married woman whose portrait he painted several times in her youth, and who he saw into his old age.[80] Other women he treated as divinities—as was the case with the opera singer Rose Caron. His female contemporaries wrote clear-eyed accounts of him, tinted with affection, and Madeleine Zillhardt wrote, 'I never noticed that Degas detested our sex.'[81] Mme Alexandre Jeanniot—the painter Jeanniot's mother—hearing him on the subject of women, sighed and said to the artist: 'Monsieur Degas, to speak so ill of them you must have loved them very much!'[82]

Alice Michel described the artist's difficult sessions with his intelligent and good-natured model Pauline, late in his life. It had not always been like that. In the later 1860s, Degas had enjoyed the company of Emma Dobigny (who had also delighted Corot) and had written affectionately to her. In the 1870s he was more compassionate than his fellow artists towards one of his former models, Valérie Roumi, who was ill and destitute, and died in the hospital where Degas had managed to find a place for her. We also know from Jeanne Baudot that in 1896–97 Renoir had passed a beautiful model on to her, who he also recommended to Degas. Renoir and Baudot dropped the model when she proved visibly pregnant, but Degas retained her.[83]

Berthe Morisot, whose mother hoped Degas might propose, was terrified in the early days by his criticism of her painting, as was Mary Cassatt later. Both women admired his work—Mary Cassatt more so—and he grew to admire both as artists. His letters abound with the adjective '*formidable*' ('awesome' in English) in connection with his impressive female connections. While he treated his women friends with deference and occasional amusement, Degas believed artists had no gender, and he evidently discussed art with Morisot and Cassatt as if they were male students, when they wanted to be treated as ladies. Deep down, Mary Cassatt seems to have never forgiven him for this, but she alone, when he was old and infirm, took matters in hand and from a distance organised his family affairs. The less lady-like Suzanne Valadon—for Degas the '*terrible* Maria' or 'illustrious Valadon'—his former model and now herself a great artist, let him admire her drawings without fuss. When Valadon was unwell, he worried enough to write: 'How are you, my poor Maria? Give me some news of yourself.'[84] Berthe Morisot

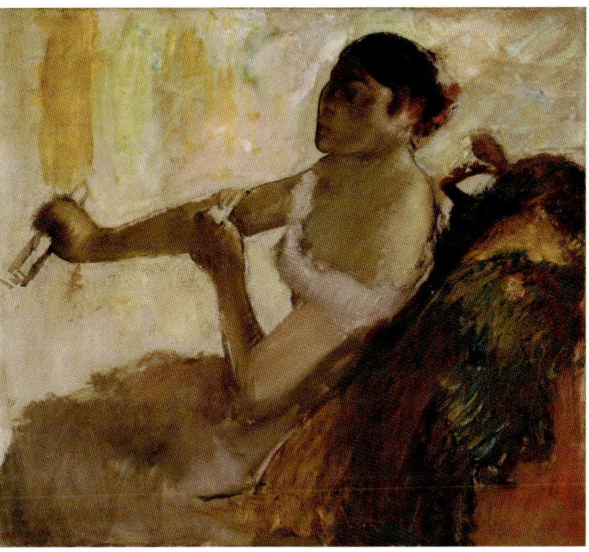

Rose Caron c 1885–90
oil on canvas, 76.2 x 82.5 cm
Albright-Knox Art Gallery, Buffalo
Charles Clifton, Charles W Goodyear and Elisabeth H Gates Funds, 1943
Lemoisne 862

knew him well enough to pay him the compliment, before her premature death, of appointing him, with Renoir and Stéphane Mallarmé, as a 'family council' to look after her young orphaned daughter, Julie Manet. Few have remarked on how extraordinary a gesture this was, towards a man reputed to be 'nasty'. The young Julie Manet left interesting observations in her diary, recording how thrilled she was to be treated by Degas almost as an adult. The artist was manifestly fond of his friends' children, and they remained devoted to him to the end. Hortense Valpinçon, even after she married, went on asking him to stay at Ménil-Hubert, where pantomimes were staged for the benefit of a photographer (see over page).

Degas spoke a good deal about marriage—increasingly in later life when his friends were happily paired. A sense of his complex psychological make-up is evident in a letter Degas addressed on 21 August 1884 to the painter Henry Lerolle (a recent addition to his circle), and quoted by the mezzo-soprano Jeanne Raunay who was a friend of Degas. It presumably followed some contretemps Degas had with the Lerolles:

> If you were single and aged fifty (which I turned a month ago) you would have this kind of reaction, when you shut yourself like a door and not only on your friends. You suppress everything around you, you annihilate yourself and you finally kill yourself out of disgust.
>
> I conceived too many projects and here I am, blocked and powerless. And I lost the thread. I always thought I would have time; what I didn't do, that which I was prevented from doing, in the midst of all my troubles, and in spite of my incompetence with life, I never once despaired that I'd get there one fine morning. I locked all my plans into a cupboard and always had the key with me but now I've lost it.[85]

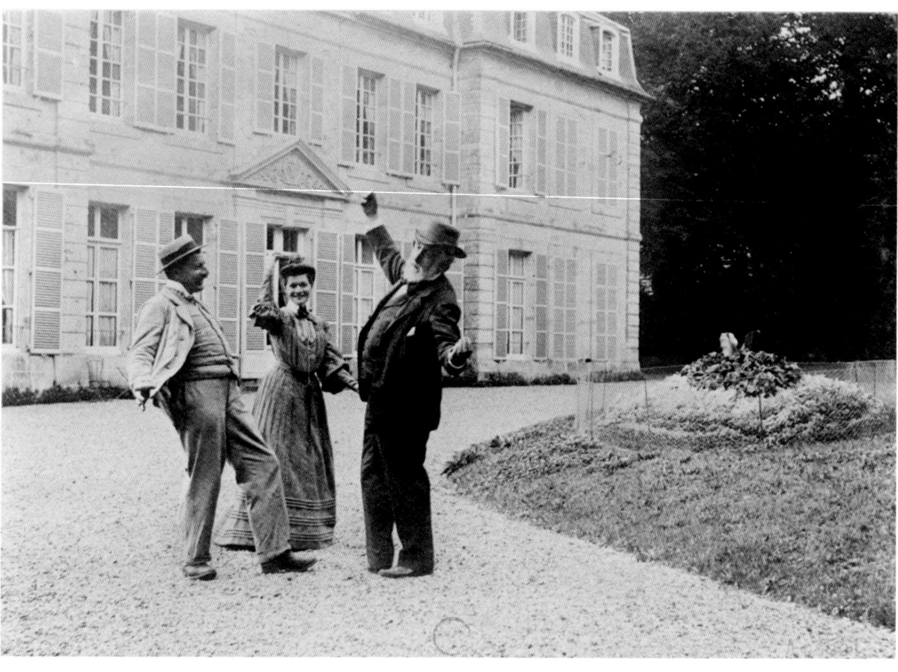

Unknown photographer
*Degas with M. and Mme Jacques Fourchy, née Hortense Valpinçon, in the park of the château at Ménil-Hubert (Degas, M. et Mme Jacques Fourchy, mimant des petites scènes dans le parc de Ménil-*Hubert)
c 1895
gelatin silver photograph
Bibliothèque nationale de France, Paris

The matter of his solitude evidently bothered the artist. In 1890, when he visited the Jeanniots at Diénnay with Bartholomé, he was troubled and wrote to Paul Lafond: 'You don't seem to notice that I am no longer myself […] I repeat, I am not quite certain about what goes on in my head and I am afraid.'[86] Nobody quite knew why Degas undertook this long buggy-and-horse trip with Bartholomé. After Degas and Bartholomé left, Jeanniot reassured Lafond but observed: 'Confidentially, I believe Degas is haunted by ideas of marriage and perhaps he wanted to take a breather before plunging that awesome head of his into the unknown.'[87] If true, nobody knows who the woman was. In 1898, at the wedding of Eugène Rouart with Yvonne Lerolle—in which Degas had played a part—he conspired with Julie Manet to arrange the marriage of her cousin, Paule Gobillard, to Paul Valéry (Degas had introduced the couple). At the same time, he contrived the marriage of Julie Manet to Ernest Rouart, Eugène's brother; it later took place at the same time as the Gobillard–Valéry wedding, on 31 May 1900. Amidst this matrimonial activity, in 1898, at Julie Manet's, Degas met Jeanne Baudot, a charming and very bright young student of Renoir's. She was 21. Degas asked Julie: 'What if I married Mamzelle Baudot! … It would be a strange marriage.'[88] When Julie relayed the message, more or less jokingly, a Baudot family servant observed that Degas was too old; Jeanne Baudot herself handled the matter with tact and humour. The following summer, at a dinner party in Degas' apartment—when it emerged that Jeanne loved duck but disliked chicken, whereas Degas liked chicken but not duck—Degas' young friends told the artist that the match would never work.[89]

Degas' reluctance to exhibit and have his work published without his consent also extended to interviews, dedications or articles his friends wrote about him. The rule was strict. His old friend George Moore, the Irish novelist, and Jacques-Emile Blanche (who published a portrait he'd made of Degas), were never spoken to again.[90] Oddly, as he liked poetry—he sometimes wrote letters to Paul Lafond in verse—Degas didn't mind circulating among friends his sonnets, his obsession of 1888–89, and allowed their publication in a small edition in his lifetime.[91] The sonnets' subjects mostly corresponded to those of his art—dancers, horses, and the opera.

Degas was by no means averse to the idea of reproduction, however, if he was directly involved. In 1888 he agreed to the publication of an album of 15 transfer lithographs after his work commissioned by Theo van Gogh for the Boussod, Valadon & Cie Gallery he directed. The work was entrusted to George William Thornley, who later worked also with Pissarro and Monet. The printing, in black and white and colours, was carried out at Bequet's shop for the Goupil firm. Degas was unhappy with the proof of *At the milliner's* (Museo Thyssen-Bornemisza, Madrid; Lemoisne 729) and stopped the printing, but changed his mind about retouching Thornley's transfer drawing himself and waited instead for Thornley to return from his honeymoon to tend to it. Several individual plates were shown at van Gogh's gallery in 1888 and some non-edition prints occasionally have both Degas' and Thornley's signature.[92] The album, issued in an edition of 1000 copies with the title *15 lithographies d'après Degas par GW Thornley*, was ready in February 1889 (though widely advertised only in 1890). It sold for 100 francs and the plates were signed by Thornley.[93]

A second project followed in the later 1890s. This was Degas' rare album *Vingt dessins (Twenty drawings) 1861–1896*, an altogether different proposition as it involved photography. Degas had already experimented with photography himself. In this instance, a colour photo-aquatint system adapted by Degas' friend, Michel Manzi, was used. The set, published by Boussod, Manzi, Joyant & Cie in an edition of 100 copies, each signed by Degas, came out in 1897. Degas chose the drawings very carefully, and again the Goupil firm was involved. The publication took more than a year to produce and each plate was presented in a mat; the facsimiles were of such quality as to pass at first glance for originals—as they sometimes do today. The costs had been high. In the event, each album was priced at 1000 francs.[94] The early plates included five variations on figures for *Semiramis building Babylon* (Musée d'Orsay, Paris; Lemoisne 82) and the beautiful *Hélène Hertel* (cat 3)—the only portrait included. Pissarro saw the album in January 1898, and thought it splendid. He wrote: 'It is there that you can see Degas is truly a master, it is more beautiful than Ingres and, gosh, it is modern.'[95] Manzi was a trusted friend and belonged in a group with Albert Bartholomé and Paul Lafond. His oil portrait by Degas, showing him preparing an acid bath (Paris, Musée d'Orsay, MNR 848), is generally dated to 1889 but perhaps dates from this time.[96] The *Vingt dessins* publication not only conveys a sense of how Degas wanted to be seen by the public but gives a rare glimpse of how he perceived his evolution as a draughtsman over a period of 35 years—from his studies for *Semiramis*, to the latest bather. In anticipation of the publication Degas sifted through his old drawings, dated some (occasionally wrongly) and had cause to revisit others in his new work. A number of studies of bathers from 1896 onwards are obvious variations on the studies for the tortured nudes he made in 1866–67 for *Scene of war in the Middle Ages* (Musée d'Orsay, Paris, Lemoisne 124).[97]

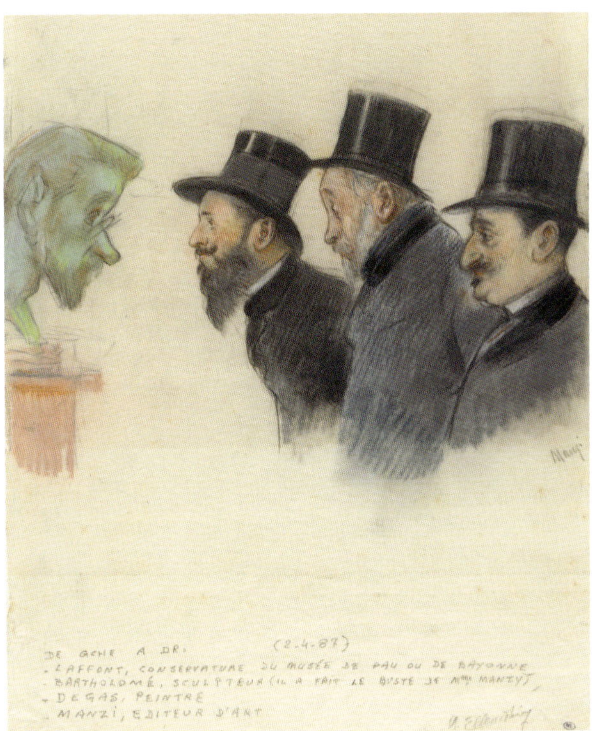

(above)
Michel Manzi
Albert Bartholomé, Degas and Michel Manzi looking at a bust of Paul Lafond (Trois hommes contemplant la tête d'un homme barbu) 1887
pastel and black chalk with white highlights on tracing paper
41.3 x 28.4 cm
Musée du Louvre, Département des arts graphiques, Fonds du Musée d'Orsay, Paris

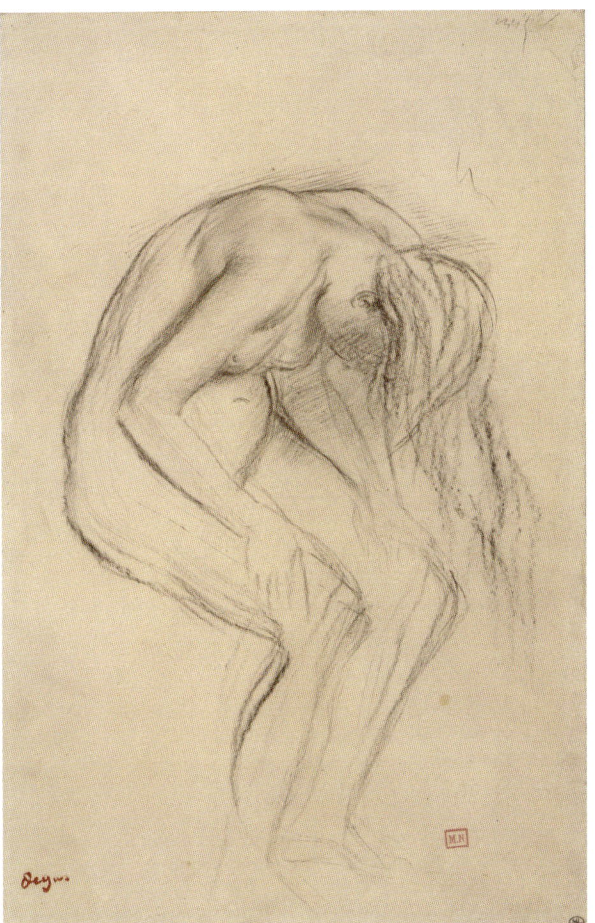

(below) **Edgar Degas**
Nude dishevelled woman leaning forward (Femme nue échevelée penchée en avant à droite)
crayon noir, 36 x 22.9 cm
Musée du Louvre, Département des arts graphiques, Fonds du Musée d'Orsay, Paris

Later years

Degas' old age in the 1890s—failing vision aside—was less unhappy than he imagined it might be. Most first-hand published accounts of Degas emanate from this period. Friends and their children, writers, poets, opera singers, musicians, all climbed the steps to his apartment and ate his insipid food—he believed in healthy, plain fare. Paul Lafond, on errands in Paris, would stay at the 'Hôtel Ingres'—Degas' house. Among artists, Degas saw Berthe Morisot (until her premature death), and Renoir. He also frequently saw Bartholomé and Jean-Louis Forain, whose satirical graphic work he collected, and Forain's wife, Jeanne Bosc, who enchanted him. Louis Braquaval and his family, and the Jeanniots, visited when in Paris. He was also asked out, but sometimes tired of the intellectual dinners given by Geneviève Halévy (widow of Georges Bizet, and now Mme Emile Straus), who was Marcel Proust's muse; or lamented the marble-covered surroundings of the collector, Countess de Béhague, at whose house his works were hung with famous drawings by Leonardo da Vinci.[98] Degas also travelled—several times to Naples, over the never-ending question of the settlement of the De Gas estate—and in 1889 to Spain and Tangiers, with Giovanni Boldini. (He clearly didn't expect to be entirely inactive there, and asked Boldini to go to a well-known establishment to purchase condoms: 'Buy a *fair quantity*. There may be seduction, first for you and then even for me.'[99]) Degas also travelled within France with friends, or went on water cures, like every good bourgeois. Away from his studio, the tone of his letters became amused and chatty.

Over the years, Degas had grown comfortable in the space he occupied at 37 rue Victor-Massé, in Montmartre. On the street side, the windows gave onto the Bal Tabarin, and at the back onto a walled garden. On the first floor was the reception area with his collection of works of art—his 'museum'. On the second were the dining room, and his bedroom where Zillhardt once saw an El Greco leaning on a chair, half-covered by the artist's underclothes.[100] There was a studio full of his canvases on the third floor, but the actual working studio was on the fourth floor above, where—as Valéry wrote—light and dust were equally happy. There, visitors saw:

> the tarnished tin bathtub, the worn bath-robes, the wax dancer with her real gauze tutu in its glass case, easels laden with creatures drawn in charcoal, cramped, twisted, holding a comb about their hair stretched by the other hand . Along the skylight vaguely rubbed by sun ran a narrow shelf cluttered with boxes, bottles, pencils, bits of pastel and nameless things that one day might be of use.[101]

In the studio Degas dressed the part, and looked like a pauper. He thought of bequeathing his collection as a gallery, until he saw Gustave Moreau's museum–studio nearby: 'It is truly sinister … you would think you're in an ancient tomb.'[102] From 1894, owing to the Caillebotte bequest, Degas was represented in the national collection at the Musée du Luxembourg with three small works: two pastels over monotypes, and a pastel of a dancer. He preferred that they were not there. It was only in 1911 that Count Isaac de Camondo's gift to the nation redressed the balance with 11 of Degas' best-known paintings, including *The racecourse (Amateur jockeys close to a carriage)* (cat 15) and *The dance class* (cat 53).

Meanwhile, the rest of the De Gas family had a harder time. In 1893, when Degas' brother Achille was ill in Switzerland, the artist brought him back to Paris, where he died. Marguerite, who in 1889 had settled with her family in Argentina, died in 1895. René returned to France from America, and by 1897 there was a reconciliation between the brothers. Thérèse, who Degas helped financially, was a widow in Naples. By this time, however, Degas' true family—as he often wrote—was Henri Rouart's.[103]

Though Degas was now better off financially, purchases for his growing collection of other artists' work pressed him to sell more of his own. The dealers, however, often preferred his early paintings. As his technique evolved over the years, he sought advice about materials and fixatives for pastels from specialists such as Luigi Chialiva (1842–1914).[104] This was also the time when he had to restore or retouch his poorly stored and sometimes deteriorated earlier paintings, such as *Interior* (*The rape*) (Philadelphia Museum of Art; Lemoisne 348).[105] He was, however, competent about the preparation of canvases, as can be seen in a letter of October 1897; and he was careful about varnishes, an issue which is documented both first-hand and from analysis of his work.[106] Conservation was indeed an interest, and he became the scourge of the administration of the Louvre with his protests over what he considered abusive restorations of old masters.

Degas' late paintings and pastels took an astonishing turn in their intense colour—as if to contradict the prevailing idea that he was primarily one of the great draughtsmen of all times. Before he knew Degas, Valéry wrote to André Gide: 'Degas has just exhibited some absolute stunners at Durand-Ruel's. Dancers, it is clear, but coming from a most extraordinary *planet*. One [work] in particular, a bright orangey thing, has positively stunned me!'[107] Valéry was to learn (from a notebook kept by Berthe Morisot) of a rare observation Degas made on colour when at a dinner with Mallarmé: 'Degas says: orange colours, green neutralises, violet throws a shadow.'[108] As everyone knew, Degas was prone to sudden enthusiastic leaps into the unknown, as had been the case with his immersion in monotypes in 1876. In 1895, he developed a similar interest in photography, which he could feed, at least technically, through his art-and-photography supplier Tasset and Lhote. The passion lasted mostly over that year and, as with everything Degas did, it was all-consuming. Photography was the only artistic activity he performed more or less in public—with willing models, who for the most part were friends. Sculpture, at which he had worked sporadically, also increasingly preoccupied him. He never handled the essential matter of armature (supportive framework) properly, presumably because he wanted freedom to change the movement of the form—as recent scientific examination has shown. Bartholomé recommended casting to the artist, but Degas was reluctant; though a few attempts were made. The last record of Degas at work comes from Alice Michel's account of the model Pauline posing for him, mainly for a version of *Dancer looking at the sole of her right foot* (Czestochowski and Pingeot 32), from around 1910–11.[109]

In the autumn of 1911, modernity unexpectedly forced itself on the artist, when the owner of the building in which he lived announced it was scheduled for demolition. Degas was overwhelmed by the news. On his birthday in July, he had told Madeleine Zillhardt: 'I am 76 today! You can't imagine, can you, what it is like to be 76 years old? I think only of that!'[110] Fortunately, Suzanne Valadon found an apartment for him at 6 boulevard de Clichy. Unfortunately, it was on the fifth floor, but his legs were still good. On 1 December 1911, Mary Cassatt wrote to Mrs Havemeyer: 'Degas is almost out of his mind for he has come to move & he hasn't even dusted his pictures for years. His temper is dreadfully upset.'[111] A few days later, Ambroise Vollard told René Gimpel:

> he was due to move, he was furious. I went to him, kindly, to help him. As I arrived he was piling up pastels on the floor. 'Be careful', I said, 'you will damage them. You must cover every canvas with waxed paper secured at the back with tacks.' As an answer, Degas began to kick the stretchers, pushing them and shoving them from behind with his feet until he got them to lean against the wall in a frightful cloud of pastel and dust.[112]

Degas' last years coincided with his recognition as being perhaps the greatest living artist of his time. On 10 December 1912, at the sale that followed the death of his friend Henri Rouart, Degas' *Dancers at the bar* (Lemoisne 408, The Metropolitan Museum of Art, New York) sold for 435 000 francs—500 000 after premiums—the highest price paid to date for a painting at auction. Even people who knew the art scene observed: 'The world is mad, others say it is a consortium formed by Durand-Ruel with a capital of 20 million which plays on the names of a few painters promoted by the journalists. In any event, it is inexplicable and absurd.'[113] Renoir was not present at what he called (writing to Paule Gobillard) Degas' 'apotheosis', but the almost-blind Degas was there, by himself, standing apart from the dealers, amateur collectors and journalists. Daniel Halévy heard a voice say, 'Degas is there', and found him in a side room. Degas told him, 'It is strange, paintings I sold for 500 francs'[114]—before Daniel helped Degas make the walk to Louise Halévy's. A few days later, Daniel Halévy again noted his impressions of Degas at the sale:

> Degas still so beautiful. That semi-withdrawal which announces death. But as soon as he is spoken to, the presence, the energy, the clarity in his eyes and his voice.
>
> Madame Ganderax says in front of his painting:
> —Bravo, Degas ! This Degas we love, he is not the one of the [Dreyfus] Affair.
> —Madam, it is the whole Degas that I wish to be loved.
> They ask him:
> —Nevertheless, you are not unhappy with this painting?
> —I believe that the one who made it is not an ass; but surely the one who paid so much is an idiot.
> They congratulate him for the price. He shrugs his shoulders.
> —I am a race-horse, he says. I run the great-stakes races but am satisfied with my ration of oats.[115]

Although Degas lived until 1917, his studio was never installed in his new apartment. In December 1912 he told Daniel Halévy, 'I don't work anymore since I moved ... It is funny: I haven't sorted anything, everything stands there against the walls ... I don't care, I give up everything ...'[116] Long walks, sometimes to his old address, where he'd stare at the gaping hole that had been his studio, became a routine habit. But he saw his old friends who visited him and walked with him—he was still sprightly. In 1913, Sacha Guitry, who was producing a film on great men of France, and had obtained an interview from Renoir, asked Degas to participate. Degas refused. As he went for his walk on the Boulevard de Clichy with his niece Jeanne Fevre, cameramen chased after them and managed to film him until he noticed.[117]

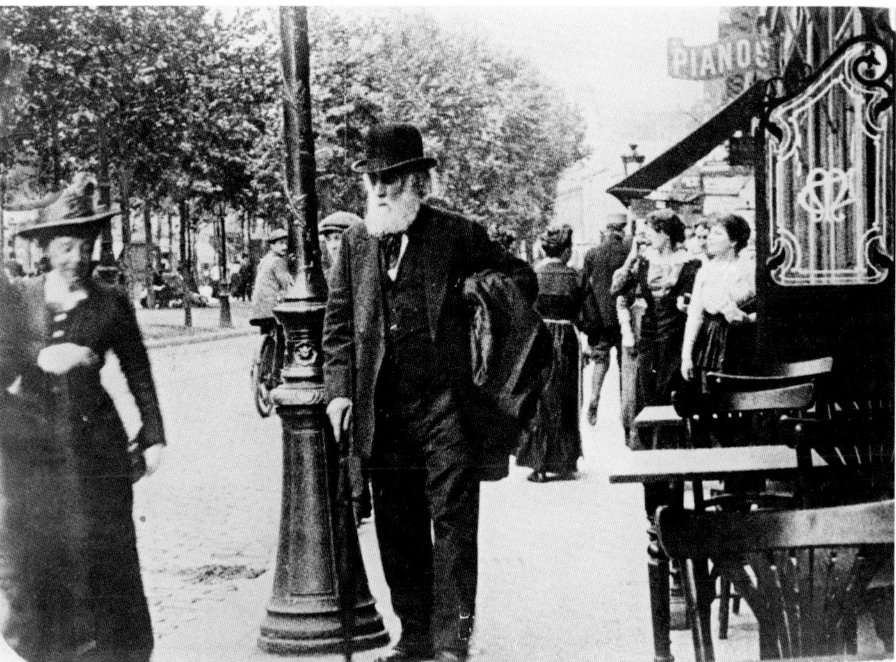

Sacha Guitry
Degas walking along the Boulevard de Clichy (Degas marchant, boulevard de Clichy) 1914–15
modern print, still from Guitry's film *Ceux de chez nous,* 1915
Bibliothèque nationale de France, Paris

When Degas had moved apartments in 1912, Vollard had bought some works from him, including many drawings. Predictably, the transaction is not well documented, but it soon became public knowledge. In early 1913, Mary Cassatt wrote to Mrs Havemeyer:

> It seems the price of the 'Danseuses à la barre' has temporarily stopped the sales of Degas pictures. No matter what you ask, amateurs say, 'Oh of course you want a big price after the Rouart sale'. Vollard says he has some of the finest Degas pastels. As for old M. Durand-Ruel he groans over Vollard buying Degas, thinks it dreadful of Vollard, but Degas is the one to blame.[118]

Vollard's boast was reasonably true, and in 1914 he suggested to Degas a volume of reproductions of works in his stock. The now almost blind Degas agreed, with the same proviso as for earlier publications—he had to have control. In a manner of speaking, it was the artist's last project. Vollard knew perfectly well how difficult Degas could be in matters of copyright—the artist was ahead of the most stringent laws. He submitted to Degas the photographic prints

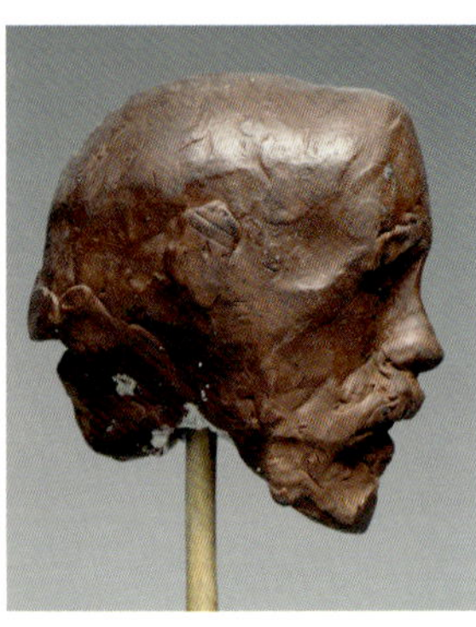

Paul Valéry
Edgar Degas 1910
wax, 10.2 x 6.5 x 9.1 cm
Musée d'Orsay, Paris
Don de Mme Paul Rouart
et M. François Valéry, 1994

mounted on board, before they were sent to the printer, and the artist verified each one and signed it.[119] The publication came out in 1914, under the title, *Degas—peintures, dessins et estampes* (*Degas—paintings, drawings and prints*). Only six paintings were reproduced, but the volume was the most substantial corpus of reproductions of Degas' works to date, being mostly late works on paper.

Edgar Degas died at midnight on 27 September 1917. The funeral, on a sunny day, was a quiet event. Old and younger friends came, including Mary Cassatt, who was in Paris, and Monet from nearby Giverny. Both had additional agendas on their minds: Mary Cassatt wanted to make certain that her great friend, Mrs Havemeyer, would have the *Little dancer aged fourteen*, and Monet wanted to make certain that his own dealer, Bernheim—who Degas detested—would share in the sale of the contents of his studio. Monet's letter of condolence to René Degas mentioned Bernheim, but for the time being René did not answer.[120]

After Degas' death, the fate of his studio was in the hands of his family and dealers. A dispute over two contradictory wills, one in favour of René alone, was mediated by Mary Cassatt and others and resulted in equal shares for all descendants. Everything was to go under the hammer, in wartime Paris. There was no question about sorting through the studio as Degas intended it. The firm Bernheim-Jeune took a part in the process and Ambroise Vollard was of course involved. Durand-Ruel undertook the careful inventory and had everything photographed—the negatives are invaluable today for art historians and conservators. Vollard had the sculpture photographed. Degas' private collection of other artists' work was sold first, in March 1918, followed by two further sales in November.[121] German cannons could be heard during the March sale, and a shell hit the building at 15 rue Lafitte, across from Durand-Ruel's, where Degas' works were stored. The first of the four studio sales took place in May 1918, and the sales continued through November and December, up until April 1919.[122] The prints by Degas were auctioned off by the firm of his late friend Manzi in November 1918, and the sale allowed Loÿs Delteil to produce the first catalogue raisonné (comprehensive catalogue) of Degas' prints, in record time.[123]

The reaction to the first studio sale among Degas' younger friends was of particular interest. The sale consisted of both early and late works, giving the effect of irreconcilable polarities. *Mlle Fiocre* (cat 45), with the oil study (cat 47), *Giovanna and Giulia Bellelli* (cat 9) and the portrait of Hélène Hertel (cat 3) were there; but so were the late *A group of dancers* (cat 76) and *After the bath* (cat 125)—along with other, unfinished works. Daniel Halévy saw them as they were sorted, and again in the exhibition on 4 and 5 May. He watched the expressions of shock people showed in front of the late works, and was in fact shocked himself—they gave him an impression of disaster.[124] He remembered old Degas like a shabby Prospero (his term), and his saying, not so long before: 'How easy it would be if people only left us in peace … Journalists bore the public with our works and bore us with their articles, their phrases … They want to explain everything, always explain … One explains nothing … How silly to bring people before what we do … Beauty, beauty is a mystery.'[125]

A different notion of shock, and of catastrophe, haunted Paul Valéry. He had grown fond of Degas, had seen him often enough and had modelled a wax portrait of him. He wrote to André Gide:

> Disaster. The Degas sale exhibition. It is treason. The family displayed everything, everything. When one thinks that [Degas] planned to entrust Ernest [Rouart] to sort out his studio, to burn a lot … Senility set in, they made for him every testament they wished and once dead he suffered everything he hated most: his collection sold, B[ernheim] charged with the sale; his rough sketches on view and auctioned off.[126]

Gide answered sensibly, on 8 May 1918:

> What you tell me of the Degas [sale] exhibition does not surprise me. One saw it coming, which doesn't make it any less painful […] But why did Degas keep his doodles? There could have been no more delicate a mission than the one that was put to Ernest. I am so very sorry for Degas but happy that Ernest did not have to assume this responsibility.[127]

The first studio sale opened with the great *Dancer with bouquets* (cat 77), which sold for 70 000 francs. Unsold works were bought back by the heirs and formed the object of sales, or gifts, until the later part of the twentieth century. The artist's wax sculptures, found in a sorry state, were set aside: some models could be cleaned and restored with the help of Bartholomé. The rest—nothing but crumbling dust—were destroyed. In 1919, arrangements were made with the firm Hébrard to produce casts from the remaining 73 models; an additional sculpture, *The schoolgirl* (Czestochowski and Pingeot 74) was cast only in or after 1956. By an innovative process of rubber moulds devised by Albino Palazzolo, a set of bronze casts was made, but four of the wax models were destroyed in the process. The bronze casts served as models for the published edition—72 numbered works and the *Little dancer aged fourteen* (cat 67). Both the wax originals and bronze models were left in the foundry's storehouse, where they were uncovered only after World War II. The wax sculptures were purchased in 1955 by Paul Mellon and are largely now in the National Gallery of Art, Washington—with the exception of models given by Mellon to the Musée d'Orsay (Paris), the Virginia Museum of Fine Arts (Richmond, Virginia), and the Fitzwilliam Museum (Cambridge, England).

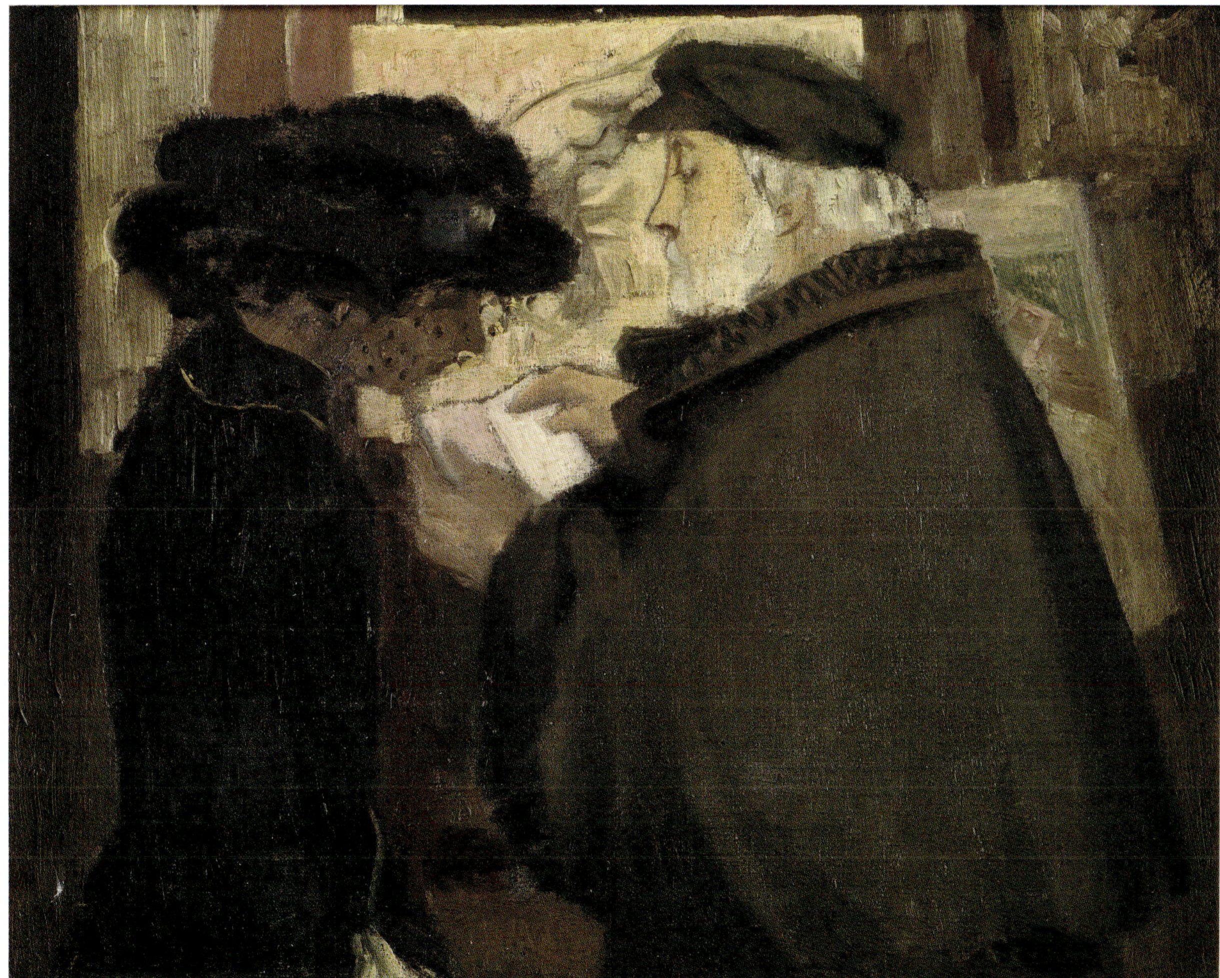

Maurice Denis
Degas and his model (Degas et son modèle) c 1906
oil on canvas, 38 x 46 cm
Musée d'Orsay, Paris

The stored bronze models for the published edition were firmly identified in the mid 1970s. The surviving 71 casts (two were missing) were purchased in 1976 by Norton Simon and are now in the Norton Simon Museum (Pasadena, United States).

Vollard had shown Maurice Denis—who around 1906 had painted an irresistible portrait of Degas in old age—the works before the sale. Unlike Valéry or Halévy, who were not artists, Denis saw the unfinished paintings in a different light. He noted in his diary:

> What strikes one first: the will, the need to be decisive, to affirm outlines with a heavy line, or retouches with essence, on flat tones. Then one discerns that this will is the expression of an observant spirit, curious, eager for originality, seeking the unexplored detail. At the beginnings of a composition there is only a kind of short-hand based on sensation, on sharp observation. Movement, cinematography; to capture movement, to capture the elusive moment which passes. How far it is from Cézanne and the classics! This comes from Ingres. First, patience and attention to detail. Then, as sight is less able to analyse, the line becomes less careful, the purpose more synthetic; Degas no longer does heads and hands, nor any of the details he rendered with such perfection and flavour, but a gesture surrounded by specks, like a bouquet; the outline of a torso, incomplete forms but agitated […] This broadness [of brushstroke] is not the effect of a more abundant imagination but the result of a more fierce honesty, a more brutal and more highly focused effort. He rejects everything that is extraneous to the object of his study, he doesn't fuss about, and, in so doing, he carries it off.[128]

Many years before his death, in a conversation about epitaphs, Degas had jokingly suggested that the phrase 'He loved drawing' might be a suitable one for him. One suspects he would also have enjoyed: 'He captured the elusive moment that passes.'

Notes

Unless otherwise indicated, all translation from the French is by the author.

1 For Degas and his family in Naples see Ricardo Raimondi, *Degas e la sua famiglia in Napoli, 1793–1917*, SAV, Naples, 1958; Jean Sutherland Boggs, 'Edgar Degas and Naples,' *The Burlington Magazine*, vol 105 (June 1963), pp 273–76, with a good deal of archival material; and Henri Loyrette, *Degas*, Fayard, Paris, 1991, pp 10–19, who deals also with the origins of the family. The recent work by Rosa Spinillo, *Degas e Napoli: gli anni giovanili*, Plectica, Salerno, 2004, adds little except documents related to the sale in the 20th century of family pictures by Degas and a supposed pastel portrait attributed to Degas.

2 See Roy McMullen, *Degas: his life, times, and work*, Houghton Mifflin, Boston, 1984, p 16; Jean Sutherland Boggs, 'Degas et la maternité,' in *Degas inédit* (Actes du Colloque Degas, Musée d'Orsay, 18–21 Avril 1988), La Documentation Française, Paris, 1989, pp 35–45; and Loyrette 1991, pp 19–20.

3 Author's translation. Degas' two pages of notes, with a transcription are reproduced in Colta Ives, Susan Alyson Stein and Julie A Steiner, et al, *The private collection of Edgar Degas: a summary catalogue*, The Metropolitan Museum of Art, New York, 1997, p 117.

4 See notebook 5, p 33, in Reff 1985, vol I, p 49; the translation, with slight modifications, is from Kendall 1993, p 8.

5 See Richard Kendall, *Degas landscapes* (exhibition catalogue, The Metropolitan Museum of Art, New York, and The Museum of Fine Arts, Houston), Yale University Press, New Haven and London, 1993, pp 8–13 (translation p 9), 21, 23, 39–40, 43, 48, 272.

6 See Frits Lugt, *Les marques de collections de dessins & d'estampes*, Vereenigde Drukkerijen, Amsterdam, 1921, pp 437–38, and Frits Lugt, *Les marques de collections de dessins & d'estampes. Supplément*, Martinus Nijhoff, The Hague, 1956, p 344. The marks of the Soutzo collections are as follows: Lugt 2340 belongs to Nicholas J Soutzo, Grégoire Soutzo's first cousin, who formed while in his twenties a collection which included *Agar in the desert* by Camille Corot, now in the Metropolitan Museum of Art, New York; there were three sales of his collection in Paris: the vente Prince S ..., 28 February 1876, the vente Prince Nicolas J Soutzo, 7 April 1876, and an anonymous sale in Paris, 9 November 1875. Lugt 2341 is Grégoire Soutzo's mark; he collected prints, sold after his death in Paris, Hôtel Drouot, on 5 March 1869. The unidentified posthumous sale of a Soutzo collection in Paris, on 17–19 December 1877, was that of prince Alexandre Soutzo (1830–1877), a first cousin of Grégoire's and Nicolas, who died in Paris on 7 May 1877.

7 See Adhémar in Jean Adhémar and Françoise Cachin, *Degas: the complete etchings, lithographs and monotypes*, Chartwell Books, Hong Kong, 1974, p 261, followed in Theodore Reff, *The notebooks of Edgar Degas*, new rev edn, Hacker Art Books, New York, 1985, pp 49, 50, 51, 58 and 98.

8 The identification, by the present author, was introduced in Sue Welsh Reed and Barbara Stern Shapiro, *Edgar Degas: the painter as printmaker* (exhibition catalogue), The Museum of Fine Arts, Boston, 1984, pp ix, 2 and adopted in subsequent literature.

9 For the Soutzo family see Eugène Rizo-Ranghabé, 'Famille Soutzo' in *Livre d'or de la noblesse Phanariote et des familles princières de Valachie et de Moldavie*, 2nd edn, S Vlastos, Athens, 1904, pp 213–226, 258f–258h; Mihail-Dimitri Sturdza, 'Soutzo' in *Dictionnaire historique et généalogique des grandes familles de Grèce, d'Albanie et de Constantinople*, 2nd edn, The Author, Paris, 1999, pp 418–25; and Alexandre Negresco-Soutzo, *Livre d'or de la famille Soutzo*, The Author, Paris, 2005. We retained for the name the form 'Soutzo,' the most common outside Romania and Greece.

10 Notebook 18, pp 227, 229, in Reff 1985, vol I, p 101, vol II, fig Nb 18, p 229.

11 The Caradja circle in Pisa included in 1821 Percy Bysshe Shelley and Mary Shelley. In 1827, Lady Blessington gave a dinner for Soutzo in Pisa and remarked that she 'had never known a more interesting family than his, nor one in which talent and worth were so united'; See Richard Robert Madden, *The literary life and correspondence of the Countess of Blessington*, Harper & Brothers, New York, 1855, vol II, p 529–30.

12 See Sturdza 1999, ill on p 424; Grégoire is shown second from the right.

13 The young Charles Gounod (1818–1893) was among visitors and lent Michel his score of Weber's *Der freichutz* before he left to study in Rome. Frederick Chopin (1810–1849) played the piano with Grégoire's sisters but particularly with Catherine Soutzo (1820–1874), his brother Jean's wife, to whom Chopin dedicated the *Fantasia in F minor, Op 49*. Franz Liszt (1811–1886) and Hector Berlioz (1803–1869) also frequented Catherine's musical salon.

14 The current title of the work, *Ruins in a mountainous landscape (Mount Hymettus)/(Ruines dans un site montagneux (le Mont Hymette)*, partly derived from the Degas sale catalogue, is misleading as the view represents the Acropolis at Athens (the title used by Degas), seen from the West, with the Altar of Zeus in the foreground.

15 Notebook 6, pp 43–42, in Reff 1985, vol I, p 51, vol II, ill Nb 6, p 14. Loyrette supposed it was after a print: see Loyrette 1991, p 76. On his part, Kendall has argued that a painting served as model: see Kendall 1993, p 277, n 49.

16 Lemoisne, vol I, p 18.

17 See, most recently, *Charles Atencio: monotypes*, Galerie La Bouvèche, Orsay, 2007, p 3: 'Ce nom fût suggéré par le graveur Grégoire Soutzo à Edgar Degas.' In any event, the term 'monotype' came in use only in the 1880s.

18 The other was given to Philippe Burty; see Loyrette 1991, p 103.

19 The works are *The dancing class (Classe de danse)* (Lemoisne 297; The Metropolitan Museum of Art, New York) and *A laundress (Une blanchisseuse)* (Brame and Reff 62; Musée d'Orsay, Paris).

20 For the Degas-Moreau relationship see Phoebe Pool, 'Degas and Moreau,' *The Burlington Magazine*, vol CV (June 1963), pp 251–256, and Loyrette 1991, pp 109–121.

21 Author's translation, letter from Degas to Gustave Moreau, 21 September 1858, Florence to Venice; cited in Loyrette 1991, p 136.

22 For Degas' artistic connection in Florence with the 'Macchiaioli' and his subsequent relation with them in Paris, see Pietro Dini, *Dal caffè Michelangiolo al caffè Nouvelles Athènes, I Macchiaioli tra Firenze e Parigi* (exhibition catalogue, Azienda Autonoma di Cura e Soggiorno, Montecatini Terme), Turin, Umberto Allemandi & C, 1986; Ann Dumas (ed), *Degas e gli italiani a Parigi* (exhibition catalogue), Palazzo dei Diamanti, Ferrara, 2003, and the version in English by Ann Dumas, *Degas and the Italians in Paris* (exhibition catalogue), National Gallery of Scotland, Edinburgh, 2004.

23 Letter, Auguste De Gas to Degas, 4 January 1859, Paris to Florence, cited in Loyrette 1991, pp 80–81.

24 For the painting, see Hanne Finsen, *Degas og familien Bellelli* (exhibition catalogue, Ordrupgaardsamlingen, Charlottenlund), Ordrupgaard, Copenhagen, 1983; Henri Loyrette in *Degas*, 1988, pp 77–83; and Mario Ursino (ed), *Degas: La famiglia Bellelli* (exhibition catalogue, Galeria Nazionale d'Arte Moderna, Rome), Electa, Rome, 2005.

25 For Degas' portraits see Jean Sutherland Boggs, *Portraits by Degas*, University of California Press, Berkeley/Los Angeles, 1962; Felix Baumann and Marianne Karabelnik (eds), *Degas portraits* (exhibition catalogue, Kunsthaus Zurich and Kunsthalle, Tubingen), Merrell Holberton, London, 1995; and, recently, Werner Hofmann, *Degas: a dialogue of difference*, Thames & Hudson, London, 2007, pp 83–117.

26 See Henri Loyrette in *Degas* 1988, pp 140–42.

27 The letter, Degas to Adèle Dietz-Monnin, is undated but likely 1878, Paris to Paris, see Guerin 1947, p 60, no 37; for the painting in the Art Institute of Chicago, see Richard Brettell's analysis in Richard R Brettell and Suzanne Folds McCullagh (eds) *Degas in the Art Institute in Chicago* (exhibition catalogue), The Art Institute of Chicago and Harry N Abrams Inc, New York, 1984. The portrait by Henner is in the Musée du Petit Palais, Paris.

28 For *Mme Jeantaud before a mirror* (Lemoisne 371; Musée d'Orsay, Paris) see Michael Pantazzi in *Degas* 1988, pp 147–49; a second portrait is *Mme Jeantaud on a chaise-longue with two dogs* (Lemoisne 440; Staatliche

Kunsthalle, Karlsruhe). A third painting, *The woman with an umbrella* (National Gallery of Canada, Ottawa, Lemoisne 463) was identified by Henri Loyrette as a portrait of Mme Jeantaud.

29 The portrait is *Mary Cassatt* (The National Portrait Gallery, Washington, DC, Lemoisne 796) of c1884; see Gary Tinterow's catalogue entry in *Degas*, 1988, pp 442–43. The letter, in French, Mary Cassatt to Paul Durand-Ruel, undated but late 1912, Grasse to Paris, is cited in Lionello Venturi, *Les archives de l'Impressionnisme*, Durand-Ruel, Paris–New York, 1938, vol II, p 129.

30 Letter, Auguste De Gas to Michel Musson, 21 November 1861, Paris to New Orleans, cited in Loyrette 1991, p 157.

31 Edmond Duranty, *La nouvelle peinture*, reprinted in *The new painting: Impressionism 1874–1886* (exhibition catalogue) San Francisco and Washington, 1986, p 478.

32 For Degas' period in New Orleans, see Marilyn R Brown, 'Degas and a cotton office in New Orleans,' *The Burlington Magazine*, vol CXXX (March 1988), pp 216–221; Marilyn R Brown, 'The De Gas–Musson Papers at Tulane University, *The Art Bulletin*, vol LXXII, March 1990, pp 118–130; Marilyn R Brown, *The De Gas–Musson family papers: an annotated inventory*, New Orleans, 1991; Christopher Benfey, *Degas in New Orleans*, Alfred A Knopf, New York, 1997; an earlier essay version, 'Degas in New Orleans,' was published in *The American Scholar*, vol 65, Autumn 1996, pp 579–86; and Gail Feigenbaum, Jean Sutherland Boggs, et al, *Degas and New Orleans: a French Impressionist in America* (exhibition catalogue), New Orleans Museum of Art, New Orleans, 1999, and the Danish version at Ordrupgaard, *Degas et la Nouvelle-Orléans* (exhibition catalogue), Ordrupgaard, Copenhagen, 1991, with a different essay by Jean Sutherland Boggs.

33 Letter from Degas to Désire Dihau, 11 November 1872, New Orleans to Paris, in Guérin (ed), 1947, p 15, no 2.

34 For Deschamps see Jeremy Maas, *Gambart: prince of the Victorian art world*, Barrie & Jenkins, London, 1975.

35 Cited in the exhibition catalogue by Henri Loyrette, *Degas e l'Italia*, Accademia di Francia a Roma (exhibition catalogue, Villa Medici, Rome), Fratelli Palombi Editori, Rome, 1984, pp 171–72.

36 See *Degas*, 1988, p 58.

37 See the two letters from Pierre Auguste Renoir to Claude Monet, 20 August 1900 and 23 August 1900, Louveciennes to Giverny, in Jeanne Baudot, *Renoir, ses amis, ses modèles*, Editions Littéraires de France, Paris, 1949, pp 49–50.

38 For the exhibitions, see Brown 1994, pp 83–116, and Marc Le Cœur, 'Le Salon annuel de la Société des amis des arts de Pau, quartier d'hiver des impressionnistes de 1876 à 1879,' *Histoire de l'art*, no 35/36, October 1996, pp 57–70.

39 For the identification of the works shown by Degas in the Impressionist exhibitions, see Gary Tinterow and Anne MP Norton, 'Degas au expositions 'impressionnistes' ', in *Degas inédit*, Actes du Colloque Degas, Musée d'Orsay, 18–21 April 1988, La Documentation Française, Paris, 1989, pp 289–351, and Berson 1996, vol II, pp 7–8, 34–36, 72–74, 109–112, 147–48, 180, 240–41.

40 Letter, Degas to Albert Bartholomé, 22 August 1892, Ménil-Hubert to Paris, in Guérin (ed), 1947, p 183, no 185; Guérin, 1997, p 194, no CLXXII.

41 Letter, Degas to Henri Lerolle, 18 December 1897, Paris to Paris, in Guérin (ed), 1947, p 206, no 227; Guérin 1997, p 219, no CCX.

42 See *Degas*, 1988, p 203.

43 See Frances Weitzenhoffer, *The Havemeyers: Impressionism comes to America*, Harry N Abrams, New York, 1986, p 81.

44 See Michael Pantazzi, 'Degas and Faure,' in *Degas*, 1988, pp 221–23.

45 See *Degas* 1988, cat 205.

46 See Lillian Browse, *Degas dancers*, Faber and Faber, London, 1949, p 380, no 127, pl 127.

47 See Browse 1949, p 387, no 151, pl 151; also, Jill DeVonyar and Richard Kendall, *Degas and the dance* (exhibition catalogue), Harry N Abrams, New York, 2002, p 146, fig 161.

48 For this aspect of Whistler's theories, see the last chapter of Deanna Marohn Bendix, *Diabolical designs: paintings, interiors, and exhibitions of James McNeill Whistler*, Smithsonian Institution Press, Washington/London, 1995, pp 206–268. A reconstitution of Whistler's exhibition concepts was carried out at the Art Institute of Chicago by the curators of the exhibition *Songs on stone: James McNeill Whistler and the art of lithography* in 1998.

49 See Gustave Goetschy's review, 'Exposition des artistes indépendants,' *Le Voltaire*, 3 April 1881, p 1, in Berson 1996, vol I, pp 144–45.

50 For Degas' frames, see Isabelle Cahn, 'Les cadres impressionnistes,' in the special issue devoted to frames of *Revue de l'art*, no 76, 1987, pp 57–59; Isabelle Cahn, *Cadres des peintres*, Réunion des Musées Nationaux / Hermann, Paris, 1989, pp 70–72, fig 22, 35–37, col pl 8–9, on the occasion of the exhibition held at the Musée d'Orsay, *Or et couleur: le cadre dans la seconde moitié du dix-neuvième siècle*, 19 June – 24 September 1989 (with a fold-out catalogue; Degas paintings in original frames were nos 64, 65 and 66); and Isabelle Cahn, 'Edgar Degas. Gold or colour,' in the catalogue of the exhibition held in 1995 at the Van Gogh Museum, Amsterdam and the Kunstforum, Vienna, *In perfect harmony: picture + frame 1850–1920*, Wanders Uitgevers, Zwolle, 1995, pp 129–38. Elizabeth Easton, ' "Pictures properly framed": Degas and innovation in Impressionist frames', *The Burlington Magazine*, vol CL, no 1266, September 2008, pp 603–611.

51 Letter, Degas to Paul Durand-Ruel, undated, Paris to Paris, in Caroline Durand-Ruel Godfroy, 'Lettres de Degas conservées dans les archives Durand-Ruel', in *Degas inédit 1989*, letter ND 15, p 506.

52 See *Degas* 1988, no 214.

53 See Isabelle Cahn in *Perfect harmony: picture + frame 1850–1920*, Wanders Uitgevers, Zwolle, 1995, fig 116 on p 133.

54 Author's translation. Letter, Degas to Paul Durand-Ruel, 13 August 1885, Paramé to Paris, in Caroline Durand-Ruel Godfroy, 'Lettres de Degas conservées dans les archives Durand-Ruel' in *Degas inédit 1989*, letter D15, p 443.

55 Cited in Madeleine Octave Maus, *Trente années de lutte pour l'art. Les XX, La Libre esthétique, 1884–1914*, Editions Lebeer Hosmmann, Brussels, 1980, p 43.

56 See Marcel Guérin (ed), *Degas: letters*, Bruno Cassirer, Oxford, 1947, p 212; the French version is in *Lettres de Degas*, Bernard Grasset, Paris, 1945, letter CCXXIII, p 227. Oddly, Albert Ludovici (1852–1932), the International Society's agent in Paris and recipient of the letter addressed to the organising committee, published in his memoirs a similar letter but differently and more strongly worded. See A Ludovici, *An artist's life in London and Paris, 1870–1925*, RF Unwin, London, 1926, p 121. Did Degas send two similar letters, one to Ludovici, the other to the committee?

57 Author's translation. See Denys Sutton and Jean Adhémar, 'Lettres inédites de Degas à Paul Lafond et autres documents', *Gazette des Beaux-Arts*, April 1987, p 1975.

58 Author's translation. Letter, Albert Bartholomé to Paul Lafond, c1900, in Sutton-Adhémar, 1989, p 175.

59 See Philip Hale, 'Art in Paris,' *Arcadia*, vol I, no 16, 15 December 1992, p 326.

60 Reproduced in *The Impressionist & modern art—evening* sale catalogue at Sotheby's, New York, 3 May 2006, p 38. The works shown at left are *Landscape (The hills) (Paysage (Les collines))* (private collection, Lemoisne 1047/Janis 303) and, below, *Landscape (Paysage)* (private collection, Lemoisne 1039/Janis 314). At the centre of the photograph are shown, on the lower register of the wall, *Landscape (Paysage)* (private collection, Lemoisne 1044/Janis 288,) , at left; *Rocky Coast (Côte rocheuse)* (private collection, Lemoisne 1035/Janis 293), at centre; and *Landscape (Paysage)* (Mohammed Al Fayed collection, Lemoisne 1036), at right.

61 See Lillian MC Randall (ed), *The diary of George A Lucas, 1857–1909*, Princeton University Press, Princeton, vol I, 1979, p 755.

62 On 4 December 1892, in a letter giving news to the Fevres; cited in Jeanne Fevre, *Mon oncle Degas*, P Cailler, Geneva, 1949, p 102; On 10 November, Durand-Ruel wrote in a letter that 25 landscapes were shown; See Kendall 1993, pp 183, 288, n 1.

63 The sale was recorded on 3 June 1893 at the price of 1000 francs each. A tabulation of the records, kindly communicated by Caroline Durand-Ruel in 1987, and the later history of the works, shows that the landscapes purchased were Lemoisne 633, 1034, 1035, 1036, 1037, 1038, 1039, 1040, 1041, 1045, 1046, 1047, 1048, 1049, 1051, 1052, 1055, 1059, 1060, Brame and Reff 127, 134, 136, Janis 278 and Kendall 4. The two supplementary landscapes must have been drawn among five signed works, three of which belonged to Jeanniot and Bartholomé, friends connected with the excursion to Diennay: Lemoisne 1042 and 1063, sold by Mme Jeanniot to Durand-Ruel on 3 August 1905, and Cachin 201, inscribed to Bartholomé and left by him to the Louvre. Two landscapes inscribed to Georges Charpentier, Lemoisne 413 and 632, seem less likely candidates but cannot be ruled out.

64 Author's translation, in *Degas inédit* 1989, p 449.

65 Transcript kindly communicated by Sona Johnston; an excerpt was published in Sona Johnston's exhibition catalogue *In Monet's light: Theodore Robinson at Giverny*, The Baltimore Museum of Art, Philip Wilson, Baltimore, 2004, p 193.

66 See Guerin (ed), 1947, p 36, no 9, wrongly dated 8 August 1873; for amended date see Pantazzi, 1988, p 131, no IV.

67 See Durand-Ruel Galleries, New York, *Paintings and drawings by Degas*, 16 February – 2 March 1901 and *Exhibition of paintings and pastels by Degas*, 24 February – 16 March 1909.

68 Letter of 30 June 1906, author's translation. See Jean Claude (ed), *Correspondance André Gide – Jacques Copeau (Cahiers André Gide 12)*, Gallimard, Paris, 1987, p 193.

69 Richard Kendall, 'Degas and the Contingency of Vision,' *The Burlington Magazine*, vol CXXX, March 1988, pp 180–197.

70 See Pantazzi 1988, p 126, no 4.

71 Letter to Mme Jeanniot, 4 March 1896, (in the Elliott Galleries, New York, 1980s) and to Louise Halévy, 12 March 1896 (Bibliothèque de l'Institut, Paris, no 347), both unpublished.

72 Author's translation. In Georges Jeanniot, 'Souvenirs sur Degas,' *La revue universelle*, vol LV, 15 October 1933, p 158.

73 Letter from Degas to Albert Bartholomé, 9 September 1888, Cauterets to Paris, in Guérin (ed), 1947, p 129, no 107 (undated), French original in Guérin 1997, p 132, no CVII, dated 9 September, year given in Pantazzi 1988, p 132; author's translation, letter from Degas to Paul Paulin, Paris, undated, in *Degas inédit* 1989, p 404; letter, Degas to Evariste de Valernes, 26 October 1890, Paris to Carpentras, in Guérin (ed), 1947, p 171, no 170; author's translation, letter, Degas to Thérèse Morbilli, 26 March 1892, Valorbes to Naples, in Pantazzi 1988, p 127, no 5.

74 *Portraits at the stock exchange (Portraits à la bourse)* (Musée d'Orsay, Paris, Lemoisne 499), which May bequeathed to the Louvre. For the issue of Degas' anti-Semitism, see Linda Nochlin, 'Degas and the Dreyfus Affair: a portrait of the artist as an anti-semite,' in Norman L Kleeblatt (ed), *The Dreyfus affair: art, truth & justice* (exhibition catalogue), The Jewish Museum, New York, 1987, pp 96–116; May's portrait is discussed pp 99–101.

75 Author's translation, letter from André Gide to Eugène Rouart, 24 January 1898; see André Gide and Eugène Rouart, *Correspondence 1893–1901*, vol I, Presses Universitaires de Lyon, Lyon, 2006, p 450.

76 See Maurice Denis, *Journal (1905–1920)*, vol II, La Colombe, Paris, entry for 7 January 1907, p 50.

77 Letter from Degas to Mme Alexis Rouart, 1884 or 1885, Paris to Paris, in Guerin (ed), 1947, p 101, no 84.

78 Author's translation, letter from Joseph Tourny to Degas, 13 August 1858, Ivry to Florence, cited in Lemoisne 1946–1949, vol I, pp 227–28 (with wrong date) and Loyrette 1991, p 104.

79 Author's translation, letter from Auguste Renoir to Jeanne Baudot, December 1912, Grasse to Paris, cited in Jeanne Baudot, *Renoir, ses amis, ses modèles*, Editions littéraires de France, Paris, 1949, p 105.

80 Madeleine Zilhardt, *Louise-Catherine Breslau et ses amis*, Editions des Portiques, Paris, 1932, pp 69–70; for Degas and Mme Camus, see Pantazzi, 1988, pp 124–125, and Raunay 1931, pp 627–628.

81 Author's translation. See Zillhardt 1932, p 69.

82 Author's translation. See Georges Jeanniot, 'Souvenirs sur Degas,' *La Revue universelle*, vol LV (15 October 1933), p 161.

83 Jeanne Baudot, *Renoir, ses amis, ses modèles*, Editions littéraires de France, Paris, 1949, p 67; the model was called by Renoir 'The Venus of Villejuif'—Villejuif was a suburb of Paris. Baudot indicates the event took place before Renoir as he undertook the double portrait of *Christine and Yvonne Lerolle at the piano* (fig XX, Musée de l'Orangerie, Paris) which Julie Manet saw finished in October 1897. The model may well have posed for the pregnant figure in red, in *Combing the hair (La coiffure)* (National Gallery, London, Lemoisne 1128), painted in c1896 according to some scholars, or the *Pregnant woman (Femme enceinte)* (Czestochowski and Pingeot 24), dated by John Rewald to 1896–1911.

84 Author's translation; letter unpublished, Degas to Suzanne Valadon, [27?] July 1895, Paris to Paris, unpublished, The Getty Center for The History of Art and the Humanities, Los Angeles, inv 850250.

85 Author's translation. See Jeanne Raunay, 'Souvenirs anecdotiques sur Degas', pt I, *Revue de France*, 15 March 1931, p 265.

86 Letter of 7 October 1890, in Sutton and Admémar 1987, p 166; for the date assigned, see Pantazzi 1988, p 134.

87 Letter of 18 October 1890, in Sutton and Adhémar 1987, p 166; for the date assigned, see Pantazzi 1988, p 134.

88 See Julie Manet, *Journal 1893–1899*, Scala, Paris, 1987, entry for 3 November 1898, p 148.

89 See Julie Manet's diary entry for 6 June 1899 in *Manet* 1987, p 172.

90 For the Blanche incident, in which Degas took back from him a pastel, see the exhibition catalogue on that pastel, Maureen O'Brien, *Edgar Degas: six friends at Dieppe*, Rhode Island School of Design, Providence, 2001, p 113, citing a letter of Daniel Halévy who dates the incident to c1910. The event took place in early 1904: Blanche's portrait of Degas, painted in June 1903 after he promised not to published it, was reproduced full-page in *The Studio*, vol XXX, no 123, December 1903, p 195.

91 Degas, *Sonets*, privately printed in an edition of 20 by AS Rouart, 1914—meaning Alexis Stanislas Rouart (1869–1921), Henri Rouart's eldest son; four of the sonnets are dedicated to the poet José-Maria de Heredia, the painter Mary Cassatt, the dancer Marie Sanlaville and the singer Rose Caron; the poems were reprinted in a limited edition by Jean Nepveu-Degas as *Huit sonets d'Edgar Degas*, La Jeune Parque, New York, Wittenborn/Paris, 1946, with a commentary, notes and illustrations of 19 previously unpublished drawings by Degas from his collection.

92 For the project, see Reed and Shapiro 1984, pp lvii–lix, with amplifications by Sabine de Vignan in *Degas, Boldini, Toulouse-Lautrec … Portraits inédits par Michel Manzi* (exhibition catalogue), Musée Toulouse-Lautrec, Albi, 1997, pp 88–92, no 27.

93 The archives of the Goupil firm show that only 17 sets were sold between 1889 and June 1895; see Sabine de Vignan in *Degas, Boldini, Toulouse-Lautrec* 1997, p 92.

94 See Sabine de Vignan in *Degas, Boldini, Toulouse-Lautrec 1997*, pp 93–96, no 29.

95 Author's translation, letter from Camille Pissarro to his daughter Esther, 23 January 1898, in Janine Bailly-Herzberg (ed), *Correspondance de Camille Pissarro*, vol IV, Editions du Valhermeil, Paris, 1989, p 439; Georges Jeanniot also wrote about the album and in particular of the portrait of Hélène Hertel; see Georges Jeanniot, 'Souvenirs sur Degas,' *La Revue universelle*, vol LV (1 November 1933), pp 298–99.

96 This is surely the same work as that mistakenly described by Lemoisne (Lemoisne 995) and others as a pastel.

97 This similarity was variously observed by Jean Sutherland Boggs, Richard Thomson and Richard Kendall; see Boggs in *Degas* 1988, p 557, no 347; Richard Thomson, *Degas: the nudes*, Thames & Hudson, London, 1988, pp 205, 207; and Richard Kendall, *Degas: beyond Impressionism* (exhibition

catalogue, National Gallery, London, and The Art Institute of Chicago), National Gallery, London, 1996, p 174.

98 For Degas' comic description of a visit to Martine de Béhague, to whom Paul Valéry dedicated his *Degas, danse, dessin*, see Henri de Régnier, *Les cahiers inédits, 1887–1936*, Pygmalion, Paris, 2002, pp 837–38.

99 Author's translation. Letter from Degas to Giovanni Boldini, August 1889, Pau to Paris, in *Degas Inédit* 1989, p 418.

100 See Zillhardt 1932, p 74–76.

101 Author's translation. See Valéry 1983, pp 29–30.

102 See Valéry 1983, p 49.

103 For the Rouart family, see Rebecca R DeMuth, 'Edgar Degas, Henri Rouart: art and industry,' MA thesis, University of Pittsburgh, 1982; Agathe Rouart-Valéry (1906–2002), 'Degas, ami de ma famille,' in *Degas inédit* 1989, pp 23–34; Jean-Marie Rouart, *Une famille dans l'impressionnisme*, Gallimard, Paris, 2001; and Solange Thierry, Dominique Bona, François Chapon et al, *Au cœur de l'impressionnisme. La famille Rouart* (exhibition catalogue), Musée de la Vie Romantique, Paris, 2004.

104 See the letter to Julia Braquaval, who prepared her the canvases of her husband, Louis Braquaval, written on Tasset et Lhote stationery, 18 October 1897, in *Degas inédit* 1989, pp 389–90.

105 See *Degas* 1988, p 145.

106 For the technical aspects of Degas' work, see *Art in the making* (exhibition catalogue), National Gallery, London, 2004, with extensive bibliography, to which one may add Anne Maheux, 'Disegnare con il colore. Le tecnica del pastello, in De Nittis e Zandomeneghi,' in Ann Dumas (ed), *Degas e gli italiani a Parigi* (exhibition catalogue), Ferrara Arte, Ferrara, 2003, pp 147–70. For the old paintings he retouched, see his letter to Charles Ephrussi, undated, Paris to Paris: 'Don't forget, I beg you to place the canvas outside and in daylight in order for the retouches to dry well'; and to Durand-Ruel, undated, Paris to Paris: 'Take note that this head must not be varnished, the repainted parts will take a long time to dry', in *Degas inédit* 1989, p 378, and letter ND 15 on p 506.

107 Author's translation. See letter from Paul Valéry to André Gide, 11 March 1898, in André Gide and Paul Valéry, *André Gide–Paul Valéry: correspondance 1890–1942*, Gallimard, Paris, 1955, p 314. For a pioneering analysis of Degas' late works, see Richard Kendall, *Degas: beyond Impressionism* (exhibition catalogue), National Gallery, London, 1996.

108 See Valéry 1983, p 127.

109 See Michel 1919, and Anne Pingeot and Frank Horvat, *Degas, sculptures*, Réunion des Musées Nationaux, Paris, 1991, p 168, no 32.

110 Author's translation. See Zillhardt 1932, p 72.

111 See Mary Cassatt's letter to Louisine Havemeyer, 1 December 1911, Nice to New York, unpublished, Archives of the Metropolitan Museum of Art, New York.

112 See René Gimpel, *Journal d'un collectionneur marchand de tableaux*, Calmann-Lévy, Paris, p 92, entry for 16 December 1911.

113 Author's translation. See Marguerite de Saint-Marceaux, *Journal 1894–1927* (ed Myriam Chimènes), Fayard, Paris, 2007, entry for 11 December 1912, p 729.

114 Letter reproduced in Baudot 1946, p 105.

115 Author's translation. See Halévy 1995, entry for 25 January 1912, pp 191–92 .

116 Author's translation. In Halévy 1995, p 189.

117 Sacha Guitry's account is given in Loyrette 1991, pp 667–69.

118 Letter from Mary Cassatt to Louisine Havemeyer, Nice to New York, 30 March 1913, unpublished, Archives of The Metropolitan Museum of Art, New York.

119 The mounted photographs occasionally appear on the market with the suggestion, because of the authentic signature, that they are by Degas.

120 See Mary Cassatt's letter to Louisine Havemeyer, 2 October 1917, in Nancy Mowll Matthews (ed), *Cassatt and her circle: selected letters*, Abbeville Press, New York, 1984, p 328; Claude Monet's letters to J Durand-Ruel, 15 October 1917, and to G Bernheim-Jeune, 20 October 1917, are reproduced in Daniel Wildenstein, *Claude Monet: biographie et catalogue raisonné*, Bibliothèque des arts, Lausanne, 1985, vol IV, p 398, nos 224 and 225.

121 See Galerie Georges Petit, *Catalogue des tableaux modernes et anciens: aquarelles, pastels, dessins … composant la Collection Edgar Degas*, Paris, 26–27 March 1918; Hôtel Drouot, *Catalogue des estampes anciennes et modernes … composant la Collection Edgar Degas*, Paris, 6–7 November 1918; and Hôtel Drouot, *Catalogue des tableaux modernes et anciens: aquarelles, pastels, dessins anciens et modernes … faisant partie de la Collection Edgar Degas*, Paris, 15–16 November 1918.

122 See Galerie Georges Petit, *Catalogue des tableaux modernes: pastels, aquarelles, dessins par Edgar Degas et provenant de son atelier…* Paris, 6–8 May 1918; 2nd sale, 11–13 December 1918; 3rd sale, 7–9 April 1919; 4th sale, 2–4 July 1919.

123 See Galerie Manzi-Joyant, Paris, *Catalogue des eaux-fortes, vernis-mous, aquatintes, lithographies et monotypes par Edgar Degas et provenant de son atelier…* ; the exhibition was on 21 November 1918 and the sale on 22 and 23 November 1918; The now famous Cardinal monotypes, kept with all related material as a single group, failed to sell, and were sold only much later; see Pantazzi in *Degas* 1988, p 280.

124 See Halévy 1995, diary entries for 2, 4 and 5 May 1918, pp 195–200.

125 Author's translation. In Halévy 1995, p 197, and in Halévy 1995, p 219.

126 Author's translation. See André Gide and Paul Valéry, *Correspondance 1890–1942*, (ed Robert Mallet), 2nd edn, Gallimard, Paris, 1955, p 316.

127 Author's translation. See André Gide and Paul Valéry, *Correspondance 1890–1942*, (ed Robert Mallet), 2nd edn, Gallimard, Paris, 1955, p 471.

128 Author's translation. See Denis 1957, vol II, pp 201–02.

CHRONOLOGY
EDGAR DEGAS AND HIS TIMES

This chronology provides the key events in Degas' life with the significant events of the artist's time in coloured text.

The chronology is based on Jean Sutherland Boggs et al, *Degas*, Metropolitan Museum of Art and the National Gallery of Canada, New York and Ottawa, 1988 (reproduced with permission), with additions compiled by Niki van den Heuvel.

1830 King Charles X is overthrown during the July Revolution. Louis-Philippe I ascends the throne.

1832 14 July
Degas' parents, Laurent Pierre Augustin Hyacinthe De Gas (b Naples 27 September 1807) and Marie Célestine Musson (b New Orleans 10 April 1815) are married at the church of Notre-Dame-de-Lorette, Paris.

1833 Establishment of the Le Jockey Club, Paris.

1834 19 July
Birth of Hilaire Germain Edgar De Gas, 8 rue Saint-Georges, Paris. Although the artist's father and siblings adopted the upwardly aspiring spelling of the family name, De Gas, Edgar instead chose to use the form Degas, as used by his grandfather and extended family.

15 May
Inaugural race at Chantilly racecourse on the Champ de Mars, Paris.

16 October
Burning of the Houses of Parliament, London.

1836 10 June
The artist's grandfather, René Hilaire Degas, establishes the company Degas Padre e Figli with his sons Henri, Edouard and Achille, in Naples.

March 1836 – October 1838
Publication of Charles Dickens' first novel, *The Pickwick papers* in monthly parts, London.

1838 16 November
Birth of the artist's brother Achille De Gas, Paris.

1839 French artist and chemist, Louis Daguerre, exhibits the daguerreotype. The first successful photographic image is produced on a silver-coated plate.

1840 8 April
Birth of the artist's sister, Thérèse De Gas, Naples.

1841 Invention of tube paints by American painter John G Rand.

1842 2 July
Birth of the artist's sister, Marguerite De Gas, Passy.

31 August
Degas' aunt, Laura Degas, marries Baron Gennaro Bellelli, Naples.

1845 6 May
Birth of the artist's brother, René De Gas, Paris. René would later spell his name using a lower-case participle. The spelling de Gas implied an aristocratic background, which the Degas family did not in fact possess.

5 October
Degas begins attendance at the Lycée Louis-le-Grand, along with Paul Valpinçon and Ludovic Halévy.

1847 5 September
Death of the artist's mother, Célestine De Gas, in Paris.

1848 Revolutions throughout Europe.

21 February
Publication of Marx and Engels' Communist manifesto, London.

In France, February Revolution ends the reign of King Louis-Philippe I and Orléans rule. Establishment of the Second Republic.

15–16 May
The artist's cousin, Gustavo Morbilli, is killed during the Italian Revolution, Naples.

10 December
Birth of the artist's cousin, Giovanna Bellelli, Naples.

20 December
Louis Napoléon Bonaparte begins office as first President of the French Republic.

Publication of Alexandre Dumas' La Dame aux camélias.

1851 1 May – 15 October
London's Great Exhibition is housed in Joseph Paxton's specially designed Crystal Palace.

13 July
Birth of the artist's cousin, Giulia Bellelli, Naples.

2 December
France's Second Republic is ended, and the French Empire restored. Louis Napoléon Bonaparte becomes Emperor Napoléon III.

19 December
Death of JMW Turner, London.

Publication of John Ruskin's *The stones of Venice*.

1853 6 March
Verdi's opera *La Traviata*, based on Dumas' *La Dame aux camélias*, debuts at the Teatro la Fenice, Venice.

23 and 27 March
Degas obtains his baccalaureate and leaves Lycée Louis-le-Grand.

7 and 9 April
Degas receives permission to copy at the Louvre and the Cabinet des Estampes at the Bibliothèque nationale de France.

1853–56 Crimean War between Russia and an alliance of forces from France, the United Kingdom, Sardinia and the Ottoman Empire.

1855 Degas accompanies art collector and father of his friend, Edouard Valpinçon, to meet his Idol, Jean-Auguste-Dominique Ingres, at his studio on the Quai Voltaire in Paris.

5 and 6 April
After ranking thirty-third in the March competitions for admittance into the Ecole des Beaux-Arts, Degas registers as a student in the painting and sculpture section.

May 15 to November
The first Exposition Universelle des produits de l'Agriculture, de l'Industrie et des Beaux-Arts de Paris 1855 is held on the Champ de Mars, Paris. The event includes a large representation of works by Ingres, Eugène Delacroix and Théodore Rousseau.

Gustave Courbet withdraws 11 paintings from the Exposition and exhibits works in his own Pavilion du Realisme, following the rejection of his *A burial at Ornans* 1849–50 and *The painter's studio* 1854–55, now held in the Musée d'Orsay, Paris.

May – July
Degas visits the Exposition and makes copies of works by Ingres.

July – September

Degas travels to Lyons, Arles, Sète, Nîmes and Avignon.

Late September 1855 – mid July 1856

Degas continues copying at the Louvre.

1856 17 July
Degas arrives in Naples from Marseilles, where he copies works in the Museo Nazionale.

7 October 1856 – late July 1857
Travels to Rome by sea. Studies at night, at the academy of the Villa Medici. He draws copies of artworks in churches and in the Vatican. During this time he also becomes acquainted with Emile Lévy, Camille Clère, Elie Delaunay and Henri Chapu.

Invention of pasteurisation by the French chemist, Louis Pasteur.

1857 27 April
Inaugural race at Longchamp racecourse, at the Bois de Boulogne, Paris.

1 August
Travels to Naples and stays at René Hilaire Degas' villa at San Rocco di Capodimonte.

Late October
Degas returns to Rome.

Delacroix is elected an academician at the Académie des Beaux-Arts, L'Institut de France.

1858 January
Meeting of Degas and Gustave Moreau, Rome.

24 July
Degas travels from Rome to Florence via Viterbo, Orvieto, Perugia, Assisi, Spello and Arezzo.

4 August 1858 – March 1859
Degas stays at the Bellelli's apartment in Florence, and makes various copies of works in the Uffizi.

31 August
Death of the artist's grandfather, Hilaire René De Gas, Naples.

November
Degas begins portraits of Laura, Giulia and Giovanna Bellelli.

1859 Late March – early April
Degas leaves Florence for Paris, travelling via Livorno, Genoa, Turin, Mont-Cenis, Saint-Jean-de-Maurienne, Lac du Bourget and Mâcon.

April
Stays at his father's apartment, 4 rue de Mondovi.

1 October
Moves to 13 rue de Laval, Paris.

24 November
Publication of Darwin's *On the origin of species*, London.

1860 Degas makes sketches after Delacroix's *Christ on the Lake of Gennesaret* c 1853, now in the Metropolitan Museum of Art, New York, and *Mirabeau and Dreux-Brézé* 1830, now in the Musée national Eugène Delacroix, Paris.

21 March
Travelling from Marseilles, Degas arrives in Naples where he stays with his aunt, the Marchessa di Cicerale and Duchessa di Montejasi. The artist's sisters Thérèse and Marguerite are also present.

2 April
Degas leaves Naples for Livorno, before travelling to the Bellilli's in Florence.

May
Unification of Italy under Victor Emmanuel II.

Degas returns to Paris.

1861 September – October
Degas spends three weeks at the country estate of his childhood friend, Paul Valpinçon, in Ménil-Hubert, Normandy.

1861–65 American Civil War

1862 Degas meets Edouard Manet at the Louvre, while copying the work *Infanta Margarita*, attributed at the time to Diego Velázquez.

1863 November
Degas encourages his brother René to leave their father's business and move to America.

Napoleon III instigates the establishment of the Salon des Refusés as an exhibition venue for works rejected by the Official Salon Jury. The inaugural Salon includes works by Manet, Camille Pissarro, Johan Barthold Jongkind, Armand Guillaumin, James McNeill Whistler, Henri Fantin-Latour and Paul Cézanne.

13 April
Death of Eugène Delacroix, Paris.

1864 Degas attends a small exhibition of Ingres' work, held at the artist's studio.

22 August
Establishment of the First Geneva Convention, or Convention for the Amelioration of the Condition of the Wounded in Armies in the Field.

1865 1 May
Degas' *Scene of war in the Middle Ages* c 1863–65 (Lemoisne 124), now in the Musée d'Orsay, Paris, is exhibited at the Salon.

Courbet, Monet, Whistler and Charles-François Daubigny paint at Trouville in Normandy.

Publication of Leo Tolstoy's *War and peace.*

1866 1 May
The steeplechase 1866 (Lemoisne 140), now in the National Gallery of Art, Washington DC, is exhibited at the Salon.

12 November
Premiere of the ballet *La Source* at Le Théâtre de l'Académie Royale de Musique, the Opéra, at rue Le Peletier.

Fyodor Dostoevski's *Crime and punishment* is published in 12 monthly instalments in the literary magazine, *The Russian Messenger.*

Mary Cassatt moves to Paris.

1867 15 April
Two portraits of the Bellelli family are exhibited at the Salon: *The Bellelli family* 1858–67 (Lemoisne 79), now in the Musée d'Orsay, Paris; and *The Bellelli sisters* c 1865–66 (Lemoisne 126), now in the Los Angeles County Museum of Art.

14 January
Death of Ingres, Paris.

A major retrospective exhibition of Ingres' work is held at the Ecole des Beaux-Arts.

April – October
The second Exposition Universelle, is held at the Champ de Mars, Paris. Courbet and Manet exhibit their art in specially erected pavilions nearby the Exposition.

31 August
Death of Charles Baudelaire, Paris.

26, 28 November and 3 December
Baudelaire's *Le Peintre de la vie moderne* is published in three instalments, in *Le Figaro.*

1868 Spring
A group of artists centred around Manet begins to meet at the Café Guerbois, 11 grande rue des Batignolles. Along with Degas, regular attendees at the café include Emile Zola, Fréderic Bazille, Louis Edmond Duranty, Henri Fantin-Latour, Claude Monet, Pierre-Auguste Renoir and Alfred Sisley.

March
Degas registers for the last time as a copyist at the Louvre.

1 May
Degas exhibits one work at the Paris Salon, *Mlle Fiocre in the ballet 'La Source'* 1867–68 (Lemoisne 146), now in The Brooklyn Museum, New York.

1869 1 May
Degas exhibits one painting at the Salon, *Mme Gaujelin* 1867 (Lemoisne 165), now in the Isabella Stewart Gardener Museum, Boston.

July – August
Degas visits Etretat, Villers-sur-Mer. Also visits Manet in Boulogne-sur-Mer.

31 December
Birth of Henri Matisse, at Le Cateau-Cambrésis, France.

1870 12 April
Paris-Journal publishes Degas' letter to the Salon jury proposing a number of improvements to the way works are displayed.

May
Degas exhibits one oil painting and a pastel at the Salon: *Mme Camus in red* 1870 (Lemoisne 271), now in the National Gallery of Art, Washington DC; and *Mme Théodore Gobilard* 1869 (Lemoisne 214), now in the Metropolitan Museum of Art, New York.

Publication of Ludovic Halévy's 'Madame Cardinal' in *La Vie Parisienne.*

19 July 1870 – 10 May 1871
Franco–Prussian War

September 1870
Degas volunteers for the National Guard, and is assigned to an infantry company. During rifle practice at Vincennes he reveals that he cannot see a target clearly with his right eye. After this time he is assigned as an artilleryman and gunner.

4 September 1870
France's Napoleon III is deposed following defeat by the Prussians and their allies at the Battle of Sedan.

The French Third Republic is proclaimed.

19 September 1870 – January 1871
The Siege of Paris

Around this time Degas is beset by acute discomfort and troubles with his eyesight, and begins to fear that he will become completely blind.

Early October 1870
Degas is posted to the Bastion 12 fortifications, north of the Bois de Vincennes, under command of his friend Henri Rouart.

1871 23 January
German unification under the Prussian Chancellor, Otto von Bismarck.

March – May
The Paris Commune, a socialist government of Paris, is established on 18 March. It fails on 27 May, suppressed by the National Assembly in a battle in which 33 000 people die.

Gustave Courbet, as president of the Commune Art Commission, is involved in the destruction of the Vendôme Column and is subsequently imprisoned.

The orchestra of the opera c 1870 (Lemoisne 186), now in the Musée d'Orsay, Paris, is exhibited at Lille, northern France.

October
Degas and his brother René De Gas travel to England to make arrangements for their passage to America.

While in London the artist possibly sees the Second Annual Exhibition of the Society of French Artists, organised by the French art dealer Paul Durand-Ruel at 168 Bond Street.

1872 January
Durand-Ruel purchases three works from Degas for the first time.

Summer
Two Degas paintings are exhibited in London at the Fourth Exhibition of the Society of French Artists: *The false start* 1866–68 (Lemoisne 258), now in Yale University Art Gallery, New Haven; and *The ballet from 'Robert le Diable'* 1871 (Lemoisne 294), now in the Metropolitan Museum of Art, New York.

12–24 October
Edgar and René travel to New Orleans from Paris, via Liverpool, England.

2 November
Degas exhibits two paintings at the Fifth Exhibition of the Society of French Artists in London: *At the races in the countryside* 1869 (Lemoisne 281), now in the Museum of Fine Arts, Boston; and *Dance class at the Opéra* 1872 (Lemoisne 298), now in the Musée d'Orsay, Paris.

1873 9 January
Death of Napoleon III

Late March
Degas returns from New Orleans to Paris and takes up residence at 77 rue Blanche.

November
Degas joins his ill father, Auguste, in Turin.

27 December
Degas, Monet, Pissarro, Sisley, Cézanne, Berthe Morisot and others form the Société Anonyme des Artistes.

28–29 October
The Opéra on rue Le Peletier is destroyed by fire.

1874 23 February
Death of the artist's father, Auguste De Gas, Naples.

March
Degas recruits participants for the first exhibition of the Société Anonyme des Artistes.

4 April
Auguste De Gas' estate is divided equally among his five children. His inventoried effects amount to Fr 4918.

15 April – May
Opening of the first exhibition of the Société Anonyme des Artistes—the first of eight exhibitions which came to be known as the Impressionist exhibitions—at the photographer and balloonist Nadar's studio, 35 boulevard des Capucines, Paris.

Degas exhibits 10 works, three of which are for sale.

15 May
Plagued by bad press, poor attendance and lack of sales, the exhibition closes. The Société Anonyme des Artistes is dissolved.

Mary Cassatt exhibits at the Salon, where her work is noticed by Degas.

1875 15 January
Charles Garnier's newly constructed Palais Garnier on Place de l'Opéra is formally inaugurated. Construction of the Paris Opéra was begun in 1862.

28 February
Degas travels to Naples, following the death of his uncle, Achille Degas. The deceased's estate is divided up among his family and is settled only in 1909.

19 August
The artist's brother, Achille De Gas, wounds Victor-Georges Legrand after being attacked by Legrand, the husband of his former mistress, Thérèse Mallot.

24 September
Achille is sentenced to six months in prison, a conviction later reduced to one month in prison and a fine of Fr 50.

10 December
The question of Auguste De Gas' estate and his firm's debts becomes pressing. Edgar's uncle, Henri Musson, writes from Paris to New Orleans requesting that René De Gas repay a loan he received from the firm in 1872.

End of 1875

Members of the dissolved Société Anonyme des Artistes plan a second exhibition to be held in spring 1876.

1876 30 March
The second Impressionist Exhibition opens at Galerie Durand-Ruel, 11 rue Le Peletier.

Degas' work, which consists of 22 catalogued items as well as additional photographs, receives mixed reviews.

June
Degas visits Naples with his brother Achille, in a final attempt to raise funds from creditors.

End June
Degas returns to Paris.

28 August
René De Gas leaves Paris for New Orleans, with his debt to Henri Musson left unpaid. Achille De Gas notifies his uncle, Michel Musson, that their bank has been closed and that his brother's failure to repay his loan has forced his siblings to live on a bare subsistence to honour their debts.

Alexander Graham Bell invents the telephone.

1877 Following two unsuccessful attempts, one of Degas' works is accepted at the annual Salon of the Société Bérnaise des Amins des Art, Pau.

4 April
Opening of the third Impressionist Exhibition, 6 rue Le Peletier. After this time the artists begin to gather at the Café de la Nouvelle-Athènes, on Place Pigalle.

Degas exhibits approximately 23 paintings and pastels, and three groups of monotypes which receive mixed reviews. Several critics praise his café-concert scenes.

August
Degas visits the Valpinçons at Ménil-Hubert.

October
By the end of the month Degas has rented an apartment at 50 rue Lepic, Paris.

Summer
The Grosvenor Gallery in London holds its first show.

1878 March
The Musée des Beaux-Arts in Pau acquires *A cotton office in New Orleans* 1873 (Lemoisne 320) for Fr 2000. The painting is Degas' first work to enter a public collection.

13 April
René De Gas deserts his wife (and cousin) Estelle Musson and their five children in New Orleans, eventually settling in New York, and causing a rift with Edgar.

4 December
Gaston Tissandier presents a discussion of the work of English-born photographer, Eadweard J Muybridge.

1 May – 10 November
The third Exposition Universelle is held at the Champ de Mars.

25 November
Libel suit of Whistler versus Ruskin.

The Yablochkov candle is used for the first public street lighting, Paris.

Inventors Sir Joseph William Swann and Thomas Edison invent incandescent light bulbs independently of one another.

1879 January
Degas attends performances at the Cirque Fernando, making serval studies for *Mlle La La at the Cirque Fernando* 1879 (Lemoisne 522), now in The National Gallery, London.

10 April
Opening of the fourth Impressionist Exhibition, 28 avenue de l'Opéra.

Degas invites Mary Cassatt to exhibit with the group.

Although the catalogue lists a group of 20 paintings and pastels by him, as well as five painted fans, Degas exhibits less than a dozen works.

20 June
Henri Degas, Edgar's last surviving paternal uncle, dies in Naples.

Muybridge invents the Zoopraxiscope, an early device for displaying motion pictures.

1880 March
In an argument with Gustave Caillebotte over the poster for the fifth group exhibition, Degas insists that it not list the names of the exhibitors. Writing to Bracquemond, the artist remarks that: 'I had to give into him and let them appear. When will we stop playing at being stars?'

1 April
Opening of the fifth Impressionist Exhibition, 10 rue des Pyramides.

Although Degas' catalogued works include eight paintings and pastels, two groups of drawings, a group of prints and a sculpture, in fact a number of works are not displayed, including *Little dancer aged fourteen* 1879–81 (cat 67), now held in the National Gallery of Art, Washington DC.

9 April
Death of Edmond Duranty
Degas and Emile Zola are named executors of Duranty's will.

27 December
Durand-Ruel buys a work from Degas for the first time in six years.

1881 24 January
Caillebotte withdraws from the forthcoming sixth Impressionist Exhibition, following a disagreement with Degas on the nature of the exhibition and the contributors Degas recruited.

28-29 January
A fundraising sale organised by Degas and Zola for Duranty's companion, Pauline Bourgeois, produces disappointing results.

2 April
Opening of the sixth Impressionist Exhibition, 35 Boulevard des Capucines.

Degas' section of the exhibition contains four portraits, two of the three drawings entitled *Criminal physiognomy* (based on the Abadie trial), and a *Laundress*.

A glass vitrine intended for the *Little dancer aged fourteen* is left empty until 16 April. Its eventual display unleashes controversy among critics, with Joris-Karl Huysmans, Jules Arsène Arnaud Claretie, Nina de Villard, and Paul de Charry praising the work as a masterpiece.

25 October
Birth of Pablo Picasso, Málaga, Spain.

26 November
Muybridge demonstrates his photographic proof of 'true' animal motion.

1882 1 February
The crash of the Catholic bank Union Général has grave ramifications for gallery-owner, Durand-Ruel.

1 March
Opening of the seventh Impressionist Exhibition, 251 rue Saint-Honoré.
Degas refuses to participate in the exhibition.

Summer
Durand-Ruel's exhibition at White's Gallery in London includes four works by Degas.

Late July
Degas visits the Halévys at Etretat, on the Normandy coast.

1883 April
Seven works by Degas exhibited at Durand-Ruel's exhibition at Dowdeswell and Dowdeswell's in London are received favourably.

30 April
Death of Edouard Manet, Paris.

August
Degas makes studies for a portrait of Hortense Valpinçon at Ménil-Hubert.

September
Durand-Ruel organises a series of one-man shows in his new gallery.
Degas declines to participate.

1884 6 August – October
Degas continually delays returning to his studio in Paris, staying with the Valpinçons at Ménil-Hubert.

Late October
Visits the Halévys at Dieppe.

1885 March – December
Degas attends numerous performances at the Paris Opéra, including: *Rigoletto, Le Tribut de Zamora, L'Africaine, Coppélia, La Korrigane, Guillaume Tell, Rigoletto, Faust, Hamlet, La Farandole, La Favorite, Sigurd, Les Huguenots, La Juive, Robert le Diable* and *Le Cid*.

16 March – 15 April
Delacroix exhibition at the Ecole des Beaux-Arts.

Death of the artist's uncle, Michael Musson, in New Orleans.

June
Three works by Degas are sold at an exhibition of Impressionist works organised by Durand-Ruel in Brussels.

22 August – 21 September
Degas visits the Halévys at Dieppe. Walter Barnes photographs Degas' parodic orchestration of Ingres' *Apotheosis of Homer*.

Frédéric Auguste Bartholdi's *Liberty enlightening the world* ('Statue of Liberty') is shipped from Paris to New York, where it is erected the following year.

American inventor George Eastman creates flexible photographic film.

1886 French writer, Octave Mirbeau, bases a character, Eugéne Lirat, on Degas for his novel *La calvaire*.

January – December
Degas attends performances of *Sigurd, Robert le Diable, Le Cid, La Favorite, Les Jumeaux de Bergame, Les Huguenots, L'Africaine, Guillaume Tell, Rigoletto, La Juive, Henri VIII, La Korrigane, Faust, Le Freischutz, Les deux pigeons* and *Patrie* at the Paris Opéra.

March
As plans advance for the next (and eighth) Impressionist exhibition, Degas obstinately insists on the inclusion of certain artists for reasons of friendship while rejecting others.

April May
Twenty-three works by Degas are exhibited in a New York exhibition organised by Durand-Ruel.

15 May
Opening of the eighth Impressionist Exhibition, 1 rue Laffitte. This is the last of the Impressionist exhibitions.

Of his 15 catalogued works, Degas appears to have exhibited no more than 10. His nudes create a sensation, as they are not idealised.

Summer
Degas and Cassatt exchange their respective works: Degas' *Woman bathing in a shallow tub* 1885 (Lemoisne 816), now in the Metropolitan Museum of Art, New York; and Cassatt's *Girl arranging her hair* 1886, now in the National Gallery of Art, Washington DC. Cassatt's work can be seen in photographs taken of Degas' sitting room during the 1890s.

18 September
Jean Moréas' Symbolist manifesto is published in *Le Figaro*.

Emile Zola publishes *L'Oeuvre*, a fictionalised account of his friendship with Cézanne.

1887 Publication of Muybridge's *Animal locomotion*. Degas presumably obtains a copy.

February – December
Degas attends performances of *Patrie, Sigurd, Rigoletto, Les deux pigeons, Les Huguesnots, Aïda, La Favorite, Faust, Le Prophète, Le Cid, Robert le Diable, Guillame Tell, Don Juan* and *Coppélia* at the Paris Opéra.

1888 Degas moves from 21 rue Pigalle to 18 rue de Boulogne (now rue Ballu) sometime between 1888 and 1890.

Durand-Ruel opens a gallery in New York, following a recovery from financial disasters of 1882–84.

January
Works by Degas are shown at Galerie Boussod et Valadon, in a small exhibition arranged by Theo van Gogh, Paris.

March – December
Degas attends performances of *Aïda, Henri VIII, Sigurd, Faust, La Favorite, La Korrigane* and *Roméo et Juliette* at the Paris Opéra.

August
Degas spends time at the town of Cauterets, in the Hautes-Pyrénées of Southwestern France, for his first 'cure'.

Winter 1888–89
Degas writes eight sonnets, drawing inspiration from the subjects that occupied him at the time.

1889 Huysmans' *Certains* is published. It includes a chapter on Degas' nudes in the 1886 Impressionist exhibition.

January – December
Degas attends performances of *Roméo et Juliette, La Favorite, La Korrigane, La Tempête, Henri VIII, Le Prophète,* and *Lucie de Lammermoor.*

6 May – 31 October
The Eiffel tower is erected for the Exposition Universelle on the Champ de Mars.

14 July
100th anniversary of the Storming of the Bastille.

13 June
In a letter to the French painter and sculptor Paul-Albert Bartholomé, Degas mentions that he is working on a sculpture, *The tub* 1888–89 (Czestochowski and Pingeot 56), now in the National Gallery of Art, Washington DC.

29 August
Degas returns to Cauterets for a health cure.

8 September
Degas arrives in Madrid with Italian portrait painter Giovanni Boldini.

18 September
Writes to Bartholomé from Tangiers, Morocco, remarking how 'Delacroix passed here'.

The Moulin Rouge opens on the Boulevard de Clichy near Montmartre, Paris.

1890 March – October
Degas attends performances of *Ascanio, Salammbô, Coppélia, Zaïre, Le Rêve, L'Africaine* and *Sigurd* at the Paris Opéra.

29 April
In a letter to Bartholomé, Degas writes that he has visited the Exhibition of Japanese Prints at the Ecole des Beaux-Arts.

May
Attends a performance of *Salammbô* in Brussels, starring Rose Caron.

August
At Cauterets for a further health cure. Travels to Geneva to see his brother Achille De Gas.

Late September
Degas produces his first landscape, during a trip to Burgundy.

October
Degas is offended by publication of personal details about his family, and a quote about Whistler, in an article by George Moore in the *Magazine of Art*.

29 July
Death of Vincent van Gogh

American inventor Thomas Edison and his French rivals Auguste and Louis Lumière, introduce the first moving pictures.

1891 Degas invites Bartholomé to attend a Buddhist mass at the Musée Guimet, Paris.

January – October
Attends performances of *Sigurd, Aïda, Robert le Diable* and *Lohengrin* at the Paris Opéra.

6 July
Writes to Valernes that he is planning a series of lithographs depicting nudes and dancers.

1892 Attends performances of *Guillaum Tell* and *Faust* at the Paris Opéra.

25 March
Travels to Geneva to visit Achille De Gas.

28 March
Travels to Carpentras via Grenoble, Valence and Avignon.

27 August
During a visit to Ménil-Hubert, the artist paints two canvases of the Valpinçons' billiard room.

September
The first of two known exhibitions devoted to Degas' landscapes (in his own lifetime) is held at Galerie Durand-Ruel.

October
In a letter to Evariste de Valernes, the artist makes mention of an 'ominous contraption' worn to strengthen his eyes.

1893 Ambroise Vollard opens a small gallery at 37 rue Laffitte, Paris.

March
Display of *In a café (The absinthe drinker)* 1875–76, now in the Musée d'Orsay, Paris, at the Grafton Galleries in London causes a sensation.

31 August
Degas visits his sister Thérèse and her husband Edmondo Morbilli in Interlaken, Switzerland.

13 October
Death of Achille De Gas, Paris.

1894 October
Death of Paul Valpinçon.

22 December
Captain Alfred Dreyfus, a French Officer of Jewish origin who is falsely accused of treason, receives a conviction of life imprisonment for selling military secrets to Germany.

December
Degas purchases Gauguin's *Day of the god (Mahana no atua)* 1894, now in the Art Institute of Chicago.

1895 18 February
Degas purchases eight works at a Gauguin sale. As well as an oil painting *Woman of the mango (Vahine no te vi)* 1892, now in the Baltimore Museum of Art, the artist acquires a group of seven monotypes, including: *The bath, Tahitian hut, Tahiti (Te fare maorie)* 1894, *Standing woman, Seated woman* and two works titled *Words of the devil (Parau no varua)* 1984.

2 March
Death of Morisot, Paris.

June
Degas obtains Delacroix's portrait, *Louis-Auguste Schwiter* 1826–30, now in the National Gallery, London.

11 August
Degas writes the first of several letters to Guillaume Charles Tasset, a colour merchant and framer who is assisting him with his photographic experiments.

18 August
Degas goes to Mont-Dore, hoping for a cure from bronchitis.

Late August
Spends five days at Saint Valéry-sur-Somme.

October
Death of Degas' sister Marguerite Fevre, Buenos Aires.

29 November
Degas attends the Cézanne exhibition at Ambroise Vollard's and purchases the still life, *Apples* 1875–77, now on loan to the Fitwilliam Museum, Cambridge.

22 December
Degas shows recently acquired works to Daniel Halévy, including works by Delacroix, van Gogh and Cézanne.

28 December
Degas undertakes a long photographic session at the Halévy's.

French brothers Louis and Auguste Lumière demonstrate their Cinématographe, the first motion-picture apparatus capable of recording and projecting images.

1896 January, March and May
Degas purchases three works by Cézanne from Ambroise Vollard: *Two fruits* c 1885, now in Galerie Yoshii, Tokyo, *Glass and apples* 1879–92, now in the Rudolf Staechelin Family Foundation, Basel, and a portrait, *Victor Chocquet* c 1877, now in the Virginia Museum of Fine Arts.

23 January
Durand-Ruel buys Ingres' portraits of Jacques-Louis Leblanc and Mme Leblanc (now at the Metropolitan Museum of Art, New York) on behalf of Degas at the Hôtel Drouot auction.

March
Degas, Monet and Renoir organise a small posthumous exhibition of Morisot's work at Durand-Ruel.

September
Degas acquires El Greco's *Saint Dominic in prayer* c 1605, now in the Museum of Fine Arts, Boston, for Fr 3000.

1897 20 March
Degas invites Louis Braquaval and his wife to dinner with René De Gas and his family. This is the first written mention of a reconciliation between Edgar and his brother.

16 August
Visits the Musée Ingres at Montauban with Bartholomé.

November–December
Degas' anti-Semitic sentiments estrange him from the liberal, bourgeois and partly Jewish Halévy family.

25 November
Publication of Zola's first article supporting Captain Dreyfus, in *Le Figaro*.

13 December
Zola's pamphlet *Letter to youth* calls on young intellectuals to rally in support of Captain Dreyfus.

1898 22 August

Degas stays at Saint-Valéry-sur-Somme.

10 September
Death of Stéphane Mallarmé.

13 January
Zola's open letter *J'accuse*, accusing the French army of covering up the Dreyfus conviction, is published on the front page of *Aurore*.

Discovery of radium by French physicists Marie Curie, Pierre Curie and George Henri Becquerel.

1899–1902 Boer War between British and Boer republics, South Africa.

1899 28 January
Degas refuses a request by Julie Manet to provide a drawing for a publication of Mallarmé's poems, because the publisher is a Dreyfusard.

1 July
Degas purchases two works by Delacroix at the Chocquet sale: *The death of Charles the Bold at the Battle of Nancy* 1828–29, now in Ny Carlsberg Glyptotek, Copenhagen, and *Hercules rescuing the Hesione, study for the Old Hôtel de Ville* 1852, now in Ordrupgard, Copenhagen.

19 September
Captain Dreyfus is pardoned.

1900 31 May
Degas attends the double wedding of Julie Manet to Ernest Rouart, and Jeannie Gobillard to Paul Valéry.

Count Ferdinand von Zeppelin of Germany invents the Zeppelin aircraft.

George Eastman invents the first hand-held camera for amateur users.

1901 22 January
Death of Queen Victoria. Succession of Edward VII.

An estrangement occurs between Degas and Bartholomé, following the latter's second marriage to a young model, Florence Letessier.

1903 8 May
Death of Paul Gauguin, on the Island of Hiva Oa in the Marquesas Islands.

13 November
Death of Pissarro, Eragny-sur-Epte, Oise.

American inventor Orville Wright travels 40 yards (36.5 metres) in the first successful powered flight.

1904 May
Daniel Halévy is shocked by Degas' appearance when he visits the artist, who has been ill with intestinal grippe for two months.

August
Degas spends time at Pontarlier for a cure for gastritis, travelling via Epinal, Gérardmer, Alsace, Munster, Colmar, Belfort, Besançon and Ornans.

1905 Thirty-five works by Degas are displayed alongside works by Cézanne, Eugène Boudin and other Impressionists at Durand-Ruel's Grafton Galleries exhibition, London.

Albert Einstein publishes his theory of relativity.

1906 Eruption of Vesuvius, Naples
Degas writes to his sister Thérèse on 18 April that he is relieved that his Neapolitan relatives were unaffected by the eruption.

22 October
Death of Cézanne, Aix-en-Provence, Southern France.

Late October – December
Degas travels to Naples.

1908 8 May
Death of Ludovic Halévy, Paris.

1909 Death of Degas' cousin, Lucie, in Naples.

1911 April
Degas' second one-man show is held at the Fogg Art Museum at Harvard University, Cambridge, Massachusetts.

May
Degas attends an exhibition of Ingres' work at Galerie Georges Petit, Paris.

1912 2 January
Death of Rouart, Paris.

The artist's apartment at rue Victor-Massé is to be demolished. Degas is forced to move to another apartment, at 6 boulevard de Clichy.

July
Death of the artist's sister, Thérèse Morbilli, at Naples.

1913 Degas' health deteriorates.

The Frankfurt Städel Museum purchases *Orchestra musicians* c 1870–71/74–76 (Lemoisne 295) from Durand-Ruel.

1916 Summer
Degas visits the Bartholomés at Auteuil.

1917 27 September
Edgar Degas dies in Paris.

28 September
Following a service at the church of Saint-Jean-l'Evangeliste, the artist is buried in the family vault at Montmartre cemetery.

SELECT BIBLIOGRAPHY

Books and exhibition catalogues

Adhémar, Hélène, Dreyfus-Brühl, Madeleine and Sérullaz, Maurice et al. *Catalogue des peintures, pastels, sculptures impressionnistes exposés au Musée de l'Impressionnisme, Jeu du Paume des Tuileries,* Musées Nationaux, Paris, 1958

Adhémar, Hélène and Dayez, Anne (eds). *Musée du Jeu du Paume*, Editions des Musées Nationaux, Paris, 1973

Adhémar, Hélène and Dayez-Distel, Anne (eds). *Musée du Jeu du paume*, 4th edn, Editions des Musées Nationaux, Paris, 1979

Adhémar, Jean and Cachin, Françoise. *Degas: the complete etchings, lithographs and monotypes,* translated by Jane Brenton, Thames & Hudson, London, 1974

Armstrong, Carol. *A Degas sketchbook: with a postscript by David Hockney,* J Paul Getty Museum, Los Angeles, 2000

Armstrong, Carol. *Odd man out: readings of the work and reputation of Edgar Degas,* The University of Chicago Press, Chicago, 1991

Asano, Shūgō and Clark, Timothy. *The passionate art of Kitagawa Utamaro,* Asahi Shimbun, Japan, 1995

Bailly-Herzberg, Janine (ed). *Correspondance de Camille Pissarro,* vol 1, 1865–1885, Presses Universitaires de France, Paris, 1980

Baudelaire, Charles. *The painter of modern life and other essays,* translated and edited by Jonathan Mayne, Phaidon, London, 1964

Baumann, Felix Andreas and Karabelnik, Marianne (eds). *Degas: portraits,* Merrell Holberton, London, 1994

Bazin, Germain. *Trésors de l'impressionnisme au Louvre,* Editions Aimery Somogy, Paris, 1958

Bernheimer, Charles. *Figures of ill repute: representing prostitution in nineteenth century France,* Duke University Press, Durham, 1997

Berson, Ruth. *The new painting: Impressionism 1874–1886: documentation,* 2 vols, Fine Arts Museum of San Francisco, San Francisco, 1996

Blanche, Jacques-Emile. *Propos de peintre: de David à Degas,* 9th edn, Emile Paul Frères, Paris, 1927

Boggs, Jean Sutherland. *Portraits by Degas,* University of California Press, Berkeley, 1962

Boggs, Jean Sutherland. *Drawings by Degas,* City Art Museum of Saint Louis, Saint Louis, 1966

Boggs, Jean Sutherland, Druick, Douglas W and Loyrette, Henri et al. *Degas,* The Metropolitan Museum of Art, and the National Gallery of Canada, New York, 1988

Boggs, Jean Sutherland. *Degas at the races,* National Gallery of Art, Washington, 1998

Boggs, Jean Sutherland and Maheux, Anne. *Degas pastels,* Thames & Hudson, London, 1992

Boime, Albert. *The academy and French painting in the nineteenth century,* Phaidon, London, 1971

Bomford, David, Herring, Sarah and Kirby, Jo et al. *Art in the making: Degas,* National Gallery Company, London, 2004

Bouret, Jean. *Degas,* translated by Daphne Woodward, Thames & Hudson, London, 1965

Bowlby, Rachel. *Just looking: consumer culture in Dreiser, Grissing and Zola,* Methuen, New York, 1985

Brame, Philippe and Reff, Theodore. *Degas and his work (Degas et son oeuvre): a supplement,* Garland Press, New York, 1984

Breeskin, Adelyn D. *The graphic work of Mary Cassatt: a catalogue raisonné,* H Bittner & Co, New York, 1948

Brière, Gaston. *Catalogue des peintures exposées dans les galeries,* vol 1, Ecole Française, Editions des Musées Nationaux, Paris, 1924

Brown, Marilyn. *Degas and the business of art: a Cotton Office in New Orleans,* Pennsylvania State Press, Pennsylvania, 1994

Browse, Lillian. *Degas dancers,* Faber and Faber, London, 1949

Buchloh, Benjamin H D, Guilbaut, Serge and Solkin, David (eds). *Modernism and modernity: the Vancouver conference papers,* The Press of the Nova Scotia College of Art and Design, Nova Scotia, 1983

Cabanne, Pierre. *Edgar Degas,* translated by Michel Lee Landa, Pierre Tisné, Paris, 1958

Callen, Anthea. *The spectacular body: science, method and meaning in the work of Degas,* Yale University Press, New Haven, 1995

Callen, Anthea. *Techniques of the Impressionists,* Orbis Publishing Limited, London, 1982

Catalogue des estampes anciennes et modernes oeuvres de Bracquemond, Mary Cassatt, Daumier ... et al: Collection Edgar Degas... à Paris à l'Hôtel Drouot, Salle no 6 les Mercredi 6 et Jeudi 7 Novembre 1918... Hôtel Drouot, Paris, 1918

Catalogue des tableaux modernes pastels, aquarelles, dessins anciens et modernes par Brandon-Braquaval ... faisant partie de la Collection Edgar Degas [2me vente], Hôtel Drouot, Paris, Novembre 1918

Catalogue des tableaux, pastels et dessins par Edgar Degas et provenant de son atelier: dont la [1e-4e] vente aux enchères publiques, après décès de l'artiste, aura lieu à Paris / Galerie Georges Petit ... [Imp. Lahure], Paris, 1918–1919

Clair, Jean (ed). *The great parade,* National Gallery of Canada, Ottawa, 2004

Clarke, Mary and Crisp, Clement. *Ballet: an illustrated history,* Adam and Charles Black, London, 1973

Clayson, Hollis. *Painted love: prostitution in French art of the Impressionist era,* Yale University Press, New Haven, 1991

Compin, I and Roquebert, Anne. *Catalogue sommaire illustré des peintures du Musée du Louvre et du Musée d'Orsay: Ecole Française,* 3 vols, Editions de la Réunion des Musées Nationaux, Paris, 1986

Cooper, Douglas. *The Courtauld collection,* University of London, Athlone Press, London, 1954

Coquiot, Gustave. *Degas,* Ollendorff, Paris, 1924

Correspondance de Berthe Morisot, Quatre Chemins-Editart, Paris, 1950

Crouzet, Marcel. *Un méconnu du réalisme: Duranty (1833–1880), l'homme, le critique, le romancier,* Librairie Nizet, Paris, 1964

Czestochowski, Joseph S and Pingeot, Anne. *Degas sculptures: catalogue raisonné of the bronzes,* International Arts and Torch Press, Memphis, 2002

Daniel, Malcolm. *Edgar Degas: photographer,* The Metropolitan Museum of Art, New York, 1998

Dean, Sonia. *European painting of the 19th and early 20th centuries in the National Gallery of Victoria,* National Gallery of Victoria, Melbourne, 1995

Degas en blanc et noir, Fondation Angladon – Dubrujeaud, Avignon, 2004

Degas e gli italiani a Parigi, Palazzo dei Diamanti, Ferrara, 14 September – 16 November 2003

Degas inédit: Actes du Colloque Degas, Musée d'Orsay, 18–21 April 1988, La Documentation Française, Paris, 1989

Degas's Atelier at auction 1918 – sales I + II [Vente atelier Edgar Degas 1918 – ventes I + II], Alan Wofsy Fine Arts, San Francisco, 1989

Degas's Atelier at auction 1919 – sales III + IV [Vente atelier Edgar Degas 1919 – ventes III + IV], Alan Wofsy Fine Arts, San Francisco, 1989

Delteil, Loÿs, *Edgar Degas, Le peintre-graveur illustré*, vol 9, privately printed, Paris, 1919

DeVonyar, Jill and Kendall, Richard. *Degas and the art of Japan*, Reading Public Museum, Reading, 2007

Dunlop, Ian. *Degas*, Harper and Row, New York, 1979

Dumas, Ann. *Degas's Mlle. Fiocre in context: a study of Portrait de Mlle. EF ... à propos du ballet "La source"*, The Brooklyn Museum, Brooklyn, 1988

Dumas, Ann and Brenneman, David A. *Degas and America: the early collectors*, High Museum of Art, The Minneapolis Institute of Arts, Minneapolis, 2000

Dumas, Ann (ed). *Inspiring Impressionism: the Impressionists and the art of the past*, distributed by Yale University Press for Denver Art Museum, New Haven, London, 2007

Duranty, Edmond. *La nouvelle peinture: à propos du groupe d'artistes qui expose dans les galeries Durand-Ruel*, E Dentu, Paris, 1876

Ellis, Andrew. *Oil paintings in public ownership in Cambridgeshire: the Fitzwilliam Museum*, Public Catalogue Foundation, London, 2006

Fénéon, Félix. *Oeuvres plus que complètes* (edited by Joan U Halperin), 2 vols, Librairie Droz, Geneva, 1970

Fernandez, Rafael and Murphy, Alexandra R. *Degas in the Clark collection*, Sterling and Francine Clark Art Institute, Williamstown, 1987

Fevre, Jeanne. *Mon oncle Degas* (edited by Pierre Borel), Pierre Cailler, Geneva, 1949

Feigenbaum, Gail. *Degas and New Orleans: a French Impressionist in America*, New Orleans Museum of Art, New Orleans, 1999

Flint, Kate (ed). *Impressionists in England: the critical reception*, Routledge and Kegan Paul, London, 1984

Fontaine, Gérard. *Charles Garnier's Opéra: architecture and exterior décor*; translated by Ellie Rea in collaboration with Barbara Shapiro-Comte, Centre des monuments nationaux / Editions du Patrimoine, Paris, 2000

Goncourt, Edmond de and Goncourt, Jules de. *Journal: mémoires de la vie littéraire*, edited by Robert Ricatte, 4 vols, Fasquelle, Flammarion, Paris, 1956

Goncourt, Edmond de and Goncourt, Jules de. *Paris and the arts, 1851–1896: from the Goncourt journal*, edited and translated by George J Becker and Edith Philips, Cornell University Press, Ithaca and London, 1971, Guérin, Marcel. *Dix-neuf portraits de Degas par lui-même*, privately printed, Paris, 1931

Guérin, Marcel (ed). *Edgar Germain Hilaire Degas letters*, translated by Marguerite Kay, Cassirer, Oxford, 1947

Guest, Ivor. *Jules Perrot: master of the romantic ballet*, Dance Books, London, 1984

Halévy, Daniel. *Degas parle ...* , La Palatine, Paris, 1960

Halévy, Daniel. *My friend Degas*, translated and edited by Mina Curtiss, Wesleyan University Press, Middletown, 1964

Haverkamp-Begemann, Egbert, Lawder, Standish D and Talbot Jr, Charles W, *Drawings from the Clark Art Institute*, 2 vols, Yale University Press, New Haven/London, 1964

HO Havemeyer Collection: catalogue of paintings, prints, sculptures and objects of art, privately printed, New York, 1931

Havemeyer, Louisine W. *Sixteen to sixty: memoirs of a collector*, privately printed, New York, 1961

Heim, Jean-François, Béraud, Claire and Heim, Philippe. *Les Salons de peinture de la révolution française 1779–1799*, CAC Sarl, Paris, 1989

Hertz, Henri. *Degas*, Paris: Librairie Félix Alcan, Paris, 1920

Howard, Michael (ed). *The Impressionists by themselves*, The Chancellor Press, London, 1992

Huit Sonnets d'Edgar Degas, preface by Jean Nepveu-Degas, La Jeune Parque, Paris, 1946

Huyghe, René. *La relève du réel: impressionnisme, symbolisme*, Flammarion, Paris, 1974

Huysmans, Joris-Karl. *Certains: G Moreau, Degas, Chéret, Whisthler [sic], Rops, Le Monstre, Le Fer, etc*, Tresse et Stock, Paris, 1889

Huysmans, Joris-Karl. *Oeuvres complètes*, vol 10, Les Editions G Crès and Cie, Paris, 1929

Iskin, Ruth E. *Modern women and Parisian consumer culture in Impressionist painting*, Cambridge University Press, New York, 2007

Ives, Colta, Stein, Susan Alyson and Steiner, Julie A et al. *The private collection of Edgar Degas: a summary catalogue*, The Metropolitan Museum of Art, New York, 1997

Jamot, Paul. *Degas*, Editions de la Gazette des Beaux-arts, Paris, 1924

Janis, Eugenia Parry. *Degas monotypes: essay: catalogue and checklist*, Fogg Art Museum, Cambridge, 1968

Kelley, David. *Baudelaire: Salon de 1846*, Clarendon Press, Oxford, 1975

Kendall, Richard (ed). *Degas 1834–1984*, Manchester Polytechnic, Manchester, 1985

Kendall, Richard (ed). *Degas by himself: drawings, prints, paintings, writings*, Little, Brown and Company, Boston, 1987

Kendall, Richard (ed). *Monet by himself: paintings, drawings, pastels, letters*, translations by Bridget Strevens Romer, Macdonald Orbis, London, 1989

Kendall, Richard. *Paintings, pastels and drawings by Edgar Degas*, David Bathurst Ltd of The St James's Art Group, London, 1991

Kendall, Richard. *Degas landscapes*, Yale University Press in association with the Metropolitan Museum of Art, New York and the Museum of Fine Arts, Houston, New Haven, 1993

Kendall, Richard (ed). *Degas in time*, Ordrupgaardsamlingen, Ordrupgaard, 1994

Kendall, Richard. *Degas: beyond Impressionism*, National Gallery Publications, London, 1996

Kendall, Richard. *Degas and the little dancer*, Yale University Press in association with Josyln Art Museum, New Haven, London, 1998

Kendall, Richard and Pollock, Griselda (eds). *Dealing with Degas: representations of women and the politics of vision*, Pandora Press, London, 1992

Kessler, Marni Reva. *Sheer presence: the veil in Manet's Paris*, University of Minnesota Press, Minneapolis, 2006

Kinsman, Jane, Bascou, Marc and Gott, Ted et al. *Paris in the late 19th century*, National Gallery of Australia, Canberra, 1996

Lafond, Paul. *Degas*, 2 vols, H Floury Editeur, Paris, 1918–1919

Lassaigne, Jacques. *Edgar Degas*, Editions Hypérion, Paris, 1945

Lemaire, Gérard-Georges. *Histoire du Salon de peintre*, Klincksieck, Paris, 2004

Lemoisne, Paul-André. *Degas et son oevre*, 4 vols, Paul Brame and CM de Hauke, Arts et métiers graphiques, Paris, 1949

Leprieur, P and Demonts, L. *Catalogue de la collection Isaac de Camondo*, 2nd edn, Musée national du Louvre, Paris, 1922

Leymarie, Jean. *Les Degas au Louvre*, Librairie des Arts Décoratifs, Paris, 1947

Lipton, Eunice. *Looking into Degas: Uneasy images of women and modern life*, University of California Press, Berkeley, 1986

Lobstein, Dominique. *Les Salons au XIXe siècle: Paris, capitale des arts*, Editions de la Martinière, Paris, 2006

López-Rey, José. *Velázquez: catalogue raisonné*, Wildenstein Institute and Taschen, Köln, 1999

Louys, Pierre. *Mimes des Courtisanes: dialogues of the courtesans*, translated by Guy Daniels, Cercle des éditions privées, [Paris], 1973

Loyrette, Henri and Roquebert, Anne. *L'album Degas: Galeries nationales du Grand Palais, Paris, 9 février-16 mai 1988, Musée des beaux-arts du Canada, Ottawa, 16 juin-28 août 1988, The Metropolitan Museum of Art, New York, 27 septembre 1988–8 janvier 1989*, Editions de la Réunion des musées nationaux, Paris, 1988

Manson, J B. *The life and work of Edgar Degas*, Studio, London, 1927

Marmor, Michael F *Degas through his own eyes: visual disability and the late style of Degas*, Somogy éditions d'art, Paris, 2002

Mathieu, Pierre-Louis. *Gustave Moreau*, New York Graphic Society, Boston, 1976

Mathews, Nancy Mowll (ed). *Cassatt and her circle: selected letters*, Abbeville Press, New York, 1984

Mathews, Nancy Mowll. *Mary Cassatt: a life*, Yale University Press, New Haven and London, 1994

Maupassant, Guy de. *La Maison Tellier*, Vollard, Paris, 1934

McMullen, Roy. *Degas: his life, times and work*, Secker and Warburg, London, 1985

Meier-Graefe, *Degas*, R Piper, Munich, 1920

Meier-Graefe, Julius. *Degas*, translated by J Holroyd-Reece, Ernest Benn, London, 1923

Merlhés, Victor (ed). *Correspondance de Paul Gauguin: documents, témoignages*, vol 1, Fondation Singer-Polignac, Paris, 1984, p 12

Meyers, Jeffrey. *Impressionist quartet: the intimate genius of Manet and Morisot, Degas and Cassatt*, Harcourt, Orlando, 2005

Millard, Charles W. *The sculpture of Edgar Degas*, Princeton University Press, Princeton, 1976

Minervino, Fiorella. *Tout l'oeuvre peint de Degas* (introduction by Jacques Lassaigne), Flammarion, Paris, 1974

Moffett, Charles S. *Degas: paintings in the Metropolitan Museum of Art*, The Metropolitan Museum of Art, New York, 1979

Moffett, Charles S. *Impressionist and Post-Impressionist paintings in the Metropolitan Museum of Art*, The Metropolitan Museum of Art, New York, 1985

Moffett, Charles S, Berson, Ruth and Williams, Barbara Lee et al. *The new painting: Impressionism 1874–1886*, Richard Burton SA, Publishers, Geneva, 1986

Mongan, Agnes and Sachs, Paul J. *Drawings in the Fogg Museum of Art*, 3 vols, Harvard University Press, Cambridge, 1940

Monnier, Geneviève. *Pastels du XIXe siècle*, Editions de la Réunion des Musées Nationaux, Paris, 1985

Moore, George. *Impressions and opinions*, Scribner's, New York, 1891

Moreau-Nélaton, Etienne. *Manet raconté par lui-même*, 2 vols, H Laurens, Paris, 1926

Muybridge, Eadweard. *Muybridge's complete human and animal locomotion: all 781 plates from the 1887 Animal Locomotion*, 3 vols, Dover Publications Inc, New York, 1979

Naef, Weston, *Experimental photography: the painter–photographer*, J Paul Getty Museum, Malibu, California, 1989

Nochlin, Linda. *Representing women*, Thames & Hudson, London, 1997

Nochlin, Linda and Bolloch, Joelle. *Women in the 19th century: categories and contradictions*, The New Press, New York, 1997

Passeron, Robert. *Impressionist prints*, Dutton, New York, 1974

Pickvance, Ronald. *Degas: 19 juin – 21 novembre 1993*, Fondation Pierre Gianadda, Martigny, 1993

Pingeot, Anne, Le Normand-Romain, Antoinette and Margerie, Laure de. *Catalogue sommaire illustré des sculptures*, Editions de la réunion des musées nationaux, Paris, 1986

Pittaluga, M and Piceni, E. *De Nittis*, Bramante, Milan, 1963

Raimondi, Riccardo. *Degas e la sua famiglia in Napoli: 1793–1917*, SAV, Naples, 1958

Reed, Sue Welsh and Shapiro, Barbara Stern. *Edgar Degas: the painter as printmaker*, Museum of Fine Arts, Boston, 1984

Reff, Theodore. *Degas: the artist's mind*, The Metropolitan Museum of Art and Harper and Row, New York, 1976

Reff, Theodore. *The notebooks of Edgar Degas: a catalogue of the thirty-eight notebooks in the Bibliothèque nationale and other collections*, 2 vols, 2nd edn, Hacker Art Books, New York, 1985

Rewald, John. *The history of Impressionism*, Museum of Modern Art, New York, 1973

Rewald, John. *Degas sculpture*, Abrams, New York, 1956

Rewald, John (ed). *Camille Pissarro: letters to his son Lucien*, translated by Lionel Abel, 4th edn, Routledge and Kegan Paul, London, 1980

Rewald, John. *Studies in Post-Impressionism*, edited by Irene Gordon and Frances Weitzenhoffer, Harry N Abrams, New York, 1986

Rich, Daniel Catton. *Degas*, Harry N Abrams, New York, 1951

Rivière, Georges. *Mr. Degas, bourgeois de Paris*, Floury, Paris, 1935

Rivière, Henri. *Les dessins de Degas*, Editions Demotte, vol 1, Paris, 1922, vol 2, Paris, 1923

Roberts, Keith. *Degas: with notes by Helen Langdon*, Phaidon, Oxford/Dutton, New York, 1976

Roberts, Rosalind de Boland and Roberts, Jane (eds). *Growing up with the Impressionists: the diary of Julie Manet*, Sotheby's Publications, London, 1987

Roskill, Mark. *Van Gogh, Gauguin and the Impressionist circle*, New York Graphic Society, Greenwich, 1970

Rothenstein, Sir William. *Men and memories; recollections 1872–1938 of William Rothenstein*, abridged with introduction and noted by Mary Lago, Chatto & Windus, London, 1978

Rouart, Ernest. *Degas à la recherche de sa technique*, Floury, Paris, 1945

Rouart, Ernest. *Degas monotypes*, Quatre Chemins Editart, Paris, 1948

Rouart, Ernest (ed). *The correspondence of Berthe Morisot*, translated by Betty W Hubbard, Lund Humphries, London, 1957

Scharf, Aaron. *Art and photography*, Penguin, Baltimore, 1972

Spate, Virginia. *Claude Monet: the colour of time*, Thames & Hudson, London, 1992

Sterling, Charles and Adhémar, Hélène. *Peintures, Ecole française: XIXe siècle*, vol 2, Editions de la réunion des musées nationaux, Paris, 1959

Sterling, Charles and Salinger, Margaretta M. *French paintings: a catalogue of the collection of the Metropolitan Museum of Art*, vol 3, nos 19–20, New York Graphic Society, Greenwich, 1967

Sutton, Denys. *Edgar Degas: life and work*, Rizzoli, New York, 1986

Terrasse, Antoine. *Edgar Degas*, Thames & Hudson, London, 1974

Terrasse, Antoine. *Edgar Degas*, Ullstein Bücher, Frankfurt, Berlin, and Vienna, 1981

Terrasse, Antoine. *Degas et la photographie*, Editions Denoël, Paris, 1983

Thomson, Richard. *Degas: the nudes,* Thames & Hudson, London, 1988

Thore, Théophile. *Salons de W Bürger 1861 à 1868,* 2 vols, Paris, 1870, p 369

Thornley, George William. *Quinze lithographies d'après Degas* Boussod et Valadon, Paris, 1889

Tinterow, Gary and Lacambre, Genivième (eds). *Manet/Velázquez: the French taste for Spanish painting,* The Metropolitan Museum of Art, New York, 2003

Tinterow, Gary and Loyrette, Henri. *Origins of Impressionism,* The Metropolitan Museum of Art, New York, 1994

Tucker, William. *Early modern sculpture: Rodin, Degas, Matisse, Brancusi, Picasso, Gonzalez,* Oxford University Press, New York, 1974

Valéry, Paul. *Degas, Manet, Morisot,* translated by David Paul, Pantheon Books, New York, 1960

van Zanten, David. *Building Paris: architectural institutions and the transformation of the French capital 1830–1870,* Cambridge University Press, Cambridge, 1994

Venturi, Lionello. *Les archives de l'impressionnisme,* 2 vols, Durand-Ruel, Paris/New York, 1939

Vollard, Ambroise. *Degas: quatre-vingt-dix-huit reproductions signées par Degas,* Vollard, Paris, 1914

Vollard, Ambroise. *Degas: an intimate portrait,* translated by Randolph T Weaver, Greenberg Publisher, New York, 1927

Vollard, Ambroise. *Recollections of a picture dealer,* translated by Violet M Macdonald, Constable, London, 1936

Vollard, Ambroise. *En écoutant Cézanne, Degas, Renoir,* Grasset, Paris, 1938

Weitzenhoffer, Frances. *The Havemeyers: Impressionism comes to America,* Harry N Abrams, New York, 1986

Wildenstein, Georges. *Gauguin,* Les Beaux-arts, Paris, 1964

Wilson-Bareau, Juliet. *Correspondence & conversation Manet by himself: paintings, pastels, prints & drawings,* Little, Brown and Company, London, 1991

Articles and essays

Adam, Paul. 'Peintres impressionistes', *La Revue contemporaine: littérarire, politique et philosophique,* vol 4, April 1886, pp 541–51

Ajalbert, Jean. 'Le Salon des Impressionnistes', *La Revue Moderne,* Marseilles, 20 June 1886, pp 385–93

Alexandre, Arsène. 'Collection de M. le Comte Issac de Camondo', *Les Arts,* vol 83, November 1908, pp 22–26, 29, 32

Alexandre, Arsène. 'La Collection Henri Rouart', *Les Arts,* vol 132, December 1912, pp 2–32

Alexandre, Arsène. 'Degas: graveur et lithographe', *Les Arts,* vol 15, no 171, 1918, pp 11–19

Alexandre, Arsène. 'La collection Havemeyer: Edgar Degas', *La Renaissance de l'Art Français et des industries de luxe,* vol 20, no 10, October 1929, pp 479–86

Alexandre, Arsène. 'Degas: nouveaux aperçus', *L'Art et les artistes,* vol 29, no 154, February 1935, pp 145–73

Allen, William G. untitled review of 'Correspondance générale by Théophile Gautier' in *The French Review,* vol 72, no 4, March 1999, pp 756–75

Baignères, Arthur. 'Exposition de peinture par un groupe d'artistes, rue le Peletier, 11', *L'Echo universel,* 13 April 1876, p 3

Barazzetti, S. 'Degas et ses amis Valpinçon', *Beaux-arts,* vol 190, 21 August 1936, pp 1, 3

Barazzetti, S. 'Degas et ses amis Valpinçon', *Beaux-arts,* vol 191, 28 August 1936, pp 1, 4

Barazzetti, S. 'Degas et ses amis Valpinçon', *Beaux-arts,* vol 192, 4 September 1936, pp 1–2

Bazin, Germain. 'Degas: sculpteur', *L'Amour de l'art,* 12th year, vol 7, July 1931, pp 292–91

Beaulieu, Michèle. 'Les sculptures de Degas: essai de chronologie', *La Revue du Louvre et des Musées de France,* 19th year, vol 6, 1969, pp 369–80

Bénédite, Léonce. 'La collection Caillebotte et l'école impressionniste', *L'Artiste,* vol 8, August 1894, pp 131–32

Bertall. 'Les Impressionnalistes', *Les Beaux-arts,* 1876, pp 44–45; *Le Soir,* 15 April 1876, p 3

Bigot, Charles. 'Causerie artistique: l'exposition des "intransigeants"', *La Revue politique et littéraire,* 8 April 1876, pp 349–52

Boggs, Jean Sutherland. 'Edgar Degas and the Bellellis', *Art Bulletin,* vol 37, no 2, June 1955, pp 127–36

Boggs, Jean Sutherland. 'Degas' notebooks at the Bibliothèque nationale, vol 1, group A, 1853–1858', *Burlington Magazine,* vol 100, no 662, May 1958, pp 163–71; vol 2, group B, 1858–1861, vol 100, no 663, June 1958, pp 196–205; 'vol 3, group C, 1863–1886', vol 100, no 664, July 1958, pp 240–46

Boggs, Jean Sutherland. 'Edgar Degas and Naples', *Burlington Magazine,* vol 105, no 723, June 1963, pp 273–76

Boggs, Jean Sutherland. '*Danseuses à la barre* by Degas', *The National Gallery of Canada Bulletin,* vol 2, no 1, 1964, pp 1–9

Broude, Norma. 'An early friend of Degas in Florence: a newly- identified portrait drawing of Degas by Giovanni Fattori', *The Burlington Magazine,* vol 115, no 848, November 1973, pp 726–35

Broude, Norma. 'Degas's "misogyny"', *Art Bulletin,* vol 59, no 1, March 1977, pp 95–107

Browse, Lillian. 'Degas's grand passion', *Apollo,* vol 85, no 60, February 1967, pp 104–14

Buerger, Janet F. 'Degas' solarized and negative photographs: a look at unorthodox Classicism', *Image,* vol 20, no 2, June 1978, pp 17–23

Buerger, Janet F. 'Another note on Degas', *Image,* vol 23, no 1, June 1980, p 6

Burroughs, Bryson. 'Drawings by Degas', *The Metropolitan Museum of Art Bulletin,* vol 14, no 5, May 1919, pp 115–17

Burroughs, Louise. 'Degas in the Havemeyer Collection', *The Metropolitan Museum of Art Bulletin,* vol 27, no 5, May 1932, pp 141–46

Burroughs, Louise. 'Degas paints a portrait', *The Metropolitan Museum of Art Bulletin,* vol 21, no 5, January 1963, pp 169–72

Burty, Phillipe. 'Exposition de la société anonyme des artistes', *La Republique française,* 25 April 1874, p 2

Cabanne, Pierre. 'Degas chez Picasso', *Connaissance des Arts,* vol 262, December 1973, pp 146–51

Callen, Anthea. 'Jean-Baptiste Faure, 1830–1914: a study of a patron and collector of the Impressionists and their contemporaries', unpublished MA thesis, University of Leicester, 1971

Cardon, Emile. 'Avant le Salon', *La Presse,* 28 April 1874, p 3

Cardon, Emile. 'Avant le Salon: L'exposition des révoltés', *La Presse,* 29 April 1874, pp 2–3

Carjat, Etienne. 'L'exhibition du boulevard des Capucines', *Le Patriote français,* 27 April 1874, p 3

Castagnary, Jules-Antoine. 'Exposition du boulevard des Capucines: Les Impressionnistes', *Le Siècle,* 29 April 1874, p 3

'Causerie artisque: L'exposition des "intransigeants"', *La Revue politique et littéraire,* 8 April 1876, pp 349–52

Chevalier, Frédéric. 'Les impressionnistes', *L'Artiste,* 1 May 1877

Claretie, Jules. 'Le mouvement parisien: L 'exposition des impressionnistes', *L'Indépendance belge,* 15 April 1877, p 1

Claretie, Jules. 'La vie à Paris: les artistes indépendents', *Le Temps,* 5 April 1881, p 3 and variant in *La vie* à *Paris: 1881,* Victor Harvard, Paris, 1881, pp 148–151

Crimp, Douglas. 'Positive/Negative: a note on Degas's photographs', *October,* vol 5, summer 1978, pp 89–100

[Dell, Robert E] RED. 'Arts in France', *Burlington Magazine,* vol 22, no 19, February 1913, pp 295–98

'Degas: chronology of the artist's life', viewed August 2008, metmuseum.org/explore/Degas

Fénéon, Félix. 'Les Impressionnistes en 1886 (VIIIe exposition impressionniste)', *La Vogue,* 13–20 June 1886, pp 261–75, Paris: Hermann, 1966, pp 64–67

Frantz, Henry. 'The Rouart Collection', *Studio international,* vol 50, no 199, September 1913, pp 184–93

Gedo, Mary Mathews. 'Retreat from an artistic breakthrough: Gauguin's nude study (Suzanne sewing)', *Zeitschrift für Kunstgeschichte*, vol 58, no 3, 1995, pp 407–16

Geffroy, Gustave. 'Degas', *L'Art et les Artistes*, vol 4, no 37, April 1908, pp 15–23

Gerstein, Marc. 'Degas's fans', *Art Bulletin*, vol 64, no 1, March 1982, pp 105–18

Giese, Lucretia H. 'A visit to the museum', *Boston Museum of Fine Arts Bulletin*, vol 76, 1978, pp 43–53

Goetschy, Gustave. 'Indépendants et impressionistes [sic]', *Le Voltaire*, 6 April 1880

Gruetzner, Anna. 'Degas and George Moore: some observations about the last Impressionist exhibition', *Degas 1834–1984* (edited by Kendall, Richard), Manchester Polytechnic, Manchester, 1985, pp 32–39

Guérin, Marcel. 'Notes sur les monotypes de Degas', *L'Amour de l'art*, 5th year, March 1924, pp 77–80

Guérin, Marcel. 'Trois portraits de Degas offerts par la Société des Amis du Louvre', *Bulletin des Musées de France*, 7 July 1932, pp 106–107

Hauptman, William. 'Juries, protests and counter-exhibitions before 1850', *Art Bulletin*, vol 67, no 1, March 1985, pp 95–109

Hemmings, FWJ. 'Zola, Manet, and the Impressionists (1875-80)', *PMLA*, vol 73, no 4, September 1958, pp 407–17

Hermel, Maurice. 'L'exposition de peinture de la rue Laffitte,' *La France Libre*, 27 May 1886

Hourticq, Louis. 'E Degas', *Art et Décoration*, suppl, vol 32, October 1912, pp 97–113

Huth, Hans. 'Impressionism comes to America', *Gazette des Beaux–arts*, vol 29, April 1946, pp 225–52

Huyghe, René. 'Degas ou la fiction réaliste', *L'Amour de l'Art*, 12th year, July 1931, pp 271–82

Huysmans, Joris-Karl. 'L'Exposition des indépendants en 1881' *L'art moderne*, G Charpentier, Paris, 1883, pp 225–57

Isaacson, Joel. 'Constable, Duranty, Mallarmé: Impressionism, plein air, and forgetting', *The Art Bulletin*, vol 76, no 3, September 1994, pp 427–50

Jacques [pseud]. 'Menu propos: exposition impressionniste', *L'Homme libre*, 12 April 1877

Jamot, Paul. 'La collection Camondo au Musée du Louvre: les peintures et les dessins', pt 2, *Gazette des Beaux-arts*, vol 684, June 1914, pp 441–60

Jamot, Paul. 'Degas', *Gazette des Beaux-arts*, vol 14, April – June 1918, pp 123–66

Janis, Eugenia Parry. 'The Role of the monotype in the working method of Degas – I' *The Burlington Magazine*, vol 109, no 766, January 1967, pp 20–29

Janis, Eugenia Parry. 'The role of the monotype in the working method of Degas – II', *The Burlington Magazine*, vol 109, no 767, February 1967, pp 71–81

Janis, Eugenia Parry. 'Degas and the "Master of chiaroscuro"', *Museum Studies, The Art Institute of Chicago*, vol 7, 1972, pp 52–71

Janneau, Guillaume. 'Les sculptures de Degas', *La Renaissance de l'Art Français*, vol 4, no 7, July 1921, pp 352–53

Jeanniot, Georges. 'Souvenirs sur Degas', *La Revue Universelle*, vol 55, 15 October 1933, pp 152–74, 1 November 1933, pp 280–304

Kendall, Richard. 'Degas and the contingency of vision', *Burlington Magazine*, March 1988, pp 180–97

Kinsman, Jane. 'Developing character: Gavarni's lithographs for *Paris 1852–1853*', *Extrait de la Gazette des Beaux-arts*, 1990

Koshkin-Youritzin, Victor. 'The irony of Degas', *Gazette des Beaux-arts*, vol 87, January 1976, pp 33–40

Lebensztejn, Jean-Claude. 'Framing classical space', *Art Journal*, vol 47, no 1, spring 1988, pp 37–41

Lemoisne, Paul-André. 'Degas', *Beaux-arts*, 75th year, new series, vol 219, March 1937, pp A–B

Leroy, Louis. 'L'expositoin des impressionistes', *Le Charivari*, 25 April 1874, pp 79–80

Liere, Eldon N van. 'Solutions and dissolutions: The bather in nineteenth century French painting', *Arts Magazine*, May 1980, pp 104–14

Lipton, Eunice. 'The laundress in late nineteenth century French culture: Imagery, ideology and Edgar Degas', *Art History*, vol 3, no 3, September 1980, pp 295–13

Lipton, Eunice. 'Degas' bathers: The case for realism', *Arts Magazine*, May 1980, pp 94–97

Mallarmé, Stéphane. 'The Impressionists and Edouard Manet', *Art Monthly Review and Photographic Portfolio*, 30 September 1876, pp 117–22

Malte, C. de. 'Exposition de la société anonyme des artistes peintres, sculpteurs, graveurs et lithographes', *Paris à l'eaux-fortes*, 19 April 1874, pp 12–33

Mantz, Paul. 'L'exposition des peintres impressionnistes', *Le Temps*, 22 April 1877

Mantz, Paul. 'Exposition des œuvres des artistes indépendants', *Le Temps*, 23 April 1881

Marx, Roger. 'Cartons d'artistes: Degas', *L'Image*, vol 11, October 1897, pp 321–25

Mathieu, Pierre-Louis. 'Gustave Moreau en Italie (1857–1859) d'après sa correspondance inédite', *Bulletin de la Société de l'Histoire de l'Art Français*, 1974, pp 173–91

Mauclair, Camille. 'Artistes contemporains: Edgar Degas', *Revue de l'Art Ancien et Moderne*, vol 14, no 80, November 1903, pp 381–98

Mayne, Jonathan. 'Degas's ballet scene from Robert le Diable', *Victoria and Albert Museum Bulletin*, vol 2, no 4, October 1966, pp 148–56

Michel, Alice. 'Degas et son modèle', *Mercure de France*, 16 February 1919, pp 457–78, 623–39

Michel, J M. 'Exposition des impressionnistes', *La petite gazette*, 18 May 1886

Mirbeau, Octave. 'Exposition de peinture', *La France*, Paris, 21 May 1886, pp 1–2

Monet, Claude. 'Mon histoire', *Le Temps*, 26 November 1900

Mongan, Agnes. 'Portrait studies by Degas in American collections', *Bulletin of the Fogg Art Museum*, vol 1, no 4, May 1932

Mongan, Agnes. 'Degas as seen in American collections', *Burlington Magazine*, vol 72, no 423, June 1938, pp 290–302

Monnier, Geneviève. 'Les dessins de Degas du Musée du Louvre: historique de la collection', *La Revue du Louvre et des Musées de France*, 19th year, no 6, 1969, pp 359–68

Monnier, Geneviève. 'La genèse d'une œuvre de Degas: Sémiramis construisant une ville', *La Revue du Louvre et des Musées de France*, 28th year, vols 5–6, 1978, pp 407–26

Montifaud, Marc de. 'Exposition du boulevard des Capucines', *L'Artiste*, 1 May 1874, pp 307–13

Moore, George. 'Degas: the painter of modern life', *Magazine of Art*, vol 13, 1890, pp 416–25

Moore, George. 'Degas in Bond Street', *The Speaker*, London, 2 January 1892, pp 19–20

Moore, George. 'Degas', *Kunst und Künstler*, vol 31, 6th year, 1907–1908, pp 98–108, 138–151

Moore, George. 'Memories of Degas', *Burlington Magazine*, vol 32, no 178, January 1918, pp 22–9; vol 32, no 179, February 1918, pp 63–5

Moreau-Nélaton, Etienne. 'Deux heures avec Degas', *L'Amour de l'art*, 12th year, July 1931, pp 267–70

Newhall, Beaumont. 'Degas: amateur photographer, eight unpublished letters by the famous painter written on a photographic vacation', *Image*, vol 6, June 1956, pp 124–26

Nora, Françoise. 'Degas et les maisons closes', *L'Oeil*, vol 219, October 1973, pp 26–31

Pica, Vittorio. 'Artisti contemporanei: Edgar Degas', *Emporium*, vol 26, no 156, December 1907, pp 405–18

Pickvance, Ronald. 'Henry Hill: an untypical Victorian collector', *Apollo*, vol 76, no 10, December 1962, pp 789–91

Pickvance, Ronald. 'Degas's dancers 1872–1876', *Burlington Magazine*, vol 105, no 723, June 1963, pp 256–66

Pickvance, Ronald. 'Some aspects of Degas's nudes', *Apollo*, vol 83, no 47, January 1966, pp 17–23

Pothey, Alexandre. 'Beaux-arts', *Le Petit Parisien,* 7 April 1877, p 2

Reff, Theodore. 'Degas's copies of older art', *Burlington Magazine,* vol 105, no 723, June 1963, pp 241–51

Reff, Theodore. 'New light on Degas's copies', *Burlington Magazine,* vol 105, no 735, June 1964, pp 250–59

Reff, Theodore. 'The chronology of Degas's notebooks', *Burlington Magazine,* vol 107, no 753, December 1965, pp 606–16

Reff, Theodore. 'Some unpublished letters of Degas', *Art Bulletin,* vol 50, no 1, March 1968, pp 87–93

Reff, Theodore. 'The pictures within Degas's pictures', *Metropolitan Museum Journal,* vol 1, 1968, pp 125–66

Reff, Theodore. 'More unpublished letters of Degas', *Art Bulletin,* vol 51, no 3, September 1969, pp 281–89

Reff, Theodore. 'Degas and the literature of his time- part 1', *The Burlington Magazine,* vol 112, no 810, September 1970, pp 575–89

Reff, Theodore. 'Degas and the literature of his time- part 2', *The Burlington Magazine,* vol 112, no 811, October 1970, pp 674–88

Reff, Theodore. 'Further thoughts on Degas's copies', *The Burlington Magazine,* vol 113, no 822, September 1971, pp 534–43

Reff, Theodore. 'Tableau de Genre', *The Art Bulletin,* vol 54, no 3, September 1972, pp 316–37

Reff, Theodore. 'Degas, Lautrec, and Japanese Art', in *Japonisme in art: art international symposium,* edited by The Society for the study of Japonisme, The committee for the year 2001, Tokyo, 1980, p 189

Reff, Theodore. 'Degas: a master among masters', *The Metropolitan Museum of Art Bulletin,* vol 34, no 4, spring 1977

Rewald, John. 'Degas and his family in New Orleans', *Gazette des Beaux-arts,* vol 30, August 1946, pp 105–26

Rewald, John. 'Theo van Gogh, Goupil and the Impressionists', *Gazette des Beaux-arts,* vol 81, January 1973, pp 1–64. February 1973, pp 65–108

Rivière, Georges. 'L'exposition des impressionnistes', *L'Impressionniste,* 6 April 1877, pp 1–4, 6

Rouart, Ernest. 'Degas', *Le Point,* 1 February 1937, pp 5–36

Shapiro, Michael Edward. 'Degas and the siamese twins of the café-concert: The Ambassadeurs and the Alcazar d'Eté', *Gazette des Beaux-Arts,* vol 95, no 1335, April 1980, pp 153–64

Shapiro, Michael Edward. 'Three late works by Edgar Degas', *The Bulletin, Museum of Fine Arts, Houston,* spring 1982, pp 9–22

Sickert, Walter. 'Degas', *The Burlington Magazine,* vol 31, no 176, November 1917, pp 183–92

Silvestre, Paul-Armand. 'Chronique des Beaux-arts: physiologie du refusé — L'Exposition des révoltés', *L'Opinion nationale,* 22 April 1874, pp 2–3 Silvestre, Paul-Armand. 'Le monde des arts: Les Indépendants', *La Vie moderne,* 1 May 1879, p 38

Smith, George. 'James, Degas, and the Emersonian gaze', *Novel: a forum on fiction,* vol 25, no 3, spring 1992, pp 360–86

Sutton, Denys and Adhémar, Jean. 'Lettres inédites de Degas à Paul Lafond et autres documents', *Gazette des Beaux-arts,* vol 109, no 1419, April 1987, pp 159–80

Thomson, Richard. 'The Degas exhibition in Ottawa and New York', *The Burlington Magazine,* vol 131, no 1033, April 1989, pp 293–96

Thomson, Richard. 'Degas in Edinburgh', *Burlington Magazine,* vol 121, no 919, October 1979, pp 674–77

Thomson, Richard. 'The drinkers of Daumier, Raffaelli and Toulouse-Lautrec: Preliminary observations on a motif', *Oxford Art Journal,* vol 2, Art and Society, April 1979, pp 29–33

Thomson, Richard. 'Degas's nudes at the 1886 Impressionist exhibition', *Gazette des Beaux-Arts,* no 108, November 1986, pp 187–90

Tietze-Conrat, Erika. 'What Degas learned from Mantegna', *Gazette des Beaux-arts,* no 26, December 1944, pp 413–20

Tinterow, Gary and Mirbeau, Octave. 'Mirbeau on Degas: a little-known article of 1848', *The Burlington Magazine,* vol 130, no 1020, March 1988, pp 229–30

Tucker, Paul Hayes. 'The first Impressionist exhibition and Monet's Impression, sunrise: a tale of timing, commerce and patriotism', *Art History,* vol 7, no 4, December 1984, pp 465–76

Villars, Nina de [sic]. 'Variétés: Exposition des artistes indépendants', *Le Courrier du Soir,* 23 April 1881, p 2

Walker, John. 'Degas et les maîtres anciens', *Gazette des Beaux-arts,* no 10, September 1933, pp 173–185

Wehle, H B. 'The exhibition of the H. O. Havemeyer collection', *The Metropolitan Museum of Art Bulletin,* no 25, March 1930, pp 54–76

Werner, Alfred. untitled review of 'Drawings by Degas' by Jean Sutherland Boggs, 'Degas: a critical study of his monotypes' by Eugenia P Janis in *Art Journal,* vol 29, no 1, autumn 1969, pp 140-42

Wick, Peter A. 'Degas' Violinist', *Boston Museum of Fine Arts Bulletin,* vol 57, no 309, 1959, pp 87–101

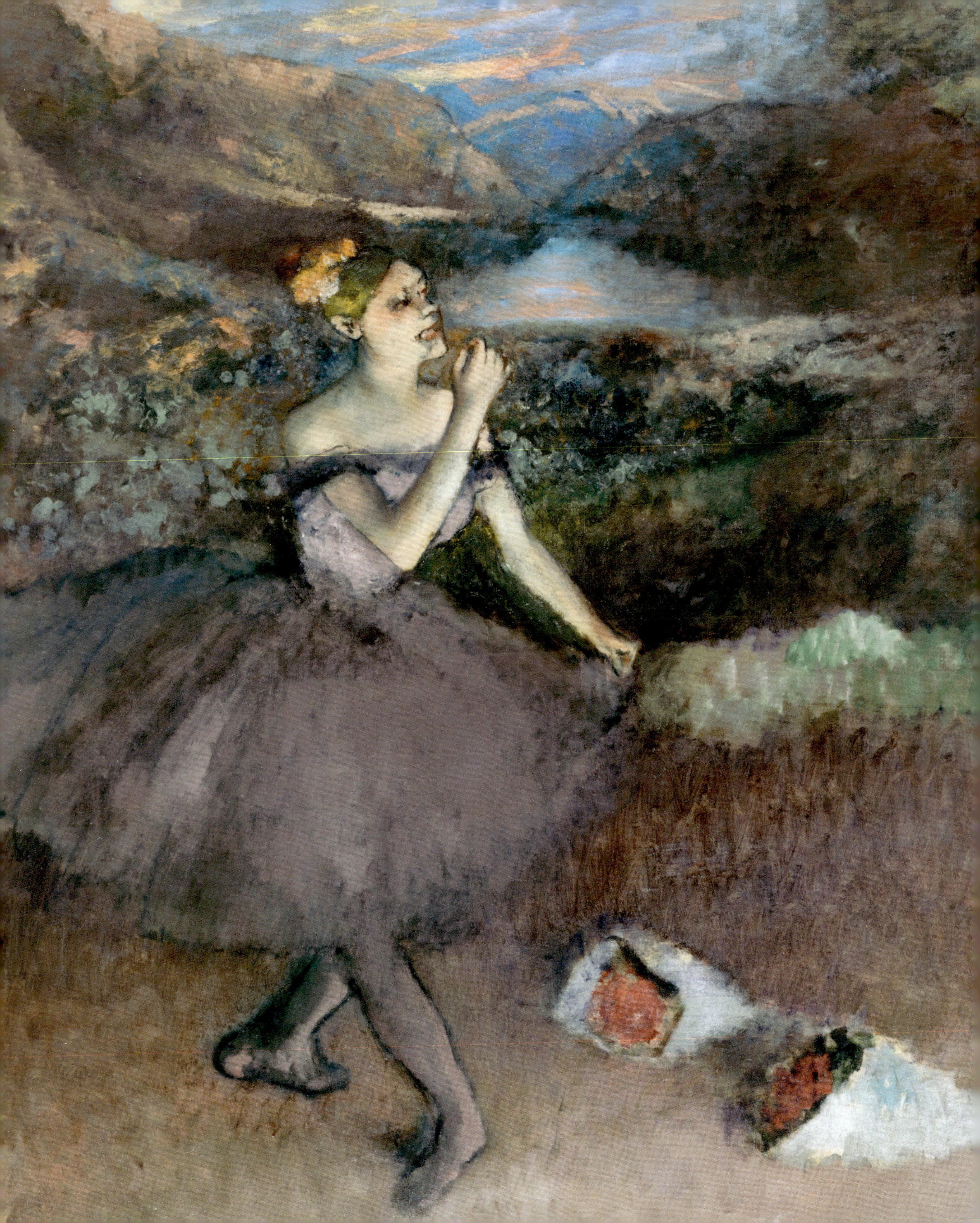

ACKNOWLEDGMENTS

An exhibition of the scale and importance of *Degas: master of French art* can only be achieved with the assistance and cooperation of many people and institutions in Australia and overseas. We would like to express our appreciation in particular to the private collectors and the directors and their staff in the 38 international and national institutions for agreeing to lend their precious art works for our exhibition. In particular those lenders—such as Musée d'Orsay Paris, The Metropolitan Museum of Art, New York and Bibliothèque nationale de France—which have lent a substantial number of works to the exhibition and to the Saint Louis Art Museum which most generously allowed their prize sculpture *Little dancer aged fourteen* to make the journey to Australia for the first time. The National Gallery would also like to thank the private lenders who also have so generously given up their much prized art works in their personal collections for the benefit of many.

The Gallery acknowledges the support of the Gallery's activities through the Minister for the Environment, Heritage and the Arts, the Hon Peter Garrett, AM, MP, and the Department of the Environment, Water, Heritage and the Arts.

Exhibitions of this scale cannot be realised without the generous financial assistance of our sponsors. The Gallery would particularly like to thank Michael Costello, Chief Executive Officer of our principal partner ActewAGL, for his support of this exhibition as the latest in their long association with the Gallery. Our supporting sponsors WIN TV, *The Canberra Times*, Adshel, Mantra on Northbourne, Champagne Pol Roger and Yalumba Wines have all contributed to the staging of this exhibition through in-kind or financial support.

We are extremely grateful to the Australian Government's indemnification scheme, Art Indemnity Australia, through which loans to the exhibition have been indemnified. Without this generous assistance such a groundbreaking exhibition could not have been realised.

The Gallery is indebted to the eminent Degas scholar, Michael Pantazzi, based in Ottawa, who has contributed a major biographical essay on the artist. Acknowledgment and thanks goes to Art Exhibitions Australia and Carol Henry for their support of the exhibition in its initial planning phase.

Many of the National Gallery of Australia staff have been involved or worked directly on the exhibition, public programs, this publication and the website. We acknowledge the support so strongly given by the Gallery's Council and its executive—Alan Froud, Simon Elliott, Shanthini Naidoo and Adam Worrall.

For close involvement, special thanks goes to Mark Henshaw, Curator of International Prints, Drawings and Illustrated Books, for his eloquent French translations; Dr Louise Maurer from the Australian National University for translation of loan correspondence; Pauline Green for her efforts in research and editing this publication; International Art Senior Curator Christine Dixon; Exhibition Assistants Simeran Maxwell and Niki van den Heuvel; Administrative Assistants Sophie Ross, Lucinda Shawcross and Emilie Owens; Conservation staff including David Wise, Andrea Wise, Beata Tworek-Matuszkiewicz, Sarah Mchugh, Cathy Collin, Fiona Kemp, James Ward, Jael Muspratt and Lisa Addison; Registration staff Sara Kelly, Jane Marsden, Kate Buckingham and Lesley Arjonilla; Exhibition Designer Patrice Riboust; Exhibition Coordinator David Turnbull, the installations crew and the art handlers; Julie Donaldson Head of Publishing, Senior Designer Kirsty Morrison and Senior Editor Paul Cliff; Research Librarian Helen Hyland; Education and Public Programs staff Peter Naumann, Katie Russell, Denise Officer, Frances Wild, Adrienne Boag and Jo Krabmann; Maryanne Voyazis and Membership staff; current and outgoing Head of Marketing and Communication Kirsten Downie and Alison Wright and the Marketing staff; the Online team Andrew Powrie, Rebecca Chandler and Owen Carroll; Nick Nicholson in Rights and Permissions; John Tassie and Eleni Kypridis from Imaging Services; Craig O'Sullivan and Security staff; and the Gallery's voluntary guides for their time and effort in revealing the pleasures and depth of the exhibition to our many visitors.

On a more personal note, Jane Kinsman acknowledges the support and patience of her daughter Bella Counihan.

Ron Radford and **Jane Kinsman**

(opposite)
Dancer with bouquets
1895–1900
(detail cat 77)

LENDERS TO THE EXHIBITION

Lenders and their members of staff who have contributed to the success of this exhibition

Albright-Knox Art Gallery, Buffalo
Director Louis Grachos, Tom Hughes and Amber Uptigrove

Auckland Art Gallery Toi o Tamaki, Auckland
Director Chris Saines, Geoffrey Heath and Rachel Walmsley

Baltimore Museum of Art, Baltimore
Director Doreen Bulger, Mandy Bartram, Brianna Bedigian, Jay M Fisher, Melissa McCready and Katy Rothkopf

The Barber Institute of Fine Arts, University of Birmingham, Birmingham
Director Professor Ann Sumner, Yvonne Locke and Dr Paul Spencer-Longhurst

Bibliothèque nationale de France, Paris
Director Bruno Racine, Sylvie Aubenas, Céline Boudot, Franck Bougamont, Nathalie Léman, Marie-Cécile Miessner, Brigitte Robin-Loiseau, Christine Semence, Françoise Simeray and Valerie Sueur-Hermel

Birmingham City Museum and Art Gallery, Birmingham
Director Rita McLean, Brendan Flynn, Tom Heaven and Varshali Patel

Borough Museum and Art Gallery, Berwick-upon-Tweed
Director Chris Green

The British Museum, London
Director Neil MacGregor, Stephen Coppel, Antony Griffiths and Philippa Kirkham

Brooklyn Museum, New York
Director Arnold L Lehman, Charles Demarais, Judith Dolkart, Ruth Janson and Katie Welty

Chrysler Museum of Art, Norfolk
Director William J Hennessey, Jeff Harrison and Erin Lopater

Collection Jacques Doucet, Paris / Bibliothèque de l'institut national d'histoire de l'art, Paris
Director Martine Poulain, Dominique Morelon and Nathalie Muller

Corcoran Gallery of Art, Washington DC
Director Paul Greenhalgh, Philip Brookman, Ila Furman, Dare Myers Hartwell and Andrea Romeo

Detroit Institute of Arts, Detroit
Director Graham W J Beal, Alfred Ackerman, George Keyes, Sylvia Inwood, Michelle S Peplin, Michelle J Smith and MaryAnn Wilkinson

Fitzwilliam Museum, Cambridge
Director Dr Timothy Potts, Nick Dunmore (Bridgeman Art Library), Jane Munro, David Scrase, Liz Woods

The Henry and Rose Pearlman Foundation, Princeton / Princeton University of Art Museum, Princeton
Director Dr Susan M Taylor, Alexia Huges, Karen Richter and Betsy J Rosasco

Hirshhorn Museum and Sculpture Garden, Smithsonian Institution, Washington DC
Director Kerry Brougher, Valerie Fletcher, Amy Snyder and Keri Towler

Galerie Neue Meister, Staatliche Kunstsammlungen Dresden
Director (Staatliche Kunstsammlung Dresden) Max Hollein, Director (Galerie Neue Meister) Dr Ulrich Bishoff, Yvonne Brandt (SKD), Dr Felix Krämer and Ute Wenzel-Förster

The J Paul Getty Museum, Los Angeles
Director Dr Michael Brand, Scott Allan, David Bromford, Jaklyn Burns, Karen Hellman, Lee Hendrix, Sally Hibbard, Judith Keller, Weston Naef, Scott Schaefer and Stephanie Schrader

Kunsthaus Zürich
Dr Christoph Becker

Los Angeles County Museum, Los Angeles
Director Michael Govan, Patrice Marandel, Piper Severance, Nancy Thomas and Amy Wright

The Metropolitan Museum, New York
Director Philippe de Montebello, Kit Basquin, Lucy von Brachel, Lisa Cain, Caitlin Corrigan, Malcolm Daniel, James David Draper, Beatrice Epstein, Roger Haapala, Colta Ives, Gary Tinterow, Saskia Verlaan, Frances Redding Wallace, Ian Wardropper and Julie Zeftel

Mildura Arts Centre Collection, Mildura
Director Julian Bowron and Jillian Peterson

Minneapolis Institute of Art, Minneapolis
Director Kaywin Feldman, Michele Callahan, DeAnn Dankowski, Tanya Morrison, Patrick Noon and Mathew Welch

Musée des Beaux-Arts, Pau
Mayor of Pau Yves Urieta, Director Guillaume Ambroise, Dominique Vazquez

Musée d'Orsay, Paris
President Guy Cogeval, Françoise Heilbrun, Virginie Lagane, Fatima Louli (RMN), Caroline Mathieu, Marianne Mathieu, Odile Michel, Edouard Papet, Sylvie Patry, Marie-Pierre Sale and Carel van Tuyll van Serooskerken (the Louvre)

Museum of Fine Arts, Boston
Director Malcolm Rogers, Kim Pashko, Erin Schleigh, George T M Shackelford and John Steigerwald

Museum of Fine Arts, Springfield
Director Heather R Haskell, Joanna Hanna and Wendy Stayman

National Gallery of Art, Washington DC
Director Earl A Powel III, the late Philip Conisbee and Barbara C G Wood

National Gallery of Scotland, Edinburgh
Director Michael Clarke, Dr Frances Fowle, Janice Slater and Rachel Travers

National Gallery of Victoria, Melbourne
Director Gerard Vaughan, Janine Bofill, Ted Gott, Catherine Leahy, Jennie Moloney and Megan Patty

New Walk Museum and Art Gallery, Leicester
Director Nick Gordon and Simon Lake

Philadelphia Museum of Art
Director the late Anne d'Harmoncourt, Holly Frisbee and Joseph Rishel

Queensland Art Gallery, Brisbane
Director Tony Ellwood, Kylie Timmins and Kathryn Weir

Reading Public Museum and Art Gallery
Director Ronald C Roth, Vasti F DeEsch

Saint Louis Art Museum, Saint Louis
Director Brent Benjamin, Charlotte Eyerman and Pat Woods

Toledo Museum of Art, Toledo
Director Don Bacigalupi, Lawrence W Nichols, Nicole Rivette and Patricia J Whitesides

UCLA Grunwald Center for Graphic Arts, Hammer Museum, Los Angeles
Director Cynthia Burlingham, Kate Bergeron, Claudine Dixon and Portland McCormick

Virginia Museum of Fine Arts, Richmond
Director Alex Nyerges, Mitchell Merling, Howell Perkins and Mary L Sullivan

Private collections

Tony and Carol Berg, Sydney

James and Katherine Goodman, New York

Margaret Olley, Sydney

Stephen Ongpin, London

Richard Owens, Sydney

and other private collectors

INDEX